BL
3131-

D1267093

PRIVATE
INTERNATIONAL LAW

PRIVATE
INTERNATIONAL LAW

PRIVATE
INTERNATIONAL LAW

BY

MARTIN WOLFF

SECOND EDITION

OXFORD
AT THE CLARENDON PRESS

Oxford University Press, Amen House, London E.C.4

GLASGOW NEW YORK TORONTO MELBOURNE WELLINGTON
BOMBAY CALCUTTA MADRAS KARACHI LAHORE DACCA
CAPE TOWN SALISBURY NAIROBI IBADAN ACCRA
KUALA LUMPUR HONG KONG

FIRST EDITION 1945

FIRST EDITION 1945
SECOND EDITION 1950
REPRINTED LITHOGRAPHICALLY IN GREAT BRITAIN
AT THE UNIVERSITY PRESS, OXFORD
FROM SHEETS OF THE SECOND EDITION
1962

PREFACE
TO THE FIRST EDITION

THIS book deals with English Private International Law. It attempts to draw on foreign legal systems where the problems under review have apparently not been the subject of English decisions or where their judicial solution has left room for doubts and difficulties.

The content of the present volume owes much to my son Victor Wolff, LL.M., barrister-at-law of the Inner Temple, who died on 30 May, 1944. He helped me greatly by his critical reading of the manuscript and by fruitful discussions on numerous legal problems. Linguistically manuscript and proofs were supervised by my wife, whose assistance has been untiring and invaluable.

That I was able to undertake the writing of this book I owe to the kindness and understanding of

THE WARDEN AND FELLOWS

OF ALL SOULS COLLEGE,

OXFORD

to whom in gratitude I dedicate it.

M. W.

OXFORD,
October 1944

CONTENTS

PART I. INTRODUCTION

CHAPTER I. THE SCOPE OF PRIVATE INTERNATIONAL LAW 1

1. The problem. 2. Reasons given for the application of foreign law: Protection of vested rights? 3. Comity of nations? *Ius gentium*? 4. Harmony of laws? 5. Definition of private international law. 6. Private international law and unified municipal laws. 7. Private international law and jurisdiction. 8. Private international law and rules on nationality. 9. Private international law and treatment of aliens. 10. The name Private International Law (Conflict of Laws).

CHAPTER II. NATIONAL OR SUPER-NATIONAL LAW? . 11

11. General aspect of the problem. 12. Conflict rules common to several states. 13. Private and public international law. 14. Comity as a basis of private international law? 15. *The société internationale des individus*. 16. Obstacles to a unification of conflict rules.

CHAPTER III. HISTORICAL SURVEY . . . 19

1. *Roman Law*
   17. Silence of the Roman legal sources.
2. *From the Sixth to the Eleventh Century*
   18. The domain of the personal law of origin.
3. *The Statute Theory (or Theories)*
   19. The beginning: Master Aldric. 20. Bartolus; the different kinds of statutes. 21. The *consuetudo Angliae*. 22. The *locus ordinarius*. 23. The French school of the sixteenth century. 24. The Dutch doctrine: Huber and John Voet. 25. Germany and France in the seventeenth and eighteenth centuries. 26. Summary.
4. *English Law to the Middle of the Eighteenth Century*
   27. Early English Law.
5. *The first Attempts at Codification*: 1756 to 1811
   28. The Bavarian and the Prussian Codes. 29. The French and the Austrian Codes.
6. *The Doctrines of the Nineteenth Century*
   30. Introduction. 31. Story. 32. von Savigny. 33. Mancini. 34. The attitude of modern jurists.

PART III. GENERAL RULES ON CONFLICT OF LAWS

PART IV. LAW OF PERSONS AND FAMILY LAW

PART VI. LAW OF PROPERTY

PART VII. SUCCESSION UPON DEATH

LIST OF CASES

LIST OF STATUTES

GENERAL BIBLIOGRAPHY

For the bibliographies of special studies see the end of the respective chapters.

The following books are quoted by the names of their authors.

I. ENGLISH LAW

DICEY and J. H. C. MORRIS (with seven specialist editors), *Conflict of Laws*, 6th ed. 1949.

WESTLAKE (and BENTWICH), *A Treatise on Private International Law*, 7th ed. 1917.

FOOTE (and BELLOT), *Private International Law*, 5th ed. 1925.

G. C. CHESHIRE, *Private International Law*, 3rd ed. 1947.

M. GWYER (and others), in *Halsbury's Laws of England* (2nd ed.), VI, 191, 1932.

R. PHILLIMORE, *Commentaries upon International Law*, vol. IV: *Private International Law*, 1889.

SCHMITTHOFF, *English Conflict of Laws*, 1945.

GRAVESON, *The Conflict of Laws*, 1948.

JOHN FOSTER, 'La théorie anglaise du droit international privé', 65 *Recueil des Cours de l'Académie* (1938, III), 399.

D. J. LLEWELYN DAVIES, 'Règles générales des conflits de lois', 62 ibid. (1937, IV), 427.

WORTLEY, *General Principles of P.I.L.*, 71 *Rec.* (1947, IV).

T. BATY, *Polarized Law*, 1914 (meaning private international law; the expression is taken from mathematics, where polarity is said to exist if a single element has constantly varying moments according as it is referred to one pole or another).[1]

Collection of Cases: W. N. HIBBERT, *Leading Cases in Conflict of Laws*, 1931. Notably: J. H. C. MORRIS, *Cases on Private International Law*, 1939. H. NELSON, *Selected Cases on Private International Law, with a Commentary*, 1889.

II. SCOTTISH LAW

W. GARRET, in *Encyclopædia of the Laws of Scotland*, VIII, 381.

MACKINNON, *Leading Cases in the International Private law of Scotland*, 1934.

III. BRITISH DOMINIONS

R. W. LEE, 'Cases on the Conflict of Laws from the British Dominions', in *Journal of Comparative Legislation*, 1934, 104; 1936, 101; 1939, 27.

1. *Canadian Law*

W. S. JOHNSON, *Conflict of Laws with Reference to Quebec*, 3 vol., 1933–7.

E. LAFLEUR, *Conflict of Laws in Quebec*, 1898.

---

[1] Bustamante, *Derecho internac. privado*, I. 18, rightly calls this comparison *oscuro y inexacto*.

E. FABRE-SURVEYER, 'Conception du droit international privé au Canada', 53 *Recueil des Cours de l'Académie* (1935, III), 83.

J. D. FALCONBRIDGE, *Essays on the Conflict of Laws*, 1947 (1923–47).

J. D. FALCONBRIDGE, *Selection of Cases on the Conflict of Laws*, 2nd ed. 1931.

J. D. FALCONBRIDGE, in *Giurisprudenza comparata*, 1938, 149.

2. *South African Law*

R. W. LEE, *Introduction to Roman-Dutch Law*, 4th ed. (1946), pp. 455–6.

R. E. DE BEER, *South African Law Journal*, 27 (1910), 390, 551; 28 (1911), 36, 188, 336.

W. POLLAK, *The South African Law of Jurisdiction*, 1937.

3. *Other British Territories*

Cases from India, Burma, and the Far East, reported by S. VESEY FITZ-GERALD, *Journal of Compar. Legisl.*, 1934, 116; 1935, 220; 1940, 57.

On Zanzibar: ABRAHAMS, ibid., 1941, 169.

IV. LAW OF THE UNITED STATES OF AMERICA

Restatement of the Law of Conflict of Laws, 1934.

J. STORY, *Commentaries on the Conflict of Laws*, 1834; 8th ed. by BIGELOW, 1883.

R. C. MINOR, *Conflict of Laws*, 1901.

WHARTON (and PARMELE), *Treatise on the Conflict of Laws*, 3rd. ed. 1905.

H. F. GOODRICH, *Handbook of the Conflict of Laws*, 2nd ed. 1938. (The 3rd ed., 1949, was not available to the present writer.)

J. H. BEALE, *Conflict of Laws* (a commentary to the American *Restatement*), 3 vol., 1935.

G. W. STUMBERG, *Principles of Conflict of Laws*, 1937.

E RABEL, *The Conflict of Laws, a Comparative Study*, 2 vol., 1945, 1947 (unfinished).

A. K. KUHN, *Comparative Commentaries on Private International Law*, 1937.

A. NUSSBAUM, *Principles of Private International Law*, 1943.

P. WIGNY, *Essai sur le droit international privé Américain*, 1932.

W. W. COOK, *Logical and Legal Bases of the Conflict of Laws*, 1942.

E. J. LORENZEN, *Selected Articles on the Conflict of Laws*, 1947.

CHEATHAM, *American Theories of Conflict of Laws*, 58 Harvard L.R. (1945), 361 et seq.

Collections of *Cases on Conflict of Laws* published by BEALE (2nd ed. 1928), and E. G. LORENZEN (4th ed. 1937).

V. CONTINENTAL LAWS

A complete bibliography up to 1932: MAKAROV, in the *Rechtsvergleichendes Handwörterbuch*, IV, 320. See also BEALE, *Conflict of Laws*, I, pp. xviii–cxii, and RABEL I. 661, II. 595. Some of the more important text-books are mentioned here; others have not been available to the present writer.

1. France[1]

E. FOELIX, *Traité de droit international privé*, 2 vol., 4th ed. by DEMANGEAT, 1886.

Ch. BROCHER, *Nouveau Traité de droit international privé*, 1876 (a Swiss treatise based on French law).

AUDINET, *Principes élémentaires de droit international privé*, 1906.

COMTE DE VAREILLES-SOMMIÈRES, *La synthèse du droit international privé*, 2 vol. 1897.

DESPAGNET, *Précis de droit international privé*, 5th ed. by DE BOECK, 1909.

ANDRÉ WEISS, *Traité théorique et pratique de droit international privé*, 6 vol., 2nd ed. 1908.

ANDRÉ WEISS, *Manuel de droit international privé*, 9th ed. 1925 (Supplement, 1928).

J. VALÉRY, *Manuel de droit international privé*, 1914.

A. PILLET, *Traité pratique de droit international privé*, 2 vol. 1923.

A. PILLET, *Principes de droit international privé*, 1903.

Mélanges Antoine Pillet, 2 vol. 1929, containing articles by PILLET, ARMINJON, GAUDEMET, LAPRADELLE, and NIBOYET.

P. ARMINJON, *Précis de droit international privé*, 3 vol.; 1st vol. in 3rd ed. 1947, 2nd vol. in 2nd ed. 1934, 3rd vol. 1931.

P. ARMINJON, *Précis de droit international privé commercial*, 1948 (without Maritime Law).

NIBOYET, *Manuel de droit international privé* (this is the 2nd edition of a *Manuel* by PILLET and NIBOYET), 1928 (suppl. 1936).

NIBOYET, *Traité de droit international privé*, 5 vol. 1938–48.

E. BARTIN, *Principes de droit international privé*, 3 vol. 1930–5.

LEREBOURS-PIGEONNIÈRE, *Précis de droit international privé*, 4th ed. 1946.

BATIFFOL, *Traité élém. de droit international privé*, 1949.

MAURY, 'Règles générales des conflits de lois', 57 *Recueil des Cours de l'Académie* (1936 III), 329.

SURVILLE, *Cours élémentaire du droit international privé*, 7th ed. by JULLIOT DE LA MORANDIÈRE and BATIFFOL, 1925–9.

R. PLAISANT, *Les règles de conflit de lois dans les traités*, 1946.

2. Belgium

LAURENT, *Droit civil international*, 8 vol. 1880 ('diffuse and choleric, but interesting', as Beale rightly says).

ROLIN, *Principes de droit international privé belge*, 3 vol. 1897.

POULLET, *Manuel de droit international privé*, 2nd ed. 1928.

3. Germany[2]

F. K. VON SAVIGNY, *System des heutigen römischen Rechts*, VIII, 1849 (English translation by Guthrie).

---

[1] Leading: Arminjon, Niboyet, Lerebours-Pigeonnière, Batiffol.
[2] The treatises written by Savigny, v. Bar, Lewald, and Melchior should be given prominence.

L. von Bar, *Theorie und Praxis des internationalen Privatrechts*, 2 vol. 2nd ed., 1889 (Engl. translation by Gillespie).

L. v. Bar, *Lehrbuch des internationalen Privat- und Strafrechts*, 1892.

L. v. Bar, Internationales Handelsrecht, in *Ehrenberg's Handbuch des Handelsrechts*, I, 327 (1913).

L. v. Bar, in *Holtzendorff's Encyklopaedie*, 7th ed. II, 225 (1915).

Otto Gierke, *Deutsches Privatrecht*, I (1895), 209.

Hans Lewald, *Deutsches Internationales Privatrecht*, 1931.

G. Melchior, *Die Grundlagen des deutschen Internationalen Privatrechts*, 1932.

E. Zitelmann, *Internationales Privatrecht*, 2 vol., 1897, 1912.

L. Raape, Commentary on the Introductory Law to the Civil Code (in Staudinger's *Kommentar zum Bürgerlichen Gesetzbuch*, VI, 2, 1932).

Nussbaum, *Deutsches Internationales Privatrecht*, 1932.

E. Frankenstein, *Internationales Privatrecht*, 4 vol. 1926–35.

H. Lewald, *Règles générales des conflits de lois*, 1941.

E. Riezler, *Internat. Zivilprozessrecht*, 1949.

Franz Kahn, *Abhandlungen zum Internationalen Privatrecht*, ed. by Lenel and Lewald, 2 vol., 1928.

Short introductory books for the use of beginners by Gutzwiller (in *Stammler's Encyklopädie*, 1930, p. 1521), Raape, third ed. 1950, and M. Wolff, 2nd ed., 1949.[1]

4. Austria

Walker, *Internationales Privatrecht*, 4th ed., 1926.

5. Switzerland

Meili, *Internationales Civil- und Handelsrecht*, 2 vol. 1902 (English translation by Kuhn, 1905).

Ad. Schnitzer, *Internationales Privatrecht*, 2nd ed., 1944.

Ad. Schnitzer, *Internationales Handelsrecht*, 1938.

M. Schoch, 55 *Harvard Law Review* (1942), 738.

6. Italy

Pasquale Fiore, *Diritto internazionale privato*, 4th ed., 4 vol. 1907–15 (French translation, 1909).

P. Fiore, *Elementi di diritto internazionale privato*, 1905.

Diena, *Principî di diritto internazionale*, Parte II (2nd ed.), 1917.

Diena, 'Conception du droit international privé en Italie', *Recueil des Cours de l'Académie* (1927, II), 347.

Diena, *Trattato di diritto commerciale internazionale*, 3 vol. 1900–6.

Gabba, *Introduzione al diritto civile internazionale*, 3 vol. 1906–11.

---

[1] M. W.'s introd. book is a summary of the fundamental problems of Private International Law and a description of the particular provisions of German law dealing with it; the present treatise therefore covers different ground and is neither a translation nor a new edition of the German study.

M. UDINA, *Elementi di diritto internazionale privato italiano*, 1933.
PACCHIONI, *Elementi di diritto internazionale privato*, 2nd ed. 1935.
FEDOZZI, *Diritto internaz. privato*, 1935.
R. AGO, *Teoria del diritto internazionale privato, parte generale*, 1934 (on this book, see MELCHIOR, in *Rabel's Zeitschrift* 9, 333).
R. AGO, 58 *Recueil des Cours de l'Académie* (1936, IV), 247.
GEMMA, *Appunti di diritto internazionale privato*, 1936.

7. *The Netherlands*

The influence of the great Dutch jurists of the seventeenth century on the development of English and American law justifies the inclusion of some old treatises here.

PAUL VOET, *De statutis eorumque concursu*, 1661.
JOHANNES VOET, *Commentarius ad Pandectas*, lib. I tit. IV, 1698.
ULRICUS HUBER, *De conflictu legum diversarum in diversis imperiis* (appendix to his *Praelectiones juris civilis*, II lib. 1, tit. 3, no. 10), 1684. See 18 *Brit. Year Book* (1937), 64.

Modern writers:

Jos. JITTA, *Internationaal Privaatrecht*, 1916.
J. M. C. ASSER, *Schets van het internationaal Privaatrecht*, 1879 (German translation by Cohn, 1880; French translation by Rivier, 1884).
KOSTERS, *Het internationaal burgerlijk Recht*, 1917.
MULDER, *Inleiding tot het Nederlandsch Internat. Privaatrecht*, 1927–8.

8. *Scandinavia*

O. A. BORUM, *Personalstatutet efter dansk og fremmed Ret*, 1927.
W. MICHAELI, *Internation. Privatrecht* (Swedish law) written in German. Stockholm, 1948.

9. *Russia*

A. N. MAKAROV, *Précis de droit international privé, d'après la législation et la doctrine russes*, 1933.
A. N. MAKAROV, 35 *Recueil des Cours de l'Académie* (1931, I), 477.

10. *Greece*

STREIT and VALLINDAS, Ἰδιωτικὸν διεθνὲς δίκαιον, 2 vol. 1937.
Under the same title: MARIDAKIS I, 1950.
STREIT, 'Conception du droit international privé en Grèce, 20 *Recueil des Cours de l'Académie* (1927, V), 5.
GOGOS and AUBIN, *Das IPR im griech. Ziv. GB.* (1940) in 15 *Rabel's Z.* 240.
NIKOLETOPOULOS, 23 *Tulene LR.* 452.

VI. LATIN AMERICA

A. S. BUSTAMANTE y SIRVÉN, *Derecho internacional privado*, 3 vol., 2nd ed., Habana, 1934.

VII. PERIODICALS

British Year Book of International law, since 1920.
Journal of Comparative Legislation, since 1879.
Transactions of the Grotius Society, since 1916.
International Law Quarterly, since 1947.
American Journal of International Law, since 1907.
Journal du droit international (privé), founded by CLUNET, 1874.
Revue de droit international et de législation comparée, founded 1869 in Ghent, ed. by DE VISSCHER.
Revue de droit international privé, founded 1905 by DARRAS, ed. by LAPRA-DELLE till 1933, then continued as
Revue critique de droit international (privé), since 1934, ed. by NIBOYET.
Nouvelle Revue de droit international privé, since 1934, ed. by LAPRADELLE.
Annuaire de l'Institut de droit international, since 1877.
Recueil des Cours de l'Académie de Droit International, since 1923.
Travaux du Comité français de droit international privé, 1934–9.
Rivista di diritto internazionale, founded 1908 by ANZILOTTI.
Rivista italiana di diritto internazionale privato e processuale, founded by FEDOZZI, 1931.
Zeitschrift für internationales Privat- und Strafrecht (later: *Zeitschrift für internationales Recht,*) founded by BÖHM, 1891, continued by NIEMEYER.
Zeitschrift für ausländisches und internationales Privatrecht, founded by RABEL, 1928; and its *Beihefte: Die deutsche Rechtsprechung auf dem Gebiete des deutschen internationalen Privatrechts.*
Zeitschrift für ausländisches öffentliches Recht und Völkerrecht, founded by VICTOR BRUNS, 1929.

VIII. ENCYCLOPAEDIC WORKS

LAPRADELLE and NIBOYET, *Répertoire de droit international,* 10 vol., 1929 et seq.

Rechtsvergleichendes Handwörterbuch, vol. IV (1933), p. 320 et seq. (includes comparative studies on Private International Law, by various authors).

MAKAROV, *Die Quellen des Internationalen Privatrechts,* 1929 (contains the text of all statutes and conventions concerning Private International Law).

BURGE, *Commentaries on Colonial and Foreign Laws Generally and in their Conflict with each other and with English Law,* 1838; new edition by RENTON, PHILLIMORE, and BEWES, vol. I–IV, 2; 1907–28.

ABBREVIATIONS

American J.	= American Journal of International Law.
Annuaire	= Annuaire de l'Institut de droit international.
Arch.	= Archiv.
Böhm's Z.	= Zeitschrift für internationales Privat- und Strafrecht.
Br.Y.B.	= British Year Book of International Law.
Bruns' Z.	= Zeitschrift für ausländ. öffentliches Recht u. Völker-recht.
c.c. (or C.C.)	= Civil Code.
Grotius Soc.	= Transactions of the Grotius Society.
Int. L.Q.	= International Law Quarterly.
IPRspr.	= Rechtsprechung auf dem Gebiete des deutschen in-ternationalen Privatrechts (Beihefte to Rabel's Z.).
J. Clunet	= Journal du droit international.
J. Comp. Leg.	= Journal of Comparative Legislation.
Jur. W.	= Juristische Wochenschrift.
L.J.	= Law Journal (Cambridge, Yale, &c.).
L.Q.R.	= Law Quarterly Review.
L.R.	= Law Review (Harvard, Columbia, Michigan, &c.), or Law Reports.
Mod. L.R.	= Modern Law Review
Nouv. Rev.	= Nouvelle Revue de droit international privé.
Rabel's Z.	= Zeitschrift für ausländisches und internationales Privatrecht.
Rec.	= Recueil des Cours de l'Académie de droit Inter-national.
Répert.	= Répertoire de droit international privé.
Rev. crit.	= Revue critique de droit international.
Rev. Darras	= Revue de droit international privé.
Rev. Ghent	= Revue de droit international et de législation com-parée.
Riv.	= Rivista.
R.S.C.	= Rules of the Supreme Court.
RvglHWB.	= Rechtsvergleichendes Handwörterbuch.
Trav. d. Com. fr.	= Travaux du Comité français de droit international privé.
Z.	= Zeitschrift.

PART I

INTRODUCTION

CHAPTER I

THE SCOPE OF PRIVATE INTERNATIONAL LAW

1. WHEN certain events which may entail legal con- 1. The sequences take place in England—an agreement between problem two persons, for example, or an assault; the completion of a person's twenty-first year, or his death—and when all the persons concerned are British subjects domiciled in England; when, further, such events may be expected to take effect in this country (the performance of the agreement, for example), and an action is brought in an English court, no one thinks it necessary to mention that English law applies. The question what law is applicable does not arise because the answer to it would be obvious. But if in the facts of a case there is some foreign element—if one of the parties is of foreign nationality or has a foreign domicile; if the events or some of them have happened in France or are expected to take effect in France—then its legal repercussions can only be examined when the preliminary question as to the applicable law has been answered. It is the task of Private International Law to find that answer.

At first sight one might be inclined to ask: why should an English court be obliged to apply any foreign law under any circumstances? Why not let it apply English law and nothing but English law, thus avoiding any problems of Private International Law? English law is what the English judge knows, and if English law is good enough for purely English lawsuits, why pay any attention to other legal systems which the court does not know and which may be inferior to the English rules? The answer is that this simple solution would lead to grave injustice. If two Frenchmen have concluded a contract in Marseilles to be performed there, and if an action on that contract is, for some reason, brought in an English court, the parties are entitled to expect that the court will decide it according to French law; were English law to be applied, the effect of the contract might be altered contrary to the intention of the contracting parties. Or again: suppose an English registrar were to marry two Bulgarians, both domiciled in Sofia, although they are first cousins and therefore debarred from marriage with each other. By so doing he would assist in a marriage that would be invalid in the country of the parties' domicile. Or, to take another example. Under German law the ownership of stolen goods sold in market overt to a *bona-fide* purchaser does not pass to him; the right of the original owner is not extinguished when the purchaser brings the goods to England. It would be unjust in such a case to apply the English rule according to which ownership of stolen goods is transferred to the *bona-fide* purchaser by sale in market overt.

2. Reasons given for the application of foreign law: protection of vested rights? From time to time attempts have been made to find an exhaustive formula covering all the reasons for which justice may require foreign law to be applied. None of these attempts has proved satisfactory because, owing to the varied nature of the claims, such reasons are too manifold and complex to be included in a simple formula.

Three examples of these attempts are the following:

1. Some writers think that the applicability of foreign law depends on the principle of *protection of vested rights*.[1] It is—so runs their argument—one of the tenets of justice that rights acquired in one country must be recognized and legally protected in others. No such general principle exists however, nor would it in every case explain the application of foreign law.[2]

(*a*) The protection of vested rights (*iura quaesita*) was first claimed and developed in intertemporal law[3] where

---

[1] Horst Müller, *Der Grundsatz des wohlerworbenen Rechts im I.P.R.*, 1935.

[2] Thus notably P. Arminjon 44 *Rec.* (1933 II), 5; Arminjon, *Précis* I, 127 et seq.; G. C. Cheshire 46–52.

[3] The law of conflicts between old and new law was first called 'Private Intertemporal Law' by a Swiss author, Affolter, *Das intertemporale Privatrecht*, 1901.

it is expressed in the principle that new laws shall not have retroactive effect. But it should not be transferred from that field to Private International Law. The error in such analogy is apparent from the following reasoning. When the law of the country X has granted a person a certain right, it would seem unjust for the same country to deprive him of that right by a new law without paying him adequate compensation; the country X is as it were estopped by its previous conduct. It does not follow that another country Y is bound to recognize such person's right.

(*b*) Not all rights acquired under a foreign law are protected elsewhere, nor is their protection always desirable or even possible. This is particularly the case when one has to choose between the vested right of one person A arising under a law x, and the vested right of another person B created by a law y and incompatible with A's right.

Example: A German domiciled in Scotland dies intestate, leaving a widow and a brother: his movable property is worth £10,000. Under German law his widow succeeds to half the estate, under Scots law she can only claim a sum of £500. The English court would apply Scots law as the law of the domicile and thus refuse to recognize her right to one-half, which under German law is her 'vested right'. An Italian court, on the other hand, would apply the national law of the deceased and consequently deny the brother's right, acquired under Scots law, to the whole estate minus £500.

(*c*) The law protects not only vested 'rights' constituted abroad, but often also foreign legal relationships, capacities, or powers out of which rights, or the extinction of duties and charges, or the invalidity of acts may arise. Thus the American divorce of an English couple domiciled in America will be recognized here although it has not created a 'right' but merely the capacity to conclude another marriage and the extinction of rights (to maintenance, &c.).

(*d*) Finally, the 'protection' of rights and other interests is not the only consideration to be taken into account. The issue very often is whether a *disability* existing under one law should be maintained by a foreign court. Take the example given above: a Bulgarian wants to marry his cousin, though under Bulgarian law marriages between relations up to the seventh degree are prohibited. The question arising in England or France (or wherever they are resident) will then be whether the Bulgarian rule should apply or whether the marriage is to be allowed. As the Bulgarian provision is not intended to protect any private 'rights' but to secure obedience to a religious behest, its application here does not come under the head of 'protection of vested interests'.

3. Comity of nations? *Ius gentium?*

2. Other authors have said that the application of foreign legal systems in cases involving foreign elements is necessary because their non-application would constitute a disregard of foreign sovereignties, a lack of 'comity' towards foreign states.[1] It has even been thought that there are principles of *ius gentium* (public international law) according to which every state is under a legal obligation to its fellow states to apply foreign law in certain circumstances. In section 13 it will be explained that there are no such rules of public international law, and that it is not the interest of the various states as such that demands the application of foreign laws. If the courts of any given country X were to apply exclusively the law prevailing in X, they would act unjustly not against any other country (state), but against the individual parties, and it would make no difference whether the parties were subjects of country X or of any other country.

4. The 'harmony of laws'?

3. Finally, some writers regard as the reason for the application of foreign law the desire to establish what has been called 'harmony of laws all over the world'.[2] If every court were to apply only the *lex fori*, the outcome of any action would depend entirely on where it is brought. Often the plaintiff may start proceedings at his own choice in one of several countries: he may choose the defendant's domicile or his place of business or the country where the defendant happens to be when the action is launched, &c. It would be unjust to allow the plaintiff to choose not only between several *fora* but, through this choice, between the legal systems of several countries. Justice requires that the decision be the same wherever the claim is brought.

[1] See *infra*, ss. 14, 24.   [2] See *infra*, s. 15.

This reasoning is sound though not exhaustive. Even where a plaintiff has no choice of forum, it might be contrary to justice for the court entertaining the action to apply its own law.

II. It is thus the function of Private International Law to determine which of several simultaneously valid legal systems is applicable to a given set of facts. Four points in this definition are important.

5. Definition of Private International Law

1. Like all other rules of law the rules of Private International Law apply to certain given *facts*, to facts not previously touched by law, not characterized as creating some legal relationship. For only a legal system can determine whether a certain set of facts has produced any legal relationship or not, and it is for Private International Law to elucidate the operative legal system in the individual case. That truism has sometimes been overlooked, and the task of Private International Law has been defined as the determination of the legal system applicable to a given *legal relationship*. As we shall see later that mistaken formula has sometimes entailed mistakes in connexion with the doctrine of classification.

2. The selection of legal systems open to the court is limited to those *simultaneously valid*. Where the law in any given country has been changed—as, for example, English divorce law by the Matrimonial Causes Act, 1937—the question arises whether facts which took place before the change, such as an act of cruelty committed by a husband in 1936, are to be governed by the old law or the new law. The answer is often given by statutory provisions. If it is not the court will have to apply certain general principles, such as the principle of non-retroactivity of new laws.

3. The legal systems between which the choice lies are mostly those prevailing in different *countries*, that is either in different states (French law, German law), or in different parts of one state (English law, Scots law, borough-English; legal rules in force in one of the occupied 'zones' of Germany).[1] Sometimes, however, two

---

[1] 'Interzonal law.' See on this: Ernst Wolff, in *Raape-Festschrift* (1948), p. 181; Dölle, ibid., p. 149.

or more legal systems are simultaneously in force within the same country. Thus in Egypt, in Syria, in Palestine, in Arabia, in Iran, in India, and in most colonies different legal rules apply to natives, Hindus, Muhammedans, Europeans, Jews, and other groups of persons classified according to their race[1] or religion. This is especially true of marriage, succession, and land law. In Europe, too, such distinctions are to be found in those Balkan states in which the laws of marriage, divorce, and separation are entirely regulated by religion. Before 1938 this was also the case in Austria, where the Civil Code of 1811 laid down divergent rules for the marriage of Roman Catholics, of other Christians, and of Jews. The legal rules determining the incidents of the varying 'personal' systems, e.g. in the case of mixed marriages, may be called *Private Interpersonal Law*.[2] Most of the rules of Private International Law can be applied here analogously.

4. The legal effects of a certain set of facts are not always determined by *one single* legal system. It is sometimes necessary to apply several systems, either cumulatively or alternatively.

(*a*) *Cumulatively.* It may happen that a given set of facts produces legal effects only if certain conditions common to two legal systems are fulfilled. Thus an act committed abroad gives rise to an action for tort in this country only if such act constitutes an actionable tort according to English law and is not justifiable under the law of the country where it was committed.[3] Or, a given set of facts may produce several legal effects each of which is governed by a different legal system.

Examples: When a contract concluded in New York is to be performed in London, it may be that the contract as a whole is governed by the law of New York, but that English law, as the *lex loci solutionis*, applies to the manner or sufficiency of performance or to excuses for non-performance.[4] In international loan contracts the lender often stipulates for an *option de change*, i.e. that repayment is to be effected either in London in English

---

[1] On 'inter-racial' law: J. Lewin, *J. Comp. Leg.* 1938, 16.
[2] Cf. on this particularly Arminjon, *J. Clunet* 39 (1912), 698, 1025; 40 (1913), 34, 435, 812; and Giesker-Zeller, *Die Rechtsanwendungsnorm* (1914), 36 et seq.
[3] *The Halley* (1868), L.R. 2 P.C., 193. See *infra*, s. 470.
[4] Thus U.S.A. Restatement, §§ 332, 338.

money or in Amsterdam in Dutch money at his choice; in that case the contract frequently contains a clause to the effect that all questions as to the amount and mode of payment are to be decided according to the law of the country he chooses.[1]

(*b*) *Alternatively*. In England, for example, capacity to conclude mercantile contracts is governed alternatively by the law of the contracting party's domicile or the law of the place where the contract is made. If either of these two systems declares him capable of contracting the contract is valid.[2]

If therefore a 20 year old domiciled Swiss and a 22 year old Hungarian make a contract in London, such contract is valid, because the Swiss has attained majority under Swiss law (at 20), though not under English law, while the Hungarian has attained it under English, though not under Hungarian law (at 24).[3]

III. Private International Law must also be distinguished from those rules of private law which have become common to many countries as a result of international conventions. The law introduced in the various countries by reason of such conventions is in the nature of ordinary substantive 'internal' or 'municipal' law; it is not concerned with the application of foreign laws. Indeed, where such unified internal laws have been created, all problems of Private International Law disappear—unless the agreed rule is variously interpreted in the countries concerned.

6. Private International Law and unified municipal laws

International conventions of this kind are very numerous. Of those which Great Britain has ratified the most important are the Convention of Paris for the Protection of Industrial Property of 1883, modified by the additional Acts of Brussels, 1900, Washington, 1911, the Hague, 1925, and London, 1934;[4] a series of Maritime Conventions of Brussels, since 1910, establishing uniform rules

---

[1] Cf. for example *Rex* v. *International Trustee*, [1937] A.C. 500, 574. See *infra*, s. 445.

[2] Cf. *infra*, s. 261 et seq.

[3] Cf. Cheshire, *International Contracts*, 1948, p. 48 et seq.

[4] Its subject is the protection of patents, designs, models, trade marks, and trade names, the protection of indication of origin, and the repression of unfair competition. It has been put into force in England by a series of Acts of Parliament, such as the Patents &c. (International Conventions) Act 1938 (1 & 2 Geo. VI, c. 29).

with respect to collisions at sea, assistance and salvage at sea, and certain other subjects;[1] the Berne Convention, 1885, for the Protection of Works of Art and Literature, amended in Paris, 1896, in Berlin 1908, and in Rome, 1928;[2] the Warsaw Convention of 1929 for the Unification of certain rules relating to International Carriage by Air,[3] and others. Certain rules concerning carriage of goods by sea were recommended in two international conferences held at Brussels in 1922 and 1923, on the basis of the 'Hague Rules' drafted at the 1921 meeting of the International Law Association. Great Britain and other states have adapted their internal laws to these provisions.[4] Some important international conventions, on the other hand, though accepted by nearly all European and by several extra-European states, have not been ratified by Britain, nor, for that matter, by the United States of America. These are the Geneva Conventions concerning a Uniform Law for Bills of Exchange and Promissory Notes, 1930, and a Uniform Law for Cheques, 1931. Great Britain has only accepted the two Conventions on Stamp Laws in connexion with Bills of Exchange, Promissory Notes, and Cheques.

None of these matters are relevant to a book dealing with Private International Law, though the conventions referred to establish rules of private law bearing an international character.

IV. There are three subjects which, though not directly concerned with the application of foreign law, are usually dealt with in text-books on Private International Law.

---

[1] See Maritime Conventions Act, 1911 (1 & 2 Geo. V, c. 57). On the unification of the law of the sea: Gutteridge, *J. Comp. Leg.* 1934, 246; Cleminson, ibid. 1941, 163.

[2] These conventions do not establish a uniform law of copyright; the unification is limited to a certain number of particular points. Their main subject is the protection of the copyrights of foreigners. They have no force of law in England, and the rights of foreigners are governed only by Orders in Council made under s. 29 Copyright Act, 1911.

[3] Put into force in Great Britain by the Carriage by Air Act, 1932 (22 & 23 Geo. V, c. 36). A second International Convention on Air Law of 1933 has not been ratified by Great Britain. See R. Coquoz, *Le droit privé international aérien* (1938).

[4] Carriage of Goods by Sea Act, 1924 (14 & 15 Geo V, c. 22).

1. All English and American writers on Private International Law begin by expounding the circumstances in which English or American courts have *jurisdiction* in a suit that contains a foreign element. The same practice will be followed here. For it is usually in lawsuits that problems of private international law come under discussion. It must, however, be stressed that the necessity of determining the applicable law does not arise only in the course of litigation. The same questions come up where a person seeks legal opinion on his position, possibly without any intention of starting proceedings, or where a registrar has to make up his mind whether or not to allow two persons of different domicile or nationality to be married before him, notwithstanding a bar existing in one of the legal systems involved; or where the Land Registry has to decide whether to make an entry based on a foreign will valid according to the law of the deceased's domicile, but not according to the *lex situs*.

7. Private International Law and jurisdiction

2. All French and some English writers on Private International Law deal with the rules governing *acquisition or loss of nationality*, because in many countries, such as France and Germany, all questions relating to the status of a person and to family law are decided according to the law of the person's nationality. The same reasoning does not apply in this country and therefore the subject will not be discussed here.[1]

8. Private International Law and rules on nationality

3. Many authors, notably all French authors, reckon among the subjects of Private International Law the *Legal Treatment of Aliens* according to the internal law of a country. Under this heading the rights and duties of those who are not subjects of the state are discussed. Are aliens capable of becoming guardians, of owning or buying land, of concluding labour contracts? How, if at all, can commercial, industrial, and mining companies guard against the possibility of alien control? It is merely a question of terminology and arrangement of the subject-matter whether one treats problems of that kind under the head of Private International Law or not. In all these cases the foreign nationality of any person concerned constitutes a

9. Private International Law and the treatment of aliens

---

[1] Cf., however, *infra*, s. 122 et seq.

'foreign element'. But the problem that they raise is not: Which country's internal law is applicable? It is: How does the internal law of a particular country provide for problems such as those mentioned here, problems which are both legally and politically very different from those concerned with the applicable law? It has therefore been found preferable to exclude them from this study.[1]

10. The name 'Private International Law' ('Conflict of Laws')

V. The usual titles of our subject are 'Private International Law'[2] or 'Rules on Conflict of Laws'.[3] Both are open to objection. The first seems to suggest that there are two kinds of International Law, public and private, while Private International Law to-day is not international but national law (cf. *infra*, p. 11). The second term is no more satisfactory, because it is the task of this branch of law to choose between several legal systems and thus to avoid conflicts. As, however, both titles are used throughout the world and as nobody has found a better one,[4] it hardly seems worth while to devote further thought to this merely terminological issue.

[1] See on this subject: Lauterpacht, *Internat. Law*, 6th ed. i. 619 et seq.

[2] In Scotland: 'International Private Law', corresponding to the continental terms: *Droit international privé, Internationales Privatrecht, Diritto internazionale privato*, &c. This designation was introduced by Foelix, 1843.

[3] In German: *Kollisionsrecht*. The French expression *Conflit des lois* covers only one of the three parts of *Droit international privé*, excluding the rules on nationality and on the legal treatment of aliens.

[4] The name 'Demarcation Law' (*Grenzrecht*) which some German authors have tried to introduce, and which makes one think of boundary-stones, fences, and hedges, may be mentioned only as a diverting terminological exercise. On the term 'Polarized Law' see General Bibliography, p. xxxviii, *ad nom*. Baty.

BIBLIOGRAPHY

JOS. JITTA, *La méthode du droit internat. privé* (1890), 32 et seq. P. ARMINJON, 'L'objet et la méthode du dr. i. p.', 21 *Rec.* (1928 I). ARMINJON, 56 *Rev. Ghent* (1929), 680 et seq. ARMINJON, 'La notion des droits acquis en dr. i. p.', 44 *Rec.* (1933 II), 5 et seq. PILLET, 'La théorie générale des droits acquis', 8 *Rec.* (1925 III), 489. KAECKENBEECK, 17 *Brit. Y. B.*, 1936, 1; 59 *Rec.* (1937 I), 321. GIESKER-ZELLER, *Die Rechtsanwendungsnorm* (1914). W. E. BECKETT, *Brit. Y.B.*, 1926, 73. NEUNER, 20 *Canadian Bar Rev.* (1942), 481.

CHAPTER II

NATIONAL OR SUPER-NATIONAL LAW

1. To-DAY undoubtedly Private International Law is national law. There exists an English private international law as distinct from a French, a German, an Italian private international law. The rules on the conflict of laws in the various countries differ nearly as much from each other as do those on internal (municipal) law.

11. General aspect of the problem

Private International Law, however, was not always looked on as purely national. When it was born—in the Italian city-states of the Middle Ages[1]—it was thought of as a super-national law; there were no separate systems of private international law for Florence, Bologna, and Modena, but one law common to all states and of a common origin. The idea of a super-national law was maintained also in the doctrines developed in France and Holland from the sixteenth century onwards (in spite of the importance then attached to the conception of sovereignty) and in those developed later by the school of Natural Law. Not till the epoch of the great continental codes did the idea of a super-national law disappear.

There are, no doubt, many rules on conflict of laws common to all, or at any rate to a number of countries. But to-day they are no longer considered super-national. They are looked upon as part of their respective national legal systems. Identical rules of this kind arise in three different ways.

12. Conflict rules common to several states

1. Some of the rules which made up the super-national medieval doctrines of the Italian jurists retained their force everywhere. Examples are the rule *locus regit actum*, according to which contracts are formally valid if they are in the form prescribed by the law of the place where the contract is concluded; and the rule of the *lex situs* in the case of a transfer of immovables *inter vivos*.

2. Some rules have become a law common to a number of countries by spontaneous adoption. Thus the (scanty)

---

[1] Cf. *infra*, s. 19 et seq.

provisions in the French Civil Code, art. 3, have been copied by many other codes. The more detailed rules of the German Code have been reproduced by an even greater number of foreign statutes. Nearly all the English conflict rules have been taken over by Scottish, Canadian, and South African decisions, and many English rules have been followed in the United States of America.

3. Finally, some rules of Private International Law have become common to several countries as the result of international conventions.[1] Such conventions merely create an obligation on the part of the contracting Powers to introduce the rules agreed on. Enactment by the legislative bodies of the states concerned transforms these rules into national law of the respective states, which thus contains rules common to all the parties to the convention.

13. Private and Public International Law II. This leads to another question, that of the relationship between Private International Law and Public International Law, or, as the latter is shortly called, 'International Law' (*droit des gens, Völkerrecht*). Are the various states, apart from State Treaties, under any obligation towards each other to make their rules on conflict of laws conform to certain principles?

Wishful thinking has induced many authors to answer this question in the affirmative. They believe that certain general principles of Private International Law may be derived from fundamental conceptions embodied in Public International Law.[2] This is hardly tenable. In recent decades public international law has certainly developed some rules relative to the treatment of aliens. In particular, it has been laid down by several decisions in international jurisdiction that a state, though it may expropriate the private property of foreigners as well as of its own nationals, is not at liberty to do so without just compensation.[3] But

---

[1] Cf. *infra*, s. 39 et seq.

[2] Some decisions of the Mixed Arbitral Tribunals established by the Peace Treaties, 1919, likewise assert that there are 'general principles' of private international law, independent of the national conflict rules of the various states. Cf. *Recueil des décisions des tribun. arbitraux mixtes*, 4. 9; 6. 975; 1. 162.

[3] See Erich Kaufmann, *Règles générales du droit de la paix* (1936), 121. Permanent Court of Internat. Justice, Decision No. 7, 23 May 1926. (*Chorzów*

these rules do not affect the problem of choosing the system of law applicable to facts containing a foreign element, and there is no evidence that Public International Law has so far laid down any rules on this subject. There is no such thing as a principle of international law embodying a 'distribution of competences' in the field of private law, i.e. a demarcation of the respective spheres of legislative competence of the various states. Ernst Zitelmann attempted to prove the existence of such a principle.[1] His starting-point was the idea that every state has dominion over all things situate in its territory and over all persons who are its nationals. If this were true, the English system of applying to persons not their national law, but the law of their domicile would be contrary to international law— but no state has ever raised any objection to it.[2]

There are, however, certain generally recognized principles of international law concerning the obligations of sovereign states towards each other and resulting from their co-existence. All states are, for example, bound to respect the independence, the territorial supremacy, and the dignity of other states, to permit intercourse between them and to act on the principle of the equality of states. Can it then be said that any of these fundamental obligations entails a duty on the part of the various nations to

---

Case, 'Le principe du respect des droits acquis fait partie du droit international commun'). Permanent Court of Arbitration, 1922, in *Norway* v. *United States of America* (17 *Amer. J.* 362): 'Just compensation is due to the claimants under the municipal law of the United States as well as under the international law based upon the respect of private property.' When *Italy* nationalized the Italian life insurance companies, it was recognized that the Italian state was bound to compensate foreign nationals equitably even if it did not compensate its own nationals. Arbitral Decision by M. Huber, 1924, in *Great Britain* v. *Spain* (*Annual Digest* 1923–4, 157, 163): 'il peut être considéré comme acquis qu'en droit international un étranger ne peut être privé de sa propriété sans juste indemnité.' Arbitral Decision by M. Fazy, 1928, in *Goldenberg* v. *German Reich*: 'Si le droit des gens autorise un État, pour des motifs d'utilité publique à déroger au principe du respect de la propriété privée des étrangers, c'est à la condition sine qua non que les biens requisitionnés seront équitablement payés le plus rapidement possible.' (*Bruns' Z.* I. 2, p. 94.) General Claims Commission in the *de Sabla* controversy (concerning the applicability of the agrarian laws of Panama to aliens) between the *U.S.A. and Panama, Bruns' Z.* IV. 925. 28 *Amer. J.* (1934), 602.

[1] Similarly Frankenstein in his work on Private International Law.
[2] Cf. Melchior, *Grundlagen*, p. 36; Maury, p. 31.

lay down particular rules of private international law? Hardly. A given state X is by no means jeopardized in its 'territorial supremacy' if another state Y decrees that succession to immovables situated in X shall be governed, not by the law of X, but by the law of the last domicile of the deceased. The 'dignity' of a state is not affronted when some of its rules are considered by a second state to be incompatible with the public policy of such second state or with its conception of the requirements of *boni mores*.[1] The Soviet Union has not objected to the statement of an English judge[2] that what Russia calls a marriage is not a marriage in the Christian sense; and Germany could not protest if other countries refused to apply the Nuremberg Laws concerning racial purity of marriages. It would be pure fantastic speculation to discuss a possible rule whereby the courts would be debarred from applying any foreign law or the law of a particular foreign country; no state has ever made a rule of this kind, and it is not likely that any state will. Of course, if any state were to make a conflict rule directed against well-founded rights or interests of aliens, or leading to the violation of such interests—say, a rule to the effect that contracts between the state's nationals and foreigners shall be governed by that law which is more favourable to the national—this would infringe the rule of international law mentioned above concerning the treatment of aliens. But, again, conflict rules of that kind do not exist.

14. Comity as a basis of Private International Law? III. Some authors, though rejecting public international law as the basis of private international law, would substitute for it the notion of *comity*. The word comity is ambiguous.[3] Often it is used simply as an equivalent of the term 'conflict of laws'. More frequently its meaning is restricted to the notion of a voluntary concession to other states—the application of foreign laws and recognition of rights created under foreign law do not depend

[1] See, however, Scrutton, L.J., in *A. M. Luther v. Sagor & Co.*, [1921] 3 K.B. 532, 558, 559. *Infra*, s. 169.

[2] Hill, J., in *Nachimson v. Nachimson*, 142 L.T.R. 329 (overruled by the Court of Appeal, [1930] P. 217).

[3] Cf. Beale I, 53 et seq.; Goodrich, p. 9.

on a legal obligation existing under public international law, but are acts of courtesy dictated by a *comitas gentium*. This opinion, which goes back to the Dutch authors of the seventeenth century, is still upheld by some authors in the United States of America and in England. Sometimes it is the courts of a country,[1] sometimes the legislatures, that are said to extend such courtesy to the corresponding institutions in another country. Both these conceptions are dangerous and both are erroneous. They are dangerous because they tend to make the application of foreign law and the recognition of foreign judgments dependent on 'reciprocity'—as if the valueless decisions pronounced by corrupt or ignorant judges in Ruritania could be rendered innocuous in England by the fact that the courts of Ruritania recognize wise decisions pronounced by English judges. And the doctrine is erroneous because it is based on the idea that any state has an interest in the application of its law by the courts of other states. Suppose that the true proper law of a contract concluded in Italy between two Frenchmen is Italian law, but that the English court which entertains an action arising out of that contract wrongly holds that French law applies and therefore dismisses the action—then it is only the plaintiff who suffers—the Italian state is indifferent. How little it matters to any state whether its legal system is applied abroad or not becomes very manifest in war. Never has any belligerent state decreed that during the war its courts should exclude from application all the legal rules of the enemy state. Even national-socialistic Germany did not forbid the application of English law by its courts during the war. If the application of foreign law were founded on *comitas gentium*, surely it should cease with the outbreak of hostilities.

IV. Although thus no rule of international law and no postulate of comity prevents a country from introducing whatever rule of private international law it may see fit, justice demands that every country in making such rules

15. The *société internationale des individus*

---

[1] Cf. for example, *Simpson* v. *Fogo* (1863), 1 Hemm. & M. 195, 247. See also *Szalátnay-Stacho* v. *Fink*, [1947] 1 K.B. 1.

should consider how they will affect social and economic intercourse between any persons, be they its own nationals or aliens. The community, the interests of which must be borne in mind by the lawgiver, is neither the community of his own nationals nor that of the various states or nations, but the community of all individuals, of mankind, the *société internationale des individus*, as a Dutch author, Josephus Jitta, puts it. A system of conflict rules which neglected this super-national view would be contrary to justice. Rules, in particular, that can only be dictated by a desire to increase the power of his own legal system would not be compatible with the object of a lawgiver on Private International Law. His aim must be to establish such rules *as he can reasonably wish to see introduced by the legislators or courts of other countries*. Private International Law is not itself international, but it should certainly be drawn up in an international frame of mind.

The ultimate goal would seem to be the attainment of uniformity in the conflict rules of all countries, of 'Harmony of Laws', as it has been called by Franz Kahn.[1] If this aim were achieved every lawsuit could be decided under the same 'internal' (municipal) laws irrespective of the courts in which it is brought. And where the parties do not want to bring an action in any court but simply to be advised about their legal position, their lawyer would be able to give an unambiguous answer, whereas now he might be obliged to say: 'My answer depends on whether the claim is brought in a court of country X or of country Y. According to the conflict rules of X the internal law of, say, Switzerland is applicable, under which the claim in question is well-founded; according to the conflict rules in Y the internal French law is decisive, and under this the claim is groundless.' If, then, the parties insist that they do not want to bring an action anywhere, but only to know which of them 'is right', then even the most learned and able lawyer must reply: 'There is no possible answer to your question though there is not the least doubt about the law.'

The final goal—uniformity of conflict rules throughout

---

[1] See *supra*, s. 4.

the world—is, however, very distant and will possibly never be attained as long as independent states exist. In particular it seems improbable that all states will reach an agreement as to whether the status of a person should be determined by his national law or by the law of his domicile.[1] Further, no state will be prepared to apply foreign law if that leads to a result incompatible with fundamental principles of its own legislation. Unsatisfactory though this may be, it can, on the other hand, not be denied that the importance of the 'harmony of laws' has sometimes been somewhat over-stressed. Harmony is very desirable both where a lawsuit can be brought in courts of several countries[2] and where it is probable that the effects of an act (e.g. a marriage, a divorce, or a contract) will become operative in more than one country. But suppose a Yugoslav has lived twenty years in London, never wants to return to his country, and has neither property nor relatives there; if he marries in London before the registrar all that matters to him and to others is that this marriage is valid under English law. He would not be disturbed if he were told that in Yugoslavia his marriage is considered as non-existent.

16. Obstacles to a unification of conflict rules

The attainment of harmony of laws is particularly often obstructed by the *preference* both of legislatures and of courts for the application of the *law of their own country*. This tendency is to be found in every country. In so far as it is based on a nationalistic desire unfairly to extend the natural scope of their law's ascendancy it is not defensible from the point of view of justice. Sometimes, however, the reasons are different. A conscientious judge will be glad if the rules of Private International Law allow him to apply the law of his own country. That is the system with which he is familiar, and in applying it he is sure not to overlook new statutes or recent decisions of the courts. If he has to apply foreign law, he will be dependent for the most part on what expert witnesses tell him, never knowing for certain whether their evidence is accurate. Even if he knows the foreign language he is never sure that his interpretation of, say, a foreign code is correct

---

[1] Cf. *infra*, ss. 93–6.   [2] Cf. *supra*, ss. 4, 15.

and that all the essential statutes, decisions, and text-books are at his disposal. He is acting as a judge, but he knows no more and often less about the foreign law than first-year students in the country in question. Courts and legislatures are therefore not entirely to blame if they are inclined to favour the application of their own law. This tendency explains a series of phenomena to be found in many countries:

1. the *Renvoi* doctrine; cf. *infra*, s. 194.

2. the presumption in English Law that foreign law is the same as English Law; cf. *infra*, ss. 208, 209;

3. the excessive application under French Law and those systems based on it of the conception of *ordre public*; cf. *infra*, s. 159;

4. Everywhere the procedure of the court is governed by the *lex fori*. The courts of this country go very far in their definition of 'procedure', to which English Law is to be applied. Thus limitation of actions, set-off, measure of damages, and sometimes even burden of proof, are treated here as matters of procedure; cf. *infra*, s. 218 et seq.

5. The desire of the legislature to extend the application of its own laws beyond the limits allowed by the 'harmony of laws' has been quite openly expressed in some modern codes. Thus the German Introductory Law to the Civil Code[1] lays down that if a husband or if the parents lose their German nationality German law shall nevertheless continue to apply to certain family relationships, provided the wife or the child respectively have remained German nationals. There is no question in such cases of *protecting* persons of German nationality—for German law applies even if it is less favourable to the German subject than foreign law.

---

[1] Introd. Law, 1896, art. 14, § 2; art. 17, § 3; art. 19 and 20.

BIBLIOGRAPHY

BURCKHARDT, *Festgabe by Berne Law Faculty to E. Huber* (1919), 263. JITTA, loc. cit. 69. V. BRUNS AND SCHINDLER, *Mitteil. d. Deutsch. Gesellsch. für Völkerrecht* 12 (1933), 47, 57. FACHIRI, *Brit. Y.B.*, 1925, 159. KAECKENBEECK, ibid. 1936, 1. NIBOYET, 40 *Rec.* (1932 II), 157.

CHAPTER III

HISTORICAL SURVEY

I. ROMAN LAW

PRIVATE International Law in our epoch is national law, and its sources are statutes, custom, and precedents. It was not so in its infancy. It started as a super-national law and its source was legal science.

Its origin is to be found neither in the writings of the great Roman jurists from Mucius Scaevola to Modestin nor in the Byzantine law of the sixth century. The *Corpus iuris civilis*—which either answers, or suggests an answer to practically every conceivable legal question—says next to nothing on the subject of the application of foreign laws. Justinian, in dealing with the different kinds of law, twice repeats the didactic passage from Gaius' Institutes that all peoples governed by laws and custom use partly their own law and partly the common law of mankind; the former, the *ius proprium civitatis*, he calls *ius civile*, as opposed to the latter, the *ius gentium*.[1] But neither Gaius nor Justinian indicates whether under any circumstances a Roman court or a *praeses provinciae* would apply that foreign law, nor do they explain whether *ius gentium* is used only to fill in the gaps of the foreign *ius civile* or whether conversely the primary law is the *ius gentium*, and *ius civile* merely supplementary. Most of the passages in the Corpus iuris which are usually quoted by medieval writers have nothing whatever to do with the determination of the applicable law, but deal with the jurisdiction of the *praeses provinciae*, the *duumviri*, and other officials, or with the distribution of powers between two guardians, the activity of each being limited to a particular territorial area, and the like.[2] When in some places the Digest states that certain points are to be decided by the *mos* or *consuetudo regionis* or *loci* or *provinciae*[3] that does not imply a

[1] *Gai Inst.* i. 1. *Iust. Inst.* i. 2. 1 and *Dig.* i. 1. 1. 4.
[2] Cf. e.g. *Dig.* 26. 5. 1. 2; 26. 5. 27; 26. 7. 47; 2. *Cod.* 8. 48 (49). 1.
[3] Cf. *Dig.* 33. 1. 21. pr.; 26. 7. 7. 10; 30. 39. 1; 17. 1. 10. 3; 25. 4. 1. 15; 2. 12. 4; 26. 7. 32. 6.

reference to any customary 'law', but only to factual customs, local usages which the judge takes into account in order to fill gaps in contracts and wills. Moreover, the sole point of interest, i.e. the question which of two conflicting local customs is to predominate, is mentioned in one passage only. In *Dig.* 21. 2. 6 it is said that, if a piece of land has been sold, the question whether and how the seller should *cavere pro evictione* must be answered according to the custom of the place where the contract was made. It would be a mistake to derive from a passage like this a general rule to the effect that a sale of immovables is governed by the *lex loci actus*, and not by the *lex situs*.[1] From sources outside Roman Law books it seems that in questions of liberty and serfdom, of manumission, of marriage and matrimonial property, of *patria potestas*, guardianship, and inheritance the *lex originis* of the person in question was applied in Roman courts. But no Roman jurist even mentions this practice. This complete silence may be due to the fact that private international law can only establish itself where respect is shown for foreign law, where there is an atmosphere of equality such as pervaded legal thinking in the Italian city-states from the twelfth century onwards. Roman jurists were very far from entertaining this conception. Their justifiable admiration for their own law may have induced in many of them such a contempt for all foreign law, including the Greek, that it never even occurred to them to set up rules for the application of such inferior productions. Cicero may have expressed the common feeling of all educated Romans of his time when, in comparing Roman law with that of Lycurgus, Draco, and Solon, he exclaims, 'incredibile est quam sit omne ius civile praeter hoc nostrum inconditum ac paene ridiculum'.[2]

[1] However, legal writers from the Middle Ages to the eighteenth century quoted this passage, time and again, to support their doctrine that the *locus actus* was decisive for the construction to be put on contracts.

[2] Cicero, *De oratore* i. 44. 197.

BIBLIOGRAPHY

L. MITTEIS, *Reichsrecht und Volksrecht* (1891), 102; H. LEWALD, *Conflits de lois dans le monde grec et romain, Archeion idiotikou dikaiou* 13 (1946).

2. FROM THE SIXTH TO THE ELEVENTH CENTURY

No theory of Private International Law was developed **18. The** under the Barbarian laws. Wherever a person went he **domain of the** carried the law of his origin with him;[1] thus the Salian **personal** would live under Salic law, the Saxon under Saxon law, **law of origin** and so on. This became a universal principle. In countries with a mixed population, such as Italy, it was the custom to designate in contractual instruments the law under which the contracting parties lived. The seller, for example, is designated as one 'qui profitetur se lege salica vivere'. In judicial proceedings, too, the judge might ask the plaintiff or the defendant *qua lege vivis?*[2] and a Royal Ordinance of the end of the eighth century exhorts the *missi dominici*[3] to ask the litigants 'quale habeant legem ex natione'.[4] Sometimes the parties seem to have been at liberty to state, not the law under which they lived, but the law under which they wished to live. This is the first deviation from the principle of the personal *lex originis*, the first example of a choice of law by the contracting parties.[5] In the Frankish Empire the ordinances promulgated by the King—the *Capitularia*—applied to the whole of his Empire; they were territorial in character, not personal.[6]

From the tenth century onwards, at least in France and Germany, the old 'personal' laws of the various peoples, the Salians, the Ripuarians, the Burgundians, and so on, sank into oblivion and the law of the country replaced the law of the person.

3. THE STATUTE THEORY (OR THEORIES)

Private International Law was a product of the Italian **19. The** universities of the thirteenth century. The law of the **beginning. Master** Italian city-states—Genoa, Pisa, Milan, Bologna, Venice, **Aldric** Florence, Parma, Siena, Amalfi, and others—was contained in 'statutes'. A *statutum* was in the main a declara-

---

[1] The *lex Ripuaria*, c. 31 § 3, speaks of the 'lex loci ubi natus fuit'.
[2] Brunner, *Deutsche Rechtsgeschichte* i (2nd ed.), p. 396.
[3] i.e. royal administrative supervisors and judges of assizes (on circuit).
[4] Brunner, loc. cit. 398, n. 72.
[5] Meijers, *Histoire des principes*, p. 17.
[6] Brunner, loc. cit. 411, 548.

tory restatement of older customary law of the city and its commercial communities—'statutum est arbitraria mundi norma que a vulgari hominum consuetudine procedit', according to a definition by Buoncampagni about 1215;[1] but many statutes also embodied new legal rules. Commercial intercourse between the various cities, and between Italy on the one hand and Syria, Arabia, Spain, and Southern France on the other, called for rules governing the choice of the applicable legal system. It seems that at first all the judges confined themselves to applying the law of their own cities. This practice was thought to be justified partly by a passage in the Digest (which says nothing of the kind)[2] and partly by the idea that parties in choosing their judge implicitly choose his legal system: 'iudicem illum eligendo videntur eligere statuta et consuetudines suas', as Iacobus Balduini formulated it.[3] As the numerous treaties concluded between the various cities never dealt with the question of the choice of law, the first problem was not that of the applicable law but of determining which judge had jurisdiction. The real problem of private international law was raised, however, in the works of the Glossators. According to Neumeyer's careful studies[4] the first to bring up this problem was a Magister ALDRICUS, who discussed it at the end of the twelfth century. He asked very precisely, 'Quaeritur si homines diversarum provinciarum quae diversas habent consuetudines sub uno eodemque iudice litigant, utram earum ... iudex sequi debeat'. Aldric's answer was unsatisfactory and ambiguous: the judge should apply that law which seems to him the better and more useful, 'potior et utilior'; 'debet enim iudicare secundum quod melius ei visum fuerit'. It is doubtful whether the better and more useful law means the law which has the most real connexion with the subject of litigation,[5] or whether Master Aldric was referring to the quality of the law itself. The second answer would seem the more probable.

[1] Levin Goldschmidt, *Universalgeschichte des Handelsrechts,* i (1891), p. 151, n. 29.
[2] *Dig.* 4. 8. 21, § 10.   [3] Cf. Neumeyer, ii, p. 58 et seq.
[4] Neumeyer, ii, p. 66 et seq.
[5] That is what Gutzwiller, *Le développement historique,* p. 14 et seq., believes.

One principle of Private International Law seems to have been fully developed by the beginning of the thirteenth century, viz. the rule that laws imposed by any prince or city are binding only on subjects of that prince or city: *Imperator non imposuit legem nisi suis subditis. Subditos tantum ligat consuetudo cuiusque civitatis.*[1] About the same time a distinction—one of the most essential in Private International Law—began to be drawn between substantive law (*consuetudo ad litem decidendam*) and law of procedure (*consuetudo ad litis ordinationem introducta*). Questions of procedure were decided according to the law of the forum, questions of substance according to the law of the place *ubi contractum est.*[2] This distinction, which was inaugurated by Jacobus Balduini, was disapproved by many Italian writers of the time but accepted by such eminent French jurists as James of Révigny (*d.* 1296) and Peter of Belleperche (*d.* 1308),[3] and this may have contributed to its final acceptance in Italy. Such was the inception of the rule *locus regit actum* which was destined to be adopted all over the world. The rule was not then restricted to questions of form, as it now is in many countries; it governed also the substantive conditions for the validity of any act and its effects. The narrower rule *locus regit formam actus* seems to be of French origin.[4] Another early rule concerns property: the *lex situs* is decisive, and this was first applied both to immovables and to those movables which by their origin belong to the territory, the *res in territorio natae.*

Then came BARTOLUS DE SAXOFERRATO, who in spite of a short life (1314–57) had a greater influence on the subsequent fate of Roman law in Europe than any other thinker. It may be that his merits in the field of private international law have been slightly over-estimated, since his forerunners had done more than merely prepare the way for him.[5] But it was he who laid bare all the manifold

20. Bartolus. The different kinds of statutes

---

[1] See Meijers, loc. cit., p. 52.

[2] The rule of the *lex loci actus* was partly derived from *Dig.* 21. 2. 6 (cf. *supra,* s. 17, p. 20) and from *Dig.* 50. 17. 34 (which says nothing at all on the subject).

[3] Meijers, pp. 53, 54.

[4] William of Cuneo, fourteenth century. Cf. Meijers, p. 58.

[5] Meijers, p. 60 et seq. The text of Bartolus' writings on private international

potentialities inherent in private international law and broke new trails in regard both to individual problems and to the method of their solution. For nearly five centuries jurists followed his way of dealing with the subject. He did not ask, What legal system applies to a given set of facts?, but, What groups of relationship fall under a given rule of law? Thus his starting-point was the grouping not of legal relationships between persons, but of the rules of law existing in any given country, such as those contained in the statutes of the various Italian city-states. Similarly in France, Holland, and Germany the school of Bartolus attempted to classify the numerous provincial and local customs (*coutumes*) and later in Germany the enormous bulk of laws and ordinances promulgated by more than 1800 'reigning' sovereigns and sovereign cities. A distinction was drawn between statutes—or rather statutory and customary rules—concerned with persons (*statuta personalia*) and those relating to things (*statuta realia*). Personal statutes governed the legal status of persons having their domicile or their origin[1] in the country where the statute was in force. Real statutes dealt with all rights to immovables situate in that country. In regard to movables the school of the Statute Theory accepted the view expressed in Brittany at the beginning of the fourteenth century:[2] 'les meubles suivent la personne, mobilia personam sequuntur';[3] thus the statutes in any country relating to movables were applicable to all movables belonging to, or in the possession of, subjects of that country. Bartolus improved on the theory by setting up a third group of rules. These concern the form of contracts and their immediate, natural effects, as opposed to those resulting from a breach of contract. These rules,

---

law was reprinted in *Böhm's Z.* 4, pp. 260, 340, 446. There, too, is to be found what Bartolus' great pupil Baldus de Ubaldis (1327–1400) has written on the subject; see p. 455 et seq. On Baldus see: Meijers, 35 *Rev. Crit.* 205 et seq. and Meijers' edition of Baldus' *Repetitio super lege Cunctos populos* (Cod. 1. 1. 1.), 1939.

[1] The connexion between origin and domicile still obtains in the English conception of a domicile of origin. Cf. *infra*, ss. 94, 100.

[2] Meijers, pp. 45, 96, has shown that the rule was not invented by Baldus but is probably of French origin.

[3] Accursius' much earlier glossa contained the curious formula *mobilia ossibus inhaerent*, but there it referred to incorporeal things only. Cf. Meijers, pp. 97, 98.

which were later called *statuta mixta*, applied to all contracts concluded within the country where the statute was
in force, while rules on the effects of breaches of contract
were to apply to all contracts to be performed in the
country of the statute. The notion of *statuta mixta*, however, lacked precision, and in later periods it was often
used to denote rules which concern both persons and
things.[1]

The greatest difficulty in the application of the Statute
Theory lay in deciding whether a given rule was personal
or real in character. This difficulty became particularly
apparent in respect of the so-called English custom, the
consuetudo Angliae, that is, the law of primogeniture.
Bartolus himself saw no other way of solving this particular problem than by a very crude literal interpretation.
He argued that the solution depended on the order of the
words in the statute. If the statute read 'primogenitus
succedat in immobilia', then *primogenitus* was the governing word and the statute therefore personal, whereas if the
text ran 'bona decedentium veniant in primogenitum',
then the emphasis was on *bona* and the statute was 'real'.
During five centuries this solution was ridiculed. Bertrand
d'Argentré, the great scholar of Brittany, even wrote:
'pudeat pueros talia aut sentire aut docere', thus condemn-
ing a greater scholar than himself merely for not having
broken away from the narrow methods of his epoch.[2]

Bartolus and his followers, just as the glossators had
done, all discussed the problems of private international
law with reference to the same passage of the *Corpus iuris
civilis*, viz. the first words of the *Codex*, which at that time
were read as follows: 'Cunctos populos quos clementiae
nostrae regit imperium.'[3] (*Cod.* I, 1 *de S. Trinitate*, c. 1.)
This passage afforded an opportunity for explaining that
a person who was not subject to a Sovereign's 'mild rule'
was not amenable to any law of his. For many a century
the passage quoted remained the *locus ordinarius* of the
doctrines on conflict of laws, 'par singerie et indiscrète

21. The consuetudo Angliae

22. The locus ordinarius

---

[1] Savigny, *System*, viii, p. 122. (Guthrie's translation, p. 141.)
[2] On this see Lainé, i, p. 154 et seq.
[3] Better version: *temperamentum*.

imitation', as the French jurist Gui Coquille called it, thus adopting the contemptuous manner in which learned authors—of the sixteenth century—liked to refer to each other. Actually such conservatism where a purely systematic point is in question accords with the typically juristic manner in which the Theory of Statutes was evolved: though all that the great Italians expounded was new and nothing was derived from Roman law, yet they pretended that they only developed rules latent in the *Corpus iuris*.[1] Every one of their ideas had to be supported by passages from the *Codex*, the *Digest*, or the *Corpus iuris canonici*,[2] which in actual fact did nothing to strengthen them.

23. The French school of the sixteenth century

In the sixteenth century it fell to the French jurists further to develop the Italian Statute Theory. Eminent amongst them was CHARLES DUMOULIN (MOLINAEUS).[3] It was he who was primarily responsible for the doctrine that the contracting parties could choose the law that was to govern their agreement.

BERTRAND D'ARGENTRÉ (1519–90), while retaining the Statute Theory, deliberately turned aside from the doctrines of the Italians and of Dumoulin. His feudalist views led him to pronounce the opinion that whenever there was any doubt as to whether a statutory rule was personal or real, or wherever a rule was partly real and partly personal it was to be deemed real. *Omnia statuta in dubio realia*. According to him personal statutes are only those which deal with questions of status or capacity or with property in chattels (he does not discuss contracts and torts). His views on the law of succession became particularly important. There was an old controversy as to whether it followed from the doctrine of 'universal succession' as developed in Roman law that succession is governed by one and only one law, or whether it is con-

[1] In this the Italians can be compared with English judges who create new law under the guise of showing merely what is already law.

[2] Meijers, loc. cit., p. 84.

[3] He lived from 1500 till 1566. It may be mentioned that his pre-eminence was not restricted to private international law. His commentary on the Paris custom, his insistence on the desirability of making a common code for the whole of France, and his money doctrine—which possibly is the basis of the modern nominalistic theory of money—are his main contributions to legal science.

sistent with that doctrine that if a person leaves immovables
in various countries the laws of the countries concerned
are to be applied respectively to the immovables therein
situated. True to his feudalistic point of view d'Argentré
decided in the latter sense, and this decision has been
adopted not only by English and Anglo-American law—
which have not accepted the Roman idea of universal
succession—but even in many countries which in respect
of their internal law follow the Roman principle, such as
France, Belgium, Austria.

D'Argentré's doctrine[1] had its first success not in
France, but in the Netherlands. The Dutch authors modified it by bringing in the conception of *sovereignty*. Besides
many other writers, such as Nicolaus Burgundus (*d.* 1649),
Christian Rodenburgh (*d.* 1668), and Paul Voet (*d.* 1677),[2]
there are two in particular who helped to build up the
new doctrine: the Frisian ULRIC HUBER (1636–94) and
Paul Voet's son John (1647–1714).[3] Huber in his short
article *De conflictu legum diversarum in diversis imperiis*[4]
laid down three principles: (1) The laws of every state
operate within the territorial limits of such state and are
binding on all its subjects but not beyond (those limits);
(2) Subjects of a state are all those who are found within
the limits of its territory, whether they reside there permanently or whether their presence there is only temporary; (3) The sovereigns of the states act by comity
(*comiter agunt*) to the effect that the laws of every people
after having been applied within the limits of their own
country retain their force everywhere; provided that the
powers or rights of another sovereign or of his citizens
are not thereby prejudiced.

The first two of these principles embody the doctrine
of pure territoriality; according to strict law every legal
rule is applicable only within the country where it is in
force. Under the third rule an extra-territorial effect may
be obtained through the application of *comitas gentium*.

24. The
Dutch
doctrine;
Huber and
John Voet

---

[1] See Barbey, 'Le sort du système de d'Argentré', *Rev. historique d. droit
franç*, 1940/41, 397.
[2] Kollewijn, loc. cit., pp. 16, 52, 78.   [3] Kollewijn, pp. 109, 131.
[4] See on Huber: Lorenzen, *Selected Articles*, 136–80 (with a reprint of H.'s
article). Cf. also Davies, 18, *Br. Y.B.*, 49

JOHN VOET expressed similar views; he stressed particularly that the principle of territoriality of laws applies even if, in the traditional terminology, the statute is not a 'real' but a 'personal' or a 'mixed' statute.

At first sight this would appear to contain a retrograde step, a reversion to the law as it stood before Master Aldric's time, when every judge was bound to apply exclusively the internal law of his country. But that would be a mistaken view. What the Dutch school intended to do was to establish the following rule on conflict of laws. Every state is at liberty to lay down its conflict rules at its own discretion. It may instruct the judges of its territory to apply no foreign law at all, or again to apply certain rules under conditions which the state fixes. The freedom of choice of the state is in no way hampered by rules of inter-state law; the Dutch writers derive this from the concept of sovereignty (*imperium*). No state will, however, make use of its right to the extent of choosing the law arbitrarily. Up to this point legal thinking of the twentieth century in all countries of the world unreservedly follows the Dutch doctrine: all private international law is national law; it is for the sovereign of each country to determine under what conditions his judges shall apply foreign laws, and there are no rules of public international law in existence which would bind him in this respect. The conception of *comitas* or *comitas gentium*, which nowadays means courteous and benevolent conduct based on reciprocity, was used by Dutch authors to designate the acts of a legislature not bound by superior orders (from a sovereign). *Comitas* was identical with *ratio legis*, with equity and utility and opposed to something *incongruum et iniquum*.[1]

25. Germany and France in the seventeenth and eighteenth centuries

The Dutch doctrines influenced the German jurists of the seventeenth and eighteenth centuries, such as Henry de Cocceji (1644–1719) and John Nicholas Hert (1652–1710); they form, as will be seen later, one of the scientific foundations of English law, and, united to the doctrines of the French statutists, they helped to bring about a new development in France, where in the eighteenth century

---

[1] Thus v. d. Keessel; see Meijers, 35 *Rev. crit.* 215; Meijers, *Tractatus Duo*, p. xii. Differing Story's view; see Lorenzen, *Select. Articles*, 158.

three outstanding practitioners, the advocates L. Froland
(*d.* 1746) and Boullenois (*d.* 1762) 'and the president of
the Parliament of Burgundy, Bouhier (*d.* 1746), without
evolving fundamentally new ideas, used their knowledge
of legal practice to advance the treatment of conflicts of
laws in numerous points of detail.

This book will not deal in detail with the history of the 26. Sum-
statute theory in Italy, France, Holland, and Germany. ^{mary}
It should, however, be clearly understood that the so-called
statute 'theory' was not in fact 'one' theory with a single
definite content. It may seem so to us who regard it from
our present-day standpoint; just as a climber, from the
summit of a mountain, fails to see in the valley below all
its undulations, all its by-ways and thickets. In truth,
there are the greatest possible differences between one
'statutist' and another, differences in terminology,[1] in
method, in the questions they raise, and in the answers
they give. Thus the scholastic method of the fourteenth
century was an alien outmoded instrument in the hands
of the sixteenth-century jurists. Thus also the political
opinions of jurists and contemporary events brought about
many modifications in the theory.[2] Another factor was
the development of public international law; Grotius'
doctrines in particular contributed largely to the form of
the theory adopted in Holland. And finally philosophic
conceptions, such as the doctrine of the Law of Nature,
could not fail to influence the statute theory in their sweep
across Europe. D'Argentré's comment on the Italian
school, 'Incerti magistri incertiores lectores dimittunt',
applies equally to himself and his school. Two things,
however, are common to all statutists, from Bartolus down
to the nineteenth century:

1. They all examine the individual *legal rule* itself and
consider the question whether it is restricted in its application to the state which enacted it, or whether it is equally
valid extra-territorially.

---

[1] Concerning the term *statuta mixta* see *supra*, s. 20 *in fin.*

[2] Dumoulin, for example, fought for monarchy and against feudalism,
ecclesiastical jurisdiction, and the ecclesiastical ban on lending money at interest.
D'Argentré, the commentator of the *Coutume* of Brittany, struggled to preserve
the privileges of nobility.

2. They all try to evolve principles which are to apply super-nationally, super-provincially, super-locally.

BIBLIOGRAPHY

CATELLANI, *Il diritto internazionale privato e i suoi recenti progressi* (2nd ed.), 2 vols. 1895, 1902. GUTZWILLER, 'Le développement historique du droit inter-nat. privé', 29 *Rec.* (1929 IV), 291. LAINÉ, *Introduction au droit international privé contenant une étude historique et critique de la théorie des statuts*, 2 vols. 1888, 1892. K. NEUMEYER, *Die gemeinrechtliche Entwicklung des internationalen Privat-und Strafrechts bis Bartolus*, 2 vols. 1901, 1916. E. M. MEIJERS, *Bijdrage tot de Geschiedenis van het internat. Privaat-en Strafrecht in Frankrijk en de Neder-landen*, 1914. MEIJERS, 'Histoire des principes fondamentaux du droit int. pr', 49 *Rec.* (1934 III), 574. MEIJERS, 35 *Rev. Crit.* (1946), 203. MEIJERS, *Tractatus Baldi et van der Keessel de vi et potestate statutorum*, Haarlem 1939. KOLLEWIJN, *Geschiedenis van de nederlandse wetenschap van het internat. priv. r.*, 1937. NIBOYET, *Traité* III, 40 et seq. ARMINJON I, 71–140.

4. ENGLISH LAW TO THE MIDDLE OF THE EIGHTEENTH CENTURY

27. Early English law

Under English law the problem of conflict of laws was non-existent until the end of the seventeenth century. Every court applied its own laws exclusively. The administration by English courts of the law merchant was no exception to this rule, at least from the time when the law merchant had become part of English common law.[1] Instead of conflicts of laws only 'conflicts of jurisdictions'[2] were to be found in this country: the issue was not: which law has the court to apply to a given case? but: which court has competence to adjudicate upon the case?

The first approach to the application of foreign law was the recognition of judgments of foreign courts based on foreign law. As early as 1607[3] it was held by English courts that they were bound to give effect to foreign judgments under the rules of the law of nations or of international comity. 'It is against the law of nations', pronounced Lord Nottingham in *Cottington's Case*,[4] 'not to give credit to the judgments and sentences of foreign countries. For what right hath one Kingdom to reverse

---

[1] A. N. Sack, in *Law, A Century of Progress*, 1937 (New York), iii. 342, 375–8; G. C. Cheshire, 36–42.
[2] Sack, ibid. 356.
[3] *Wiers Case*, I Rolle Abridgmt. 530, 12 (Sack, 440, n. 292).
[4] [1678] 2 Swans. 326 (Sack, 383, 384).

the judgment of another? And what confusion would
follow in Christendom if they should serve us so abroad,
and give no credit to our sentences?'

From the end of the seventeenth century English courts,
without declining jurisdiction, sometimes refused to apply
English law and replaced it by the *lex loci actus*[1] or the
lex situs.[2] In 1752 an eminent judge, Sir E. Simpson,[3]
exclaimed, 'Why may not this court *take notice*[4] of foreign
laws, there being nothing illegal in doing it?' And in 1760
Lord Mansfield declared that the 'general rule' according
to which 'the place where the contract is made is decisive'
is 'established *ex comitate et iure gentium*', and that 'this
rule admits of an exception where the parties had a view
to a different kingdom'.[5] The English rules on conflict
of laws, which have been developed since the middle of the
eighteenth century, appear to be only slightly influenced
by the doctrines of the statutists, apart from the theories
of the famous Dutch writers.

5. THE FIRST ATTEMPTS AT CODIFICATION
(1756–1811)

The emphasis which the Dutch school and its followers
laid on the sovereignty of the state as the source of all
rules on conflict of laws prompted continental legislators
from the middle of the eighteenth century to establish
such rules and incorporate them in their codes of civil law.

28. The Bavarian and the Prussian codes

The first of these codes was the Bavarian code, the
Codex Maximilianeus Bavaricus of 1756, which reproduced
some general principles laid down by the statute theories.
It is remarkable for one thing only, viz. that it declines
to accept the rule that movables follow the person, and

---

[1] See the cases *Blankard* v. *Galdy* (1693), 2 Salk. 411; *Dungannon* v. *Hackett*
(1702) I Eq. Cases Abridgmt. 289. See Sack, loc. cit. 387.

[2] See the case *Smith* v. *Brown & Cooper* (1706), 2 Salk. 666: sale concluded in
England of a slave who was in Virginia; under the law of Virginia the contract
was valid, not so under English law.

[3] In *Scrimshire* v. *Scrimshire*, [1752] 2 Hagg. Con. 395, 416.

[4] The judge was careful not to speak of 'application' of foreign law or
'adjudicating' under foreign law.

[5] *Robinson* v. *Bland*, 2 Burrow 1077.

replaces it by the provision that the *lex situs* shall prevail 'without any distinction between immovables and movables and between corporeal and incorporeal things'.[1]

The *Prussian General Code* of 1794 was much more original and explicit. True, it adopted many rules of the statute theoreticians and left many problems unsolved, particularly those concerned with the substantial validity and the effects of contracts. But it developed some remarkable rules of its own. An example is furnished by the way in which the principle of *res magis valeat quam pereat*[2] was applied to private international law. Firstly, if a person has two domiciles (which is possible under many continental laws),[3] that domicile is decisive under the law of which the contract or other act in question is valid. Secondly, if a person domiciled abroad concludes a contract within Prussian territory relating to chattels situate there, and if he is capable so to contract under the law of his domicile and not under the *lex loci actus*, or vice versa, then the law under which the contract is valid is to be applied—a very sound idea contributing both to the *favor negotii* and to the protection of commercial intercourse.

29. The French and the Austrian codes More important for the development of private international law was the *French Civil Code* of 1804. It contains only one single article on the subject. This article, far from being exhaustive, is not even quite unambiguous. But it embodies one far-reaching new rule: it replaces the law of the domicile of a person by the law of his nationality.[4]

The last great code of the beginning of the nineteenth century was the *Austrian Civil Code* of 1811; it adopted the French principle of nationality as governing personal status and capacity.[5] Apart from this its scanty rules on private international law are not remarkable.

[1] *Cod. Maximil.* i. 2, § 17.

[2] Or, to use the phrase of Roman law, *ut res in tuto sit* (*Dig.* 45. 1. 80).

[3] See *infra*, s. 99.

[4] See *infra*, s. 95. On French conflict rules on the eve of the civil code: Delaume, 36 *Rev. crit.* (1947), 370 et seq.; Niboyet, *Traité*, iii. 110 et seq.

[5] Cf. on this point Steinlechner and Strisower in the *Festschrift zur Jahrhundertfeier des österreichischen Gesetzbuchs*, 1911, ii, pp. 55, 97.

6. THE DOCTRINES OF THE NINETEENTH CENTURY

In continental jurisprudence it came to be recognized **30. Intro-**
more and more clearly that the attempt made in the **duction**
statute theories to solve all questions of private international law on the basis of a few general principles had
failed. It became apparent that most of the particular
rules derived from them were equivocal and gave rise to
violent controversies. Moreover, as the doctrines of the
school of Natural Law had been the main source of private
international law in the seventeenth and eighteenth centuries, most of the rules faded away when this school of
thought disappeared.

Private international law owes its development during
the nineteenth century mainly to three men, an American
judge, a German professor, and an Italian statesman.

JOSEPH STORY,[1] the American, published his famous **31. Story**
Commentaries on the Conflict of Laws in 1834. By de-
voting himself to the study of precedents and by refusing
to be prejudiced by pseudo-scientific axioms he showed
European lawyers the superiority of his method of interpreting and expounding the law as it is administered. In
Europe continental writers of that time were not accustomed to proceed in this way. Books on conflicts of laws,
or, for that matter, on any other legal subject, abounded
in quotations from doctrines which the author criticized
or approved, but references to judicial decisions were few
and far between. This was partly due to the influence
of the law of nature, partly to a certain contempt for court
judgments often found in learned men of that epoch.[2]
Story did not build his book entirely on English and
American decisions; he also made use of the works of
continental writers, such as Ulric Huber, Voet, father
and son, and other Dutch authors, as well as some French
writers of the eighteenth century. From them he took the
leading principles that the rules on conflict of laws are

---

[1] 1779 to 1845. See on Story: Lorenzen, *Select. Articles*, 181 et seq.

[2] Cf. for example, what in 1810 an eminent legal writer, Anselm Feuerbach,
wrote in his text-book on criminal law, p. ix: 'The author thinks that he has
acted wisely in not entirely passing over judicial decisions much though he hates
that cushion of literary indolence, that support of blind arbitrariness.'

part of the national law and that the application of foreign law is a matter of comity—principles he handed on to English lawyers. His numerous quotations from older authors were, so to speak, ornamental, just as passages of the *Corpus iuris* quoted by the post-glossators in order to support their doctrines had been ornamental. As a whole Story was rather sceptical of the value of what his precursors had written. He thought their 'theoretical distinctions served little other purpose than to provoke idle discussions' and that their 'metaphysic subtleties perplex if they do not confound the inquirer'. Story's way of approaching the issues was the reverse of that familiar to continental scholars. He avoided establishing principles of too general a character; his method was rather inductive than deductive. His common sense and his practical turn of mind were such as to earn for his work the admiration not only of American lawyers—a great many of his views have been adopted by American law and are now firmly established in the legal practice of the American courts[1]— but also that of English jurists and judges. As Cheshire says very aptly, 'he brought about what can only be described as the renaissance of the subject'.[2] His worth was acknowledged even by continental writers, including J. J. C. Foelix,[3] who in 1843 published a treatise on conflict of laws based entirely on Story's doctrines, and Savigny.

32. von Savigny

In 1849 FRIEDRICH CARL VON SAVIGNY published the eighth volume of his system of modern Roman law, which deals with Private International Law. This work, though written by a septuagenarian, revealed the unbroken creative power of his genius. It did more for the development of the law—not only in Germany—than any other work devoted to law as it stands. To some extent the ground had been cleared for him. C. G. VON WÄCHTER, who has rightly been called one of the greatest German jurists of all time,[4] had some years before torn the statute theory

---

[1] For example, the rule that the capacity of contracting parties is governed not by the law of the domicile but by that of the *locus actus*.

[2] Cheshire, 56.

[3] On Foelix see: de Lapradelle 10 *Nouv. Rev.* (1943), 16 et seq.

[4] E. Landsberg, *Geschichte der deutschen Rechtswissenschaft*, iii. 2, 386 (1910).

to pieces and swept up its ruins.[1] Then Story's method, his refusal to build a legal system on theories of natural law, the 'rich collection of materials'[2] which his book contains, made a great impression on the founder of the continental Historical School and had a certain influence on his work. Savigny's starting-point, however, was opposed to both Wächter's and Story's views. Wächter had seriously warned legal thinkers not to confound the judicial and the legislative standpoint. Savigny replied to that: 'What he (i.e. Wächter) assigns to the legislative standpoint certainly falls in a great measure within the judicial in a *matter which legislation has left very much to scientific development*.'[3] This observation is of the utmost importance for the setting up of legal rules in a branch of law which in Savigny's time was, and in this country still is, incomplete and unsettled. Wächter thought that the incompleteness of the rules on conflict of laws could be cured simply by a maxim that the court ought to fill in gaps by applying its own (internal) law.[4] Savigny firmly rejected this view. On the other hand, he disapproved equally of Story's way out of the difficulties, viz. the reference to comity between states.

Savigny started from the conception that it is 'expedient' that in cases containing a foreign element 'the same legal relations have to expect the same decision whether the judgment be pronounced in this state or in that'. Therefore, in his view, it is essential to bear in mind the existence of 'an *international community of nations having intercourse with one another*'. And rightly he adds the famous words: 'This view has in the course of time always obtained wider recognition, under the influence of a common Christian morality and of the real advantage which results from it to all concerned.'[5] Thus it is not only and not even primarily the respect due from one sovereign state to other sovereign states on which the application of foreign

[1] In four articles in the *Archiv für civilistische Praxis*, vol. 24, 25 (1841, 1842).
[2] Savigny, loc. cit. Preface, p. iv.
[3] Savigny, loc. cit., p. 71, note g (in Guthrie's translation).
[4] Wächter, loc. cit. 24, p. 265 et seq.
[5] Savigny (Guthrie), 68, 69.

law is based. Its true basis is rather the benefit it brings
'to all concerned', i.e. both states and individuals. This is
one of the principal distinctions between Savigny's opinion
and that of the Dutch writers and Story.

Savigny also broke new ground in posing the initial
question of private international law. He no longer asked
as the statute theoreticians ('the statutists') had done, what
is the nature of this or that legal rule? Is it concerned with
persons, things, or acts? Instead, he set out to classify
legal relationships, and it was his aim 'to ascertain for
every legal relation that law to which, in its proper nature,
it belongs or is subject',[1] and thus to find out where a
relationship has 'its seat', as he calls it.[2] He performed this
task by examining nearly every type of legal relationship
known to continental laws of Roman origin and assigning
to it the place to which it 'belongs'. Legal relations foreign
to Roman law or to modern laws based on Roman law,
such as trusts or other equitable institutions of English
law, were not included in his study, though he was well
acquainted with Story's work.

The principles and most of the particular rules established by Savigny have been adopted by German judicial
practice and have thus become common German law. It
even happened that some of the older statutory rules
(with unambiguous provisions incompatible with Savigny's
views) were distorted so as to allow of their interpretation
in accordance with Savigny's opinions.[3] Outside Germany
Savigny's doctrines have largely influenced Austrian,

---

[1] The value of this change may perhaps have been overrated.

[2] Savigny (Guthrie), 70, 133.

[3] An example of how lawyers wrenched from the clear text of the Prussian
Code of 1794 a meaning it was never intended to have may be seen in connexion
with ss. 28 and 32 of the Introduction to the Code. There it is said that the law
of the domicile governs the 'movable property' (*bewegliches Vermögen*) of a
person and the law of the situs his immovable property. The courts and the
doctrine of the nineteenth century have altered the clear sense of these provisions;
the Code's rule about movable property was applied only to the 'whole' of the
movable property, for example, of a deceased person, not to single movables,
while conversely the rule on immovable property was considered to govern
merely single immovables, but not the immovable property of a deceased as
a whole! Thus Savigny's rule was in effect substituted for the rule of the Prussian
Code. Cf. Eccius, *Preussisches Privatrecht*, i. 59, 66; Dernburg, *Preussisches
Privatrecht*, i. 53.

French,[1] Italian, and Greek law and legal literature. In England and the United States of America, particularly under the influence of Dicey and Westlake, Savigny became one of the highest authorities, second only to Story. His cool reasoning and the practical good sense shown in every individual suggestion that he made, the absence of all barren doctrinairism, the tranquil flow of his arguments—these could not fail to impress English lawyers and courts. Moreover, Savigny was a strong supporter of the principle prevailing in English law that the status of a person should be tested by his domicile and not by his nationality.

There has been and still is much opposition to his formula of the 'local seat' which has to be found for every relationship. It was stressed that this is pure metaphor and that it leads to juristic 'impressionism' (Niboyet). How-ever, it is not always possible for the jurist to argue without making use of metaphors, and a good metaphor often enables the reader to attain the mental attitude necessary to observe and weigh the phenomena he is studying. True, the word 'seat' is possibly too vague. It was a further step forward when Gierke, who in the main adopted Savigny's doctrines, replaced it by the term 'centre of gravity', and still more when Westlake, ignoring any territorial implications, simply spoke of the *law* with which a relationship 'is most closely connected'.[2] None of these phrases is entirely correct. But jurists are not mathematicians; they are often bound to operate with concepts that are less than absolutely clear-cut.[3] Naturally

[1] Particularly Valéry, Despagnet, and Bartin. French authors sometimes justified their admiration for Savigny by stating that they believed him to be of French stock. One eminent French scholar even thought that Savigny 'doit peut-être à cette origine le don de la clarté qui distingue ses ouvrages'.

[2] The connexion is not always a local one. Whether a person living in India is governed by Hindu or Muhammedan or English law does not depend on the place where he is resident. Further: it may happen that a contract is closely connected with English law though not with England. A French and a Scottish merchant living in China in a settlement mainly inhabited by Englishmen conclude a contract performable in China and subject it to English law, because this is usually applied in contracts of that kind by their English rivals; it is justifiable to say that English law is for economic reasons the law with which the contract is most closely connected. See *infra*, s. 402.

[3] Examples: 'Remoteness' of causation, 'effective control' as a test of possession.

it is frequently open to doubt where the 'seat', the 'centre of gravity' of a certain relationship is to be found, particularly in the case of contractual obligations and of *res in transitu*. Be that as it may, Savigny showed the way as far as one can do so by a general formula.

33.
Mancini

The third leader in Private International Law was PASQUALE STANISLAO MANCINI, the Neapolitan exile who had fled to Piedmont and who in January 1851 made his famous speech at the University of Turin on 'Nationality as Basis of the Law of Nations'.[1] In glowing words and with the southerner's fervent passion he defended the thesis that the 'rational basis' of (public) international law is not the state[2] but the nation and the *nazionalità*; components of nationality, he said, are the landscape of the country, the climate, the religion, the customs of life, the language, the race of the people, its historical traditions— all these create a spiritual unity through the common consciousness (*coscienza*) of nationality. The personality of the individual too is, according to Mancini, determined by his nationality only. Recognition of a personality is possible only by way of recognition of his nationality. This doctrine was far more than a juristic theory, and it certainly did not aim at establishing a basis for Private International Law. Nevertheless, it largely inspired Italian and French jurists and was made the foundation of a new, so-called Italian, theory of private international law, which was developed in Italy by Esperson and Fiore, in France by André Weiss, and in Belgium by Laurent. According to this theory there are in every legal system two kinds of rules, those created in the interest of private individuals, and those for the protection of public order, *ordine pubblico*. Rules of the former group are thought to be applicable to all persons who belong to the country by their nationality (not by their domicile), wherever they are;[3] and every state is bound not by mere comity but by

[1] Mancini's speech is reprinted in his *Diritto internazionale, Prelezioni*, 1873, p. 5 et seq.; cf. particularly pp. 27, 35 et seq.

[2] Italy at that time was not yet a 'state'.

[3] The adherents of this doctrine are able to cite in its support Montesquieu's *Esprit des lois*, i. 3, § 14. He, too, knew that there is a close relation between the laws of a country on the one hand, and religion, customs of living, climate,

international law to respect this and consequently to apply
to aliens the law of their own country. This theory has
not been adopted by international law, and the English
rule that it is the domicile and not the nationality that
matters has never been regarded as a violation of principles
of international law. The rules of the other group, those
relating to public order, have territorial effect; they are
binding both on the state's own nationals and on aliens
as long as they are present in the country; they have no
effect beyond the limits of the country even with regard
to its nationals. Savigny, too, had recognized that every
legal system contains some rules that in the public interest
have to be applied within the territory, whether the persons
concerned are or are not domiciled in that country; but
Savigny treated rules of this kind as anomalous, as exceptions to the principles of private international law. Mancini
and his school consider the territoriality of all rules on
public policy as one of the two fundamental principles of
that part of the law. The Italian school finally added to
the two 'principles' of 'nationality and sovereignty' a third,
the 'principle of liberty', meaning the freedom of contracting parties to choose the law which is to govern their
contract.

The influence of the Italian school on continental law
was considerable. In the first place it broadened the conception of *ordre public*, particularly in France and Belgium,[1]
and it seems secondly to have contributed to the substitution by some modern codes of the national law for the
law of the domicile. True, the French and the Austrian
civil codes had, as we have seen, introduced the national
law in place of the *lex domicilii* long before Mancini. But
the Italian Code of 1865, which was possibly influenced
by ideas such as Mancini had developed,[2] went farther
than the French Code in declaring the national law
decisive, first for all questions of succession, even in

temperament, and other natural qualities of a people or a country on the other;
for example, in respect of the rules on majority and puberty, which may be
based on experience regarding the physical maturity of men and women.

[1] Cf. *infra*, s. 160.

[2] This is not beyond doubt. See Baron de Nolde, *La codification du droit
international privé* (1936), p. 24 et seq.

respect of immovables situate abroad; and secondly, for contracts where both contracting parties are nationals of the same foreign state.[1] On English and American law the Italian school had no influence at all. No wonder; its magniloquent pomposity, plainly manifest in the high-sounding terms 'nationality, sovereignty, and liberty', is most unlikely to appeal to cool, clear-headed thinkers.

Of much greater importance perhaps than his influence on Private International Law was Mancini's struggle (after 1866) for international agreement on the fundamental rules of Private International Law. He developed his programme in a Memorandum which he laid before the *Institut de Droit International* in 1874. He called it, 'On the Advantages of making binding on all States by means of one or more International Conventions a certain number of General Rules of Private International Law in order to secure the Uniform Solution of Conflicts between the various Civil and Penal Laws'. His ideas were received with enthusiasm and put into practice in Latin America (cf. *infra*, s. 42).

34. The attitude of modern jurists
In the last seventy or eighty years it has come to be recognized more and more that the coining of general formulae, often by deceptive methods, is not very helpful, and that Private International Law, like any other branch of private law, can only be culled from custom, statutes, precedents, and the requirements of the various human communities.

Occasionally, however, some isolated scholar reverts to the old practice, arguing that the principles he formulates are founded either on Public International Law, or on basic conceptions of law (legal philosophy). The two German scholars who took this course, Ernst Zitelmann and Ernst Frankenstein, have had no following.[2] Both

[1] *Disposizioni sulla pubbl.*, art. 8, 9. The same rules are to be found in the new Italian Civ. Code (1938, 1942); *Disposiz. sull' applicazione*, art. 15, 16.

[2] Against Zitelmann's attempt to construct a system of Private International Law on the basis of principles of Public International Law, rightly: German Supr. Court, *Offic. Coll.* 95, 165. Frankenstein even thinks that it is possible to establish 'axioms *a priori*' to the effect that the English, Danish, Norwegian, American rule connecting the status of persons with the law of their domicile constitutes a 'forced association (*gewaltsame Anknüpfung*) which in the eyes of the law is non-existent' (i, p. 34).

have made valuable contributions to the solution of particular problems, the value of which in no way depends on the truth of their axioms. More successful was the French jurist Antoine Pillet. His views were adopted by a number of younger lawyers, particularly by J. P. Niboyet, who, however, has done much to improve them by considerable modifications. Pillet's two leading ideas are the following: First, he considers it vital to make a sharp distinction between questions of conflict of laws, which in his opinion are those concerned with the acquisition of rights, and problems dealing with the protection of vested rights. It may be open to discussion whether such a distinction is useful, as the conception of vested rights lacks clarity and was extended by Pillet to all kinds of legal situations, such as powers, interests, and even disabilities.[1] Pillet's second leading idea is the distinction between two groups of legal rules: those which are 'general' and therefore unrestrictedly applicable to everybody present in the territory (but not outside the territory), and those which are 'permanent', i.e. effectual everywhere with regard to all nationals of the country, but do not affect foreigners— in other words, have a limited effect both territorially and extra-territorially. Such a distinction between various groups of legal rules is reminiscent of the Statute Theories; but while these distinguished between legal rules according to their subject (persons, things, acts), Pillet makes the touchstone their social aim (*'leur but social'*). If the aim of a rule is the protection of personal interests, the rule belongs to the second group, i.e. to the 'permanent' rules having an extra-territorial effect. If on the other hand the social aim of the rule is the protection of general interests, of interests of the community, as Pillet puts it, then this rule is 'general', i.e. has unlimited territorial effect. This distinction is hardly tenable. Practically every rule of private law aims at protecting both private and public interests. Pillet gives several examples, amongst them the rules on immovable property and those on marriage. For the first he asserts that their social aim is to protect interests of the community; for the second he sees the

[1] See *supra*, s. 2.

social aim in the personal protection of the future spouses. The opposite may be asserted with equal force: if marriages could be validly contracted by infants or by persons already married or under the influence of threats, that would be detrimental to the social and religious interests of the community; while the rule of English Property Law that 'nemo dat qui non habet', protects the owner and may even be regarded as militating against the public interests of commercial intercourse.

BIBLIOGRAPHY

GUTZWILLER, *Der Einfluss Savignys auf die Entwicklung des IPR*, 1923. BARON B. NOLDE, 'La codification du droit international privé', 55 *Rec.* (1936 i) 303. C. G. v. WÄCHTER, in *Archiv f. d. civilistische Praxis*, 24 and 25 (1841, 1842). KRČMAR, 'Beiträge zur Geschichte des I.P.R.' in *Festschrift z. Jahrhundertfeier des österr. allg. bürgerl. Gesetzbuchs* (1911 ii) 133. A. D. GIBB, 39 *Jurid. Rev.* (1927), 369. D. J. L. DAVIES, 'Influence of Huber', 18 *Br. Y.B.* (1937), 49. CATELLANI, 'Les maîtres de l'école italienne au 19e siècle', 46 *Rec.* (1933 iv), 709. J. DONNEDIEU DE VABRES, *L'évolution de la jurisprudence française en matière des conflits des lois depuis le début du XXe siècle*, 1938. LORENZEN, *Selected Articles*, 136–80, 203–27.

7. MODERN LEGISLATION

35. Influence of the French Civil Code Of the early codes that dealt with Private International Law only the French Civil Code of 1804 had any considerable influence on later legislation.[1] The very scanty rules which its Art. 3 contains were adopted or imitated by nearly all those countries which modelled their civil law on the French Code, such as the Netherlands (1829) or Roumania (1865). The codes of Italy (1865),[2] Portugal (1867), Spain (1888), and numerous statutes of Latin-American states were also largely drafted under the influence of French law, though they are much more complete than their model.

36. The German Civil Code Germany codified a great part of her Private International Law in the Introductory Law to the Civil Code of 1896, but intentionally left certain gaps, particularly in respect of the law of contracts and quasi-contracts, because on this subject it seemed impossible to draw up satisfactory general rules. German law has influenced the

[1] Some of the Swiss cantonal laws were influenced by Austrian law.
[2] On the new Italian Code of 1938, 1942, see *infra*, s. 37.

legislation of Japan (1898) and China (1918). In 1891 Switzerland promulgated a Federal Law dealing with inter-cantonal law and with the law applicable to aliens resident in Switzerland and Swiss citizens resident abroad. This law, though supplemented by the Swiss Civil Code of 1907, is still very incomplete and its interpretation doubtful.

Among the most recent codifications of Private Inter-national Law there are five which deserve particular attention:[1]

37. The latest codes

1. The Brazilian Civil Code of 1916, modified by a law of 1942, which lays down some remarkable, though not exhaustive, rules on Private International Law.

2. Two Polish statutes, both of 2 August 1926. One of them is a code of private international, the other a code of private inter-local law. Both are complete codifications, the first ever drawn up in Europe. The necessity for a code of inter-local law arose out of the fact that Poland did not possess a uniform law.[2]   In some parts the German Civil Code was applicable, in others the Austrian Code of 1811, in others again Hungarian customary law or a code of 1825, together with the second and third book of the Code Napoléon; finally, in some districts the old Russian Civil Law, that is, the Svod Zakanov, had remained in force.

3. Italy created a new Civil Code (1942) under the ascendancy of Fascist conceptions, the first part of which was promulgated on 12 December 1938. Its introductory *Disposizioni sull' applicazione delle legge* embody rules on Private International Law which differ from the rules of the older code of 1865 only in some minor particulars.

4. The Greek code was promulgated 15 March 1940,

---

[1] Other European codes: (*a*) the Civil Code of Canton Zurich (1853), now superseded by the Swiss codification, embodied six very precise rules on conflict of laws, based partly on Savigny's doctrines. (*b*) The Saxonian Civil Code (1863) abolished by the German codification of 1896, and under its influence the Baltic Code of 1864, which is still in force in parts of Esthonia and Lithuania. (*c*) The rules on private international law made in the small Principality of Liechtenstein, 1926 and following years. (*d*) The Latvian Code of 1937, art. 8–25, partly based on German, partly on Baltic law. Baron Nolde, *La codification du droit international privé*, p. 20 and in *Bulletin de la Société de législ. comparée*, 1938.

[2] The Law of Obligations was unified by a Code of 27 Oct. 1933. Other parts of private law have been unified more recently.

after having been in preparation for a whole century. Its articles 11 and following constitute a complete code of private international law. Having regard to the very high standard of modern Greek jurisprudence, whose most outstanding representatives drafted or helped to draft the text, the student of comparative law should study the new Greek rules with great care.[1]

5. Czechoslovakia promulgated a code of Private International and Inter-local Law on 10 April 1948.[2]

38. The territories without a code No attempt has been made to codify private international law in the Scandinavian States and Finland, in the Union of the Soviet Republics, in the British Empire, and in the United States of America.

1. The law of the Scandinavian States and Finland is customary law. Swedish and Finnish rules on conflict of laws on the one hand, Danish, Norwegian, and Icelandic rules on the other, differ considerably from each other. Since 1931 the five states have concluded a series of treaties in order to establish a certain uniformity of rules. Such uniformity, however, is very limited, as the rules apply only in cases where all persons concerned are subjects of one of those five states.[3]

2. The Soviet Union and the separate Soviet States have made very few rules on conflict of laws. These rules relate to certain specific matters: maritime law, cheques, capacity of foreign legal persons, and one or two others. The enormous gaps thus existing are, of course, not filled by former Russian law. As far as possible, Soviet law is applied, even to the status or the marriages of aliens residing in Russia, or of nationals of one of the Soviet Republics when residing outside Soviet territory. This extravagant extension of the application of Russian law is founded on the idea that there is no 'intellectual community' between the Soviet States and the bourgeois states, that any foreign law must be considered as 'coming from a hostile camp'.[4]

---

[1] Cf. Maridakis, *Rabel's* Z, ii, pp. 111 et seq. Streït and Vallindas, i, p. 218 et seq.

[2] On this see Drucker, 2 *Internat. L.Q.R.* (1948), 473–5.

[3] Cf. *Rabel's* Z, 8. 627; 9. 266, 513; 10. 712.

[4] Makarov, *Conception du droit international privé d'après la doctrine et la pratique russes* (1932), pp. 28, 126, 127.

3. The laws of the British Commonwealth are not codified, except in the Province of Quebec, where the Civil Code of 1866 contains a few rules on conflict of laws derived from the French Code. There are no civil codes in the territories governed by English law, by Scots law, or by Roman-Dutch law; and until the middle of the nineteenth century Private International Law was hardly developed at all. Judicial decisions were rare[1] and often half-hearted and vague. No doctrines had been developed, as it is unusual in this country for the text-book writer or theoretician to take the initiative. Under the influence of growing international commerce and increasing mobility of mankind (journeys abroad, service in foreign branches of commercial or industrial enterprises, emigration) sets of facts with a foreign element have become much more frequent. Nevertheless, English private international law is even now far less fully developed than any other branch of English law.[2] Therefore, in this section of the law the courts will frequently have to consult and often follow foreign, particularly American, decisions and also the well-known text-books, amongst which Dicey's *Conflict of Laws* has achieved a special prominence.[3]

4. In the forty-nine legal systems of the United States of America, where the rules on conflict of laws are very similar to those of England, there exists no 'Code' in the proper sense of the term, but an unofficial 'Restatement of the Law of Conflict of Laws', which is very similar to a code. The Restatement is the private work of the American Law Institute, and particularly of its appointed Reporter, Professor Joseph H. Beale, of Harvard Law School, and his advisers, amongst whom were the most famous American teachers of private international law. Its aim is to present 'an orderly statement of the general

---

[1] Cf. *supra*, s. 27, and Holdsworth, *History of Engl. Law*, xi. 270.

[2] Some English Statutes contain rules on private international law, in particular: the Wills Act, 1861 (Lord Kingsdown's Act), the Bills of Exchange Act, 1882, s. 72, the Foreign Marriages Act, 1892, the Bankruptcy Act, 1914, s. 1 & 4, the Legitimacy Act, 1926, s. 8, the Companies Act, 1948, s. 406, the Arbitration (Foreign Rewards) Act, 1930, the Foreign Judgments (Reciprocal Enforcement) Act, 1933, and some others.

[3] See, however, J. Foster's remarks on Dicey's work, before it was taken over by J. H. C. Morris, 16 *Brit. Y.B.* (1935), p. 102.

common law of the United States'. It is based on the recognition that

the ever-increasing volume of the decisions of the courts, and the numerous instances in which the decisions are irreconcilable are so increasing the law's uncertainty and lack of clarity that this will force the abandonment of the common law system of expressing and developing law through judicial application of existing rules to new fact combinations and the adoption in its place of rigid legislative codes, unless a new factor promoting certainty and clarity could be found.[1]

This 'new factor', the Restatement, is what in the Middle Ages would have been called a *speculum*,[2] a *Mirror*.[3] But sometimes, though not often, it is used in practice as a source of law.[4]

39. International Conventions

National legislation has been supplemented in some countries by international conventions concerning private international law. The conclusion of such conventions had been recommended even before Savigny, and since Mancini (1874) the movement towards international regulation has grown. Most successful amongst the European supporters of this tendency was the Dutch jurist, Professor Asser. Under his influence the Dutch Government in 1892 invited the principal European states to a conference in order that they might agree on an international codification of the rules of conflict of laws. Six conferences were held at the Hague in the years 1893, 1894, 1900, 1904, 1925, and 1928. Great Britain took part in those held in 1925 and 1928. The results, however, were disappointing. Many projects covering the conflict rules on marriage, divorce, guardianship, interdiction of incapables, succession and wills, civil procedure, bankruptcy, recognition and execution of foreign judg-

---

[1] Restatement, pp. viii, ix.

[2] At the end of the ninth century it was said of a *regula* written by Pope Gregory: 'melius et verius speculum nuncupari potuisset'; Dümmler, *Formelbuch des Bischofs Salomo* (of Constance), iii. 71. See also the *speculum iudiciale* by William Durantis (1271).

[3] What the author of the Saxon Mirror said of his book (about 1230), 'This law I have not invented, it has been brought to us from old times by our good ancestors', was to a certain degree the aim of the Restatement.

[4] See, however, the critical review of the Restatement by Lorenzen, 48 *Harvard L. R.* (1935) 15; Heilman, 83 *Univ. of Pennsylv. L. Rev.* (1925) 555; Cook, *passim*; Nussbaum l.c.; Barbey, *Rev. Crit.* 1936, 86; on the other hand: De Sloovère, 41 *Harv. L. R.* (1928) 421.

ments, were discussed and a vote taken thereon; some of them were passed by the delegates, but the number of resolutions which were put into force and the number of states which adopted them was very small, and subsequently some of the states which had first introduced the rules withdrew their consent.

The Hague Conventions which came into force concern: **40. In particular. The Hague Conventions**

1. the *Conclusion of Marriage*. The Convention (of 12 June 1902) is now valid for eleven states, viz., Germany, Danzig, Italy, Luxemburg, the Netherlands, Poland, Portugal, Roumania, Sweden, Switzerland, and Hungary. France and Belgium withdrew their agreement.[1]

2. *Divorce and Separation*. This Convention (of 12 June 1902), since the withdrawal of Switzerland (1929), Germany and Sweden (1934), has been valid only for eight countries; they are the same as sub (1).

3. *Guardianship* (of 12 June 1902)—in force now in thirteen countries: the same as sub (1), together with Spain and Belgium, while France withdrew in 1914.

4. *The Effects of Marriage* (of 17 July 1905)—in force, after the withdrawal of France and Belgium (1917 and 1922 respectively), only in eight countries: Germany, Danzig, Italy, the Netherlands, Poland, Portugal, Roumania, and Sweden.

5. *The Interdiction of Incapable Persons* (of 17 July 1905)—valid in nine countries, namely, the same as sub (4) and Hungary.

6. Finally, a Convention (of 17 July 1905) concerning several minor points of *Civil Procedure*, such as service of judicial documents and security for costs, to which twenty-two states adhere. It will not be discussed in this book.

None of these Conventions have been put into operation either by Great Britain or by Russia; none of them are in force outside Europe.

Of much greater importance are the conflict rules in matters of Bills of Exchange and Cheques, established in Geneva in 1930 and 1931 respectively. Parties to these conventions are twenty-one European states (Austria, **41. The Geneva Conventions**

---

[1] For the reasons see s. 43 and s. 167.

Germany, Belgium, Danzig, Poland, Denmark, Norway, Finland, Sweden, France, Italy, Spain, Portugal, Luxemburg, the Netherlands, Switzerland, Czechoslovakia, Yugoslavia, Turkey, Hungary, and Greece) and five extra-European countries (Brazil, Colombia, Ecuador, Peru, and Japan). Neither Great Britain nor any of her Dominions—nor for that matter the Soviet Union—has adhered to these conventions.

Finally, two Geneva Conventions of 1923 and 1927 concerning Arbitration Clauses and the Execution of Foreign Arbitral Awards[1] have been ratified by most European states, this time including Great Britain and Northern Ireland,[2] and by some extra-European countries (New Zealand, Newfoundland, &c.).

42. The Latin-American Conventions

The movement towards the unification of Private International Law has made greater progress in Latin America than in Europe. Three conventions should be mentioned in this connexion:

1 and 2. Two Treaties of Montevideo of 12 February 1889 (revised 14 March 1940) on Civil International Law and on Commercial International Law. They were concluded under the leadership of that energetic Uruguayan jurist, Gonzalo Ramirez. Parties to them were five South American states which follow the domicile principle, viz. Argentine, Bolivia, Paraguay, Peru, and Uruguay. Those states which did not wish to abandon their system of testing the status of persons by their nationality, such as Brazil (before 1942) and Chile, remained outside. Both treaties are exhaustive codifications of Private International Law.

3. The *Código Bustamante* of 1928. It took its name from its author, the well-known Cuban jurist, Antonio Sanchez de Bustamante y Sirvén. This code covers the whole of Private International Law, including commercial law, criminal law, and procedure. It was accepted by the sixth Pan-American Conference of Havana, 1928, at which twenty-one states were represented. It has since

---

[1] Nussbaum, 56 *Harvard L. R.* (1942) 219.

[2] Arbitration Clauses (Protocol) Act, 1924 (14 & 15 Geo. V, c. 39) and Arbitration (Foreign Awards) Act, 1930 (20 Geo. V), c. 15.

been ratified by six South American states (Brazil, Chile, Venezuela, Ecuador, Bolivia, and Peru)[1] and by all the nine states of Central America and the West Indies. None of the North American states (Canada, Mexico, and the United States) have ratified the Código Bustamante. This code, much praised and much condemned, is particularly remarkable because it does more than attempt to establish a few fundamental principles; it contains very detailed rules which are intended to provide the judge with an answer to any question that may arise. The first two books, dealing with Civil and Commercial International Law, contain as many as 295 sections. There are thirty-five sections concerning international property law, 'a subject which till then had seemed to be quite adequately covered by a single rule'.[2] Nevertheless, the code does not create a true unity of conflict rules. For in one of the most crucial questions, viz. whether the status of persons (including marriage, divorce, guardianship, paternal power) is to be tested by their domicile or by their nationality, the code simply leaves the answer to the particular states.[3] There is, however, no reason why an agreement on a great number of subordinate points should be rejected merely because there is no agreement on essential points.

It is worth mentioning that the Código Bustamante is to a certain extent based on conceptions of the Italian school. This is manifest in particular in s. 3, where all legal rules are divided into three groups, corresponding to the Italian principles of 'Nationality, territorial Sovereignty, and Liberty': the *leyes personales* which follow the person wherever he goes, the *leyes territoriales*, binding on everybody within the territory, and the *leyes voluntarias*, or of 'private order', which obtain only if they have been adopted by the parties.

What, then, are the prospects of a really 'international' Private International Law?

43.
Prospects

1. It will hardly be possible to reach an agreement

---

[1] The only South American state which is not a party either to the Montevideo Conventions or to the Código Bustamante is Colombia.
[2] Baron Nolde, p. 66.   [3] Código Bust., s. 7.

between the countries governed by Common Law (England, United States of America, Australia, &c.) and the Civil Law countries. The simple fact that the former are opposed to codification is prohibitive.

2. The experience gained on the European continent in connexion with the Hague Conventions, in particular those concerning marriage and divorce, makes the unbiased observer somewhat sceptical. Thus the Hague Convention on Marriage provides that all impediments to marriage existing under the national law of one of the parties shall be respected wherever the marriage is concluded; no state shall disregard such an impediment as contrary to its own public policy. Under German law 'military persons' may be married only with the consent of the military authority, and this was made applicable to the numerous German deserters who escaped into France or Belgium and wished to be married there. The French and Belgian authorities were debarred by the text of the Convention from allowing the conclusion of such marriages on their respective territories. That was why these states withdrew from the Convention. The Hague Convention on Divorce brought other predicaments in its train. It allows a divorce only if it is not forbidden by the national law of the spouses. Numerous Swiss, German, and Swedish women who had married Italian citizens, thereby acquiring Italian nationality, and who then left their husbands for some reason which under Swiss, German, or Swedish law would constitute a ground of divorce (adultery, cruelty, &c.), were unable under the Convention to obtain it because divorce is inadmissible under Italian law. Switzerland, Germany, and Sweden consequently denounced the Divorce Convention. If, on the other hand, the Conventions had refrained from establishing rigid rules or had mitigated them by a general clause such as : no state is bound to apply the rules laid down by the Convention if such application be contrary to its public policy, then the whole Convention would be of little value since it would be left to the contracting states to decide how widely they should extend the elastic conception of public policy.

3. One must bear in mind that not only in England but also in the continental countries Private International Law is an unfinished section of the law, much less complete than any other, and that therefore all legislative experiments in this field, even those made in single states, suffer from a certain immaturity. The imaginative reflections and writings of scholars can never succeed in bringing unknown contingencies to light to the same extent as a centuries-old body of case law. Matters of comparative unimportance will be apt to bulk largely in the foreground, while those likely to be of practical value in human affairs may be overlooked. Seen in this light the creation of a synthetic world-code—a juristic Esperanto—would appear to be a goal unattainable to-day and perhaps undesirable at any time.

4. Even where an international agreement can be attained—on limited points—the danger exists that unless an International Supreme Court is established the courts of the various states will interpret the rules of the Convention in different ways, so that the apparent unity of the law falls to pieces. In particular they will be prone to construe an ambiguous term in the sense in which it is understood by their own law. A distinguished French author, E. Bartin, is even in favour of this;[1] but his opinion is hardly reconcilable with the fact that a Convention is more than a juxtaposition of two unilateral declarations.

5. In spite of these stumbling-blocks Conventions on Unification of particular conflict rules are not entirely useless. They achieve a certain though very modest progress on special points, and the very fact that attempts are made to reach agreement creates a healthy tendency to relegate to the background the isolationist conception that one's own law should be applied as widely as possible.

---

[1] Cf. on this subject: Bartin, *Principes* i. 105 et seq.; Streit and Vallindas i. 163, n. 13; Vallindas, *Rabel's Z*, 7. 170; Vallindas, *Rev. Darras*, 27 (1932), 727–30; Ténékides, *Revue génér. d. dr. internat. public*, 1933, 114 et seq.; *Annuaire*, 25 ii. 305; 39 ii. 305; Bioux, *Bruns' Z*, 4. 702, 753; Joki, *De l'interprétation des traités normatifs d'après la doctrine et la jurisprudence internationales*, Paris (1936). See German Supreme Court, *Seuffert's Archiv*, 85, 137; Hamburg Court of Appeal, *IPRspr.* 1932, 131; 1933, 35. (Oppenheim-)Lauterpacht, *Internat. Law* (6th ed.), i. 861. See *infra*, s. 133.

PART II

JURISDICTION OF THE ENGLISH COURTS

CHAPTER IV

DELIMITATION OF JURISDICTION

44. 'International' and 'local' jurisdiction As we have seen, the need to choose one out of several legal systems mostly arises in the course of judicial proceedings. It is therefore desirable to pave the way for the discussion of these questions by determining the conditions under which the courts of a given country have jurisdiction.

This problem must be distinguished from two others:

1. from the question *which* of the courts of a certain country, e.g. England, is competent to entertain a particular action. Is it the High Court, or a County Court, and which of the County Courts? Is it the court of the district where the defendant resides, or the court of the place where the contract on which the action is based was made or was to be performed? Such questions of *intra-territorial competence* have no relation to international law. When an internally incompetent court, e.g. the tribunal at Toulouse instead of that at Marseilles, has entertained an action, its judgment has the same effect in England as if it had been delivered by the competent tribunal, unless under French law the lack of local jurisdiction impeaches the validity of such judgment. We are concerned in this book not with the question which of a country's courts is competent, but of which country the courts are competent?

Italian authors distinguish aptly between jurisdiction and competence. The *giurisdizione* is the international, the *competenza* the intra-territorial, competence. In France, it is usual to oppose the *compétence générale*, the jurisdiction of a country as a whole, to the intra-territorial *compétence spéciale*.[1]

[1] E. Bartin, *J. Clunet*, 28, p. 1 et seq. Cf. Neuner, loc. cit., p. 6.

2. from the question of the effect in one country of judicial proceedings that have taken place in another; in particular, from the question whether foreign judgments are to be recognized and executed elsewhere. This is undoubtedly a question of international law, and it will be treated later (*infra*, s. 231). But it is different from the problem which is the subject of the present chapter. Here we are dealing only with the jurisdiction of the courts of country X as it exists according to the law of X. Later we shall have to deal with the jurisdiction of the courts of country Y as it is recognized by the law of X.[1] In both cases the issue is the delimitation of jurisdiction. French jurists speak in the first case of *compétence générale directe*, in the second of *compétence générale indirecte*. Unfortunately the delimitation of jurisdiction is very different in the two cases. Every state is inclined to concede to its own courts a wider jurisdiction than it is prepared to recognize in foreign courts, and no rule of international law prevents states from establishing such discordance. A distribution of judicial competence among the different states by international conventions or unwritten international law does not exist, apart from the rules on immunity of foreign states, sovereigns, and diplomatic representatives.[2] Thus every country is at liberty to decide in which cases it will itself assume jurisdiction (and whether it claims exclusive or merely concurrent jurisdiction), and in which cases it will recognize foreign jurisdiction (again, either exclusive or concurrent).

45. Jurisdiction of foreign courts

[1] See *infra*, s. 228, 231 et seq.
[2] See *infra*, s. 47 et seq.

BIBLIOGRAPHY

R. NEUNER, *Internationale Zuständigkeit* (1929). A. D. GIBB, *Law of Jurisdiction in England and Scotland* (1926). DUNCAN AND DYKES, *The Principles of Civil Jurisdiction* (1911) (Scott. Law).

THE PERSONS SUBJECTED TO THE JURISDICTION
OF ENGLISH COURTS

Under English law any person, whether a British subject or an alien, may sue or be sued in English courts. This conforms to a general principle of all modern laws. The French rule under which actions between two aliens are admitted only in exceptional cases[1] is unknown in this country.

46. Enemy aliens I. Any person can sue. Unlike most continental laws, English law does not require an alien plaintiff to furnish security for costs (*cautio iudicatum solvi*).[2] English courts, however, again unlike continental courts, have no jurisdiction to entertain an action brought by an enemy alien. Enemy alien is:[3]

1. every person of enemy nationality unless resident in Great Britain by permission of the Crown, or (apparently) in an allied or neutral country.[4] Is in the latter case permission of the sovereign of that country material? Probably not.

2. a British subject or a subject of an allied or neutral state 'who is voluntarily resident or who is carrying on business in hostile territory'.[5] Territory which has been occupied by the enemy is to be treated as hostile if the

---

[1] Code civil, art. 14, 15. See Pillet, *Traité prat.* i. 394 et seq.

[2] The court, however, can in its discretion compel any plaintiff, whether he be an alien or a British subject, to give such security, in particular if he resides permanently outside England. Rules of the Supr. Court, Order 65, 4, 6, 6A, 6B; *Republic of Costa Rica* v. *Erlanger* (1876), 3 Ch.D. (C.A.) 62, 68; *The Newbattle* (1885), 10 P.D. (C.A.) 33. The obligation of aliens to give security is to be found in France, Germany, Austria, and many other countries. The Hague Convention on Civil Procedure, 1905, art. 17, has abolished it in favour of those nationals of one of the contracting states who are residents in one of these states and bring an action in a court of another.

[3] The definition of this term by the Trading with the Enemy Act, 1939 (6 & 7 Geo. VI, c. 89), s. 2 does not apply here.

[4] *In re Mary Duchess of Sutherland* (1915), 31 T.L.R. 394; *Janson* v. *Driefontein Consol. Mines Co.*, [1902] A.C. 484, 505, 506. It is not sufficient that he carries on trade in a neutral country; *The Hypatia*, [1917] P. 36; *The Clan Grant* (1915), 31 T.L.R. 321; *The Flamenco* (1915), 32 T.L.R. 53.

[5] *Porter* v. *Freudenberg*, [1915] 1 K.B. (C.A.) 857, 869; *Johnstone* v. *Pedlar*, [1921] 2 A.C. 262; *Princess Thurn and Taxis* v. *Moffitt*, [1915] 1 Ch. 58. Cf. *Netz* v. *Chuter Ede*, [1946] Ch. 224. *R.* v. *Bottrill*, [1947] K.B. 41 (C.A.).

enemy has 'effective control' and 'is exercising some kind of government or administration over the area'; a slighter occupation, merely 'incidental to military operations', would not suffice.[1]

Just as the enemy alien cannot sue he cannot counterclaim when sued, but he can plead a set-off, as this is purely defensive.

II. Anybody can be sued. Exceptions to this exist under the law of nations in favour of foreign states, foreign sovereigns, and diplomatic representatives of foreign states. Many states, however, have gone farther in granting immunity from jurisdiction than they are bound to go by the law of nations. In Great Britain the law of nations—which forms part of the common law—is supplemented by the Diplomatic Privileges Act, 1708,[2] and by the Diplomatic Privileges (Extension) Acts 1941,[3] 1944, and 1946.[4] The following rules are recognized.

47. Immunities

[1] *Soufracht* v. *Van Udens Scheepvaart en Agentuur Maatschappij*, [1943] A.C. 203, 211 (*per* Lord Simon, L.C.). Lord Wright (ibid. 219) contrasts the merely 'enemy-occupied' country with the 'enemy-subjugated'. Lord Porter emphasizes that no single answer can be given which applies to all these cases; 'the solution depends on the quality of the occupation, to be judged by the time it endures, the amount of control exercised, and the extent to which the former government is superseded' (ibid. at p. 240). Cf. *In re Anglo-International Bank*, [1943] 1 Ch. (C.A.) 233, 238, 240. In *The Pamia*, [1943] 1 A.E.R. 269 a Belgian company domiciled in Belgium had commenced an action in the English court before Belgium was invaded, but had transferred its head office to the United States (after the invasion). The court held that the company was not to be regarded as enemy alien.

[2] (7 Anne, c. 12.) This Act is merely declaratory of the common law; *Novello* v. *Toogood* (1823), 1 B. & C. 554, 562; *In re Suarez*, [1918] 1 Ch. (C.A.) 176, 192. See J. M. Jones, *J. Comp. Leg.*, 1940, 19.

[3] This Act (4 & 5 Geo. 6, c. 7) extends the immunity of foreign envoys to members of the governments of foreign Powers established in the United Kingdom, and to certain other persons.

[4] These Acts (7 & 8 Geo. 6, c. 44, and 9 & 10 Geo. 6, c. 66) grant immunity from suit and legal process to any 'organization' declared by Order in Council to be an organization of which the Government is a member, and for the holders of certain high offices of such organizations. Examples: the United Nations Organization and its high officers, the Judges of the International Court of Justice, the Food and Agriculture Organization, the International Monetary Fund, the Bank for Reconstruction and Development, &c. Other classes of officers of such organizations and servants enjoy immunity from suit and legal process only 'in respect of things done or omitted to be done in the course of the performance of official duties'. See (Oppenheim-)Lauterpacht, *International Law* (6th ed.), i. 734 et seq.; Schwelb, 8 *Modern L.R.* (1945), 50.

Immunity is granted

48. Of States

1. to foreign sovereign states. Non-sovereign states such as member-states of a federal state (Bavaria, the Canton of Berne, Connecticut)[1] are not exempted from jurisdiction; they are incapable of exercising any rights of sovereignty in the international sphere. The immunity exists only in favour of those states which have been recognized as such in this country. If the court is in doubt as to the defendant's quality as a sovereign state, it may apply for information to the Foreign Office, and the resulting information is then conclusive.[2] The recognition of a state must not be confused with that of a government. The latter is concerned with the question: Who is entitled to act on behalf of the state?

The immunity of a sovereign state is effective not only where the state itself has been made a party to an action brought in an English court. It has some effect also where the sovereign state is only indirectly affected by the action. 'The court should not so exercise its jurisdiction as to put a foreign sovereign to election between being deprived of property..., or else submitting to the jurisdiction of the court.'[3]

It occurs frequently that a state creates, e.g. for a commercial purpose, a separate legal entity, in law distinct from the state. Examples are many companies under state control, the state possessing all or practically all the shares in the company. Such a corporation does not benefit from the immunity of the state, unless it has been constituted a 'department of the state'.[4]

---

[1] See the decision of the Court of Appeal of Colmar in the case of *Dorr* v. *the Brazilian State Céara*, of 27 June 1928 in *Bruns' Z*, i. 2, 217; *Annual Digest of Public Internat. Law Cases*, 1927-8, p. 39, 40; *J. Clunet*, 1929, 1040. See *D'Archer de Montgascon* v. *Céara*, Ann. Dig. 1931-2, 162-3, and *Annual Dig.* 1938-40, p. 242, no. 3.

[2] See, e.g., *Duff Development Co.* v. *Government of Kelantan*, [1924] A.C. 797, 805; *Bank of Ethiopia* v. *National Bank of Egypt*, [1937] 3 A.E.R. 8; *The Arantzazu Mendi*, [1939] A.C. 256, 264. Cf. *Engelke* v. *Musmann*, [1928] A.C. 433, 442, and 40 *American J.* (1946) 205. The certificate issued by an ambassador stating that the defendant state-agency constitutes a mere department of the state is not conclusive but creates a rebuttable presumption. *Krajina* v. *Tass Agency*, [1949] 2 A.E.R. 274 (C.A.), following *Compania Mercantil Argentina* v. *United States Shipping Board*, 131 L.T. 388.

[3] *Dolfuss Mieg* v. *Bank of England*, [1949] 1 Ch. 946.

[4] See *supra*, note 2 i.f. American cases: *United States* v. *Société Commerciale*

State immunity covers all state property. Even an action relative to immovables that belong to a foreign state but are situate in this country cannot be entertained by an English court; herein English law differs from French and many other continental laws.[1]

Does the immunity cover exclusively acts of a state in the exercise of its sovereign rights (*acta iure imperii*) and property *publicis usibus destinatum*? Or does it extend to acts done by the state in its private capacity, such as trade contracts, liabilities arising from torts (*acta iure gestionis*), and to the state's private property? The question has been discussed notably for governments trading as owners of merchant vessels.[2] The decision in *The Porto Alexandre*[3] took the wider view: a trading ship, requisitioned[4] by the Portuguese government and then used for trading purposes was regarded as entitled to immunity. The House of Lords, however, criticized this view *obiter* in the case of *The Cristina*,[5] where Lord Maugham convincingly stated that states trading as shipowners should be subjected to the same actions as any other shipowner. If, however, a state ship is used for carrying both the public mails and merchandise, its immunity is not lost 'by reason of the ship having been used for trading purposes'.[6] A Convention concluded at Brussels in 1926 and amended in 1934

des Potasses d'Alsace (1929), 31 Fed. Rep. 2nd ser. 199; *Ulen & Co.* v. *Bank Gostpodarstwa Krajowego* (N. York, Supr. C.), in 36 *American J.* (1942), 695. In *Hafiz Habib-ul-Heq* v. *Gaekwar Baroda State Railways* (1938), 107 L.J.P.C. 46, the Judicial Committee of the Privy Council held that the suit was directed against the Sovereign (Gaekwar) in fact, though not in form, since the defendants (State Railways) were not a separate legal person.

1 De Lapradelle, *Rev. Darras*, 1910, 784.

2 See van Praag, *Rev. Ghent*, 1934, 562; 1935, 100; Brookfield, *J. Comp. Leg.* 1938, 1; Brinton, *American J.* 1931, 50; Feller, ibid. 83; Fox, ibid. 1941, 632; Hackworth, *Digest of Internat. Law*, ii. 480; F. A. Mann, 59, *L.Q.R.* (1943) 46; Kuhn, 40 *American J.*, 1946, 376; Colombos, 21 *Brit. Y.B.* 101. Sanborn, 39 *Amer. J.* (1945), 794 et seq. Anon. on the Russian-American controversy in respect of *Lorina* v. *The Rossia*, 58 *Yale L. J.* 1949, 176.

3 [1920] P. 30.—On the practice of Swedish Courts: Jägerskjölt, 42 *Amer. J.* 601.

4 On temporary requisition by a foreign state, see also *The Tervaete*, [1922] P. 259; *The Cristina*, [1938], A.C. 485.

5 l.c. See also the Irish decision in *Zarine* v. *Owners of S.S. Ramara*, [1942] Ir. Rep. 148, 165, which granted immunity only to such state vessels as are 'publicis usibus destinatae'.

6 *The Parlement Belge* (1880), L.R. 5, P.D. 197.

excluded from immunity commercial vessels and their cargoes belonging to states; this Convention was ratified by nine states, but not by Great Britain.

49. Of heads of states

2. Immunity is further granted to sovereigns and other heads of sovereign states, such as the president of a republic. They are immune even in respect of acts done in their private capacity. Thus the Sultan of Johore who, while living in England under the name of Baker, had promised to marry an English woman, could not be sued for breach of promise.[1]

50. Of diplomatic agents

3. Finally, immunity is accorded to diplomatic representatives of a foreign state, such as ambassadors accredited to the Crown. Commercial agents, e.g. consuls, are immune from jurisdiction only in respect of their official functions.[2] Ambassadors accredited not to the British Crown but to some other state cannot claim immunity on British territory. In Great Britain and most other countries the immunity of diplomatic agents extends to their private sphere, contracts as well as torts.[3] In *The Amazone*[4] the wife of a Belgian councillor at the London Legation issued a writ against her husband, claiming ownership of a motor yacht which he had in possession; the court held that he could not be sued. English law does not even allow an action concerning immovables situate in England to be brought against them in an English court,[5] and it grants these privileges even to such diplomatic agents of a foreign state as are themselves of British nationality (the so-called *agents régnicoles*). In both points it differs from most continental laws.[6] As immunity is accorded to a diplomatic agent 'in order that he may transact his Sovereign's

---

[1] *Mighell* v. *The Sultan of Johore*, [1894] 1 Q.B. (C.A.) 149. In France there is a controversy as to whether private acts of sovereigns are covered by their immunity. Cf. Pillet, *Traité prat.* i, p. 374.

[2] W. E. Beckett, 21 *Brit. Y.B.* (1944), 34, 38. Cf. *Cour d. Cass., J. Clunet*, 1927, 408; 1929, 1043.

[3] Italian courts have often taken a narrower view: *Riv. d. dir. internaz.* 9 (1915), 215; 14 (1924), 173; 23 (1931), 563.

[4] [1939] P. 322; [1940] P. (C.A.) 40.

[5] *Contra*: German law (Courts' Organization Act [*Gerichtsverfassungsgesetz*] of 1924 s. 20).

[6] *Macartney* v. *Garbutt* (1890), 24 Q.B.D. 368. Cf. Morelli, *Riv. d. dir. int.* 26 (1934), 42.

business', it extends to his 'personal family', that is his wife and children living with him, and his 'diplomatic family' (councillors, secretaries, clerks), and even to his domestic servants.[1] These members of the 'suite', however, do not themselves possess the right to immunity—it pertains to the ambassador or other agent, who may exercise or waive it without their consent.[2]

The immunity of foreign states, sovereigns, and diplomatic agents is immunity from local jurisdiction, and not immunity from legal liability. If, for example, a diplomatic agent has by careless motoring injured a person, he is bound to pay damages, though he cannot be sued for them; if he pays voluntarily he does not make a gift but fulfils a legal obligation, so that he is entitled to recover the amount paid from his insurer.[3]

51. No immunity from liability

The foreign state, its sovereign, and its diplomatic agents may waive their privileges and submit to the jurisdiction of the court.[4] For such submission the diplomatic agent needs his sovereign's consent.[5] But his declaration of waiver is presumed to be in accordance with his instructions.[6]

52. Waiver and extinction of immunity

The submission may be made expressly or by implication, and an implied submission to the jurisdiction of the court is to be found when the state, the sovereign, or the ambassador brings an action in that court. Such submission is, however, restricted to the particular action and—apparently—to actions concerned with the same matter; it does not cover a counterclaim not connected with the claim.[7]

The immunity ceases in the case of foreign sovereigns when the sovereign abdicates or is dethroned, in the case of a diplomatic agent when his functions are terminated

---

[1] *Engelke* v. *Musmann*, [1928] A.C. 433. An exception to immunity of domestic servants (under the English Act of 1708) is made when they engage in trade. Jones, *J. Comp. Leg.* 1940, 19.

[2] *R.* v. *Kent*, [1941] 1 K.B. 454.

[3] *Dickinson* v. *Del Solar*, [1930] 1 K.B. 376.

[4] *Taylor* v. *Best* (1854), 23 L.J. C.P. 89, 93.

[5] *In re Republic of Bolivia Exploration Syndic.*, [1914] 1 Ch. 139. *In re Suarez*, [1918] 1 Ch. (C.A.) 176, 191-4.

[6] *In re Suarez*, loc. cit.

[7] *South African Republic* v. *La Compagnie Franco-Belge du Chemin de Fer du Nord*, [1898] 1 Ch. 190. Cf. German Supreme Court, Offic. Collect. 111, 380.

and a reasonable period for winding up the affairs of his embassy and preparing to leave the country has elapsed.[1]

[1] *Magdalena Steam Navigation Co.* v. *Martin* (1859), 2 E. & E. 94, 111; *Musurus Bey* v. *Gadban*, [1894] 2 Q.B. 352. Cf. Sir C. Hurst, loc. cit., 237.

BIBLIOGRAPHY

SIR C. HURST, 'Les immunités diplomatiques', 12 *Rec.* (1926 II), 119. G. G. PHILLIMORE, 'Immunité des États au point de vue de la Juridiction', 8 *Rec.* (1925 III), 417. FITZMAURICE, 'State Immunity', 14 *Brit. Y.B.* (1933), 101. BROOKFIELD, 19 *Brit. Y.B.* (1938), 151. LOURIE, 42 Michigan L.R. (1943), 516. LYONS, 23 *Brit. Y.B.* (1946), 240. DICEY–(MORRIS), 131 et seq. SANBORN, 39 *Amer. J.* (1945), 794 et seq.

PRINCIPLES GOVERNING THE COMPETENCE OF THE COURTS

The question to be answered here is: on what circumstances does any given state make the competence of its courts dependent? Is competence determined by the nationality of the parties or of one of them, or their domicile, or their residence, or their presence within the country, or the place of performance of the obligation in issue?[1] Every state answers this question in accordance with the view it takes of the fundamental purpose of its jurisdiction.

53. Jurisdiction destined to protect nationals?

I. A country may consider it to be the primary task of its courts to serve its own nationals and not, or only exceptionally, the citizens of foreign states. This is the starting-point of French law.[2] French courts always have jurisdiction where the plaintiff is of French nationality, even though the defendant may be an alien neither domiciled nor resident nor present in France, and even where the facts on which the claim is based have no relation to

[1] The further question of the effect of proceedings in foreign courts, particularly of foreign judgments, is discussed *infra*, s. 230 et seq.

[2] French *Civ. C.*, art. 14, 15. Art. 14 says: 'The alien even when not resident in France . . . can be brought before the French tribunals with regard to obligations contracted by him in a foreign country towards Frenchmen.' Art. 15: 'A Frenchman can be brought before a French tribunal with regard to obligations contracted by him in a foreign country towards an alien.' On the interpretation of these ambiguous rules see Pillet, *Traité prat.* i. 354; Niboyet, *Manuel*, p. 884 et seq.

France. When an alien wishes to sue a French national
the defendant can always demand that the action be
brought in a French court. France here claims exclusive
jurisdiction, even where the basic facts are not in any way
concerned with France, and irrespective of the parties'
domicile and residence. Finally, if both parties are aliens,
the rule is that French courts have no jurisdiction to
entertain the action.[1] These 'exorbitant and intolerable
rules'[2] have met with severe and well-founded criticism
everywhere. They establish an inequality between French
nationals and aliens which is in harmony with the chau-
vinistic attitude of the authors of the Civil Code, but can
hardly be justified by any rational, social, or economic
consideration. Italy, too, bases her rules of jurisdiction
mainly on nationality, but avoids the exaggeration of
French law.[3]

2. Conceivably a country might take the view that the
task of its courts is to apply and develop its own law.[4] If
that were so the courts of any country would entertain
such actions, and such actions only, as according to their
conflict rules are governed by the internal law of the forum.
No court, however, has adopted such a rule, and this
rightly. There is certainly a close connexion between the
delimitation of jurisdiction and the applicable law. A
clause in a contract to the effect that the courts of a
particular country are to decide any question arising
thereunder is often considered to be an implied submission to the law of that country; 'qui eligit iudicem
eligit ius'.[5] Furthermore, when a contract is governed by
English law, an English court can at its discretion give
leave to serve notice of a writ on an absent defendant and

*54. Juris-
diction as
a means to
develop
own law?*

---

[1] This principle, however, is subject to many exceptions developed by the
courts. See Pillet, loc. cit. i. 394.

[2] Niboyet, *Manuel*, p. 888. See the discussions in the French 'comité de droit
internat. privé', printed in the *Trav. d. Com. franc.*, iii. (1937), 43 et seq.

[3] *Cod. di procedura civile*, art. 105, 106 (which gave rise to much controversy).
Cf. Udina, *Elementi*, p. 69 et seq.

[4] This view was taken by von Bar, ii. 427 (Engl. translat., p. 907, 908) and
the Institute of International Law, *Annuaire*, i. 125, 126. It prevailed in English
law until the eighteenth century. See *supra*, s. 27.

[5] See, e.g., German Supreme Court, *Jur. W.* 1906, 452, and 1928, 1197.
Decision of the Bavarian Supreme Court in *IPRspr.* 1934, 45.

thus assume jurisdiction.[1] But this connexion between applicable law and jurisdiction must not be exaggerated, or to quote Savigny's warning, 'must not be supposed to amount to complete identity'.[2]

55. Jurisdiction and the interests of the parties

3. Practically all modern laws dealing with jurisdiction rightly take the consideration of the *conflicting interests* of the parties as their starting-point and, particularly in cases of status, also take into account the *public interest* involved.

(*a*) The *plaintiff's* interest is to bring his action in the courts of that country in which he can at that time reasonably expect to be able to enforce the judgment he hopes to obtain. It is obvious that this is not necessarily the country of which the defendant is a national. A German who has left Germany and settled in America may not have any property in Germany and will probably be more vulnerable in America. Thus jurisdiction will be given to the courts of that country where the defendant is ordinarily resident, or where without being resident he has some property which the creditor may seize. In the case of a claim to chattels or immovables the *forum situs* will be most appropriate. Where the plaintiff seeks an injunction it would seem sensible to choose the forum at one of the places where the defendant would be likely to commit the acts sought to be prohibited. Dicey speaks rightly of a 'principle of effectiveness'[3] as determining the limits within which the courts have jurisdiction. The plaintiff will, moreover, not only desire to obtain an effective judgment; it is also to his interest that his action should be entertained by a court easily accessible to him, a court, that is, of the country where he and his witnesses are, or to which they can travel without difficulty.

(*b*) This latter interest, however, will not be protected where it conflicts with the *defendant's interest*. In such cases the defendant's interest to be sued in a court which is easily accessible to him and his witnesses must prevail— this follows from the general maxim that a defendant can

---

[1] R.S.C. Order XI, r. 1 (e) (iii). Cf. also Order XI, r. 1. (d) (execution of trusts of any written instrument which ought to be executed according to the law of England).

[2] Savigny, viii, § 360, 1, § 361, note k (Guthrie's transl., pp. 134, 144, note (k)).   [3] Dicey–Morris, pp. 22, 23.

claim greater protection than his aggressor. Therefore the law cannot allow the plaintiff to choose the court solely to suit his own convenience. The principle *actor forum rei sequitur* is rightly recognized everywhere.[1] The defendant's, not the plaintiff's, domicile, residence, or presence is the test for the competence of a court to entertain an action.

(*c*) Every country has regulated the details of the juris- 56. Jurisdiction of its courts by specific rules: the decision has diction and nowhere been left entirely to the court's discretion. As of the the strictness of the rules may in many instances entail parties some unfairness, all legal systems allow the parties to grant jurisdiction to any court by *agreement*, either before or after the dispute has arisen. Such agreement will be implied when the defendant submits to proceedings in a court which would otherwise have no jurisdiction to deal with them. Furthermore, English law—in contradistinction to the continental systems—has added to the strict rules a certain number of cases in which the court has a discretionary power to assume jurisdiction at the plaintiff's request, or again, to stay actions at the defendant's request.

(*d*) The *public interest* is involved in proceedings affect- 57. Jurisding the status of a person, such as suits for divorce, for diction and judicial separation, for declaration of legitimacy, or of the public nullity of marriage. Under many legal systems questions interest on property rights over land are included in this category; *omnis fundus patriae pars*. In all these cases the law determines the appropriate forum by compulsory rules and does not allow the parties to choose their forum by agreement.[2] In the case of status proceedings the right forum is to be found at the centre of the person's life, i.e. either his domicile or his ordinary residence. Actions concerning rights to land belong to the *forum situs*.

---

[1] On the exceptions under French and Italian law see *supra*, s. 53.

[2] *Hyman* v. *Hyman*, [1929] P. 30 (*per* Scrutton L.J.): 'The Divorce Court does not, as other courts do, act on mere consents or defaults of pleading or mere admissions of the parties.' The same is true for all continental systems. See, for example, French Civil Code, art. 235; German Code of Civ. Procedure, s. 606 et seq.

BIBLIOGRAPHY

H. C. GUTTERIDGE, 'Le conflit des lois de compétence judiciaire', 44 *Rec.* (1933 II), 115; GUTTERIDGE, 19 *Brit. Y.B.* (1938), 19 (*Rev. Ghent*, 1938, 1).

CHAPTER V

ENGLISH RULES ON ACTIONS
IN PERSONAM

58. The two kinds of actions ENGLISH law distinguishes between actions *in rem* and actions *in personam*. Though both terms are of Roman origin, their meaning differs from that of the same words in Roman and modern continental law.[1] In Roman law *actio in personam* designated an action arising from an obligation (*ex contractu*, *ex delicto*, &c.), *actio in rem* an action protecting a *ius in rem*, such as ownership, servitudes, or pledges,[2] and similarly modern laws speak of *actions personnelles* or *réelles*, of *dinglicher* or *persönlicher Anspruch*, thus pointing to the kind of right from which the action arises.

English lawyers call actions *in personam* all those actions which aim at 'determining the rights of parties *inter se* in the subject-matter',[3] and it makes no difference whether they spring from an obligation (contract, tort) or from a *ius in rem*: the owner's action for delivery of chattels detained by the defendant, or for the recovery of land, or any proceedings aiming at settling questions of title as between the parties, are actions *in personam*. It has been rightly said that it would be preferable to call all these actions actions *inter partes*.[4]

Actions *in rem*, on the other hand, are all those which aim at a decision effective for and against everybody. Some of these decisions are of a constitutive character in so far as they create a new legal situation or extinguish an

---

[1] Often, however, English lawyers use them 'without attaching any definite meaning to those phrases', Blackburn, J., in *Castrique* v. *Imrie* (1870), L.R. 4, H.L. 429.

[2] Examples of *actiones in rem* were the *rei vindicatio*, the *actio negatoria*, the *actio confessoria*, the *actio Publiciana*, the *hereditatis petitio*; Inst. 4, 6, 1 et seq. The immediate object of the *actio in rem* was the *res* itself irrespective of the person possessing it; in the classic epoch the name of the defendant was (mostly) not contained in the *intentio*, and no obligation rested on him to *defendere rem* (cf. *Dig.* 50. 17. 156 pr.; 6.1.80). In the case of *res indefensa* he was obliged to surrender the *res* without a decision of the *ius in rem*.

[3] Vaisey and Meyer in *Halsbury*, xiii, p. 405.

[4] Vaisey and Meyer, loc. cit.

existing one, such as a divorce decree, a decision for
revocation of a patent, or an order of discharge in bankruptcy; others are merely declaratory, such as a decision
establishing the validity of a will, the nullity of marriage,[1]
the legitimacy of a person, or the character of a piece of
land as part of a highway. These decisions are effective
not only *inter partes* but *adversus omnes*.[2]

In an action *in personam* the English courts have jurisdiction if at the time when the writ is served the defendant
is present in England or Wales. Mere physical presence
is sufficient. He need not be domiciled or ordinarily resident in this country. His presence for however short a
period establishes jurisdiction. If an Irishman flying from
Dublin to Amsterdam stops at Croydon for ten minutes
he may there be served with a writ and English jurisdiction would thereby be established. Nor does it matter
whether the defendant is in this country voluntarily or is
brought here as a prisoner of war. It makes no difference,
finally, whether the facts of the case have any relation to
England or not.[3] This fundamental rule of English jurisdiction—unknown in continental laws[4]—has often and
rightly been criticized as unfair to a defendant not resident
in England. On the other hand, in some extreme cases
of unfairness the court has power to interfere by staying
or dismissing an action 'whenever there is vexation and
oppression'.[5]

59. Presence in England or Wales of the defendant

[1] See, however, on this point, *infra*, s. 74.

[2] Thus not all actions *in rem* are based on a *ius in rem* (just as not all actions
based on a *ius in rem* are actions *in rem*; see *supra*). The reason why acts effective
against everybody are called *in rem* is to be found in an error in logical reasoning:
because all *iura in rem* are effective against everybody all legal facts effective
against everybody are called *in rem*. It is, therefore, submitted that Lord
Dunedin's reasoning in *Salvesen* v. *Administrator of Austrian Property*, [1927]
A.C. 641, 662, was hardly necessary. He tried to explain that as the action for
nullity of marriage is an action *in rem* the status of marriage is a *res*. He admits,
however, that it 'is not strictly a *res*', but he adds that 'it, to borrow a phrase,
savours of a *res*, and has long been treated as such'.

[3] *Jackson* v. *Spitall* (1870), L.R. 5, C.P. 542, 549.

[4] Except Italian *Cod. proc. civ.*, art. 106, no. 2, where the jurisdiction in
respect of a foreign defendant is declared dependent on his being either resident
in Italy or present to be served personally with a writ.

[5] Bowen, L. J., in *McHenry* v. *Lewis* (1882), 22 Ch.D. (C.A.) 397, 407, 408.
See *infra*, s. 229.

An example of this:[1]

An American domiciled in India executed a deed of separation from his wife under which he promised to pay her a certain annuity. A solicitor domiciled and resident in India was made trustee under the deed. The husband failed to perform his obligations, and the solicitor neglected to take proceedings against him; thereby the wife suffered some damage. While she and the solicitor were temporarily in England, she brought an action against him and served him with a writ. Thereafter she went to America and the solicitor returned to India. On his application the court dismissed the action.

60. Companies and partnerships as defendants   If the defendant is a legal person, such as a limited company, it is impossible to speak of its presence in or absence from England in the true sense of these terms. The company is, however, to be treated as being 'present' in this country if it is either incorporated here or carrying on business in England.[2]

When an action has to be brought against the members of a partnership, the English court has jurisdiction if the partnership carries on business in England, irrespective of whether any of the partners are or are not present here; it is sufficient that the writ is served 'either upon any one or more of the partners at the principal place of business . . . or upon any person having at the time of service the control or management of the partnership business there'.[3] This rule reflects the sound idea that a partnership, without being a 'legal person' different from the sum of the partners, is *in some respects* to be treated as if it were a legal person. French and Italian law go even farther; they regard commercial partnerships as genuine legal persons. German law takes practically the same view as English law in recognizing a certain independent personality of partnerships, though only for some restricted purposes.[4]

61. Defendant absent: discretionary power of court   Under common law the English courts have no jurisdiction to entertain an action against a defendant who

[1] *Egbert* v. *Short*, [1907] 2 Ch. 205, 211. Cf. *In re Norton's Settlement*, [1908] 1 Ch. (C.A.) 471; *Logan* v. *Bank of Scotland*, [1906] 1 K.B. (C.A.) 141; *Watkins* v. *North American Land & Timber Co.* (1904), 20 T.L.R. (H.L.) 534.

[2] Dicey–Morris, p. 174. See Companies Act, 1948, ss. 437, 412. Order IX, rule 8. *Dunlop Pneumatic Tyre Co.* v. *Actien-Gesellschaft für Motor*, &c., [1902] 1 K.B. (C.A.) 342. *La Bourgogne*, [1899] A.C. 431.

[3] Order XLVIII A (1891), rules, 1, 3.

[4] See *infra*, ss. 277, 283.

being absent from England cannot be served with a writ
here. The obvious hardship of this principle has been
mitigated by *Rules of the Supreme Court* (R.S.C.), based
on the Common Law Procedure Act, 1852.[1] These rules
empower the court upon the plaintiff's application in
certain circumstances to permit the service of notice of a
writ upon a defendant absent from England, and thus to
assume jurisdiction.[2] This power is discretionary—the
court may exercise it or refuse to do so. It will refuse, e.g.,
when the defendant is an alien living abroad in a country
possessing an impartial and satisfactory legal procedure,[3]
if it would be unjustifiable to put him to 'the inconvenience
and annoyance of being brought to contest his rights in
this country'.[4]

The discretionary power of the courts to assume jurisdiction against an absent defendant exists only in a
strictly limited number of cases. It is a long list, but an
exhaustive one. Studying the particular cases included in
the list one finds many of those 'connecting factors'[5] that
give rise in continental systems to regular jurisdiction,
i.e. to a jurisdiction which is not dependent upon any discretion of the courts. There are seven of these connecting
factors:

1. The *situs rei*. Subject to the discretion of the court, 62. The
all claims relating to land situate in England, including *forum situs*
actions for the recovery of rent, can be brought in an
English court as the *forum situs* even if the defendant is
not present in England.[6] We are speaking here of actions

---

[1] 15 & 16 Vict., c. 76. The rules were made in 1883 and have been supplemented several times.

[2] Under a rule of 1941 (R.S.C. Ord. IX, r. 14b) the court may even entirely
dispense with service of a writ on any defendant who is an enemy, if prompt
personal service on such defendant is impossible or (if effected) could not be
proved, and if the applicant produces a statement of claim and an affidavit
showing that he is entitled on merits to succeed in the action. This rule, however,
does not apply in matrimonial causes (divorce proceedings, &c.); *Read* v. *Read*,
[1942] P. (C.A.) 87.

[3] *Oppenheimer* v. *Louis Rosenthal & Co.*, [1937] 1 A.E.R. 23. Cf. also *George
Munro Ltd.* v. *American Cyanid Corp.*, [1944] 1 K.B. 432, 437.

[4] *Société générale de Paris* v. *Dreyfus Bros.* (1885), 29 Ch.D. 239, 242. *Rosler*
v. *Hilbery*, [1925] Ch. 250, 259. *In re Schintz*, [1926] Ch. 710, 716.

[5] Or 'points of contact'. Cf. on this conception *infra*, s. 91.

[6] Order XI, r. 1 (a) & 1 (b); cf. also part of r. 1 (f).—R. 1 (a) allows service

in personam only. But as actions for the recovery of land, actions of ejectment, proceedings for preventing or removing a nuisance on land, foreclosure of mortgages, relief for disturbance of easements are personal actions,[1] jurisdiction to entertain them against an absent defendant is not given merely by the fact that the piece of land is situate in England; it can only be established by special leave of the court. In the case of movables—or, to be exact, of personal property[2]—the court of the situs is competent to entertain proceedings between mortgagor and mortgagee when one of the parties seeks relief of a certain kind.[3] Finally, the *forum situs* of personal property has jurisdiction—by leave of the court—'whenever the action is for the execution (as to property situate within the jurisdiction) of the trusts of any written instrument of which' the defendant is a trustee irrespective of whether the testator or settlor has or has had his domicile in England or abroad, provided that the trust 'ought to be executed according to the law of England'.[4]

63. *Fora domicilii et mansionis*

2. The *domicile* or the *ordinary residence* of the defendant. With leave of the court claims of any kind can be brought against a defendant absent from England but either domiciled or ordinarily resident here.[5] These two *fora domicilii* and *habitationis* (*seu mansionis*) are to be found with slight differences of detail in all continental systems,

out of England 'whenever the whole subject-matter of the action is land situate within the jurisdiction; or the perpetuation of testimony relating to land within the jurisdiction'; R. 1 (b): whenever 'any act, deed, will, contract, obligation, or liability, *affecting* land or hereditaments situate within the jurisdiction is sought to be construed, rectified, set aside, or enforced in the action'. (The term 'affecting land' has given rise to many doubts; cf. *Agnew* v. *Usher* (1884), 14 Q.B.D. 78, 80; *Kaye* v. *Sutherland* (1887), 20 Q.B.D. 147; *Tassell* v. *Hallen*, [1892] 1 Q.B. 321).—R. 1 (f) allows jurisdiction 'whenever any injunction is sought as to anything to be done within the jurisdiction, or any nuisance within the jurisdiction is sought to be prevented or removed, whether damages are or are not sought in respect thereof'.

[1] *Supra*, p. 64.

[2] The distinction between personal and real property, which in private international law has been displaced by the division of property into movables and immovables, here retains a certain importance; *infra*, s. 486.

[3] (Order XI, r. 1 (h)) viz., 'sale, foreclosure, delivery of possession by the mortgagor, redemption, re-conveyance, delivery of possession by the mortgagee'.

[4] Order XI, r. 1 (d) second part.

[5] Order XI, r. 1 (c).

where indeed they are regular and ordinary, not exceptional *fora*.[1] The last domicile of a deceased person in England and Wales suffices to create a discretionary jurisdiction 'whenever the action is for the administration of the personal estate' of the deceased—corresponding to the *forum hereditatis* known in continental laws.[2]

3. The English court can assume jurisdiction as *forum* *contractus* in four cases,[3] viz.: **64. Forum contractus**

(*a*) If the contract was made in England: *forum loci celebrationis*, corresponding to the *lex loci celebrationis* in English Conflict Law.

Most modern laws have decided against the jurisdiction of this forum, though until the nineteenth century many continental writers adopted it, founding their opinion (wrongly) on some passages in the *Digest*.[4] As, however, in England such jurisdiction depends on the discretion of the court, there can be little doubt that when a contract has no internal relation to England the fact that it happened to be signed on English soil would not be regarded as a sufficient reason for assuming jurisdiction.

(*b*) if the contract was made abroad but 'through an agent trading or residing' in England 'on behalf of a principal trading or residing out of England'. That does not mean that the agent must have concluded the contract; it is sufficient that he has sent the offer to the principal or has negotiated the contract even if the acceptance was made by the principal himself.[5]

(*c*) if the contract 'by its terms or by implication is to be governed by English law';[6]

(*d*) if the action is brought in respect of any breach committed in England.[7] It does not matter whether it is

[1] Under French law competence is determined by the defendant's domicile, and if he has no domicile by his residence (the French conception of domicile, however, differs from the English; see *infra*, s. 98). Under German law by the defendant's domicile and if he has none by the place of his sojourn; if this cannot be ascertained, by his last domicile.

[2] Order XI, r. 1 (d) first part. Cf. German Code of Civ. Proced., s. 28. As to the history, see Wach, *Civilprocessrecht*, i. 429, note.

[3] Order XI, r. 1 (e).

[4] In particular on *Dig.* 5. 1. 19. 2. See Savigny, § 370 *ad not.* (a).

[5] *National Mortgage & Agency Co.* v. *Gosselin* (1922), 38 T.L.R. 832.

[6] See *Ocean Steamship Co.* v. *Queensland*, [1941] 1 K.B. (C.A.) 402; *N. V. Kwik Hoo Tong Handel Maatschappij* v. *Finlay & Co.*, [1927] A.C. 604; *Kadel Chajkin Ltd.* v. *Mitchell, Cotts & Co.*, [1947] 2 A.E.R. 786.

[7] See further Order XI, r. 1 (h); Dicey–Morris, p. 197.

a substantial breach or one concerning a merely subsidiary obligation.[1]

As the place where a contract is broken is in most cases identical with the place where it ought to have been performed, this forum usually coincides with the continental *forum loci solutionis*.[2]

In the four cases mentioned the court is not allowed to assume jurisdiction as a *forum contractus* if the defendant is domiciled or ordinarily resident in Scotland; jurisdiction is then left to the Scottish courts.

65. *Fora delicti et actus*

4. The *locus delicti commissi*. Where the action is founded on a tort committed in England the court may assume jurisdiction. If the tort was committed abroad the assumption of jurisdiction by the English court presupposes that the tortfeasor is domiciled or ordinarily resident in this country.[3]

While most continental laws reject the *forum delicti*, German and French law allow it without restrictions[4]—which is hardly justifiable. As under German (and possibly under French) law a tort is committed everywhere where either the wrongful act is done or its effects come into existence, there may be several *fora delicti*, for example, in cases where copies of a newspaper containing a defamatory statement have been sold in two or more countries.[5] English law therefore seems to have done wisely in giving the court discretion to assume or refuse jurisdiction.[6]

5. The place where anything is 'to be done, or any nuisance to be prevented or removed'. When that place is in England the court may assume jurisdiction to grant an injunction.[7]

66. *Forum connexitatis*

6. The substantial *connexity* of actions. If an action has been 'properly brought' against a person duly served in England, and if another person out of England is 'a necessary or proper party' to that action the court may

[1] The contrary doctrine laid down in *Johnson* v. *Taylor Bros.*, [1920] A.C. 144, 147 has been abandoned. See *Oppenheimer* v. *Louis Rosenthal & Co.*, [1937] 1 A.E.R. 23.

[2] See, for example, German Code of Civ. Proced. (1933), s. 29. The rather tortuous way in which English law has framed its rule is to be found on the continent too; Wach, *Civilprocessr.* i. 451, n. 20.

[3] Order XI, r. 1 (ee) added in 1920, and r. 1 (a).

[4] German C. of Civ. Proc., s. 32; French C. of Civ. Proc., art. 59 *in fine* (since 1923).

[5] See *infra*, ss. 477, 478.

[6] See *Kroch* v. *Rossell & Co.*, [1937] 1 A.E.R. 725 (C.A.).

[7] Order XI, r. 1 (f) and *Rosler* v. *Hilbery*, [1925] Ch. (C.A.) 250.

at its discretion assume jurisdiction to entertain the connected claim against the absent person as a *litis consors* of the first.[1]

This *forum connexitatis*, as it was called by medieval writers, is appropriate particularly when two persons are joint debtors under a contract or joined tortfeasors, and when only one is present in England. There is, however, a risk that the plaintiff may first bring an action against a bogus defendant, that is, a defendant 'against whom no plausible cause of action exists'[2] and who is present in this country, in order that he may then cite with him the substantial defendant living abroad. In such a case the action is not 'properly brought'. The decisive test is, as Lord Esher put it, 'supposing both parties had been within the jurisdiction, would they both have been proper parties to the action? If they would and only one of them is in this country, then the rule says that the other may be served.'[3]

The English rule, as it is formulated, has two defects: (*a*) The court can allow service out of England only after the party present in England has been served with the writ;[4] thus the plaintiff is in the unfortunate position of having to decide whether to bring the action in an English or a foreign court before he knows whether the English court will allow the extension of the action to the absentee. (*b*) The court cannot allow extension to the connected action if both defendants are out of England and one of them has been served with an English writ under Order XI; for example, because he is domiciled or ordinarily resident in England.[5]

7. Finally, the English court can assume jurisdiction against an absent air carrier in the case of an international transport of goods or persons by air.

67. Jurisdiction against Air Carrier

This was introduced by the Carriage by Air Act, 1932, which put into force an International Convention of 1929.[6] Under this Convention actions

---

[1] Order XI, r. 1 (g). See *Bloomfield* v. *Serenyi*, [1945] 2 A.E.R. 646 (C.A.); Wach, loc. cit., p. 495, n. 13.

[2] *Witted* v. *Galbraith*, [1893] 1 Q.B. (C.A.) 577, 579.

[3] *Massey* v. *Heynes* (1888), 21 Q.B.D. (C.A.) 330, 338. See *The Washburn Co.* v. *The Cunard Steamship Co.* (1889), 5 T.L.R. 592; *The Duc d'Aumale*, [1903] P. 18, 22. *Ellinger* v. *Guinness*, [1939] 4 A.E.R. 16. It is, on the other hand, not necessary that the present defendant should be 'the principal defendant or at least as much a substantial defendant' as the absent. That was the formula framed by Pearson, J., in *The Yorkshire Tannery Co.* v. *The Eglinton Co.* (1884), 54 L.J. Ch. 81, 83.

[4] *The Yorkshire Tannery Co.* v. *The Eglinton Co.*, loc. cit.

[5] On this, see Dicey–Morris, p. 195[46].

[6] 22 & 23 Geo. V, c. 36; and Order XI, r. 1 (i).

for damages can be brought 'at the option of the plaintiff in the territory of one of the High Contracting Parties either before the court having jurisdiction where the carrier is ordinarily resident, or has his principal place of business, or has an establishment by which the contract has been made, or before the court having jurisdiction at the place of destination'.

68. *Forum patrimonii?*   Apart from these seven exceptions the rule stands; jurisdiction of the English court depends on the defendant's presence in England. The court is, in particular, not at liberty to entertain an action against an absentee merely on the ground that he has some *property* in this country. That is a regrettable gap. When a domiciled Englishman has a claim against a foreigner who is neither present nor domiciled nor resident here, out of a contract made and broken abroad, he cannot bring an action here though the debtor possesses a bank account at an English bank sufficient to satisfy the claimant.

This rule differs from some continental laws, from Scottish law and from the law of several states of the U.S.A. German law[1] certainly goes too far in allowing the action even if the property situate in Germany is practically of no value or cannot be seized by the creditor (such as tools and implements of the debtor's trade). Scottish law distinguishes the case where the defendant possesses immovables in Scotland from the case where he has only movables there; in the first case the Scottish court has jurisdiction; in the second, the plaintiff must first 'fix' the movables by arrestment, whereby jurisdiction is founded.[2] The same principle obtains in the United States, where jurisdiction can be founded by attachment.[3] An alteration of the legal situation in England and an adoption of the Scottish system was considered by the Government. But the Committee on British and Foreign Legal Procedure rejected the reform plan in 1919.[4]

69. *Forum prorogatum*   Like Roman law,[5] Scottish law, and all continental laws, English law too recognizes an agreement of the parties as to the competence of the court.[6] Such an agreement creating a *forum prorogatum (seu conventionale)* can be made only if the cause of action arises from a contract.[7] There

---

[1] German Code of Civil Proc. (1933), s. 23.

[2] This system of *arrestum ad fundandam iurisdictionem* was taken over from Holland. Cf. Duncan and Dykes, *Principles of Civil Jurisdiction*, p. 71 et seq.; Burnet, *Jurid. Rev.* i (1889), 54 et seq. (on the lawsuit *Parnell* v. *The Times*).

[3] Beale, i. 449 et seq.; *Rest.* §§ 106–8.

[4] Gutteridge, 19 *Br. Y.B.* (1938), 29, 51, 61.

[5] *Dig.* 5. 1. 1.

[6] Cf. Graupner, 59 *L.Q.R.* (1943), 227.

[7] Order XI, r. 2 (a). Continental laws do not restrict *prorogatio fori* so much.

is, however, another rule which practically covers all non-contractual cases. If a person by his conduct voluntarily submits to the jurisdiction of the court he is precluded from objecting to it.[1] The submission may be expressed or implied.[2] Thus a plaintiff submits to the court's jurisdiction to entertain a cross-action against him if there is any connexion between his claim and the cross-action.[3] A counter-claim not *ex eodem negotio* but *eiusdem generis* would probably be insufficient in England to establish submission, though admitted by Scottish law.[4]

[1] *The Gemma*, [1899] P. 285. *The Dupleix*, [1912] P. 8. *Schibsby* v. *Westenholz* (1870), L.R. 6 Q.B. 155. *Copin* v. *Adamson* (1875), 1 Ex.D. (C.A.) 17.

[2] Must the parties have known that the court to which they submit has no jurisdiction? Yes, under Roman law (*Dig.* 5. 1. 2 pr.); no, under English law.

[3] *Yorkshire Tannery* v. *Eglinton Co.* (1884), 54 L.J.Ch. 81, 83.

[4] Thus Inglis, L.J.Cl., in *Thompson* v. *Whitehead* (1862), 24 S.C. 331, 339.

CHAPTER VI

ACTIONS OR OTHER PROCEEDINGS *IN REM*

1. AGAINST A SHIP

70. Against a ship THE English court is competent, as *forum situs*, to entertain an action against a ship or things connected with a ship—such as cargo—if the ship or the things are in England or in English waters. The action must be one which before the coming into force of the Judicature Act, 1873, would have been brought in the Court of Admiralty. Examples of this are claims to ownership or possession of an English ship, claims for damage done or suffered by an English or foreign ship, claims of a maritime lien, for salvage, wages, pilotage, and others.[1]

2. DIVORCE PROCEEDINGS

71. The rule The English court has jurisdiction if at the beginning of the proceedings the parties are domiciled in England. Neither their residence nor their presence in England nor their nationality matters. In this, English law is less complicated than most of the continental systems. Under these the substantive law to be applied in divorce cases is usually determined by nationality; the lawgiver is therefore inclined to make jurisdiction dependent on nationality too, relegating the domicile to a position of secondary importance.[2] In particular, the Hague Divorce Convention, 1902;[3] established an intricate system: the action can be brought at the plaintiff's choice either in the court competent according to the national law of both

---

[1] Dicey–Morris, pp. 205–15. On the jurisdiction of maritime courts established by Allied and Associated Powers see 4 & 5 Geo. VI (1941) c. 21.

[2] See, for example, the German rules (Code of Civ. Proced., s. 606): In principle jurisdiction is tested by the husband's domicile; if he has no domicile, by the place of his sojourn, and if this cannot be established, by his last domicile. But if he is of German nationality, or if he was a German and his wife is still German, or if both spouses have lost their German nationality without acquiring any other, then there is always a German court competent to entertain divorce proceedings. Finally, when both spouses are aliens an action for divorce can be brought in a German court only if according to the husband's national law German courts have jurisdiction.

[3] See *supra*, s. 40.

spouses or in the court of the domicile of both; if under their national law they have not the same domicile, the domicile of the respondent is decisive.[1] Under English law there is complete harmony between the conflict rule and jurisdiction, the *forum domicilii* corresponding to the *lex domicilii*. This would be a very sound solution if the English conception of domicile were satisfactory. A foreigner who has never been in this country but who has his domicile of origin here (because at the time of his birth his father had an English domicile) can sue and be sued in divorce in the English court.[2] It is a sound principle to give jurisdiction to the country where the spouses have their real home, the centre of their life; but that centre is not always their domicile and is more likely to be the place of their ordinary residence.

The principle that divorce jurisdiction lies exclusively at the court of the domicile is now firmly established, subject, however, to certain qualifications and exceptions.[3]

(1) As English law does not recognize separate domiciles for husband and wife, the husband's domicile (the so-called 'matrimonial domicile'[4]) is decisive. This presupposes, however, that the marriage is valid. Where according to the law of the husband's domicile (though not according to English law) the marriage is void, his 'wife' is under *his* law a *feme sole* and therefore capable of having a domicile of her own. If, for example, a domiciled Greek marries an Englishwoman in England before the registrar, his marriage though valid under English law is void under Greek law because no Greek priest was present at the ceremony; in the view of Greek law, therefore, the wife has not acquired a Greek domicile by the marriage. In two

72. Anomalous cases

---

[1] Art. 5–7 Hague Convention. That is the principle. There are some exceptions, but they are without interest here.

[2] See on this *infra*, s. 121.

[3] *Le Mesurier* v. *Le Mesurier*, [1895] A.C. 517 (which, in fact, overruled the majority decision in *Niboyet* v. *Niboyet* (1878), 4 P.D. 1); *Salvesen* v. *Administr. of Austrian Property*, [1921] A.C. 641, 666; *H.* v. *H.*, [1928] P. 206, 212; *Herd* v. *Herd*, [1936] P. 205, and others. (See Cook, *Logical and Legal Bases*, 457–68.) Scots law is different; there jurisdiction is tested by residence. American laws follow English law in giving jurisdiction to the court of the domicile; in some states, however, residence is required; as to what is meant thereby, see Beale, i. 116.   [4] Lord Haldane in *Lord Advocate* v. *Jaffrey*, [1921] 1 A.C. 146, 152.

such cases[1] the court allowed the wife here to sue for divorce since she had had an English domicile. But later decisions abandoned this view.[2] The solution now seems to be the following: When the court of the husband's domicile (a Greek court) has pronounced a decree of nullity[3] this will be recognized by the English court (though under English law the marriage was valid); the foreign nullity decree is looked upon as having destroyed the marriage *adversus omnes*, it has—to use a continental expression—transformed the *matrimonium claudicans* into a *matrimonium non existens*. There is therefore no room for divorce proceedings.

It is submitted that this solution does not remove the hardship caused to the wife. Though her English marriage was valid in England, she has no right to retain her marriage name, her children are not legitimate, and she is deprived of the economic advantages she might have had if her marriage had been dissolved by divorce on the ground, for example, of her husband's adultery.

73. Desertion and deportation

(2) A graver situation arises where a wife has been deserted by her husband, who immediately before the desertion had been domiciled in England but has changed his domicile since the desertion. Under the law as it stood before 1938 she could not sue for divorce in an English court. Divorce jurisdiction was exclusively with the court of the husband's new domicile,[4] and if this happened to be a country in which no divorce is permitted—such as Italy—the wife was debarred from suing for divorce anywhere; in the court of the husband's new domicile she would be able to obtain nothing but a judicial separation. The Matrimonial Causes Act, 1937,[5] has improved the

---

[1] Viz. in *Stathatos* v. *Stathatos*, [1913] P. 46; and *De Montaigu* v. *De Montaigu*, [1913] P. 154.

[2] *Salvesen* v. *Administrator of Austrian Property*, [1927] A.C. 641; *De Massa* v. *De Massa*, 48 *L.Q.R.* 13. See the Scottish case *Watson* (or *Mangrulkar*) v. *Mangrulkar*, [1939] Sess. C. 239, 245; G. C. Cheshire, pp. 473, 474, and 13 *Brit. Y.B.* (1932), 169, 170.

[3] If the (Greek) court of the husband's domicile has not yet made a nullity decree, the wife would be regarded in England as having her husband's Greek domicile and could for this reason not sue for divorce in an English court. See *Watson* v. *Mangrulkar*, loc. cit.

[4] See *H.* v. *H.*, [1928] P. 206; *Herd* v. *Herd*, [1936] P. 205.

[5] (1 Edw. VIII & 1 Geo. VI, c. 57), s. 13. Similarly in Canada under the Canad. Divorce Jurisdiction Act, 1930; Read, *Recognition and Enforcement of Foreign Judgments* (1938), 218; Johnson, *Confl. of Laws*, ii. (1934), 91.

wife's situation. It gives the English court divorce jurisdiction when she has been deserted and when the husband was 'immediately before the desertion' domiciled in
England. It treats in the same way the case where the
husband had been deported from the United Kingdom
under any law relating to the deportation of aliens.[1]

(3) This rule, however, does not cover those cases where
the husband changed his domicile before he deserted his
wife or where there is no desertion at all.

A new law, the *Law Reform (Miscellaneous Provisions)
Act*, 1949,[2] further extends the jurisdiction of the English
court in divorce proceedings. If a husband is not domiciled in the United Kingdom, the Channel Islands, or the
Isle of Man, and if the wife is resident in England and
has been ordinarily resident there for three years immediately preceding the divorce proceedings the English
Court has jurisdiction in proceedings where the wife is
the petitioner.

If, for example, a domiciled English couple establishes a new domicile
in Italy, and the husband commits adultery, his wife can obtain in Italy
only a judicial separation; but when she returns to England and resides
there for three years the English court has jurisdiction to entertain divorce
proceedings.

Several continental laws have dealt with the problem in a similar
way. A famous decision of the French Court of Cassation held that a
Frenchwoman by birth who has married an Italian can bring divorce
proceedings in the French court provided that she has obtained a separation
decree according to Italian law and has re-acquired French nationality.[3]
Switzerland, Germany, and Sweden have followed this sound rule.[4]

---

[1] In *H.* v. *H.*, [1928] P. 206 at p. 212, it was stated that 'authority to decree
divorce cannot . . . co-exist at the same time in two sovereign states'. This is no
longer true, the wife having the choice between the English court and the court
of her husband's new domicile.

[2] 12, 13 and 14 Geo. VI, c. 100 s. 1.

[3] *Arrêt Ferrari, J. Clunet*, 1922, 714 (*Dalloz*, 1922, 1, 139). This doctrine is now firmly established; *J. Clunet*, 1928, 382; 1929, 1258, though it has
met with strong opposition on the part of some eminent French scholars
(Pillet, *Traité prat.*, i. 607; Audinet, *J. Clunet*, 1930, 329). See Rabel, ii.
442–5.

[4] See German law of 24 Jan. 1935: German law is applicable if only the wife
is German and the husband is the subject of a state which does not allow divorce;
she can sue for divorce in a German court. As to Switzerland, see the decision
of the Swiss Federal Court, 3 May 1932 (*Official Coll.*, 1932, ii. 93; *Rabel's Z.*,
7, 630). This situation has led to the denunciation of the Hague Divorce Convention of 1902 by Switzerland, Sweden, and Germany; see *supra*, s. 43.

The jurisdiction of the English court in divorce proceedings brought by the husband on the ground of his wife's adultery extends to the co-respondent, no matter where his domicile or residence may be, or whether he is present in England or not.[1]

It has been thought that the jurisdiction of the English court to entertain the husband's suit for damages against the co-respondent depends on the husband's domicile in England. There is nothing to support this view.[2]

3. NULLITY OF MARRIAGE PROCEEDINGS

The various kinds of Defective Marriages

74. Void, voidable, and non-existent marriages   Under all modern laws a decree of nullity can be pronounced either because a marriage is *void ab initio* or because it is *voidable*. Examples of the first type are to be found in marriages within prohibited degrees, or in bigamous marriages, or in marriages concluded in religious form in a country where civil marriage is obligatory.[3] Examples of the second kind exist where the marriage has been concluded under the influence of fraudulent misrepresentation or by a person of unsound mind or suffering from a venereal disease in communicable form.[4] Voidable marriages, as opposed to void marriages, are, under English as well as under all continental laws, valid marriages until they are avoided by the party entitled to nullify them.[5] Therefore they have all the effects of

---

[1] According to the Matrim. Causes Act, 1857 (20 & 21 Vict., c. 28), the husband 'shall' make the alleged adulterer a co-respondent.

[2] *Jacobs* v. *Jacobs*, [1950] 1 A.E.R. 96. Dicey–Morris, pp. 228⁹⁰, 229 *in fine*.

[3] As is the case in Belgium, France, the Netherlands, Luxemburg, Germany, Switzerland, Hungary, Portugal, Esthonia, Turkey, and in some of the Latin-American states (Argentine, Brazil, Chile, Cuba).

[4] See Matrim. Causes Act, 1937, s. 7 (1) (b) & (c).

[5] The notion of voidable marriages is not very old. Lord Coke (see *infra*, p. 80⁴) used the term 'voydable' where he meant void marriages. The conception of a marriage that is first valid and then becomes retroactively void through the act of one of the spouses has at all times been rejected by Canon law as incompatible with the character of the marriage as a sacrament. The Protestant doctrine introduced the notion of voidable marriages (on this see: Heyer, *Staats-Lexicon der Görres-Gesellschaft*, i, 4th ed., 1911, pp. 1405, 1419). All modern state laws have adopted the category of voidable marriages (*mariage annulable,*

non-defective marriages: The wife acquires the husband's domicile. She has the same rights to maintenance, pensions, and allowances as any wife. The defect of her marriage may disappear without having led to annullation, e.g. if the party entitled to avoidance dies before exercising his or her right. But if the entitled party petitions for a nullity decree and obtains it, the voidable marriage becomes void with retroactive effect. Maintenance or allowances have never been due. If in consideration of the marriage a payment of money has been promised, the consideration fails.[1] If, however, the jurisdiction of the English court to entertain nullity proceedings is founded on the English domicile of both spouses the nullity decree, in spite of its retrospective character, can hardly destroy the domicile, that is, the basis on which the jurisdiction rests.

Both the void and the voidable marriage should be distinguished from the 'non-existent' marriage. Nobody would call a concubinage a void marriage, even if the couple pretended to be married. The question whether a given act is void or valid presupposes its existence. In a country where marriage requires a declaration before a registrar or priest a private and secret declaration of consent does not create any link of marriage, not even a void one. The difference between a *matrimonium nullum* and a *matrimonium non existens* has been very clearly worked out by Canon law[2] and is recognized in nearly all

anfechtbare Ehe) as distinct from void marriages (*mariage nul, nichtige Ehe*). Only the new German Marriage Law of 1938 has abolished the 'voidable' marriage and the (post-Hitler) Marriage Law of 20 Feb. 1946, ss. 28–37, has maintained the abolition. Instead it speaks of *Aufhebung*, dissolution of marriages. This *Aufhebung* does not destroy the validity of the marriage with retroactive effect; it extinguishes the marriage *ex nunc* and has thus the effects of divorce. In fact, it is a divorce, though not based on post-nuptial facts, but on ante-nuptial facts, or on facts simultaneous with the celebration of the marriage. From the standpoint of private international law it has to be treated in the same way as other cases of marriage extinction for initial defects. Under English private international law, therefore, a German marriage which is subject to *Aufhebung* (e.g., for fraudulent misrepresentation or coercion) is equivalent to a voidable marriage, not to one that may be dissolved by divorce.

[1] *In re Ames' Settlement*, [1946] Ch. 217.

[2] In Canon law the distinction is particularly important with regard to the question: Who is entitled to allege the defect of the marriage? In the case of a *matrimonium nullum* the *ius accusandi matrimonium* belongs only to the parties and an ecclesiastical official (*promotor iustitiae*), while other persons can do no

modern continental laws.[1] There a *matrimonium nullum* has
prima facie all or at least some effects of a valid marriage;
the woman shares the domicile of the man. When, on the
other hand, a marriage is non-existent the union is without
any of the legal effects of a marriage; the woman is a *feme
sole* and may have a separate domicile. Where there is a
void marriage the rules on maintenance and matrimonial
property are at first applicable as in the case of a valid
marriage. Children conceived in a void marriage are
under many laws treated as legitimate unless both parents
are in bad faith;[2] while children of a non-married couple
are everywhere illegitimate irrespective of what the parents
believed. In the case of a void marriage a nullity decree
may be granted; not so if the marriage is non-existent.
Here it is only possible to apply for a declaratory judgment
stating that no marriage exists.[3]

75. English law   This distinction—though never consciously and fully
developed—is to be found also in early English law. Lord
Coke, in dealing with bigamous marriages, said that such
marriage *de facto* 'is a marriage in judgment of the law until
it be avoided'.[4] An avoidance by nullity proceedings, on
the other hand, cannot take place where the parties have
not even gone through an ecclesiastical or civil marriage
ceremony, but have taken up community of life after
mutual declarations that each intends to marry the other.[5]

---

more than inform the authorities; *codex iur. canonici*, 1917, c. 1971. Not until
the death of one of the parties or the nullity decree is it possible to treat the
marriage *incidenter* as void. In the case of a non-existent marriage there is no
room for a nullity decree.

[1] On the French distinction between *mariage nul* and *mariage non-existent*
see Planiol and Ripert, *Traité*, ii. no. 252. On the German and Swiss distinction
between *nichtige Ehe* and *Nicht-Ehe*: von Tuhr, *Allgemeiner Teil*, ii. 1, 295, and
(Enneccerus, Kipp and) Wolff, *Lehrbuch d. bürgerl. Rechts*, iv. (7th ed., 1931),
p. 83 et seq.

[2] See *infra*, s. 362.

[3] Thus, for example, German law (Code of Civ. Proced., s. 606, 631, 638)
distinguishes very precisely the *Nichtigkeitsklage* from the *Klage auf Feststellung
des Nichtbestehens einer Ehe*. The latter is, up to a certain point, similar to a suit
for 'jactitation of marriage' brought under English law against a person who
persistently alleges marriage with the petitioner.

[4] Coke, *Inst.*, p. 88 *ad v.*, 'being married'; Cheshire (2nd ed.), p. 337, n. 1.
See *Dodworth* v. *Dale*, [1936] 2 K.B. 503, 512, 519.

[5] In those countries in which a valid marriage may be concluded without any
religious or civil ceremony, either *nudo consensu* (as is the case in some states of

Modern English law—in contradistinction to modern continental laws—has abandoned the distinction between void and non-existent marriages. A marriage called 'void' is in every respect treated as if it did not exist.[1] By concluding a void marriage a woman does not acquire her partner's domicile;[2] the children conceived or born in a void marriage are illegitimate even if the parents believe in the validity of the marriage.[3] A nullity decree does not change the status of the couple; it merely 'declares' a legal relationship to be non-existent. If there is no nullity decree the nullity of the marriage can be alleged '*incidenter*' in any law-suit by any third parties, e.g. in litigation concerning intestate succession. An incidental statement of the court that the marriage is a nullity, however, has effect between the litigating parties only, while a nullity decree pronounced by the Probate, Divorce, and Admiralty Division is effective *in rem*, i.e. *contra omnes*.

The English court has jurisdiction to entertain nullity proceedings if the spouses have their domicile in England. This corresponds to the rule on divorce jurisdiction (*supra*, s. 71). But the rule of jurisdiction is much less rigid in nullity proceedings than in the case of divorce: apart from the domicile of both spouses there are several other connecting points on which English jurisdiction may be founded, such as residence, or the place of celebration of the marriage. Discussion of these points has not yet clarified them sufficiently. Though a considerable number

76. *Forum domicilii*

---

the U.S.A. and in Russia, and as was legal in Scotland until 1939) or 'by habit and repute' (thus still under the Marriage (Scotland) Act, 1939) the marriage cannot be 'void' for lack of form; for if the marital consent has not been declared and (in Scottish cases) if habit or repute are lacking the union is nothing but a concubinage, a 'non-existent marriage'.

[1] *Niboyet* v. *Niboyet* (1878), 4 P.D. 1, 9. *Newboult* v. *Att.-Gen.*, [1931] P. 75, 77. *Ogden* v. *Ogden* (1908), P. (C.A.) 46, 78 (where it was denied that even a merely voidable marriage effects a change of the woman's domicile). *White* v. *White* (1937), P. 111 (one of the reasons for assuming jurisdiction was that through a void marriage the woman did not acquire the foreign domicile of the respondent but retained her English domicile); see also *Easterbrook* v. *Easterbrook*, [1944] P. 10.

[2] According to the Court of Appeal in *De Reneville* v. *De Reneville*, [1948] P. 100.

[3] There is no protection in England of children born in void 'marriages' as there is in Scotland and in most continental countries.

of the judges of the courts of first instance have dealt with these problems, their views have been far from unanimous, and there are only two decisions by higher courts, one by the House of Lords,[1] and one by the Court of Appeal.[2]

1. Undoubtedly the English court has nullity jurisdiction if *both* spouses have their *domicile* in this country.[3] That is true both for void and for voidable marriages. In the case of a voidable marriage the wife's domicile is always identical with the husband's. By concluding a void marriage the woman does not acquire that domicile *ipsa lege*, but in most cases she acquires it by choice.[4]

In one group of voidable marriages jurisdiction can *only* be based on the English domicile of the spouses: that is, where the marriage is alleged to be voidable on the ground of impotence or wilful refusal to consummate the marriage. At least, that was the view expressed by Bateson, J. in the case of *Inverclyde* v. *Inverclyde*.[5]

77. Inverclyde v. Inverclyde   In that case the facts were as follows: The marriage between the parties had been celebrated in England, where the petitioner (the wife) resided. The respondent resided sometimes in England and sometimes in Scotland. The wife petitioned for a decree of nullity on the ground of the respondent's impotence. Bateson, J. held that he had no jurisdiction to entertain the petition. He said: 'If the principle is sound that in a suit for dissolution of marriage divorce jurisdiction depends on domicile it must equally so depend in a suit for dissolution of marriage on the ground of impotence.' He stresses the fact that the difference between these two kinds of dissolution is a 'mere difference of form'; he adds that in such cases the usual relief in the United States of America is 'dissolution and not nullity' and quotes a Scottish judge's dictum that 'impotence is not a bar to the constitution of marriage but a means of setting it aside or . . . a resolutive condition of the contract'.[6]

[1] *Salvesen* v. *Administrator of Austrian Property*, [1927] A.C. 641.
[2] *De Reneville* v. *De Reneville*, [1948] P. 100.
[3] See notably the *Salvesen* case, the *De Reneville* case, l.c., and *Inverclyde* v. *Inverclyde*, [1931] P. 29 at p. 42.
[4] See *infra*, ss. 118, 119.
[5] [1931] P. 29.
[6] The decision in *Inverclyde* v. *Inverclyde* was opposed by Hudson, J. in *Easterbrook* v. *Easterbrook*, [1944] P. 10, and by Pilcher, J. in *Hutter* v. *Hutter*, [1944] P. 95. The Court of Appeal in *De Reneville* v. *De Reneville* neither approved nor rejected it. *Casey* v. *Casey*, [1949] P. 420 approves it. It is submitted that the Inverclyde doctrine makes good sense, since in some countries impotence and wilful refusal render the marriage void, in others they make it voidable, and in others again they constitute grounds for divorce.

The learned judge's view seems to have been this: in the case of impotence or wilful refusal the true reason for the destruction of the marriage is not the (ante-nuptial) fact that there is impotence, but the (post-nuptial) fact that owing to that impotence the consummation of the valid marriage did not follow, just as if the ground for non-consummation were the wilful refusal of one party to consummate the marriage. The latter case—undoubtedly of a post-nuptial character—has been put on the same footing as the case of non-consummation for impotence by the Matrimonial Causes Act, 1937,[1] and it is indeed a mere technicality of form when in both cases the law declares the marriage to be voidable instead of allowing a divorce.[2] The historical basis for this particular form may be found in the older ecclesiastical idea that a marriage though validly concluded by consent of the parties can only become a sacrament by consummation.[3]

It would hardly be justifiable to extend a rule established for a non-consummated to other voidable marriages merely because in the case of impotence or wilful refusal the marriage is styled voidable.

2. The English court, further, has jurisdiction if only the petitioner is domiciled in England, while the respondent has a foreign domicile. This can happen where the marriage is alleged to be void, not if it is voidable. It is immaterial whether petitioner is the husband or the wife.

---

[1] 1 Edw. VIII & Geo. VI, ch. 57, s. 7, subs. (1) (a). This juxtaposition of impotence and refusal, which reminds us of the old scholastic phrase 'casus impotentiae involvit casum noluntatis' is unknown to all continental laws. Cf. the dictum of Cozens-Hardy, M.R. in *Napier* v. *Napier*, [1915] P. 184, 186.

[2] Modern codes recognize wilful refusal as a ground for divorce.

[3] This has been discussed very often since the ninth century. Hincmar of Rheims wrote: 'Nec habent nuptiae in se Christi et Ecclesiae sacramentum . . . si se nuptialiter non utuntur, i.e. si eas non subsequitur commixtio sexuum.' And Gratian taught: 'coniugium desponsatione initiatur, commixtione perficitur.' Pope Alexander III (1180) distinguished between sacramental marriages, which require *copula carnalis* and cannot be dissolved, and non-sacramental marriages, which can be dissolved *quoad vinculum*. The principal foundation of this theological doctrine is Gen. ii. 24 (*erunt duo in una carne*). Cf. Esmein, *Le mariage en droit canonique* (2nd ed., 1929), i, pp. 70, 119 et seq. Even now the Church allows divorce in the case of a *matrimonium non consummatum*; *Cod. iur. can.* (1917), c. 1118, 1119.

The jurisdiction of the English court is based on *White* v. *White*,[1] as explained by the Court of Appeal in *De Reneville* v. *De Reneville*,[2] and on the curious case of *Metha* v. *Metha*,[3] where a domiciled Englishwoman, not knowing the language and wishing to become a Hindu by religion, went through a religious ceremony making her a Hindu and containing an act of marriage with a Hindu; she did not know that she had thus been 'married'. Under English law the marriage was void *ab initio*;[4] the woman retained her English domicile and was entitled to sue in England, though her 'husband' was a domiciled Indian.

78. Forum of residence?

3. Residence of both parties in England seems to be a sufficient basis for the English court's jurisdiction to entertain nullity proceedings. At least this was the view of the court in *Easterbrook* v. *Easterbrook*[5] and *Hutter* v. *Hutter*,[6] although in both cases the fact that the marriage had been celebrated in England may have been of considerable weight.[7] The Court of Appeal expressly refused (in the *De Reneville* case) to give an opinion on the point.

The contention that residence is sufficient is based on the former practice of the ecclesiastical courts, which were, however, concerned with questions not of international jurisdiction but of local competence.

Residence of the petitioner alone, or of the respondent alone cannot furnish a ground for nullity jurisdiction.[8] Only if the wife has been ordinarily resident in England for three years can she bring a nullity petition in this country.[9]

In contrast to many continental systems a petition for nullity of marriage cannot be brought in an English court on the ground that both parties are of British nationality.

78 a. Forum loci celebrationis

4. Whether the fact that the marriage has been celebrated in England is or is not a sufficient ground for the jurisdiction of a British court is debatable, but the prevail-

---

[1] [1937] P. 111.

[2] [1948] P. 100, at p. 117. See Cheshire, 453-5.

[3] [1945] 2 A.E.R. 690.

[4] Under most continental laws the marriage would have been voidable; see, for example, German *BGB*. s. 1332.

[5] [1944] P. 10.   [6] [1944] P. 95.

[7] On the Northern-Irish case *Mason* v. *Mason*, [1944] N. Ir. 134, see Morris, 61 L.Q.R. 341.

[8] The opposite view held in *Roberts* v. *Brennan* ([1902] P. 143) and *Robert* v. *Robert* ([1947] P. 164) was expressly rejected by the Court of Appeal in the *De Reneville* case, [1948] P. 117.

[9] Law Reform (Miscellaneous Provisions) Act, 1949 (12, 13 and 14 Geo. VI, c. 100), s. (1), subs. (2).

ing opinion allows such jurisdiction.[1] This is supported by a considerable number of decisions[2] and by a (rather weak) 'rational' or 'logical' consideration: some jurists argue that a defective marriage should be destroyed by the country in which it was concluded, an argument based on the old fallacy that what has been done by an act can be undone by an *actus contrarius*.

5. Under s. 13 of the Matrimonial Causes Act, 1937, the English court has nullity jurisdiction if the husband has deserted his wife or has been deported from the United Kingdom, having been domiciled in England immediately before such desertion or deportation. It does not matter whether the wife is or is not resident in England. **78 b.** Desertion and deportation

BIBLIOGRAPHY

G. C. CHESHIRE, *Nullity of Marriage and Conflict of Laws*, 32 *Grotius Soc.* (1947), 68–86. CHESHIRE, *P.I.L.*, pp. 435, 440–70. DICEY(–MORRIS), pp. 244–68. GARNER, *Jurisdiction and Choice of Law in Nullity Suits*, 63 *L.Q.R.* (1947), 486–90. MORRIS, 61 *L.Q.R.* 341 et seq. NOWACK, 8 *Mod. L. R.* (1945), 203–19. HAMILTON, 26 *Can. B. R.* (1948), 875 et seq. FALCONBRIDGE, 26 *Can. B. R.* (1948), 907 et seq. G. C. CHESHIRE, *The International Validity of Divorces*, 61 *L.Q.R.* 352–72. LATEY, 11 *Mod. L. R.* (1948), 70–1.

4. JURISDICTION CONCERNING JUDICIAL SEPARATION AND RESTITUTION OF CONJUGAL RIGHTS

I. Do proceedings for *judicial separation* aim at a change in the 'status' of the parties? The term status is ambiguous. While there is certainly a status of marriage and a status of celibacy it is open to discussion whether the position of persons judicially separated can be described as a status. This is, however, purely a question of terminology. The effects of judicial separation are not the same in all countries. Canon law, where the historical **79.** Separation from bed and board

---

[1] Dicey(–Morris), 250; Cheshire, 448; Differing: Falconbridge, *Essays* 627, and 26 *Can. B.R.* 914, and others.

[2] *Simonin* v. *Mallac* (1860), 2 Sw. & Tr. 67. *Sottomayor* v. *De Barros* (1877), 3 P.D. 1 and (1879), 5 P.D. 94. *Linke* v. *Van Aerde* (1894), 10 T.L.R. 426. *Hay* v. *Northcote*, [1900] 2 Ch. 262 (in this case the marriage was solemnized before the British consul at Bordeaux in accordance with the Foreign Marriage Act, 1892, and was therefore equivalent to a marriage celebrated in England). *Ogden* v. *Ogden*, [1908] P. (C.A.) 46. *Valier* v. *Valier*, [1925] 133 L.T. 830. *Hussein* v. *Hussein*, [1938] P. 159. Cf. *Cooper* v. *Crane* (1891), P. 369 and the remark made by Brett, L.J. in *Niboyet* v. *Niboyet* (1878), 4 P.D. (C.A.) at p. 20.

root of the institution is to be found, calls it a *solutio* of the *communicatio vitae conjugalis*, which in the case of adultery relieves the innocent party of the obligation to re-admit the other party to community of life, while in other cases both are under the obligation to re-establish their common life as soon as the reason for the separation ceases.[1] In many countries separation has the effect of loosening the marriage tie to a far greater extent than under Canon law. In Scandinavian laws[2] judicial separation is employed as a preliminary step towards divorce; after the lapse of a year (or several years) it is permissible for either of the spouses to demand that the separation be transformed into full divorce. The German Civil Code went so far as to lay down that the judicial separation had all the effects of divorce, except that neither of the parties could marry a third person and that both could re-establish their common life without any formalities. This gave rise to a good deal of discussion whether under German law a judicial separation was not more like a divorce than a separation in the canonical sense.[3]

The fact that separation is thus something like an intermediate status between full marriage and full celibacy as produced by divorce comes to the fore in the British rules on jurisdiction.

(*a*) A suit for separation can be brought in the English courts when the parties have their *domicile* in England. In this respect separation is assimilated to divorce.[4]

(*b*) On the other hand, an English *residence* of both parties is sufficient.[5] And even less than that: if they had

---

[1] *Cod. iur. can.*, c. 1128 et seq. Until 1917 it was usual to speak of a 'separatio a thoro [*sic*] et mensa', and that is still the English custom, though the *Cod. iur. can.* has replaced it by better Latin in dropping the senseless *h* and speaking of 'separatio tori, mensae et habitationis'.

[2] Sweden, Marriage Act, 1915, VI, §§ 1, 3, 4; Norway, Marriage Act, 1918, §§ 41–3; Denmark, Marriage Act, 1922, §§ 52–4; Finland, Marriage Act, 1921, § 76. Similarly Czechoslovakian Marriage Act, s. 13 (i), 15.

[3] German Civ. C., 1896, s. 1586, 1587. The German Marriage Act, 1938, and the Act of 20 Feb. 1946 (s. 78) have abolished this rule and (s. 48) imitated the Scandinavian rules.

[4] *Eustace* v. *Eustace*, [1924] P. 45. (C.A.)

[5] *Armytage* v. *Armytage*, [1898] P. 178, 186; *Anghinelli* v. *Anghinelli*, [1918] P. (C.A.) 247. *Sim* v. *Sim*, [1944] P. 87. If the husband has neither residence nor domicile in England, the magistrates have no jurisdiction under the Sum-

a common residence in England at the time when they
parted it seems to suffice that the petitioner alone still has
an English residence.[1] This mitigation is particularly
important in the interest of a wife who does not follow her
husband abroad because he has ill-treated her. She needs
the protection of the court against unwelcome visits he
might pay her at her English home.

II. Suits for restitution of conjugal rights must be
mentioned here, though there is no question of status
involved. Like separation suits they are often a preliminary to divorce proceedings and are therefore treated
in the same way. Jurisdiction is tested either by domicile
or by the husband's residence.[2]

80. Restitution of conjugal rights

5. DECLARATION OF LEGITIMACY AND
OF VALIDITY OF MARRIAGE

I. The English court has jurisdiction to declare by a
decree valid *adversus omnes* the legitimacy of a person if

81.

   1. this person is British-born or his right to be treated
as British-born depends on his legitimacy or on the
validity of a marriage, *and*

   2. the person is either domiciled in England (or
Wales) or in Northern Ireland or claims (real or personal)
property situate in England or Wales.[3]

   A person who fulfils these two conditions can apply for
one or more of the following three declarations: a declara-

mary Jurisdiction (Separation and Maintenance) Acts, 1895–1925. *Forsyth* v.
Forsyth, [1948] P. 125 (C.A.). *Macrae* v. *Macrae,* [1949] P. 272; [1949]
2 A.E.R. (C.A.) 34.

   [1] Cf. *Perrin* v. *Perrin,* [1914] P. 135. True, this case does not deal with
separation but with a suit for restitution of conjugal rights. See further
Raeburn v. *Raeburn* (1928), 44 T.L.R. 384.

   [2] *Thornton* v. *Thornton* (1886), 11 P.D. 176. *Dicks* v. *Dicks,* [1899] P. 275.
Perrin v. *Perrin,* [1914] P. 135. *Yelverton* v. *Yelverton* (1859), 1 Sw. & Tr. 574.
Firebrace v. *Firebrace* (1878), 4 P.D. 63. In *Milligan* v. *Milligan,* [1941]
2 A.E.R. 62, 66, the husband had failed to set up a joint home; thereby he 'had
ceased cohabitation'. His real residence, or, as Henn Collins, J. put it, his
'physical home', was therefore immaterial and had to be replaced by the place
'where he ought to have set up the joint home'. This place must be treated as
his residence. A highly satisfactory solution.

   [3] Supreme Court of Judicature (Consolidation) Act, 1925 (15 & 16 Geo. V,
c. 49), s. 188; Brit. Nationality Act, 1948, s. 31.

tion of the petitioner's legitimacy, a declaration of the validity of his marriage or of the marriages of his parents or grandparents, and a declaration of his British nationality. The court has jurisdiction to make these declarations. They are effective *in rem*, that is, binding upon everybody, except those persons who are interested in the decree and have not been cited.[1] If the decree has been obtained by fraud it may be set aside.

II. A comparison of the rules on a declaration of legitimacy or marriage validity with the rules on marriage nullity proceedings shows considerable differences which it seems impossible to justify. In legitimacy and marriage validity cases the test of jurisdiction is neither domicile alone nor residence—as is the case in suits for nullity of marriage—but a combination of either domicile and nationality or *situs rei* and nationality. At first sight this seems surprising: a foreigner domiciled in England is allowed to apply in this country for a declaration of the nullity of his marriage but neither for a declaration of its validity, nor of his legitimacy. This inconsistency, however, does not do him much harm, as he is not barred from asserting his legitimacy or the validity of his marriage (or for that matter of any marriage) *incidenter* in any judicial proceedings where the issue depends on these facts, for example, when he claims a share in the intestate succession of his parents. But such assertion can never procure for him a declaration *in rem*, i.e. effective *inter omnes*. Continental laws do not draw this distinction between the various kinds of status proceedings.

III. More startling is another differentiation made by English law. Where a person alleges that he has been legitimated by the subsequent marriage of his parents under his personal (English or foreign) law he may apply for a judicial declaration of his legitimation, or of the legitimation of one of his parents or ancestors. The jurisdiction of the court to make such declaration *in rem* then depends neither on his English domicile nor on his

<hr />

[1] See Dicey(–Morris), p. 272.

British nationality. He may be a foreigner domiciled abroad.[1]

Thus there is no restriction in respect of the jurisdiction of the English court. But that does not mean that every illegitimate child—whatever his nationality, wherever his domicile—is legitimated by the subsequent marriage of his parents. Whether he is so legitimated is answered—under English private international law—by the law of the father's domicile.[2]

If a legitimation is not made by subsequent marriage, but by recognition or by the Sovereign or the state (see *infra*, s. 371), the English court has no jurisdiction to make a declaration *in rem* of such legitimation.

6. INFANTS AND LUNATICS

I. *Infants*. English courts[3] have jurisdiction to appoint **82. Infants** a guardian for an infant and to supervise, remove, and replace a guardian if the infant is either present in England or a British subject.[4] Neither domicile nor residence matters. The fact that an infant has property in England does not by itself suffice to establish the jurisdiction of the English court;[5] but if under the particular circumstances of the case the infant's property situate in England requires protection, the competence of the English court will hardly be denied. This seems to follow from the fact that English courts have assumed jurisdiction in cases where lunatics who were not present in this country possessed property situate here which demanded protection;[6] a court would not refuse protection to an infant which it grants to a lunatic.[7]

II. *Lunatics*. Jurisdiction in lunacy of the English court **83. Luna-** is also tested by the presence of the lunatic in this country, **tics** irrespective of whether he is domiciled or resident here. This is even more urgent in the case of lunacy than it is in

---

[1] Legitimacy Act, 1926 (16 & 17 Geo. V, c. 60), s. 1, 2, 8.

[2] See Dicey(–Morris), pp. 274, 275.

[3] On the appointment by the Secretary of State of guardians for refugee children, see Guardianship (Refugee Children) Act, 1944, 7 and 8 Geo. VI, c. 8.

[4] See on this in particular *Hope* v. *Hope* (1854), 4 De G.M. & G. 328, 345; *Re D. (Infant)*, [1943] 1 Ch. 305; *In re Willoughby* (1885), L.R. 30 Ch.D. 324; *In re Pavitt*, [1907] Ir. L. Rep. 234. Cf. further, *infra*, s. 391.

[5] *Brown* v. *Collins* (1883), 25 Ch.D. 56, 60, 61.

[6] *Ex parte Southcot* (1751), 2 Ves. Sen. 401. *Re Scott* (1874), 22 W. Rep. 748.

[7] Of course, it is within the discretion of the court to assume jurisdiction or to refuse it.

that of infants, as it is not only the lunatic's welfare that has to be considered, but the danger to public safety.

It has not yet been decided whether British nationality by itself suffices to constitute English lunacy jurisdiction. The answer would probably be in the negative.[1]

Finally, the fact that the lunatic possesses property in England might be a reason for the English court to assume jurisdiction, provided that the property needs the protection of the court.[2]

7. BANKRUPTCY JURISDICTION, AND WINDING-UP OF COMPANIES

84. Bankruptcy
I. The court has bankruptcy jurisdiction on the petition either of the debtor himself or of a creditor, provided in both cases that the debtor has committed an 'act of bankruptcy', such as a fraudulent conveyance of his property or a notice to a creditor that he has suspended payment.[3] Jurisdiction is, however, more extended in the first than in the second case.

1. If it is the debtor who initiates the proceedings the English court has jurisdiction if at the time when he committed an act of bankruptcy he was either present in England, or had a place of residence here, or was carrying on business in this country (personally or by an agent or manager, alone or as a member of a partnership).[4] He need neither be a British subject[5] nor be domiciled in England.

2. If it is a creditor who presents the petition, mere presence of the debtor in England is not sufficient. In such case the jurisdiction of the English court requires either that the debtor be domiciled in England or that within a year before the presentation of the petition he had ordinarily resided, or had a dwelling-house or place of business in England, or had carried on business in Eng-

---

[1] See Cheshire, 540.

[2] See also *re Burbidge*, [1902] 1 Ch. (C.A.) 426; *re Bariatinski (Princess)* (1843), 1 Ph. 375; *re Sottomaior* (1874), 9 Ch. App. 677. *Infra*, s. 270.

[3] Bankruptcy Act, 1914 (4 & 5 Geo. V, ch. 59), s. 1.

[4] Ibid., ss. 1, 3, 6, 18.

[5] It was different before 1913, when English bankruptcy law applied only to debtors who were British subjects.

land (personally or by an agent or manager, alone or as a member of a partnership).[1]

This distinction seems somewhat arbitrary. Why, for example, pay attention to the domicile in the second and not in the first case? Why attach significance to the possession of an English dwelling-house in the second case? Continental laws test jurisdiction in both cases by the debtor's ordinary residence (domicile in the continental use of that term)[2] or his place of business.

Under all legal systems it may happen that a debtor is made bankrupt in more countries than one. The English court retains the right to adjudge a debtor bankrupt even when this has been done already by a foreign court. But as the court's jurisdiction in bankruptcy is discretionary, the fact that the debtor has been made bankrupt abroad may be a good reason for refusing a petition here.[3]

II. Jurisdiction to wind-up companies or other associations **85. Winding-up** of individuals, irrespective of whether they have legal personality or not, lies with the English court if the association is registered in the United Kingdom. Such jurisdiction extends[4] to all other associations, in particular to foreign companies registered outside Great Britain, if the court is of opinion that it is 'just and equitable' that they should be wound up, for example, if they are unable to pay their debts or have ceased to carry on business in this country.

Russian companies—banking, insurance, industrial, and shipping companies—have been dissolved under Soviet law and have ceased to exist. Many of them had branches in this as well as in other countries. In respect of their English property the English court has jurisdiction to wind them up as if they were still existent.[5]

[1] Bankruptcy Act, 1914, s. 4, subs. (I) (d).   [2] See *infra*, s. 98, 130.
[3] *Ex parte McCulloch* (1880), 14 Ch.D. (C.A.) 716, 719. *Ex parte Robinson* (1883), 22 Ch.D. 816, 818.   [4] Companies Act, 1948, s. 399.
[5] See *Russian and English Bank* v. *Baring Bros.*, [1932] 1 Ch. 435. *Re Russian and English Bank*, [1932] 1 Ch. 663. *Re Russian Bank for Foreign Trade*, [1933] Ch. 745. *In re Tovarishestvo Manufactur Liudvig-Rabenek*, [1944] 1 Ch. 404. See also *Re N. V. Handelsmaatschappij Wokar*, [1946] Ch. 98. Cf. *infra*, s. 287.

BIBLIOGRAPHY

CHESHIRE, 626–36. BALDWIN, *Law of Bankruptcy* (11th ed.), p. 98. DICEY (-MORRIS), pp. 276–96. LIPSTEIN, 12 Mod. L.R. (1949), 454–76.

8. FOREIGN IMMOVABLES

86. Foreign immovables AN English court has no jurisdiction to adjudicate upon rights to immovables situate outside England.[1] The same principle obtains on the continent. Actions on rights of this kind belong exclusively to the *forum rei sitae*.

Further, in the case of trespass to foreign land, English law denies jurisdiction to the English court to entertain actions for damages, while continental laws do not treat the *forum rei sitae* as exclusively competent to adjudicate upon such actions.[2]

On the other hand, actions which are based, not on proprietary rights in foreign land as such, but only on contracts creating a personal duty to transfer proprietary rights, may be entertained by an English court. The same is true where the action is based on an equity between the parties, since equity acts *in personam* only.[3] Thus the English court can give judgment for specific performance of an agreement to create a mortgage on foreign land[4] or for redemption or foreclosure of a mortgage on land abroad[5] or for relieving the plaintiff of a charge on foreign land obtained by the defendant's fraud.[6] In particular the court can entertain an action brought by a *cestui que trust* to enforce a trust concerning foreign land against the trustee.[7] In all these cases jurisdiction of the English court depends on the presence of the defendant in this country or on the consent of the court (under Order XI) to service out of jurisdiction.

---

[1] *Mostyn* v. *Fabrigas* (1775), 1 Cowp. 161 (Smith, *Leading Cases*, 13th ed., pp. 642, 659). See von Bar II. 431 et seq.; Dicey(–Morris), pp. 141–4; Cheshire, pp. 716–21.

[2] *British South Africa Co.* v. *Companhia de Moçambique*, [1893] A.C. 602. (Cf. *The Tolten*, [1946] P. 135, and Graveson, 10 Mod. L. R. (1947), 306–11.) Under German law an action for damages for trespass to land can, but need not, be brought in the *forum situs*; German Code of Civ. Proced., s. 26.

[3] *Ewing* v. *Orr-Ewing* (1883), 9 A.C. 34, 40. *Deschamp* v. *Miller*, [1908] 1 Ch. 863, 864.

[4] *Penn* v. *Lord Baltimore* (1750), 1 Ves. Sen. 444.

[5] *Toller* v. *Carteret* (1705), 2 Vern. 494. *Paget* v. *Ede* (1874), L.R. 18 Eq. 118.

[6] *Arglasse* v. *Muschamp* (1682), 1 Vern. 75.

[7] *Jenney* v. *Mackintosh* (1886), 33 Ch.D. 595.

PART III

GENERAL RULES ON CONFLICT OF LAWS

CHAPTER VII

PRELIMINARY OBSERVATIONS ON CONFLICT RULES

I. In any country the courts, the land registry, the superintendent registrars, and other state officials, when legal questions arise, are required to apply the conflict rules of their own country. An English court applies English conflict rules, a French court French conflict rules. Only exceptionally, in cases of *renvoi*,[1] are foreign conflict rules applied. 87. Application of the conflict rules of the court

It goes without saying that the Judicial Committee of the Privy Council applies the private international law of the court below, for example, Canadian or Australian conflict rules. The House of Lords when sitting in Scottish cases applies Scottish private international law. The conflict rules of the various parts of the British Empire, however, are mostly based on English common law.[2]

II. It may happen that the tribunal appointed to decide a case has no system of conflict rules at all. This occurs when the tribunal has been established by an international convention between two or more states, such as the Mixed Arbitral Tribunals created by the Peace Treaties of 1919,[3] or the Permanent Court of International Justice.[4] The 88. Conflict rules of international courts and arbitral tribunals

---

[1] *Infra*, s. 178 et seq.

[2] Not only have Scottish courts adopted English conflict rules, but conversely also some decisions in Scottish cases are treated as authorities by English law; for example, *Bell* v. *Kennedy* (1868), L.R. 1, Sc. App. 307, *Udny* v. *Udny* (1869), L.R. 1, Sc. App. 441, *Ramsay* v. *Liverpool Royal Infirmary*, [1930] A.C. 588.

[3] M. Gutzwiller has made an interesting study of the private international law developed by these Mixed Arbitral Tribunals. See *Internationales Jahrbuch f. Schiedsgerichtswesen*, 3 (1931), 123, and Lipstein, 27 *Grotius Soc.* (1942), 149.

[4] Cf. for example, the judgments in the cases of the Serbian and Brazilian loans No. 14, 15, in *Collect. of Judgments of the Perman. Court*, Series A, No. 20/21.

same difficulty arises when a court of arbitration is either
set up by an agreement between private parties or created
by commercial bodies as an element in their organization
to which any merchants or industrialists may submit the
differences arising under their contracts. Such arbitral
tribunals have, for example, been instituted by the
American Chamber of Commerce, the International
Chamber of Commerce in Paris, and at many stock
exchanges. If, then, the international convention or the
private arbitration agreement contains no rule concerning
the applicable law, the difficult task of finding such rule
devolves on the court of arbitration. In many cases it is
not necessary to answer the question as to which law
applies, viz. when all the municipal laws between which
the choice lies either have identical rules on the relevant
points, or lead to the same decision in spite of differing
rules. Where the difficulties cannot be solved in this way
the arbitration court will have to investigate the systems
of private international law prevailing in the countries with
which the case before them is connected. In these systems
the court will often find such similarity as enables it to
apply common conflict rules. In cases of contractual
claims practically all legal systems make the decision
dependent on the intention of the contracting parties,
either express or implied or presumed.[1] When the ownership of some piece of land is in issue, the court will apply
the *lex situs*, as provided by all systems of private international law. Or again, when in an action between a
Frenchman and a Swiss there is doubt about the capacity
of one of them to conclude the contract, the arbitrator will
decide the point according to the national law of that
party, because both French and Swiss law make nationality the test of capacity. When, however, this method of
careful comparisons does not lead to a solution, when, for
example, the action lies between a Swiss domiciled in
England and an Englishman domiciled in Denmark and
the status of one of them is in doubt, the arbitral tribunal
finds itself in difficulties. It may either

  (*a*) adopt the following rule laid down by the Anglo-

[1] See *infra*, s. 393 et seq., 411 et seq.

German Mixed Arbitral Tribunal. It is to apply 'the law which would have been normally applied if the war and the Treaty had not intervened'.[1] It will therefore examine which regular court of law would have had jurisdiction to entertain the action. If (apart from war and the Peace Treaty) only one court has jurisdiction, it is sound to apply the private international law prevailing at that court, because any other choice of law would possibly entail an alteration of the rights and duties of the parties. When, on the other hand, several courts have jurisdiction, the Anglo-German Mixed Arbitral Tribunal held it 'most adequate to ascertain the applicable law by following the private international law of the place of domicile of the debtor'. This rule, it is submitted, is both obscure and arbitrary. It is obscure first because the term 'domicile' has a different meaning according to its use in English, French, or German law; secondly, because the rule does not say which debtor's domicile is decisive when there is more than one debtor. And it is arbitrary to suppose that had there been no war and no treaty the plaintiff would have selected from the various competent courts those of the debtor's domicile; probably he would have chosen that court the conflict rules of which would operate most favourably for his claim and afford the best chance of a quick and successful execution of a judgment.

Or, (b) The arbitral tribunal may endeavour to fill in the gap in the same way in which judges everywhere are accustomed to fill gaps in municipal law.[2] It falls outside the scope of this book to show how the very divergent formulae used to find a solution lead in the main to the same results. It does not matter whether one says that *silente lege* the judge must be guided by 'natural justice' or whether one follows the famous Swiss rule: 'The judge has to decide according to the rule he would establish as legislator.'[3] In any case the arbitral tribunal will try to find out where the relationship in question has its 'local seat', as Savigny puts it, or its 'centre of gravity' (Gierke),

---

[1] *Büsse* v. *British Manufacturing Stationery* (1927), *Recueil des décisions des tribun. arbitraux mixtes*, 7, 345, at p. 348.
[2] See s. 90.   [3] Swiss Civil Code, art. 1, § 2.

or with which legal system it has 'the most real connection' (Westlake). This may be what is meant by the obscure and magniloquent statement contained in certain decisions of the Mixed Arbitral Tribunals that the solution is to be found by the tribunal 'd'après les principes généraux du (?) droit international privé'.[1]

'One-sided' and 'All-sided' Conflict Rules

89. The two kinds of conflict rules   Any rule on conflict of laws in any country X may be framed in one of two ways. Either it may restrict itself to determining the conditions under which the internal (municipal) law of X governs the case. Or it may also state which foreign law is applicable if the law of X is not. The first system of so-called 'one-sided' conflict rules has been adopted by the French Civil Code and some codes based on French law,[2] by most of the provisions of the German Introductory Law to the Civil Code,[3] and by a very few English statutes, such as the Legitimacy Act, 1926.[4] The second system of 'all-sided' rules is that developed by English common law as well as by most modern codes, such as those of Italy, Portugal, Greece, Brazil, China, and Japan.

Prevailing legal doctrine rightly favours the second system. Some Swiss and German authors, however, have praised and recommended to legislators the other, the system of one-sided conflict rules.[5] They reason that the task of the national lawgiver is confined to the delimitation of the area of his own internal rules and that he would be encroaching on foreign legislation if he were to state

[1] See, for example, *Recueil des décisions*, 6, 247, and Gutzwiller, loc. cit. p. 135 et seq.

[2] French c.c., art. 3; Belgian c.c., art. 3; Roumanian c.c., art. 2, §§ 1, 2; Spanish c.c., art. 8, 9; Quebec c.c., art. 6, §§ 1 and 3; Chilian c.c., art. 15, 16; Peruvian c.c., Introduct., Title IV, V, and others.

[3] Introd. Law (1896) art. 8–10, 14–16, 18–20, 22–24. Curiously, this same law has adopted the better system (of all-sided rules) in art. 7, 11–13, 17, and 21. No reason can be found for the distinction.

[4] 16 & 17 Geo. V, c. 60, s. 1 and 8.

[5] Schnell, 5 *Böhm's Z.* (1895), 337; Niedner, *Einführungsgesetz* (Commentary), p. 13; Hugo Neumann, in *Verhandlungen des 24. Deutschen Juristentags*, 1897, I, 169; Enneccerus, *Lehrbuch d. bürg. Rechts*, I, § 59. Recently an American author, Sohn, 55 *Harvard L.R.* (1942), 978, and some French authors, notably Niboyet III, 243 et seq., have adopted this view.

which of several foreign laws is applicable when his own law is not. This attitude is hardly justifiable. It is for him to tell the judges of his country what law to apply in any proceedings they may entertain. Behind his seeming 'modesty' in narrowing his task to a restricted group of problems there may be hidden an unreasonable wish to make his municipal law more widely applicable than is compatible with the so-called 'harmony of laws'.[1]

The first system, then, is defective. The gaps it leaves must be filled in by the courts in some way, and it is worthy of note that wherever it prevails on the Continent (for example, in France and Germany) the courts apply the principle underlying the one-sided rules by analogy to relationships not governed by the country's own law.[2]

90. Filling in of gaps

For example, art. 3, §§ 2 and 3, of the French Civil Code is applied as if it ran: 'Immovables are governed by the law of the country where they are situate. The laws concerning status and capacity govern the nationals of that state in which these laws prevail, even in respect of persons resident in a different country.'[3]

This does not, however, mean that the system of conflict rules is anywhere complete. Even in those countries where, as in France, Germany, Italy, or Switzerland, the legislator endeavours to lay down a complete system of rules on municipal law, he does not attempt to reach

---

[1] See on this *supra*, ss. 4 and 15.

[2] The attitude of the English court in interpreting ss. 1 and 8 Legitimacy Act (16 & 17 Geo. V, c. 60) in *Collins* v. *Att.-Gen.* (1931), 145 L.T. 551, is not quite clear. See on this Mendelssohn-Bartholdy, *Renvoi*, p. 30 et seq.

[3] The champions of the first system, in particular H. Neumann, do not deny that the gap their system leaves has to be filled. They concede, too, that for that purpose it is necessary to gather the appropriate answer from the one-sided conflict rule. But such answer, they say, is not an answer to the question as to which *municipal* law is applicable, but to the question: Which country furnishes the appropriate *conflict* rule ? In the case, for example, of art. 3, § 3, French Civil Code, they would not say that status and capacity are governed by the (municipal) law of the country of which the person is a national, but that that country determines (by its *conflict* rules) which law governs status and capacity: if the person, for example, is an Englishman domiciled in Switzerland, the French rule would be that English law has to decide which law is applicable, and as under English law status is tested by domicile, the French judge has to apply Swiss law. Thus the doctrine of one-sided conflict rules results in a system of all-sided conflict rules with recognition of an automatic *renvoi* system. It is submitted that though the *renvoi* doctrine is sound in the main (cf. *infra*, ss. 192, 193), it ought to be based not on such fragile academic reasoning but on its substantial usefulness.

completeness in the sphere of private international law. It goes without saying that in England, where practically all law is uncodified, there is not as yet anything like a complete system of conflict rules. Further, where conflict rules have been developed, they are often inconsistent with each other,[1] and it is sometimes difficult to recognize the legal principle on which the court has based a particular decision. In all countries,[2] then, the gaps left in private international law are much more numerous than those existing in municipal law. How are they to be filled?

The question how a case is to be decided when there is no authoritative direction by precedent or statute has often been discussed within the sphere of pure municipal law. The English judge looks for analogies within his own legal system, he takes into account the merits of the case and, by following his sense of justice, evolves a new principle as closely as possible cognate to the whole of his municipal law. He is seldom—perhaps too seldom—inclined to look at modern codes of foreign countries, though he may occasionally test his solution by the eternal wisdom of the Roman jurists, by great lawyers such as Savigny or Story, and by decisions of the courts of the United States, of Scotland, or of South Africa. If it may be said that he acts as if he were a legislator, this is true with a certain reservation. He is a legislator *malgré liu*, anxious not to reform the law, a legislator who adds but, if possible, does not alter. All this applies equally to the judge who has to fill in a gap found in the Conflict Rules. Here, however, a new element enters into consideration: it is his task to contribute to the attainment of a substantially international character in conflict rules, bearing in mind the ideal of the so-called harmony of laws.[3] He may therefore be bound to consider, to a greater extent than when he fills in a gap in his municipal law, any rules of foreign private international law dealing with the problem before him.

---

[1] Examples of this are to be found in the doctrine of *renvoi*, in the rules on the proper law of contract, in the determination of the law applicable to questions of capacity, and many others.

[2] With the exception of Poland, and the States Signatories of the Conventions of Montevideo and the Código Bustamante.　　　[3] Cf. *supra*, ss. 4 and 15.

CHAPTER VIII

THE POINTS OF CONTACT

In every set of facts one or more circumstances are present that may serve as possible 'tests' for the determination of the applicable law. If, for example, a British subject domiciled in Italy makes a will in France and dies leaving immovable property in Switzerland, the circumstances which may turn out to be decisive are his British nationality, his Italian domicile, the French *locus actus*, and the Swiss *situs rei*. Continental jurists call these test factors *Anknüpfungspunkte*, *points de rattachement*, *momenti di collegamento*. The American Restatement speaks of *points of contact*. In this book either the American term will be used or the expressions '*test factor*' or '*connecting factor*'. *91. Meaning of this term*

The most important of these points of contact are the following: *92. The main points of contact*

1. The domicile of a person, his nationality, his residence, his place of sojourn, his origin, and in interpersonal law[1] the personal group to which he belongs (Hindus, Muhammadans, &c.). These test factors will be dealt with in the following sections. They are of importance for determining status, capacity, succession, the validity of marriage, &c.

2. The seat of a legal person; it may be determined in various ways.[2]

3. The *situs* of a thing, that is, the place where it is, or is deemed to be,[3] situate. In particular the *lex situs* is decisive when *iura in rem* are in question.

4. The flag of a ship. This takes the place of the nationality of persons and the *situs* of things. It is decisive for practically all legal relationships of the ship and of its master or owner as such. It also covers contractual relationships, particularly contracts of affreightment, unless the parties intended to exclude the law of the flag.[4] When

---

[1] See *supra*, s. 5, sub. (3).
[2] See *infra*, ss. 279–81.
[3] Thus, e.g., in the case of the *quasi-situs* of a *chose in action* (a debt, &c.).
[4] *Lloyd* v. *Guibert* (1865), 1 Q.B. 115, 125. *The Gaetano & Maria* (1882),

a ship is not entitled to carry the flag which it carries or when it hoists the flag of a state consisting of several countries, it is the law of the country of registry that is decisive.[1]

5. The place where an act has been done—for example, a contract has been made, a marriage celebrated, a will signed, a tort committed. The *lex loci actus* is particularly important in contracts and torts.

6. The place where an act is intended to come into effect; thus, the place of performance of contractual duties, or the place where a power of attorney is to be exercised.

7. The agreement of contracting parties on the law which is to govern their contract.[2]

8. The place where judicial proceedings are instituted or other official acts done, such as inscriptions in a land registry, or the grant of privileges, concessions, or patents. The law of the *forum* is particularly important because all 'procedure' is governed by it, and because it applies whenever the content of the otherwise applicable foreign law cannot be ascertained, or when that foreign law is excluded from application for reasons of public policy.

DOMICILE AND NATIONALITY AS POINTS OF CONTACT

93. The problem

Which is the most appropriate law for determining the status of a person and his capacity, and for regulating his marriage or divorce, the succession to his movable property, and any other point of his personal situation? Is it the law of his domicile, or of his place of origin, or of his nationality? This question has been discussed very often by jurists and legal philosophers of all countries, but no consensus has been reached in a positive sense, though it would seem that the place of origin as a test is rejected unanimously—and justly so.

94. The *lex originis* principle

There can be no doubt that the conception of 'origin' should have no place here. It is a survival from an age when a fully developed notion of the state as a corporate

---

7 P.D. (C.A.) 137. *The Industrie*, [1894] P. (C.A.) 58, 76. *The Njegos*, [1936] P. 90, 106. *The Adriatic*, [1931] P. 241, 246. See *infra*, s. 416.

1 See Dicey–Morris, Rule 146, p. 664.

2 See on this (*lex voluntatis*), *infra*, ss. 394–405.

body of citizens, and consequently of nationality as membership of this corporation, did not exist. The forerunner of the conception of nationality was the Roman notion of membership of a *civitas*, of a community of *municipes*. Here, indeed, membership was founded on the *origo* within the *civitas*, the term designating not the place of birth of a person but the place to which his father, or in the case of an illegitimate child his mother, belonged.[1] This notion of *origo* as a test for personal rights survived in Prussian law[2] until 1900. It is still to a certain degree maintained by English and Anglo-American law, where it has been merged with the conception of 'domicile', just as German and Dutch authors since the seventeenth century have combined the two notions in speaking of a *domicilium originis*.[3] The conception of *origo* has furthermore retained a certain importance as an auxiliary conception in the interlocal law of some modern states, such as Yugoslavia and (until 1949) Czechoslovakia, where different legal systems prevail in the various parts of their territory: there the personal rights of nationals are tested not by domicile but by origin.[4] Apart from these remnants the origin test has disappeared entirely, and the choice lies between nationality and domicile.

It was a momentous event in legal history when the French Civil Code introduced the principle of nationality. Most modern states have followed this model.

95. Countries with the nationality principle

Belgium, Luxemburg, Monaco, simply by accepting the French code; other states by building their own codes on the basis of the French code, such as Haiti (1825), the Netherlands (1829), the Dominican Republic (1845), Greece (even before 1856),[5] Italy and Roumania (1865), Portugal (1867), Spain (1888), or on the basis of Spanish or Portuguese law, such

---

[1] 'Civitas ex qua pater naturalem originem ducit', *Dig.* 50. 1. 6. 1. See also *Dig.* 50. 1. 1. 2 and Savigny VIII, § 351.

[2] *Allgemeines Landrecht* (1794), Introduct. ss. 23–5. The Prussian provisions were similar to English law; they may therefore be quoted here: 'The personal qualities and rights of a man are governed by the laws of the jurisdiction where he has his proper domicile. A mere departure from his jurisdiction does not change his personal rights or duties unless his intention of choosing another domicile is ascertained beyond doubt. As long as a person has no fixed domicile his personal rights and duties are tested by the place of his origin.'

[3] Savigny, § 359, note q.; See Cassin, *Rec.*, loc. cit.

[4] von Caemmerer, *RVgl.HWB*, IV, 347.

[5] See Vallindas, *Rabel's Z.*, 10, 1013.

as Ecuador (1843, 1887), Chile (1855), Salvador (1860), Venezuela (1867, 1922), Uruguay (1868, 1914), Colombia (1873), Dominican Republic (1884), Costa Rica (1887), Cuba (1888), Honduras (1906), Panama (1916), Mexico (1926). The principle of nationality has further been adopted by Austrian courts, by Swiss law (1881, 1891, 1907),[1] by the German Civil Code, 1896, by Hungary, Liechtenstein, Czechoslovakia, by Bulgaria, Yugoslavia, Albania, Turkey, by Finland and Sweden, and by the Polish Statute on Private International Law (1926). In Asia the nationality principle has been introduced by Japan (1898), China (1918), Iran (1928), and Siam (1939). Many international treaties have adopted it, in particular the Hague Conventions on Family Law of 1902 and 1905, and the Geneva Conventions concerning Bills of Exchange and Cheques of 1930 and 1931.

In some countries—fortunately few—the nationality principle has been adopted only for citizens of the country to the effect that these are governed by their national law even if living abroad, whereas foreigners present in the country are subject to the law of their domicile (Austria,[2] Peru, Venezuela), or even to the territorial law of the country (Soviet Russia).[3] It is obvious that this attitude of discrimination in favour of its own nationals is incompatible with the duty of a state to bear in mind the goal of an international harmony of laws. And yet in France a new political movement led by Professor Niboyet champions just such ideas.[4]

96. Countries with the domicile principle

Under the other existing system personal status and personal rights are tested by *domicile*. This principle, which prevailed everywhere in Europe before the French code, still obtains in Denmark, Iceland, Norway,[5] the Baltic States,[6] in those South American States which are parties to the Convention of Montevideo (Argentine, Bolivia, Paraguay, Peru, and Uruguay),[7] in Brazil (since 1942),[8] also in two states of Central America (Nicaragua,

[1] There are, however, some exceptions under Swiss law in favour of the domicile principle. Cf. Carasso, *Des conflits de lois en matière de capacité civile*, 1938; Rabel, *Confl. of Laws*, I. 115.

[2] This, at least, is the view of the best Austrian authors (Unger, *System des österr. Privatrechts*, 1876, I. 164, Pfaff & Hofmann, *Excurse*, I. 106), and it is covered by the text of ss. 4, 34 of the Austrian Civil Code (1811). The question is, however, doubtful, and the courts often apply the nationality principle in the case of foreigners also.

[3] As to the personal law of aliens outside Russia, Russian law gives no hint. Similar to Russian law: Mexican code of 1928; see Audinet, *Répert.* VII. 653, no. 117.

[4] See Rabel, loc. cit., I. 152²⁰⁴.

[5] In Sweden and Finland it applies only to inter-Scandinavian relations.

[6] Even the Latvian Civil Code of 1937, s. 8, still enjoins application of the law of the domicile.

[7] With regard to Uruguay, the domicile principle prevails only in so far as relations with the other contracting states are concerned. Apart from that, the test factor there is nationality.   [8] Rabel, loc. cit., I. 151²⁰⁰.

1903; Guatemala, 1926), and particularly, though in a very peculiar form, in the United Kingdom, the British Commonwealth, and the United States of America.

Both systems have their advantages and their defects. **97. Advantages and defects** The domicile system looks on the status of a person, his capacities, and his personal rights, as something closely connected with his personal home and his family, this being the centre of his life. It allows a person to change the law governing his personal situation by his own private act, that is, by changing his domicile. It is, so to speak, an individualistic and liberal system. It considers it inequitable that a man who for economic or political reasons has left his country should, nevertheless, in marrying, in educating his children, in making a will, be subject to a legal system which he disowns and which he no longer recognizes as his law. Its foundation is the desire to preclude interference by the state with the personal affairs of such of its members as have left its territory and settled abroad. The system of nationality, on the other hand, is based on the idea that man is more deeply rooted in his nation than in his home, that, to use Mancini's phrase, personality is recognized by nationality. The view is often advanced that if a person leaves his country without severing his national tie he should remain subject to all the laws of his state and should not be able by a 'private' act of emigration to alter his status and capacities. This justification of the principle of nationality does not seem very convincing, particularly if we consider the incessant stream of emigrants from Eastern and Central Europe and from Italy which the political and racial persecutions of recent years have brought about. It seems unreasonable to subject millions of refugees to the law of a state from which, and from the legal system of which, they have fled, and to justify such subjection by the argument that they have not yet been released from their nationality.[1] The conditions of the present age have thus

---

[1] The national law of a country has often been applied even to those who have ceased to be its nationals without acquiring a new nationality (stateless persons). Thus: the German Introductory Law to the Civil Code, 1896, s. 29 (altered in 1938).

shown that the domicile principle possesses some advantages. Its main defects are: first, it is often much more difficult to determine with certainty a person's domicile than his nationality, since domicile depends largely on an intention which it may be hard to prove,[1] while a change of nationality can nearly always be verified by official documents. Further, the notion of domicile not only differs widely in various states, but even within one state often gives rise to grave controversies, while the conception of nationality is free from ambiguity. Finally, where the domicile principle prevails there is always the danger of a feigned change of domicile, made with the purpose of concluding a marriage which under the law of the true domicile is not permissible, of obtaining a divorce, or the like. Where nationality is decisive such evasion is hardly possible.

From the point of view of the two states concerned—the state to which a person belongs by nationality and the state of domicile—it is evident that states with a very mixed population, such as the principal immigration countries in both Americas, may be said to need the domicile principle in order to attain a certain fusion of their population and to avoid the necessity of applying a different law to practically every case.[2] In these states the nationality system could be tolerated only if the state were to facilitate naturalization more than is desirable, or were even, as did Venezuela in 1850, and Brazil in 1889, to impose its nationality upon all persons resident in the country, thus disguising the domicile system under the system of nationality. Those states, on the other hand, from which large numbers of citizens emigrate, such as Germany, Austria, and Italy, are often inclined to preserve the nationality system in order to maintain as long and as effectually as possible the relationship between their nationals and the mother-country. It may, however, be open to discussion whether this interest deserves pro-

---

[1] See *May* v. *May*, [1943] 2 A.E.R. 146.

[2] Even in France, where in the last thirty years large numbers of refugees from Soviet Russia, Fascist Italy, Nazi Germany, and Spain have found a (temporary) home, the movement in favour of the domicile system is increasing. See Niboyet, *Traité* III, pp. 211–22, V, p. 243; Cassin, in 34 *Rec.* (1930 IV), no. 50 et seq.

tection; it savours of *sacro egoismo* and covers a desire for expansion and for the exercise of a certain control within the sphere of foreign countries.

The domicile principle would, further, seem preferable for countries that have different municipal laws in the various parts of their territory, such as the United Kingdom, Canada, the United States of America, and some of the new states created during or after the war of 1914–18, such as Czechoslovakia and Yugoslavia. If some of these states—for example, Poland—have, nevertheless, adopted the nationality system they need an auxiliary system to establish the status of their own nationals, and that will best be built up on the domicile test. Finally, all states that have adopted the nationality principle have to decide which nationality is conclusive in the case of persons who have more than one nationality, and what shall be the point of contact in the case of stateless persons. In both respects the law will then take into account the domicile (or the residence) of the person concerned.

According to a very rough calculation made by the Argentine jurist, Zeballos, 500 millions of men lived (in 1909) in countries governed by the domicile principle, while 460 millions were subject to the nationality system.

BIBLIOGRAPHY

CHAMPCOMMUNAL, *Rev. Darras*, 1909, 536; 1910, 57, 712. JORDAN, ibid. 1922, 672. BUSTAMANTE, ibid. 1927, 375. SIMONS, 15 *Rec.* (1926 V) 525. CASSIN, 'La nouvelle conception du domicile', 34 *Rec.* (1930 IV), 737. C. v. SCHILLING, in *Rabel's Z.* 5 (1931), 633. *Annuaire.* 36, I, 163, 182; II, 69, 237; 37, 186, 425, 566. NEUNER, 20 *Canadian Bar Rev.* (1942), 493 et seq. G. C. CHESHIRE, 61 *L.Q.R.* (1945), 363 et seq.; CHESHIRE, *Private International Law*, 199 et seq. DICEY–MORRIS, 77–128. COOK, 194–210. GOODRICH, 25–69. BATIFFOL, *Traité*, 397–410.

CHAPTER IX

THE DOMICILE

98. The notion of domicile

A PERSON's domicile is the country which is considered by law to be the centre of his life, his 'centre of gravity, as it were'.[1] This notion is common to all legal systems; but they have very different ways of determining the place to be looked on as such centre.

1. Whether a place is the centre of life of a given person in the eyes of the law is decided *by law*, while the notion of 'habitual or ordinary residence'[2] depends solely on facts in which the law plays no part.[3] Thus a wife may have her habitual residence anywhere in the world quite independently of her husband's residence; according to law, however, the centre of her life is deemed to be at the husband's domicile, even if she has never so much as seen it and is neither bound nor willing to live there.

'Residence', for that matter, does not require actual presence. 'A seaman ordinarily absent from this country is resident in the home which he provides here for his wife. So is a man of business whose employment keeps him abroad.'[4]

2. On the other hand, under all legal systems the notion of domicile is closely connected with that of habitual residence, and there are strong grounds for reducing the distinction between them to a minimum. Habitual residence is the basis on which the conception of domicile by choice (*domicilium voluntarium*) is built up, and even where a domicile is established by operation of law (a *domicilium necessarium*), as in the case of a wife, such domicile coincides in the great majority of cases with residence.

3. The domicile is to be found in a certain 'country'. The place where a person resides within that country may be an

---

[1] *Att.-Gen.* v. *Dame Yule* (1931), 145 L.T. 9, 11 (per Rowlatt, J.).

[2] Another expression frequently used is 'permanent home'. But if the London house which belongs to *A* and where he lives has been destroyed he has no longer a 'home' in London, though he may retain his 'habitual residence' there.

[3] Cf. Lord Westbury in *Bell* v. *Kennedy* (1868), L.R. 1 H.L. Sc. 307, 320: 'Domicil is an idea of law. It is the relation which the law creates between an individual and a particular locality or country.'

[4] *Raeburn* v. *Raeburn* (1928), 44 T.L.R. 384, 386.

ascertained house, a flat, a single room, or even a tent, a caravan, or a vessel.[1] Sometimes, however, it is impossible to designate a fixed dwelling-place, and for the purpose of private international law this does not matter. It suffices to ascertain the 'country' in which a person is domiciled, to find, for example, that his domicile is in 'England and Wales',[2] and not in Scotland. But it is unimportant whether he is resident in London, Birmingham, or Cardiff, and if in London in which part.[3]

Even if it is certain that he has no particular dwelling-place in a country he can have a domicile there. In the Scottish case *Arnott* v. *Groom*,[4] the judge said: 'Many old bachelors never have a house they can call their own. They go from hotel to hotel and from watering-place to watering-place, careless of the comfort of more permanent residence. . . . There was the case of a nobleman who always lived at inns, and would have no servants but waiters; but he did not lose his domicile on this account.' The same is true for English and American law.[5] It makes a difference, of course, if the hotels in which he is accustomed to live are all situate in various countries, unless there are reasons for attributing a preponderance to one of them.

Under English law every man has a domicile.[6] Persons who have no habitual residence, no permanent home, are by law provided with a fictitious home which thus becomes their legal domicile and by which their personal status is tested. The English rule has been adopted by American law,[7] while it was unknown to Roman law and is unknown to all modern continental legal systems.

99. Everybody has one domicile and only one

English and American law, furthermore, do not allow a person to have more than one domicile at the same time.[8] On this point English law agrees with French law and all modern laws derived from French law. According to the French Civil Code[9] a person is domiciled at the place where

---

[1] Restatement, § 17 (domicile is 'the place where the vehicle regularly remains for a considerable time each year and for a longer time than it regularly remains in any other place').

[2] England and Wales are one country.

[3] A consequence of this becomes manifest if the 'place' where he resides is annexed by a foreign state. See *infra*, s. 106.

[4] (1846), 9 Sess. C. 142, 150.

[5] *In re Craignish*, [1892] 3 Ch. (C.A.) 180, 192 (per Chitty, J.); Westlake, p. 343; Beale, I, 126, n. 1.

[6] See the Scottish case *Udny* v. *Udny* (1869), L.R. 1 Scot. & Div. App., 441, 453, 457.

[7] Restatement, § 11.

[8] *Udny* v. *Udny*, loc. cit.; Restatement, § 11.   [9] Art. 102.

he has his *principal établissement*. Difficulties in determining which of two establishments is the 'principal' have, however, induced some French jurists to recommend *de lege ferenda* the system of plurality of domicile.[1] The plurality system, which prevailed in Roman law[2] and is still in force in Germany,[3] may indeed be preferable in so far as jurisdiction is concerned; where the law allows the creditor to bring his action in the court of the debtor's domicile—as is the case in all continental laws—it is certainly justifiable to give the creditor the choice between the debtor's various establishments and thus to relieve him of the difficulty of finding out which of these is the 'principal' establishment. But in private international law the plurality system is embarrassing.

BIBLIOGRAPHY

J. G. FOSTER, 16 *Brit. Y.B.*, 1935, 84. FOSTER, *Théorie anglaise*, 30. BENTWICH, *Rabel's Z.*, 5 (1931), 57; 6 (1932), 715. BENTWICH, 49 *Rec.* (1934 III), 377. V. TEDESCHI, *Il domicilio nel diritto internazionale privato*, 1933. RHEINSTEIN, in *Giurisprudenza comparata*, I, 1932 (1936), 141. J. H. C. MORRIS, *Br. Y.B.*, 1937, 32. LEVASSEUR, *Le domicile et sa détermination en droit international privé*, 1931. GRUNBERG-VINAVER, 'Domicile', *Répert.* V. Cordier, *J. Clunet* 1937, 970. BARBOSA DE MAGALHAES, 23 *Rec.* (1928 III), 5. H. W. HOLT, 39 *Michig. L.R.* (1941), 689. FARNSWORTH, 59 *L.Q.R.* (1943), 219. NIBOYET, *Traité* I, 552–622. COOK, 194–210.

I. DOMICILE OF ORIGIN

100. The domicile of origin According to English and Anglo-American law[4] every person acquires at birth a so-called domicile of origin. This is neither the country where he is born nor that in which his parents are resident, but the country in which his father is domiciled at the time of the child's birth. If the father is dead or if the child is illegitimate its domicile follows that of the mother.[5]

The father may have a domicile of choice; this then becomes the child's domicile of origin. In the frequent

---

1 See Josserand, *Cours de droit civ.*, I, no. 238.
2 *Dig.* 50. 1. 5; 6, § 2; 27, § 2.
3 German Civil Code, s. 7, § 2.
4 Restatement, § 14.
5 *Udny* v. *Udny* (1869), L.R. 1, Sc. & Div. App. 441, 457. *Re Wright's Trusts* (1856), 25 L.J.Ch. (N.S.) 621. *Urquhart* v. *Butterfield* (1887), 37 Ch.D. 357.

cases where the father has never established a domicile of choice his domicile of origin is decisive. This sometimes makes it necessary to ascertain the grandfather's domicile of origin or to delve even farther back into the child's ancestry. It follows that a person may by birth have his domicile in a country with which he himself has no factual connexion. Not only is the word 'domicile' inappropriate in cases of this kind, but the rule itself is open to objection.[1] The archaic and feudal idea that a man belongs to the land to which his ancestors belonged has lost its meaning in an age of migratory populations.

A difficulty arises when it has to be decided whether a child is legitimate or illegitimate; for under English law this depends on the law of the domicile of the child,[2] while the domicile depends on the child's legitimacy. This vicious circle can be broken by the following reasoning: A child is illegitimate if there is no man on earth who according to the law of his domicile is its legitimate father. Therefore if under the law of the 'father's' domicile the child is legitimate that domicile is assigned to it, and it does not matter whether under the law of the mother's domicile the child would be considered legitimate or not. Conversely, if under the father's law the child is not legitimate (and if there is no other man who might be the legitimate father), the child takes the mother's domicile irrespective of whether under the law of that domicile it would be regarded as legitimate or not.

101. Domicile and legitimacy

Example: A domiciled Greek marries a Greek girl domiciled in Paris before the French registrar without going through a religious ceremony; the marriage is void under Greek, valid under French law. After a few months they separate; the husband continues to live in Athens, the wife returns to her antenuptial home in Paris. There a child is born. Its domicile is France. According to the law of the father's domicile (Greek law) the child is not born in wedlock and therefore illegitimate, though under the law of the mother's domicile (French law)[3] the child was born in wedlock.

The domicile of origin can be replaced either by a

[1] Cf. Foster, *Théorie anglaise*, p. 32.

[2] *Doe d. Birtwhistle* v. *Vardill* (1835), 2 Cl. & Fin., 571, 574. *In re Don's Estate* (1857), 4 Drew. 194, 197.

[3] As according to the law of her 'husband's' domicile she was not married, she was able to have a domicile of her own.

domicile of choice (II) or by a domicile by operation of
law (III).

II. THE DOMICILE OF CHOICE

102. Domicile of choice: capacity and residence

Its acquisition requires three factors: capacity, residence, and intention.

1. *Capacity*. Persons under disability, such as infants, lunatics, or married women, are not able to acquire a domicile of their own choice. See *infra*, ss. 112, 118, 120.

If a person is an infant under the law of his domicile though not under English law—e.g. if he is 22 years old and domiciled in Hungary, where majority is not attained till the age of 24—he will, it is submitted, not be capable of acquiring a domicile in England by his own choice, because his capacity is governed by the law of his domicile.[1]

2. *Residence* may be defined as habitual physical presence in a place.[2] It is more than sojourn (physical presence) and less than domicile. It is a purely factual conception and requires no legal capacity. A minor can acquire a residence different from his father's. A wife may have a residence of her own. Though no one can have more than one domicile, anyone can have an unlimited number of residences. Furthermore, residence requires 'habitual' presence merely, while domicile presupposes the intention of indefinite residence. In both cases, however, it depends on intention whether presence can be designated as habitual or not; therefore a temporary interruption of presence does not destroy residence.

It may be mentioned that residence alone—i.e. not amounting to domicile—is in some particular cases regarded by English law as a sufficient point of contact. Thus bankruptcy jurisdiction and jurisdiction concerning judicial separation or restitution of conjugal rights can be based on residence.[3] Residence in enemy territory invests a person with the character of an enemy alien.

103. Intention

3. *Intention of 'permanent' (indefinite) residence.*[4] In this,

[1] *Contra*: Dicey–Morris, p. 90[65].   [2] See Dicey–Morris, p. 77.

[3] See *supra*, ss. 84, 79, 80.

[4] This has been developed in two leading Scottish cases: *Bell* v. *Kennedy* (1868), L.R. 1 Sc. & Div. App., 307, 318, 319; *Udny* v. *Udny* (1869), ibid., 441, 449.

English law is very different from all continental laws. On the Continent capacity and habitual presence (residence) are sufficient to establish a domicile, and no intention of permanency is necessary.[1] Where an international convention is bilingual, the French word *domicile* is rendered in the English version not by 'domicile' but by 'habitual residence'.[2] It is not quite correct to call the intention required by English law an *animus manendi*; it is an *animus semper manendi*. It is directed towards living in the chosen country for an unlimited time and without limitation to definite purpose. The intention of staying until one has made a fortune does not suffice.[3] It needs the will to 'live and die' in that country, as it has been rather loosely put.[4]

The intention of permanent residence presupposes and includes that of permanent abandonment of the old domicile, the *animus relinquendi*. Though a person not infrequently leaves his domicile with the *animus relinquendi* without intending to reside permanently elsewhere, the converse is not possible, for no new domicile can be established without the destruction of that which exists. The question thus arises as to what is required for such destruction. English law—different in this from continental laws and perhaps from American law[5]—distinguishes sharply between the case where the domicile to be abandoned is the domicile of origin and that of any other domicile (of choice or by operation of law). It is easy to abandon such other domicile, while there is a very stringent presumption that the domicile of origin is retained.[6] This distinction works in two directions. First:

104. The animus relinquendi

---

[1] French Civ. Code, art. 102; German Civ. Code, s. 7; Swiss Civ. Code, art. 23 (as interpreted by the Federal Supreme Court; cf. *Off. Coll.* of its decisions, 41, III. 54; 49, I. 429).

[2] *Example*: Treaty of Versailles, art. 91: *ressortissants allemands domiciliés sur les territoires*, &c. (German nationals *habitually resident* in territories, &c.).

[3] *Jopp* v. *Wood* (1864), 34 L.J.Ch. 212. See *May* v. *May*, [1943] 2 A.E.R. 146.

[4] *In re Steer* (1858), 3 H. & N. 594, 599 (per Pollock, C.B.).

[5] Thus according to Beale and the Restatement. The question has, however, given rise to some controversy. Cf. Lorenzen, 37 *Yale L.J.* 1127; Coudert, 36 *Yale L.J.* 949; Lorenzen, *Répert.* VI, no. 56.

[6] *Aikman* v. *Aikman* (1860), 3 Macq. 854, 863, 877; *Udny* v. *Udny*, loc. cit.; *Bell* v. *Kennedy*, loc. cit.; *Jopp* v. *Wood*. loc. cit., at p. 219.

105. Domicile of origin 'in reserve'

(*a*) The domicile of origin continues to exist until a domicile of choice is in fact established; a domicile of choice is only retained until it is abandoned.[1] If such abandonment has taken place without the establishment of a new domicile (of choice) the domicile of origin is resumed. This domicile 'always remains, as it were, in reserve, to be resorted to in case no other domicile is found to exist'.[2]

Example: A woman having a Scottish domicile of origin establishes a domicile of choice in England and marries there a domiciled Englishman. After his death she and her twenty-two-year-old son decide to leave England for good and to settle in New York. During their voyage from Liverpool to New York both die, the son as a domiciled Englishman, while his mother when leaving England had lost her English and resumed her Scottish domicile. A surprising and unsatisfactory result, which seems to show some inadequacy in the English rule.

106. Change of sovereignty at the domicile of origin

A delicate problem confronts us when the place where the domicile of origin lies has undergone a change of sovereignty, either by cession of the territory to another state or by the foundation of a new state, while the person concerned had a domicile of choice elsewhere. Suppose that he had a domicile of origin at Poznán, which he abandoned in 1910 by establishing a domicile of choice in England, and that in 1925 he abandoned his English domicile without acquiring a new domicile of choice. Is he then a domiciled Pole or a domiciled German? It is suggested that the second alternative is correct, since by settling in England he had abandoned a German domicile.[3]

107. Ramsay v. Liverpool Royal Infirmary

Secondly, (*b*): Because a domicile of origin is 'in its character more enduring, its hold stronger, and less easily shaken off',[4] the courts usually require stronger evidence in the case of a change from a domicile of origin than in that of a change from a domicile of choice.[5] A striking

---

[1] Dicey, rule 8 (2).

[2] Per Lord Chelmsford in *Udny* v. *Udny*, loc. cit., at pp. 454, 455. See *King* v. *Foxwell* (1876), 3 Ch.D., 518, 521.

[3] See *supra*, s. 98 (3).

[4] *Winans* v. *Att.-Gen.*, [1904] A.C. 287, 290 (*per* Lord Macnaghten).

[5] *Ross* v. *Ross*, [1930] A.C. 1. *Fowler* v. *Fowler* (1930; on this: Bentwich in *Rabel's Z.* 5 (1931) 58). *Att.-Gen.* v. *Dame Yule* (1931); 145 L.T. 9. *Ramsay* v. *Liverpool Royal Infirmary*, [1930] A.C. 588. *Wahl* v. *Att.-Gen.* (1932), 147 L.T. 382.

example of this is to be found in the Scottish case *Ramsay* (or *Bowie*) v. *Liverpool Royal Infirmary*.[1]

The testator left a will valid under Scottish, but invalid under English law. His domicile of origin was Scottish, but for the last thirty-five years of his life he lived in Liverpool, where he stayed with his mother, his brother, and his sisters. He had no real attachment to Liverpool but for the presence of these members of his family. He remained there, however, even after their death. He never went to Scotland, but 'he would have followed his family had they returned to Scotland'.[2] In his will he named a Glasgow writer as trustee and directed that his bequests to three Glasgow infirmaries and one Liverpool infirmary should be given anonymously as from 'a Glasgow man'. He had told people that he was proud to be a Glasgow man and had subscribed to a Glasgow weekly newspaper. The Scottish Courts and the House of Lords held that he had retained his Scottish domicile because an intention to abandon it 'is not to be inferred from an attitude of indifference or disinclination to move',[3] and because he had not intended to achieve a 'complete severance of ties with the domicile of origin'.[4] Professor Cheshire rightly calls this decision 'a little startling' and adds[5] that it is 'difficult to conceive of a clearer example of a fixed intention to remain permanently in a country'. It may however be that the decision was influenced by the unexpressed wish of the court to uphold the deceased man's will.

The reason for the differentiation between the domicile of origin and other domiciles is the deceptive idea that a man belongs to the country of his origin much more than to a country of his choice, and that it is difficult to suppose that he is determined to strip himself of 'his birthright in the place of his original domicile'.[6]

The intention of a person to make a country his permanent residence does not require his knowledge that he is thereby changing his domicile. The intention is directed merely towards a factual change in life, not towards a legal change. Conversely, an express declaration of a person that he intends to abandon his domicile of origin and acquire a

108. Intention and knowledge

---

[1] [1930] A.C. 588.   [2] loc. cit., at p. 593.
[3] See *Winans* v. *Att.-Gen.*, [1904] A.C. 287, 291.
[4] *Ross* v. *Ross*, [1930] A.C. 1, 24.   [5] At p. 220.
[6] *Moorhouse* v. *Lord* (1863), 10 H. L.Cas. 272. *Marchioness of Huntly* v. *Gaskell*, [1906] A.C. 56, at p. 66. It is not however necessary that he should have the intention of 'stripping himself of his nationality', as was suggested in *Moorhouse* v. *Lord*, loc. cit., though it is true that it is easier to assume a change of domicile from one country to another under the same sovereign (from Scotland to England) than a change from one state to another state (from England to France). *Whicker* v. *Hume* (1858), 7 H.L.Cas. 124, at p. 159. Cf. *Wahl* v. *Att.-Gen.* (1932), 147 L.T. 382.

domicile of choice is not conclusive. It is no more than an *indicium* of his intention and, as Dr. Lushington puts it, the 'lowest species of evidence';[1] on the other hand, it must 'not be discarded but duly weighed together with the rest of the evidence adduced'.[2]

109. 'Present' intention

It has been said that the intention of a person to make a certain country his permanent residence must be a 'present' intention.[3] Thereby is meant his will immediately to make the country his permanent residence. The fact of physical presence in a country and the intention of staying there indefinitely need not be simultaneous. It may be that the intention precedes, or again that it follows arrival in a country.

If it precedes arrival, domicile is not established until he has in fact arrived. A person who has left his English domicile intending to settle in Ontario has during the voyage not yet constituted an Ontario domicile.[4] He constitutes it by arriving in Ontario, provided he has still the intention of staying there permanently. If, on the other hand, he does not decide to make his home there until after his arrival, he becomes domiciled upon taking such decision; from a visitor he changes to a domiciled resident through intention alone.[5]

Once his domicile of choice is established it does not matter whether he retains the will to live there, or for any reason decides to leave the country again, so long as he does not actually leave. Events following the apparent establishment of a domicile may be of importance as evidence of the person's previous intention, i.e. they may show that no settled intention of perpetual residence ever existed. But otherwise they are immaterial. If, for example, doubts are raised as to where a husband was domiciled at the time when divorce proceedings were instituted, it is

1 Hodgson v. *De Beauchesne* (1858), 12 Moore P.C. 285, 325. Cf. *Re Steer* (1858), 3 H. & N. 594, 599.

2 Sir C. Creswell in *Crookenden v. Fuller* (1859), 1 Sw. & Tr. 441, 450. *Bryce* v. *Bryce*, [1933] P. 83, 86. *Gulbenkian* v. *Gulbenkian*, [1937] 4 A.E.R. 618, 627.

3 See Cheshire's criticism, pp. 216 et seq.

4 A different view, according to which a new domicile may be acquired *in itinere* (*Munroe* v. *Douglas* (1820), 5 Madd. 379, 405), seems to have been abandoned; *In the Goods of Raffenel* (1863), 32 L.J., P.M. & A. 203; Dicey-Morris, p. 98.

5 *May* v. *May*, [1943] 2 A.E.R. 146. The situation is similar to the acquisition of possession *corpore et animo*, where the *corpus* may follow the *animus* or precede it, so that by mere change of will the *detentor* may become a *possessor*.

not necessary to ascertain the husband's intention at the time of the suit; it suffices to show his intention at the time of changing residence or at *any* subsequent moment; a later change of intention does not destroy domicile unless it is accompanied by an actual change of residence.

It has often been said that there can be no choice of permanent residence where there is no liberty of choice:[1] 'the word "choose" indicates that the act is voluntary'.[2] Complete exclusion of choice, however, does not exist, except in the case of physical coercion, for example where a prisoner is transported to a foreign country.[3] Apart from that there is always some alternative open to the person concerned.[4] The fugitive from justice[5] could have stayed to face the consequences of his crimes. The New York debtor who escapes to Canada has chosen between dishonest flight and submission to law. The invalid who is told by his doctor that there is no hope for his recovery, but that he may live a few months longer in another climate,[6] may choose between going to Egypt and staying in England to face an earlier end or to learn that his doctor was wrong. In all cases of this kind the simple issue is whether he would wish to return to his former residence if the reason for his going abroad should disappear, i.e. if his crime should cease to be punishable, if he should make a fortune and pay his creditors, if he should recover *adversus medicum*, &c.

Whether the German refugee from Nazi oppression resident in this country acquires a domicile here depends on similar considerations.[7] If he intends never to return to Germany whatever her future government may be[8] and

110. Want of liberty of choice

---

[1] On the following see Cheshire, pp. 222–8; Dicey(–Morris), p. 118.

[2] Sir G. Jessel in *King* v. *Foxwell* (1876), 3 Ch.D. 518, 520. *Cruh* v. *Cruh*, [1945] 2 A.E.R. 546.

[3] *Burton* v. *Fisher* (1828), Milward's Rep. 183, 191.

[4] Cf. *Urquhart* v. *Butterfield* (1887), 37 Ch.D. 357, 385 (per Lopes. L.J.).

[5] Cf. *In re Martin, Loustalan* v. *Loustalan*, [1900] P. (C.A.) 211, 233.

[6] Cf. *Hoskins* v. *Matthews* (1856), 25 L.J.Ch. 689. *Moorhouse* v. *Lord* (1863), 10 H.L.Cas. 272, 292. *Johnstone* v. *Beattie* (1843), 10 Cl. & Fin. 42. 139.

[7] *De Bonneval* v. *De Bonneval* (1838), 1 Curt. 856. Cf. *In re Lloyd-Evans*, [1947] 1 Ch. 695. See E. Kahn, 65 *South Afric. L. Journ.* (1948), 220 et seq., and Anonym. 42 *Columbia L.R.* 640.

[8] *May* v. *May*, [1943] 2 A.E.R. 146. There are indubitably many who share

not to settle in a third country, he has undoubtedly established an English domicile. If he hopes—i.e. wishes and believes—that he may be able to return to a changed Germany, he certainly retains his German domicile. If, finally, he fears that this will not happen, his intention is permanently to live in England though he would prefer living in Germany: wish and will point different ways.

Those persons who as public servants of their or of a foreign government reside abroad to fulfil duties as consuls, colonial judges, and the like, cannot as a rule be said to have changed their domicile, unless there is evidence that they intend to stay abroad after retiring from office.[1]

III. DOMICILE BY OPERATION OF LAW[2]

111. Domicilium necessarium　　　Under all legal systems a domicile is established by law (not by a voluntary act of the domiciled person) in the case of dependent persons or of certain categories of such persons. Everywhere these categories include infants (minors) and married women, in most countries also lunatics and persons placed under guardianship. Some legal systems recognize a *domicilium necessarium* also for house-servants[3]—a relic of the time when they belonged to the 'family' of the householder and were under his domestic control (*mundium*)—for soldiers, civil servants, or certain groups of officials,[4] and for prisoners.[5] English

the feeling expressed by a certain Professor J. H. Gilchrist about his mother-country, in which, as he wrote in 1825, he had suffered 'a blow which dissolution cannot efface from a conscious retrospective mind, wherever it may wing its flight, and one that impels me to disown and deny my country as a tyrannical stepmother, to whom . . . I owe nought save the deepest disgust'. (*Whicker* v. *Hume* (1858), 7, H.L.Cas. 126.)

[1] *Att.-Gen.* v. *Pottinger* (1861), 30 L.J.Ex. 284. *Att.-Gen.* v. *Rowe* (1862), 1 H. & C. 31. *Re Macreight* (1885), 30 Ch.D. 165. *Sharpe* v. *Crispin* (1869), L.R. 1, P. & D. 611. *Urquhart* v. *Butterfield* (1887), 37 Ch.D. 357, at p. 382. See also *Donaldson* v. *Donaldson*, [1949] P. 363.

[2] This term is used in the United States; Restatement, § 26 et seq. Obviously the domicile of origin is an example of 'domicile by operation of law'.

[3] French, c.c., art. 109. Nearly all modern laws have cancelled a corresponding provision.

[4] French law (art. 107): all officials appointed for life. German law (civ.c., s. 9): professional members of the armed forces, not civil servants. Swiss law: only certain Federal officials, viz. Federal Judges, the Federal Chancellor, Federal Councillors.　　　　[5] Brazil Civil Code, art. 40.

and American law reject this extension of the·concept of
necessary domicile, and the same sound tendency is to be
found in certain modern legal systems, such as the Swiss
Civil Code, the Italian Code, and the Montevideo Convention.

English law establishes legal domicile:

I. *for infants*. We have dealt (*supra*, s. 101) with their
domicile of origin, which comes into existence at the
moment of their birth. The question arises how this
domicile can be changed during the period of minority.
A change by the infant's own voluntary act takes place
in one case only, that is, when a female infant marries and
thereby acquires her husband's domicile.[1] Apart from
that the infant's domicile of origin is changed:

(a) in the case of a legitimate child by a change of the
father's domicile. During minority the child shares compulsorily the father's changing domicile. It makes no
difference whether the child follows the father to his new
domicile or stays with the mother. Even when the court
has declared the father unfit to have the custody of the
child it takes the father's domicile. On this point American
laws are well ahead of the English provisions. When, in
America, an infant's parents are divorced or separated, the
child has the domicile of the parent to whom it has been
entrusted or with whom it lives.[2]

112.
(1) Infants.
Principle:
father's
domicile

Neither under English nor under American law can the father change
his child's domicile without changing his own. If, for example, he places
his son in charge of a business abroad where the son in fact lives, this does
not affect the latter's domicile.[3] The reason for this incapacity may be found

---

[1] The question has been raised whether an infant 'tacitly emancipated' under
Roman-Dutch law is capable of changing its domicile by its own choice, and
whether its father loses his capacity to change his son's domicile; *Ochberg* v.
Ochberg's Estate, [1941] South Africa L.R. Cape Prov. D., 15, 36, 37. The
answer depends on the nature of tacit emancipation. If such emancipation has
the effect of making the infant come of age, the answer would be in the affirmative.
But if its effect is merely to empower the infant to carry on business abroad on
its own behalf and therefore to conclude contracts connected with the business,
this hardly includes a change of domicile. (In the quoted South African case
the question was not decided.)

[2] Restatement, § 32; Beale, I, 215. Similarly under Swiss law: Civ. Code, s. 25;
the domicile of the parent who has the 'parental power' is decisive.

[3] Beale, I, 211, n. 6. On the rules of the various states of U.S.A. concerning

in the fact that though the father may establish a separate residence for his son, he cannot form on behalf of a person who will be independent on coming of age an intention *permanently* to reside in any particular country.

113.
Mother's
domicile

(*b*) After the father's death the legitimate child retains his last domicile until the mother adopts a new one; then it shares the mother's domicile, just as an illegitimate child does from birth. In both cases, however, the child's domicile changes only if and so long as the child lives with its mother.[1] Unlike the rule prevailing in the case of the legitimate child during its father's life-time the rule that the child follows the mother's domicile is not compulsory.

The change in the child's domicile, then, as Stirling, J., stated,[2] 'is not to be regarded as a necessary consequence of change of the mother's[3] domicile but as the result of the exercise by her of a power vested in her for the welfare of the infants, which in their interest she may abstain from exercising'. This differentiation between the father's and the mother's domicile is particularly startling because it seems to grant the mother a 'power' which it denies to the father, though in both cases the infant's interest is the same. American laws have abolished such unjustifiable differentiation—which, for that matter, is not to be found in any law of the European continent.

114. Influ-
ence of
mother's
marriage

With regard to the question how the mother's marriage affects the child's domicile, two cases must be considered:

(i) If, after the father's death, the mother remarries, the domicile of the infant is not automatically changed. When, however, she changes her residence in fact by going to live at her second husband's domicile, and takes her children with her, they, too, acquire their stepfather's domicile.[4]

(ii) The same rule applies if the mother of an illegitimate infant marries. Only if she marries the infant's father and if, according to the law applicable to legitimation, the child becomes legitimate by subsequent marriage does it thereby acquire the father's domicile. Under most continental laws the legitimation has no retroactive effect.[5]

the domicile of infants: Vernier, *Family Laws* (1938), V, 227–40. *Contra*: German law (civ.c., s. 8) and—though this is not quite certain—Swiss law. See Brodtbeck & Daeppen, *Bundesgerichtspraxis zum ZivGB* (1934), art. 25, n. I 2.

[1] *In re Beaumont*, [1893] 3 Ch. 490. *Potinger* v. *Wightman* (1817), 3 Merivale's Ch.R. 67.   [2] *In re Beaumont*, loc. cit., at p. 496.

[3] Restatement, § 38 c.   [4] *In re Beaumont*, loc. cit.

[5] The contrary statement in Beale, II, 707, seems to be based on some misunderstanding. Compare *infra*, s. 373 n., 374, n.

Where, however, such effect is provided—as, for example, in Hungary[1], or Ontario,[2] or formerly in Canon law,[3] and now possibly under English law[4]—the child acquires by legitimation the paternal domicile as from its birth. This domicile then becomes the domicile of origin.

(c) If the child stays with its mother who is not the guardian, it has the mother's and not the guardian's domicile. If, on the other hand, it does not reside with its mother and therefore does not share her domicile, it seems doubtful where its domicile lies. It is certain that no child acquires the guardian's domicile. Probably it retains its last domicile, which may be the domicile of origin.

115. Guardian's domicile?

Whether the guardian can change his ward's domicile is doubtful,[5] but as even a father is not able to do so without changing his own domicile such power can hardly be attributed to the guardian. Continental laws allow a change of a minor's domicile by his legal representative, be it the father or a guardian.[6]

(d) English law makes no provision for the domicile of an *adopted* infant. The Adoption of Children Act, 1926,[7] speaks merely of 'rights, duties, obligations and liabilities' of the parents or guardians 'in relation to the future custody, maintenance and education of the adopted child' and provides that they 'shall be extinguished' and 'vest in and be exercisable by and enforceable against the adopter as though the adopted child was a child born to the adopter in lawful wedlock'. It does not mention the child's domicile either explicitly or by implication. Nor does the Adoption of Children Act, 1949.[8] But there can be little doubt that in respect of domicile the adopter replaces the parents. The adopted child therefore acquires the

116. Adopter's domicile?

---

[1] Almási, *Ungar. Privatrecht*, I, 214, n. 8.

[2] Johnson (Canad.), *Conflict of Laws*, I, 344.

[3] Esmein, *Le mariage en droit canonique* (2nd ed.), II, 43.

[4] According to Scott, L.J., in *Re Luck*, [1940] Ch. 864, 898, 899. But is this view correct in spite of the unambiguous wording of ss. 1, 8, of the Legitimacy Act?

[5] Dicey(–Morris), p. 102[30].

[6] Cf. for example, German Civ. C., s. 8. 11. According to the American Restatement (s. 37) the guardian cannot change the domicile of the ward to a state other than the one in which he was appointed.

[7] 16 & 17 Geo. V, c. 29, s. 5.

[8] 12, 13 & 14 Geo. IV, c. 98. See *infra*, s. 378.

adopter's domicile by operation of law. In Continental laws and in the United States the same rule prevails.[1] If the adopter dies, his wife's domicile becomes the infant's domicile only if the application for the adoption order had been made by both spouses jointly, not if it had been made by the husband alone though with his wife's consent.[2] As 'adoption imitates nature',[3] it would seem justifiable to apply by way of analogy to the acquisition of a female adopter's domicile all the rules—defective as they may be—on the acquisition by a child of its own mother's domicile.

117. New domicile acquired during infancy

(e) In those cases in which an infant's domicile changes—for example, by change in the father's domicile or by adoption—is the new domicile to be considered as its 'domicile of origin'? The point is important when a person acquires a domicile of choice and after some time abandons it without establishing a new domicile of choice; then his domicile of origin revives. The answer is not quite certain.[4] In principle it should be in the negative; the child's new domicile is not to be treated as its domicile of origin, except in those cases where the change has a retroactive effect.

Example: The divorced husband of the child's mother effectively disputes the legitimacy of the child and thereby creates for it a status of illegitimacy from birth.[5]

118. (2) Married women

2. *Married women.* When a valid marriage is concluded the wife immediately loses her domicile and

---

[1] Restatement, § 35. German Civ. Code, s, 11. In Swiss law the same is to be assumed from Civ. Code, art. 268, in French law from art. 352 C.C. (though neither provision speaks of domicile); see Egger in his *Commentary on the Swiss Code* (2nd ed., 1930), I, p. 211; Josserand, *Cours de droit civil*, I, no. 232 ad. 1; Italian *Codice civ.* (1938), art. 42, 299.

[2] Adoption of Children Act, 1926 (16 & 17 Geo. V, c. 29), s. 1 (3), s. 2 (4).

[3] Justinian's *Instit.*, 1, 11, 4.

[4] Cf. *Firebrace* v. *Firebrace* (1878), 4 P.D. 63; and *Urquhart* v. *Butterfield* (1887), 37 Ch.D. 357, at pp. 384, 385 (*per* Lopez, L.J.). See J. G. Foster, *Brit. Y.B.* 1935, 87.

[5] According to most modern laws a child conceived during wedlock and born after divorce is prima facie a legitimate child of the mother's divorced husband, and therefore takes his domicile. When he brings proceedings for disputing the legitimacy and succeeds in proving that he cannot be the father, the child becomes illegitimate *ex tunc* and is deemed to have acquired at birth its mother's domicile, which after divorce may be different from the husband's. Cf., for example, Swiss Civ. Code, art. 252–4. Another example of retroactive change of domicile has been mentioned above, p. 118, *ad. n. 5*.

acquires that of her husband, and if later he changes his domicile she shares the new one. English law does not allow any exception to this rule. Even if the husband deserts her and establishes a domicile in a foreign country, or if the spouses are judicially separated, she acquires his domicile in countries to which she neither goes nor is bound to go.[1] Not until the marriage is dissolved by death or by a decree of divorce (recognized in this country[2]) is she able to establish a domicile of her own.

Where a voidable marriage is concluded, the wife acquires her husband's domicile just as if it were a fully valid marriage, and although a nullity decree has retrospective effect, this does not mean that after the decree the wife is to be treated as if she had never acquired the husband's domicile.

Where the marriage is not voidable but void *ab initio*, it now seems settled (by the decision of the Court of Appeal in *De Reneville* v. *De Reneville*[3]) that the marriage has no effect on the woman's domicile: even if she has gone through a marriage ceremony, the husband's domicile does not pass to her by operation of law; she may, of course, establish in fact a domicile of choice at his domicile.

It is submitted, with great respect, that the different treatment of void and voidable marriages is highly unsatisfactory. As we have seen,[4] the void marriage should not be confused with a non-existent marriage. A marriage, even if void, has at least the effect of creating a rebuttable presumption in favour of the existence of the marriage. This presumption may be refuted either *incidenter* with effect only between the litigating parties or *in rem*, as against everybody, by a nullity decree pronounced by the Probate, Divorce and Admiralty Division, while in the case of a non-existent marriage, where the parties have not even gone through a marriage ceremony, no presumption of this kind exists, no nullity decree can be pronounced, and the person who asserts that there is a marriage has the burden of proof. Where there has been a marriage ceremony—and where therefore a rebuttable presumption exists that the parties are married—such ceremony should be regarded as creating a new 'status' differing from that of unmarried persons, and it would not be too bold to assume that the 'wife' acquires her husband's

---

[1] *Warrender* v. *Warrender* (1835), 2 Cl. & Fin. 488, 523, 561. *Dolphin* v. *Robins* (1859), 7 H.L.Cas. 390, 420, 423. *Yelverton* v. *Yelverton* (1859), 1 Sw. & Tr. 574, 584. *In re Mackenzie*, [1911] 1 Ch. 578, 591. *Lord Advocate* v. *Jaffrey*, [1921] 1 A.C. 146, 152, 168 (discussed in 20 *Michig. L.R.* 86). *Att.-Gen. for Alberta* v. *Cook*, [1926] A.C. 444, 453.

[2] See Lewald, p. 72, n. 1.   [3] [1948] P. 100.   [4] pp. 79–81.

domicile by operation of law. True, the nullity decree destroys the effect of a void marriage retrospectively. But so does a nullity decree in the case of a voidable marriage. And if it is permissible to disregard that retroactivity with regard to the wife's domicile in cases of voidable marriages, it should be equally permissible to disregard it for void marriages.

119. No exceptions

The strictness of the rule under which the wife takes her husband's domicile is a remnant of the doctrine of coverture, of the old fiction that husband and wife are one person.[1] Continental laws rightly recognize exceptions to the wife's *domicilium necessarium*. Under French law the wife in case of judicial separation 'ceases to have as her legal domicile the domicile of her husband'.[2] German law gives her the right to establish a separate domicile 'if the husband establishes a domicile in a foreign country at a place to which the wife neither follows him nor is bound to follow'.[3] Italian law allows her a separate domicile if the spouses are judicially separated, or the husband is placed under guardianship or transfers his domicile to a foreign country.[4] A better solution[5] seems to be that of the Swiss Civil Code, according to which 'the wife who is entitled to live separately may have a domicile of her own', even if she has not applied for a judicial separation.[6] In the United States of America, too, the courts have mitigated the English rule; they recognize a separate domicile of a wife, first if she lives apart from her husband without being guilty of desertion, and secondly upon judicial separation; in a few decisions a separate domicile has even been admitted where the wife has abandoned her husband without cause.[7]

120. Lunatics

3. There are no English rules with regard to the domicile of *lunatics*. If a person who has attained full age becomes mentally incompetent so that he is unable to choose

---

[1] Possibly the 'fear of subjecting English husbands to the more lax divorce laws of other countries' (40 *Harvard L.R.* 135) may have been of some influence.

[2] Code Civil, art. 108 (3) (added by a statute of 1893, which however merely laid down what had already been recognized by the courts).

[3] German Civ. C., s. 10. The wife is not bound to follow if the husband's demand 'constitutes an abuse of his right', or if she is 'entitled to claim a divorce' (s. 1353).   [4] Codice civile (1942), s. 42.

[5] Unless one decides entirely to reject the *domicilium necessarium* of married women (which would be the soundest solution).

[6] Swiss Civ. C., art. 25, § 2.

[7] Restatement, §§ 28, 29. Beale, I, p. 208.

a domicile, he retains the domicile he had before he became a lunatic, and it seems that this domicile cannot be changed; in particular, not by his guardian.[1]

The same rule prevails in the United States,[2] at least in so far as the guardian cannot transfer the lunatic's domicile to a state other than the one in which he has been appointed guardian. Continental laws differ from this. Under French law the ward shares the guardian's domicile;[3] under Swiss law the ward's domicile is to be found where the competent authority has its seat.[4] German law[5] recognizes that it ought to be within the guardian's power to alter not only the residence but also the domicile of his ward, and that this need not depend on a simultaneous change of the guardian's own domicile, which is not necessarily shared by the ward.

Where a child is born insane or becomes insane during infancy, it shares its father's changing domicile, like any other infant, and it seems that even a change made by the father after the lunatic's coming of age alters the lunatic's domicile.[6]

IV. The English doctrine of domicile has met with grave criticism. The principle itself, however, of testing personal law by domicile and not by nationality seems satisfactory, though this too is open to doubt.[7] The main defects of the English doctrine are the following:

1. The way in which the conception of 'domicile of origin' is determined, in that it is referred not only to the father's domicile but sometimes to that of the grandfather and even of more distant ancestors. The parental, not the

121. Defects of the English rules

---

[1] *Urquhart* v. *Butterfield* (1887), 37 Ch.D. 357, 382. *Sharpe* v. *Crispin* (1869), L.R. 1 P. & D. 611. Cheshire, p. 238.   [2] Restatement, § 40.
[3] French C.C., art. 108, § 2.   [4] Swiss Civ. Code, art. 25, § 1.
[5] German Civ. Code, s. 8.   [6] *Sharpe* v. *Crispin*, loc. cit., at p. 618.
[7] J. G. Foster, *Brit. Y.B.*, 1935, p. 85, recommends in the first place the adoption of the continental doctrine of nationality. But the number of opponents to the nationality principle on the continent itself is increasing, particularly in France (see *supra*. p. 104[2]). Alternatively he proposes certain concessions to the nationality principle, viz. application of the law of domicile only in the case of British subjects and persons domiciled in the British dominions; all other persons to be governed by the law of their nationality, but if the conflict rules of their national state point to the law of domicile such *renvoi* should be accepted. Thus a Frenchman domiciled in Denmark (and a Danish subject domiciled in France) would be governed by French law. It is submitted that it would be sufficient to 'relax some of the rigid rules of domicile at present applied by the English courts', as Morris, *Cases on Private International Law* (1939), p. 22, proposes. See notably Cheshire, 61 *L.Q.R.* (1945), 363-4.

ancestral home is the place where the normal centre of the life of a child lies.

2. The difficulty any person has in ridding himself of his domicile of origin, which necessitates the loosening of all ties connecting him with such domicile.

3. The rule that the domicile of origin revives when a domicile of choice is given up and no new domicile of choice has been established. The American rule that any domicile once established continues until it is superseded by a new domicile is a considerable improvement.[1] Even the solution given by the Conventions of Montevideo and the Código Bustamante seems preferable to the English rule: there the factual residence of a person who abandons his domicile, or even the place of his transitory sojourn is treated as his domicile until a new domicile has been created.[2]

4. The principle that the establishment of a domicile of choice needs the intention of 'permanent' residence, that consequently habitual residence is not sufficient, though it suffices under all continental systems.[3]

5. The strictness of the two rules according to which (*a*) a wife shares her husband's domicile even if she is entitled to a separate life, and (*b*) the children have their father's domicile even if he has no right to their custody. In these respects American law has improved on English law.

6. The undeniable incompleteness and uncertainty with regard to the domicile of lunatics, infants under guardianship, and of married women in the case of a void marriage.

---

[1] Restatement, § 23.

[2] *Montevideo Conv. on Private Internat. Law* (see *supra*, p. 48), s. 9; *Código Bustamante*, art. 26.

[3] There is one group of cases, however, where the necessity of that intention has proved highly satisfactory, that is where a person of European civilization settles in a country with a wholly different way of living (unless in that country the status of persons is governed by different laws according as they are natives or persons of European descent). The English rule saves such settlers from being subject in respect of status, marriage, wills, and so on, to legal rules repugnant to the European mind. Cf. *In re Tootal's Trusts* (1883), 23 Ch.D. 532, 534. *Maltass v. Maltass* (1844), 1 Rob. Eccl. C. 67, 80, 81. *Casdagli v. Casdagli*, [1919] A.C. 145.

CHAPTER X

NATIONALITY AS A POINT OF CONTACT

I. Though under English law a person's status is pri-122. The questions tested by nationality marily tested by his domicile, there are a few situations in which it is to some extent affected by his nationality. They are the following:

1. Marriages of British subjects abroad are formally valid (a) if concluded in a foreign country before a British ambassador, consul, or other marriage officer, or on board a British ship before the commanding officer. It is sufficient if one of the parties is a British subject.

(b) if concluded in the forms of English law in a place where there is no local form, or where the local form is utterly foreign to those of European countries, or one closely connected with a particular religion or confession, and therefore not accessible to the couple. Again, it is sufficient if one of them is a British subject. See ss. 326, 327.

2. Marriages of aliens.

(a) They are formally valid if concluded at the Embassy of their state in England, provided that both parties belong to the same foreign state.[1]

(b) It is doubtful whether aliens domiciled in a country where they cannot avail themselves of the local form or where there is no local form can marry in the form of their national law. It is believed that the answer is in the affirmative provided that their national law (or laws) recognize such marriage.[2]

3. The Adoption of Children Act, 1926,[3] was (before 1950) applicable only if the child was a British subject.[4]

---

[1] *Pertreis* v. *Tondear* (1790), 1 Hagg. Consist. 136, 138, 139.

[2] There are further privileges in Asiatic countries in favour of Europeans living within the limits of a factory or a trade settlement; British subjects may marry within the British factory in British form, if they are English therefore in English form; French subjects in a French factory in French form, &c. Dicey–Morris, p. 769. See *infra*, s. 326 c.

[3] 16 & 17 Geo. V, c. 29, s. 2 (5).

[4] Altered by the Adoption of Children Act, 1949, 12, 13 & 14 Geo. VI, c. 98, s. 1 (subs. 2).

4. The Wills Act, 1861 (known as Lord Kingsdown's Act),[1] ordains that a will made by a British subject shall be formally valid if executed according to the law of the country where it is made (or in certain other forms). This does not apply to persons of foreign nationality domiciled in the United Kingdom. Cf. *infra*, ss. 561–4.

5. English courts have often pronounced, though only *obiter*, that foreign judgments *in personam* are to be recognized if, at the time of the judgment, the defendant was a subject of the country of the adjudicating court.[2] This rule, however, raises grave doubts;[3] and not only because nationality is not the normal point of contact in English private international law. Even those continental countries which test the status of a person by his nationality and not by his domicile—such as France or Germany—have no rule of this character. English law does not provide that the defendant's British nationality alone is enough to render him amenable to the *British* court's jurisdiction. Thus it would seem surprising to find that nationality is considered sufficient to give jurisdiction to a *foreign* court. It has been argued in favour of the doctrine that a 'subject is bound to obey the commands of his sovereign and therefore the judgments of his sovereign's courts'.[4] Even if this were entirely true with regard to subjects residing abroad it would not follow that it is the duty of another sovereign to see those commands obeyed.

123. Which law decides on nationality? II. In all these cases, where the applicable law depends on nationality, there is a series of problems to be solved.

1. The question whether a given person is the citizen of a certain state can only be decided by the law of that state. This principle of international law has been asserted

---

[1] 24 & 25 Vict., c. 114, ss. 1, 2.

[2] *Douglas* v. *Forrest* (1828), 4 Bingh. 686, 702, 703 (here limited to the case of 'natural-born subjects of any country'). *Schibsby* v. *Westenholz* (1870), L.R. 6, Q.B. 155, 161. Notably: *Rousillon* v. *Rousillon* (1880), 14 Ch.D. 351, 371. *Emanuel* v. *Symon*, [1908] 1 K.B. (C.A.) 302, 309. *Phillips* v. *Batho*, [1913] 3 K.B. (C.A.) 25, 29. *Harris* v. *Taylor*, [1915] 2 K.B. (C.A.) 580, 591. Cf. also American Restatement, § 77 (1) (c).

[3] See Atkin, J., in *Gavin Gibson & Co.* v. *Gibson*, [1913] 3 K.B. 379, 388, and Cheshire 788, 789.

[4] Dicey, pp. 405, 406 (5th ed.). Against it: Morris in 6th ed., p. 357.

by the Hague Convention concerning certain Questions relating to the Conflict of Nationality Laws of 12 April 1930[1]; further by English courts,[2] and by the Court of International Justice: 'La qualité de ressortissant d'un État ne peut se fonder que sur la loi de cet État.'[3] If a German marries an American woman, German law decides whether she acquires German nationality by marriage (she does), and the law of the United States decides whether she loses her American nationality (she does not).

The principle that no state is entitled to determine the conditions on which a person becomes a citizen of a foreign state has been disregarded by the Naturalization Act, 1870, and by some continental codes.

The *Naturalization Act*, 1870 s. 10 (1) ordered: 'A married woman shall be deemed to be a subject of the state of which her husband is for the time being a subject.' See also, with regard to the nationality of children, s. 10 (3) of the Act. Not till the *British Nationality and Status of Aliens Act*, 1914, s. 10[4], was the mistake corrected: it ran, '. . . the wife of a British subject shall be deemed to be a British subject, and the wife of an alien shall be deemed to be an alien'.

The French Civil Code in its original text (1804) established the rule that a French woman marrying an alien shares her husband's nationality,[5] and though French law later abolished this provision, many other codes based on the French Code have preserved it.[6] Similar mistakes are sometimes to be found in rules on the nationality of illegitimate children. Thus a French law of 26 June 1889 provided that 'the illegitimate child whose parentage has been established during its minority follows the nationality of that one of its parents with regard to whom the facts have first been established'. Under this rule the illegitimate child of an English woman, when born abroad, would be considered as of British nationality—which undoubtedly is untrue according to English law. The French rule was rightly abolished in 1927; but an identical rule still prevails in Belgium.[7]

[1] Ratified by Great Britain, Belgium, Netherlands, Norway, Sweden, Poland, Australia, Canada, India, Morocco, Brazil, China—J. M. Jones, pp. 22 et seq. According to Jones, p. 17, it has been ratified by all members of the British Commonwealth.

[2] *Stoeck* v. *Public Trustee*, [1921] 2 Ch. 67, 82. *Re Chamberlain's Settlement*, [1921] 2 Ch. 533, 544.

[3] *Publications de la Cour Permanente*, *Série B*, No. 10, p. 19. See also the decision *Sér. B*, No. 4, p. 24, and Melchior, loc. cit., p. 442.

[4] (4 & 5 Geo. V, c. 17) and 1933 (23 & 24 Geo. V, c. 49) s. 10 (1).

[5] Civil Code, art. 19.

[6] For example, Luxemburg Civ. Code, art. 19; Spanish *Código Civil* (1889), art. 22; Dutch law of Dec. 12, 1892, art. 5, and others.

[7] Belg. law of May 15, 1922, art. 2. See also the erroneous decisions of the French Court of Cassation, *Rev. Darras*, 1909, 249; Melchior, p. 442, n. 4.

Such provisions, though binding on the courts of the state which made them,[1] will be disregarded by the courts of any foreign country.

A peculiar situation arises in cases like this: A German woman marries a British subject; in normal circumstances she would thereby lose her German and may acquire British nationality by registration. Suppose, however, that the marriage is considered void by German and valid by English law, e.g., because it was concluded within the precincts of the British Embassy in Switzerland. Then the wife does not lose her German though she acquires British nationality.[2]

In all these respects nationality differs from domicile. Any legal system may validly determine the conditions upon which domicile depends. It may hold the domicile to have been established in a foreign country, though the law of that country regards the domicile as established elsewhere.[3] The law of a given country can answer the question 'where is the domicile of X?' It cannot answer the question 'of which state is he a citizen?', but merely: 'is he a citizen of my state?' Therefore English law may prevent a person from being without domicile or from having more than one domicile in the sense of English law. It cannot prevent him from having two or more nationalities[4] or from having none.

124.
Examples of dual nationality

Examples of 'dual' (or plural) nationality—*sujets mixtes*. Dual nationality may exist from birth: a legitimate child born in England of a German father is German in virtue of *ius sanguinis* and British in virtue of *ius soli*. Or it may result from a marriage: an American woman married to a British subject remains an American and may become a British subject. Or it may be produced by a formal and voluntary act: a German subject acquiring a foreign nationality may retain his German nationality if he

---

[1] In some cases, however, it may be possible to prove that the 'legislator' (or the draftsman) made a mistake in formulating the text, since it is difficult to suppose that he really wished to interfere in foreign nationality legislation.

[2] See Decisions of the German Supreme Court (Offic. Coll.), 70, 139; 105, 364. Cf. Lewald, *Renvoi*, p. 72.

[3] See *In re Annesley*, [1926] 1 Ch. 692, 703 (*per* Russell, J.), and *infra*, p. 136[2].

[4] Nevertheless some laws, and even some Constitutions, lay down that 'nobody shall be simultaneously a citizen of the state and of any other state'. See Poland, Constit. of March 17, 1921, art. 87; Lithuania, Constit. of 15 May 1928, art. 10; Latvian Law of 2 June 1927, no. VIII, and others. This is ineffective. A state can prevent dual nationality only by prescribing loss of nationality for any subject acquiring or possessing nationality of a foreign state.

has obtained the permission of the German authority to remain a German subject.[1]

Examples of stateless persons (*apatrides*). Stateless from birth: an illegitimate child born in France of a British mother; English law regards it as not British, French law as not French. Or a legitimate child of a stateless father, born in France. Statelessness may further arise from marriage: a German woman marrying an American or a stateless person becomes stateless. Finally, hundreds of thousands of Russian and German refugees have in the last twenty years lost their nationality through Soviet and Nazi decrees.

125. Examples of statelessness

2. Though no state can positively determine the conditions on which a person becomes a national of a foreign state, it does not follow that the rules established by that state as to its nationals are always to be recognized abroad. Art. 1 of the Hague Convention on Conflict of Nationality Laws, 1930, allows non-recognition in so far as the rules are inconsistent 'with international conventions, international custom', or 'the principles of law generally recognized with regard to nationality'. Only Germany can establish rules on German nationality; but not all rules she establishes must be accepted by other states.[2] If Germany were to declare that all persons of German race are from now on German nationals, irrespective of whether they have Swiss, Dutch, Brazilian, Chilean, or Argentinian nationality, no state would be prepared to accept this and to recognize that its nationals had thus acquired a second, the German nationality.[3] When the Brazilian law of 4 December 1889 declared all persons resident in Brazil on 15 November 1889 to be Brazilian subjects unless they lodged an objection within six months, this was treated by some French decisions as contrary to international law and therefore invalid.[4] Deprivation of nationality likewise, though generally allowed to any state (in cases of emigration, of treason, of marriage, &c.), may

126. Non-recognition of foreign nationality

[1] This was possible under the notorious German *lex Delbrück* (German Law of 22 July 1913, s. 25, § 2). On the political dangers of this provision see A. Weil, *Rev. Darras*, 11 & 12 (1916), 142; Flournoy, *American J.* 1914, 477. Cf. on the other hand, the observations of G. Schwartz, *Das Recht der Staatsangehörigkeit* (1925), p. 153 et seq.

[2] *Kramer* v. *Att.-Gen.*, [1922] 2 Ch. 850, 877 (*per* Younger, L.J.).

[3] See on this: Triepel, *Bruns' Z.*, 1, 185, 196.

[4] *Rev. Darras*, 11 & 12 (1916), p. 67, and Melchior, 443, n. 2.

include a violation of international law, for example, if made on purely racial grounds, since this is likely to entail mass emigration and the inundation of foreign countries with aliens, apart from its inconsistency with tenets of humanity and morality.[1] Sometimes it is the interpretation of internal law which leads to the non-recognition of a foreign nationality.

A British subject cannot, for example, divest himself of his nationality to acquire that of the enemy; if he does, this is treason and he remains liable to all the obligations of a British subject.[2] The writer H. St. Chamberlain, a British subject, acquired German nationality during the war (1916), and the question arose whether this should be recognized by the English court. The answer was to the effect that 'for the purpose of the Treaty of Versailles' he was German, but 'for all other purposes' he was not.[3] Therefore s. 13 of the British Nationality and Status of Aliens Act, 1914,[4] which provides that 'a British subject who, when in a foreign country . . . by any voluntary and formal act becomes naturalized therein, shall thenceforth be deemed to have ceased to be a British subject' would not be applicable to him. He would remain a British subject because the German nationality he had acquired by treason could not be recognized by the court.

127. *Sujets mixtes* in the cases of s. 122

3. The rules applicable to British nationals only, that is, the rules mentioned *supra*, s. 122, apply even in the case of British *sujets mixtes*, i.e. persons having two nationalities one of which is British. If, for example, a man both of British and Portuguese nationality marries a Portuguese woman before the British ambassador in Lisbon, the marriage is valid in the view of English law. Similarly foreign nationals may rely on the law of their state even if they have more than one foreign nationality (unless they are British subjects).

Example: An American who is also Portuguese marries an American woman within the precincts of the American Embassy in London; the marriage is valid in the eyes of English law; if both parties are Portuguese as well as American they may marry in London at their choice in the

---

[1] It may be objected that foreign countries are not legally bound to receive would-be immigrants. Nevertheless, for humanitarian reasons, they may feel morally bound to do so. See Jennings, 20 *Br.Y.B.*, 111.

[2] *R.* v. *Lynch*, [1903] 1 K.B. 444; *Ex parte Freyberger*, [1917] 2 K.B. 129, 133.

[3] *In re Chamberlain's Settlement*, [1921] 2 Ch. 533, 544. See J. M. Jones, l.c., 201.

[4] 4 & 5 Geo. V, c. 17.

Embassy of the United States or in the Portuguese Embassy (or in any form provided by English municipal law). But if one of them is American and British, their marriage concluded in the American Embassy is formally void; for Great Britain, like any other state, treats her own subjects solely as such and disregards their allegiance to a second state.

4. Where British nationality is decisive it is often difficult to ascertain which of the manifold legal systems prevailing in the British Empire applies, since there is no 'British' law, but only English, Scottish, Manx law, and so forth. This problem arises in particular if a British subject concludes a marriage, either with another British subject or with an alien, on board a British merchant ship on the high seas. It has been suggested that in such a case the law of the country where the parties are domiciled applies; when, for example, before the Marriage (Scotland) Act, 1939, both spouses had a Scottish domicile and married on board a British ship outside territorial waters, such marriage would be valid if concluded by *verba de praesenti*. This solution seems justifiable; but it is restricted to the case in which both parties have the same domicile. If they are domiciled in different countries of the British Empire or if neither of them is domiciled in any part of the Empire, it is not unreasonable to apply the law of the country where the ship is registered; though a Glasgow ship on the high seas is certainly not a detached part of Scottish soil, it is more closely connected with Scotland than with any other country.

128. The application of 'British' law

Dicey[1] advocated the doctrine that in case of doubt a British subject is deemed to be governed by English law. The reason for this opinion, which is rather unfair to Scottish people, was that in several other respects English law has developed into 'a species of imperial law'. Dicey referred to the principle that British subjects settling in a newly discovered country carry with them the law of England (even if they are Scottish), and he mentions several British statutes pointing to such predominance of English law, in particular the Foreign Marriage Act, 1892, s. 4, where it is said that a marriage under this Act requires such consent as is required for marriages solemnized in England. Dr. Morris in Dicey's sixth edition abandoned this view.

5. Several problems concerning nationality arise in connexion with *renvoi* (*infra*, s. 178).

129. Renvoi and Nationality

[1] (5th ed.), p. 741, n. (u).

(a) If the *propositus* has more than one nationality the *renvoi* to his 'national law' does not answer the question as to which of the several nationalities is decisive.

Example: The English court entertains an action concerning the distribution on intestacy of movables situate in England and left by *X* who had his domicile in Italy but was of German and Dutch nationality. Has the English court to apply Italian, German, or Dutch law? If there were no *renvoi*, Italian law, as the law of the last domicile of the deceased, would be applicable. But since English law has accepted the doctrine of *renvoi* (see s. 183) the Italian conflict rule will have to answer the question to which of the two national laws it refers. If the Italian rule is silent on this point—as indeed it is—the English judge himself should find an appropriate solution corresponding to the Italian view. It is suggested that he should examine which of the two nationalities, the German or the Dutch, is the *nationalité effective ou active*, as it has been called, i.e. the nationality with which the deceased was the more closely connected.

The judge will take into account all the circumstances of the particular case: has the deceased travelled more frequently to one of the countries than to the other? Did he reside there for some time? Had he business or family relations in the country? Has he done military service in either of the countries? Did he know the language? and so forth.[1]

(b) The second problem is similar to the first. The *propositus* has only one nationality, viz. British, and is domiciled outside the Commonwealth, say, in Italy. Under the English conflict rule the domiciliary Italian law would be applicable if there were no *renvoi*. The *renvoi*, however, points to the national 'British law'. As there is no such thing, and as the Italian conflict rule does not indicate which of the several legal systems within the British Commonwealth (English, Scottish, Maltese, &c.) is to apply, the court, as in the case of the first problem, will choose that law with which the deceased was most closely connected. In making this choice all the circumstances of the particular case will be taken into consideration.

In two cases, the *Re Johnson*[2] and the *Re O'Keefe*,[3] the judge chose the deceased's former domicile of origin, although that domicile had long been abandoned and replaced by a domicile of choice. This was particularly unfortunate in the *O'Keefe* case where the deceased woman had been

---

[1] See art. 21 (2) of the Aliens Order, 1920 (S.R.O. 1920, No. 448); Jones, l.c., p. 16. Cf. the case in the Hungarian–Serbian Mixed Arbitral Tribunal, 12 July 1926 (*Rec.* VI 499, 502); Makarov, l.c., 297.

[2] [1903] i Ch. 821.   [1940] Ch. 124.

settled in Naples for 47 years and her domicile of origin had to be traced back to her father's origin. The decision has been sharply criticized.[1]

If the facts are such that it is impossible to find a country within the British Commonwealth with which the *propositus* is closely connected, the *renvoi* becomes too vague to be effective: a person who is not connected with an ascertainable country in the British Commonwealth must, for the purpose of *renvoi*, be treated as a stateless person.[2] Therefore it seems adequate to apply by way of analogy the Italian rule concerning the personal statute of stateless persons,[3] according to which the law of the residence of such person—not the law of his domicile[4]— is applicable.

[1] Falconbridge, 19 *Can. Bar Rev.* (1941) 323. J. H. C. Morris, 56 *L.Q.R.* 144–7. Cheshire, 111–13. Rabel, I, 132.

[2] This was rightly suggested by De Nova, *Il caso in Re O'Keefe e la determinazione della lex patriae di un cittadino britannico domiciliato all' estero*, in *Festschrift f. Raape*, 1948, p. 67 et seq.

[3] Art. 29, *disp. prel. cod. civ.*

[4] As Dr. Morris and Dr. Cheshire recommend.

BIBLIOGRAPHY

MAURY, *Répert.* IX (1931) 238. ZEBALLOS, *La nationalité au point de vue d. droit comparé*, 5 vol. 1914–19. FLOURNOY & HUDSON, *A Collection of Nationality Laws*, 1929. J. M. JONES, *British Nationality, Law and Practice*, 1947. A. N. MAKAROV, *Allgemeine Lehren des Staatsangehörigkeitsrechts*, 1947. J. FOSTER, *Théorie anglaise*, p. 48 et seq. H. TRIEPEL, 'Internationale Regelung der Staatsangehörigkeit', in *Bruns' Z.* I. 1, 185. GUTZWILLER, *JurW.*, 1930, p. 1818, 1819. DE GERMINY, *Les conflits de nationalités devant les juridictions internationales*, 1916. P. LOUIS-LUCAS, 'Conflits des nationalités', 64 *Rec.* (1938 II) 5. TH. BATY, *Rev. Ghent*, 1926, 622. ANCEL, *J. Clunet*, 1937, 19. OPPENHEIM (Lauterpacht), *Internat. Law*, 6th ed., I. 606 et seq. J. P. A. FRANÇOIS, 'Le problème des apatrides', 53 *Rec.* (1935 III) 287. AUDINET, *J. Clunet*, 1925, 882. SECKLER & HUDSON, *Statelessness*, 1934. LOEWENFELD, 27 *Grotius Soc.* 59. KOESSLER, 'Subject, Citizen, National', 56 *Yale L.J.* (1946) 58 et seq. FALCONBRIDGE, 204 et seq.

CHAPTER XI

APPARENT IDENTITY OF POINTS
OF CONTACT

**130. The
various
cases**

I. SOMETIMES the rules on conflict of laws in two countries seem at first sight to use identical conceptions for testing legal relationships. Thus in both countries the validity of a will or of a marriage may be tested by 'domicile', the effects of a contract may be determined by the law of the 'place of contracting'. It might then appear as if a desirable harmony between the two laws had been secured. But closer examination may reveal that the identical terms designating the point of contact cover divergent meanings. Thus:

1. 'Domicile' under French law is not the same as under English law. A man may still have his domicile of origin (in the English sense) in one country though he has constituted an *établissement permanent*, and therefore a 'domicile' in the French sense, in a different country.[1] German law, furthermore, has a conception of domicile differing both from English and from French law, in particular by allowing a plurality of domiciles.[2]

2. The 'place of contracting' is determined differently in different legal systems. Under English law the contract is made at the time when the letter of acceptance is posted, and it can be inferred from this (by way of analogy) that it is made at the place where that letter is posted.[3] Under

[1] Before 1927 French law distinguished between a legal domicile and a mere *domicile de fait*. A legal domicile on French soil could be acquired only by official authorization; art. 13 c.c. (abrogated 10 Aug. 1927). In the famous case of *Carlos de Marchi della Costa, Nouv. Rev.*, 1938, 143, the deceased was of Argentine nationality and had in France only a *domicile de fait*. Under French law Argentine law was applicable. But the Argentine *Código civ.* declares the domiciliary law to be decisive. The French Appeal Court was prepared to accept a *renvoi* to the law of the domicile, but did not consider a mere unofficial domicile in France adequate within the meaning of the Argentine conflict rule. This view was hardly correct, but the *Cour de Cassation* was powerless to revise the interpretation of foreign law by the lower court. Cf. on that case: J. Donnedieu de Vabres, 66 *Rev. Ghent*, 1939, 167.

[2] See *supra*. s. 99.

[3] *Household Fire Insurance Co.* v. *Grant* (1879), 4 Ex.D. 216; *Henthorn* v.

German law the place of contracting lies where the letter reaches the addressee.[1] In French law the problem is not settled, and the decisions of the Supreme Court sometimes adopt the system of *déclaration*, sometimes that of *expédition* (which is the English system), sometimes the German system (*réception*) or even the rule that the contract is made when and where the offerer learns of the acceptance.[2]

3. The 'place of performance' of contractual obligations is under some laws the debtor's residence at the time of performance (French, Italian, Spanish, Portuguese, Polish laws), under others his residence at the time of contracting (German, Swiss, Austrian, Scandinavian laws), under yet others the creditor's residence (Netherlands).[3] Under English law in the case of sale of goods the seller is bound to deliver them at his place of business and, if he has none, at his residence; 'if the contract be for the sale of specific goods which to the knowledge of the parties when the contract is made are in some other place, then that place is the place of delivery'.[4] The Indian Contract Act[5] fixes the place of delivery of any goods sold at the place at which they are at the time of the sale, irrespective of whether the parties had knowledge thereof or not; if the goods are not yet in existence the delivery must be made at 'the place at which they are produced'. Some countries establish special rules for the performance of money obligations; thus English and Swiss law determine as place of performance not the debtor's, but the creditor's residence (or place of business).[6]

Fraser, [1892] 2 Ch. 27, 33; *Benaim* v. *De Bono*, [1924] A.C. 514, 520. Cf. Rabel, *Conflict of Laws*, II, 453, 454. Similarly, but with some differences, American Restatement of the Law of Contracts, ss. 64–9.

[1] German Civ. Code, s. 130. The same rule prevails in Swiss, Austrian, Hungarian, Polish, and Soviet law.

[2] The same controversy is to be found in Italy and the Netherlands. The French-Italian Project of a Law of Obligations, 1928, art. 2, § 1, declared that a contract is concluded when the offerer 'knows of the acceptance'. Does this mean that the place where he acquires such knowledge is decisive?

[3] Rabel, *Recht des Warenkaufs*, I (1936), p. 324.

[4] Sale of Goods Act, s. 29 (1). The same rule prevails in the United States under the Uniform Sales Act, s. 43 (1).   [5] S. 94.

[6] *Robey* v. *Snaefell Mining Co.* (1887), 20 Q.B.D. 152, 154. *The Eider*, [1893] P. 119, 128, 131, 134. *Charles Duval* v. *Gans*, [1904] 2 K.B. 685. Swiss Code of Obligations, 1911, s. 74. *Contra*: French, Italian, and German law.

II. The question which of several definitions of the point of contact shall be adopted in any given case has often been regarded as a problem of 'classification', or again as a problem of *renvoi*. It has, however, nothing to do with either of those thorny problems.

1. It must be distinguished from *classification*, with which it is often confused.[1] The difference between these two problems may best be illustrated by an example. Take the English rule: succession on death to movables is governed by the law of the last domicile of the deceased. This gives rise to two questions of different character. First, which law determines the place at which the domicile of the deceased is to be found? Secondly, which legal rules belong to the category designated 'succession on death'? (Are, for example, rules under which a will becomes invalid by the testator's marriage rules on succession, or rules on marriage?) The second question is concerned with 'classification'.[1] The first question is concerned with the determination of the point of contact, and the answer to it is easy. It is to be found in that system of private international law which the court will apply. As the English court usually only applies its own private international law, it determines the domicile according to English rules on the subject.[2] The same is true for any other point of contact. Where under an English conflict rule the law of the place of contracting or that of the place of performance is to govern the case, the question as to where that place is to be found must be decided by English law.

2. The relationship between the determination of the point of contact and the *renvoi* doctrine[3] is obvious, though

---

[1] See *infra*, s. 138 et seq.

[2] *In re Annesley*, [1926] 1 Ch. 692, 705 (*per* Russell, J.): 'The question whether a person is or is not domiciled in a foreign country is to be determined in accordance with the requirements of English law as to domicile irrespective of whether the person in question has or has not acquired a domicile in the foreign country in the eyes of the law of that country.' See: *In re Martin*, [1900] P. (C.A.) 211, 227. *Contra*: *In re Johnson*, [1903] 1 Ch. 821 and *In re Bowes* (1906), 22 T.L.R. 711. *In re Johnson* was criticized by Scrutton, L.J., in *Casdagli* v. *Casdagli*, [1918] P. 98, 109, and has been rejected by *In re Annesley*, loc. cit. On American law, see Restatement, s. 11.

[3] See *infra*, s. 178 et seq.

sometimes a dangerous error creeps into the discussion. The rule on *renvoi* is to the effect that if the conflict rules of the forum X order the application of a foreign law Y, and if the conflict rules of Y declare applicable the law of either the forum X or of a third country Z, the court respects such remission or transmission and therefore applies the municipal law of X or Z respectively. It goes without saying that this *renvoi* rule cannot become operative until a point of contact has been found according to the law of the forum X. But when that point of contact has been established, a second point of contact may be found according to the conflict rule of Y, and it may happen that the conflict rule of Y designates the point of contact by using words like domicile or place of contracting, which occur also in the conflict rules of X, but have there a different meaning. Such words have then to be interpreted according to the legislation of Y.[1] Two contrasting illustrations may show the issue.

(*a*) A British subject, domiciled in Copenhagen from birth, had his ordinary residence (his 'domicile' in the Danish sense of the term) in England, but without loosening all ties binding him to Denmark. In a lawsuit concerning the succession to his movables the English court will apply English law; for this reason: The English conflict rule declares the law of the last 'domicile' (in the English sense) to be decisive, that is, Danish law. The Danish conflict rule declares that the law of the ordinary residence (what the Danes call 'domicile') governs succession, and as the ordinary residence was English, the Danish court would apply English law. Under the rule of *renvoi* the English court has to apply the Danish conflict rule; therefore the English municipal law obtains.

(*b*) A Dutch subject, domiciled (in the English sense) in Sweden, but ordinarily resident in Copenhagen, dies leaving movables in England. The English court will first consider Swedish (and not Danish) law as the the law of the domicile. The Swedish conflict rule, however, refers to the national law of the deceased, that is Dutch law, and as the Netherlands too follow the nationality principle, the English court in accepting the *renvoi* will have to apply Dutch law. It is immaterial that Swedish law regards as the 'domicile' of a person his factual residence, in this case Denmark; for under Swedish private international law domicile is not the point of contact. There is, therefore, no *renvoi* from Swedish to Danish law. The view here expounded undoubtedly corresponds to the prevailing English law; this has been finally settled by the decision *in re Annesley*.[2] The opposite view is

[1] See Lewald, *Théorie du renvoi*, at p. 564, n. 2, Melchior, 175 et seq., Tedeschi, *Il domicilio*, 52. German Court of Appeal, Karlsruhe *IPRechtspr.*, 1930, No. 89. Cf. *supra*, p. 134, n. 1.   [2] [1926] 1 Ch. 692, 705.

taken by the Convention of Montevideo, art. 5, and the Código Bustamante, art. 22. According to these conventions the law of the country in which a person happens to be decides whether he has a domicile in that country. An eminent German scholar, Zitelmann, tried to justify this view. He advanced the opinion that the rules on nationality ought to apply by way of analogy to the issue of domicile.[1] Such analogy is not unassailable. It is for the state, and only for the state, to grant citzenship. to determine which persons are its members.[2] But it does not infringe the sovereignty of any state if the law prevailing outside that state treats a person as domiciled in its territory, though the state itself has a different conception of domicile.[3]

132. The interpretation of conflict rules by resorting to municipal law

III. We have seen that the court fixes the place where the point of contact lies by applying its own conflict rules. Their interpretation, however, depends most frequently on the internal law of the country. Where, for example, the validity of a contract is to be tested by the law of the place of contracting, it is internal English law which answers the question as to where the contract has been made.[4] The same is true for the place of performance. Attention has been drawn to the fact that the conflict rules of a country sometimes use a term in a different sense from that in which it is used by purely internal law. It goes without saying that in such cases the interpretation in the conflict rule is decisive.[5] Such divergence, however, between the meaning of terms in the conflict rules and in internal law respectively is rare.[6] Terms like place of contracting, place of performance, place of committing a tort, domicile, have the same meaning whether used in English private international law or in English internal law.

133. Interpretation of points of contact in international conventions

IV. When international conventions on private international law, such as the Hague Conventions or those of Montevideo or the Código Bustamante, designate points of contact by terms which in the various contracting states have different meanings, sometimes the convention itelf

[1] Zitelmann, I. 279.   [2] See *supra*, s. 123.
[3] On this point: V. Tedeschi, *Il domicilio*, 61 et seq.; Melchior, 162 et seq.; von Caemmerer, *RVgl.HWB*, IV. 350.
[4] Cf. *Benaim* v. *De Bono*, [1924] A.C. 514, 520.
[5] Rabel in his *Zeitschr.* 5, p. 248.
[6] An example of such divergence is to be found with regard to the *situs* (or quasi-*situs*) of intangibles. See *infra*, s. 515.

defines the term.[1] If not, the term must be interpreted in a uniform way; it would be contrary to the tendency of the convention if the courts of the particular countries were allowed to construe ambiguous expressions in the sense of their own internal laws.[2] It seems desirable that the text of conventions should be so framed as to avoid any words possessing a technical juridical meaning; instead of the conception of domicile, for instance, the term 'habitual residence' should be employed.

[1] The following is an example. Cód. Bustamante, art. 23, 24, in dealing with the domicile by operation of law of dependent persons. The Hague Convention on Conflict Rules with regard to Divorce, art. 5, no. 2, on the other hand, speaks of domicile without giving a definition. It seems that here the concept of domicile is to be determined according to the national law of the parties. Cf. Melchior, p. 180, n. 3.

[2] On this, *supra*, s. 43. See Permanent Court of Internat. Justice, *Publications Series B*, no. 7 (concerning the term 'domiciliés' in the Treaty between the Allies and Poland, of 28 June 1919) and no. 10 (concerning the term 'établi' in the Greek-Turkish Treaty of 30 Jan. 1923).

BIBLIOGRAPHY

F. KAHN, *Abhandlungen*, I. 92. NEUNER, *Rabel's Z.*, 8, 81. J. DONNEDIEU DE VABRES, 66 *Rev. Ghent* (1939) 167. See *infra*, s. 157, the books on classification, in particular A. H. ROBERTSON, *Characterization in the Conflict of Laws*, 92 et seq.

CHAPTER XII

FRAUDULENT CREATION OF
POINTS OF CONTACT

134. The problem A PERSON who by a compulsory legal rule is prevented from achieving his aims often tries to evade it by establishing in an abnormal way a set of facts to which the legal rule does not apply and which nevertheless secures the economic or social result he has in mind. Such *fraus legi facta* may occur within the boundaries of internal law, and legal history in every country abounds in examples of the 'inexhaustibility of the resource and cunning devoted to frustrating the law'.[1] In English law the most famous example was the invention of the trust designed to elude the Statute of Uses, 1535. In the area of private international law such evasions are very frequent. The parties who wish to produce a certain legal effect forbidden by the law of country *X* establish in an artificial and unusual way a point of contact in country *Y* where the law is favourable for their purpose. The following are some illustrations:

1. A company which intends to carry on business solely in England is incorporated in another country where the rules are less stringent or income tax is lower than in this country.[2]

2. A marriage between first cousins, forbidden by Spanish law to which the parties are subject, is solemnized in a country where such prohibition is unknown. This kind of evasion is particularly frequent in the United States, where the prevailing rule of private international law is to the effect that a marriage valid where celebrated is valid everywhere.[3]

---

[1] Jhering, *Geist des römischen Rechts*, III. 257.

[2] Numerous companies having their real centre of management in New York have been incorporated under the easier law of Delaware. Tax-dodging English or other European companies are to be found in Monaco, Luxemburg, the Channel Islands, the Swiss canton of Vaud, and above all in the Lilliput state of Liechtenstein, where the number of legal persons is possibly greater than that of natural persons.

[3] Restatement, § 121.

3. A married couple wishes to obtain a divorce, though their personal law renders it impossible. They therefore transfer their domicile to another country or even adopt a new nationality.

Examples were the famous 'Klausenburg marriages' and the 'Fiume marriages'. Scores of Austrian Catholics when separated from bed and board went to Klausenburg in Hungary, where they obtained under Hungarian law the divorce denied them under Austrian law, and then concluded new marriages. Many Italians in order to obtain divorces acquired the nationality of Hungary or of the Free State of Fiume (which existed from 1920 to 1924), either by naturalization or by adoption. This enabled them to obtain divorce decrees, which cannot be given under Italian law.[1] 'Migratory divorces', as they have been called, are particularly frequent in the United States. Persons who at their genuine domicile cannot obtain a divorce decree owing to the strictness of their domiciliary law, travel to Nevada or any other state that allows divorce under less severe conditions and reside there for a certain time.[2]

4. A domiciled Scotsman establishes an English domicile of choice in order to frustrate the Scottish rule according to which a testator is restricted in favour of his children in his liberty to dispose of his property by will.[3]

5. A pregnant unmarried woman before her confinement changes her domicile with the purpose of having her or her child's claim against the father governed by a more favourable legal system.

6. In making a contract the parties subject it to a legal system which considers as valid certain clauses that under the normally applicable law would be void.

7. A Frenchman residing at Evian-les-Bains on the French shore of the lake of Geneva desires to promise a gift. As French law requires a deed attested by a notary public, and Swiss law declares a written document to be

---

[1] See also the French case Vidal, *J. Clunet*, 1878, 268.

[2] The question under what conditions the divorce decree thus obtained must be recognized in every other state of the U.S.A. according to the 'full faith and credit clause' of the American Constitution (art. IV) was controversial. The answer is in the negative if neither spouse had a domicile in the state granting the divorce. Where, however, only one of them had constituted such domicile, the other being served by publicity only, the non-recognition was allowed by a majority decision (Holmes, J., dissenting) in *Haddock* v. *Haddock* (1906), 201 U.S. 562. In 1943 the Supreme Court overruled this decision in *Williams* v. *North Carolina*, 317 U.S. 287. See also the second decision of the Supreme Court in this lawsuit, [1945] 325 U.S. 226. Cf. Lorenzen, 402–27; Holt, 41 *Mich. L.R.* (1943), 1013.   [3] See the Italian case, *J. Clunet*, 1898, 969.

sufficient, he crosses the lake and makes his promise at Ouchy in Swiss form in order to save the notary fees.

135.
Means of
stopping
evasion

Is there any rule against evasions of this kind?

In a small number of cases it is possible to declare the creation of the ostensible foreign point of contact to be contrary to the true intention of the parties and therefore inoperative. Thus a court will hardly be inclined to believe that a person who changes his place of sojourn with the purpose of facilitating his divorce or of making a will unhampered by restrictions really intends to establish a new permanent home.[1] In some other cases the creation by contracting parties of an artificial point of contact fails under all those continental laws which prescribe that a contract can only be subjected to a legal system with which it has a real connexion.[2] There are also in some states certain special cases regulated by particular statutory rules. In the United States[3] the National Conference of Commissioners on Uniform State Laws drafted (in 1912) a *Marriage Evasion Act* concerning 'marriages in another state or country in evasion or violation of the laws of the state of domicile', which, however, was introduced only in a few states.[4] Another Uniform Act regulating *Annulment of Marriage and Divorce*, 1907, made jurisdiction in nullity and divorce cases dependent on the condition that either party 'was a *bona-fide* resident of this state and has continued so to be' during a certain period.[5] The Swiss Civil Code of 1907 pronounces that 'a marriage concluded abroad is void if the transference of the act to a foreign country was made with the manifest purpose of eluding the nullity grounds of Swiss law'.[6]

---

[1] This covers the examples 3, 4, and 5, *supra*, p. 141.

[2] See *infra*, s. 399. This covers case 6, *supra*, p. 141 (under continental laws, though possibly not under English law); see *infra*, s. 400.

[3] On American law: 42 *Columbia L.R.* (1942), 1022.

[4] Vermont, Massachusetts, Louisiana, Wisconsin, Illinois; Rabel, I. 253[32], 290 (on the reason for the failure). See Beale, II. 682 et seq. As to Quebec, see the Quebec Code (1865), s. 135.

[5] This act was introduced only in Delaware, New Jersey, and Wisconsin; Rabel, I. 505.

[6] Civ. Code Final Title, art. 61, s. 7 f. A German law of 15 Sept. 1935, s. 1, adopted a similar rule, though only for the case of a marriage concluded in disregard of racial prohibitions.

These rules do not cover all types of artificially created points of contact. They do not, for example, include a fraudulent change of nationality, or, in cases where the *lex loci actus* is decisive, the arbitrary establishment of a *locus actus* in some foreign country. French law, therefore, has developed an all-embracing doctrine on the basis of an old and ambiguous adage *fraus omnia corrumpit*. Any 'fraudulent' exclusion of a legal rule by establishing a foreign point of contact is regarded in France as invalid, and therefore the excluded rule applies as if it had not been excluded.[1] An act is considered as fraudulent if it suffers from a *défaut de sincérité*—a rather vague formula. The French courts have mostly followed this doctrine.

136. The French rule

> When the *Société du Moulin Rouge* was established with a nominal seat in London by incorporation there as a company limited, though the real seat of business and management was in Paris, the French tribunal declared the constitution of the English seat to be fraudulent.[2] When French couples in order to evade certain marriage formalities required by French law went to England and solemnized their marriages there, the French courts declared such marriages to be void, and justified this by the conception of *fraude à la loi*.[3]

The same view has been taken by Italian courts when an Italian subject had acquired a foreign nationality with the purpose of evading the Italian prohibition of divorce.

English law, and for that matter German law, has never adopted this doctrine. The famous Gretna Green marriages concluded on Scottish soil by eloping English couples have always been upheld in England.[4] The choice of a place for concluding any contract has never been regarded by English law as a fraudulent manœuvre even if made in order to elude the laws of another country. It is indeed difficult to understand why an act like that in the Evian-Ouchy example[5] should be considered fraudulent, since the aim of the French Civil Code art. 931, which declares all promises of gifts void unless made before

137. English law

---

[1] See Niboyet, *Traité*, III, 630 et seq. Much narrower: Arminjon, I, 248 et seq.
[2] *Tribunal de la Seine, Dalloz Pér.* 1913. 2. 165.
[3] *Cour de Cass., Dalloz*, 54. 1. 201; 67. 1. 13; 75. 1. 482, and others.
[4] *Compton* v. *Bearcroft* (1769), 2 Hagg. Cons., 430.
[5] See *supra*, p. 141, example no. 7.

a notary public, is not to bring fees to the notary or taxes to the state.

From the point of view of English law, the doctrine of *fraus legi facta* is unavailing in cases like that in example (2). In England the capacity to inter-marry is not governed by the law of the place where the marriage is solemnized, but by the law of the domicile; there can therefore be no such thing as a fraudulent choice of a particularly favourable *locus actus*. Finally, in cases like that of example (1) the English solution is very simple. A company incorporated in a foreign country is a 'foreign' company. If it has its centre of management in England it is subject to all those rules that govern any true and honest foreign company with a place of business or assets in England. In particular, the English court is empowered to wind it up, like any other unregistered company which is trading in England. It is immaterial whether the incorporation abroad was made with a fraudulent purpose or not.[1]

It has been said that there is one single case in which the change of domicile, if made with a fraudulent purpose, is ineffective: that is where the mother or the guardian changes the minor's home in order to alter the distribution of the minor's estate in case of his death. True, in *Potinger* v. *Wightman*[2]—quoted to support this exception[3]—such rule was alleged and founded on the continental (Dutch and French)[4] doctrine of *fraus*; but the case was not decided on this point, and Grant, M.R., stated that 'there never was a case in which there could be less suspicion of fraud'. It is submitted that where a child is stricken by a mortal illness and its mother shifts the place of her abode

---

[1] Companies Act, 1948 s. 399.

[2] (1817), 3 Mer. 67.

[3] Dicey–Morris, p. 106 *in fine*; Cheshire, p. 237.

[4] John Voet, in his commentary on the *Digest*, dealt with the case of a change of domicile from South Holland, where the *Schependomsrecht* prevailed, to North Holland governed by a different system of succession, the *Aasdoms-recht* (cf. Lee, *Introduction to Roman-Dutch Law*, p. 397), and stated that only if the change was made *bona fide*, if the parent had a 'justa et probabilis causa migrandi', is the change valid. Pothier said, in adopting the doctrine of fraud, that the surviving mother's domicile 'quelque part qu'elle juge de le transférer sans fraude doit être celui de ses enfans. Il y auroit fraude s'il ne paroisoit aucune raison de sa translation de domicile que celle de procurer des avantages dans les successions mobiliaires de ses enfans.' Cf. *Potinger* v. *Wightman*, loc. cit., at pp. 74, 76.

with a fraudulent view to succeeding to its estate she has no true intention of altering her domicile.

BIBLIOGRAPHY

OTTOLENGHI, *La frode alla legge e la questione dei divorzi fra Italiani*, 1909. ARMINJON, *Précis* I, 248–70, and *J. Clunet*, 1920, 409; 1921, 64. TRAVERS, *Rev. Darras*, 1910, 24, 362. NIBOYET, *Rev. Ghent*, 53 (1926), 485. NIBOYET, *Traité*, III, 630–69. REGIS RIVOL, *Les divorces de Fiume*, 1925. MORELLI, 3 *Rabel's Z.* (1929), 338. GRAVESON, 19 *J. Comp. Legisl.*, 1937, 21. VETSCH, *Umgehung des Gesetzes* (Zurich, 1917) 146. LIGEROPOULO, *Le problème de la fraude à la loi*, 1928, and in *Répert.*, VIII, 439. JOHN FOSTER, *La théorie anglaise*, p. 118. PLAISANT, *Règles de Conflits*, pp. 112–20.

CHAPTER XIII

CLASSIFICATION

**138. Intro-
duction**
I. EVERY legal system confers a particular legal character on the relationships regulated by law. Property
rights given by law to a widow may be regarded as rights
of succession *ab intestato*, as is the case in English law,[1]
or they may spring from a special system of matrimonial
property such as the French *communauté légale*,[2] or again
they may be general effects of marriage such as the right
of maintenance under German law.[3] The English rule
that a will made by an unmarried person becomes void if
he marries has been considered to be a part of matrimonial
law,[4] while the German rule that a will becomes voidable
in such a case undoubtedly belongs to the law of succession.[5] Nearly everywhere the property of a person who
dies intestate without inheritable blood belongs to the
state or the Crown; but this right is sometimes regarded
as a genuine right of inheritance (German, Italian law),
sometimes as a quasi-feudal right of escheat (English law
before 1926), or a *ius in bona vacantia* (modern English
law).[6] All continental laws regard the consent of parents
or guardians to the marriage of their child or ward as
belonging to the substantive conditions of marriage;[7]
English law classifies rules requiring such consent under
those dealing merely with 'formalities'.[8] The breach of a
promise to marry is characterized by English and German
law as a breach of contract,[9] by French law as a legal

---

[1] Engl. Administration of Estates Act, 1925, s. 46, subs. (1) (i); French C.C.,
art. 767 (*succession irrégulière*); German Civ. C., s. 1931, 1932.

[2] French C.C., art. 1400 et seq. Or the German statutory or contractual régimes,
Civ. C., s. 1363 to 1557.

[3] Cf., for example, German Civ. C., s. 1360, 1361, 1615. French C.C., art. 212.

[4] *In re Martin*, [1900] P. 211, 240.

[5] German Civ. C., s. 2079.

[6] Cf. s. 46 (1) (vi) and s. 45 (1) (d) Administr. of Estates Act, 1925. German
Civ. C., s. 1936.

[7] Cf. French C.C., art. 148–50, 154, 159, 182.

[8] *Simonin* v. *Mallac* (1860), 2 Sw. & Tr. 67. Cf. *infra*, s. 306.

[9] In German law the question is controversial; the Supreme Court however,
applies the rules of contract; Decis. (Off. Coll.) 61, 268.

nullity unless the conditions of a 'delict' are fulfilled.[1]
Limitation of action belongs under all continental laws to
substantive law; English law looks upon it as pertaining
to procedure.[2] In most legal systems a person who con-
ducts the business of another without his request is under
certain circumstances responsible for damage arising from
such conduct; this duty is sometimes regarded as 'quasi-
contractual',[3] sometimes as delictual.

What do these 'classifications' or 'characterizations'[4] mean?

139. The various aims of classification

1. Sometimes their aim is merely to establish a system
to bring order into the immense bulk of legal rules. This
kind of classification is immaterial here and may be
ignored.

Examples: The famous question whether possession is to be regarded
as a right or as a fact, or the problem whether the right of a lessee is to
be characterized as a *ius in rem* in those legal systems where 'lease goes
before sale' (as is the case in Germany).

2. Sometimes they cover one or other of the rules on
conflict of laws. An example of this is the English classification of limitation of action as a procedural institution.
This is a short expression for the provision of private
international law that the English court is to apply the *lex
fori* to answer the question whether a claim is barred by
lapse of time or not. Another instance is the rule that in
marriage the consent of parents is a 'formality', which
means that it is governed by the law of the place where
the marriage is celebrated. Classifications of this kind
must be taken into account by a foreign court where that
court is bound by way of *renvoi* to apply foreign private
international law.

3. Most classifications embody legal rules that are part
of the municipal law of the country. Their object is to give
a large number of rules of municipal law in a condensed

---

[1] Planiol & Ripert, *Traité prat.*, II (1926), 72 et seq.

[2] Cf. *British Linen Co.* v. *Drummond* (1830), 10 B & C., 903; *Huber* v. *Steiner*
(1835), 2 Bing. N.C., 202. Cf. *infra*, s. 219.

[3] *Negotiorum gestio*. Cf. German Civ. C., s. 678.

[4] On the continent one speaks of 'qualifications', a term first used by E.
Bartin and adopted by all authors writing in French, Italian, German, or
Spanish.

form. Classification has the effect of avoiding repetitions. Instead of first laying down rules on the conclusion of a contract of sale and then repeating them over and over again in dealing with barter, partnership, service contracts, &c., the law establishes general rules on contracts and then classifies the various kinds of agreements by stating that they are or are not contracts. Instead of first explaining that transfer of ownership operates against third parties and then making the same statement in speaking of easements, mortgages, pledges, usufruct, the law characterizes all of them as *iura in rem*. A rule giving the widow a share in the deceased's property may be classified as part of the régime of matrimonial property or as part of the law of succession upon death; in the first case it means that the deceased could not dispose of it by will, that his creditors cannot seize it, that a testamentary executor has no share in its administration, &c.; in the second case it means that the widow's share can be excluded or restricted by will, that the property to which she succeeds was owned exclusively by the *de cuius* and is liable for his debts, that the rules on acceptance and disclaimer of estates are applicable, &c. Classification may be compared with the mathematical process of placing a factor common to several numbers outside the bracket.[1]

Therefore a judge applying foreign internal law is bound to apply all those foreign rules that result from the classification embodied in that foreign law and to refrain from applying any foreign legal rules which would be applicable if the classification were different. If, for example, an English court entertains an action by a workman against his employer for compensation in respect of an accident he had suffered in France it has, in applying

[1] Sometimes classification of the same rule or institution varies within one legal system. In one sphere, for example in private law, the power given by the owner of a chattel to another person to dispose of it in his own interest is characterized as a mere agency, while the rules of tax law often treat such power (which economically amounts to ownership) as ownership in a legal sense. Or again, what in one section of the law is designated as 'formality' may under another section of the same law be a matter of 'substance'. In German law, for example, the rule that marital consent cannot be declared under a condition is classified as a matter of form, while the rule that a set-off cannot be declared under a condition is a substantive one. See *infra*, s. 324. Cf. Cook, 214 et seq.

French law, to take into account that French law classifies the employer's liability as contractual and not as resulting from a delict or quasi-delict (as does English law),[1] and therefore if the contract happens to be void to give judgment for the defendant.

II. All this presupposes, however, that there is no doubt as to which law applies. Difficulties arise if this very question *depends on the classification (characterization)* of the legal rules which may be applicable to the facts and if such characterization differs in the various laws concerned. The famous French case *Anton* v. *Bartolo*[2]—which caused E. Bartin to start his study of *qualifications*—may serve to illustrate the issue.

140. The applicable law depending on classification. The Maltese case

A Maltese couple domiciled in Malta before 1870 ultimately settled in (French) Algeria, where the husband acquired land and died in 1889. His widow claimed—apart from one moiety of the common property, about which there seems to have been no doubt—the *usufruct* of one quarter of the property left by the deceased. Her claim was justifiable under Maltese law as it stood at the time of the marriage,[3] though not under French law. Which of the two applied?

The answer depended on the classification of the rule of Maltese law. If this rule was part of the matrimonial *régime des biens* the claim was well-founded, because under the French conflict rules the matrimonial régime was governed by the law of Malta as the *first* matrimonial domicile. If, on the other hand, the Maltese rule was part of the succession law the claim was baseless, since under the French conflict rule succession to movables was governed by French law as the law of the *last* domicile of the deceased, and succession to immovables by the *lex situs*, i.e. again French law. Now under Maltese law the widow's right to the usufruct of one quarter was classified as part of the matrimonial régime, the rule being found not in the

---

[1] Cf. Beckett, loc. cit., pp. 62, 63, n. 2.

[2] *J. Clunet*, 1891, 1171. The case is usually called the 'Maltese case'.

[3] *Code Rohan*, art. 17, 18: after the death of one of the spouses the surviving spouse receives half of the goods 'qu'ils auront acquis pendant le mariage par leur travail et leur industrie', and in case of poverty the usufruct of one quarter of the property of the deceased.

chapter on successions but in that dealing with marriage. Under French municipal law the Maltese rule (if such a rule were known to French law) would be classified in the same way as under Roman law,[1] as belonging to succession law. Which of the two classifications was the French court to adopt?

Surely the correct answer should be found in the conflict rule itself. But a survey of the conflict rules in all countries shows that this is very rarely the case.[2] The reason is this: in most countries conflict rules make use of only a small number of general conceptions, such as capacity, form of legal acts, conclusion of marriage, divorce, matrimonial property, succession on death, legitimacy, legitimation, adoption, guardianship, delicts, contracts, *iura in rem*. As no legislator is able to state exhaustively which institutions and legal rules of foreign countries are covered by this that or the other of these general conceptions, he is bound to leave a vague area. Each general conception has a firm and stable nucleus but an indistinct periphery, and it would be practically impossible for any legislator or court to establish a rigid and precise delimitation. The legislator cannot lay down catalogues of all the rules of foreign legal systems which deal with what he calls matrimonial property, and then of those concerned with what he designates as form, and so forth. He is obliged to leave the answer to the court and the doctrine. It is for them to fill in the gaps. By what principles are they to be guided?

141. The prevailing doctrine (Kahn, Bartin)

1. The prevailing opinion, established by Kahn and Bartin, recommends that the question should be answered by the *internal* law of the *forum*. As the general conceptions operating in private international law are simply taken from rules of internal law and their classification,

---

[1] The *quarte du conjoint pauvre* of Roman law (Nov. 53, c. 6, 117, c. 5) which before the *code civil* was the law in the *pays de droit écrit*, was always looked on as a right of inheritance.

[2] An example of a conflict rule providing the required answer is to be found in *Huntington* v. *Attrill*, [1893] A.C. (P.C.) 150, 155: According to an English conflict rule foreign 'penal' law is excluded from application by an English court. The question as to which foreign laws are penal is to be answered not by the law of the state where the foreign legal rule has been enacted but by the English conflict rule. See on this: Cheshire, 176 et seq.

this solution seems at first sight comprehensible. Some illustrations may show to what results it leads:

(a) The *Maltese* case (*Anton* v. *Bartolo*); cf. p. 149. Here Bartin proposes that the usufruct of the fourth part granted by Maltese law to the widow be classified not according to Maltese law, but to French internal law—although no such right exists under French law. The Algiers Appeal Court rightly decided against this doctrine.

(b) The German Civil Code deals under the heading 'Matrimonial Property' with the 'Continuance of Community of Goods' after the death of one of the spouses between the survivor and the issue, irrespective of whether they are of age or minors. Under Dutch law such a continued community exists only in favour of minors and is considered and treated as resulting from the 'Relationship between Parents and Children'. Suppose that a Dutch court has to adjudicate upon the continuance of a community and that at the time of marriage the couple was of German, at the death of the husband of Dutch, nationality. Undoubtedly matrimonial property is governed by German law, the relationship between parents and children by Dutch law. From the point of view of Bartin the continuance of the community would be subjected to Dutch law, to the effect, for example, that if there are no minor children there could be no continuance. And what, according to Bartin, would be the correct attitude of an English court if it had to decide the case?

(c) A domiciled Italian, illegitimate, dies intestate and unmarried. His mother had predeceased him. Part of his estate is a bank deposit with an English bank. According to English (and for that matter Italian) private international law, Italian internal law has to designate the 'heir' to this property. Under Italian internal law the Italian state is the heir[1] and the state's right is in every respect treated as a right of inheritance. When an English court has to adjudicate upon an action brought by the Italian state against the bank, the court, if Bartin were right, would reason as follows: The right of the English Crown to be the 'ultimate recipient' of movable property is

---

[1] *Codice civile*, art. 586.

characterized by internal English law not as a right of inheritance but as a *ius in bona vacantia*.[1] This classification must be carried over into English private international law and applied to all 'similar' rights of any state in the world. Though under Italian law the property is not a *bonum vacans*, the state being the heir just as if it had been appointed by will, it has to be treated as 'heirless', therefore *bonum vacans* and subject to the law of the situs. The result is that the bank deposit goes to the English Crown —even if there are persons in existence who under English law of succession would be entitled to succeed.[2]

142. Criticism It is submitted that there is no foundation for this solution. Bartin emphasizes that the rules on conflict of laws and those on internal law of a given country form part of the same legal system, and that the legal conceptions of this system are the basis of the juridical training of both the judges and the lawgiver. This is true and it explains why in formulating rules on conflict of laws the legislator and the courts use the terminology developed in internal law. This community of terms allows us to assume that a term, such as form or inheritance, used by a conflict rule, has probably the same meaning as in internal law, provided that the conflict rule merely delimits the area of application of the *internal* law of the country. But that does not help much.[3] It does not furnish any answer to the question which rules of *foreign* law belong to which category. It does not justify the bringing of an institution of foreign internal law into the domain of a particular conflict rule of the forum in cases where the foreign institution is 'similar' to an institution of the internal law of the forum. In English internal law, for example, there is no such thing as community of property between spouses, and there is nothing similar to it, apart perhaps from a partnership agreement. Does that prevent an English court from classifying a community of foreign spouses as a special type of matrimonial property system,

---

[1] Administration of Estates Act, 1925, s. 46, subs. (1) (vi).

[2] For example, persons instituted by a will that is void under Italian law but would be valid under English law.

[3] J. Donnedieu de Vabres l.c. (supra p. 41) p. 752 rightly speaks of the '*détermination brutale de la prépondérance de la lex fori*'.

which under English conflict rules is governed by the law of the domicile?[1] Or again, in a purely English marriage the consent of the parents is a matter of 'formality'. Must therefore an English court in adjudicating upon a marriage concluded in England between two domiciled French subjects take it that the consent of the parents is to be treated as a formality in the sense of English conflict law, to the effect that the significance of that consent is to be decided by the *lex loci celebrationis*, though French law regards the consent as a matter of capacity and therefore subject to the law of the domicile?[2]

2. While Bartin and his adherents wrest foreign legal rules from their connexion with the foreign legal system as a whole, Dr. Rabel and, independently of him, W. B. Beckett, advocate a solution to be found by means of *comparative legal studies* and *analytical jurisprudence*. Every rule of every legal system should be compared with corresponding rules of other legal systems with the aim of establishing an exhaustive system of fundamental conceptions of an 'absolutely general character' (Beckett). Some of these conceptions, such as the *iura in rem* and *in personam*, the notions of contract and delict, of universal and particular succession, have been developed since the Middle Ages by the glossators, by the post-glossators, and

143. The doctrine of analytical jurisprudence

---

[1] Bartin's reasoning in the Maltese case would possibly induce him to say that the English court ought to treat the case as one of contractual partnership and therefore apply the conflict rules on partnership. (*Quaere.*)

[2] In *Ogden* v. *Ogden*, [1908] P. 46, the Court of Appeal applied the doctrine of classification according to the *lex fori*; but the authority of this decision has been impugned by many writers. (See Rabel, I. 267[95].) The decision was (perhaps) tolerable because it helped to uphold a marriage. The facts were these: a Frenchman had married in England without the consent of his parents, and a French court, in accordance with art. 148 *Code civ.* had pronounced the nullity of that marriage. The English court declared its validity. It may be asked: what would the English court do if the facts were slightly changed as follows? The Frenchman married after 1927 without his father's, but with his mother's, consent and the marriage was celebrated in Germany (not England). A French court would declare the marriage valid, because since 1927 the consent of one of the parents is sufficient. A German court would deliver the same decision, because under a German conflict rule French law applies. But an English court (if it adopted Bartin's doctrines) would regard the marriage as voidable. It would transfer the English classification of the consent as a matter of formality to the sphere of private international law. It would, therefore, apply the rule on consent of the *lex loci celebrationis*, i.e. of German municipal law (Bartin rejects *renvoi*)— and German law does not allow the father's consent to be replaced by the mother's!

by the general doctrines of 'jurisprudence' established by modern continental, and (since John Austin) by English and American jurists. This school of analytical jurisprudence should continue, improve, and complete its work till it has built up a framework with numerous compartments, a system of legal categories, in which every legal rule (or every legal institution?) would have its proper place. The plan is attractive, and there is no doubt that more could be done along these lines than has yet been achieved.

It may be pointed out in particular that the American Restatement has begun to do away with some of the difficulties arising from different classifications. On the other hand, the European rules on private international law are still very incomplete.

Even if it were possible to invent an exhaustive system of legal categories—covering all existing institutions in the world and leaving empty compartments to be filled by future institutions—this could hardly be achieved without alteration in the laws themselves. To give some examples: Greek law grants the *quarta viduae* as a right of inheritance in the case of intestacy, while in Maltese law the rule on the *quarta* is part of the matrimonial property system. French and Italian law forbid the making of joint wills;[1] in French law this is a rule concerning 'form', in Italian law a rule on the 'intrinsic validity' of the act.[2] How could the most erudite 'comparer' of laws or the most incisive 'analyst' remove such differences of classification without thereby altering the law? For the divergence of classifications is not jurisprudential in character, it connotes a difference in the law.

In particular the function of comparative law with regard to co-ordination of classifications would seem to be overestimated. Comparison of various legal systems with each other enlarges the lawyer's view by presenting a survey of the manifold solutions of a given problem and by pointing the way to well-founded criticism, but cannot by itself create a uniformity of classifications.

144. Classification of a rule according to the legal system to which it belongs

3. It is therefore preferable to start from the view that every legal rule takes its classification from the legal system *to which it belongs*. French law classifies French

---

[1] French code civ., art. 968; Italian c.c., art. 761.
[2] Diena, *Principî*, II. 215; Rabel, loc. cit., 49.

legal rules, Italian law Italian rules, and an English court examining the applicability of French rules will have to take the French classification into consideration. Of course, an English rule on conflict of laws can either expressly or implicitly forbid the court to accept the foreign classification. Such exclusion may be based, for example, on principles of justice or morality.[1] But this will be a rare exception. To examine the applicability of foreign law without reference to its classifications is to fail to look at foreign law as it is. Bartin and his followers shut their eyes to good portraits and rest satisfied with a collection of caricatures.

The view suggested here[2] would possibly have found more adherents if it had not been repeatedly criticized in respect of the vicious circle in which it seems to be caught up. 'If the law which is finally to regulate the matter (i.e.

---

[1] *Ogden* v. *Ogden*, [1908] P. 46 may be explained in this way. The court may have thought that it would be unjust to have a marriage annulled which had been concluded on English soil and would have been valid under English municipal law.

[2] Held by Despagnet, Valéry (p. 500, n. 2), Surville (p. 19, n. 3), Neuner, and others. Cheshire and Robertson steer a middle course between this view and the *lex fori* doctrine. They distinguish between 'primary' and 'secondary' classification. First—so they say—the general 'issue', or the 'factual situation', must be 'allocated to its correct legal category', e.g. characterized as being a contract or a tort, a matter of matrimonial property or a case of succession, and so on. Such primary classification would be made in accordance with the law of the forum (on certain exceptions see Robertson, *Characterization*, pp. 75, 76). When the *lex fori* has conclusively decided that the problem is one, say, of matrimonial property, the conflict rule of the forum would indicate the applicable law—for example, French law as the law of the first matrimonial domicile of the deceased. Then comes the secondary classification, its aim being to solve a conflict of classification between *lex causae* and *lex fori* (Cheshire, p. 72) in order to determine how much of the *lex causae* is to apply. It is difficult to justify such distinction. The questions: Is French law applicable and How much of it is applicable? should be answered by the same legal rule. Take the following situation. A married man dies leaving a widow and a child; his first matrimonial domicile was country X; his last domicile country Y; the widow claims some part of the property in a court of country Z. Is this claim one under matrimonial property law, or one of succession? Suppose the law of the forum Z characterizes the facts as relative to matrimonial property, and the conflict rule of Z in respect of matrimonial property points to the law of the first matrimonial domicile, i.e. of X. By this primary classification the law of Y is definitively excluded from application (if I understand Mr. Robertson rightly). This may lead to injustice. Suppose the law of X gives the widow no share at all in the matrimonial property, but the law of Y would give her a right of succession. Then the primary classification would debar her from claiming such right (in the court of country Z).

the *lex causae*) depends upon classification, how can a classification be made according to that law?'[1] In my opinion this criticism does not hold good, but is based merely on the peculiar way in which conflict rules are framed. To give examples: 'The effect of marriage on the property of the spouses is governed by the law of their first matrimonial domicile.' More correctly phrased this rule would run thus: 'If two persons are married to each other the court has to apply all those rules operative at their first matrimonial domicile which according to the law there prevailing regulate the effects of marriage on the property of spouses.' Similarly the rule 'Inheritance (succession on death) is governed by the law of the country where the *de cuius* was domiciled at the time of his death' would, if phrased more correctly, run as follows: 'When a person dies the court applies all those rules prevailing at his last domicile which according to the law of that domicile are characterized as parts of the law of inheritance.'

Illustrations in point:

145. Illustrations:
(a) Continuance of community

(*a*) A domiciled German couple concluded a matrimonial contract establishing 'community of all goods'. Later they emigrated to the Netherlands, where they became naturalized. Then the husband died. Was the community of goods to be 'continued' between the widow and the only son (who was of full age)? The answer is: yes, if German law is applicable—no, if Dutch law governs the case.[2] Now, German law classes the continuance as part of the matrimonial property régime, Dutch law as part of the law of parents and children. How has the Dutch court to classify the continuance system? According to Dutch conflict rules it has to apply German rules on matrimonial property and Dutch provisions on the relationship between parents and children. As it has to accept the German classification of German rules it will hold that the German continuance of community takes place and that the views of Dutch municipal law on its similar system are immaterial.

---

[1] Cheshire (2nd edition), p. 34; (3rd ed.), p. 64.
[2] The Dutch system of continuance of community supposes minority of the children; art. 182, *Burgerl. Wetboek*.

(b) In the case of the Italian state claiming succession to the English bank deposit as heir (mentioned above, p. 151 (c)) the following reasoning is submitted. The English court will first apply the English conflict rule according to which inheritance is governed by the *lex ultimi domicilii* —which in this case is the law of Italy. Under Italian law the property is not heirless, because the Italian state is an heir *ab intestato*. Therefore judgment will be given for the plaintiff. Had it been heirless according to the law of the last domicile, for example, had the deceased been a domiciled Austrian or Turk, the decision would be different; this was the case in *re Barnett's Trusts*[1] and in *The Estate of Musurus*.[2]

146. (b) The state as heir or as entitled to bona vacantia?

(c) A German national domiciled in Germany makes a will; later he marries, and the couple enters into a contract introducing separation of goods. After some years the spouses emigrate to England, where they become naturalized and acquire a domicile. He dies, and his widow argues that his will has either become void under English law through the subsequent marriage of the testator,[3] or voidable under German law because the will passes over a person entitled to a 'compulsory portion' (viz. the widow), whose title arose later than the date of the will.[4] Whether the widow brings an action in an English or in a German, or for that matter in a French, court the decision would be the same. The Englishr ule that a will is revoked by marriage is by English law classified as a rule of matrimonial law.[5] According to the conflict rules of England, Germany, and France the case before the court is to be governed by German not by English matrimonial law; therefore the English rule quoted does not apply. The German rule, on the other hand, is classified by German law as part of inheritance law; it is not limited to the case of marriage, but applies also to cases of a son born subsequently to the making of a will. Under the conflict rules of all the countries

147. (c) Effect of marriage on a will

---

[1] [1902] 1 Ch. 847.
[2] [1936] 2 A.E.R. 1666.
[3] Wills Act, 1837 (7 Will. IV and 1 Vict. c. 26), s. 18.
[4] German Civ. Code, s. 2079.
[5] *In re Martin*, [1900] P. 211, 240 (*per* Vaughan Williams, L.J.).

mentioned inheritance is regulated by the personal law of
the testator at the time of his death, that is, English, not
German, law. Hence the German rule does not apply
either. The will consequently stands.[1] If Bartin were
right the English court would classify the German rule
in accordance with the *lex fori* as part of matrimonial law
—which would mean falsifying it. The German court
would conversely treat the English rule—contrary to
In re Martin[2]—as part of testamentary law, thus rendering
the will void; and what a French court would do is difficult
to guess, because under French municipal law there is no
provision corresponding either to the German or to the
English rule.

148. (d)
Parental
consent to
marriage as
concerning
'form or
'capacity'?

(*d*) In *Ogden* v. *Ogden*[3] a domiciled Frenchman had
married a domiciled English girl in England without the
necessary consent of his parents. If such case were to be
decided by a German or Italian court the marriage would
have to be annulled. The reasoning would be as follows:
The form of the marriage and the result of a defect of
form are governed by English law as the *lex loci celebrationis*; under English law the consent of the parents
belongs to the 'form'; its absence does not make the marriage void or voidable. But the capacity to marry and the
intrinsic validity of the marriage are tested by the personal
law of the parties, i.e. French law; under French law the
consent of the parents creates full 'capacity', which otherwise is lacking; its absence makes the marriage voidable.
If this is true, the decision in *Ogden* v. *Ogden* is assailable.

---

[1] Is this decision sound ? It is believed that it is. There would be no reason for
applying a (rather surprising) English rule to a purely German marriage
concluded in Germany between Germans; why should such marriage affect the
validity of the will ? Suppose, for example, that the wife had died before her
husband emigrated to England. Then the will would indubitably have been valid
under German law. Its voidability under the German rule depends on the fact
that at the time of the testator's death his wife was still living (and still married
to him). But at that time the couple was under the domain of English law, under
which the testator has full liberty to make a will irrespective of the interests of
the widow. This may be criticized as an unjust rule; but as long as this is the
law it is not unjust to apply it to the will of a man who dies as a domiciled
Englishman.

[2] [1900] P. 211, 240.

[3] [1908] P. 46. See, on this decision, *supra*, pp. 81[1], 153[2], 155[1], and *infra*,
s. 306.

(e) *De Nicols* v. *Curlier*[1] was decided on the lines proposed here, that is, by classifying in accordance with the *lex causae*. The facts were as follows: A domiciled Frenchman married a domiciled Frenchwoman in France without making a contract as to their property. Some years later they came to London and established a small restaurant which eventually developed into the Café Royal in Regent Street. The husband died domiciled in England, having made a fortune of £600,000. The widow claimed the share to which she would be entitled under the French rules on *communauté des biens*. The English rule of private international law tests the rights of husband and wife in respect of their movable property

(i) where there is a marriage contract, by such contract and in case of doubt by the law of the *first* matrimonial domicile;

(ii) where there is no contract, by the law of the *actual* matrimonial domicile, i.e. if the domicile was changed during the marriage, by the law of the *new* domicile.[2]

The widow's claim was justifiable if the first, unjustifiable if the second alternative was adopted. The decision therefore depended on whether the application of French internal law can be based on a marriage 'contract'. The House of Lords answered this question in the affirmative by following a curious classification of French law; though the French code distinguishes between the *communauté légale* and the *communauté conventionnelle*, French doctrine and courts have often characterized the *communauté légale* as based on an implied contract and therefore as a kind of *communauté conventionnelle*.[3]

(f) In the case of *Anderson* v. *Equitable Assurance Society of the United States*[4] the defendant owed a sum of German marks under a contract governed by English law; when the debt fell due the value of the mark had considerably diminished. Were the German rules on revalorization to be applied? The answer was: yes, if they were part of the

Margin notes:
149. (e) *De Nicols* v. *Curlier*

150. (f) Revalorization laws: currency law or proper law of the contract?

---

[1] [1900] A.C. 21.   [2] See Dicey–Morris, pp. 786, 796. *Infra*, ss. 339, 346.
[3] This is important with regard to art. 1395 c.c., according to which the *conventions matrimoniales* cannot be changed after the celebration of the marriage. See, however, *infra*, s. 338 in fin.
[4] (1926), 134 L.T. (C.A.) 557, 566.

German currency law; no, if they were part of the German law of obligations. As here an English contract was to be performed by the payment of German currency, it was necessary to choose between the two classifications. The Court of Appeal tried to find out how *German* law classifies its revalorization rules (and correctly answered that they are part of the German law of obligations). The Court did not attempt to classify the German rules according to English law—which indeed would have been difficult, for English law does not possess any revalorization laws.[1]

151.
Difficulties and uncertainty of classification

III. As a result of these considerations it is submitted that in principle a foreign rule should be classified with reference to the whole of the foreign legal system. The task is easy where modern codes have established a complete system, or where analytical jurisprudence has been so much developed as to facilitate classification. It is more difficult to classify English legal rules according to English law, since the English way of thinking is not favourable to establishing a complete system of general conceptions and assigning within it a definite place to every rule. The main doubts arise when we try to classify rules on such institutions as are unknown to continental laws, such as trusts and other equitable institutions. Is, for example, the right of a *cestui que trust* to be characterized as a *ius in personam* or as a *ius in rem*? Dr. Hanbury is probably right in calling it a hybrid conception standing midway between the two.[2] But this characterization is not, and is not intended to be helpful for the purpose of classification in private international law.

The ultimate aim of classification is to determine the conflict rule of the forum to which a given rule of foreign internal law is related. Sometimes it happens that the foreign classification, when found, is of little use for this purpose. There is, for example, an English conflict rule to the effect that succession to immovables is governed by the *lex situs*, succession to movables by the law of the domicile. Is a debt secured by a mortgage or 'hypothec'

---

[1] F. A. Mann, *The Legal Aspect of Money* (1938), p. 205, n. 1.
[2] Hanbury, *Essays in Equity*, p. 27.

on a German piece of land movable or immovable? The German Civil Code in dealing with the matrimonial régime of community of movables classifies both hypothecs and debts secured by them as movables in the sense of that community system.[1] But it would be unreasonable automatically to transfer a classification set up for a very restricted purpose into the realm of private international law.[2]

If the court finds no appropriate classification in the foreign law, as in the just mentioned case of German hypothecs, the gap must be filled in the usual way, for instance by looking for analogies, by considering solutions possibly to be found in kindred legal systems, ultimately by reverting to the law of the forum.

Classification according to the *lex causae* sometimes leads to a result inconsistent with fundamental tenets of the forum.

Example: In Greece marriage requires the co-operation of the Church; this requirement, which in England, France, and Germany is considered a matter of 'form', is regarded in Greece, where the Orthodox creed prevails, as bound up with the sacramental character of marriage and therefore with its 'substance'. In England, France, and Germany classification according to these Eastern standards must be disregarded.

There are also cases where the classification discovered **152. Absurd results** by the judge in foreign law leads to absurd results if adopted mechanically. In such cases, as in all parts of the law, common sense, that great guardian, teacher, and corrector, must give the answer. A famous example of this is furnished by a decision of the German Supreme Court of 1882.[3] The plaintiff suing in a German court claimed payment of promissory notes issued by the defendant in Tennessee and governed by the law of that state. Under the law of Tennessee the recovery of the debt is barred by lapse of six years; if German law were applicable the period of limitation would be three years.[4] American like English law classifies the rules on limitation of action as procedural; German law, like all other continental laws,

---

[1] German Civ. Code, s. 1551, § 2.
[2] See Wengler, *Rabel's Z.*, 8 (1934), 183, 184.   [3] *Offic. Collect.*, 7, 21.
[4] In the case before the court more than six years seem to have elapsed from the date of maturity.

regards them as substantive. Procedure is determined by the *lex fori*, the substance of rights by the proper law of the contract. The German Supreme Court correctly classified the German rule on limitation as substantive and therefore not applicable here. On the other hand, it followed (rightly) the Tennessee classification of the American limitation rule, but drew from this the conclusion that the defendant in a German court was not allowed to adduce a procedural rule of foreign law. Therefore the court gave judgment for the plaintiff.[1] The mistake in this absurd judgment was that the court misunderstood the classification of the Tennessee rule. When American or English law characterizes a rule as 'procedural' this means that it has to be applied in all cases brought in an American or English court and that divergent rules of any foreign system are to be disregarded.[2] But this does not prevent a foreign court from applying the rule. English courts use the word 'procedure' in a wider sense than that in which French, Italian, and German law speak of *procédure, procedura, procedimento, Prozess*. The right to bring an action in court is in the continental terminology, as opposed to the English, not a part but the basis of procedure. Everywhere it is this right of action, and not the proceeding in court, that is affected by limitation. To call the fact that the right of action is barred and that consequently judgment will be given for the defendant, a matter of procedure must be one of two things: either an error in reasoning or a use of the word procedure that differs from continental terminology. It follows that a continental court must not simply translate the English expression by a similar continental expression used in a narrower sense.

153. Gaps in the conflict rules   IV. Sometimes the difficulty in which the court finds itself does not lie in the search for an appropriate classification in the foreign law, but in the fact that there is a

---

[1] Later decisions have abandoned the principle on which the decision of 1882 was founded. Cf. in particular a decision of 1934 (*Off. Coll.* 145, pp. 121, 128 et seq.), which, however, decided the case on the basis of the *lex fori* doctrine.

[2] *British Linen Co.* v. *Drummond* (1830), B. & C. 903. *Huber* v. *Steiner* (1835), 2 Bing. N. C., 202.

gap in its own conflict rules. Then the court fills in the gap by looking for analogies.

Examples: (*a*) Under Californian law a child has been legitimated by acknowledgment, or has been adopted. The father who has acknowledged the child, or the adopter respectively, was domiciled in England at the date of the child's birth, and in California at the time of the legitimation or adoption. The English court, in which these facts have been stated, had no difficulty in classifying the rules on legitimation by acknowledgment or on adoption either according to Californian or to English law. But there is no rule in English private international law deciding which law is to govern such legitimation or adoption. The Court of Appeal applied to a case of legitimation by acknowledgment a rule analogous to the conflict rule on legitimation by subsequent marriage.[1] It has, however, not yet established which law applies in the case of adoption.[2] Gaps of this kind are not rare in English private international law. The incompleteness of this branch of law will only be cured very slowly owing to what one might describe as a monopoly possessed by the English courts of the solution of hitherto undecided questions. Such gaps are less frequent in continental laws, where legal problems not yet decided by the courts are constantly discussed by a great number of jurists, and where the appearance of an unforeseen gap in the law almost constitutes a reproach to legal science for not having seen and studied the problem and found the means of solving it.

(*b*) The conception of *ultra vires agere* in company law is unknown outside English and American law. How should a continental court deal with this peculiar kind of limitation of capacity? Its English classification is easy; but none of the 'capacities' known to continental conflict rules is appropriate here—neither the capacity to *have* rights (*Rechtsfähigkeit, capacité de jouissance*) nor the capacity to *dispose* of them by an act-in-law (*Geschäftsfähigkeit, capacité d'exercice*), nor the capacity to create obligations by committing a delict. The restriction imposed on the second of these types comes nearest to the English restriction, though there are material differences. It would therefore seem appropriate to apply by way of analogy the conflict rules concerning the capacity to dispose of rights.

V. The views developed here show that one set of facts often has to be considered from the standpoint of more than one legal system. There is nothing surprising in this. Quite apart from any reasoning on classification, private international law not rarely demands a readiness to consult several legal systems. In this respect the need of classification leads to two kinds of problems. It may happen that the concurrence of two legal systems entails the application

154. Adjustment where several systems are to be considered

[1] *In re Luck*, [1940] Ch. 864; *infra*, s. 375.
[2] F. A. Mann, 57 *L.Q.R.* (1941), 123, 124.

of both of them, or, conversely, that neither of them proves applicable. The result is in the first case a cumulation of applicable rules, in the second a vacuum.

155. In cases of cumulation

1. Cases of cumulation.

Examples: (*a*) The defendant, a domiciled Englishman, has made a promise of marriage to the plaintiff, an Englishwoman. Later he takes up residence and establishes a domicile in Paris; she follows him there. While in Paris he breaks his promise and marries another woman. Then he returns to England, where the plaintiff brings an action against him. The question is not whether her claim should be classified as based on contract *or* tort. She may found her action on English law, i.e. on the breach of an English contract, *and* on French law, that is, on a delict, provided that the defendant's behaviour in France amounted to a delict in the eyes of French law. The second ground, however, will be of no use to her in an English court; if she cannot succeed on the first ground—for example, if the defendant was only twenty years old when he promised to marry her—his act, though constituting a delict where committed, would not give her a right to bring an action for tort in an English court.[1] Had she brought the action in a French court, she could have sued for delict (if the defendant's act constituted a delict), but not for breach of contract, because it would be against French public policy to regard under any circumstances a promise of marriage as a legally binding contract and thus to endanger the 'liberty of consent'.[2]

(*b*) A Swedish couple when marrying made an agreement to live under the legal matrimonial régime. This régime is a system of separation of property with two peculiarities; first, each spouse in administering his or her property needs for certain acts of disposal the consent of the other; secondly, at the dissolution of the marriage by divorce or death the property of both becomes common to them or to the survivor and the heirs of the deceased. The survivor receives half of this common property not as heir but as co-owner in virtue of the matrimonial régime. If the pre-deceased spouse died intestate leaving issue the survivor has no right of 'inheritance.' Suppose that some years after the marriage the Swedish couple went to Switzerland where they became domiciled, that then the husband died intestate and left a large amount of movable property mostly deposited with an English bank, while his wife had been penniless. The widow brings an action in an English court. The problem is not whether her claim should be classified as based on matrimonial property *or* on inheritance law. She is entitled on both grounds. Under Swedish matrimonial law she has acquired the right to half of the present and future property of her husband and is consequently co-owner of all he leaves. The property open to inheritance consists merely of the other moiety.[3] The succession of this property is under English private international law governed by Swiss law, which

---

[1] See *The Halley* (1868), L.R. 2, P.C. 193; *Phillips* v. *Eyre* (1870), L.R. 6, Q.B. 1. See *infra*, s. 471.

[2] See also Rabel, I, 201.   [3] Apart from certain personal goods.

grants the widow at her choice either ownership of a quarter or usufruct of one-half of the inheritance (s. 762, civ. c.). The fact that under Swedish law she would 'inherit' nothing is immaterial, since Swedish law does not grant her the moiety of the matrimonial property as a substitute for a non-existent right of succession. She is *ab intestato* in the same position as if the deceased had given her by will all the rights which the Swiss Civil Code gives her without a will.

2. Cases of a vacuum. These seem to entail greater difficulties.   156. In cases of a vacuum

(*a*) A promise of marriage has been made in Paris between two domiciled French parties. Later both become domiciled in England; the defendant breaks his promise by marrying another woman in England. The plaintiff brings an action in the English court. As the promise of marriage was not governed by English law it had not the character of a contract; the English rules on breach of contract do not apply, since they presuppose a valid contract. Neither do French rules on delict apply, a delict in the sense of French law having been committed only in England; even if they were applicable in France they would not be so in England owing to the rule in *The Halley*.[1] It is therefore probable that an English court would give judgment for the defendant, unless circumstances permitted of the assumption that after coming to England the parties had by their behaviour made a new implied contract to be married. The result is not unsatisfactory, at least not more so than when in a purely English case of breach of promise the promise proves to be legally invalid.[2]

(*b*) A domiciled Swiss couple living under a contractual system of separation of property[3] ultimately becomes domiciled and naturalized in Sweden, where the husband dies intestate leaving a child. His personal property consists mainly of a large bank deposit with an English bank. His widow cannot claim the Swiss portion of a quarter, as Swiss inheritance law does not apply. Is she entitled to the Swedish moiety of the united property? Prima facie it would seem that she is not, because this moiety is part of the Swedish system of matrimonial property, which system does not apply to the couple. Under Swedish inheritance law, on the other hand, she has no right. Thus she would apparently receive nothing. This unsatisfactory result will be corrected by a reasonable construction of Swedish internal law. A Swedish widow has no right of inheritance because the law assumes that she is provided for by her moiety of the united matrimonial property. But when this safeguard fails because Swedish matrimonial law does not apply, it seems reasonable to suppose that Swedish law will give her as 'hereditary' portion all she would have received as matrimonial property if Swedish matrimonial law had been applicable. In other words,

---

[1] (1868), L.R. 2, P.C. 193. See *infra*, s. 471.

[2] As to the case of a promise made by an infant and the effect of ultimate ratification on the one hand, and a new promise on the other hand, see Infant Relief Act, 1874 (37 & 38 Vict. c. 62), s. 2; *Coxhead* v. *Mullis* (1878), 3 C.P.D. 439; *Ditcham* v. *Worrall* (1880), 5 C.P.D. 410.

[3] Swiss Civ. Code, s. 241, subs. (2).

Swedish law in classifying the moiety rule as part of matrimonial law includes a subsidiary classification of that rule as an inheritance rule when through the non-applicabililty of Swedish matrimonial law the widow would have no share in her husband's property.

(*c*) A domiciled Englishman dies intestate leaving movable property in Germany. His next of kin is a cousin of his father's. According both to English and German conflict rules inheritance is governed by English law. As under this law the father's cousin is not entitled to succeed, the property becomes 'heirless', *bona vacantia*.[1] The English Crown, the Duchy of Lancaster, and the Duke of Cornwall have no right of 'succession', and their right to *bona vacantia* is (probably) not applicable to property situate outside England and Wales. German inheritance law under which the father's cousin would succeed as 'heir' is certainly not applicable. The right to take *bona vacantia* is governed under English and German conflict rules by the *lex situs*, which is in this case German internal law. That law, however, presents a difficulty. The Roman principle *res nullius cedunt occupanti* has been adopted by German law.[2] But as it cannot be the intention of German law to abandon the ownerless property of a deceased person to pillage, to treat it like mussels on the seashore, there is a gap in German internal law which has to be filled by way of analogy. As in the case of jetsam or stranded goods, or in that of the German state taking over the succession to a deceased German's property if there is nobody else to succeed, so here, too, the German (Hessian, Bavarian, &c.) state in whose geographical area the ownerless goods are to be found is entitled to acquire them.

157.
Summary

To sum up, the problems to which differences of classification lead are not so insoluble as is sometimes suggested and do not need the chaotic interpretation built up by the *lex fori* doctrine. The true difficulties consist in the adjustment of several internal legal systems working together in respect of the same set of facts. The questions arising in this domain, however, are not concerned with private international law but with the correct interpretation of internal legal rules. They cannot arise where only one legal system applies, but emerge solely where facts containing foreign elements are at issue.

---

[1] Administration of Estates Act, 1925 (15 Geo. V. c. 23), s. 46 (1) (VI).
[2] s. 958, German Civ. Code.

BIBLIOGRAPHY

F. KAHN, in *Jhering's Jahrb.*, 1891, 1 (reprinted: *Abhandlungen*, I. 92). E. BARTIN, *J. Clunet*, 1897, 225, 466, 720; *Études de droit int. pr.*, 1; *Principes*, I. 221; 31 *Rec.* (1930 I), 565. DESPAGNET, *J. Clunet*, 1898, 253. LORENZEN, *Selected Articles*, 80–135; RABEL in his *Z.*, 5. 241. LEA MERIGGI, 28 *Rev. Darras* (1933), 201. W. E. BECKETT, 15 *Brit. Y.B.*, 1934, 46. G. C. CHESHIRE, pp. 58 et seq. J. D. FALCONBRIDGE, *Essays*, 35–108, 157–86. A. H. ROBERTSON, 52 *Harvard L.R.*, 1929, 747. ROBERTSON, *Characterization in the Conflict of Laws* (1940). (See on this book CHEATHAM, 55 *Harvard L.R.* 164). CHEATHAM, 21 *Cornell L.Q.R.* (1936), 570. W. W. COOK, 211–238, 284 et seq. DICEY(– MORRIS), pp. 62–73. HANCOCK, *Torts in the Conflict of Laws* (1942), 65 et seq. NEUNER, *Der Sinn der internat.-privatrechtl. Norm*, 1932 (see on this: LEWALD, *JurW.*, 1932, 2253). J. UNGER, 19 *Bell Yard* (1937), 3. MAURY, 57 *Rec.* (1936 III), 508. NIBOYET, *Traité* III. 343–96. ARMINJON I. 309–51. REYAN HAKKI, *Les conflits de qualifications*, 1934. W. NIEDERER, *Die Frage der Qualifikation*, Zürich, 1940 (see on this: GUTZWILLER, *Schweiz. Juristenzeitg*, 37, 143). WIGNY, *Rev. crit.*, 1936, 392. BATIFFOL, *Traité*, 310 et seq. NIBOYET, 'Le problème d. qualifications sur le terrain d. traités diplom.', *Rev. crit.*, 1935, 1. PLAISANT, *Conflits dans les Traités*, 47–60. LIPSTEIN, 21 *Brit. Y.B.* (1944), 257.

CHAPTER XIV

EXCEPTIONS TO THE APPLICATION
OF FOREIGN LAW

158.
Savigny's
doctrine

I. In certain cases a foreign legal rule normally applicable is excluded for special reasons. Such exceptional non-application occurs particularly where the application would lead to a result inconsistent with some fundamental principle of the law of the forum. No country can do without such occasional overruling of the normal conflict rules: a contract, for example, which is valid under its proper law, but contrary to *boni mores* as understood in this country, cannot be upheld by the English courts.

It was Savigny who clearly showed that the rules of an absolute, imperative character (the *ius cogens*) to be found in any legal system are of two kinds.[1] There are first those rules 'that are enacted merely for the sake of persons who are the possessors of rights', such as laws limiting the capacity to act on account of age or sex, or laws concerning the transfer of property; and secondly the rules that are not made solely for the benefit of single individuals but rest on moral grounds or on the 'public interest' (*publica utilitas*), 'whether they relate to politics, police or political economy'. As to the first group of rules, though they cannot be put out of operation by contract—*ius cogens privatorum pactis mutari non potest*—they become inapplicable where according to private international law a foreign legal system governs the case. The laws belonging to the second group, on the other hand, are intended to be applied in all circumstances, even though the applicable foreign system does not know them or allows 'free scope to the individual will'.

159. *'Ordre*
public
interne' and
'ordre
public inter-
national'

A Swiss jurist[2] has given to these two categories of compulsory rules somewhat misleading names, and many French writers have adopted them. He called the first type *lois d'ordre public interne*, and the second *lois d'ordre*

---

[1] Savigny, *System d. röm. R. VIII*, 35 (English translation by Guthrie, p. 78).
[2] Brocher, *Nouveau traité*, 1876, no. 141. See A. Weiss, *Traité*, III. 94; Despagnet, p. 362, and others. *Contra*: Niboyet, III. 490, Bartin, I. 269.

public international; he wished to indicate thereby that the laws of the first category are applicable only where the internal municipal law of the forum applies, while the second group imperatively demands application even in the sphere of the private international law of the country.1 The expression *ordre public international* says 'nearly the opposite of what it intends' (Bartin), since it has in view an *ordre public national* operative in the international sphere.2

Savigny mentions further another group of exceptional cases in which foreign law must be excluded. They concern foreign 'legal institutions of which the existence is not recognized at all in our law and which therefore have no claim to the protection of our courts'. He gives as examples civil death, known at that time in French and Russian law, and slavery.

Savigny's views had a certain influence on English and German law. Both uphold the conception that the exclusion of foreign law is an exception to the leading principles of private international law. In this Mancini and his adherents differ from Savigny; they regard the rules excluding foreign law not as anomalous but as following from the principles of private international law.3 Their opinion has largely contributed to the unfortunate extension of the domain of law exclusion4 and thereby increased the danger that the courts may look on laws that differ from compulsory rules of the forum as inconsistent with the *ordre public* of the country and reject them for that reason. French courts, in particular, go far in allowing

160. Mancini and his influence

---

1 To understand this startling terminology one has to consider art. 6, French c.c.: One cannot by private agreements set aside the laws *qui intéressent l'ordre public*. This, of course, points only to the compulsory rules working within the sphere of internal law, the *ius cogens*. (See also art. 1133, c.c.) But it is correct that among them there are some rules which take effect not only against private contracts but also against foreign laws.

2 *Ordre public externe* would be the appropriate term.

3 See *supra*, s. 33.

4 The hope uttered by Savigny (VIII. 38, English translation, p. 80): 'it is to be expected that these exceptional cases will gradually be diminished with the natural legal development of nations' was too optimistic. Modern short-sighted nationalism has on the contrary considerably enlarged the number of these 'exceptional rules' and thus seriously impaired the value of private international law as a body of rules tending towards international regulation.

the operation of *ordre public*. In divorce cases governed by foreign law they pronounce no divorce decree for any reason unknown to French law. In the case of a domiciled Englishman marrying the English mother of his illegitimate child they applied the French rule of legitimation by subsequent marriage, though English law at that time did not admit any legitimation. And conversely: the legitimation of a child born in adultery is not recognized in France, even if under the personal law of the parents and the child, for example, under German law adultery between the parents is no bar to legitimation by subsequent marriage.[1] French law does not recognize a hypothec (that is, a pledge without delivery of possession) on movables, even if constituted abroad according to the *lex situs*.[2] The French Supreme Court also excludes the application of a foreign rule denying to father and child any claim for maintenance against each other.[3] As long as French law did not allow an illegitimate child to claim recognition by its natural father (viz. until 1912), French courts refused to foreign children likewise the right to bring such an action against their foreign father, and since 1912 *recherche de la paternité* has been admitted only within the limits of the new art. 340.[4] Italian courts, too, though not Italian doctrine, have adopted the conception of *ordine pubblico internazionale* in the wide sense favoured by French courts.

161. The German provision   German law has maintained Savigny's leading idea that the exclusion of foreign law must be an exception, but German courts màke many more such exceptions than Savigny would have allowed. The most characteristic points in the German rule on public order are the two following:

---

[1] Paris Appeal Court, *J. Clunet*, 1927, p. 77. See Mann, 57 *L.Q.R.* (1941), 14, n. 6. English law does not take the same view: s. 1, subs. (2) and s. 8, Legitimacy Act, 1926 (16 & 17 Geo. V, c. 60). See *In re Askew*, [1930] 2 Ch. 259, and Morris, *Cases on Priv. Int. L.*, 207.

[2] Code civil, art. 2119: 'les meubles n'ont pas de suite par hypothèque.'

[3] *J. Clunet*, 1922, p. 115.

[4] Art. 340 now allows declaration of paternity by judgment only in cases of elopement, rape, seduction by means of deception, by abuse of authority or promise of marriage; further in the case of notorious concubinage, or where the father has admitted his paternity in writing and unequivocally, or has contributed to the maintenance and education of the child in his capacity as its father.

1. German law distinguishes between foreign rules which would, if applied, produce a result contrary to *boni mores*, and those which, though unobjectionable *per se*, would entail an inconsistency with 'the purpose of a German legal rule'.[1] In the first case the 'accent'[2] is laid on the repugnant feature of the foreign rule, in the second on the imperative character of a German rule from which no deviation is admissible. Similarly for English law the problem may arise in these two forms. The distinction is of no great practical value.

2. Even those foreign rules which in themselves are open to objection from the point of view of European civilization may be applied if in the particular circumstances their application does not lead to an objectionable result. It is not for the courts of any country to criticize foreign rules as such; it is sufficient for them critically to examine the effect of their application in the particular case.

II. Sometimes the doctrine of *ordre public* has been used to justify the exclusion of foreign *public law* from application. This is hardly correct. True, no state would be prepared to enforce foreign constitutional or administrative law, particularly revenue law, or foreign penal law. But the reason for this is not to be found in its own 'public policy', but in the consideration that these branches of the law have, or according to the law of nations should have, a strictly territorial character, since —generally speaking—it is no part of the task of any sovereign state to protect the interests of a foreign sovereign state as such. {162. Exclusion of foreign public law}

In the area of private international law the exclusion of foreign public law operates as follows:

1. Foreign *penal* law is inapplicable.[3] This not only means that the courts cannot found a conviction for criminal offence on the breach of a foreign penal rule, but {163. (1) Penal law}

---

[1] s. 30 of the Introductory Law to the Civ. Code.

[2] Zitelmann, I. 326.

[3] In the American case *The Antelope* (quoted in *Huntington* v. *Attrill*, [1893] A.C. (P.C.) 150, 156), Marshall, C.J., stated the rule 'The courts of no country execute the penal laws of another'. See *Banco de Vizcaja* v. *Don Alfonso de Borbon y Austria*, [1935] 1 K.B. 140, 144.

also implies that they will refuse to enforce foreign judgments given in penal proceedings.[1] Thus an action for the
recovery of pecuniary penalties imposed by a foreign court
cannot be brought in an English court. Penal law in the
strict sense of the term means a law imposing punishment
for an offence against the community (state, nation, township, &c.) or its representatives (government). Where the
punishment consists in a fine the destination of the money
makes no difference to the nature of the rule under which
the fine is imposed; it is penal whether the money goes to
the state or to a state official or to an informer, or even if
some of it is paid to a private person adversely affected by
the crime. Private penalties, however—such as the doub-
ling of the amount of a claim in cases where the debtor
wrongly denies the debt[2]—are not of a penal character,[3]
'in the sense of the English conflict rule', and penalties
payable for non-performance of a contract and imposed by
the contracting parties may be recognized by an English
court as valid and enforceable under foreign law, though
they are invalid under English municipal law.[4] Where
there is a criminal offence such as adultery, the punishment
may consist in a prohibition of marriage after a divorce:
thus Swiss law forbids the guilty party to remarry during
a certain period,[5] and the law of Cape Colony prohibited
his or her remarriage for so long as the injured party
remained unmarried. Neither of these rules is regarded as
applicable abroad.[6] English private international law has

---

[1] *Huntington* v. *Attrill*, loc. cit.; *Raulin* v. *Fischer*, [1911] 2 K.B. 93.

[2] Roman law: *lis infitiatione crescit in duplum. Dig.* 9. 2. 2. 1; *Inst.* IV. 6, 19, 23, 26.

[3] See *Huntington* v. *Attrill*, loc. cit., pp. 157, 159. *Contra*: numerous American decisions; see Goodrich, pp. 13, 14.

[4] *Law* v. *Local Board of Redditch*, [1892] 1 Q.B. 127, 133; *Wall* v. *Rederi-aktiebolaget Luggude*, [1915] 3 K.B. 66, 72.

[5] Swiss Civ. C., art. 150. See the decision of the Berlin Court of Appeal in *IPRechtspr.*, 1932, p. 179.

[6] *Scott* v. *Att. Gen.* (1886), 11 P.D. 128; van Leeuwen, *Commentaries on Rom.-Dutch Law* (2nd ed., 1921), I. 117. See *Warter* v. *Warter* (1890), 15 P.D. 152, 155. *Quaere*: Is this Roman-Dutch rule really of a penal character? The so-called divorce (in that law) is something between a genuine divorce (i.e. dissolution of all ties) and judicial separation; it is a judicial separation giving the innocent party the right of remarriage. Not until he exercises this right is his former marriage dissolved *quoad vinculum*.

given to the term 'penal' a very wide application, or, as Romer J.[1] put it, a law may not be 'penal in the strict sense' (that is in the sense of *Huntington* v. *Attrill*[2]) but may be 'regarded in the same light as penal laws'. The confiscation of the property of the ex-King Alfonso of Spain during the Spanish revolution was characterized as penal.[3] So was the French law of 1901 on the contract of association in so far as it restricted religious congregations and enjoined the liquidation of the property of non-authorized congregations.[4] Nazi decrees placing Jewish businesses in the hands of state officials were treated as penal[5] because of their confiscatory character. The status of an adjudicated prodigal[6] is regarded as penal. Other examples of penal or quasi-penal relations are slavery, civil death, infamy, and all disabilities caused by religious vows, religious belief, race, or caste. An English court will therefore not recognize the impediments to marriage based on *disparitas cultus* or *mixta religio* and developed by Canon law. It would further (probably) refuse to apply the so-called Nuremberg Laws of the German Third Reich[7] which forbade male Jews to employ female Aryan-Germans under the age of thirty-five as domestic servants and prohibited the conclusion of marriages between Aryan-Germans and Jews (of any nationality).[8]

[1] In *Frankfurther* v. *Exner*, [1947] 1 Ch. 629, 636.

[2] See *supra*, p. 170[1].

[3] *Banco de Vizcaja* v. *Don Alfonso de Borbon y Austria*, [1935] 1 K.B. 140, 144.

[4] *Lecouturier* v. *Rey*, [1910] A.C. 262, 265.

[5] *Frankfurther* v. *Exner*, l.c.

[6] *Worms* v. *De Valdor* (1880), 49 L.J.Ch. 261. *In re Selot's Trust*, [1902] 1 Ch. 488.

[7] Of 15 Sept. and 14 Nov. 1935.

[8] Most countries refused to apply the Nuremberg rules as being contrary to *ordre public* unless they, too, have adopted marriage prohibition on racial grounds—as most of the southern states of the U.S.A. have done in respect of marriages between white and black persons (see Restatement, s. 132, Beale, II. 691). Difficulties, however, arose for the Netherlands and Switzerland, which are bound by the Hague Convention on Conflict of Laws in respect of Marriages, 1902. Under this Convention the Signatory States are not allowed to disregard for reasons of *ordre public* any impediment established by the national law of the spouses, except only those impediments that are based on *religious* grounds; art. 2. Some decisions of Dutch courts have disregarded the Nuremberg impediment, partly because the conception of racial distinction is unknown to Dutch law, partly because of Dutch *ordre public* (?). See: *Rabel's Z.* 11 (1937), 206; Sichel, 45 *Yale L.J.* 1936, 1463; Janowski & Fagen, *International Aspects of German Racial*

164.
(2) Admi-
nistrative
law

2. Foreign *administrative law* is territorial in character and therefore not enforceable in England. This refers in particular to foreign *revenue* law, such as tax law,[1] law on local rates,[2] claims of foreign local authorities (arising under Poor Law) against relatives of poor persons for contributions to the costs of maintenance, and the like. It goes without saying that the enforcement of military duties or duties created by a foreign police order is left entirely to the authorities of the foreign territory in which they originated. But it would be an exaggeration to say— as has often been said—that foreign public law is excluded from any 'application' owing to its territorial character.

Examples:

165.
Validity of
foreign
state acts

(*a*) The question frequently arises whether a certain statute of a foreign state has been validly enacted, in particular whether it is consistent with the constitution of that state—for example, in the case of a foreign Refugee Government in London, issuing Orders in this country.[3] The answer to such questions can only be given by the constitutional law of the foreign state. The English court will have to examine the constitutionality of the foreign statute in the same way as the foreign court would undertake such examination according to the law of its country.

(*b*) In the case of a contract concluded between an English company and a foreign state, foreign administrative law decides whether the person acting on behalf of the state had power to do so.

(*c*) If an insurance contract is void according to its proper law because at the time of contracting the insurance company was not duly licensed by the appropriate administrative authority,[4] then this effect of a violation of foreign administrative law on the validity of the contract must be respected by an English court.

Policies, N. York, 1937; Foster, *Théorie anglaise,* p. 129 (partly differing from Cheshire) Schröder, *Nouv. Rev.* 4, 275. Feist, 24 *Grotius Soc.* 81. Rowson, 10 *Modern L.R.* 345; Gutzwiller, *Geltungsbereich der Währungsvorschriften,* 128[15]. Cf. also 6 *Nouv. R.* (1939), 387.

[1] *Holman* v. *Johnson* (1775), Cowp. 341, 343. *Foster* v. *Driscoll,* [1929] 1 K.B. 470, 496, 518. *Queen of Holland* v. *Drukker,* [1928] Ch. 877, 884.

[2] *Municipal Council of Sydney* v. *Bull,* [1909] 1 K.B. 7, 12: 'the action is analogous to an action brought in one country to enforce the revenue laws of another'.

[3] *In re Amand,* [1941] 2 K.B. 239, 252; Fedozzi, 27 *Rec.* (1929 II) 221; F. A. Mann, 59 *L.Q.R.* (1943), 53, 155.

[4] Cf. the decision of the Hamburg Appeal Court, *Veröffentlichungen des Aufsichtsamts für Privatversicherung,* vol. VII (1907), Annex, p. 37, no. 372.

(*d*) Laws prohibiting the importation of certain goods (wine, spirits, narcotic drugs) have to be taken into account by foreign courts adjudicating on a contract concluded for delivery or shipping of the prohibited goods into the prohibiting country. If the proper law of the contract is the law of that country the contract is void, and the court is bound to recognize its nullity. But even if the contract is governed by a different law, either the *lex fori* or the law of a third country, English law will refuse enforcement of the contract, because an English court 'will not assist or sanction the breach of the laws of other independent states'.[1]

166. Foreign trade restrictions

No such rule seems to exist in other European countries.—On the continent, generally speaking, contracts violating foreign import restrictions are held to be valid unless there are special reasons for considering them contrary to *boni mores*. German law, for example, regards the contract as void where the import restriction is based on considerations of public health, as is the case with anti-alcoholic laws, and as valid where the law forms part of the state's economic policy.[2]

(*e*) A problem which at first sight seems similar arises in the case of foreign exchange regulations prohibiting the export of money, the disposal of foreigners' bank deposits, the importation of domestic bank notes, and other transactions liable to endanger the rate of exchange. If the law that has established such restrictions is the proper law of the contract, these restrictions will be applied in principle. Do considerations of public policy result in their non-application? On this see *infra*, s. 456.

(*f*) Another famous illustration of the applicability of foreign administrative law concerned the marriages of members of the German armed forces. Such persons required a marriage licence granted by their superior officers. The Hague Convention of the Private International Law of Marriage embodies the rule that marriage conditions are governed by the national law of the parties. Was the French or Belgian registrar precluded from allowing marriages of German deserters who had, of course, no such licence? In Germany the question was answered in the affirmative; France and Belgium opposed this view,[3] because the application of German military

167. Foreign military law

---

[1] *Ralli Bros.* v. *Compañia Naviera Sota y Aznar*, [1920] 2 K.B. 287, 304 (*per* Scrutton, L.J.); *Foster* v. *Driscoll*, [1929] 1 K.B. 470.

[2] German Supreme Court, *Jur.W.* 1927, 2288.

[3] The three states mentioned were among the Signatories of the Convention. See *supra*, s. 40. France withdrew in 1914, Belgium in 1919.

law was not within the scope of a Convention on private international law. The wording of the Convention supported the German, its spirit the French view.

168.
Infringe-
ments of
foreign
rules

(*g*) The 'territorial character' of foreign public law does not prevent a person who infringes the foreign rule within the foreign country from becoming liable to pay damages in this country, provided the wrong committed would have been actionable under English law had it been done here.[1] It even happens, though rarely, that the law of country *X* expressly provides that the violation of certain administrative rules of other countries creates a liability in *X*.[2]

(*h*) Though English courts do not directly enforce obligations to pay taxes or stamp duties, they have recognized the nullity of written contracts where the instrument had not been stamped according to the revenue law of the place of execution.[3]

169. Public
policy.
Principle

III. The continental conception of *ordre public* as excluding the application of foreign law reappears in England under the name of *public policy*.[4] But the part it plays in this country is smaller and less important than on the continent. English courts hesitate to raise the question whether any foreign rule is or is not consistent with English principles of justice.

As Scrutton, L.J., put it: 'it appears a serious breach of international comity, if a state is recognized as a sovereign independent state, to postulate that its legislation is contrary to essential principles of justice and morality; such an allegation might well with a susceptible foreign government

---

[1] See *infra*, s. 470.

[2] *Example:* German Commercial Code, 1897, s. 515: 'If the master of a ship does not observe abroad the legal rules prevailing there, in particular the police laws, tax laws and custom laws he shall make reparation for the damage arising out of such failure' (for example, to the ship-owner or charterer). See Neumeyer, *Internat. Verwaltungsrecht*, III. 1, 177; IV. 193.

[3] See, for example, *Alves* v. *Hodgson* (1797), 7 T.R. 241; *Clegg* v. *Levy* (1812), 3 Camp. 166; *Bristow* v. *Sequeville* (1850), 5 Ex. 275, 279.

[4] Where there are both English and French authentic texts of a State Treaty the terms 'ordre public' and 'public policy' are used as equivalents. *Example:* Geneva Convention on the Execution of Foreign Arbitral Awards, 1927, art. 1 (e).

become a *casus belli*[1] and should, in my view, be the action of the Sovereign through his ministers, and not of the judge'.[2]

Another reason for this attitude of the courts lies in the fact that in many cases the regular English conflict rules suffice to attain the result reached on the continent by the use of the vague conception of *ordre public*.

1. English courts treat as *procedural* many institutions which it would be more correct to regard as substantive.

170. Its English substitutes

The German Supreme Court relied upon the principle of *ordre public* to exclude from application a Swiss provision under which certain debts are not barred by limitation of action.[3] Similarly the Swiss Supreme Court excluded the rules on limitation embodied in the proper law of the contract, and applied Swiss law.[4] English law obtains a similar result by ruling that limitation of actions is a matter of procedure,[5] hence governed by the *lex fori*.[6]

2. The exclusion of foreign law for reasons of *ordre public* in the continental sense is furthermore partly achieved in this country by the very wide application of the concept *penal law*. See on this *supra*, s. 163.

3. The English rules on *jurisdiction* entail in some cases the non-application of foreign substantive law. Thus in divorce proceedings English courts have no opportunity of deciding whether any grounds of divorce, recognized in foreign legal systems but unknown to English law, are against the public policy of this country.

Under French law divorce is governed by the national law of the spouses, and if according to that law a divorce is permissible on the ground of mutual consent or of the respondent's insanity, the French courts need the

---

[1] Apart from the obvious exaggeration contained in these words, it may be submitted that when an English court states that a given foreign provision is inconsistent with 'essential principles of justice and morality', it has in view the English conceptions of these qualities and is not treating divergent foreign opinions with contempt. The court may believe that the foreign conception is inferior to the English. But it would hardly object to foreign judges conversely emphasizing their belief in the superiority of their own conception of justice and morality.

[2] In *A. M. Luther* v. *Sagor & Co.*, [1921] 3 K.B. 532, 558, 559.

[3] German Supr. Court, *Off. Coll.*, 106, 83.

[4] In *Compagnie Tangeroise* v. *Comp. Grainière Soc. anon.* 4 (Schweizerisches) *Jahrbuch f. internat. Recht*, 1947, 216, and Gutzwiller, ibid., p. 221.

[5] See Husserl, *Virginia L.R.*, Nov. 1939, 47 et seq.

[6] On further so-called procedural rules of English law which exclude the application of foreign law, see *infra*, ss. 218–27.

conception of *ordre public* for excluding such grounds from application in France. In England the question does not arise because the English court has divorce jurisdiction only if the husband has an English domicile,[1] and in that case English law applies exclusively.

Another example: in Massachusetts the courts have no jurisdiction to entertain an action concerning property between husband and wife even if the (substantive) 'right' which one spouse seeks to enforce against the other has arisen validly in a foreign state. Beale states generally, as a rule prevailing in the United States, that 'if the law of the forum does not provide a *form of action* appropriate for the enforcement of the foreign right the action may not be maintained'.[2] The same seems to be true for English law, though 'forms of action' belong to the past.[3] English courts in distinguishing between rights and 'remedies'[4] do not invent new remedies in order to entertain an action based on a foreign right.[5] Three examples may illustrate the issue:

(*a*) A German court in pronouncing a divorce decree does not necessarily fix the amount of maintenance which under German substantive law[6] the adulterous wife has to pay her innocent husband who is unable to maintain himself. Suppose that after the divorce both parties emigrate to England, where they reside without founding a domicile, and that the former husband wishes to sue his former wife for maintenance. Has the English court jurisdiction? It seems probable that it has not.

(*b*) A bastard sues his father residing in England, though domiciled in Germany, for alimony due to him under German law. Can the English court entertain the suit though the bastard would have no action if the father were a domiciled Englishman? French law, for reasons of *ordre public*, denies to a foreign bastard any right which internal French law does not confer on French bastards.

---

[1] Apart from s. 13 Matrimonial Causes Act, 1937; see *supra*, s. 73.

[2] Beale, III. 1631. Cp. Restatement, s. 608.

[3] Lord Wright said in *Fibrosa* v. *Fairbairn*, [1943] A.C. 32, 63: 'Yet the ghosts of the forms of action have been allowed at times to intrude in the ways of the living and impede vital functions of the law.'

[4] See on this (ambiguous) notion *infra*, s. 215.

[5] *In re Macartney*, [1921] 1 Ch. 522, 528 (following an American decision).

[6] Marriage and Divorce Law (1946), s. 58.

It would seem that the same result is correct here, not on account of public policy, but because the court has no jurisdiction.[1]

(c) A domiciled Frenchman resident in this country lives with his wife under the French system of community of goods. Under French law she can sue him for judicial separation of goods if her dowry is endangered by his mismanagement.[2] Can she bring an action to this effect in an English court, though no action of this kind, apart from dissolution of partnerships, is known to English law?[3] It seems doubtful whether the court would find it had jurisdiction in such a case.

IV. There remain a few cases where the application of foreign law is excluded for reasons of *public policy*. A clear and unambiguous definition of this vague and slippery conception has often been sought, but without success.

171.
Cases of public policy

The German Supreme Court holds that German public policy is jeopardized 'where the difference between the political and social conceptions on which rest respectively the foreign and the German law is so substantial that the application of the foreign law would directly threaten the bases of German political and economic life'.[4] This formula is faulty, even apart from the fact that it leaves the notion it attempts to explain practically as vague as it was before. It cannot matter on what political conceptions the foreign rule is based. Its basis may be the same as that of German law, but the means by which the aim is to be attained may be so different that the application of the foreign rule is inconsistent with German public interest. The German code of 1896 and French law are based on nearly identical political, social, and economic ideas, i.e. the conceptions of a socially tinged liberalism; nevertheless French courts would, for example, not admit an action for breach of a promise to marry given by a German to a German woman in Germany.

English law is at any rate opposed to the view that public policy in the sense of 'political expedience, or that which is

---

[1] Or because internal English bastardy law is mainly part of the pauper legislation, that is of administrative law, and foreign administrative law cannot be enforced here? In my belief this reasoning is untenable unless the foreign law likewise regards the obligation of a father to maintain his bastard as based on the idea that the child should not become a charge on the parish, a view which has been adopted by the law of the United States (Beale, II. 1430).

[2] French Civil Code, art. 1443.

[3] See Partnership Act, 1890 (53 & 54 Vict., c. 39), s. 35 (b) to (f).

[4] Supr. Court, *Offic. Coll.*, 60, 300; 63, 19; 93, 183; 110, 173; 119, 259.

best for the common good of the community', should be taken into account by a court of law.

On this subject Parke, B., said in *Egerton* v. *Earl Brownlow*:[1] 'there may be every variety of opinion according to the education, habits, talents and disposition of each person who is to decide whether an act is against public policy or not. To allow this to be a ground of judicial decision would lead to the greatest uncertainty and confusion. It is the province of the statesman and not of the lawyer to discuss, and of the legislature to determine, what is the best for the public good.' A similar view is expressed in other decisions.[2]

The cases, therefore, in which English courts exclude foreign law by invoking the doctrine of public policy are not very frequent.

The conception of public policy serves in particular two purposes:

172.
Foreign provisions *contra bonos mores*

1. The courts refuse the application of foreign law where this would lead to an infringement of *boni mores*, of morality in the wider sense of the term as understood in this country. This includes in the first place contracts which though valid under their proper law, would be considered illegal or immoral if they were governed by English law. Examples: a contract with a courtesan for the price of her prostitution,[3] the sale of wine to be consumed in a brothel,[4] a champertous agreement made in France (where it was held valid) with regard to litigation in England,[5] a contract between spouses to facilitate divorce and by which the husband abandons the custody of his children to his wife;[6] a marriage brokerage contract. In the famous case *Santos* v. *Illidge* (1860)[7] a contract for the sale of slaves concluded in 1858 between an English slave-

[1] (1853), 4 H.L.C. 1, 123.

[2] *Fender* v. *St. John-Mildmay*, [1938] A.C. 1, 12 (*per* Lord Atkin): 'The doctrine of public policy should only be invoked in clear cases in which the harm to the public is substantially incontestable and does not depend upon the idiosyncratic inferences of a few judicial minds.' In *Janson* v. *Driefontein Consol. Mines*, [1902] A.C. 484, 491 (*per* Lord Halsbury): 'I deny that any court can invent a new head of public policy.'

[3] See the *dictum* in *Robinson* v. *Bland* (1760), 2 Burr. 1077, 1084; *Pearce* v. *Brooks* (1866), L.R. 1 Ex. 213.

[4] *Taylor* v. *Chester* (1869), L.R. 4 Q.B. 309.

[5] *Grell* v. *Levy* (1864), 16 C.B. (N.Ser.) 73.

[6] *Hope* v. *Hope* (1857), 8 De G.M. & G. 731. The German Marriage Law, 1946, s. 72 allows such contracts.

[7] 8 C.B. (N.Ser.) 861.

owner and an alien to be performed in a country where slavery was still recognized was adjudged valid;[1] in our time it would undoubtedly be regarded as void. An undertaking by a father to confer on his illegitimate child a right to perpetual maintenance effective even after the father's death, which was valid according to the applicable Maltese law (and would be valid under any continental law), was declared void as contrary to English public policy.[2] A contract unassailable as to its content but concluded under duress, undue influence, or fraud will not be enforced in this country, even if under its proper law the contract is valid.[3]

In respect of wagering contracts the attitude of English law is peculiar. (a) Since they are not 'illegal' under English law, the English courts allow actions for recovery of money won at play or lent for gambling purposes if the foreign law governing the contract permits recovery by action.[4] It is submitted that this hardly seems compatible with the rule that the 'remedy', the right of a person to recover his claim by action, is a matter of procedure and therefore governed by the *lex fori*.[5] (b) If the debtor of a foreign gambling debt has given a security, for example a cheque, for the amount of the debt, and if the security is subject to English law, the debtor cannot be sued upon the security; but as giving a cheque is not payment—*delegatio non est solutio*—the creditor may sue on the gambling debt itself.[6]

173. Wagering contracts

[1] Two judges of the Exchequer Chamber (Pollock, C.B., and Wightman, J.) and the court of Common Pleas (Willes, Williams, and Byles, J.J., 6 C.B., N.Ser., 841) dissenting.

[2] *In re Macartney*, [1921] 1 Ch. 522, 527 (there were, however, two other reasons for the decision).

[3] *Kaufmann* v. *Gerson*, [1904] 1 K.B. 591.

[4] *Robinson* v. *Bland* (1760), 2 Burr. 1077; *Quarrier* v. *Colston* (1842), 1 Ph. 147; *Saxby* v. *Fulton*, [1909] 2 K.B. 208, 232. A different view has been taken by French and German law. See Pillet, *Traité prat.*, II. 240; Raape, *Comment.*, p. 826, no. 8; German Supr. C., *Seufferts Arch.*, 86 (1932), p. 299. The courts are in particular often concerned with the question whether contracts on gambling on the Stock Exchange are actionable (Raape, loc. cit., 830). American law: Beale, III. 1649.

[5] See *supra*, s. 170 (3) (a).

[6] *Moulis* v. *Owen*, [1907] 1 K.B. 746. *Société anonyme des Grands Établissements du Touquet* v. *Baumgart*, [1927], W.N. 78.

174. Vital interests of the State   2. Foreign law is excluded from application if such application endangers vital interests of the British State.[1] The main examples for this are cases where the application would lead to help for the King's enemy[2] or jeopardize the good relations between this country and a friendly state. A contract for the raising of a loan to further a revolt against a foreign government in a friendly state X is void if governed by English law;[3] it may be valid if governed by the law of a foreign state Y, for example if Y is at war with X. But in this case it would be contrary to English public policy to allow the contract to be enforced by an English court. The same is true of a contract for the import of wine into a prohibitionist country. Such contract is void under English internal law, if this is the proper law of the contract;[4] under English private international law it is not enforceable in England, even if valid under the foreign proper law.

In all these cases the conception of public policy (or distinctive English policy) has been used for the purpose of *excluding* foreign law. In the war it was invoked to justify the *application* of foreign rules which normally might have been excluded. In the case of *Lorenzen* v. *Lydden & Co.*[5] the interest of the state and of its policy urgently demanded the recognition of a certain expropriation decree of a foreign state, which *possibly* went beyond the normal powers of that state; but it is submitted that the decision can be defended by a different reasoning. (See on this *infra*, s. 501.)

175. Limits to the exclusion of foreign law   V. The exclusion of foreign law for reasons of public policy does not go farther than is necessary in the public interest. This leads to two limitations:

1. Not all consequences of the application of an objectionable rule are necessarily themselves objectionable. An example is furnished by marriages between father-in-

---

[1] See Cheshire, 191, 192.

[2] *Robson* v. *Premier Oil & Pipe Line Co.*, [1915] 2 Ch. (C.A.) 124, 136; *Dynamit Aktiengesellschaft* v. *Rio Tinto Co.*, [1918] A.C. 202, 294.

[3] *De Wütz* v. *Hendricks* (1824), 2 Bing. 314.

[4] See *Foster* v. *Driscoll*, [1929] 1 K.B. 470. See *supra*, p. 175 (d).

[5] [1942] 2 K.B. 202, 214.

law and daughter-in-law. Soviet-Russian law allows such marriages; so did German-Nazi law. A marriage of this kind would offend against English public policy, and no English registrar would allow such persons to marry before him. But if they were married at their foreign domicile and later established an English domicile, the marriage would (probably) be treated as valid[1] and their children as legitimate.

Niboyet speaks aptly of the different 'intensity' of *ordre public*; sometimes it is only the creation of a right that is contrary to public policy, but if the right has been validly created abroad its effects need not offend against public policy.[2]

2. Where a foreign legal rule is excluded its place is in most cases filled by the *lex fori*. But this substitution should be restricted as far as possible. If the foreign law normally applicable contains a rule *x* which is unobjectionable, but which is subject to an exception *y*, and if *y* is contrary to English public policy, its exclusion does not entail the application of English law but that of the foreign main rule *x*.

An illustration of this is to be found in a decision of the German Supreme Court.[3] Swiss law exempts certain debts from the general rules on limitation and makes them enforceable *in perpetuum*. This exemption is deemed to be contrary to German public policy and is therefore not applied in a German court; the court held that the normal Swiss and not the normal German period of limitation was to apply in such case.[4] Another example: a contract governed by and valid under German law in all its parts contains one clause inconsistent with English public policy which is therefore treated as void by the English court. The question whether thereby the whole of the contract becomes void must be decided not by the English *lex fori* but by German law as the proper law of the contract.[5]

[1] At any rate the court will allow a claim for maintenance, though probably not for restitution of conjugal rights, because a right to incestuous intercourse would hardly be enforced in this country.

[2] Niboyet, III. 543 et seq. Cf. the German formula in art. 30 Introduct. Law; *supra*, p. 171.

[3] *Offic. Collect.*, 106, 85.

[4] This case would raise no problem in an English court, where limitation of action is regarded as a matter of procedure. See *infra*, s. 219.

[5] According to *Pickering* v. *Ilfracombe Railway Co.* (1868), L.R. 3 C.P. 235, 250, the answer of English municipal law would be to the effect that where the illegal can be separated from the legal part, one may reject the bad part and retain the good. Under German law the whole of the contract is *in dubio* void. To retain the 'good part' it must be proved that the parties would have concluded the

176.
Foreign
ordre public

VI. Every court applies rules of its own public policy only; it does not take into account any foreign *ordre public*. With one exception however: where the court applies foreign private international law (by way of *renvoi*)[1] it must not disregard the rules on public policy embodied in that law.

Illustration:[2] In 1930 an Austrian of Christian faith domiciled in Italy married an Austrian Jewess before the English registrar. He brought a suit for nullity of the marriage in an English court. Under English private international law the validity of the marriage falls to be decided by the law of the domicile, i.e. Italian law. According to Italian private international law the validity depends on the national law of the spouses, i.e. Austrian law. The Austrian Civil Code declares marriages between Christians and non-Christians to be void; but Italian law regarded (at that time) the *impedimentum disparitatis cultus* as incompatible with Italian *ordine pubblico*. The English court would probably accept this disqualification irrespective of whether its own public policy is or is not opposed to the application of the Austrian rule. (See *infra*, s. 317).

177. Public
policy in
the case of
inter-
national
courts and
of the
Privy
Council

VII. It is difficult to say what rules an International Court or an International Arbitral Tribunal is allowed to disqualify as contrary to public policy. The court need certainly not consider either the public policy of the country where it has its seat or that prevailing in the countries to which the members of the court belong. It is submitted that the court should take into account only the law applicable in the case (for example, the proper law of the contract). If more than one law is concerned and one of them embodies a rule repugnant to all the others—and only then—the court would be justified in rejecting it.[3]

Finally, it may be mentioned that the Judicial Committee of the Privy Council does not possess one uniform standard for deciding whether a given rule is compatible

good part alone if they had known that the other part was invalid; Germ. Civ. C., s. 139.

[1] See *infra*, s. 178 et seq.
[2] Taken from a famous case decided by the German Supreme Court, *Off. Coll.* 132, 416 (here slightly modified).
[3] It must be doubted whether there exists any such thing as what Niboyet (*Répert.*, X, no. 439 et seq.) calls 'ordre public vraiment international', unless this expression means rules of public policy which are common to all countries of European civilization. Niboyet's views are different from those indicated here.

with public policy or not. An institution like the polygamous marriage of Hindu or Muhammedan law cannot be disregarded in Indian cases as it must be in European lawsuits.

BIBLIOGRAPHY

F. KAHN, *Abhandl.* I. 161. DE VAREILLES-SOMMIÈRES, *Des lois d'ordre public*, 1899. PILLET in *Mélanges Pillet*, I. 407. BARTIN, *Études*, 189. H. LEWALD in *Mitteilungen d. d. Gesellsch. f. Völkerrecht*, 7 (1926), 47; and 23 *Rev. Darras* (1928), 149; and *Règles génér.* 120. LOUIS-LUCAS, *Rev. Darras*, 1933, 393. SOLODOVNIKOFF, *La notion de l'ordre public*, 1936. TH. H. HEALY, 9 *Rec.* (1925 IV), 411. NIBOYET *Traité* III. 488–586. BATIFFOL, *Traité*, 374–89. ARMINJON, I. 218 et seq. KNIGHT, 38 *L.Q.R.* (1922), 207. LORENZEN, *Select. Art.* 1–18. GOODRICH 14–20. FOSTER, *La théorie anglaise*, p. 107. DICEY(–MORRIS), pp. 17–22, 152–60. NUSSBAUM, 49 *Yale L.J.* (1940), 1027. KUHN, *Rec.* 21 (1928 I), 214. PLAISANT, *Conflits dans les Traités* 90–111. HANCOCK, *Torts in Confl. of Laws*, (1942), 65 et seq. GUTZWILLER in *Mélanges Streit*, 1939. GUTZWILLER, *Geltungsbereich der Währungsvorschriften*, 1940, 114 et seq. On MADSEN-MYGDAL, *Ordre public og Territorialitet* (Danish), 2 vol. 1946; see *Rabel's Z.* 15, 173 et seq.

CHAPTER XV

RENVOI

178. The problem I. Where the private international law of a country X indicates that the court should apply the law of a foreign country Y, the meaning of the term 'law of the country Y' needs clarification. There are two possible solutions, viz.:

1. 'Law of the country Y' means the *internal* (municipal) law prevailing in Y. At first sight this would seem to be the natural solution, and many jurists and some courts consider that it is the only one.

2. 'Law of the country Y' may mean the *whole* law of Y and therefore first and foremost its private international law. Y's municipal law only applies when its private international law so directs. X's private international law must therefore be confirmed by Y's before Y's municipal law can be applied. It needs two lawgivers to make the Y law applicable. Where there is no such harmony between the two sets of private international law, it may be either:

(*a*) that the conflict rule of Y refers back to the law of X. This is what French lawyers have called a *Renvoi* in the strict sense of the word, and the term has been adopted everywhere. In Germany the word *Rückverweisung* is used, in England and the United States *Remission*.[1]

Or (*b*) that the conflict rule of Y refers to the law of a third country Z. This, too, is a *Renvoi* (the word being used in a wider sense), though it is rather a *transmission* than a remission, a *Weiterverweisung*, not a *Rückverweisung*.[2] Whether the conflict rules of Z too have to be taken into consideration is an open question.

The problem is best illustrated by a few examples:

179. Illustration: cases of succession (i) A British subject born in England, domiciled first in England, later in Italy, dies intestate leaving movable property in England. An English court has to adjudicate

---

[1] 14 *L.Q.R.* (1898), 231. 232. In Italy the term *rinvio indietro* is used.
[2] Italian: *Rinvio altrove*.

between *A* and *B* as claimants to the succession. *A* bases his claim on Italian inheritance law, *B* contends that he should succeed under the English Administration of Estates Act. Under English private international law the law of the domicile of the deceased, i.e. Italian law, is decisive. If the court rejects the doctrine of *renvoi* it simply applies Italian internal law and decides in favour of *A*; if on the other hand it accepts that doctrine—as in fact English law does—it first ascertains the Italian rule of private international law concerning succession, and as this rule refers back to the national law of the deceased, it applies English internal law (as that 'British' law with which the deceased is more closely connected than with any other law prevailing in the British Commonwealth)[1] and gives judgment for *B*: case of *remission*.

(ii) The same example, except that the deceased was a German subject domiciled in Italy. Then the *renvoi* doctrine leads to the application by the English court of German internal inheritance law, since this is the national law to which the Italian conflict rule refers: case of *transmission*.

(iii) An example of the *lex domicilii* referring to the *lex loci actus*. Before English law adopted the rule *locus regit actum* in the case of wills—that is, before the Wills Act, 1861—a British subject domiciled in France made a will in England in correct English form, and not in French form. The court considered French law to be the law of the domicile and accepted the remission from French private international law to the *lex loci actus*, that is to English internal law; thus it recognized the validity of the will.[2] If in the same case the will had been made in Switzerland and in Swiss form the English court would probably have accepted the transmission from French to Swiss law.

(iv) Remissions and transmissions from the national law to the law of the domicile have also to be taken into consideration; a German court, for example, entertains an action concerning succession to the movable property of a

---

[1] *See supra*, p. 131–3.
[2] Cf. *Laneuville* v. *Anderson & Guichard* (1860), 2 Sw. & Tr. 24, 38.

British subject domiciled in Germany: German private international law points to English law as the national law, and English private international law refers back to German law as the law of the domicile. The German court then has to accept the *renvoi* and to apply German internal law.[1]

(v) It may further happen that the law of the domicile in the English sense of this term refers to the law of a different 'domicile', viz. where the term 'domicile' is used for two different conceptions in the two countries concerned.

An example of this has been given, *supra* s. 131 (2) (a): the case of an Englishman who has his domicile (in the English sense) in Denmark but is ordinarily resident—and therefore domiciled in the Danish sense—in England (or Italy). As under Danish private international law succession is tested by ordinary residence (called domicile), the English court will apply English law (remission) or Italian law (transmission) respectively.

(vi) Sometimes a *renvoi* is made from the *lex situs* to the national law of the deceased or to the *lex loci actus*. Thus a testamentary disposition of immovables may be void under the internal law of the country where the immovables lie; but the conflict rules of that country refer to the law of the place where the will was made. In cases of this kind even American law, which as a rule rejects the *renvoi* doctrine, recognizes an exception in its favour.[2]

(vii) Lastly, an example of reference from the *lex loci actus* to the national law. Under the Wills Act, 1861, a will is formally valid if made by a British subject in accordance with the 'law of the place where it was made'. In the case *In Goods of Lacroix*[3] the court held that this means the law which the courts of the country where the will was made deem applicable to the particular case; the will was made in France by a British subject in English form, and the *renvoi* from the *lex loci actus* to the national law was admitted.

180. Other cases   All the examples hitherto given have been concerned with succession. The problem of *renvoi* may however arise

---

[1] German Introductory Law to the Civil Code, art. 27.
[2] Restatement, § 8 (i).
[3] (1877) 2 P.D. 94, 96, 97.

in any branch of private law, for example, where the validity of a marriage or of a decree of divorce or again of a legitimation by subsequent marriage[1] is in issue, or where the validity of a bill of exchange or a cheque depends on the capacity of the person who has signed or endorsed it,[2] or where the requirements for the assignment of a debt have to be ascertained,[3] or where the transfer of ownership is in dispute.

II. The conception of *renvoi* was developed in the nine- **181. His-** teenth century. It had precursors in certain decisions by **tory up to** the Parliament of Rouen of 1652 and 1663. These were dis- **1879** cussed by the French jurist Froland, who thus became the first author on the subject.[4] In the nineteenth century the first decisions to apply *renvoi* (though without using the expression and without theoretical consideration) were three judgments by English courts (1841, 1847, and 1877) and one by a German court (1861). In the first of these, *Collier* v. *Rivaz* (1841),[5] the issue was whether a will made by a British subject domiciled in Belgium was valid. The court held that this was to be answered by English law, since English private international law pointed to the law of the domicile, that is, to Belgian law and (in the view of the English judge) a Belgian court would have applied

---

[1] *In re Askew*, [1930] 2 Ch. 259; *Collins* v. *Att.-Gen.* 145 L.T.R. 551.

[2] Geneva Conventions on Private International Law concerning Bills of Exchange (1930), s. 1; concerning Cheques (1931), s. 1.

[3] Cf. the very strong case in favour of *renvoi* mentioned by Melchior, p. 245. The creditor of a debt which is governed by French law though the debtor is a domiciled German, assigned that debt to a third person without giving notice to the debtor, and the assignee brought an action against the debtor in a German court. Under German private international law the validity of an assignment depends on the law that governs the debt itself, here French law. According to French municipal law the assignment would be void because the *signification* to the debtor is wanting. But French private international law subjects the assignment of a debt to the law of the debtor's domicile, and under this (German) law the assignment is valid. It would seem unjustifiable for the German court to regard the assignment as void on the basis of French law when under the French conflict rule it turns out to be valid.

[4] Froland seems to have admitted *renvoi* in one case only, namely, where *renvoi* serves as a basis for excluding the application of an 'extraordinary' (anomalous) custom and deciding the case by the *Coutume de Paris*. See on all this: Niboyet, 21 *Rev. Darras* (1926) 15; *Traité* III. 438. Cf. Lewald, *Renvoi*, p. 19.

[5] 2 Curteis, 855.

the national law of the deceased.[1] In *Frere* v. *Frere*,[2] a British subject domiciled in Malta had made a will in England which was valid under English but not under Maltese law. The court held that Maltese law governed the case as *lex domicilii* and that Maltese private international law referred the case back to English law as the law of the place at which it was executed. A similar situation arose in the third clear case of *renvoi*, in *The Goods of Lacroix*, 1877.[3] Legal doctrine, however, paid no attention to these English decisions, nor for that matter to the striking German decision given by the Appeal Court of Luebeck in 1861.[4] No one seemed even to suspect that a problem existed.

182. Development since the Forgo case The discovery of the *renvoi* problem is due to the violent discussion which the French *Forgo* case[5] aroused. The case that produced such a storm was a simple succession suit of the same type as its English and German forerunners.

Forgo, an illegitimate child, Bavarian by nationality, domiciled in France, died intestate and left movable property in France. Who was to succeed? Under French private international law Bavarian law governed the case, and according to Bavarian municipal law certain illegitimate collaterals would have succeeded. Bavarian private international law,

[1] Mendelssohn-Bartholdy, *Renvoi*, p. 60 et seq., attempts to show that *Collier* v. *Rivaz* is no support for the *renvoi* doctrine. He argues that English law is indicated not by Belgian private international law but by Belgian municipal law, under which some of its rules apply only to Belgian nationals. He compares the situation with that where a municipal law prohibits or restricts the purchase of land by aliens. This comparison seems hardly justifiable. Where a country's law, for example Swedish law, forbids foreigners to acquire land in Sweden, the question 'which law is to be applied by the Swedish court' does not arise: it is Swedish law and can be nothing else. But when Belgian law provides that the Belgian form of wills is open only to Belgian nationals the question remains: 'What law is to be applied by a Belgian court to a will made by a foreigner?' And this question cannot be answered by Belgian *municipal* law; the answer must be sought in Belgian private international law.

[2] (1847) 5 Notes of Cases, 593. *Maltass* v. *Maltass* (1844), 1 Rob. 67, is remarkable only because it contains a reference by the judge to the decision *Collier* v. *Rivaz* and repeats the statement made there that 'law of domicile is ... the law which the country of domicile applies to the particular case under consideration'.

[3] (1877) 2 P.D. 94, 96, 97.

[4] Published in *Seuffert's Archiv*. 14, no. 107.

[5] The decision of the *Cour de Cassation* is to be found in *Dalloz Pér*. 1879, 1. 56. Cf. on this decision in particular Lainé, *Rev. Darras*, 1906, 615; Philonenko, *J. Clunet*, 1932, 281.

however, pointed to French law. The *Cour de Cassation* bowed to this remission and applied French law according to which those collaterals were not entitled to succeed and the whole of the property fell to the French state.

In spite of the weight of opposition brought to bear on the *renvoi* doctrine by many legal writers past and present in France, Italy, Holland, Germany, Switzerland, Belgium, Greece, Sweden, and the United States of America, and even by some eminent English authors,[1] the courts of most countries have adopted it, exceptions being those of Italy, Greece,[2] Sweden, Denmark, and Brazil.[3] True, the extent to which the courts recognize *renvoi* and the ways of dealing with it vary from country to country.

Thus the German Code, omitting transmission altogether, treats of remission for a limited schedule of cases only;[4] but the German courts admit both remission and transmission and have by analogy extended the *renvoi* area to cover all cases where it could conceivably apply.[5] The French courts have certainly adopted remission, apparently also transmission.[6] The same seems to be true of the Swiss Federal Court, which, however, has as yet had no occasion to decide the question definitively.[7] In Poland the Act concerning Private International Law, 1926, art. 36, adopted the *renvoi* doctrine in its widest possible form, i.e. remission and transmission wherever the Polish conflict rule points to the application of foreign law. The United States of America, though in principle hostile to the doctrine, have allowed it in two special cases,[8] namely, where title to land or the validity of a divorce decree is in question. In both cases there is remission or transmission, according to the circumstances. The two Geneva Conventions (1930, 1931) concerning bills of exchange, promissory notes, and cheques, provide that though the capacity of a person to bind himself by any of these documents depends on his national law, a *renvoi* (remission

---

[1] Particularly Dr. Cheshire, p. 88; Morris(–Dicey), p. 59. Adherents of the doctrine are, in England, Dicey and (with reservations, see *infra*, s. 191) Westlake; in the United States: Rabel, Griswold; in Germany: von Bar, Melchior, Raape, Nussbaum, Frankenstein, Enneccerus; in France: André Weiss, Lerebours-Pigeonnière, and Lepaulle; in Belgium: Poullet; in Italy: Fiore, Anzilotti; in Switzerland: Schnitzer.

[2] The new codes of both countries (Italy, 1938; Greece, 1940) reject the *renvoi* doctrine. The Greek courts, though not the Areopague, had accepted it; see Streït and Vallindas, I. 276–8.

[3] Rabel I. 82[52]

[4] German Introductory Law, art. 27.

[5] Decisions of the Supreme Court (Off. Coll.), 62, 404; 64, 393; 78, 50 and 236; 91, 139; 132, 416; 136, 365. See on this Melchior, 207 et seq.

[6] See Batiffol, *Traité*, pp. 323, 331.

[7] Schnitzer, *Handbuch d. IPR*, I. 189.

[8] Restatement, § 8.

or transmission, as the case may be) to any other law, such as the law of the domicile or the *lex loci actus*, must be followed. A similar rule is to be found in the Hague Convention on Conflict of Marriage Laws, 1902.[1]

183. The attitude of English courts

III. The attitude of the English courts is favourable to *renvoi*, although there are doubts as to the scope of the doctrine. It is certain that a great number of decisions have followed it, though sometimes only in *dicta*; in one case the judge indicated expressly that he would have preferred to reason without reference to the *renvoi* doctrine.[2] A single decision is irreconcilable with it. Finally, in many cases, particularly those dealing with commercial contracts, the problem of *renvoi* was not raised.

184. Cases where no renvoi was suggested

I. To begin with the last group: the cases in question are of various kinds.[3]

(*a*) First there are numerous cases where the court looked in the main to the express or implied intention of the contracting parties for aid in determining the proper law of a contract. It goes without saying that when such intention is directed towards the application of the law of the country *X*, it is not the conflict rules of that country, but its municipal law that is applicable. The same is true where in the absence of any real intention of the parties, the court applies the *lex loci solutionis* or the *lex loci contractus*, because such choice of law is based on the assumption that the parties would have chosen that law if they had considered the question. This explains the decisions in *Ruby Steamship Corporation* v. *Commercial Union Assurance Co.*,[4] *Broken Hill Proprietary Co.* v. *Latham*,[5] *Adelaide Electric Supply Co.* v. *Prudential Assurance Co.*,[6] and many other cases.[7]

---

[1] s. 1 of the Convention.

[2] *In re Annesley*, [1926] Ch. 692 (*per* Russell, J.).

[3] Mendelssohn-Barthody's study of English decisions unfortunately does not distinguish between two separate problems. First: If the law of domicile is decisive, what law decides where the domicile lies ? Second: Is the law of domicile decisive ? and, if not, what other law is ? Only on the second question does the *renvoi* problem arise. The first question (see *supra*, s. 131 (2)) has nothing to do with *renvoi*. Therefore cases like *Hamilton* v. *Dallas* (1875), 1 Ch. D. 257; *Wahl* v. *Att.-Gen.* (1932), 147 L.T. 382 are irrelevant here.

[4] 18 Aspinall's Mar. C. (1933) 445.

[5] [1933] 1 Ch. 373.   [6] [1934] A.C. 122.

[7] Quoted by Mendelssohn-Bartholdy, 44 et seq. This eminent jurist seems

(b) There is a rule of English law to the effect that a contract is void if it is illegal and void either under the *lex loci solutionis* or (perhaps) under the *lex loci contractus*.[1] It cannot be doubted that this means the municipal law of the place of performance or the place of contracting, not their conflict rules. This explains decisions like *The Torni*[2] or *De Béeche* v. *South American Stores*.[3]

(c) Other cases in which the *renvoi* question was not discussed in court may be explained by the consideration that English courts treat the content of foreign (municipal or private international) law as a fact, not as law. Thus where the parties do not direct the attention of the court to the conflict rules of the foreign legal system which has to be applied the court presumes that those conflict rules are the same as the English conflict rules. No argument against *renvoi* can be derived from this.

2. Decisions *hostile* to the *renvoi* doctrine. There is only one and that an early case, viz. *Bremer* v. *Freeman*,[4] which concerns the validity of a will. According to the English rule prevailing at that time (1857) the law of the domicile of the deceased governed the case; the Privy Council applied the municipal law of the domicile (French internal law) without accepting the *renvoi* from French private international law to the *lex loci actus*. The decision was rejected by later decisions beginning with *In the Goods of Lacroix*, 1877.[5] Some authors quote the case of *Hamilton* v. *Dallas*[6] as following *Bremer* v. *Freeman* in its rejection of *renvoi*; this, however, is not correct; *Hamilton* v. *Dallas* merely deals with the question of determination of domicile.

185.
Bremer v. Freeman

to have taken the view that if the *renvoi* doctrine is accepted at all, it should apply even to those cases where the applicable law is determined by the choice of the parties. That this was his opinion emerges from his observations on *The Adriatic*, [1931] P. 241; cf. p. 53 of his article, n. 1.

1 See *infra*, s. 425.
2 [1932] P. 27 and 78.
3 [1935] A.C. 148.
4 (1857), 10 Moore, P.C. 306, 359, 374. Some authors, however, think that *Bremer* v. *Freeman* is compatible with the doctrine of *renvoi*, or even that it supports this doctrine (?). Cf. on this point: Schreiber, 31 *Harv. L.R.* 542, n. 31.
5 (1877) 2 P.D. 94, 96, 97. See *infra*, s. 187.
6 (1875) 1 Ch. D. 257. See *supra*, p. 192, n. 3.

186. *Renvoi* cases: (a) transmission

3. Decisions *accepting* the *renvoi* doctrine, though in some cases merely by *dicta*. These are:

(*a*) two clear cases of *transmission*.

(α) *In re Achillopoulos*.[1] The deceased was a Greek subject who at the time of his death was possibly domiciled in Egypt. The court applied Greek municipal law to the succession because—if the domicile was in Egypt—Egyptian private international law had to be consulted, and this pointed to Greek law.

(β) In *re Trufort*.[2] Here the deceased had been a Swiss citizen domiciled in France. According to English law the succession to his movables was governed by French law, which, however, transmitted the case to the national (i.e. Swiss) law.

True, the court did not expressly pronounce that Swiss law was applicable, but hinted at it by stating that the Swiss courts were 'the proper and competent tribunals to decide. . . .' The case is one of those where conflict of jurisdictions and conflict of substantive laws are not clearly distinguished from each other.

187. (b) remission

(*b*) There are many more cases in which English courts recognize *remission*. They may be divided into two groups.

(i) The first group, beginning 1841, consists of those decisions in which the remission to English law results simply in the application of English municipal law, no further *renvoi* being considered. It is submitted that the following four decisions belong to this group: *Collier* v. *Rivaz*,[3] *Frere* v. *Frere*,[4] *Laneuville* v. *Anderson*,[5] and *In the Goods of Lacroix*.[6] All of them deal with wills made outside England and Wales in English form, and in all the *renvoi* led to affirmation of validity. In some other cases the *renvoi* doctrine was approved (partly by *obiter dicta*): for example, in *Maltas* v. *Maltas*,[7] in *Crookenden* v.

---

[1] [1928] 1 Ch. 433, 443 (*per* Tomlin, J.). Mendelssohn-Bartholdy, in his review of the various cases, does not deal with this case.

[2] (1887) 36 Ch. D. 600.

[3] (1841) 2 Curt. 855 (*per* Sir H. Jenner, P.).

[4] (1847) 5 Notes of Cas. 593 (*per eundem jud.*).

[5] (1860) 2 Sw. & Tr. 24, 38.

[6] (1877) 2 P.D. 94, 96, 97 (*per* Sir P. Hannen, P.).

[7] (1844) 1 Rob. 67.

Fuller,[1] in *Re Johnson*,[2] and in particular by Scrutton, L.J., in a dissenting judgment in *Casdagli* v. *Casdagli*.[3]

(ii) A second group of cases, beginning 1926, shows **188. Cases** *of double* the *renvoi* doctrine in a 'more refined form'.[4] The remis- *renvoi* sion to English law does not simply mean remission to English *municipal* law, but possibly remission to English *conflict rules* resulting in a second remission, a *double renvoi* to the same foreign law as before. Whether the *renvoi* is a simple or a *double renvoi* does not depend on English conflict rules but on the foreign conflict rule to be applied by the English court. This somewhat complicated theory—it has been called the *ping-pong* doctrine[5]— merely carries to its logical conclusion a principle which Sir H. Jenner, P., enunciated in *Collier* v. *Rivaz*[6] and which has since been repeated by a great number of other judges,[7] i.e. the rule that a judge applying foreign law . . . must 'consider himself sitting in the foreign country'. It results from this that he must apply the foreign conflict rules, including the *renvoi* rules which the foreign court would apply. The way in which this system of *renvoi* works is best seen by contrasting the two decisions *In re Annesley*[8] and *In re Ross*.[9] In the first case the testatrix, a British subject domiciled in France, had disposed by will of the whole of her property, leaving nothing to her son. Under English law this would be valid, while under French law her power of disposition was restricted to one-third of her property.[10] Russell, J., started from the law of domicile (French law), which remitted back to English law; but as a French court recognizes the doctrine of *renvoi* it would accept a re-remission from English to French law and

[1] (1859) 1 Sw. & Tr. 441, 460.

[2] [1903] 1 Ch. 821, 827. See *supra*, s. 129. It may be mentioned that here the court for the first time made use of the term *renvoi* and expressed its view that the doctrine of *renvoi* does not result in a *circulus inextricabilis*, as its opponents had believed. [3] [1918] P. 89, 111.

[4] (Dicey-)Morris, p. 51, speaks of 'the total renvoi theory').

[5] By J. D. Falconbridge. [6] Curt. 855.

[7] Not only by English, but also by continental judges. See, for example, the reasoning of the Appeal Court of Lübeck, 1861, *Seuffert's Archiv*. 14, no. 107, or of the German Supreme Court, *Offic. Coll*. 62, 404; 64, 393; 91, 141.

[8] [1926] Ch. 692. See decision Bentwich, 4 *Rabel's Z.*, 433.

[9] [1930] 1 Ch. 377. [10] *Code Civil*, art. 913.

therefore apply French municipal law. This, then, resulted in the application of French law by the English court. In the second case, *In re Ross*, the legal situation was the same except that here the testatrix was domiciled in Italy (not in France): as Italian courts pay no attention to foreign conflict rules, and therefore do not allow *renvoi* from foreign law to Italian law, they would be bound by their own conflict rule to apply English municipal law, and that was what the English court did.[1] In two other cases, *In re Askew*[2] and *Collins* v. *Att.-Gen.*,[3] the question was whether an illegitimate child, conceived in adultery, had been validly legitimated by the subsequent marriage of its parents. This would be answered in the negative by English, in the affirmative by German municipal law. The domicile to which the English conflict rule referred was German. According to German private international law the national (English) law was decisive, but in view of the English conflict rule German courts would be bound[4] to accept the (second) *renvoi* from English to German law, and consequently to apply German municipal law. This course was followed by the two English decisions. The decision *In re Askew*, however, introduced a new—though hardly convincing—argument in favour of *renvoi* in cases of foreign domicile, viz. that English law refers to the domiciliary law merely for the purpose of ascertaining whether a person has 'acquired rights' under that law, in which case the English court is bound to recognize such rights.[5] Further cases in which the court followed the decisions in *Re Annesley* and *Re Ross* without adding new arguments are *Re O'Keefe*,[6] *Jaber Elias Kotia* v. *Katr Bind Jiryes Nahas*,[7] and *Re The Duke of Wellington*.[8]

---

[1] *Per* Luxmoore, J.

[2] [1930] 2 Ch. 259 (*per* Maugham, J.).

[3] (1931) 145 L.T. 551.

[4] According to the German *renvoi* provision in art. 27 Introd. Law.

[5] See on this Falconbridge, 17 *Can. Bar Rev.* 386. On the exception to be taken to the doctrine of acquired rights, see *supra*, s. 2.

[6] [1940] Ch. 124.

[7] [1941] A.C. (P.C.) 403, 413. (On this decision see, however, Falconbridge, 214–22.) It is therefore no exaggeration to speak with Dicey(–Morris), p. 51, of an 'unbroken catena of English authority'. (*Contra*: Mendelssohn-Bartholdy, 77.)

[8] [1947] Ch. 506. (The decision of the Court of Appeal, [1948] Ch. 118, does

189.
Summary

To sum up: A study of English cases seems to show beyond doubt the existence of the following two rules:

1. No *renvoi* is recognized where in making a contract the parties have expressly or by implication agreed to subject their contract to a certain legal system, or where the court applies the *lex loci actus* or *solutionis* as corresponding to the assumed intention of the parties.

2. *Renvoi* is recognized where the formal or intrinsic validity of a will or of a legitimation by subsequent marriage is at issue, irrespective of whether the *renvoi* leads from the law of the domicile or from the *lex situs* to the national law of the party concerned or to the *lex loci actus*. The meaning of *renvoi* has varied. In the earlier cases it meant simply one single remission to the municipal law of the forum or one single transmission to the municipal law of a third country. In the cases since 1926 it includes a second remission (or transmission) if this leads to the law which the foreign court would have applied. This interpretation of *renvoi* has apparently replaced that which prevailed earlier.

There remains the problem of filling in the *lacunae*, for example, in cases of validity of marriage, of adoption, or of transfer of property *inter vivos*. In particular, should there be a single *renvoi* in these cases, or a repeated (double, treble) *renvoi*? Should remission and transmission cases be treated alike? The answers depend largely on the general view taken of the whole doctrine and of its various types.

IV. The objections which have been raised to the conception of *renvoi* as a whole are mainly the following:

190. Objections raised to the *renvoi* doctrine

1. It has been said that the *renvoi* doctrine is illogical and 'repugnant to the nature and purpose of rules for the choice of law'.[1] In fact, the meaning of conflict rules has been altered since 1841. Instead of stating without reserve which law is applicable to a given set of facts, the *renvoi* doctrine makes such statement dependent on the view

not deal with this problem.) See J. H. C. Morris's criticism, 64 *L.Q.R.* (1948), 264–8, and R. Jennings, ibid., 331–3.

[1] Cheshire, p. 92.

held on this question by the foreign law *to which it points*. It has been argued that the abandonment of the carefully devised conflict rules of this country merely because 'some foreign country prefers a different rule' is a 'self-effacement', which though it may be 'a fine moral gesture' is not to be recommended to a judge whose duty it is to administer the law of his country.[1] The answer to this would be that the judge does not consider the conflict rules of 'some' foreign country but those of the country to which his conflict rule points. It is his own conflict rule which he applies in the first place. Only he does not stop there.

2. It has been said that the doctrine of *renvoi* is uncertain, ambiguous, and vacillating. True, it has been developed more actively in this country than elsewhere, and its application to various branches of law is not yet quite settled. But if a certain vagueness of outline were a well-founded objection to legal principles and if we lawyers were to demand inflexible precision we should probably find a more congenial sphere in mathematics.

3. It has been said that the doctrine of *renvoi* is inconvenient from a practical point of view, because it obliges the court to study foreign private international law and this is believed to be more difficult than the investigation of foreign municipal law. This may be true in some cases. But if the court is unable to ascertain the conflict rule of the foreign law it applies the English conflict rule on the presumption that foreign law is the same as English law.[2]

191. The doctrine of 'désistement' **4.** Finally, the conception of *renvoi* has been declared to be superfluous. In particular Westlake and von Bar thought that the desired result might be obtained in another way, viz. by their theory of *désistement*:[3] if the English conflict rule, for example, leads to French law as the law of domicile, it is French municipal law that is hereby indicated; but no municipal law ought to be applied —this is Westlake's starting point—to cases for which it

---

[1] Cheshire (2nd edition), p. 59.
[2] See *infra*, s. 209.
[3] 18 *Annuaire* (1900), 35, 41. See on this doctrine, Lewald, *Renvoi*, 85 et seq.; Lorenzen, *Select. Articles*, 98.

is not intended. It is solely for this reason that the English court examines the French conflict rule. As this rule shows that French municipal law is intended to govern the status of French nationals only, the English court fills in the gap by applying its own municipal law. 'La loi (française) ne renvoie pas, elle s'abstient, elle se désinté-resse.' This theory, which in its final effect leads to remission, but never to transmission, is founded on the idea that it is only for France to determine the areas of applica-tion of its municipal law, and it has even been said that the application of French law in the teeth of French law would involve an infringement of French sovereignty. With due respect to the two great jurists I have named it is submitted that this view is not tenable. No state has ever taken exception to the adoption of its entire law by a foreign state; Switzerland was pleased, not shocked, by the Turkish adoption of the Swiss Civil Code. Why, then, should any state object to the application of some parts of its municipal law to cases in which its own courts refrain from applying it?

V. *The reasons for renvoi.* The very fact that in nearly all European countries the courts are in favour of *renvoi* in one form or another suggests that the doctrine has its justification and practical advantages. What are these? And what consequently are the limits within which it is proper to apply it?

192. The reasons for renvoi

The reasons for its application given in most European decisions are not convincing; they are not even reasons. It is argued that every rule of private international law providing for the application of foreign law points to the foreign law 'in its totality', to the whole of the foreign law'; it intends the foreign law to be applied 'dans son ensemble'; it is a *Gesamtverweisung*. The true reason for this at first sight startling interpretation of conflict rules is alluded to in another formula, and this too is to be found in both continental and English decisions: the court, so runs the formula, wishes to decide the case by the same rules as the foreign court would apply if it were seized of the matter. English courts have even evolved a curious fictitious formula to express this: the judges say they wish to give judgment *as if* they were sitting as judges in the foreign country. 'I consider myself sitting in Belgium', said Sir H. Jenner, P., in *Collier* v. *Rivaz*,[1] when he had to apply Belgian law. It is easy to ridicule this phrase. But setting aside the rather extravagant picture,[2] its meaning is plain: the English court intends to decide the case exactly as the foreign court would decide it if it were seized with the case, if it had jurisdiction, and if it had to apply English rules of procedure and of public policy.

It must, however, be stressed that this or a similar formula, though common to decisions of several countries, has for the most part not been carried to its logical conclusion. German and French courts undertake to put it into practice, but stop after the first remission; before 1926 the attitude of English courts was the same. A German court, for example, seized of a suit on succession to the property of a Norwegian subject domiciled in Germany looks quite correctly to the Norwegian conflict rule; but having ascertained that this rule refers back to the law of the domicile of the deceased (German law) it simply applies German municipal law without troubling to consider whether the Norwegian court would not by a converse *renvoi* from German to Norwegian law have applied the latter.

This continental and early English method of stopping half-way has two advantages: it never leads to an eternal to and fro, to that disturbing situation which opponents of the *renvoi* doctrine have thought to be inevitably connected with it.[3] Secondly, it leads (in the case of remission) to the application of the court's own municipal law. That this is a sound result where no harmony

---

[1] Curt. 855, 863.

[2] of an English judge sitting in a foreign country without knowing the language or the law prevailing there, dependent on what expert witnesses tell him, and, if they do not succeed in convincing him, prepared at any moment to inform the parties that he presumes the law to be the same as English law.

[3] This situation has often been compared with a *perpetuum mobile*, or international lawn tennis. It has been called a 'logical cabinet of mirrors', a 'process of ebb and flow', &c.

of decisions can be obtained will be shown below (s. 194). But when this method is adopted, it cannot be said with truth that the court is deciding the case 'as the foreign court would decide it'.

The English courts since *In re Annesley*[1] take that formula more seriously; they make a point of putting it into full practice. This method helps to establish the desired harmony of decisions,[2] at any rate between two, in the case of transmission even between three countries.[3] Its weak point is that it would not work if the other country or countries concerned were to adopt the same method. In that case an endless oscillation, or in some cases of transmission an endless rotation, would take place. The English and the foreign judge would bow to each other, each saying to all eternity 'Non monsieur, à vous l'honneur'.[4] In an old German comedy *Die deutschen Kleinstädter*, by Kotzebue, some over-polite provincials stand before an open door bowing and inviting each other to take precedence—until the curtain falls, and when the curtain rises for the next act they are still standing in the same place. It is very fortunate for the English courts that there is no country outside the British Commonwealth, either on the European continent or in America, Asia, or Africa, that has adopted the English system of (double) *renvoi*; and it is to be expected—and hoped—that the English rule will remain strictly insular. True, one must suppose that other than English courts within the Empire might follow the English rule. But as these courts have mostly adopted English private international law, apart from statutory law, particularly the English principle of testing status, marriage, divorce, and succession to movables by domicile, a *renvoi* from one of them to English law will be extremely rare. Should, however, the English *renvoi* system become universal it would break down entirely and

---

[1] [1926] Ch. 692.

[2] See *supra*, ss. 4, 15.

[3] For example, in *Re Achillopoulos*, [1928] 1 Ch. 433, 443, the courts of the three countries Egypt, Greece, and England would apply the same (Greek) municipal law.

[4] This attitude of the officers in the battle of Fontenoy is recalled by Maugham, J., [1930] 2 Ch. 267.

result in an endless circle. In such case[1] the simple *renvoi* leading to the application of the court's own (municipal) law would be justified.[2] For the time being the English solution works well.

193. Harmony of decisions

1. Thus the first and main justification of *renvoi* is to be found in the fact that in certain cases it helps to attain the chief aim of private international law: harmony of decisions irrespective of where the judicial proceedings take place. To be more exact, the cases in which the desired harmony is reached by application of any form of *renvoi* are the following:

(*a*) A remission is sound where only one of the two legal systems involved recognizes *renvoi*, while the other rejects it.

Example: the French court, owing to its conflict rule, is bound to apply Italian law as the *lex situs* to immovables situate in Italy and left by a Frenchman; under the Italian conflict rule the national law of the deceased governs the case. The French court accepts the *renvoi* to its own law; the Italian court if seized of the matter would reject any *renvoi* from French to Italian law. Consequently both countries apply French law.

(*b*) A remission is also sound, as previously explained, where one of the two countries concerned allows *renvoi* as understood on the continent (one single *renvoi*), while the other adopts *double renvoi* (England).

(*c*) A transmission to a third country produces harmony of decisions between the three countries only where the courts of the two legal systems between which the transmission is at issue would apply the same municipal law if called upon to decide the case.

A Dutch national domiciled in Italy dies, and the English court has

[1] *Example:* An English couple is domiciled in Quebec; the wife obtains a judicial separation in Quebec and returns to her pre-matrimonial English domicile. Then she dies intestate leaving movables in England. Under English law the succession to her movable property is regulated by the law of her domicile, and according to English law her domicile is Quebec. But an English court will decide 'as if sitting in Quebec', whereas under the private international law of Quebec English law applies, since in Canada a wife who has obtained a judicial separation can acquire a domicile of her own. Hence the Quebec court (if seized of the question) would 'regard itself sitting in England' and apply the law which the English court would apply (see W. S. Johnson, *Conflict of Laws*, I. 11, 144; *Quebec Code*, art. 206, 207). It seems reasonable to assume that in such a case the English court would apply English law.

[2] See *infra*, s. 194.

to decide on the succession to his London bank account. Here it is sound
to apply Dutch law, as would be done both by the Italian and the Dutch
courts. It may be doubtful whether transmission should be admitted if
the two foreign systems concerned are not in agreement. Take a Danish
national domiciled in Italy. The English conflict rule on succession points
to Italian law; the Italian conflict rule transmits the case to Danish law;
but the Danish conflict rule declares Italian law (as the law of the deceased's
domicile) to be applicable—neither Italy nor Denmark recognizes any
renvoi. Probably the English court would even then accept the transmission
from Italy to Denmark and apply Danish municipal law, because that is
what the Italian court would do. But it is submitted with great hesitation
that in such case it would be preferable to decline transmission. As no
harmony can be attained between an Italian and a Danish judgment, there
is no material reason why the English court should abandon its conflict
rule which is in perfect agreement with the Danish conflict rule.

2. Where uniformity of decision cannot be reached, the *renvoi* is nevertheless satisfactory in those cases where it leads to the application by the court of its own municipal law. This is the true reason why all continental systems which allow *renvoi* call a halt as soon as they arrive at their own law. We have spoken before[1] of the tendency of the courts of all countries to apply their own law if possible, since that is the law they know. It is not true, as has sometimes been said, that *renvoi* to the judge's own law serves merely to protect the lazy judge. A conscientious judge will be particularly disinclined to apply a foreign law, where he has to depend mainly on foreign experts. 'Such evidence from learned foreigners', said Lord Cranworth once,[2] 'is in general far from satisfactory, but it often happens that no better evidence can be obtained, and then the courts here must ascertain, from conflicting testimony, as well as they can, what the law is on which they must act.' If there were no *renvoi* a German judge, for example, when dealing with the succession to the property of an Argentine subject domiciled in Germany, would have to apply Argentine law, which he does not know, while the Argentine court would in the same case be bound to apply German law and to delve deeply into the mysteries of the German Civil Code. This result seems absurd.

194. Application of domestic law

[1] pp. 17–18.
[2] *Doglioni* v. *Crispin* (1866), L.R. 1 H.L. 301 at p. 314.

195. *Favor testamentarius ?* **3.** Is there a third group of cases where a *renvoi* may be justifiable ?[1] Many of the decisions mentioned above seem to suggest that the courts have made use of *renvoi* in order to uphold a will which would be void under the foreign municipal law to which the English conflict rule points, but valid under the municipal law that under the foreign conflict rule would govern the case. There is no doubt that sometimes either the *favor testamentarius* or the principle 'res magis valeat quam pereat' has in history influenced even the rules of private international law.[2] But it would be difficult to say that in fact either of these conceptions has formed the *ratio decidendi* of any admission of *renvoi* or that it was any more than an idea at the back of the judge's mind.[3] Even *de lege ferenda* it would be dangerous to assign to these principles a higher place than they occupy now as mere rules of construction of wills or other acts-in law. Where parties are allowed to choose the law to which they subject their acts—as is the case in contracts—the application of that law which secures the validity of their act is certainly covered by the presumptive intention of the contracting parties. But where the intention of the parties forms no point of contact in private international law, as in the case of the making or revocation of wills, it would seem unjust to allow the *favor* principle to work.[4]

---

[1] Or conversely, are there cases in which a *renvoi* though justifiable under (1) or (2) should not be applied ?

[2] Example, the Prussian Code of 1794, see *supra*, s. 28.

[3] Cf. in particular *In re Annesley*, [1926] Ch. 692, where Russell, J., put into practice the rule of double *renvoi* though this led to invalidating parts of the will, while if a single *renvoi* had been applied the will would have been wholly valid.

[4] In *Velasco* v. *Coney*, [1934] P. 143, 148, the problem was whether the revocation of a will was to be governed by English law, under which it was void, or by Italian law under which it was valid. The court held that Italian law should apply (it was no case of *renvoi*) and gave as one reason that 'the court leans always towards giving effect to the intention of the testator'. This, however, was a dictum, and one open to objection.

BIBLIOGRAPHY

CHESHIRE, 85–128. DICEY(–MORRIS), 47–61. RABEL I. 70–83. GOODRICH, 12–14. KAHN, *Abhandl*, I. 7, 124. BUZZATI, *Il rinvio* (1898). E. POTU, *La question du renvoi* (1913). H. LEWALD, 'La théorie du renvoi', 29 *Rec.* (1929 IV), 519. R. DE NOVA, 30 *Rivista d. dir. internaz.* (1938), 388, and in the *Raape-Festschrift* (1948).

LEPAULLE, *J. Clunet*, 1936, 284–96; *Droit internat. privé* 172 et seq. J. P. BATE, *Notes on the Doctrine of Renvoi*, 1904. ABBOT, 24 *L.Q.R.* (1908) 133. LORENZEN, *Selected Articles* pp. 19–79. COOK, *Logical and Legal Bases* 239–51. BATIFFOL, *Traité* 320–36. SCHREIBER, 31 *Harv. L.R.* (1918) 523. N. BENTWICH, in *Rabel's Z.*, 4, 433; 14 Canad. Bar R. (1936) 379. BATES, 16 *Cornell L.Q.* (1931) 311. FALCONBRIDGE, *Essays*, 109–222. A. MENDELSSOHN-BARTHOLDY, *Renvoi in Modern English Law* (ed. by Dr. Cheshire) 1937. DOBRIN, 15 *Brit.Y.B.* 1934, 36 et seq. GRISWOLD, 51 *Harv. L.R.* 1165. PLAISANT, *Conflits dans les Traités*, 61 et seq. NIBOYET, *Traité* III 435–87. ARMINJON I. 352–84. Further references in Rabel I 70, 71 n. 6.

CHAPTER XVI

THE APPLICATION OF FOREIGN CONFLICT RULES APART FROM RENVOI

196. 'Preliminary' question: the problem

I. The so-called 'preliminary question', better called 'incidental question'.

The question whether *renvoi* takes place arises *before* the judge has ascertained which law is to apply to the case before him. It forms part of the quest for the applicable law. Once the court—either by way of *renvoi* or without it—has determined which municipal law is applicable, there is no room for any further *renvoi*. There are however situations in which a question very similar to the *renvoi* problem presents itself *after* the determination of the applicable law, a question *within* the domain of interpretation of the foreign municipal law governing the case.

Example: A Greek subject domiciled in Greece dies intestate leaving movable property in England. There is no doubt that the English court must, both by English and Greek conflict rules, apply Greek municipal law, and no *renvoi* comes into consideration. Under Greek succession law a certain part of the property goes to the deceased's 'wife'. Is the woman *W* his wife in the eye of the English court? The answer may depend on whether the court applies its own or the Greek conflict rules on marriage. Suppose, for example, that a marriage between the deceased and *W* was celebrated in England before a registrar without any religious ceremony. If the English conflict rule applies, under which the form of marriage is governed by the *lex loci actus*, English municipal law obtains, and the marriage is valid. If, however, the Greek conflict rule is decisive the national law of the parties (Greek law) predominates: the marriage is void. The question of the validity of the marriage arises in such case only incidentally, namely, within a litigation on succession, and as succession is governed by Greek law, the English court must be justified in ignoring its own and applying the Greek conflict rule, thus denying *W*'s right to succeed to the property.

And indeed, this would be to follow the line taken by English courts in *renvoi* questions: the court is anxious to decide the suit exactly as the Greek court would decide it.

We are faced with the same problem when the 'principal' question is not one of succession but one of legitimacy or legitimation or of marriage or adoption, and when the 'incidental question'[1] is not concerned with the validity of marriage, but with an adoption or a legitimation. Examples:

(a) The legitimacy of a child depends on the validity **197.** of a marriage between its parents. If under the conflict **Examples** rule of the English forum the legitimacy is governed by the law of country X, it is the conflict rule of country X which will decide what law governs the question of the validity of the marriage.[2]

(b) Under many laws (for example, French and German law) an adoption (of C by A) is valid only if the adopter A has no legitimate issue of his own. Suppose the English court has to adjudicate on the validity of an adoption. Then the incidental question may be: is a given person B the legitimate child of the adopter A? The answer is to be found through the conflict rule of the legal system that governs the adoption, and not through the English conflict rule.

(c) The validity of a marriage between A and B, which under the conflict rule of the English forum is subject to the domiciliary law of country X, may depend on the nullity of a previous marriage concluded between A and C. Again, the conflict rule of X will decide under which municipal law the marriage A-C is to be examined.

(d) Creditor C and debtor D are both Frenchmen resident in England; their contract was made in England and is to be performed here. The parties did not determine the law governing the contract. An Italian friend S of the debtor's, living in Italy, later guarantees the debt, and the contract of suretyship is subject to Italian law. When the debt falls due, C brings an action against the surety S in an English court (S is present in England). The defendant argues that his obligation depends on the validity of the principal debt, that according to the *lex fori*

---

[1] The term 'incidental question' is preferable to the usual term 'preliminary question' (*Vorfrage, question préalable*), as it is, so to speak, 'postliminary': it arises only after the law applicable to the principal question has been ascertained.

[2] *Contra* (as it seems): *Shaw* v. *Gould* (1865), L.R. 1 Eq. 247; (1868) L.R. 3 H.L. 55, which decision will be examined *infra*, s. 364. See also Cheshire, 501 et seq.

the principal debt is governed by English municipal law (as this is the *lex loci actus et solutionis*), and that under English law the contract is void, for example, for lack of consideration. The plaintiff, on the other hand, argues that as the suretyship contract is governed by Italian law, the English court should consider itself 'sitting in Italy'—to use Sir Herbert Jenner's phrase in *Collier* v. *Rivaz*[1]—and that under the Italian conflict rule the effects of the principal obligation are determined by the national law of the contracting parties provided both belong to the same nation; therefore French law should apply, under which the lack of consideration is immaterial. Is the English or the Italian conflict rule called upon to decide the incidental point of the validity of the principal obligation? It seems safe to assume that the Italian rule is decisive, and that the plaintiff's argument is sound.

(*e*) It may happen that the answer to the main question depends not on one but on two or more 'incidental' questions. *A* dies intestate, and *S* claims a right to succession as his legitimate son; his legitimacy may depend on the validity of a marriage between his parents, and the validity of this marriage may be conditioned by the nullity or a previous marriage concluded by his father with a third person. The main question concerns succession; it is answered according to the English conflict rule by the domiciliary law of the deceased, say the law of country *X*. All the incidental questions arising within the field of the municipal law of *X* will probably be answered by the English court in the same way in which the court of *X* would decide them, and therefore not according to English conflict rules.

198. Solution   If the opinion expressed here is correct the general rule may be formulated in this way: Not the conflict rules of the forum, but the conflict rules contained in that legal system which governs the 'principal' question are to be applied to all incidental questions on which the answer to the principal question depends. The justification of this rule—as in the case of *renvoi*—lies in the fact that it helps to a certain degree to bring about harmony of

[1] (1841), 2 Curt. 855. See *supra*, s. 188.

decisions as between the courts of the forum and the courts of one or more foreign countries.

Such *international harmony* is, however, dearly bought at the price of *internal dissonance*. The question whether *W* is the lawful wife of *H* can be raised in the English court in very varied connexions. *H* may bring proceedings for the declaration of nullity of his marriage: then the court will apply the law of his domicile at the time of his marriage, say, Danish law. Or the court may be called upon to decide on a claim of his widow *W* on succession to movables: then the case is governed by the law of *H*'s last domicile, say France, and the English court has to consider (as if it were a French court) whether the French conflict rule on marriage leads to a municipal law that regards the marriage as valid; and so forth. Thus it happens that the same question (of validity of a particular marriage) might be answered in one way to-day, and in a different way to-morrow. It must be stressed, however, that a similar lack of harmony obtains in cases of purely municipal law. If, for example, a Muhammedan couple domiciled in England lives in polygamous marriage, this will not be recognized as a 'marriage' when divorce proceedings are brought, but it will probably be regarded as marriage when the legitimacy of children or rights of succession are in issue.[1]

199. Objections

Undoubtedly, however, there are cases in which such sacrifice of internal harmony to international harmony becomes intolerable. Suppose an Italian couple (Andrea and Berta) validly married under all laws concerned is domiciled in England. Berta obtains from the English court a decree of divorce under English law on the ground of her husband's adultery. Then both parties marry again in England. Later Andrea goes with his second wife (Carlotta) to Italy, acquires a domicile there, and dies intestate leaving movable property in England. The English court entertains an action concerning the distribution of this property. Under the English conflict rule (and, for that matter, also under the Italian conflict rule) Italian municipal law applies. According to this law,

200. Exceptional cases

[1] See *supra*, s. 175.

the surviving spouse (if the parents of the deceased are alive) can claim the third part of the property. The question whether Berta or Carlotta or neither is the 'surviving wife of the deceased' is incidental, the principal question being the distribution of the deceased's property. If the English court were to decide the case exactly as the Italian court would do if seized of the matter, its reasoning would run as follows: Italian law does not recognize divorce decrees between Italian subjects; therefore Berta remained Andrea's wife until his death; the marriage to Carlotta was void; the fact that Berta had brought divorce proceedings and married again (validly under English, though not under Italian law) does not deprive her of her one-third of Andrea's estate.[1] It must be doubted whether such reasoning would be adopted by the forum. An English court cannot be expected to treat a marriage as existing in spite of a divorce decree which it has itself pronounced and which was entirely correct.[2] It is therefore submitted that the English court should apply the conflict rule of the (English) forum and disregard the (Italian) conflict rules of the legal system governing the principal question. The non-recognition of the English divorce decree by Italian courts would therefore not concern the English court, which will give judgment for Carlotta.[3]

201. Withdrawal of the domestic conflict rule in favour of *lex situs* II. Another case where the private international law of the forum gives way to foreign private international law is to be found in some continental laws and in two of the Hague Conventions.[4] There we find self-effacement in favour of the *lex situs* of immovables. Under English

---

[1] Art. 585 of the *codice civile* does not apply. It runs: 'The rights of succession granted to the surviving spouse do not belong to a spouse against whom the deceased has obtained a decree of judicial separation'. Even an application by way of analogy is not admissible, since it was not the deceased who obtained the divorce decree against Berta, but Berta who obtained it against him.

[2] Cf. the decision of the German Supreme Court in *Jur. W.*, 1912, 642. This decision is based on the conception of *ordre public*. See Lewald, 118; Melchior, 250; Wengler, 225.

[3] See on the English decision in *Shaw* v. *Gould* (1868), L.R. 3 H.L. 55, *infra*, s. 364.

[4] Hague Convention on Conflict Rules concerned with Guardianship, 1902, art. 6, § 2; Hague Convention concerning the Effects of Marriage, 1905, art. 7.

private international law, as will be seen later, the succession upon death is governed by the personal law (domicile law) of the deceased with regard to his movable property only; the succession to his immovables is subject to the *lex situs*. Many continental states, such as Germany, Poland, Switzerland, Italy, Spain, Portugal, and the Scandinavian states, have declined to take this view and have carried out to the full the Roman law conception of 'universal succession' by subjecting succession on death to one law (either the *lex domicilii* or the *lex patriae*) for movables and immovables alike. Some of them, for example Italy, make a point of putting their conflict rule into practice regardless of any provision of the *lex situs*.[1] If the deceased Italian citizen has left a piece of land in England, the Italian courts, disregarding English law, will consider nothing but Italian inheritance law, powerless though they are to enforce their order. On the other hand, some continental laws, particularly German law, though not adopting the English principle, make a remarkable concession to it.[2] Where according to the *lex situs* the succession to land as distinct from the succession to movables is governed by the *lex situs*, the German law abandons its own principle and applies the law of succession prevailing at the place where the immovable is situate. If, for example, a domiciled German subject leaves land in England the German court deals with the succession to it according to English law.

English law has, of course, no rule corresponding to the German one. It does not need it.

[1] At least this is the point of view of Italian courts (since 1905). See Lewald, *Successions*, 29–31.

[2] German Introduct. Law, art. 28. Cf. Polish Statute on Private International Law, 1926, art. 16.

BIBLIOGRAPHY

MELCHIOR, *Grundlagen*, 245. WENGLER, in *Rabel's Z.*, 8 (1934) 148. DICEY-MORRIS, pp. 73–6. MAURY, *Règles générales* (1930) 230. RAAPE, 'Les rapports juridiques entre parents et enfants', 50 *Rec.* (1934 IV) 485. A. H. ROBERTSON, 55 *L.Q.R.* (1939) 565. ROBERTSON, *Characterization in the Conflict of Laws* (1940) 135. FALCONBRIDGE, 165. BRESLAUER, *Priv. Intern. Law of Succession* (1937), p. 18. NIBOYET, *Traité* III 388–91.

CHAPTER XVII

THE APPLICATION OF FOREIGN MUNICIPAL LAW

202. Cases where domestic and foreign law lead to the same result

I. The first task of the court is to decide what law is applicable: its own municipal law or a foreign law, and in the latter case what foreign law. It often happens that the law of the forum and the foreign laws concerned all lead to the same decision, either because their provisions are identical or because the differences between them have no bearing on the question at issue.

Example: Under one of the laws the plaintiff's claim is well-founded on the basis of a valid contract, while the other law considers the contract void but the plaintiff's action justified by the defendant's unjust enrichment. In such cases the court may take its decision without answering the question which law is applicable,[1] thus being spared the investigation of a possibly thorny problem. This fairly obvious course has been adopted everywhere, except by the German Supreme Court.[2]

203. Law in force. Repealed foreign laws

II. Where the court has recourse to the law of a foreign country it may only apply the law which is in force there at the time. Foreign law which has been repealed and replaced by later legal rules must not be applied, even if the modern rule is inapplicable to the case in point.

Illustration. A German rule of 1932 was repealed by a rule of 1934. The English Court rejects the 1934 rule as opposed to English public policy. It cannot apply the repealed rule. If, however, the rejected rule is no more than an exception to a general rule still in force, the court will apply the general rule even to the case for which the later (exceptional) rule is intended. See *supra*, s. 175 (2).

Russians who after the revolution of 1917 fled from Russia in order to escape from Soviet rule and settled

---

[1] See *In re Bankes*, [1902] 2 Ch. 333, 338; *In re Hoyles*, [1911] 1 Ch. (C.A.) 179, 185.

[2] The German Supreme Court does not allow the inferior courts (those of first instance or of appeal) to leave the question which law is applicable unexamined, though in its own decisions it sometimes acts on the principle it condemns. See on the one hand: German Supr. Court, *Off. Coll.*, 100, 81, and *IPRspr.*, 1929, nos. 1 and 3; 1932, nos. 38 and 122; on the other hand: *Off. Coll.*, 113, 42; 124, 148.

in England for the time being without establishing a domicile here in the sense of English law have retained their Russian domicile of origin. The normal consequence of this would be that succession upon their death is governed by Soviet law, which at first abolished any rights of succession (1919), later recognized very restricted rights (1922), and even now grants succession, either *ab intestato* or by will, only to the surviving spouse, to children, grandchildren, and persons whom the deceased maintained during the last year of his life. It would be unjust to apply any of these laws to a person whose very flight has shown his unwillingness to submit to the lack of liberty on which they are based. If the English court— like many continental courts—should for such reason decline to apply these laws to refugees, what law will apply? The old law of Czarist Russia has been suggested,[1] wrongly, since it is nowhere in force. The best solution would be to apply the law of the ordinary residence (as continental laws do) or *deficiente regula* the law of the forum.

The court must apply the *whole* law in force in the country concerned, statute law as well as customary law, law made by a *de iure* or by a *de facto* government, even by a government not recognized by the state of the court. The reason is this. Rules which are generally obeyed in a country and applied by its courts can certainly not be regarded by a foreign court as ordinances of the state concerned if made by rulers not recognized as representatives of that state, but they are law, like any other customary law based on actual practice and a general belief that such practice is law.[2]

III. If the state the law of which is to be applied by the English court has no single legal system but employs different systems either in different parts of the state territory (as is the case in Poland, Roumania, and Yugo-

204. Law of states lacking a unitary system

---

[1] Cf. for example, von Falkovsky, *Jur. W.*, 1925, 1237. See also French and Belgian decisions: Niboyet, *Manuel*, p. 555.

[2] See *Banco de Bilbao* v. *Rex*, [1938] 2 A.E.R. 253; *Bank of Ethiopia* v. *National Bank of Egypt*, [1937] 3 A.E.R. 8.—Foster, *Théorie anglaise*, p. 70 et seq.

slavia) or for different religious, racial, or social classes of the population (India), the English court will apply the law which according to the interlocal or interpersonal law of the country concerned governs the case. Conversely, a foreign court may find that it should apply the national law of a British subject; and an English court may find itself in the same position when the law of domicile through *renvoi* remits the case to 'British' law as the national law of the person concerned. As there are no inter-regional conflict rules in the British Commonwealth, the court will be concerned to discover with which country within the Commonwealth the case has the most real connexion. See *supra*, s. 129.

205.
Foreign law to be applied as it is applied by its own courts

IV. The court must apply the law of a foreign country just as a court of that country would apply it, with the following consequences:

1. It has to be shown to the court that the law on which one of the parties founds his claim or his plea is actually in force. If the dispute concerns the question whether a certain statute is invalid as infringing the constitution of the state the court has a right to examine its validity to the same extent as any ordinary court of the foreign state itself. Thus an English court may investigate the question whether an American statute oversteps the constitutional powers of the state, since such examination would be open to the American court; but it is not allowed to do the same in the case of French statutes because their application in France does not depend on their conformity with the constitution.[1] Similar questions emerge when the foreign statute is contrary to a state treaty concluded with a third state: the answer again depends on whether it has been applied or would be applied in the state in which it was made, irrespective of its incompatibility with the treaty. It is not for the court to insist in the execution of obligations that result from a convention concluded

[1] See Maury, loc. cit., 70, 71; Niboyet, *Rev. Ghent*, 1928, 771; *Traité* III. 404; F. A. Mann, 59 *L.Q.R.* (1943), 156 et seq. Cf. 60 *Harvard L.R.* (1947), 1351 et seq.

between two foreign states. If the foreign statute contravenes a convention concluded with the state of the forum
the court will disregard the statute.[1]

2. In interpreting foreign statutes the English court
follows the same principles as the foreign court observes
in regard to its own laws, not those which it applies when
construing an English statute. It is well known that
English rules on construction of statutes differ widely
from those prevailing in all other parts of Europe. Thus,
the axiom of literal or grammatical construction, abandoned everywhere on the continent, still obtains in this
country unless the text of the statute is ambiguous. This
rule must not be applied to the construction of a continental
statute. In particular the English principle that the court
must glean the intention of the legislature from the Act
itself, not from statements made during debates in the
House or from the policy of the promoters of the bill or
even from the 'general policy of the Realm',[2] is unknown
to continental courts and must therefore be excluded when
an English court is ascertaining the meaning of a foreign
statute.

3. Decisions made by foreign courts have to be taken
into account. Though the principle of binding precedents
is not known to any continental law, the decisions of the
Supreme Courts and the Appeal Courts in fact enjoy high
authority. They are generally followed in their own
countries practically to the same extent as English High
Court *dicta* and decisions of the House of Lords in Scottish cases and of the Privy Council are accepted by
English courts. Though the court is not in principle
inhibited from rejecting the interpretation of a foreign
statute by the decision of a foreign court this will hardly
ever happen, unless such interpretation has been questioned in the foreign country itself.

Only where the text of the foreign statute is identical
with that of a statute in force in the country of the forum

---

[1] For reasons similar to those for which a foreign rule is disregarded if at
variance with the public policy of the country.

[2] Cf. *Scranton's Trustee* v. *Pearse*, [1922] 2 Ch. 87, 123 (*per* Lord Sterndale,
M.R.).

is the court justified in revising a wrong construction by a foreign court.

An example of this is to be found in a decision of the former German Supreme Commercial Court of 1874:[1] the court had to apply the Bills of Exchange Act, 1848, which was common to Germany and Austria; and the bill of exchange before the court was governed by Austrian law. The Act of 1848 was therefore to be applied as Austrian, i.e. foreign, law. In a particular point the interpretation of the text by Austrian courts differed from that approved by German courts; the German Supreme Commercial Court did not hesitate to declare the Austrian interpretation of an Austrian statute erroneous. This decision seems justifiable[2] because in that case it could not be contended that the interpretation given by the Austrian courts had become part of Austrian customary law.[3]

The same view should be taken where the state of the deciding court and some foreign states have concluded a convention concerning the unification of certain rules of civil or commercial law, such as the Brussels Conventions on Maritime Law, and where the court is to apply the content of such convention as part of the law of one of the contracting foreign states. The court must be at liberty to declare a certain interpretation of that law by a foreign court to be mistaken. The convention was intended to create one law common to several states and this must carry greater weight than the fact that— formally— on the basis of the convention several laws have been created with identical texts.

206.
Foreign law is 'Law'

V. When the court 'applies foreign law', does it apply it as such? Or as part of its own law? Or finally as a mere fact? These questions have been very frequently dis-

---

[1] *Reichs-Oberhandelsgericht* (Offic. Coll.) 15, 207 et seq. See on this: Melchior, p. 91.

[2] Dissenting: Melchior, loc. cit.

[3] The result is different where (for example, in Belgium) the French civil code has been interpreted in some peculiar way for so long a period that this special interpretation may be regarded as customary law. *Example*: art. 970 *code civil* says that a holograph will is valid only 'if wholly written, dated and signed by the hand of the testator'. There can be no doubt that the 'date' thus required must be a correct date, and that is what the French Supreme Court has rightly established. Since 1857 the Belgian courts have, however, continuously taken a divergent view and have declared a mistake in the date to be innocuous. An English court examining the validity of a Belgian will would probably accept the view of the Belgian courts.

cussed, particularly in the United States and in Italy, though they suggest scholastic refinements of little practical value. The true and simple answer to them is:

1. What the court applies to the facts laid before it is 'law', not mere fact. It is meaningless to say that a judge applies a 'fact' to facts. Every judicial decision constitutes a syllogism; its major premise is a legal rule and cannot be anything else, its minor is a set of facts. The conflict rule alone does not suffice for the major: if, for example, we say: succession is governed by the law of the deceased's domicile (major premise) and X was at the time of his death domiciled in France (minor), this leads only to the conclusion that the succession to X's property is governed by French law, but not to the decision of the case before the court. It needs a second syllogism to reach the final answer, and here a rule of French municipal law constitutes the major. The fact that French law is not a law that prevails in England does not deprive it of its character as law, even in England. Thus there can be no doubt that the court in forming the second syllogism 'applies' French law as genuine law, just as it would have applied English law if X had had an English domicile.[1]

2. The law which is applied is foreign law and remains foreign law. This has been denied by some authors on the ground that law which is not in force in a country (say, Italy) cannot have any *effetti giuridici* in that country; therefore foreign law must become part of the local law of the country in which it is applied.[2] The simple truth is that the judge obeys his national conflict rule in applying foreign law but without making it in any sense part of

---

[1] All this is so obvious that to mention it needs an excuse. The excuse is that the assertion 'the English court applies foreign law as a fact' is to be found over and over again. Cf. Jacq. Donnedieu de Vabres, *Evolution* 689.

[2] The Italian view is well explained by Ago, 107, and Fedozzi, 162. Cf. Maury, 57. The American *Local Law Theory* is practically the same as the Italian doctrine, though it starts from a different point of view. Cf. notably: W. W. Cook p. 21 et seq., F. J. de Sloovère, Lorenzen, P. Wigny, loc. cit. Cook l. c. believes that the forum always applies its own law (why?), that in a case involving foreign elements it 'incorporates' some foreign legal rules into its own law, and that 'the forum models its own applicable rule of law upon the foreign rule of law'. It seems impossible to find a reason for such fictitious construction. See also Cheatham 58, *Harv. L.J.* (1945), 363.

his national law. To take an illustration from the linguistic field: the fact that many Italians living in England speak Italian in their intercourse with each other and with some of their English friends does not make Italian an 'English language'.

207. Foreign law treated as 'fact'

VI. Though the foreign law which the court has to apply remains law, it is in some respects treated very differently from the court's own law. This is because the judge cannot be expected to know it as he knows his own law. The exceptional treatment of foreign law shows itself:

1. first and above all in the manner in which the foreign law is ascertained. There is some diversity in this. In several continental countries, for example, in Germany and Austria, it is the duty of the judge to investigate the foreign law which he is to apply; this duty is based on the *nobile officium iudicis*. He may require assistance in this from litigant parties, who then (only on his request) have to prove[1] the content of the foreign law. In no case, however, is the judge limited to the legal material the parties bring him. He may supplement it by discovering foreign judicial decisions which the parties have overlooked, by delving into the legal literature of the foreign country, and the like.

Even where the parties agree on the content of the foreign law the judge is entitled to tell them that the law is different from what they think and to apply the law as it really is. The present writer has seen a case in point. Belgian law was to apply; counsel on both sides argued that Belgian law was nearly always the same as French law and that there was no reason to suppose they differed from each other in the particular case. The German judge, dissatisfied with this somewhat precarious argument, asked an opinion from a scientific Institute for Foreign Law and learned that Belgium had enacted a new statute by which the text of the civil code had been substantially changed.

208. The English doctrine

The opposite view on all these points has been taken by English law.[2] English courts treat the content of

---

[1] The German Code of Civil Procedure, s. 293, however, avoids the term *beweisen*, because evidence in the legal sense is not necessary. It speaks loosely of *nachweisen* (demonstrate, prove).

[2] French law is similar to English law, but not quite so rigid. Decisions in Maury, p. 79, n. 6. See Bartin, I. 279.

foreign law as if it were an extra-legal fact, which the judge cannot be expected to know. He does not, as for example in Germany, merely use the parties or their advocates as his assistants in establishing the content of the law; the parties have to prove foreign law in the same way as they prove pure facts. The judge takes no 'judicial notice' of foreign law.[1] If he happens to know it, such knowledge remains a purely private matter, just as when he has knowledge of facts which are not brought before him by one of the litigant parties. He is not entitled to decide the case on knowledge gained by private information. Therefore if the same legal question concerning the same foreign law arises in two actions entertained by the same court, the court is not allowed, in dealing with the second action, to refer to what it has learned from the discussions and the expert evidence in the first and thereby to avoid a tedious and expensive repetition: 'The court must act upon the evidence before it in the actual case.'[2] If the parties agree about the content of foreign law, in particular, if they agree that the foreign law is the same as English law, the court will accept their view, as it accepts (other) facts on which they have agreed.[3] The judge is, of course, entitled to draw the attention of counsel to some point of foreign law not put forward by them. But if they then do not take the hint he will hardly make use of it.

---

[1] In the United States the Federal Courts take judicial notice of the law of every state of the U.S.A. (*Restatement*, s. 624). According to a Uniform Judicial Notice Act, 1936 (which was adopted by fourteen states), State Courts must take judicial notice of the laws of the sister states; L. E. Hartwig, 40 *Michig. L.R.* (1941), 174; Taylor, 42 *Michig. L.R.* (1943), 516; as to New York see *Cornell L.Q.*, 1941, 502. The State Courts where the Uniform Act has not been adopted do not take such notice unless required by statute to do so. Beale, III. 1665.

[2] See *Lazard Bros.* v. *Midland Bank*, [1933] A.C. 289, 298. *In re Marseilles Extension Railway and Land Co.* (1885), 30 Ch.D. 598, 602, the learned judge (Pearson, J.) regretted not being able to make use of the opinion which a French lawyer had given in an earlier lawsuit; he added: 'I cannot import into this case the evidence given in another case'. See *Ottoman Bank* v. *Chakarian*, [1938] A.C. (P.C.) 260, 279, and Lewald, *Contrôle des Cours Suprêmes*, 94–6.

[3] In *Koechlin* v. *Kestenbaum*, [1927] 1 K.B. 622, the judge (Rowlatt, J.), after having heard some rather confused evidence on French law (cf. Bankes. L.J., at p. 894), pronounced: 'Although I admit that this evidence surprised me, it was not contradicted, and I accept it for the purpose of this judgment.' See Avory, J., at p. 900.

The means by which foreign law is proved is the evidence of expert witnesses. What persons are qualified to testify depends on the circumstances. Foreign advocates or other lawyers who actually have or at least have had legal practice in the country concerned are usually regarded as the best qualified witnesses;[1] academic training in the law will not suffice;[2] one American court, however, admitted evidence of English law by a lawyer who had no other knowledge of that law than that acquired by his having studied for six months in England. Another American court held a graduate law student of Paris University competent to explain French law.[3] English courts would hesitate to adopt this course. On the other hand, the expert witness need not always be a lawyer. Where business men, shipmasters, or secretaries of an insurance company are deemed to have knowledge and understanding of that part of the law which is the subject of inquiry, they are admitted as experts.[4] The whole system of treating foreign law as if it were an extra-legal fact, in particular of not admitting judicial knowledge, would seem inconsistent with the court's frequent practice when dealing with purely English law, of citing parallels from foreign laws, quoting American decisions, and basing its own decision on views expounded there. The English (and American) method of ascertaining foreign law is, to borrow an expression from an American judge, 'an anachronism which comes down from the time when statutes of other states were not readily accessible'.[5] And yet such easily accessible sources as the laws of Scotland,

[1] A certain distrust of the impartiality of foreign lawyers is, however, sometimes manifested; and Bruce, V.C., in *Guepratte* v. *Young* (1851), 4 De Gex & Sm., 217, 227, spoke of 'the expert witnesses, not unfairly described as *cupidi testes*, which honourable men may be'. See also *supra*, p. 203, Lord Cranworth's remark in *Doglioni* v. *Crispin* (1866), 1 H.L.C. 301, 314.

[2] *Bristow* v. *Sequeville* (1850), 19 L.J.Ex. 289.

[3] Beale, III, 1671, nn. 2 and 3.

[4] *Van der Donckt* v. *Thelluson* (1849), 8 C.B. 812, 824. See also Cheshire, 170, 171; Beale, loc. cit. It may, however, be asked: does a court admit as expert witnesses on medicine a chemist, an osteopath, a midwife, a masseur, or a faith-healer?

[5] In *Hammond Motor Car Co.* v. *Warren* (Kansas), quoted in Beale, III, 1666, n. 1. The treatment of foreign law as fact goes back to the times of the Statutists; Catellani, I, 341.

of South Africa, of India, Australia, and the Crown Colonies are not exempt from treatment by English courts as non-legal facts. Scots law, it is true, must be regarded as law in the House of Lords, even in English cases, but not so in the inferior courts.[1]

There is only one exception to the principle. Since 1920[2] it is no longer the jury that has to decide upon the 'fact' of foreign law; the task of determining it belongs to the judge. A first step on the way to a better system, a first recognition of the true nature of foreign law as law.

There remains the question of the court's procedure where the parties do not succeed in proving the actual content of the foreign law, which may happen in several distinguishable ways. It may be that the parties have proved what the foreign law was at a particular time in the past. In such case the court will possibly have recourse to the doubtful principle that what has existed once is presumed to continue in force unless the contrary is proved.[3] This helps the court to attain though not certainty of the law, at least probability. It is submitted that it would be justifiable for a court generally to be content with stating the probable law in cases where full certainty cannot be reached.[4] Knowing that English Common Law has greatly influenced the forty-eight common law systems of the United States, it seems reasonable both for the English and the continental courts to presume that any one of these systems embodies the same common law rules as does English law.

209. If foreign law is not ascertained

In a German case, which, however, did not result in a judicial decision, the issue was the right given by the law of Ecuador to a person who by his father's will had been deprived of his *legitima* in the father's succession. At that time—soon after the war of 1914–18—it was impossible to obtain access to the Ecuadorian civil code. The code, however, was known to be based on the Civil Code of Chile (itself framed on the model of the

---

[1] *Elliot* v. *Joicey*, [1935] A.C. 209, 236.

[2] Administration of Justice Act, 1920 (10 & 11 Geo. V, c. 81) s. 15, now replaced by the Supreme Court of Judicature Act, 1925 (15 & 16 Geo. V, c. 49) s. 102. The same rule was introduced by the American Uniform Judicial Notice Act, 1936. See *supra*, p. 219, n. 1.

[3] Gray, J., in the New York case *In re Gehrig's Estate*, 126 N.Y. 537, 27 N.E. 784 (1891); Beale, III, 1685, 1686.

[4] See Melchior, 423; Maury, p. 77.

Code Napoléon), its application would therefore be nearer to the right solution than the application of the *lex fori* (German law).[1]

It has been objected that this method of applying foreign law is arbitrary and might *possibly* lead to a wrong result. In answer it may be said that often the application of the *lex fori certainly* results in a wrong decision. If, for example, we modify the facts of the case discussed above by supposing that the action was brought in an English court, the result reached by an emergency application of English law would be even more strikingly unjust; for it is well known that English and American law alone in the world reject any form of *legitima*.

The prevailing law of most countries, however, does not follow the line proposed here. If the applicable law cannot be strictly proved the court deals with the case either

(*a*) by giving judgment against the party who bore the burden of proof and who has thus failed to discharge it; or

(*b*) by applying the law of the court.

The first solution prevails in Germany;[2] it originates in the old and wrong conception of the merely factual character of foreign law. The second solution is an emergency solution, adopted by most countries. It leads to a result contrary to the aim of private international law which is to reach harmony of decisions; but it might seem preferable to the first alternative.

English law has accepted the second method.[3] It has even, instead of leaving it in its low rank of an unavoidable though regrettable solution, raised it to the dignity of a presumption. It is 'presumed' that foreign law is the

---

[1] German Civil Code, s. 2303. Under German law the persons entitled to a *legitima* have no right to become 'heirs' of the deceased and co-owners of his estate, as is the case under French law and all legal systems derived from French law; they have only a money claim against the testamentary heirs for the value of one-half of the statutory portion they would have received in the case of intestacy. Every well-informed continental lawyer knows that this curious German (and Austrian) form of *legitima* has not been adopted by any other law.

[2] Zitelmann, *IPR*, I, 281 et seq.; Stein, *Kommentar z. Zivilprozessordnung*, § 293, n. 22. *Reichs-Oberhandelsgericht* (Offic. Coll.), 25, 53 et seq.

[3] *Male* v. *Roberts* (1800), 3 Esp. 163. See also *Earl Nelson* v. *Lord Bridport* (1845), 8 Beav. 527.

same as English law.[1] Even where everybody knows
that it differs from English law (though its exact content
is subject to controversy) it is presumed to be the same.
What this presumption really means is that if the content
of the foreign law cannot be established by the parties to
the satisfaction of the court, the court applies English law.

2. In many countries foreign law is treated as a mere
fact, inasmuch as an error with regard to it cannot be
raised before the Supreme Court of the country. This
rule is connected with the continental judiciary system:
in no states on the European continent, except the Scandinavian countries, do the Supreme Courts sit as courts of
(final) 'appeal'—as in England—but only as courts of
cassation or *revisio in iure*; they are bound to accept the
findings of fact of the inferior courts, and their task is
limited to an inquiry into the legal conclusions drawn
from the facts. In all these countries, therefore, it must be
decided whether a finding of foreign law is a finding of
fact or a ruling of law. In most countries it is treated as
a finding of fact and therefore not subject to *cassation* or
revision. This is so in particular in France,[2] Germany,
Switzerland, Spain, Greece, Belgium, and the Netherlands, the reason being that the Supreme Courts have
been created in order to secure a correct and uniform
interpretation of the law of the country. The better
method is to treat mistakes in foreign law as what they
are, viz. mistakes in law, and consequently to allow the
pourvoi en cassation. That is what Italy, Russia, Portugal,
and particularly Austria[3] have done.

For English law the problem does not exist in respect

210. Errors
with regard
to foreign
law before
the
Supreme
Courts

---

[1] *Brown* v. *Gracey* (1821), Dow. & Ry.N.P., 41, n. *Smith* v. *Gould* (1842), 4
Moore P.C. 21, 25. *Lloyd* v. *Guibert* (1865), L.R. 1 Q.B. 115, 129. *R.* v. *Naguib*,
[1917] 1 K.B. 359, 362. *Ertel Bieber & Co.* and *Dynamit Aktiengesellsch.* v. *Rio
Tinto Co.*, [1918] A.C. 260, 295, 301. *Tank of Oslo* v. *Agence Strauss*, [1940] 1
A.E.R. 40, 42. *Casey* v. *Casey*, [1949] P. 420.

[2] There is one curious exception: if by a mistaken interpretation of foreign law
a French statute on fiscal law has become inapplicable, *pourvoi en cassation* is
admitted in favour of the Treasury. Niboyet, *Manuel*, no. 482, III; *Traité* III
pp. 617, 618. See H. Lewald, 'Le contrôle des Cours suprêmes sur l'application des
lois étrangères' (57 *Rec.* (1936 II) 281).

[3] By her famous Code of Civil Procedure, 1895, s. 503. The Austrian rule has
been adopted by Czechoslovakia, Poland, and Yugoslavia; Lewald, loc. cit., p.
290 et seq.

of judgments of the High Court.[1] The House of Lords is not debarred from examining questions of fact. In several cases it has revised the application of foreign law.[2]

211. Taking account of non-applicable foreign law. Conflict of duties

VII. Sometimes the court is bound to take account of a rule of foreign law which it is not required to 'apply' under any conflict rule. This happens:

1. where the divergence of a (non-applicable) foreign law from the applicable rule throws a person into a *conflict of duties*. Such a conflict arises where a person according to the applicable law is under a duty to do something which under some other law he is obliged to refrain from doing, or vice-versa, provided that there exists a connexion between him and that other law sufficient to affect his behaviour. This connexion may arise from his nationality or from the fact that he has property in the territory of the non-applicable law, or that there exists a forum in that territory to which he is amenable. As in these cases it is impossible for him to obey both laws, he must be allowed to disobey one or other of them. Which of the two legal systems this is cannot be determined by a precise formula. It depends on the circumstances, on his duties of allegiance or his duties as a resident of a country, or his property interests. Some examples may clarify the issue.

(*a*) Before the war of 1914–18 a German concluded a contract with an English company; after the outbreak of war the company refused further delivery of goods, because this would have contravened the English Trading with the Enemy Act. The German party contended (rightly) that the contract was subject to German law and that in any case the English prohibition could not 'apply' as inconsistent with German public policy. He brought an action for damages. The German Supreme Court[3] gave judgment for the defendant. Though the English Trading with the Enemy Act was not applicable, it had to be taken into account; an English company could not be expected to contravene it. The decision would have been the same if the goods the English company was obliged to deliver had at the

[1] In the case of County Courts decisions an appeal to the Court of Appeal as to matters of fact is excluded. See *County Courts Act*, 1934 (24 & 25 Geo. V, c. 53) s. 105, and *County Courts Act*, 1850 (13 & 14 Vict., c. 61) s. 14.

[2] *Russian Commercial & Industrial Bank* v. *Comptoir d'Escompte de Mulhouse*, [1925] A.C. 112, 126. *Lazard Bros.* v. *Midland Bank*, [1933] A.C. 289, 298. Lewald, 299 et seq.

[3] German Supreme Court, *Off. Coll.*, 93, 182.

outbreak of war been situate in Switzerland, so that their delivery to the plaintiff would have been 'possible'.

(b) There is an English rule according to which a contract is or becomes invalid if the performance is or becomes unlawful by the law of the country where it is to be performed.[1] This rule[2] is not much more than a particular example of the principle here expressed. A person who under the proper law of the contract is bound to perform it, but under the *lex loci solutionis* is forbidden to do so, cannot as a rule be legally expected to try to act against that prohibition. A similar result is reached under continental laws.

(c) A German woman domiciled in Lucerne died in 1920 leaving two wills; in the first will she appointed her niece as heiress and charged her with a series of particular legacies in favour of A, B, C, and D; in the second will she repeated the appointment of her niece, made some changes in the amount of the legacies in favour of B, C, and D and added further legacies to E and F; of A she said nothing. It was doubtful whether the legacy in favour of A was to be considered as cancelled by the new will or as maintained in spite of its silence in this respect. Under internal Swiss law the first, under German law the second answer was correct.[3] The testatrix left property both in Germany and Switzerland. The testamentary executor (who lived in Germany) was at a loss what to do. In case of litigation, the German court if seized of the matter would apply the national law of the testatrix, i.e. German law, and therefore give judgment in favour of A. The Swiss court, however, would apply the law of domicile, i.e. Swiss law, and therefore decide against the validity of the legacy to A. If the executor paid the considerable sum left to A, the heiress would make him responsible in Switzerland for having violated a legal rule which he knew to be applicable to the case in Switzerland. On the other hand, if he did not pay it he was sure that A would bring an action against him in the German court, where judgment would be given for the plaintiff and the executor held responsible for all damage arising out of the delay, which (as he was again aware) constituted a breach of his obligation under German law. It was suggested to him that this conflict of duties should be solved as follows: He was to pay the legacy out of property situate in Germany; if that property was not sufficient to cover the whole amount due to A he would not be allowed to pay the difference out of the Swiss property. The reason for this is that

---

1 *Ralli Bros.* v. *Compañia Naviera Sota y Aznar,* [1920] 1 K.B. 614; 2 K.B. 287. *Foster* v. *Driscoll,* [1929] 1 K.B. 470. *International Trustee* v. *Rex,* [1936] 3 A.E.R. (C.A.), 407, 429.

2 See on it *infra*, s. 425.

3 Swiss Civ. Code, s. 511. German Civ. Code, s. 2258 (and German Wills Act, 1938, s. 36).

no state must treat as a violation of duty an act done in a foreign country in obedience to the laws of that country.[1]

**212.
Conflict
between
right and
duty**

2. The divergence between the 'applicable' law and another (not applicable) legal system leads sometimes to a different conflict: the *conflict between a right and a duty*. It would be wrong to think that in such case the duty always preponderates. If a person who according to a foreign rule is entitled to act in a certain way exercises this right in that foreign country, the court of another country cannot as a rule reproach him with having committed an offence against its own law. An example of this:

Under the Bankruptcy Act 1914,[2] all property of a bankrupt passes to his trustees in bankruptcy 'whether situate in England or elsewhere'. If one of the creditors brings an action in a French court against the bankrupt, attaches his property situate in France, and recovers payment thereof, this is certainly contrary to the English rule. But as it is permissible in France under French law he may keep what he has received, provided that he does not seek to prove in the English bankruptcy, that he 'ignores the English bankruptcy proceeding altogether'.[3]

[1] See Cockburn's (C.J.) *dictum* in *Phillips* v. *Eyre* (1869), L.R. 4 Q.B. 225, 239: 'An act might not only be lawful but might even be enjoined by the law of another country, which would be wrongful and give a right of action by our law, and it certainly would be in the highest degree unjust that an individual who has intended to obey the law binding upon him should be held liable in damages in another country where a different law may prevail.' 'To hold the contrary . . . would be altogether contrary to that comity of nations in matters of law to which effect should, if possible, be given.'

[2] 4 & 5 Geo. V, c. 59, s. 167.

[3] *Banco de Portugal* v. *Waddell* (1880), L.R. 5. App. Cas. 161, 167 (*per* Lord Cairns, quoting Lord Eldon). It is, however, doubtful whether this solution is always correct. See on this *infra*, s. 535.

BIBLIOGRAPHY

Annuaire, 8 (1886) 265; 9 (1888) 305; 10 (1892) 333. DARRAS, *J. Clunet*, 1901, 209, 442, 672. NIBOYET, *Rev. Ghent.* 1928, 753; *Traité* III, 399 et seq. ARMINJON I 385–412. APPERT, *Rev. Darras*, 1913, 338. VAN DER FLIER, *J. Clunet*, 1936, 1053. BATIFFOL, *Traité* 346–73; *Rev. Crit.*, 1936, 597. MAURY, *Règles génér.*, 52. MELCHIOR, *Grundlagen*, 81, 418. DODDS, 39 *Harv. L.R.* (1925) 533. COOK, 33 *Yale L.J.* (1924) 457. LORENZEN, ibid. 736. DE SLOOVERE, Local Law Theory, 41 *Harv. L.R.* (1928) 421. CHEATHAM, 58 *Harv. L.R.* (1945), 361. WIGNY, *Essai*, 175.

CHAPTER XVIII

ENFORCEMENT OF RIGHTS
AND PROCEDURE

SELF-HELP AND JUDICIAL PROCEDURE

THE rule in all civilized countries is that nobody is entitled to take the law into his own hands, i.e. to remedy wrongs done to him without recourse to judicial procedure. There are, however, exceptions to this rule, such as the possessor's right to expel a trespasser, to abate a nuisance, or within a time limit to resume possession of chattels of which he has been deprived. The cases in which self-help is allowed vary from country to country. German law, for instance, allows it generally where the enforcement of a right is in danger of being frustrated or materially hindered, provided 'that the assistance of the public authorities cannot be obtained with sufficient speed'.[1] English law does not go so far.

213.
Self-help

Whether the conditions are fulfilled in which a person is entitled to enforce his rights himself is determined not by the law governing the endangered right, but by the law of the place where such person attempts to enforce it; for a violent act is *prima facie* a breach of the peace and it is for the state in whose territory it is committed to say whether it is justifiable or not.

The normal way of enforcing a right is by judicial procedure. Procedure, like self-help, is regulated exclusively by the law of the country where it takes place, the *lex fori*. This rule prevails in every country. It is not always easy to distinguish procedural rules from rules of substantive law. Yet it has to be done since matters of a substantive character are governed by the *lex causae*, such as the proper law of the contract, the law of domicile, the *lex situs*, and so on. Is, for example, a rule on limitation of action or on set-off part of procedural or of substantive law? Does the burden of proof and do rebuttable pre-

214.
Judicial
procedure.
Notion of
procedure

Germ. C.C., 229. Similarly Swiss Law of Obligations, art. 52, § 3.

sumptions[1] belong to the former or to the latter group
of rules? Is estoppel a matter of evidence and therefore
of procedure? To which class does s. 4 Statute of Frauds
belong, according to which 'no action shall be brought'
on certain contracts unless they are evidenced by a note
or memorandum in writing? Or the rules on measure of
damages? Or those on specific performance? The difficulties in classifying rules and institutions of this kind are
increased by the fact that sometimes rules of an undoubtedly substantive nature are framed by the courts, or even
by legislators, as orders to the court to act in a certain way
or to take into account certain circumstances. Legal rules
on the construction of contracts (for example, the rule that
an ambiguous term in a contract is to be construed against
the party which has drawn it up) have often been expressed
in the form of instructions addressed to the courts, while
there is no doubt that in fact they are concerned with the
substantive rights of the parties to the contract.

215. Right and 'Remedy' Many jurists have tried to evolve some general and
simple formula which would enable the lawyer to recog-
nize the character of a given rule. None of these attempts
has succeeded. The most usual English formula, met
with over and over again, starts from the distinction
between right and remedy. Anything concerning the
right itself—the conditions upon which it comes into
existence; its extent; alterations caused either by agreement or by infringement; its extinction—all these belong
to substantive law, while all rules bearing upon the remedy
are procedural. But the conception of remedy is far from
being clear or unambiguous. Anson's standard work on
Contracts, for example, mentions four 'remedies' for
breach of contract:[2] the claim for *quantum meruit*, the
action for damages, the supplementary and discretionary
remedy of specific performance, and the injunction. Is it
true that the first and the second of these 'remedies' are
of a procedural character? Is there anything that distinguishes them from other genuine rights, such as exist

---

[1] Irrebuttable presumptions (*praesumtiones iuris et de iure* [*sc. probationem
contrarii non admittentes*]) are undoubtedly of a purely substantive character,
just as are legal fictions.　　　　[2] p. 361.

by virtue of some legal provision? The fact that the action is for 'unliquidated' damages can hardly be a sufficient reason for denying the claim the nature of a right. In any case there seems no doubt that where a contract is governed by foreign law that law, and not the *lex fori*, should answer the question whether an action for damages lies.

Not quite the same though a similar answer to the problem has been given by continental writers: the relationship existing between the parties themselves, in particular their duties towards each other, are governed by substantive law, while the duties and rights of the courts both to the parties and to third persons (witnesses and the like) are part of procedure.[1] This distinction, however, cannot be the true test. The actionability of a claim is regarded by some jurists as belonging merely to the relationship between the court and the parties, while others think that it concerns mainly the relationship between the parties themselves. It would be unjustifiable in a given case to make the decision dependent upon whether the court adopts the former or the latter view. Some philosophers have developed the idea that on close examination all commands of the law as such prove to be addressed not to individuals but to courts and executive bodies of the state, and that the duty of a debtor to pay his creditor is a legal duty to obey the order of the court. Should a judge who approves this view draw from it the conclusion that all rights are really remedies based on the relationship between the court and the parties, and consequently apply the *lex fori*? It would be to over-estimate the value of a system of legal conceptions, were one to make practical results ensue from them as if they were leading principles of human conduct.

216. Relationship between the parties distinct from relationship to the Court?

We have seen that justice often requires the application of foreign law in order to protect certain rights which have been acquired under a foreign law, or other legal situations deserving protection. But justice does not demand that such protection be given in exactly the same way as that in which the foreign courts would grant it. On the contrary,

217. Reason for subjection of procedure to the *lex fori*

[1] See, for example, A. Wach, *Civilprocessrecht* (1895), I. 118.

it is a postulate of justice that the courts of a given country follow their general rules of procedure irrespective of whether the subject-matter of the litigation is governed by foreign law or by the law of the country. If the law of country X allows evidence by hearsay or forbids the parties to give evidence, the English court will nevertheless follow its own divergent rules on this subject, though it has to adjudicate upon a contract governed by the law of X and though possibly the application of the procedural rules of X would lead to a different judgment from that reached by the English court. The contrary would not only be inconvenient for the English court; it would also entail injustice through the unequal treatment of the parties in the suit in question on the one hand and the parties in other lawsuits on the other. Only such foreign rules—even though framed as procedural rules—should be applied by the English court as are so closely connected with the applicable substantive rules of the foreign country that otherwise the foreign substantive law would be, as it were, adulterated.

What this means will best be shown by investigation of a number of special problems.

BIBLIOGRAPHY

MICHEL, *Rev. Darras*, 1912, 302. NEUNER, *Privatrecht und Prozessrecht*, 1925. W. W. COOK, 154–93. GOODRICH, 187–218. E. H. AILES, 39 *Michig. L.J.* (1941) 392. M. SCHOCH, *Klagbarkeit, Prozessanspruch u. Beweis*, 1934. MENDELSSOHN-BARTHOLDY, *Brit. Y.B.*, 1935, 20. GUTTERIDGE, *Rec.* 44, 115, and *Brit. Y.B.*, 1932, 49.

I. THE STATUTE OF FRAUDS

218.
Statute of Frauds

Under German law a contract of suretyship needs a written note signed by the surety; failing this the contract is void unless it is a commercial contract.[1] Under English law the contract also needs a written note, not as a requirement of validity but in order that it may be enforceable. No doubt the German rule is substantive in character, while the English rule may be called procedural because it merely refers to the insufficiency of oral evidence. The

---

[1] German Civ. C., s. 776; Commerc. C., s. 350.

function of both rules however is the same, and it would therefore seem unjustifiable if, for example, a German court in the case of an English suretyship should refuse to apply the Statute of Frauds by reason of its procedural character.

English law indeed looks on this statute as concerned with procedure, and English courts therefore apply it even where the contract is governed by foreign law[1]—for example, in the case of a German commercial suretyship which under German law is valid though made orally.

The same problem exists under French law,[2] where all contracts concerning an object valued at more than 5,000 francs must be made in writing and no evidence by witnesses is admitted. Prevailing opinion on the Continent recognizes the substantive character of this rule, and the French and Dutch courts[3] apply it if, and only if, the contract is governed by the law embodying it.

It does not follow from the characterization of the Statute of Frauds as procedural that in respect of the form of a contract the English court applies exclusively the provisions of that statute. Where, for example, a German contract has been made in Germany in the form of the English statute, but not in the form prescribed by German law the English court will not enforce it. For the Statute of Frauds merely *declines* the enforcement of certain contracts though they are valid under their proper law; it does not conversely allow the enforcement of a contract which according to its proper law is void.

[1] *Leroux* v. *Brown* (1852), 12 C.B. 801; *Morris* v. *Baron*, [1918] A.C. 1, 15. Willes, J., took the contrary view, as is shown by his *dicta* in *Williams* v. *Wheeler* (1860), 8 C.B. (N.S.), 299, 316, and *Gibson* v. *Holland* (1865), L.R. 1, C.P. 1, 8. Convincing in his criticism of *Leroux* v. *Brown*: Cheshire, p. 827 et seq.

[2] Code Civil, art. 1341. Similarly Italian, Dutch, and other laws derived from French law.

[3] See Frankenstein (who himself disagrees), I. 365; Niboyet, *Manuel*, p. 678. American law is still unsettled.

BIBLIOGRAPHY

LORENZEN, *Select. Art.* 322–351. A. H. ROBERTSON, *Characterization* (1940), 253. DICEY-MORRIS, 861. GOODRICH, 205–10.

2. LIMITATION OF ACTION

219.
Limitation of action
Under all legal systems the lapse of a specified period in some cases wholly extinguishes a person's right, while in some other cases it merely gives the debtor the right to refuse performance of his obligation.[1] In cases of the first kind the effect is undoubtedly substantive, in the latter case the Dutch school of the seventeenth century (U. Huber) treated the effect as procedural only, and English law as well as the law of the United States have concurred.[2] Most continental legal writers and legal systems have recognized that this view is defective and that a debtor's right to refuse payment affects the substance of his duty and does not merely 'bar the remedy'.[3] Indeed, the solution to which the English courts are committed hardly seems justifiable.[4] In the case of limitation of action the lapse of time destroys neither the actionability nor the substantive right. The creditor may start proceedings and even if upon his own showing the permissible period has elapsed the court will give judgment for him unless the defendant relies on his 'right' to refuse payment owing to the expiry of the period of limitation. It cannot be assumed that he will under all circumstances exercise this right if he has it. On the contrary, if he has another good defence he may prefer to rely on it rather than on the morally somewhat questionable plea of limitation.

The English view leads to an unjust result, particularly if the English period is longer than that allowed by the foreign law in issue.[5] One of the main aims of limitation

---

[1] As to French law, the *prescription* does not operate unless 'opposed by the debtor' (art. 2223 c.c.), while the *déchéance* in the case of a *délai préfix* is effective by operation of law (see, for example, Planiol, I, no. 704). Similarly German law distinguishes between *Verjährung* (which merely creates a right to refuse performance; s. 222 Civ.C.) and *Ausschluss-Frist* (the lapse of which extinguishes the duty; for example, s. 561 or 801 Civ.C.).

[2] *British Linen Co.* v. *Drummond* (1830), 10 B. & C., 903; *Don* v. *Lippmann* (1837), 5 Cl. & Fin., 1, 13; *Huber* v. *Steiner* (1835), 2 Bing N.C. 202. *Harris* v. *Quine* (1869), L.R. 4, Q.B. 653. Schlink, 9 *Rabel's Z.*, 418.

[3] *Annuaire*, 31, 159, 182. Arminjon, I. 34; Zitelmann, I. 158.

[4] Cheshire, p. 830 et seq.

[5] *Huber* v. *Steiner*, loc. cit.; *Harris* v. *Quine*, loc. cit.

of action is to make it safe for the debtor who has settled his account to destroy his receipts. A German debtor, for example, may safely throw away all commercial receipts more than two years old.[1] If he has to take into consideration that he may be sued in an English court in respect of an old debt and that the court would then apply the much longer English period, he is placed at an unfair disadvantage.

BIBLIOGRAPHY

Lorenzen, *Selected Articles*, 352–9. Falconbridge, 240–52. Goodrich, 201. E. H. Ailes, 31 *Michig. L.R.* 474. Algot Bagge, 'En preskriptionsfråga inom den internat. privaträtten' (Collection of Essays in honour of *Marks* v. *Würtemberg*, p. 19)—see *Rabel's Z.*, 5 (1931), 740. Arminjon in *Mélanges Pillet* (1929), I. 34. Philonenko, *J. Clunet*, 1936, 259. A. H. Robertson, *Characterization* (1940), 248. Dicey-Morris, 861. Kallmann, 37 *Rev. Crit.* (1948), 1 et seq.

3. SET-OFF

An equally difficult question arises in respect of the rules dealing with set-off. English courts regard this form of relief as a matter of procedure,[2] since the substantive effect of the set-off—the extinction of both claims—can be produced only by the courts, that is, by a judgment which allows the set-off and therefore dismisses the plaintiff's claim. Under continental laws the extinction of the debts is effected not by the court but by an informal unilateral, extra-judicial declaration by one of the parties, or even by operation of law, i.e. by the mere fact that the creditor owes his debtor the same amount as he is entitled to claim (*compensation de plein droit, par la seule force de la loi*).[3] The continental rules on set-off are of substantive character. Are they to be disregarded by the English court because the English set-off is procedural in character? It would be a mistake to assume this. After all, a defendant who pleads a set-off against a German or French debt in an English court does not ask for a *compensatio debiti per iudicem*, as in the case of an English claim; his plea is that the plaintiff's claim has been extinguished

220. Set-off

[1] s. 196, no. 1, German Civ. C.
[2] *Meyer* v. *Dresser* (1864), 16 C.B. (N.S.) 646, 664.
[3] See on this *infra*, s. 439.

according to the rules governing the contract in which the claim originates. The procedural nature of the English set-off entails the application of the English rules by an English court, even though under the proper law of the contract no set-off is permissible; but it does not exclude the application of foreign rules according to which the claim no longer exists.[1] Attention may be called to a dictum by Blackburne, J., in *Harris* v. *Quine*:[2] dealing with limitation of action he draws a distinction between limitation and the case where according to the foreign proper law the lapse of time 'extinguishes the right as well as the remedy'. If this test is applied here, the continental set-off would seem to fall into the latter rather than the former category.

4. THE BURDEN OF PROOF

221. Burden of proof
Rules on evidence are undoubtedly procedural. They include provisions on the competence of witnesses, on their examination, on the documents that may be adduced as proof and on what they prove, and the like.[3] But there are grave doubts whether the question of burden of proof is a matter of procedure or of substantive law. Some authors mention it among matters to be governed by the *lex fori*, and this view was adopted by Langton, J., in *The Roberta*.[4] Dr. Cheshire, on the other hand, convincingly emphasizes the opposite view, which was adopted in *Re Cohn*:[5] the question as to what facts have to be proved and which party has to prove them is a matter of substance and falls to be decided by the *lex causae*.

It is submitted that the domain of substantive law covers all those rules on the burden of proof which are closely connected with the existence or non-existence of substantive rights. Take, for example, the rule common to

---

[1] See *infra*, s. 439 in fin., in particular the case of *Allen* v. *Kemble* (1848), 6 Moore, P.C., 314, 320, 323, mentioned there.

[2] (1869) L.R. 4, Q.B. 653, 658.

[3] *In the Goods of Schulhof*, [1948] P. 66.

[4] [1937] 58 Lloyd's L.R. 159, 177 (C.A. 60 ibid. 84, 85). Cheshire, p. 837, shows however that the judge was not confronted with a question of burden of proof.

[5] [1945] 1 Ch. 5.

many continental laws that a person who claims ownership of movables need not prove the facts by which he
has acquired them if he is in possession, unless the movables have been stolen from or lost by the former owner;
and that it is for his opponent to adduce facts showing
that the possessor is not the owner.[1] Without this presumption which regulates the burden of proof[2] the true
relationship between possession and ownership would be
entirely distorted and one of the main functions which the
law attributes to possession would disappear. This becomes
even more manifest where the English court has to deal
with substantive institutions unknown to its municipal
law, for example, with a matrimonial system of community of income and profits.[3] Here a doubt often arises
whether a certain thing belongs to the separate property
of the husband or to that of the wife or to their common
property, and the codes provide that the burden of proof
lies with the spouse who claims separate property.[4] Should
this rebuttable presumption in favour of common property
be excluded from application in an English court because
the burden of proof is part of procedure? It is worthy of
note that those continental legislators who have made two
separate codes, a civil code and a code of civil procedure,
have placed all these rules in their civil codes.

There are, however, some quite general rules on the
burden of proof which are not connected with any special
provisions of a substantive character.

Examples: (1) If it has been proved that a right has come into existence
it need not be proved that it still exists; its continuation is to be presumed.
But it is open to doubt and to some controversy whether the same rule applies
where a mere fact, such as possession, has been proved and its continuance
is in issue.[5] This problem will be governed by the law of the forum.

---

[1] German Civ. C., s. 1006.

[2] All rebuttable presumptions merely establish the burden of proof.

[3] The *communauté réduite aux acquêts* (Code Civ., art. 1498), the German
Errungenschaftsgemeinschaft, &c.

[4] Code Civ., art. 1499 (since a statute of 1924); German Civ. C., s. 1527.

[5] With regard to possession the burden of proof may vary even within the
same legal system. A person contending that he has become owner by usucapion
need only prove that he was possessor at the beginning and at the end of the
period, while his adversary has the burden of proof in respect of the intermediate
time (*olim et hodie possessor, interea possessor*; see, for example, French cod. civ.,
art. 2234, German Civ. C., s. 938). But where a person relies on possession for

(2) Under English law persons who have for a long time been living together as spouses and have been so regarded by their neighbours and friends need not prove that they are married, and it is for the person who contends that they are not married to prove it.[1] This rule, unknown in modern continental laws, seems to have a procedural character.[2]

(3) Many legal systems have established presumptions, where it is doubtful whether one person has survived another—a situation which occurred very often in air raids. Thus in England there is a presumption to the effect that the older of the *commorientes* died before the younger, while in Germany it is presumed that they died at the same moment.[3] These presumptions are mainly connected with succession upon death; therefore the *lex causæ* (the domiciliary law of the deceased) applies, and not the *lex fori*.[4]

BIBLIOGRAPHY

J. H. UHL, 37 *Michig. L.R.* (1939), 1250. MORGAN, 58 *Harv. L.R.* (1944), 153 et seq., 180, 192. GOODRICH, 197-200.

5. ACTIONABILITY

**222.
Action-
ability**

Is the actionability of a claim part of procedural or of substantive law? Two kinds of cases have to be distinguished.

1. It happens that the foreign law applicable to the case does not permit an action to be brought, while English law contains no such restriction. Thus German law forbids a wife married under the statutory matrimonial régime—where the husband is obliged to manage the whole of her property—to bring an action against her husband in respect of the way in which he uses his powers of management; her claims remain in abeyance until the régime comes to an end, by death, divorce, or otherwise.[5] This rule, which may be called procedural since it con-

other purposes he has to prove that he actually has possession (or that he had it at the decisive moment). The former rule is closely connected with usucapion and therefore substantive; the latter (general) rule is procedural.

[1] *In re Shephard*, [1904] 1 Ch. 456, 463. *Re Thompson* (1905), 91 L.T. 680. *Sastry Velaider Aronegary* v. *Sembecutty Vaigalie* (1881), 6 A.C. (P.C.) 364, 371 (Roman-Dutch law). *Lyle* v. *Elkwood* (1874), 19 Equ.C.. 98, 107.

[2] Cf. Falconbridge, *Canad. Bar R.*, 1935, 317, 318.

[3] See *infra*, s. 256. Law of Property Act s. 184; German law of July 4th, 1939, s. 11.

[4] *In re Cohn*, [1945] Ch. 1, 5.

[5] There are exceptions to this rule, particularly where the husband's conduct justifies the fear that her property is seriously endangered. German Civ. C., s. 1394, 1391.

cerns her right to sue, is however closely connected with the legal matrimonial system. Under the English matrimonial régime, or the German contractual régime of separation of goods, no claims of this kind can arise. But where the law provides that the husband *shall* administer his wife's property, the provision being binding on both spouses—as is the case under the German legal system— the exclusion of judicial proceedings between them serves the purpose, as it were, of maintaining matrimonial peace. The English courts would therefore probably consider the rule to be substantive and consequently applicable though unknown to English municipal law. In doubtful cases, however, they seem inclined to regard the foreign rules as procedural in character. In *Hansen* v. *Dixon*,[1] a breach of promise of marriage case, the court held that if Danish law were to govern the broken contract, the Danish doctrine that no action for damages can be brought in court was merely procedural and therefore inapplicable. (This view was not based on principle but on a construction of Danish law given by an expert witness, and it must be doubted whether that construction was correct.)

2. The converse situation is more important.[2] As a result of the development of the English system of actions there is not always an appropriate form of action in common law, while the equitable remedy depends on the discretion of the court. If, for example, the plaintiff who owns a chattel is deprived of its possession at a time when the chattel is in France or Germany, he acquires under the continental law a right against the possessor for specific restitution of that particular chattel.[3] Or if by a continental contract he has bought a specified chattel or a certain quantity of 'fungible' things, or has under French law sold property for a certain sum in francs, he has thereby become entitled to claim transfer of ownership in the specified chattel or in chattels of the agreed *genus*

---

[1] (1906) 23 T.L.R. 56.

[2] On wagering contracts valid and enforceable under the proper law but not under English municipal law, see *supra*, s. 173. The English court gives a remedy in such cases because the proper law gives it.

[3] A right of *revendication,* a *Herausgabe-Anspruch* (see German Civ. C., s. 985).

or in French money to the agreed amount, respectively. English law, however, gives a remedy for specific performance only 'where the ordinary remedy by an action for damages is not adequate compensation'[1] and even then subject to the discretion of the court. These restrictions are possibly applicable also in the case of rights established under foreign law. But it seems probable that the court will exercise its discretion in a case where under the applicable foreign law a person is entitled to enjoy property *in specie*.[2] When a person has sold property under French law for a certain sum of francs there is no doubt that though he has acquired a 'right' to be paid in francs, he and the defendant must submit to the conversion of the francs into pounds sterling under the order of an English court.[3] Unsatisfactory though these results are, they are unquestionably correct under English law, where the actionability of a claim is regarded as a matter of procedure.

Whether merely declaratory judgments can be sought is clearly a question of procedure. Thus where according to the proper law of the contract an action could not be brought solely to obtain a 'declaration' of existing rights this would by no means prevent an English court from making a binding declaration.[4]

6. RULES DETERMINING THE PARTIES TO SUE
AND TO BE SUED

223. The party to sue   Three questions are to be distinguished: first, to whom does the right belong on which an action is based? Secondly, who is entitled to bring the action? Thirdly, in whose name is the action to be brought?

The first question must undoubtedly be classed as substantive. If *A* draws a cheque on his bank, which the latter certifies or accepts, and gives it to *B*, the law governing the cheque decides whether *B* has acquired a claim against the bank for the sum designated in the

---

[1] *Ryan* v. *Mutual Tontine*, [1893] 1 Ch. 116, 126.
[2] Cf. *In re Moses*, [1908] 2 Ch. 235.
[3] See *infra*, s. 447.
[4] See Order 25, r. 5, of the Supr. Court.

cheque, or whether this right has remained with *A*, as is the case under most continental laws.

The second question also belongs to substantive law, though this may be more doubtful. Under the German statutory matrimonial régime, for example, the wife retains all her property, the husband being entrusted with its management. Though he is not entitled to 'dispose' of it without her consent, e.g., to assign to a third person a debt due to her, it is for him, and only for him, to bring an action against a debtor in his own name.[1] Whether he brings the action in Germany or in England ought not to make any difference; the right to enforce his wife's claim is part of his powers and duties as legal manager and should not be subject to the *lex fori*.

The third question, finally, belongs to procedure. It is for the law of the forum to decide whether an assignee is allowed to sue in his own name or whether he must join the assignor;[2] or again whether an action brought by a partnership in the firm's name is to be admitted.

A similar distinction should be made in respect of the person to be sued. The question, for example, whether a partnership can be sued under the name of its firm, or whether the names of the partners have to be declared, is one that solely concerns procedure. Where however the difference between English procedure and that of the foreign country includes a difference in substantive law, particularly in respect of liability for debts, this should not be treated as a matter of purely procedural character. To give an example: in the *société en commandite* of continental laws there are two kinds of partners, those liable to the full extent of their property for the debts of the firm (the *commandités*) and those liable only for a certain amount (the *commanditaires*). The question whether a creditor can sue one of the *commanditaires* before having enforced his rights against the firm or the *commandités* is answered differently by Swiss law, where he has no direct action against a *commanditaire* before the dissolution of the

224. The party to be sued

---

[1] German Civ. C., s. 1380. (But see ss. 1400, 1405, 1407.)
[2] See *Wolff* v. *Oxholm* (1817), 6 M. & S. 92, 99; *Jeffery* v. *McTaggart*, ibid., 126.

partnership,[1] and by French and German law, where he has.[2] Is the Swiss rule a procedural one and therefore inapplicable in an English court? It is submitted that it is not, and that the procedural formula conceals a provision of substantive law. The view which the English court took in *Bullock* v. *Caird*[3] is however contrary to this. In that case the action was based on the breach of a foreign contract concluded with a foreign firm; only one of the partners of the firm was sued. Under the foreign law the plaintiff could not sue the defendant without having first sued the partners jointly and exhausted the property of the firm; under English law he could. The court applied the English *lex fori*. It would seem difficult to agree with this decision.

Dr. Cheshire[4] justifies it by distinguishing as follows. The foreign rule is applicable to English proceedings if the non-application would result in imposing 'a liability that does not exist by the proper law of the transaction. One the other hand, if the proper law admits the liability but requires . . . proceedings against other parties as a preliminary to suing the defendant, then the rule in question relates merely to the mode of process.' This distinction is not unassailable. If the law demands preliminary proceedings against the firm this constitutes under a procedural disguise the substantive rule that the liability of the defendant depends on a condition precedent, viz. on the condition that the joint property of the partners has proved insufficient. The legal situation does not differ from that of a surety sued by the creditor, though under the proper law of the contract the defendant is protected by an *exceptio excussionis personalis*, unknown to the municipal law of the forum.

7. RULES ON PRIORITIES

225. Pri-
orities

The question of the order in which creditors are entitled to be paid comes under consideration notably when the debtor is bankrupt, or when the deceased debtor's estate is being administered, or when a ship has been arrested and sold and the proceeds have been paid into court. What law is to give the correct solution?

Nowhere is it doubted that if the conflicting creditors have merely personal claims against the debtor and no

---

[1] Swiss Law of Oblig., s. 603.
[2] German Comm. Code, s. 171; *Cour de Cass.*, *Dalloz Pér.* 1865, 1, 479.
[3] (1875) 10 Q.B. 276. Following: *In re Doetsch*, [1896] 2 Ch. 836, 839.
[4] At pp. 844, 846.

iura in rem, the law of the forum is decisive. The rules according to which the court orders the property to be distributed among the creditors apply to all claims, domestic or foreign. The reason for this is that the question does not concern the nature and extent of the debt itself. A German physician who has attended a German and who in German bankruptcy would be privileged in respect of his fee,[1] is not injured by his lack of such privilege in an English bankruptcy. His right consists merely in the claim to be paid a certain sum, and if he wishes his right to be made effective against third persons, such as rival creditors, he may try to obtain a right *in rem*, a mortgage, a hypothec, a pledge, or the like, in a specific chattel or immovable. The priorities connected with rights *in rem* form part of such rights and ought therefore not to be classed as of a procedural, but rather as of a substantive character; they should be subjected to the law of the actual *situs rei*,[2] which will, however, in most cases coincide with the *lex fori*. English law does not appear to accept this distinction between secured and unsecured debts. In numerous Admiralty cases where the distribution of the proceeds of a foreign ship arrested and sold in England was in issue, the court held that it was for the *lex fori* to decide the question of priorities.[3] But as in all those cases the forum coincided with the situs of the ship or of the proceeds of its sale, the decisions, though open to objection in their reasoning, are correct in their result. The problem argued before the court was not: *lex fori* or *lex situs*? but proper law of the contract, law of the flag,[4] law of the domicile—or *lex fori*?

[1] German Bankruptcy Act, 1877, s. 61, no. 4.

[2] As to the question of what law is applicable to a *ius in rem mobilem*, see ss. 488–91.

[3] *The Milford* (1858), Sw. 362, 366. *The Jonathan Goodhue* (1859), Sw. 524, 526. *The Tagus*, [1903] P. 44. *The Colorado*, [1923] P. (C.A.) 103. *The Zigurds*, [1932] P. 113, 121, 122.

[4] Under the Maritime Conventions Act, 1911 (1 & 2 Geo. V, c. 57), s. 7, the distribution of salvage as between the owner, the master, the pilot, the crew, and other persons is made according to the law of the country to which the vessel belongs, and not according to the *lex fori*.

8. MEASURE OF DAMAGES

**226.
Measure of
damages** It has often been said that the measure of damages is a matter of procedure. So sweeping a rule—which for that matter does not exist outside Anglo-American law—contains both an exaggeration and an ambiguity. As Professor Cheshire has convincingly shown,[1] it is merely the calculation of damages which in England may be regarded as procedural. But the question whether the liability exists belongs to substantive law and may therefore be governed by foreign law. This is particularly the case with regard to the following points:

(*a*) Is the defendant's liability restricted to such damage as is the direct and natural consequence of his act[2] or to that damage which it was the aim of the broken contract or the violated legal provision to avoid;[3] or is he bound to pay compensation for consequential damage?[4] Is the answer to these questions dependent on the degree of culpability of the defendant?[5]

(*b*) Is the defendant liable for *dommage moral*, as is the case in England and France, or only for material injury or loss, as is the rule in Germany and Italy?

(*c*) In the case of a broken or annulled contract, is the plaintiff entitled to be placed, 'so far as money can do it, in the same situation with respect to damages as if the contract had been performed',[6] or can he claim only for what he would have had if the contract had not been concluded at all? This distinction was advanced particularly by Jhering, who speaks of the 'negative' as opposed to the 'positive' interest,[7] and it has been adopted by German, Austrian, Swiss, and Russian law.

(*d*) In what circumstances is the plaintiff to be com-

---

[1] pp. 850-7.

[2] Code civil, art. 1151 (*suite immédiate et directe*); art. 1150 (*suite prévisible*). The same view in *Hadley* v. *Baxendale* (1854), 9 Ex. 341.

[3] Prevailing doctrine in Austria; Ehrenzweig, *Bürgerliches Recht*, § 301: the soundest of all theories evolved on the problem of causation.

[4] Thus under French law if the defendant is guilty of malice; art. 1150 c.c.

[5] Art. 1150 c.c.

[6] *Robinson* v. *Harman* (1848), 1 Ex. 850.

[7] *Jhering's Jahrbücher*, 4, p. 16 et seq. See German Civ. C., ss. 122, 179, 307.

pensated not only for *damnum emergens* but also for *lucrum cessans*? This distinction, though for the most part abandoned by modern legislation, is still material in Austria, where the liability for lost profits is only recognized in the case of malice and wanton negligence.[1]

(*e*) Does the plaintiff's contributory negligence exclude his right to claim damages, or does it merely operate to reduce the amount payable? Total exclusion was the principle of English law before the Law Reform (Contributory Negligence) Act, 1945, as it was that of Roman law.

Continental codes leave it to the court's discretion to determine whether the defendant's liability is entirely destroyed or merely reduced by the plaintiff's negligence.[2] It is important to note that this continental rule—in spite of the fact that judicial discretion is decisive—is by no means procedural. It will therefore (probably) be applied by an English court if the liability is based on foreign law.

(*f*) Is the defendant allowed to take credit for any benefit which may have accrued to the plaintiff by the injurious act (so-called *compensatio lucri cum damno*)? Practically everywhere this question is answered in the affirmative, subject however to some exceptions in respect of which the various laws differ. Undoubtedly the problem is one of substantive law. So is

(*g*) the problem whether the plaintiff is entitled to interest and if so at what rate?

(*h*) What is the quantum of damages for non-delivery of goods sold? Is the buyer entitled to be compensated for the damage he actually suffered, is he entitled to the difference between the market value of the goods and the agreed price, or is he allowed to choose between these two forms of compensation? It is believed that this problem too belongs to substantive law.

When all these and similar questions have been answered according to the applicable foreign law, there often remain some questions which English, though not continental, courts would consider to be mainly procedural in character, so that the *lex fori* would apply.

---

[1] Austrian Civ. C., 1323, 1324, 1332.
[2] See in particular German Civ. C., s. 254. *RVgl.HWB,* VI. 130 et seq.

Examples: Under some continental laws the plaintiff is entitled to claim restitution *in natura*;[1] in the English court he can claim only a sum of money. Again: under the foreign law he has the right to be compensated for *dommage moral*; how such damage is to be estimated in money will be decided by English law. Or again: where a claim for damages arises in France and under French law, the sum will be expressed in francs; but, as will be explained later,[2] the English court cannot give judgment in a foreign currency, and the necessary conversion into sterling will be made at a rate of exchange fixed by the *lex fori*.

9. CONTRIBUTION BY A CO-DEBTOR?

227. Contribution by a co-debtor

Dicey,[3] when dealing with procedure, reckoned among the problems concerned that raised by *American Surety Co.* v. *Wrightson*.[4] An American firm took out two insurance policies, one with an American insurance company, and the other with an English one. The American insurance company had to pay the firm under the policy and then sued the English co-insurer for contribution in the English court. The court applied English law, and Dicey suggested as the reason that the equitable jurisdiction of the English court on which the action was based was a matter of procedure.

If this were true any matter which in English municipal law is regulated by equity would have to be governed by English law as the *lex fori*, and foreign law would be entirely excluded. It is, however, hardly defensible to look at the whole vast bulk of Equity as if it were part of a code of civil procedure. Fortunately the judge who decided the case (Hamilton, J.) did not say what Dicey suggested. He applied English law not as the *lex fori*, but as the *lex domicilii debitoris*, so that he must have regarded the question as one of substantive law.

PROCEDURE IN FOREIGN COURTS

It goes without saying that proceedings in foreign courts are governed by the *lex fori*. English courts may be concerned with foreign proceedings in manifold ways.

---

[1] Germany (C.C., s. 249), Austria, Russia.
[2] See s. 447.
[3] 5th edit., p. 855 (cancelled by Morris in the 6th ed.).
[4] (1911), 103 L.T. 663, 665.

1. Sometimes the English court needs the assistance of foreign judicial proceedings. Thus the High Court may make an order for the examination on commission of witnesses living abroad.[1] In such cases the foreign court, though observing the procedural rules of its own law, will follow English rules of procedure in so far as this is not inconsistent with the law of the court, for example, in respect of cross-examination or the administration of an oath in religious form; for should the foreign court act otherwise and its method be incompatible with tenets of English procedure the whole evidence taken abroad might be declared inadmissible in this country and thus rendered useless for its purpose.

228. English court assisted by foreign courts

2. What is the effect of judicial proceedings initiated abroad? It is important to distinguish their effect on procedure from that on substantive law.

229. Foreign proceedings : lis alibi pendens

(*a*) The procedural effect is to give the parties certain rights on the ground of *lis alibi pendens*. Most legal systems recognize this as a defence in cases where after starting an action in one court the plaintiff begins a second action for the same cause and against the same defendant in another court. *De eadem re ne bis sit actio*. Is the plea of *lis alibi pendens* a good defence when the first proceedings were brought in a court of a foreign country? French courts reject the *exceptio* in this case. German law allows it only where a judgment delivered in a foreign court would be recognized in the court which entertains the second action.[2] English law differs from both these views; there is no strict rule. Its answer to the question depends on whether the taking of proceedings in respect of the same subject-matter and between the same parties in different courts is 'vexatious or oppressive'.[3] If it is, the court has jurisdiction to stay or dismiss the English action or to

---

[1] See R.S.C., Order 37, r. 6, 6a, 6b, 6c. Cf. also the Hague Convention on Civil Procedure of 17 July 1905, art. 8 et seq (not ratified by Great Britian).

[2] Pillet, *Traité prat.*, II. 498. German Supreme Court, *Off. Coll.*, 49, 344. Ad. Wach, *Civilprocessrecht* (1885), I. 247. Katinszky, 9 *Rabel's Z.*, 855 et seq.

[3] *McHenry* v. *Lewis* (1882), 22 Ch.D. (C.A.) 397, 408 (*per* Bowen, L.J.). *Peruvian Guano Co.* v. *Bockwoldt* (1883), 23 Ch.D. (C.A.) 225, 232. *The Christiansborg* (1885), 10 P.D. (C.A.) 141, 155. *Cohen* v. *Rothfield*, [1919] 1 K.B. (C.A.) 410.

restrain the plaintiff from proceeding with his foreign action. While the continental *exceptio litis pendentis* is a defence only against the later (second) action, the English court is at liberty to interfere with the first action and allow the second proceedings to continue. There is another considerable difference between English practice and the continental rule in that English courts do not require the issues raised in the two actions to be identical. Two examples of this are to be found in *Cohen* v. *Rothfield*[1] and *Thornton* v. *Thornton*.[2]

> Cohen, who was engaged in commercial transactions both in England and Scotland, employed Rothfield as his agent in both countries; after a dispute between them Cohen brought an action in England, claiming an account of all money which Rothfield had received on the plaintiff's behalf, and a few days later Rothfield commenced a similar action for an account against Cohen in a Scottish court. As Cohen's claim for an account is not identical with Rothfield's claim, continental courts would have no power to stay either action. Similarly in the *Thornton* case: the husband Thornton brought a divorce suit in India, while his wife sued him in England for restitution of conjugal rights. There was no *eadem res*. In both cases the court refused to stay the action before it, not for the absence of *eadem res*, but because it had not been shown that the cumulation of actions led to vexation or oppression.

It is for the party which relies on *lis alibi pendens* to show that the commencement of two actions is vexatious or oppressive, since English law, unlike continental laws, does not object to the bringing of two actions on the same subject. The plaintiff may have good reasons for suing the defendant in two countries, for example, if the defendant has some property in each, but in neither of them enough to cover the whole of the debt sued upon; or if the plaintiff needs a quick decision and is not sure in which of two countries he can obtain it more rapidly. The term 'vexation or oppression' is very elastic. The courts, however, have repeatedly declared that it would be 'most unwise' to lay down any definition of what is vexatious or oppressive.[3] The jurisdiction of English courts to restrain one of the parties from proceeding in another country will

[1] [1919] 1 K.B. 410.
[2] (1886), 11 P.D. (C.A.) 176.
[3] *McHenry* v. *Lewis*, loc. cit. at p. 407.

be 'exercised with great caution'.¹ Only two special rules
have been evolved. First, it is *prima facie* vexatious to
bring the two actions in two different English courts,
while there is no presumption of vexation where one of the
actions has been brought in a non-British court.² Secondly,
there is presumably no vexation where the person who is
defendant in England brings a foreign action against the
English plaintiff.³

(*b*) In all legal systems based on Roman law the bringing of an action has certain effects in the realm of substantive law: it interrupts the course of prescription and
of usucapion; it produces a higher degree of responsibility
in the possessor who is sued by a person purporting to be
the owner; it creates a liability to pay interest on due
money sued on; rights of a highly personal character, such
as rights for *dommage moral*, which are as a rule extinguished by the creditor's death, pass to his successors if
the creditor dies during proceedings he has initiated.⁴
The question arises whether all, or any, of these effects
obtain if the action has been brought in a foreign court.
It is obvious that this is not a problem of private international law, but one of construction of those rules of
muncipal law which establish the effects in question.
Continental laws will as a rule answer the question in the
affirmative if, and only if, the judgment which is to be
expected in the foreign proceedings would be recognized
by the domestic courts. It is immaterial whether the substantive law prevailing in one country would attach to the
commencement of an action the same consequences as the
law of the other country. No such effects, for example, are
known to municipal English law. Nevertheless, if the
owner of a chattel sues its possessor in an English court
and if the cause of action is governed by German law,

230. Influence of foreign proceedings on substantive law

¹ *Orr-Lewis* v. *Orr-Lewis*, [1949] P. 347.
² If one of the actions is brought in England and the other in some part of the
British Empire outside England (Scotland, Canada, Malta, &c.) it is doubtful
whether to presume vexation or not. The Court of Appeal held in *McHenry* v.
Lewis, loc. cit., that vexation must be presumed in such cases; but it is difficult to
justify such presumption. See Cheshire, 165.
³ *Cohen* v. *Rothfield*, loc. cit.; *The London*, [1931] P. 14. Comp. *The Janera*,
[1928] P. 55, 57; *The Madrid*, [1936] P. 40, 46.
⁴ See, for example, German Civ. C., ss. 209, 941, 987, 989, 291, 847, 1300.

the increased responsibility of the defendant provided by German law comes into existence just as if the action had been brought in Germany.

Another illustration: Under a German contract D owes C £100; C brings an action in Germany; then both C and D emigrate to England, where C initiates new proceedings. In this case the effect of the action begun in Germany—that is, the obligation to pay 4 per cent. interest from the date of its commencement—will (probably) be taken into account by the English court.

3. The problem of the effect of foreign judgments in England deserves a chapter to itself.

CHAPTER XIX

RECOGNITION AND ENFOR EMENT
OF FOREIGN JUDGMENTS

GENERAL OBSERVATIONS

Of all problems arising in international intercourse the problem of the recognition of foreign judgments and their enforcement in other countries is possibly the most important.[1] This has always been so where foreign trade is concerned. The merchant who has obtained a favourable judgment against his debtor in one country and then learns that the debtor has not enough property in that country to cover the debt, will wish to enforce the judgment in another country where the debtor has a considerable bank deposit. To start a new action would be expensive and often inconvenient, for example, if the witnesses live far away. Apart from commercial intercourse the recognition of foreign judgments has become increasingly important during the last hundred years, because whole populations have migrated to other countries for political or economic reasons, and travel facilities have improved. In particular, the recognition in the country of the parties' residence of divorce decrees granted in another country, or of judgments on nullity of marriage or on legitimacy, have become of overwhelmimg importance.

231. Advantages and dangers

There was, for example, the famous case of *Prince Wrede*: an Austrian Roman Catholic (woman) had married an Austrian of orthodox faith who later became a Russian citizen; the Ecclesiastical Court of St. Petersburg declared the marriage void because the forms prescribed for the marriage of an orthodox Christian had not been observed. The woman then married the Bavarian Prince Wrede in Paris, where he was resident; this marriage was declared void by the Munich Court, the prince having changed his residence from Paris to Munich. The nullity decree was based on bigamy, since the Munich Court declined to recognize the validity of the St. Petersburg decree. Wrede then married another woman in Geneva, and in a

[1] The earliest English decisions on private international law deal with the recognition of foreign judgments. See Holdsworth, *History of Engl. L.*, xi, 270, and *supra*, s. 27.

French court the question was raised whether France was to recognize the St. Petersburg decree or the Munich judgment or neither.[1]

It is hardly necessary to stress the advantages to international relations resulting from the recognition of foreign judgments; if all judgments could be recognized everywhere this would give stability to individual relationships all over the world. The awkward situation in 'limping' marriages, that is, marriages valid in one country, void or dissolved in another, or again in limping legitimacies, would be cured as soon as a judgment had been delivered in any one country. New actions in other countries would become superfluous.

The dangers to which so sweeping a simplification would lead are as manifest as its advantages. A judge would produce international effects such as no legislator could ever contemplate. Furthermore, it is not advisable to trust every court in the world to administer justice irreproachably. Bribery of judges may have become so rare as to reduce this risk to a minimum; but in some countries unsatisfactory legal education, appointment of judges from political motives, and the influence which the state or some powerful criminal organization within the state, or some political party, may bring to bear on the judges are considerable obstacles to a universal recognition of judgments. Further, even where there is no danger of any kind of corruption of courts, differences between two countries in their fundamental attitude to questions of morality or public policy must often make the recognition of some individual judgments seem undesirable. Finally, general recognition might result in grave injustice where the same relationship was regarded differently by the courts of two countries. Take, for instance, a marriage celebrated between two Greek subjects in Paris before a Greek priest and therefore valid in Greece (and Germany), void in France (and England); such marriage, if the system under discussion were adopted, would become universally valid or void according as a Greek or German court on the one hand, or a French or English court on the other, first pronounced on its validity. This undesirable result could

[1] *Sirey*, 1900, 2, 40. See Pillet, *Traité prat.*, II. 606 et seq., and *infra*, p. 271.

of course be avoided by an international unification of the rules on court jurisdiction. But the hope of reaching agreement on this point is not better founded than the hope of agreement on rules of conflict of laws.

Thus recognition and enforcement of foreign judgments can certainly not be admitted without efficient safeguards. The question is: why admit them at all? Different reasons have been advanced for the view that apart from any implication of territorial sovereignty judgments delivered by the courts of one country should become operative in another. The doctrine of *comity* does not explain anything and leads to the inadequate rule of reciprocity as a condition of recognition of foreign judgments.[1] The doctrine of *acquired rights* begs the question by presupposing a right as acquired, while the problem is just whether it is acquired.[2] A doctrine of *obligation*,[3] based on the idea that the foreign judgment if made by a court of competent jurisdiction creates a contractual (or quasi-contractual) obligation, brings a fictitious contract into play and cannot justify the recognition of divorce decrees or other judgments *in rem*. H. E. Read bases the recognition of foreign judgments on 'grounds of judicial reason or ideas of social value or both' and requires a sufficient relation 'between the person, status or thing concerned and the territory of the foreign law district';[4] it is impossible not to agree with this. The recognition of foreign judgments, like the application of foreign law, is based on justice; but the question as to when justice requires such recognition and when it does not can hardly be answered by a short and simple formula. In the pursuit of justice here as elsewhere the inquirer must generally confine himself to the study of a vast number of examples and their classification into types.

There is, finally, the doctrine enunciated by von Bar, who attempts to harmonize the recognition of foreign judgments with the application of foreign laws, by calling attention to the relationship between law and judgment.

232. Various doctrines on the reasons for recognition

233. Doctrine of harmony between law and judgment

---

[1] See *supra*, ss. 3, 41.   [2] See *supra*, s. 2.
[3] *Russell* v. *Smyth* (1842), 9 M. & W., 810, 819. See Read, loc. cit., 60.
[4] Read, p. 257.

A judgment, in his view, is a *lex specialis*, a law regulating one single case.[1] This view tends to over-simplification. True, there is no great difference between the divorce decree of a foreign court and an Act of Parliament of Quebec by which a particular marriage is dissolved. In such cases, however, the judgment is not a kind of statute; the statute is a kind of judgment, and its application in England—which is identical with the recognition of a particular divorce decree—will depend on the English rules on recognition of foreign judgments and not on those on conflict of laws. If, for example, one of the spouses had had no opportunity of being heard before the Act of Parliament was passed, or if bribery or any other kind of fraud had conduced to its passing, this would in the eyes of English law cause the Act to be invalid, just as judgments are deemed invalid on the ground of fraud or of certain procedural defects.[2] But a certain amount of guidance can be obtained from the comparison between law and judgment, between the conflict of laws and the conflict of jurisdictions, as French authors call it. As the law now stands, the two classes of rules are independent of each other.[3] A judgment delivered in a foreign country will be recognized in England though it may be based on the application of a municipal law which under English conflict rules would not have been applied by an English court.

Example: Two Italian citizens domiciled in England conclude a contract in this country, to be performed here. An English court would apply English law, an Italian court Italian law.[4] An action on the contract is begun in Italy (where the defendant is living for the time being). The judgment of the Italian court is recognized in England because in the English view the Italian court had jurisdiction, though that court by applying Italian law may have come to a decision opposed to that which the English court would have given under English law.

[1] von Bar, II. 413 (Gillespie's transl., p. 895). Wharton, s. 671 (II, p. 1425). *Contra*: Pillet, *Traité prat.* II. 616, 663.

[2] See *infra*, s. 247.

[3] not only in England but in most continental countries, though in French law and some legal systems derived from the French interdependence has been considered and has influenced the courts: see Pillet, *Traité prat.*, II. 686. cf. *supra*, s. 54.

[4] According to the rule of the *Codice civile* (1938, 1942), *Dispos. preliminari* s. 15.

In order to establish a certain harmony between conflict rules and respect for foreign judgments, von Bar and the Institute of International Law[1] have proposed rules to the effect that the courts of a given country should in principle and 'as far as possible' decide on such actions as are to be decided under the municipal law of that country. This proposal is unsatisfactory; why should England refuse recognition and enforcement of an Italian judgment based on the application of German law in a case where the English court likewise would have applied German law? The view developed and partly followed in France[2] is more acceptable. It runs: a French court recognizes a foreign judgment only if that judgment has been rendered in accordance with French rules on conflict of laws. The objection to this rule is that it reduces the number of enforceable judgments below a reasonable limit.

BIBLIOGRAPHY

F. T. PIGGOTT, *Foreign Judgments and Jurisdiction* (3rd ed.), 1908. H. E. READ, *Recognition and Enforcement of Foreign Judgments in the Common Law Units of the Brit. Commonwealth*, 1938 (main work on the subject, a valuable contribution to comparative law). CHESHIRE, 736 et seq. GOODRICH, 522–62. H. C. GUTTERIDGE, *Brit. Y.B.*, 1932, 49. H. DE COCK, 36 *Rec.* (1925 V), 435; *Brit.Y.B.*, 1929, 225. H. SPERL, 36 *Rec.* (1931 II), 389. NUSSBAUM, 41 *Columb. L.R.*, 221. RENTON, 50 *South Afric. L.J.* (1933), 157.

THE DISTINCTION BETWEEN RECOGNITION AND ENFORCEMENT

There can be no enforcement of a judgment without recognition; but there may be recognition without enforcement.

234. Cases of mere recognition

1. Some judgments cannot be enforced; for example, merely declaratory judgments, divorce or nullity decrees, and all judgments dismissing an action (unless there is an order as to costs). Here the only question arising is whether they are to be 'recognized' in England or, as English jurists often put it, whether they are 'valid' in this country, particularly when relied on in a fresh lawsuit brought in an English court. Some illustrations:

[1] *Annuaire*, I (1877), pp. 125, 126; von Bar, II. 427 (Gillespie's transl., p. 908).
[2] See Pillet, *Traité prat.* II. 691.

(*a*) After a foreign divorce one of the parties concludes a new marriage. Its validity depends on the validity of the divorce and therefore on the recognition of the foreign decree.

(*b*) The foreign court dismisses an action. The plaintiff brings a new action on the same subject-matter in an English court. The foreign judgment, if recognized, is a good defence: *exceptio rei iudicatae*.[1]

(*c*) The defendant in an English action pleads a set-off. The plaintiff replies that the defendant's claim was dismissed by a foreign court. If the judgment of that court is recognized in England the plaintiff's *replicatio rei iudicatae* is a good defence.

235. Recognition requires less than enforcement

2. The recognition of a foreign judgment requires less than its enforcement. No enforcement is possible without an authoritative act of the domestic court allowing the execution of the judgment, be it an *Exequatur* after a re-trial of the case, or a new judgment given on the foreign one, or the entering of the foreign judgment in a register.[2] Mere recognition needs no act of this kind. Apart from this, however, the conditions of recognition are practically the same as those required for enforcement. Only in the countries in which enforcement depends on reciprocity[3] can a doubt arise whether mere recognition, and in particular the effects of *res iudicata*, are conditioned by reciprocity. In spite of von Bar's well-founded warning,[4] German law answers this question in the affirmative; it admits the *exceptio rei iudicatae* only if reciprocity is secured, at least where the foreign judgment is concerned with property

---

[1] If the foreign judgment was for the plaintiff, and if he nevertheless sues his debtor a second time (in an English court), not on the foreign judgment but on the original cause of action, the defendant has no *exceptio rei iudicatae*. Though under domestic English law a plaintiff who has obtained judgment in England is barred from suing again, this is not so in the case of a foreign judgment. Here the original cause of action is not 'merged' in the judgment. This distinction, though hardly justifiable, is firmly established: *Hall* v. *Odber* (1809), 11 East., 118, 124; *Smith* v. *Nicolls* (1839), 5 Bing. (N.C.) 208; *Bank of Australia* v. *Harding* (1850), 9 C.B. 661; *Bank of Australia* v. *Nias* (1851), 16 Q.B. 717. See Holdsworth, *History of Engl. L.*, xi, 273.

[2] See *infra*, ss. 250–3.

[3] Germany, Spain, Czechoslovakia, Hungary, several Swiss cantons, most of the Balkan States, and many extra-European countries.

[4] I. 286, II. 506 (Gillespie's transl., pp. 214, 974).

rights.[1] In England the question does not arise. It may be mentioned that the Foreign Judgments (Reciprocal Enforcement) Act, 1933,[2] has made reciprocal treatment a condition of registration only for the purpose of enforcement, not of recognition.

THE CONDITIONS OF RECOGNITION AND ENFORCEMENT

Under English law recognition and enforcement of a foreign judgment require that this should be a final judgment on a civil or commercial subject-matter by a court having competent jurisdiction; and the judgment must neither be inconsistent with fundamental principles of English law (public policy, natural justice) nor vitiated by fraud.

1. It must be a *judgment*, that is, a decision delivered after proceedings in which both parties have had an opportunity of being heard.[3] Judicial acts belonging to the sphere of 'voluntary jurisdiction', as contrasted with contentious jurisdiction,[4] are not judgments. They are of manifold types. Some of them are concerned with the status of persons, like the *venia aetatis* granted to a minor, or the interdiction of a lunatic, or the judicial confirmation of an adoption. Others have the effect of creating legal entities, such as the incorporation of a company or the confirmation of a 'foundation' (*fondation*, *Stiftung*). Others, again, deal with the appointment or dismissal of guardians or curators, or with the termination of a wife's legal authority[5] to contract on behalf of her husband in domestic matters. Under many legal systems, furthermore, the validity of certain contracts depends on the approbation of the court.[6] In all such cases the question arises whether and

236. Conditions of recognition and enforcement: (1) Judgment

---

[1] German Code of Civil Procedure, s. 328, no. 5. Divorce or nullity of marriage decrees are recognized irrespective of whether there is reciprocity or not.

[2] 23 Geo. V, c. 13. See *infra*, s. 253.

[3] See German Supreme Court, *Offic. Coll.*, 16, 428, and Melchior, 313 et seq.; further, Mann, 59 *L.Q.R.*, 53, 54.

[4] See Marcian in *Dig.*, 1, 16, 2 *pr.*

[5] The so-called *Schlüsselgewalt*, German Civ. C., s. 1357; Swiss Civ. Code, s. 167.

[6] *Examples*: Sale of immovable property by a minor (German Civ. C., s. 1821);

on what conditions the act of the foreign court is to be recognized in this country. Sometimes we are also faced with the problem whether an act of voluntary jurisdiction can be enforced here: under French law, for instance, a residuary legatee instituted by a holograph will can obtain possession of the property left to him only upon an order by the President of the Court (*envoi en possession*);[1] if such order has been made and part of the property is situate in England, or was brought into this country before the order was executed in France, can it be enforced in England? The answer to all these questions may be difficult and often doubtful; but it cannot be given by the rules on recognition and enforcement of foreign judgments.

It is submitted that the correct solution is to the following effect: no enforcement of foreign judicial acts of the types mentioned, but recognition if the foreign court was competent. Such competence, however, should not be determined on the lines of contentious jurisdiction, but be closely linked to the rule on conflict of laws: if, and only if, the legal relationship with which the act of the foreign court is connected is governed according to English private international law by the municipal law prevailing in the country of the foreign court, will the judicial act be recognized.[2] The power, for example, of a guardian appointed by a foreign court depends on whether the personal law of the ward coincides with the law of the country where the guardian was appointed. If this is the case his position in England is not different from that of a guardian who has obtained guardianship *ipsa lege* or by will and without any authoritative act.

237. (2) By a court of law. Arbitral awards

2. The judgment must have been delivered by a *Court of Law*. It does not matter whether it was a court established by the state, or by a smaller community (e.g. a *commune*), or by several states under an international convention, or whether it was an ecclesiastical court. Private arbitral tribunals, on the other hand, are not judicial courts in the strict sense of that term, since their decisions (awards) cannot be executed within the country where they have been delivered unless an enforcement order has been made by the court of that country. They are—as Eve, J., said,

contracts made by the husband in respect of his wife's property (German Civ. C., s. 1379) or by the wife without her husband's consent (French C.C., arts. 1535, 1538, 1556, &c.); disclaimer of inheritance on the part of one of the spouses without consent of the other (Swiss Civ. C., ss. 218, 204).

[1] *Code civil*, art. 1008.

[2] Cf. Mann, 59 *L.Q.R.* (1943), 55. See *infra*, ss. 268, 269, on *venia aetatis*, *émancipation*, and interdiction.

speaking of German awards[1]—'still-born for all practical purposes until vitality is infused into them by the Court'. On the other hand, before it is enforceable the award creates an obligation on the part of one party towards the other to do what the award orders him to do. There is no doubt that the party in whose favour the award is given can bring an action on the award without going back to the original cause of action, and that this is equally applicable to a foreign award.[2] But such action on an award is not an action on a foreign judgment given by a court of law. In the countries, for example, in which the enforcement of foreign judgments depends on reciprocity such dependence does not apply to foreign awards.[3] The common law rules on enforcement of arbitral awards have been substantially altered by legislation. Two English statutes, the *Arbitration Clauses (Protocol) Act*, 1924,[4] and the *Arbitration (Foreign Awards) Act*, 1930,[5] were passed to give effect to two Geneva Conventions of 1923 and 1927 respectively.[6]

Each of the contracting states recognizes the validity of arbitral agreements between parties subject to the jurisdiction of the various contracting states, even though the arbitration takes place in a third country. The arbitral procedure is governed by the will of the parties and by the law of the state in which it takes place; this state ensures the execution of the award. Some of the contracting states (such as France, Belgium, the Netherlands, Spain, and Roumania) have restricted their obligations to enforce awards to commercial contracts. The recognition and enforcement of foreign awards governed by the Acts require the fulfilment of certain conditions; in particular, that the arbitration agreement is valid according to the law applicable to that agreement, and that the enforcement of the award is not contrary to English public policy 'or to the law of England'.[7] The enforcement of the

---

[1] In *Merrifield, Ziegler & Co.* v. *Liverpool Cotton Association Ltd.* (1911), 105 L.T.R. 97, 106.

[2] *Norske Atlas Insurance Co.* v. *London General Insurance Co.* (1927), 43 T.L.R. 541.

[3] The plaintiff has only to prove that the parties submitted to arbitration, that the arbitration was conducted in accordance with the submission, and that the award is valid in the country where it was made; *Norske Atlas Insurance Co.* v. *London General Insurance Co.*, loc. cit.

[4] 14 & 15 Geo. V, c. 39.

[5] 20 Geo. V, c. 15.

[6] Ratified by a great number of states; catalogued in Read, loc. cit., p. 79, n. 104.

[7] Here, as on some other points, the English Act of 1930 has departed from the text of the Geneva Convention of 1927. Art. 1 (e) of the Convention speaks of a

award can be made either by an action based on the award or by a judicial order allowing execution in the same way as in the case of a judgment of a court.

238. (3) on civil or commercial matters

3. It must be a judgment on *civil* or *commercial matters*, including questions of status. A judgment of a penal nature or on matters of administrative law, such as revenue law, has no effect in England.[1] It may happen, however, that a court by one judgment imposes on the defendant both damages and a fine. Several continental laws allow such 'adhesion procedure' in certain cases. If, then, a judgment of this kind is severable its civil, though not its penal, part has extra-territorial effect and will be recognized in this country.[2]

239. (4) Competent jurisdiction (a) over actions *in personam*

4. The adjudicating foreign court must be a court of *competent jurisdiction*, that is, a court of a country in which jurisdiction on a given matter may be exercised not only according to the law of that country but also according to English law.[3] Under English law a foreign court has competent jurisdiction on the following conditions:

(a) It has jurisdiction over actions *in personam*:

(i) if the defendant was present in the foreign country at the time when the action was brought;[4] or

(ii) if he was resident in that country at that time;[5] or

(iii) if he has submitted to the jurisdiction of the foreign court, expressly or by implication, for ex-

recognition contrary to 'the principles of the law of the country in which it is sought to be relied upon'; and the French text (which is equally authentic) even limits the non-recognition to the case where the recognition is 'contraire aux principes du droit public'. It is submitted that the text of the English Act, s. 3 (1) *in fin.*, should be interpreted in accordance with the English text of the Convention, since that text, though not forming part of the English statute, was annexed to it.

[1] See *supra*, ss. 163, 164. See on *Boucher* v. *Lawson* (1734): Holdsworth, *Hist. of Engl. L*, XI. 270.

[2] See on this Pillet, *Traité prat.*, II. 576 et seq.; Bartin, *Principes*, 479.

[3] See *supra*, ss. 44, 45.

[4] *Carrick* v. *Hancock* (1895), 12 T.L.R. 59; *Schibsby* v. *Westenholz* (1870), L.R. 6 Q.B. 155, 161; *Emanuel* v. *Symon*, [1908] 1 K.B.(C.A.) 302, 309.

[5] *Schibsby* v. *Westenholz*, loc. cit.; *Rousillon* v. *Rousillon* (1880), 14 Ch.D. 351, 371. Whether residence here means more than presence is, however, doubtful (Dicey–Morris, p. 354). Under all continental laws residence is in any case a sufficient ground for jurisdiction, and as under these laws a resident can be served with a writ even if he is temporarily absent, the rule that residence constitutes jurisdiction is sound. See also Foreign Judgments (Reciprocal Enforcement) Act, 1933, s. 4 (2) (a) (iv).

ample, if he is fighting the action on its merits.[1]
Does the mere fact that he appears in the action only
in order to protest against the jurisdiction constitute submission? It would be appropriate to deny
submission in such case; but in *Harris* v. *Taylor* the
Court of Appeal unanimously and unfortunately
laid down the opposite view,[2] the defendant's protest being considered *protestatio facto contraria*.

(iv) Whether *nationality* is a sufficient ground for
jurisdiction is open to doubt.[3]

(v) Domicile certainly is not. Nor can the competence
of the court be based

(vi) on the fact that the defendant has *property* in the
country of that court,[4] or that a *contract* has been
concluded or is to be *performed* within that country,
or that a *tort* producing an obligation has been
committed there.[5]

(vii) We have seen (*supra*, s. 58) that actions *in personam* are not only those which arise from an
obligation but also those springing from a *ius in
rem*, such as the owner's action for delivery of
chattels or recovery of land possessed by the defendant, or an action aiming at determining a title to
movables or immovables as between the parties. It
seems that English law regards foreign courts as
competent to adjudicate upon such actions if the
land or chattel is situate within the country of that
court. In the case of immovables this jurisdiction
is even exclusive; the English court would not
recognize a judgment of a court of country X if
the immovable in issue is situate in England or in
country Y, and this is probably true also of actions
for damages for trespass to such immovables.[6]

---

[1] *Feyericke* v. *Hubbard* (1902), 71 L.J., K.B. 509; *Copin* v. *Adamson* (1874),
L.R. 9 Ex. 345.

[2] [1915] 2 K.B. 580, 587. *Contra* in the case of s. 4, subs. (2) (a) (1) of the
Foreign Judgments (Reciprocal Enforcement) Act, 1933. See Cheshire, pp. 786–7.

[3] See *supra*, s. 122 (5). Read, loc. cit., 151 et seq.

[4] *Emanuel* v. *Symon*, [1908] 1 K.B. 302.

[5] *Sirdar Gurdyal Singh* v. *Rajah of Faridkote*, [1894] A.C. (P.C.) 670, 684.

[6] Cf. Story, ss. 591, 592; Dicey–Morris, pp. 66, 70. A certain ambiguity in this
matter results from the fact that the term 'action *in rem*' sometimes seems to have

(*b*) Actions *in rem*, that is, having effect *adversus omnes*.[1]

(i) In the case of a tangible thing—a ship or a piece of land—exclusive jurisdiction lies with the court of the country where the thing was situate when judgment was delivered.[2]

(ii) A foreign court has jurisdiction in divorce cases if (and only if) the spouses were domiciled in the country of that court when proceedings were initiated, irrespective of the place of the marriage.[3] If a divorce decree has been obtained in a different country, for example in the country to which the parties belong by nationality, its validity in England depends on its recognition by the state of domicile.[4]

Examples: (1) A French subject, domiciled (in the English sense) in Germany, who obtains a divorce in a French court is validly divorced in England, because German law recognizes the competence of the French court.

(2) In the case of *Armitage* v. *Att.-Gen.*[5] the wife obtained a divorce decree from the court of South Dakota against her American husband who, though domiciled in New York, had resided for ninety days in South Dakota. The ground of divorce was desertion. Under the law of South Dakota, though not under that of New York, divorce for desertion was permissible. But it was proved that the New York courts would recognize the validity of the decree. Thereupon the English court held that the divorce decree was binding.

As Cheshire has shown, it would be unobjectionable to allow a divorce in the court of the country of *residence*, provided the divorce is granted for a cause recognized by the law of the domicile.[6]

been used in an untechnical sense. (Dicey–Morris, p. 366, speaks of proceedings which are not 'in strictness actions *in rem*'.) See Blackburn, J., in *Castrique* v. *Imrie* (1870), L.R. 4 H.L. 429. The Foreign Judgments (Reciprocal Enforcement) Act, 1933, s. 4, subs. (2) (b), distinguishes very clearly as follows: In the case of immovables the *forum situs* is competent if the immovables are 'subject-matter of an action', in the case of movables only if they are 'subject-matter of an action *in rem*', this term obviously used in its technical sense. On Canadian law, see Read, loc. cit., 191.

[1] See *supra*, ss. 44, 45.　　　　　[2] *Castrique* v. *Imrie*, loc. cit.

[3] *Harvey* v. *Farnie* (1880), 5 P.D. 153; (1882), 8 App. Cas. 43. *Le Mesurier* v. *Le Mesurier*, [1895] A.C. 517. *Bater* v. *Bater*, [1906] P. 209, 217. *Simons* v. *Simons*, [1939] 1 K.B. 490, 498.　　　　　[4] Dicey–Morris, p. 376.

[5] [1906] P. 135, 141. Criticism by Morris, 24 *Canad. B.R.* (1946), 73, at p. 84. Against him: Tuck, 25, ibid. (1947), 226–40.

[6] Cheshire, p. 61; *L.Q.R.* (1945), 354 et seq., 371. See Cook, *Legal and Logical Bases*, 457 et seq. See 23 *Canad. B.R.* (1945), 244.

(iii) Jurisdiction of a foreign court in suits for judicial separation or for restitution of conjugal rights is probably founded either on domicile alone or on residence, just as is the jurisdiction of an English court in these matters.[1]

(iv) The jurisdiction of a foreign court to entertain a suit for nullity of marriage is founded on the domicile of both spouses.[2] A nullity decree pronounced outside the *forum domicilii* is valid if it is held valid by the *forum domicilii*. Three questions arise:

(*a*) Is it sufficient that one of the spouses only is domiciled at the foreign forum?

(*b*) Has the foreign court jurisdiction on the ground of residence of both parties?

(*c*) Does the English court recognize nullity decrees pronounced by the foreign *forum loci celebrationis*?

The answer to the first question is probably 'yes', at least if the forum is at the petitioner's domicile,[3] since such domicile suffices to found nullity jurisdiction for an English court. 'Yes' is also the answer to question two, since this is perhaps supported by *Mitford* v. *Mitford*.[4] The answer to the third question (*forum loci celebrationis?*) cannot be based on any decision; but as 'English courts have assumed jurisdiction for themselves to determine the validity of a marriage celebrated in England . . . there is no apparent reason why they should not concede an analogous jurisdiction to the courts of a foreign country'.[5]

If the principle of *Inverclyde* v. *Inverclyde*,[6] according to which the English *forum domicilii* has exclusive jurisdiction in the case of voidability for impotence (or wilful refusal to consummate the marriage), is still correct, it is probable that it would be applied by way of analogy to nullity suits in foreign courts.

---

[1] Cheshire, p. 496 b. See *supra*, ss. 79, 80.

[2] *Salvesen* v. *Administrator of Austrian Property*, [1927] A.C. 641, 652. Where the domicile has changed after the celebration of the marriage the competent forum is determined by the domicile at the time of the lawsuit.

[3] See Cheshire, p. 464, and *supra*, pp. 83, 2.

[4] [1923] p. 130. The judge based the decision on residence of both parties in Germany and mentioned only incidentally the *forum loci celebrationis*. Convincing: Cheshire, p. 461.

[5] Dicey–Morris, p. 383.   [6] [1931] p. 29.

> (v) Under what circumstances a foreign court has jurisdiction to declare *adversus omnes* that a person is the legitimate child of his parents has not yet been settled. Probably the rules on jurisdiction of English courts[1] would be applied by way of analogy; if the national of a foreign country who is domiciled in that country or claims property situate there has been declared legitimate by a decree of a court of that country it may be assumed that English law would recognize such decree.
>
> (vi) In matters of succession to immovables the *forum situs* has competent jurisdiction, while succession to movables belongs to the jurisdiction of the forum of the domicile.[2]

241.
(5) Valid judgment

5. The judgment must be *valid* according to the law of the court that delivers it. At first sight it seems obvious that a judgment which is without effect in its own country has no effect abroad. Nevertheless, English law admits an exception to this, though the result 'sounds paradoxical', as the eminent judge who established the exception himself said:[3] a judgment which under its own law is void owing to a defect of procedure is considered valid in England, if the court had jurisdiction over the persons concerned and over the matter with which it dealt.[4]

Thus a divorce decree delivered by a competent court in Florida, where the parties were domiciled and resident, was declared valid by the English court though the procedure in Florida was improper and though one of the experts on the law of that country asserted that that defect impeached the validity of the decree. It is, however, difficult to believe that the slight mistake in the Florida proceedings would under the law of any country on this planet render the judgment null and void: means are provided everywhere to have an improper judgment set aside, annulled, or rescinded within a certain time, by way of appeal or of reopening the proceedings, and when the English court held that the foreign judgment was to be maintained in spite of what the legal expert thought was Florida law, this

---

[1] See *supra*, s. 81.

[2] *In re Trufort* (1887), 36 Ch.D. 600, 611, *renvoi* from the *forum domicilii* to the court of the national country of the deceased was admitted. See *supra*, s. 186 (3) (a).

[3] Lindley, M.R., in *Pemberton* v. *Hughes*, [1899] 1 Ch. 781, 790.

[4] *Vanquelin* v. *Bouard* (1863), 15 C.B. (N.S.) 341, 367; *Pemberton* v. *Hughes*, loc. cit.

was possibly a cautious expression of a well-founded inclination of the court to disbelieve the correctness of the expert's statement.

Judgments which are absolutely void *per se*, i.e. without an act of rescission by a court of law, are extremely rare.[1] If an ecclesiastical court which is empowered to deliver nullity or separation decrees transgresses its powers by pronouncing on financial relations between the spouses, this part of the judgment may be regarded as absolutely void. Or if a police court competent only to inflict punishment imposes on the defendant an obligation to pay damages to the injured person it may be questioned whether this is not so much *ultra vires* as hardly to be called a judgment at all. A judgment against a foreign state or sovereign may be looked upon as void. Apart, however, from such extreme cases, defective judgments are not void *ab initio*, but become void only by a rescinding decree, which in certain cases may be obtained; for example, if the judge has been bribed and punishment has been inflicted on him, or if the principal witness has been convicted of perjury.[2] By the rescinding decree the original judgment loses its internal and extra-territorial effects. As a rule, however, an error in procedure or even an intentional violation of procedural laws causes neither nullity nor voidability, but merely irregularity of the judgment, which thus remains valid. This is particularly the case in every country in respect of the 'intra-territorial competence' of a court. The distribution of jurisdiction between the various courts of a state—*ratione materiae*[3] or *ratione loci*[4]—hardly ever influences the validity of the judgment.

6. The judgment must be *final*.[5] This does not mean that it must be a *sententia quae nullo remedio attemptari*

242.
(6) Final judgment

---

[1] See, however, Ernst Wolff, *Grotius Soc.* 1944, pp. 102, 111 et seq.

[2] Cf., for example, the German reopening procedure under the Code of Civil Procedure, s. 578 et seq. As to perjury, see *Jacobson* v. *Frachon* (1928), 138 L.T. 386, 394 (per Atkin, L.J.). In the case of bribery it may be that the defence of fraud (see *infra*, s. 247) will be allowed even without a rescinding decree of the foreign court.

[3] District courts, county courts, commercial courts, &c.

[4] Paris courts, Marseilles courts, &c.

[5] The usual phrase 'final and conclusive'—see also Foreign Judgments (Reciprocal Enforcement) Act, 1933 (23 Geo. V, c. 13), s. 1, subs. (2) (a), (3)—does not seem to mean more than 'final'.

potest.[1] It may be open to appeal, to *cassation*, to revision; and even if an appeal is pending this does not prevent an English court from treating the judgment as final.[2] In this respect continental laws sometimes take a different view. German law, for example, recognizes foreign judgments only if they have become unassailable (*rechtskräftig*), that is, if there is no right of appeal or revision; and French courts mostly share this view, though the question is not firmly settled.[3] Finality of the judgment under English law means only that the judgment cannot be altered by the court which delivered it.[4] There are judgments which can be altered. Examples of this are to be found in every country. Besides the ordinary judicial proceedings all legal systems possess for certain cases some kind of summary proceedings in which evidence is restricted, the delays are shortened, and the defendant is prevented from presenting the whole of his case. Judgments made in summary proceedings are mostly capable of being executed at once, but the defendant is allowed to continue the litigation in ordinary proceedings before the same court and there to set up any defence known to the law, and to use any evidence; if he then succeeds the court sets aside the previous judgment and gives judgment in his favour.[5] In the majority of countries the most important instance of such divided proceedings is to be found in the case of bills of exchange, the holder of which is highly interested in obtaining an executive judgment as early as possible, even though it may be merely provisional.[6] Such provisional judgments of foreign courts are neither recognized nor enforced in this country. Another example of non-final

---

[1] *Dig.* 12, 6. 23, 1 *in fin.*

[2] *Scott* v. *Pilkington* (1862), 2 B. & S., 11, 41; *Beatty* v. *Beatty*, [1924] 1 K.B. 807, 815. See also Foreign Judgments (Reciprocal Enforcement) Act, 1933, s. 1, subs. (3). Different: the Arbitration (Foreign Awards) Act, 1930 (20 Geo. V, c. 15), s. 5. The pending of an appeal may, however, 'afford ground for the equitable interposition of the court . . . to stay execution'; *Scott* v. *Pilkington*, loc. cit.

[3] German Code of Civil Procedure, s. 328. French law: see Pillet, *Traité prat.*, II. 642 et seq.

[4] *Nouvion* v. *Freeman* (1889), 15 App. Cas. 1, 13 (per Lord Watson); *Beatty* v. *Beatty*, loc. cit.

[5] See *Nouvion* v. *Freeman*, loc. cit. (dealing with the distinction in Spanish law between ordinary and 'executive' (*remate*) judgments).

[6] *Example*: German Code of Civil Procedure, ss. 599, 600.

judgments are the judgments by default of appearance; in many countries the court which has delivered them is bound, or at least allowed, to set them aside if the defendant applies for such rescission within a certain period.[1] A third and very important instance occurs in respect of foreign maintenance decrees when the court which makes the decree is empowered by a legal provision to vary it later, i.e. to regulate future instalments in accordance with altered circumstances.[2] Such judgments are not recognized in England.[3]

It goes without saying that a foreign final judgment will have no more effect in England than it has in the country where it was delivered. A foreign divorce decree, for example, becomes final when delivered, but it does not dissolve the marriage until the time for appeal or revision has elapsed, or until the Appeal Court or the Supreme Court has dismissed the appeal.

7. A judgment *in personam* must be for a debt, that is, for the payment of an ascertained sum of money.[4] A foreign decree ordering the defendant specifically to perform a contract or to restore a chattel to its owner cannot be enforced in England. But can it be recognized as *res iudicata*? It is suggested that it can, though there is no authority for this. If, for example, the plaintiff brings an action in an English court claiming damages for non-performance of the obligation established by the original judgment the defendant will (probably) not be allowed to set up the defence that this judgment was wrong.

243. (7) Judgment for a debt

8. The recognition of a foreign judgment does not depend on its merits.[5] Even if the foreign court reached its decision by mistaking its own law the judgment cannot

244. (8) Judgment not contrary to (a) public policy

---

[1] See, for example, German Code of Civ. Proc., ss. 331, 338; Italian *Codice di procedura civile*, art. 474.

[2] German Code of Civ. Proc., s. 323.

[3] *Harrop* v. *Harrop*, [1920] 3 K.B. 386. *In re Macartney*, [1921] 1 Ch. 522. *Beatty* v. *Beatty*, [1924] 1 K.B. 807, 815.

[4] *Sadler* v. *Robins* (1808), 1 Camp. 253. *Henley* v. *Soper* (1828), 8 B. & C., 16, 21.

[5] *Castrique* v. *Imrie* (1870), L.R. 4 H.L. 414; *Godard* v. *Gray* (1870), L.R. 6 Q.B. 139. *Mezger* v. *Mezger*, [1936] 3 A.E.R. 130 (divorce on the ground of insulting behaviour).

be impeached on this ground. There are, however, some exceptions to this rule.

(*a*) The judgment must not be contrary to English *public policy*. See *supra*, ss. 169, 171. Example: a contract valid under French law which would be void under English law as being in restraint of trade was concluded in France between two domiciled Frenchmen; one of the parties brought an action in France against the other party for a breach of this contract committed in England and obtained a judgment for a certain amount. This judgment has no effect in England.[1]

245. (*b*) to natural justice   (*b*) It has often been said that the judgment must not be opposed to *natural* or *substantial justice*; but what is meant by this vague and elusive phrase is far from clear. It seems that it points mainly to a violation of the rule *audiatur et altera pars*. If the defendant has not been given 'a reasonable opportunity of presenting his case',[2] in particular if he has not received notice 'in sufficient time to act upon it and defend the proceedings', the judgment will not be recognized in this country.[3] On the other hand, a violation of substantive law resulting in an entirely wrong judgment, though undoubtedly contrary to justice, is not regarded as contrary to 'natural' justice, unless some legal principle common to all or practically all nations of our time has been infringed.

246. Judgment (*c*) based on an unknown cause of action?   (*c*) It is by no means clear whether English law forbids the recognition of a foreign judgment if the cause of action—on which the judgment is based—is *unknown* to English law. That such a rule exists is supported by Dicey's authority,[4] but not by any unambiguous precedent.

In a famous American case[5] it was held that a French judgment obtained by a son-in-law against his father-in-law for the payment of an allowance was not to be recognized; the cause of action on which it was based was

---

[1] See *Rousillon* v. *Rousillon* (1880), 14 Ch.D. 351.

[2] Report of the Foreign Judgments (Reciprocal Enforcement) Committee, 1932, Cmd. 4213 at 8 (n), quoted in Read, p. 287.

[3] *Rudd* v. *Rudd*, [1924] P. 72, 76. *Jacobson* v. *Frachon* (1928), 138 L.T. 386, 392. See Read, 281 et seq.

[4] Dicey–Morris, p. 408. See *supra*, s. 170 (3).

[5] *De Brimont* v. *Perriman* (1873), 10 Blatch. Cir. Ct., 436 (Beale, *Cases on Conflict of Laws*, I. 343). See Read, pp. 293–5.

a provision of the French civil code[1] under which in certain circumstances a legal duty of parents-in-law exists towards their son-in-law or daughter-in-law to maintain him or her if necessary.[2]

The English decision in *Re Macartney*[3] was based partly on this decision. A Maltese court applying Maltese law had delivered a judgment in favour of an illegitimate daughter against her father's personal representative, granting her perpetual maintenance out of her father's estate. The English court declined to recognize this judgment for several reasons, one of which, indeed, was that the claim was of a character which raises no cause of action in England. Another reason, however, was that the recognition of the permanent rights of illegitimate children would be contrary to the established policy of this country, especially having regard to the fact that the child's interest is not confined to minority. Thus it would seem possible to escape the unsound suggestion that recognition of a foreign judgment may be refused merely on the ground that the cause of action is unknown to English law.

(*d*) The old rule *fraus omnia corrumpit* is applied to foreign judgments in spite of the fact that a judgment is conclusive upon its merits. The problem whether the vitiating influence of fraud prevails against the strength of *res iudicata* has been discussed very often and in many countries. It is not a problem of private international law; for it does not matter whether the judgment in question has been delivered in a foreign or a domestic court.[4] Some continental, particularly German, writers hold that *res iudicata* should prevail under all circumstances, and that even fraud on the part of the judgment creditor ought not to operate as a defence.[5] The courts for the most part

247.
(*d*) Judgment not obtained by fraud

---

[1] Art. 206, 207.

[2] Loc. cit. (Beale, I. 436): 'The courts of this country shall be slow to hold that, whenever an American citizen shall visit France . . . his son, by a rash or imprudent marriage, can cast upon the parents the perpetual burden of an annuity for the support of the wife.'

[3] [1921] 1 Ch. 522.

[4] *Vadala* v. *Lawes* (1890), 25 Q.B.D. 310, 316. *Syal* v. *Heyward*, [1948] 2 K.B. 443 (C.A.). See on this Graveson, 12 *Mod. L.R.* (1949), 105 et seq. Cowen, 65 *L.Q.R.* (1949), 82 et seq.

[5] K. Hellwig, *System d. Zivilprozessrechts* (1912), I. 785, Oertmann, *Archiv für bürgerl. Recht*, 42, 1 et seq.

have rejected this view.[1] In English law there is no difference between the fraudulent use of judgments and the fraudulent use of statutes. A statute must not be made an instrument of fraud, and therefore the court without 'setting aside the Act of Parliament fastens on the individual who gets a title under that Act and imposes upon him a personal obligation',[2] and the court acts similarly in the case of the fraudulent use of a judgment. As early as 1615, in the Earl of Oxford case,[3] Lord Ellesmere pronounced that 'when a judgment is obtained by oppression, wrong and a hard conscience the Chancellor will frustrate and set it aside, not for any error or defect in the judgment but for the hard conscience of the party'. To-day there is no question of 'setting aside the judgment'. The creditor is merely personally obliged to refrain from making use of it.

The fraud may be of one of two types, i.e. either a *dolus praesens* or a *dolus praeteritus*. In the first case the judgment creditor commits fraud by making use of the judgment, which he has obtained without fraud, for example, where the judgment was delivered in default of appearance of the defendant, the plaintiff having promised not to enforce it, and where after winning his case the plaintiff has changed his mind and violated his promise.[4] In the second case the judgment creditor has by his fraud caused the judgment to be given in his favour; for example, where the plaintiff has bribed the judge[5] or has fraudulently induced the defendant not to appear in the proceedings, or has put in evidence forged documents knowing that they were forged,[6] or has produced a witness whom he knew to be perjured or even only biased and likely to mislead the court.[7] If the plaintiff acts in good faith during the proceedings but learns later that what his principal witness has said in court is not true, he may nevertheless enforce the judgment without laying himself open to the plea of fraud.[8]

It has been said that the defence of fraud must never result in a re-trial of the questions upon which the original

---

[1] German Supreme Court, *Off. Coll.*, 36, 249; 46, 75; 61, 359; 78, 390.

[2] *McCormick* v. *Grogan* (1869), L.R. 4 H.L. 82, 97.

[3] Reprinted in White & Tudor (9th ed.), I. 615, 619. See *Duchess of Kingston's* case (1776), Harg. State Trials, 602.

[4] See the case in German Supreme Court, *Off. Coll.*, 36, 249.

[5] Or in *Price* v. *Dewhurst* (1837), 8 Sim., 279, 305, 306, where the 'Executor's Court of Dealing' in the Danish Island of St. Croix had availed itself of legal proceedings in order to give a decision beneficial to the judges themselves.

[6] *Priestman* v. *Thomas* (1884), 9 P.D. 210. *Cole* v. *Langford*, [1898] 2 Q.B. 36.

[7] Dictum of Atkin, L.J., in *Jacobson* v. *Frachon* (1928), 138 L.T. 386, 394.

[8] *Jacobson* v. *Frachon* (1928), 138 L.T. 386, 394.

court has adjudicated.[1] This, however, is an exaggeration. In order to impeach a judgment on the ground of fraud it is sometimes unavoidable to attack it on its merits in spite of the effects of *res iudicata*. In this respect English law is firmly settled by *Abouloff* v. *Oppenheimer*[2] and particularly by *Vadala* v. *Lawes*,[3] and does not differ from the view prevailing in continental laws.

One restriction in the admission of the defence of fraud ought, however, to be considered. In cases where the foreign judgment according to the law of the country in which it was delivered can be rescinded in particular proceedings, such as the reopening procedure in German law,[4] the defence of fraud should as a rule not be admitted unless an attempt has been made to obtain rescission in the foreign country by the means indicated by the foreign law. Thus perjury of a witness or bribery of the judge is under German law a ground for rescinding the judgment if the culprit has been convicted for such perjury or bribery, or if his conviction was not possible owing to his death or absence.[5] In cases where a German judgment is to be enforced in England the plea of fraud based on the alleged perjury of a witness whom the plaintiff had procured and, as the defendant alleges, induced to commit perjury, will (probably) fail unless there has been a criminal prosecution which resulted in the punishment of the offender.

Fraud can invalidate only a judgment *in personam*. If a foreign court of competent jurisdiction has pronounced a divorce, the recognition of the divorce decree itself cannot be refused on the ground of a fraudulent act of one of the parties against the other, or of their fraudulent collusion to mislead the court.[6] The divorce decree stands in spite of fraud committed, so that the parties may conclude new marriages. This does not, however, exclude the right of that one of the parties who has been deceived by the other, to plead the fraud by which the decree was

---

[1] Cheshire, p. 814; Read, loc. cit., 275, and the Canadian cases quoted by Read.
[2] (1882), 10 Q.B.D. 295.
[3] (1890), 25 Q.B.D. 210.
[4] German Code of Civil Procedure, s. 578 et seq.
[5] Code of Civil Procedure, s. 581.
[6] See, however, *Crowe* v. *Crowe* (1937), 157 L.T. 557.

obtained in a personal action for damages, for maintenance, and the like.

CONFLICTING JUDGMENTS

248. Conflicting judgments　　It may happen, though it is fortunately a rare occurrence, that litigation between the same parties or their privies on the same subject-matter is started in the competent courts of two countries and that the courts disagree. A creditor, in order to enforce his claim on his debtor's German and French property, sues him in both countries; the German court dismisses the action, while the French court gives judgment for the plaintiff. If then the creditor seeks enforcement of the French judgment in England,[1] is the defendant allowed to plead *res iudicata*, referring to the German judgment?

In the field of internal law it has been said that if there are two divergent decisions by courts of the same country, both final and not open to appeal, the younger decision replaces the older one, just as a new statute conflicting with an older statute overrides it.[2] This is doubtful even in internal law, and it is certainly wrong in the case of conflicting judgments rendered in different countries. No court is capable of nullifying judgments pronounced in a different state. The contrary view would lead to an unsatisfactory result, because irrelevant circumstances may have led to one court's coming to an earlier decision than the other. It is suggested that the true answer in the case of two conflicting foreign judgments is to the effect that neither of them should be recognized. The situation is similar to where *A* and *B* conclude one contract while their agents acting on their behalf make a second contract on the same subject-matter but with different provisions: neither contract stands. If of the two conflicting judgments one is delivered by an English court, the other, the foreign judgment, will probably not be recognized or enforced in this country.[3]

[1] If he seeks enforcement in France he will succeed; see Pillet, *Traité*, II. 681.
[2] German Supreme Court, *Off. Coll.*, 52, 218; von Bar, II. 479, 480 (nr. 445).
[3] Though the reason given by French courts (*ordre public*) would certainly

One can speak of two conflicting judgments only if both decide the same question (*eadem res*). It is not sufficient that the subject-matter on which one court has adjudicated becomes material as an incidental problem in the second lawsuit, where a different point is to be decided. That seems to have been overlooked in the French *Wrede* case.[1]

249. The *Wrede* case

Slightly altered and simplified, the case is as follows: *H* was married to *W* in Austria; after the marriage he became a domiciled Russian subject; for reasons of Russian ecclesiastical law the Russian court declared the marriage to be void. On this, *W* concluded a second marriage in France with a domiciled German, *G*. Then *G* obtained a judgment of the German court pronouncing the nullity of the marriage *G–W*. The reason for this annulment was that the German court did not recognize the jurisdiction of the Russian court and regarded the marriage *H–W* as valid. Upon the German nullity decree *G* married in England an Englishwoman *E*. Now suppose the question whether this marriage *G–E* is valid is raised in an English court. What is this court to consider? It has been argued that it must choose between two conflicting judgments, the Russian and the German, since it cannot recognize both: if the marriage *H–W* is void, as the Russian court thought, then the marriage *G–W* is valid, and therefore the English marriage *G–E* must be regarded as void. If, on the other hand, the German court was right in upholding the marriage *H–W*, then *G* and *E* are validly married. This reasoning is hardly tenable. There are no conflicting judgments, for the Russian and the German courts have decided on the validity of different marriages: within the German judgment the point which the Russian court has *decided* is only the *ground* on which a decision upon a different point is based. The English court can and must recognize both judgments: there is no inconsistency in treating both marriages which Miss *W* has concluded as void; should she come to England she could marry here validly. But the point upon which the English court has to adjudicate at the moment is merely the validity of the marriage *G–E*, and this depends solely on the recognition of the German judgment. Whether that judgment is well founded or not does not matter since it cannot be impeached on its merits.

THE ENFORCEMENT OF RECOGNIZED FOREIGN JUDGMENTS

No state allows foreign judgments to be enforced by direct execution without the insertion of an authoritative act of the state in the territory of which the execution is to take place. The reason for this is not to be found in

250. Exequatur and *actio iudicati*

not be given by an English court. See the French case *Pavoncelli v. Mallet*, *J. Clunet*, 1892, 677; Pillet, II. 681 et seq.

[1] See *supra*, pp. 249–50.

the (often misused) conception of sovereignty, by which allegedly the courts of one state cannot give orders to the executive organs of another state, but in the fact that the question whether the judgment is to be recognized involves the examination of many thorny legal points which it would be inappropriate to leave to the executive.

The conditions on which the granting of execution depends are not the same in every country. The English system, which is very similar to the German, differs widely from that prevailing in France. Under German law a foreign judgment which fulfils the conditions of recognition can be enforced if the admissibility of execution has been pronounced by an 'executive judgment' of a German court; this judgment must be delivered without examination of the question whether the foreign court has correctly applied the law which according to its conflict rules governs the case.[1] French law, on the other hand, allows the French court before giving the exequatur (which corresponds to the executive judgment) to re-examine the case completely in order to make sure that both in fact and in law the judgment is satisfactory; the French court has power not only to grant or refuse exequatur but also to alter the judgment by reducing the amount awarded, though this is open to doubt.[2]

Under English law a foreign judgment, if it fulfils the conditions on which its recognition depends, constitutes a good cause of action. If one of the parties of the original procedure brings an action in an English court based on the foreign judgment (an *actio iudicati*), the judgment to be enforced is not the foreign judgment itself but the judgment delivered upon it by the English court. As the valid foreign judgment is conclusive as to its merits the English courts have not the right French courts have assumed to re-examine the whole case and to refuse the exequatur if they hold the foreign judgment bad.

251. Direct enforcement under (1) the Act of 1868   Direct enforcement of a foreign judgment without the necessity of previously obtaining an English judgment upon an *actio iudicati* has been allowed by three English

---

[1] Code of Civil Proced., ss. 722, 723.
[2] See Pillet, *Traité prat.*, II. 706 et seq.; Bartin, *Principes*, I. 544 et seq.

statutes, though with a very limited scope and on the basis of reciprocity:

1. The *Judgments Extension Act*, 1868,[1] applies only to judgments of the courts in England and Wales, in Scotland, and in Northern Ireland. The Act is not effective in Eire.[2] In each of the three countries concerned the court keeps a register in which certificates of money judgments rendered by courts of the two other countries may be entered. From the date of registration the certificate has the same effect in respect of execution as if it were a judgment originally obtained in the court of registration.

2. The *Administration of Justice Act*, 1920.[3] It applies to money judgments of the superior courts of those British dominions, colonies, protectorates, and mandated territories which have been brought under it by Order in Council. Here, too, a register is kept, but registration is subject to the discretion of the court. On application for registration the judgment debtor has practically all the defences which he would have under common law against an action upon foreign judgments.[4]

252. (2) the Act of 1920

3. The *Foreign Judgments (Reciprocal Enforcement) Act*, 1933.[5] It applies to money judgments given in the superior courts of any foreign country, provided that substantial reciprocity of treatment is assured. If the King is satisfied that this condition is fulfilled he may by Order in Council direct that the Act shall extend to that foreign country. At present Great Britain has concluded treaties concerning reciprocal enforcement of judgments only with France and Belgium (in 1934); the necessary Orders in Council were passed in 1936.[6] The Act of 1933 applies also to British dominions, colonies, protectorates, and mandated territories if the King, by Order in Council, directs that the Act shall have effect accordingly. In that event the Administra-

253. (3) the Act of 1933

---

[1] 31 & 32 Vict., c. 54. This Act has been extended to include inferior courts by the Inferior Courts Extension Act, 1882, 45 & 46 Vict., c. 31.

[2] *Wakely* v. *Triumph Cycle Co.*, [1924] 1 K.B. 214, 221. This is, however, not free from doubt. The Irish court took the opposite view. *Gieves Ltd.* v. *O'Conor*, [1924] 2 Ir. 182. See Read, p. 297.

[3] 10 & 11 Geo. V, c. 81; Part II.

[4] See ss. 9 and 12 of the Act.

[5] 23 & 24 Geo. V, c. 13.

[6] Stat. Rules & Ord., 1936, I., pp. 1477, 1503.

tion of Justice Act (1920) 'shall cease to have effect except in relation to those parts (of the British territories) to which it extends at the date of the Order'.[1] It seems to be 'the intention of the legislature that [the Act of 1933] shall eventually supplant the [provisions of the Act of 1920]'.[2] The enforcement of foreign judgments requires their registration, as under the Acts of 1868 and 1920. On the application of the judgment creditor registration has to be made, no discretion being left to the court. Subsequent to registration, however, the judgment debtor may apply to have the registration set aside, for example for lack of jurisdiction of the original court or for fraud. If the court is satisfied that the defence is well founded, it sets aside the registration of the judgment. It has discretion only in the case of the debtor's plea of *res iudicata*: if the matter in dispute had 'previously to the date of the judgment in the original court been the subject of a final and conclusive judgment by a court having jurisdiction in the matter' the court may set aside registration, but is not bound to do so.[3] The discretionary power of the court in this case corresponds to its discretion in staying an action on the plea of *lis alibi pendens*.[4]

The effect of registration is the same as under the older Acts of 1868 and 1920. A registered judgment has, 'for the purpose of execution, the same force and effect as if the judgment had been a judgment originally given in the registering court, and entered on the day of registration.'[5]

An important innovation was introduced by s. 6 of the Act: if a judgment *can* be registered under the Act of 1933 the creditor can enforce it only by way of registration. He is not at liberty to sue the debtor on the foreign judgment according to the rules of common law.[6]

---

[1] Sect. 7 of the Act.
[2] See Read, loc. cit., p. 209, n. 24.
[3] S. 4 (1) (a) and (b) of the Act.
[4] See *supra*, s. 229.
[5] S. 2 (2) of the Act.
[6] He may, of course, sue him on the original cause of action, since this has not been merged in the judgment debt. See *supra*, s. 234, and Read, loc. cit., p. 300.

PART IV

LAW OF PERSONS AND FAMILY LAW

CHAPTER XX

NATURAL PERSONS

A PERSON is a being capable of having rights. As slavery and civil death are no longer recognized, every human being is a person.

I. The unborn child, the child *in ventre sa mere*, has not yet become a person, it has no rights.[1] But certain rights are reserved which will pertain to the child when (if ever) it becomes a person, such as rights to succession, in some legal systems rights of compensation for pre-natal injuries,[2] or rights resulting from a contract between two persons in favour of the *nasciturus*.[3] The question what rights are reserved to the child should be governed by the *lex causae*, i.e. the law governing the legal relationship which may have produced the right in issue. The law of the domicile of the deceased, e.g. decides whether the unborn child can succeed to the former's estate; the proper law of the contract determines whether a *stipulatio alteri* is admitted, and if so, whether the third party may be an unborn child, &c. **254. The unborn child**

II. When the act of birth has been completed the person comes into existence. There are, however, some laws which require more than birth to constitute a person. According to French law and many legislations derived from the French civil code, it is necessary that the child be born *viable*, capable of maintaining life; Spanish law demands that it shall have lived for twenty-four hours after birth.[4] What law is applicable where a child is born *non-viable*? **255. The child not capable of maintaining life**

---

[1] Cf. however, Lord Hardwicke in *Wallis* v. *Hodson*, 2 Atk. R. 115, 117: an unborn child 'is a person *in rerum natura*, so that both by the rules of the common and civil law (it is) to all intents and purposes a child as much as if born in the father's life-time'.

[2] See 95 *University of Pennsylv. L.R.* (1946), p. 96 et seq.

[3] Winfield, 8 *Cambridge Law Journal* (1942), p. 76.

[4] French *code civil*, art. 725, 2; 906 §3. Spanish *Cód. c.*, art. 30.

There ought to be no doubt that the personal law is decisive, i.e. in England the law of the domicile which the child would have if it were a person. The opposite opinion, according to which the *lex causae* answers the question,[1] would lead to absurd results. Take the following example. An unmarried domiciled Frenchwoman living in concubinage with a domiciled Englishman gives birth to a non-viable child which dies an hour after birth; its English father had died before the child was born, and had left a will under which he appointed the child about to be born as residuary legatee. If the *lex causae* doctrine were correct the child could succeed, since succession is governed by the law of the domicile of the *de cuius*. But as the child under its own (French) domicile has never been a person it cannot leave property to a successor, it can have no 'heir'. Consequently, at the child's death its property becomes ownerless! The correct solution is that the child never succeeded to its father's property, because it did not become a person under French law.

256. Presumptions of death

III. The personality of a human being is extinguished by death. The various lawgivers have established differing presumptions, particularly in respect of *commorientes*. In some legal systems persons killed in a common disaster (an air-raid, a shipwreck) are presumed to have died simultaneously, with the effect that neither of them can succeed to the other's estate (German system). In other systems a complicated order in which they are presumed to have died has been established; thus in Roman and French law.[2] England has a very simple, though hardly satisfactory rule: the 'order of seniority' is decisive.[3] Which of these presumptions is to be applied if the disaster took place in a country that is not the country of the domicile of the deceased persons? Under all continental conflict rules those presumptions are treated as forming part of substantive law (inheritance law). The attitude of English

[1] von Bar, I. 373 (Engl. transl., p. 291); Zitelmann, II. 90.
[2] German civ. c. s. 20, and Law of 4 July, 1939; French civ. c. art. 720–2; Spanish civ. c. art. 33, &c. *Dig.* 34, 5, l. 9 § 1, l. 4, l. 22, 23.
[3] Law of Property Act, 1925, s. 184. See *Re Grosvenor*, [1944] 1 Ch. (C.A.) 138; *Hickman* v. *Peacy*, [1945] A.C. 304. *In re Pringle*, [1946] 1 Ch. 124. Cf., on Canadian laws, *J. Comp. Leg.* 1943, 68, 73, 75.

law was less certain, owing to the tendency in this country to enlarge the domain of 'procedure'.[1] The decision *in re Cohn*,[2] however, adopted the sound view (substantive character of the presumptions). American law seems to regard the question as procedural.[3]

Example: A German refugee couple, still domiciled in Germany, were killed in an air raid in London; the husband was some years older than the wife. Under German law it is presumed that they died simultaneously; under English law that the husband died first, so that the wife succeeded to his property and left it to her heirs. The German rule applies.

A declaration of death (or of absence),[4] however, produces under continental legal systems not only some rebuttable presumptions, but often creates some immediate and substantive effects on legal relationships between the probably deceased person and third persons, such as the wife, the 'heirs', or the life insurer. If, for example, the wife marries again, and then the first husband, who had been declared dead, returns, he has under German law to accept the fact that his marriage has been dissolved by the wife's second marriage.[5] Other legal systems answer the Enoch Arden problem in a very different way, either by pronouncing that the old marriage is to be upheld[6] or by allowing a re-marriage only subject to a previous dissolution of the old marriage by the court.[7] Which of these systems is to be applied by an English court? The answer to this is, the *lex domicilii* and not the *lex fori*.

257. Declaration of death

STATUS AND CAPACITY

I. The term *status*, though much in use, is not free from ambiguity.[8] It is mostly employed to designate the legal

258. Meaning of *status*

[1] *supra*, p. 177.   [2] [1945] 1 Ch. 5. See Morris, 61 *L.Q.R.* (1945), 340.

[3] *Restatement*, s. 595, 2.

[4] The system of declaration of death prevails in Germany and Austria; the system of declaration of absence in France, Belgium, the Netherlands, Spain, Portugal, Italy, and Switzerland.

[5] See German Civ. C., ss. 1348–51; German Law of 6 July 1938, s. 43.

[6] This is the view of most laws following canon law.

[7] Thus Swiss law (civ. c., art. 102) and English Matrim. Causes Act, 1937 (1 Edw. VIII and 1 Geo. VI, c. 57), s. 8. This 'dissolution' is not in the nature of a 'divorce', therefore the rules on divorce jurisdiction do not apply; *Wall* v. *Wall*, [1949] 2 A.E.R. 927, 931. Cp. Note, p. 609.

[8] See on status the observations by Scott, L.J., in *Re Luck*, [1940] 1 Ch. 864

category to which a person belongs owing either to his natural condition, such as unsound mind, or age, or to his legal condition, such as marriage or illegitimacy. Thus one speaks of the normal *status* of an average adult man of mental health, on the one hand, and the status of an infant, a married woman, a declared lunatic, a monk, a nobleman, on the other.

259. of 'capacity'   Status is the basis for capacity, incapacity, and restricted capacity, words which also are used ambiguously. Full capacity corresponds to the normal status of man. Where, as a result of a particular status, such as minority or lunacy, certain disabilities arise, the person concerned has no capacity or only a restricted capacity. In its proper sense capacity designates the faculty of a person to produce legal effects *by his own act*, whether by contracts, wills, assignments, or other transfers of rights, or by marriages, or adoptions, or by torts he commits. In a wider sense the term capacity also includes the faculty of a person to acquire rights otherwise than by any act of his own, for example, to succeed to the property of an intestate. Sometimes one speaks of a restriction of capacity even in cases of such disability of a person as is based on his relationship to one single other person. When under former Portuguese law first cousins could not intermarry,[1] or when under Roman and Roman-Dutch law gifts between spouses are invalid,[2] or when an auctioneer is precluded from bidding for articles at a public auction conducted by him,[3] such disabilities have been founded on a restriction of capacity. There is no objection to using this terminology, but it must be borne in mind that such relative incapacity is not based on any kind of status. To be married is a status; to be married to Mr. *X* is not. While there is no need to explain why incapacities derived from status are governed by the law regulating status (the personal law), this cannot be extended automatically to relative incapacities. True, the intermarriage of first cousins will be tested by their personal law. As to the

at p. 890 et seq., and Allen, 46 *L.Q.R.* 277; Cheshire, p. 256; Rabel, I. 105; Dicey-Morris, 465 et seq.

[1] See *Sottomayor* v. *De Barros* (No. 1), (1887), 3 P.D. 1, 5.
[2] See *Lee* v. *Abdy* (1886), 17 Q.B.D. 309.
[3] Cf., for example, German Civ. Code, ss. 456, 457.

validity of a gift between spouses there has been much controversy between those who advocate that the proper law of the gift should be applied, and those who subject the question to the personal law of the parties, the latter opinion being preferable. The incapacity of the auctioneer will certainly not be governed by his personal law.

Further cases of a merely relative incapacity are to be found where a person is restricted solely in his right to dispose of his property or part of it, particularly as a consequence of bankruptcy or marriage. The bankrupt retains the undiminished faculty to conclude contracts; therefore, strictly speaking, his 'capacity' is not affected. The married woman sometimes has full capacity (English and French systems), sometimes restricted capacity in its strict sense (French system until 1938), sometimes she is only deprived of the right freely to dispose of her property[1] (German system[2]). While capacity, restricted capacity, and incapacity are as a rule tested by domicile, restrictions on the right to dispose of property are subjected to the *lex causae*, in particular to the law governing the attempted disposal. They have nothing to do with the status of a person; to be married under a particular matrimonial property system is not a status.

II. The *status* of a person is determined by his personal law, in England by the law of his domicile. A status recognized by that law is recognized in England, even if the status is of a kind unknown to English law.[3] A disability based on a person's belonging to a certain caste or race or on his religious belief or on prodigality is disregarded in this country. See *supra*, s. 163.

260. Recognition of foreign status

III. As capacity in the strict sense of the term results from status, the law governing the status of a person governs his capacity. *Etat et capacité*[4] cohere.

261. Capacity governed by the law of the status

---

[1] French law of 22 September 1942 (*code civil*, art. 216): 'The married woman has full legal capacity. Its exercise is limited only by the matrimonial contract and by the law.'

[2] German Civ. Code, ss. 1395–9.

[3] It has often been said that a personal status unknown to English law will be disregarded by English courts. Cheshire, pp. 193–5 and Morris (Dicey) 467–9 have shown that this opinion is unfounded.

[4] Cf. the text of art. 3 §3 French *code civil*.

The subjection of capacity to the personal law, to the *statutum personale*, goes back to the statutists, and has been developed equally by Italian, French, Dutch, and German jurists. Thus it became one of the few common rules of European private international law, and it passed into nearly all modern codifications.[1] As we have seen before,[2] the personal law is in England (and some other countries) the law of the domicile.

It is a leading principle in this country that capacity should be subjected to the personal law. At least there is not much doubt that the capacity of a person to conclude marriages,[3] to make marriage settlements or wills is tested exclusively by domicile, and it is probable that the same principle applies to adoptions, to continental *pacta successoria*,[4] to unilateral repudiations by the heir of his right to succession,[5] to donations *inter vivos* or *mortis causa*, and to other legal acts concerned with family matters or succession, or, to put it negatively, with non-mercantile matters.

On the other hand, it is certain that the domicile principle does not apply: first, where the capacity concerns the disposal of immovables; secondly, where the capacity to become liable for the commission of a tort is in issue. In both cases the *lex causae* decides, i.e. in the first case the *lex situs*,[6] in the second the law of the place where the tort was committed in conjunction with the law of the forum.[7]

262. Mercantile contracts
There remains the question of capacity to conclude what are usually called mercantile contracts, that is, contracts

[1] For example, the Codes of Prussia (1794), Introduct., s. 23; France (loc. cit.); Austria (1811), s. 34; Italy (1865), art. 6 (1938 and 1942, art. 7); Portugal (1867), art. 24, 27; Spain (1889), art. 9; Switzerland (Law of 1891), art. 7; Germany (1896), art. 7; Poland (1926), s. 1; Latvia (1937), art. 3; Greece (1940), art. 7.

[2] See ss. 93, 96.

[3] See on this *infra*, s. 309 et seq.

[4] Cf. on this *infra*, s. 577.

[5] The right of the appointed heir to refuse acceptance is known to all continental laws.

[6] The capacity to alienate or to devise immovables or to charge them by mortgages or any other *ius in rem* is governed under English and American law solely by the *lex situs*. A twenty-year old Swiss citizen domiciled in Switzerland, *capax* under his personal law, *incapax* under English law, is incapable of transferring his right in an English piece of land.

[7] On this see *infra*, s. 470.

made by merchants or other business men in connexion with their business, or at any rate contracts of a business type: sales, service contracts, insurance, negotiable instruments, maritime contracts, &c. The word 'contract' here is not limited by its technical sense of agreements creating obligations; it also includes those agreements by which obligations arising from mercantile contracts are performed, such as assignation of debts, transfer of ownership.

The principle often formulated in *dicta* by eminent judges is here the same as for non-mercantile contracts: capacity is tested by domicile. On the other hand, it is undeniable that—as Lord Macnaghten said in *Cooper* v. *Cooper*[1]—'perhaps in this country the question is not finally settled, though the preponderance of opinion here as well as abroad seems to be in favour of the law of domicile'. There exist several decisions which test capacity to conclude mercantile contracts not by domicile but by the place of contracting.[2] It is submitted that this apparent inconsistency disappears if it is recognized that each of these doctrines has its appropriate place. The leading principle is to the effect that the law of the domicile is applicable. But this rule is modified in the interest of an undisturbed commercial intercourse by a rule that a contracting party cannot rely on his incapacity under the *lex domicilii* if he was *capax* under the *lex loci actus*.

The latter rule has been developed in numerous legal systems. The Prussian Code of 1794 provided that if a foreigner concludes a contract in Prussia about goods situate in Prussia he shall be deemed capable if he is capable either under the law of his domicile or under the law of the place of contracting; 'that law which is the most favourable for the upholding of the contract' applies.[3] A similar rule

263. Personal law and *lex loci actus*. History and foreign systems.

---

[1] (1888), 13 App. C. 88, 108. Cf. also Lord Halsbury in the same case at p. 99; Lord Westbury in the Scottish case *Udny* v. *Udny* (1869), L.R. 1, Scot. App. 441, 457; Cotton, L.J., in *Sottomayor* v. *De Barros* (No. 1) (1877), 3 P.D. 1, 5.

[2] *Male* v. *Roberts* (1800), 3 Esp. 163 (*per* Lord Eldon). See also the Scottish case *McFeetridge* v. *Stewarts & Lloyd*, [1913] S.C. 773, and the dictum of Sir Creswell Creswell in *Simonin* v. *Mallac* (1860), 2 Sw. & Tr. 67. The view of Story, s. 103, in favour of the *lex loci contractus* seems to have contributed largely to the expansion of this doctrine in America and England.

[3] Prussian *Allgemeines Landrecht*, 1794, Introduction, s. 35.

was contained in the famous Civil Code of the Canton of Zurich (1853–6) and in a Swiss Federal Law of 1881. The German Code of 1896 framed the rule cautiously:[1] the capacity of a person is determined by his national law, but a foreigner performing any legal act within Germany, though he is incapable or restricted in his capacity, is deemed capable of performing such legal act if he would be capable under German law. In respect of bills of exchange the same rule had been laid down as early as 1848 by the German Bills of Exchange Act, and the two Geneva Conventions on Bills of Exchange (1930) and on Cheques (1931) have likewise adopted it.[2] The German rule of 1896 has further been accepted by the Civil Codes of Japan and China,[3] by the Swiss Code,[4] by the new Italian Code (1938 and 1942),[5] and by the Greek Code of 1940.[6] France does not possess a written rule of this kind, but it has been developed by the courts on the ground of *ordre public*. In the famous *Lizardi case* the Cour de Cassation laid it down in order to protect commercial security:[7]

A Mexican citizen of twenty-two, who was a minor under his personal law, but would have been of age under French law, bought jewels in France from a French merchant and gave bills of exchange in payment. The court held that if the merchant had acted in good faith and without any negligence he deserved protection; the minor was not allowed to rely on his minority, and the transaction was upheld.

This sound decision, though much attacked even by distinguished writers, has on the whole been followed by the courts. The main difference between the solution of the French judiciary and that adopted by the continental codes is that the French courts protect only Frenchmen, while the codes extend protection to all, provided that the transaction

[1] Introductory Law to the German Civ. Code, art. 7.

[2] German Bills of Exchange Act, 1848, s. 84; Geneva Convention for the Settlement of Conflicts of Laws in connexion with Bills of Exchange, art. 3 §§ 2, 3; 'A person who lacks capacity' (i.e. under his national law) 'is nevertheless bound if his signature has been given in any territory in which according to the law in force there he would have the requisite capacity'. The same rule is to be found in the Cheque Convention, art. 2.

[3] Japanese Code, 1898, art. 3 § 2; Chinese Code, 1918, art. 5 § 2.

[4] Swiss Code, final chapter, art. 59, 7b.

[5] *Disposizioni prelim.*, art. 7 § 2.

[6] Greek Code, art. 9.

[7] *Dalloz Pér.* 1861, 1, 193.

has been concluded in their respective countries. And secondly, France insists on the good faith of the French merchant, whereas the codes protect even those merchants who knew that the other party was a foreigner lacking capacity under his personal law. The two Polish statutes of 1926 have chosen a somewhat ambiguous solution; they declare the *lex loci actus* applicable 'where the security of honest intercourse requires such application'.[1] The Institute of International Law discussed the problem several times; it recommended that the *lex loci actus* should govern capacity only if the other party was in good faith and resident in the country where the act was done and if the effects of the contract were to take place in that country.[2]

The German-Swiss solution seems preferable. 'Honest intercourse' is best protected if the law protects *any* intercourse without probing into the minds of the parties concerned. To allow evidence to be given on good or bad faith is an impediment in itself to the defence of such transactions, or at least protracts the suit.

The incompleteness of English law on this point makes it impossible to state the existing law with certainty. No more can be said than that the desirable solution is not inconsistent with the views expressed in the few precedents available.

264. The attitude of English law

1. There is no reason to assume that the law of the domicile is immaterial and that capacity is governed solely by the law of the place of contracting. The opposite view, advanced by Dicey–Morris[3] and formerly by Dr. Cheshire,[4] would seem to entail unfortunate results. If a person has full capacity under his personal law he should be able to act validly in any country. Swiss men of twenty or Swiss women married at eighteen[5] are fully capable of concluding contracts. Why should English law regard their contracts concluded in England as void or voidable? Do they need

---

[1] Polish Law on Private International Law, 1926, art. 3; Law on Interlocal Law, art. 5.

[2] *Annuaire*, 1931 (Cambridge Meeting) I. 181, II. 80; 1932 (Oslo Meeting) 213, 220. See the report in 13 *Rev. Genth* (1932) 820.

[3] p. 622.

[4] who, however, has changed his view; *International Contracts*, pp. 48–51.

[5] Under Swiss law (art. 14 § 2 of the civ. c.) 'marriage creates majority'.

protection by the English court against exploitation of their lack of experience, although their own law declares them mature? Such unwanted protection would be given at the expense of the English party to the contract, and this would be difficult to justify. If, in spite of this, English law were to apply, some troublesome questions might arise. Is it at least open to these Swiss citizens of twenty and eighteen on their return to Switzerland to ratify the contract invalidly concluded in England? Or must the parties make a new contract[1] by letter posted in Switzerland or elsewhere on the Continent?

2. If, conversely, a person is incapable or restricted in his capacity under his personal law, but would be fully capable under the law of the place of contracting, the contract is valid.[2] It does not matter:

(*a*) whether the other party knows the facts or not; this distinguishes English from French law;

(*b*) whether the contract is concluded in England or in a third country. This is considerably better than the French, German, and Swiss laws, which safeguard commercial intercourse only in the case of transactions taking place within their respective countries;

(*c*) whether the other party is domiciled in the country where the contract is made or a third country. Even if both parties are domiciled in the same country it is sufficient that they are capable of contracting under the law of the place of contracting. If two domiciled Hungarians, both twenty-two years old, that is, minors under Hungarian law, make a contract in London or New York, the English court will treat the contract as valid. This differs from the French rule as developed in the *Lizardi case*[3] and possibly from the Polish rule also, but it is in harmony with the provisions of the other continental codes. A doubt may arise whether the English court would uphold a contract if a domiciled Englishman who under English law is an infant, for example, twenty years old, concludes it in a foreign country, say Switzerland, where he would be regarded as of full age.

---

[1] Cf. the English Infants' Relief Act, 1874 (37 & 38 Vict., c. 62), s. 2.
[2] *Male* v. *Roberts* (1800), 3 Esp. 163.
[3] *Supra*, p. 282.

This point was vehemently discussed in Geneva when the Bills of Exchange Convention was concluded. German and French jurists were opposed to the application of the *lex loci actus* in cases of this kind, while Italian lawyers disapproved of any discriminatory treatment. Ultimately a compromise was accepted; the Convention itself rejected discrimination but allowed each of the contracting states to 'refuse to recognize the validity of a contract . . . entered into by one of its nationals' who under his national law lacks capacity.[1] France and Germany have made use of this power. This solution, which was mainly based on the two continental doctrines of *ordre public* and *fraus legi facta*, is hardly satisfactory, and it seems improbable that an English court would adopt it, since neither doctrine is recognized under English law.

(*d*) Finally, it does not matter whether the law of the place of contracting coincides with or differs from the proper law of the contract. It has been advocated both on the Continent and in England that capacity should be submitted entirely to the proper law of the contract.[2] Apart from the fact that there are no precedents supporting this view, either in England or in continental countries, it seems very doubtful whether such a rule would be beneficial. As the contracting parties themselves have the right to determine what law is to govern their contract they would be able to subject the question of their capacity to the law they elect, and thus to evade all the compulsory rules by which their capacity is, and ought to be, governed.

265. Proper law of the contract immaterial

3. If the capacity of a person is restricted both under his personal law and under the law of the place of contracting, another nice question comes up for consideration. It may be that under one of these legal systems the contract is absolutely void, under the other voidable, or that under one of them the defect can be cured by ratification after majority is attained or by the guardian's ratification, while the other legal system regards the defect as incurable. Or the time

266. Different views of the two applicable legal systems

[1] Geneva Convention, 1930, art. 2 § 3. In the same sense the Geneva Cheque Convention, 1931, art. 2 § 3.

[2] Zitelmann, II. 71. Cheshire, l.c., pp. 50–1. Against this view, Dicey–Morris, loc. cit., pp. 622–3; see also Morris, 54 *L.QR.* 78, with regard to marriage settlements.

within which the voidable contract is to be disaffirmed may be longer in one than in the other system. Which of the two rules is to be applied in these circumstances? Under continental conflict rules the correct answer would be, that system the application of which is the more favourable to the upholding of the contract.[1] The same answer would seem sound and logical under English law, because the application of the *lex loci actus* aims at safeguarding commercial transactions.

267. Influence of change of domicile

IV. Does a change of the personal law affect capacity? Here a distinction must be drawn between two situations:

1. A person who under his (personal) law is incapable (for instance, a domiciled Chilean citizen of twenty-two) acquires an English or French domicile. There can be no doubt that herewith he attains majority and capacity.[2]

2. The converse case is doubtful: a domiciled Swiss citizen of twenty acquires an English domicile. Does he keep the majority (and capacity) he had attained under his former law? Some continental codes answer the question in the affirmative,[3] and Austrian courts have decided in the same sense, reasoning that capacity once acquired is to be protected as an 'acquired right'.[4] Apart from the scepticism with which the doctrine of acquired rights is properly viewed,[5] it is urged that capacity is neither a right, nor even a source of rights; it is merely a faculty. At any rate, English law has developed no rule to the effect that the condition of majority is preserved in the case of a change of domicile. The result is not unfair; this becomes manifest where a particular capacity, such as the capacity to make a will or to marry, is in issue. Under German law an infant of sixteen may make a will, under English law full age is needed; if a domiciled German of sixteen becomes domiciled in England it would be difficult to uphold the doctrine that he retains the capacity acquired in Germany.[6]

---

[1] See, for example, Raape, *Commentary*, pp. 82, 83.

[2] In the English view, though not in the view of Chilean or French law, unless he has changed his nationality.

[3] German Civ. Code, Introduct. Law, s. 7 § 2; Polish Law on Priv. Int. L., s. 1 § 2; Chinese Code, art. 5 § 3; Convention of Montevideo, art. 2.

[4] Frankenstein, I. 138.   [5] See *supra*, s. 2.

[6] See *infra*, s. 557.

V. Capacity and incapacity sometimes depend on judicial or other authoritative decrees.

1. Roman law, Roman-Dutch law,[1] German, Austrian, Swiss, and several other continental laws allow the court or the sovereign to grant majority before the regular time (*venia aetatis*). In several legal systems the minor thereby acquires full capacity; in others, for example, in Roman-Dutch law, certain powers (such as the power to alienate or hypothecate immovables) are excepted. A similar effect is given by French law to an *émancipation*, which the parents or the family council may pronounce.[2] Although English law does not embody institutions of this kind, an English court would (probably) recognize and give effect to a *venia aetatis* or an *émancipation* if made by the authorities competent according to their own law, and if the courts of the country where the minor is domiciled recognize them.

268. Emancipation and venia aetatis

2. Conversely, persons may be deprived of their full capacity by a judicial or other authoritative decree of *interdiction*. All legal systems allow interdiction of persons of unsound mind; most of them, though not English law, also permit prodigals to be incapacitated. Some modern codes further admit an interdiction by the courts in case of dipsomania[3] or addiction to narcotics;[4] Swiss law even authorizes the court to incapacitate a person for 'vicious conduct of life', or for 'maladministration of property', if this exposes him or his family to poverty or endangers the safety of other persons. None of these *status*, except that of a person of unsound mind, has a place in English law. An English court, however, would probably give effect to a foreign decree creating such disabilities, if the validity of a contract concluded abroad *and* subject to foreign law is in issue; here the English court might accept the view taken by the proper law of the contract and the *lex loci actus*. If both of them recognize and give effect to the decree of incapacitation the English court will presumably follow.[5]

269. Interdiction

---

[1] R. W. Lee, *Introduction to Roman-Dutch Law*, pp. 44, 416, 417.

[2] *Code civil*, art. 476 et seq.

[3] For example, German Civ. Code, s. 6, no. 3; Swiss Civ. C., s. 370.

[4] See Italian Civ. C. of 1938 and 1942, art. 410.

[5] Very doubtful, however. See Dicey–Morris, rules 112, 113.

**270. Certi-
fication in
England**

In the case of unsoundness of mind the certification may be made in England or in a foreign country.

(*a*) The English court has the power to find a person a lunatic if he is present in England[1] or has property here which needs protection.[2] An English domicile is neither required nor sufficient to constitute lunacy jurisdiction. On the point of jurisdiction English law differs considerably from most continental systems and from the Hague Convention on *Interdiction*, 1905.[3]

The principles of the Hague Convention are the three following: (i) Jurisdiction to declare a person of unsound mind properly belongs to the national state, irrespective of domicile or residence; his case is governed throughout by his national law. (ii) A foreign state in which the lunatic sojourns temporarily may take provisional measures necessary to protect his person or property; but these measures come to an end when the national state takes the appropriate measures or pronounces the *interdiction*. (iii) Only when the national state declares that it will not take any measures may the state of sojourn decree *interdiction* and put the lunatic under guardianship.

**271. Certi-
fication
abroad**

(*b*) A person who has been certified a lunatic by a foreign court or other foreign authority will be considered to be a lunatic in England, provided that the decree was made or recognized in the country where he is domiciled. A foreign interdiction decree does not prevent the English authority from ordering a new inquisition, and the English court will abide by its result.

**272. The
legal effects
of lunacy**

The degree to which a lunatic, whether certified or not, is incapable of acting is not the same in all countries. Some laws distinguish between insane persons and persons suffering from mental infirmity, declaring only the former to be entirely incapable.[4] Under some systems the lunatic retains the capacity of concluding certain classes of contracts, or of

---

[1] *In re Houstoun* (1826), 1 Russ. 312. *In re Sottomaior* (1874), L.R. 9 Ch. 677. *In re Bariatinski (Princess)* (1843), 1 Phil. 375. *In re Burbidge*, [1902] 1 Ch. (C.A. 426.

[2] See *in re Soltykoff (Princess)*, [1898] Weekly Not. 77, no. 5. Whether British nationality of the lunatic is sufficient to constitute English jurisdiction has not yet been decided; see *supra*, s. 83.

[3] See *supra*, s. 40. Great Britain is not a signatory of this Convention.

[4] Italian law, for instance, distinguishes interdiction from *inabilitazione*, which is pronounced if the infirmity is not so grave as to deprive the person of his whole capacity (art. 409, 410). This corresponds to the German distinction between incapacity and restricted capacity.

making a will or marrying with his guardian's consent; other laws deny him this faculty. Many laws, for example English law, treat him as capable during lucid intervals even if he has been found a lunatic by inquisition, while other systems, such as German law, take no account of such lucid periods in the case of a certified lunatic. Which of these manifold rules are to be applied by an English court? There are no precedents leading to an unambiguous answer. The following solution would seem to meet the case. The degree to which a lunatic remains capable depends on the law of his domicile, even if he was certified in a country which is not the country of his domicile. As to mercantile contracts, the predominance of the *lex domicilii* is broken by the rule under which the contract is valid if it is valid according to the *lex loci actus*, even if invalid under the domiciliary law.[1] Only if an inquisition has been ordered by an English court is the result binding on the court. If, for example, a domiciled Frenchman has been interdicted in France as insane but is found sane in an English inquisition, he may marry in this country, and his marriage will be regarded as valid here though it may be void in other countries.

BIBLIOGRAPHY

C. K. ALLEN, 46 *L.Q.R.* (1930), 277. BATIFFOL, *Traité*, 415 et seq, and in *Travaux du Comité franç.*, I. 21, 36; II. 132, 169. v. CAEMMERER, *RVgl.HWB.* IV. 354. NIBOYET, *Traité*, V, 239–308, 500–57. PLAISANT, *Traités* 304 et seq. RABEL I. 174–96.

RIGHTS RESULTING FROM PERSONALITY

I. There are two kinds of *proprie nostrum*, said Donellus: that which belongs to us *in rebus externis* and that which we have in our own person, the *iura in persona cuiusque*, 'ea quae sunt personae', 'id quod quisque habet in sese'.[2] This doctrine, according to which every person has a 'right' to his life, his body, his liberty, and his reputation, has been developed and extended during the last century to other parts or manifestations of personality, particularly in Germany,

273. Preliminary observations

---

[1] See *supra*, ss. 262, 264.
[2] Donellus, *Comment.*, II. 8. See Savigny, *System*, I. § 53, note (*a*).

France, Austria, and Switzerland. Legal writers and courts have begun to recognize the 'right' of any person to his name, his image, his voice, and his personal privacy.[1] Some writers have regarded these rights as rights of property, similar to those incorporeal rights that are protected by copyright or patent laws;[2] others have classified them as rights of personality.[3] Whatever view one accepts in this respect, there can be little doubt that the question which law is applicable to them must not depend on which of these characterizations is preferable. All these rights are so closely connected with personality that the personal law, be it the law of the domicile or the national law, must govern their acquisition and their extinction. This has been recognized wherever the courts have had an opportunity to pronounce on the subject.[4]

274. English law

II. English law differs from the continental views. As far as can be gathered from English decisions this country has not yet developed the conception of rights resulting from personality in the sense that their owner would be protected against any infringement of them. Only in a few limited circumstances does interference with the above-mentioned personal interests constitute a tort. Many infringements which under continental laws give rise to an action for

---

[1] On rights to privacy, see Warren and Brandeis, 4 *Harvard L.R.* (1890) 193; Winfield, Gutteridge, and Walton, 47 *L.Q.R.* (1931) 23, 203, 219. See 40 *Michigan L.R.* (1942) 764.

[2] Cour d'App. Paris, *Dalloz Pér.* 1894, 2, 96. Cour de Cass., *Sirey*, 1912, 1, 95.

[3] ·Gierke, *Deutsches Privatrecht*, I. §§ 81, 82. Egger, *Comment.* on the Swiss Civ. Code, I (2nd ed.), pp. 233, 255.

[4] See, for example, German Supreme Court, *Off. Coll.*, 29, 127 (the Orelli case); ibid. 95, 272, against Zitelmann, I. 138, II. 819. There is, however, one remarkable case where the German Supreme Court has abandoned this view: Under German law (as well as under Austrian, Swedish, and Finnish law) a step-father may give his name to his wife's illegitimate child born before he married her; s. 1706 § 2, Civ. C. The step-father was a German, the child was Swiss, and Swiss law does not allow such change of a child's name. Which law should apply ? The Berlin Court of Appeal rightly considered that the person's name is subject to *his* personal law and therefore held that in the case before the court the change of the name by the step-father was void. The Supreme Court reversed this decision; *Off Coll.* 118, 44. It held that the personal law of the mother (who was German through marriage) ought to apply. This decision met with sharp criticism (Reichel, in *Gruchot's Beiträge*, 70, 51; Lewald *I.P.R.* 143, and others) and must be regarded as erroneous. As to the name of a divorced woman see *infra*, s. 357.

damages and particularly to an injunction are considered
here as neutral acts and not actionable.

If, for example, a bastard uses his father's name although the father has
not married the mother, continental laws give the father cause of action
against him, while English law provides no remedy unless the unauthorized
use of the name injures the father's business, profession, property, or reputation.[1]

As English law regards infringements of personal interests
only from the point of view of 'tort', the courts will probably apply the English rule on torts even if the parties are
aliens domiciled in a foreign country in which the right to
the name is protected more efficiently.

The same principle obtains where other personal interests of the plaintiff are at stake. The undeveloped and for
that matter rather uncertain English rules concerning invasion of personal privacy, publication of a photograph or of
a (good or bad) portrait or a caricature[2] determine the
extreme limit to which the plaintiff may be protected in this
country.

III. The ordinary name of a person must be distinguished
from his business name (*nom commercial*, *Firma*,[3] *ditta*),
also from the designation of his commercial or industrial
enterprise, and finally from the trade marks he uses in
business. Most countries have established strict rules on
these subjects in order to secure truth and clarity in the
public interest, rules however which also grant well-defined
rights to the merchant. In matters of detail these rules vary
considerably from country to country. In England, for
example, a merchant is allowed freely to choose his business
name and even to use the name of another person unless he
contravenes the rules on passing-off.[4] In Switzerland, conversely, the principle of 'strict truth' in business names
must be observed, so that the purchaser of a whole enterprise is precluded from using the seller's name even if the

275.
Business
name, trade
marks, &c.

[1] *Dockrell* v. *Douglas* (1899), 80 L.T. 556; *Walter* v. *Ashton*, [1902] 2 Ch. 282,
293.
[2] See Winfield, *Law of Torts*, 666 et seq.
[3] The German word *Firma* is not what in English is called a firm. It is merely
the name under which a single merchant or a commercial partnership or company carries on business.
[4] See Winfield, loc. cit., 634 et seq.

seller agrees to such use.[1] German rules represent a compromise between these two; they insist on the principle of truth, but allow for exceptions in the case of alienation of or succession to commercial enterprises.[2] The question whether a person has acquired or validly transferred the right to the name or designation of a commercial enterprise or a trade mark should be answered, not by the law of the domicile of the merchant, but by the law of the place of business. The reason is that all these rules are mainly concerned, not with his personality, but with the enterprise as such; the enterprise often becomes independent of the trader's person; it may have changed from a simple series of dealings or proceedings into a separate incorporeal 'thing', which may survive its creator as a son survives his father.

It may be mentioned that the Paris International Convention for the Protection of Industrial Property,[3] which is concerned among other matters with business names and trade marks, does not contain any rules on the applicable law,[4] but in this connexion deals merely with the treatment of aliens to the effect that with certain restrictions and under certain conditions the nationals of one state shall be treated in any other contracting state in the same way as the nationals of the latter state. But that is beyond the scope of the present work.

276. Rank, title, profession   IV. The class to which a person belongs

1. by birth, rank, or title (for example, nobility) has in modern times little influence on his legal position. It is determined by his personal law.

The class to which he belongs

2. by profession, in particular as a *merchant*, plays a much more important part under most modern laws, though not under English law. Under the leadership of France (1807) numerous commercial codes, as distinct from the civil codes, have been created in Germany,

---

[1] Swiss Law of Obligations, arts. 945, 946, 953.

[2] German Commercial Code (1897), ss. 21–4.

[3] Convention of 20 March 1883, revised in Brussels 1900, Washington 1911, the Hague 1925, and London 2 June 1934.

[4] Each of the contracting states applies its own law.

Austria, Italy, Spain, Portugal, Belgium, the Netherlands, Greece, Turkey, Bulgaria, and the Latin-American states, while in Switzerland special rules on merchants have been embodied in the general civil code. In all these countries provisions applying to merchants differ widely from the general civil law rules. Commercial transactions are subjected to fewer formalities; the rate of interest as between merchants in case of delay is usually higher than in the case of civil contracts; under French law and many other systems bankruptcy proceedings can take place only where the debtor is a merchant; commercial contracts of sale are governed by rules differing from those for non-mercantile sales, &c.

What law decides whether a given person is a merchant? According to the view prevailing on the Continent the answer should be sought not in his personal (national or domiciliary) law, but in the law of the place where the centre of his enterprise lies. This, however, needs qualification. The question whether a certain person is a merchant arises mostly as part of a wider problem: e.g., the *propositus* is accused of fraudulent bankruptcy committed in country X, and under the law of X it makes a difference whether he is a merchant or not. The answer will be given not by the law of the country where his enterprise is centred but by the law governing the bankruptcy. Or: the proper law of a contract between persons who are alleged to be merchants may be the law of country Y while one of the parties has his enterprise in country Z. Here the law of Y will decide whether under the rules of Y the parties are merchants.

It may, however, be that the law of Y does not itself answer the question but refers it to the personal laws of the parties. In that case it is not the domiciliary law but the law of the centre of the enterprise that is applicable.[1]

[1] Ficker, *RVglHWB.* IV 462–3. Melchior, *Grundlagen* 152–4. Arminjon, *Précis d. dr. intern. commerc.* 25 et seq. Rabel I. 171.

CHAPTER XXI

LEGAL PERSONS

277. The various types WIDELY differing types of legal (juristic, artificial) persons have been developed in the legal systems of the various countries. Only one of them is common to all laws, that is the corporation aggregate, a group of persons endowed with legal personality, such as a company or a municipal corporation. There are, however, great differences in respect of the conditions under which a group acquires personality. French law, for example, grants personality to any civil or commercial partnership, Italian law at least to commercial partnerships, while English, German, Swiss, and Anglo-American laws refuse to treat mere partnerships as legal entities.

Besides corporations aggregate, English law has developed a type of legal persons unknown elsewhere: the corporation sole, that is a body having perpetual succession, constituted in a single person, in right of some function. On the other hand, some types of juristic persons, unknown in this country, are to be found on the continent. An example of this is the independent institution or establishment, the *Anstalt* of German law, covering among others the foundation (*Stiftung*) created by private legal act and consisting of property established for a particular purpose but not made over to an existing person as trustee. Such establishments are legal persons, they differ from corporations in having no 'members'. Another example is the *hereditas iacens* of Roman law, i.e. the estate of a deceased between the date of his death and the date of acquisition by his successor; this is still found under Roman-Dutch law, Greek law, and the laws of the Baltic States. Hindu law attributes life and legal personality to idols, and the Privy Council in an appeal from the Court of Calcutta recognized this.[1] Finally, some primitive peoples endow animals, plants, or rivers with legal capacity.

[1] Cf. Duff, *Cambridge L.J.*, 3, 42.; and Bijan Kumar Mukherjea, *Indian L.R.* (1947), 271.

Before examining what law governs the creation, the 'life' and 'death' of legal persons, or to put it briefly, what their personal law is, it is useful to realize that conceptions used in the case of natural persons, such as nationality, domicile, residence, and presence, can be applied to legal persons only by way of analogy and not without distortion of their original and genuine meaning.[1] Yet it seems impossible to do without these conceptions. For every legal system contains some rules which attach certain consequences to a person's nationality, domicile, residence, and presence without distinguishing between natural and artificial persons. As to the nationality of legal persons, see *infra*, s. 288.

278.
Domicile,
residence,
presence of
legal
persons

Some confusion is created by the fact that the same word may cover different conceptions in the various sections of the law. Thus the word *residence* is used in a sense very different from the usual meaning when a company's liability for income-tax upon money arising abroad depends on the 'residence' of the company in the United Kingdom.[2] For the purpose of income-tax liability residence of the company is at the place 'where its real business is carried on', 'where the central control and management of the company abide',[3] and from this it has been inferred that in respect of tax-law a company cannot be resident simultaneously in two countries, while in all other respects a dual residence (as opposed to domicile) is possible.

The quasi-mathematical reasoning that 'a thing' cannot have two or three different and separate 'centres' is a playful misuse of a word, its naïve transference from one sphere of life to another. The House of Lords has accepted duality of residence in one case (*Swedish Central Railway* v. *Thompson*),[4] while most English decisions, including those of the House of Lords, have rejected duality.[5] Dr. Cheshire has made the interesting attempt to reconcile the conflicting judgments of the House of

[1] 'We ought to proceed as nearly as we can on the analogy of an individual': *De Beers Consolidated Mines Ltd.* v. *Howe*, [1906] A.C. 455, 458.

[2] See 8 & 9 Geo. V. c. 40 Sched. D. Case IV rule 2 (*a*), Case V rule 3 (*a*).

[3] *De Beers Consolidated Mines Ltd.* v. *Howe*, [1906] A.C. 455, 458; *Swedish Central Rlwy.* v. *Thompson*, [1925] A.C. 495, 508.

[4] *supra*, note 3.

[5] *Cesena Sulphur Co.* v. *Nicholson* (1876), 1 Ex.D., 428, 445; *San Paulo (Brazilian) Railway Co.* v. *Carter*, [1896] A.C. 31. *Goerz* v. *Bell*, [1904] 2 K.B. 136. *De Beers Consolid. Mines* v. *Howe*, [1906] A.C. 455. *Egyptian Delta Land, &c., Co.* v. *Todd*, [1929] A.C. 1, 19. *The Pamia*, [1943] 1 A.E.R., 269.

Lords:[1] a company engaged in active trading operations requires one and only one central control, while a company whose affairs are in a 'static' condition and where there is no 'real' business to carry on may be regarded as resident in every country where a substantial part of its purely administrative business is done. It is submitted that if the distinction between substantial and non-substantial work is decisive in the second case (of static companies) it is difficult to see why it should not be essential in the first case (of the active company).

Apart from tax law, the notion of residence is material as a test by which the *situs* of a debt due from a given corporation is determined. But this test is not always conclusive. If, for example, the corporation has several residences it will become necessary, in order to locate the *situs debiti*, to look at the place where the debt is 'properly recoverable' or where payment would 'normally be exigible'.[2]

It would be improper from the use of the term 'residence' in tax law to infer that the term must be used in the same sense where it is a question of the *situs debiti*.

The term *domicile* of a corporation is mostly used where the personal law of the corporation is to be applied. Because in respect of individuals the personal law is the law of the domicile, many writers insist on using the same term when determining the personal law of corporations. It will be seen later (pp. 297–301) what law in the case of corporations corresponds to the personal law of individuals.

In tax law the notion of domicile plays a very small part. If a person resident but not domiciled in the United Kingdom is entitled to stocks, shares, or rents in any place out of the United Kingdom, he has to pay income tax only on the income actually received in this country. If he is domiciled here he is bound to pay income tax upon the full amount of income. In the case of corporations domicile is replaced by the personal law (see *infra*).[3]

The concept of domicile becomes important in jurisdiction. The court is allowed to assume jurisdiction 'where relief is sought against any corporation domiciled or ordinarily resident' in England.[4]

Finally, the concept of *presence*. As already seen,[5] jurisdiction depends on the defendant's presence in England.

[1] Cheshire, pp. 248–9. Following: Dicey–Morris, p. 128.
[2] *Swiss Bank Corp.* v. *Böhmische Industrial Bank*, [1923] 1 K.B. 673, 678 (*per* Bankes, L.J.). *Richardson* v. *Richardson*, [1927] P. 228, 235. See also *infra*, s. 515.
[3] Cheshire, p. 254.
[4] R.S.C. Order XI r. 1 (c).
[5] *Supra*, p. 65.

A legal person's 'presence' here may be affirmed even when it has no English residence. A company, for example, which is incorporated in England but carries on business solely outside this country is present here though not resident,[1] and is therefore amenable to English jurisdiction. A foreign corporation, that is, one incorporated abroad, is present in England if it has a place of business here or carries on business in this country.[2]

I. The question as to which is the *personal law* of a legal person has been answered by courts and jurists in various countries in very different ways. The choice lies mainly between three doctrines.

279. Personal law: doctrine of siège social

1. The doctrine of the *siège social*, the centre of administration. Personal law according to this doctrine is the law prevailing at the place where the commercial business is carried on, and in the case of a non-commercial legal person, the place where 'its functions are discharged'.[3] In most cases the memorandum or statute drawn up when the legal person was created designates a particular place as its 'seat'; in the case of companies and many other types of corporations such designation is even prescribed by law. Further, it is to be presumed that the designated seat *is* the centre of management, but if the designation was fictitious or fraudulent the real seat must be the decisive test.[4] The *siège social* doctrine prevails in France, Germany, Italy, Spain, Austria, Switzerland, Poland, and most other continental countries, though in many of them dissenting opinions of jurists[5] and even dissenting decisions[6] can be found. The doctrine is sound and satisfactory; the criterion chosen is one which everybody who comes into commercial contact with the corporation can easily check, since the main

[1] *Egyptian Delta Land Co.* v. *Todd*, [1929] A.C. 1, 13.

[2] On details see Dicey–Morris, pp. 173, 174.

[3] As Dicey (5th ed.), rule 19 (p. 136), said in speaking of domicile (not repeated in the 6th ed.).

[4] This is the prevailing opinion everywhere, though the German Supreme Court has sometimes expressed a different view (*Off. Coll.*, 99, 218; 100, 210, and others); rightly; 117, 217; 83, 369; 88, 54.

[5] For example, Geiler, Frankenstein, Anzilotti.

[6] See the decisions of the Commercial Tribunal of Lille, 21 May 1908, and the Cour de Cassation, 6 July 1914, quoted by Kessler, *Rabel's Z.*, 3, 766.

administration centre can hardly be kept secret. It has been argued against the *siège social* doctrine that it does not allow the transference of a corporation from one country to another unless it is first dissolved and then re-created.[1] This seems a mistaken view: under the continental rule it depends on the law of the new seat whether the old company can continue to exist in spite of the change; if the law of the new seat precludes this, then it is that law which is open to criticism, not the doctrine of the social seat.

280.
Doctrine of the 'exploitation centre'

2. It has been proposed to replace the centre of management by the *centre of exploitation*, that is the main place where the legal person executes its purpose, carries on 'its principal physical labours',[2] exploits its coal mine, runs its sawmill or its factory. The reason for this seems to be that an enterprise is not conducted at the place where the board of directors meets and decides on how the work shall be done, or where the shareholders hold their meetings, but that it is the work itself that matters. All this may be true. The remark that 'the head and brain of the trading adventure'[3] is situate at the centre of management may sometimes embody an over-estimate of the intellectual gifts of the directors; in many an industrial enterprise the 'brain' may be found in the technical and chemical research offices attached to the factory, where the decisive discoveries and inventions are made. The doctrine which lays the seat at the centre of exploitation, however, overlooks the fact that the commercial part of the business, such as the buying of raw materials, the selling of products, the conclusion of contracts with banks, insurance companies, and so forth— briefly such acts as may mainly give rise to legal doubts—is carried on neither at the mine or factory, nor in the technical departments, but at the place of management; the trading centre lies here. Furthermore, companies often possess more than one central point of exploitation. The mining company may exploit gold mines in South Africa and in parts of America; the cars of the Sleeping Car Company

[1] Geiler, p. 180.
[2] Cf. Phillimore, J., in *De Beers Consolid. Mines* v. *Howe*, [1905] 2 K.B. 612, 631.
[3] *San Paulo (Brazilian) Railway Co.* v. *Carter*, [1896] A.C. 31, 38 (*per* Lord Halsbury).

run through a dozen continental countries. The East India Company was formed in England to do business in various foreign countries. The National Waterworks Co., the Standard Oil Co., and other great corporations created in any one of the states of the U.S.A. were from the outset destined to operate in many or all of them.

Nowhere on the continent, or in England or America, has this doctrine established itself, though a few French decisions have accepted it and many eminent scholars in France have regarded it as the best of all the solutions proposed.[1]

3. According to a third doctrine the personal law of a legal person is the law under which that person has been *incorporated*. This doctrine is rooted in the archaic conception that the grant of legal personality to an inanimate being is as it were an exceptional act of grace and that it is the granting state that imposes the law under which the artificial person shall 'live'. It has been adopted by English and Anglo-American law, by some Latin-American states (Brazil, Peru, Cuba, Guatemala)[2] also, with a slight modification, by Soviet-Russian law,[3] and many German jurists, opposed to the practice of the German Supreme Court, believe that German law likewise follows this doctrine.[4] The incorporation may be made by a special Act of Parliament or by the act of an administrative body, or by compliance on the part of the promoters with all the requirements established by a general statute, such as the Companies Act, or finally by a simple private act: a will creating a foundation under Swiss or Scandinavian law, a contract of partnership in France or Italy. It may further happen

281.
Doctrine of the place of incorporation

---

[1] Cf. the decisions mentioned by Pillet, *Traité prat.*, II. 785. Pillet, *Des personnes morales*, 52; Lyon-Caen et Renault, *Traité de droit commerc.*, II. Nr. 1167. Vavasseur, *Traité des sociétés civiles et commerciales* (1910) No. 863. A slight tendency towards the doctrine of the centre of exploitation may be found in the German Law on Companies Limited by Shares of 30 Jan. 1937, s. 5, which deals with the determination of the seat by the memorandum and gives the promoters the choice between the place of exploitation and the place of management.

[2] Rabel II. 32.

[3] Makarov, *Conception*, 58, 59.

[4] Frankenstein, I, 459 et seq., Geiler, 179 et seq.; *Commentary on the Civ. C. by Members of the German Supreme Court*, n. 4, preceding s. 21, Civ. C.

that a legal person originates without any human act of incorporation: the *hereditas iacens*,[1] for example, is incorporated by operation of law.

The law *under which* a legal person comes into existence is practically identical with the law of the place *where* it comes into existence.[2] Under Russian law the latter is decisive:[3] the deviation from the English formula is almost negligible. Much more essential is the difference between the English and the prevailing continental doctrine. Though a corporation created under the law of a certain country usually has its seat in that country, this does not necessarily follow. A company may be established under and in compliance with the law of country X, but by the wish of its promoters have its seat, the centre of its management, in country Y. Such formation of corporations under the law of one state for the purpose of acting solely in another is particularly common in the United States. The reasons why promoters who do business in their own state prefer to subject their corporation to a different law are not always very reputable: the law of their state may be more rigid with regard to their liability to shareholders or creditors than suits their purposes, or may grant them fewer powers, or require strict annual audits, or entail inconvenient publicity of their activities, or it may make the act of incorporation more expensive than the law of the other state. In all these cases the personal law of the corporation is not the law of the real seat, but the law of the state of incorporation.

This shows the weak point in the incorporation doctrine. It seems undesirable that the promoters should be in a posi-

---

[1] See *supra*, s. 277.

[2] In the case of the Suez Canal Co. the incorporation was made in Paris according to the requirements of French law; the financial administration of the company was to be carried on in Paris. But a Firman granted by the Ottoman authorities had previously defined the conditions under which the company was to be created; therefore it was doubtful whether the company was French or Egyptian. Vaux, 60 *L.Q.R.* (1944) 227, advances the latter view (?).

[3] Makarov, loc. cit., 52 et seq., on the Russian decree of 12 April 1923. The law of the place where a person comes into existence ought not to be of any importance: the place where 'the embryo company is brought to birth' (Lord Sumner in *Egyptian Delta Co.* v. *Todd*, [1929] A.C. 13) is even more immaterial than the place where a natural person is born.

tion freely to choose the law under which their child is to be born and will live, irrespective of whether there is any real connexion between the activity of the corporation and the law they choose. True, the dangers this involves can be, and often are, diminished by the provisions included in both the law of the social seat and the law of incorporation. The latter law may, for example, grant personality solely to such corporations as establish their real centre of management within the territory of the state.[1] Or the state where this centre lies may refuse recognition to a legal person created by a foreign law. However, the danger of a deception to the prejudice of the public is not removed, since the issue may depend on the attitude taken by a foreign state. One cannot fail to recognize that the continental doctrine which regards the real centre of management as the appropriate test is preferable to the English and American rule.

II. Thus English law regards corporations created under foreign law as 'foreign corporations', whereas continental laws treat as 'foreign' those corporations which have their centre of management in a foreign country. Under both systems the foreign corporation needs *recognition* of its existence. In most countries such recognition becomes operative without any particular administrative act of the recognizing country. This is so in England: English courts acknowledge the existence of all foreign legal persons if they have been duly created under a foreign law. French and German laws are less liberal. Germany demands in the case of associations of a non-commercial character special recognition by administrative act; until this is granted the association has no personality in Germany.[2] Commercial associations, such as companies limited by shares, need no such special act of recognition.[3]

282. Recognition of foreign corporations

The recognition of a foreign corporation does not transform it into a domestic corporation. It means nothing more than that the corporation is regarded as having personality in the recognizing country.

---

[1] This is, according to the predominant doctrine, the case under s. 23 German Civil Code; Lewald, p. 45 et seq.; Raape, *Commentary*, 126 et seq.

[2] German Introductory Law to the Civ. C., art. 10.

[3] As to French law see Arminjon, *Précis d. dr. int. commerc.*, pp. 110–13.

283. Scope of the personal law: (1) Formation of the legal person III. The personal law of a corporation, i.e. in England the law under which it was incorporated, governs its whole life.

1. It governs first the question whether a legal person has come into existence. The law to be applied if a given group of persons (or some institution or property designated for a certain purpose) is found to be a legal person answers the question whether it *is* a legal person. This corresponds to what we have seen previously when dealing with natural persons: whether a human being born 'non-viable' has legal personality is decided by the law that would be its personal law if it had personality.[1]

If an association has no personality according to its personal law—for example, an English or German partnership—it is nowhere a legal person, not even in a country like France, where a partnership, a *société civile*, or a *société commerciale en nom collectif*, has personality. Of course, French law can declare the contrary. But this is not to be presumed,[2] because it would be tantamount to the creation of a French legal person by France, not merely to the recognition of an existing legal relationship.

If conversely a group of persons, such as a French partnership, is a legal entity under its personal (French) law, it is generally recognized as a person even in a country where such entities are not personified. This has been at least indicated in England in the case of a French partnership,[3] and it corresponds to the prevailing doctrine in Germany.[4] Whether the same view would be taken if a continental foundation (*Stiftung*) were to act in this country it is difficult to say. The fact that persons of this kind are not known to

---

[1] See *supra*, s. 255.

[2] The opposite opinion has been based on the conception that this is a matter of classification. Cf. the observations of J. Maury on the judgment of the Italian Supreme Court in *Nizard* v. *Finanza* (29 Apr. 1933), *Giurisprudenza Comparativa di Diritto Internaz. Privato*, III., p. 23 et seq.

[3] *Von Hellfeld* v. *Rechnitzer*, [1914] 1 Ch. (C.A.) 748, 753, 754. This decision was, however, based on a mistaken view of French law. Buckley, L.J., and Phillimore, L.J., did not believe that in France a *société en nom collectif* is a legal person, though this is undoubtedly the law, at least since a decision by the Cour de Cassation of 23 February 1891 (*Dalloz P.* 91. 1. 337). It is submitted that such a surprising mistake would hardly have occurred if the English court had had the duty—like any continental court—of treating foreign law as law and not as fact.

[4] Lewald, 48; Geiler, 186. *Contra*: Melchior, 138.

English internal law would be no reason for disregarding their foreign personality. The purposes for which the *Stiftung* was created would under English law be achieved by giving the property to an existing person as a trustee. There is no necessity, however, for English courts to insist on this English method in a case where the applicable continental law does not comprise the institution of trust.[1] For similar reasons a continental court would recognize the personality of an English corporation sole, though this type of legal entity is entirely unknown in any continental law.

It would, at least in the case of partnerships, be desirable to reach uniform treatment, in particular with regard to international cartels, which are not infrequently constituted as partnerships.[2]

The personal law governs all acts which are part of the *formation* of the legal person, such as the settling of the memorandum and the articles, the determination of the share capital and the division thereof into shares of a fixed amount, the declaration by each subscriber of the memorandum of the number of shares he takes, and the like. These acts are to be distinguished from those preceding the formation of the corporation, such as contracts by which the promoters promise to join in creating the legal person (*pacta de condenda universitate*); these are subject not to the personal law of the corporation but to the proper law of the contract.

2. The personal law answers the question what rights the legal person is allowed to acquire and what contracts it may conclude. This question does not however depend solely on the personal law, but also on the law of the *locus actus*. A company created under the law of country X, when acting in country Y, cannot go beyond the scope of what is permissible under the laws of X and Y. Under English law a limited company cannot conclude a contract with a third person to the effect that a shareholder (without his consent) becomes personally liable for the company's debt; under

284.
(2) Acts of the legal person

---

[1] Whether an English court would treat a Hindu idol as a legal person (in contrast to the view taken by the Privy Council, see *supra*, s. 277) may be doubtful.   [2] See Geiler, p. 187.

the law of California the members of any company become
personally liable for debts of the company. The Californian
rule is not applicable to contracts concluded by an English
company in California.[1] Conversely a company which
according to its personal law is capable of acquiring land
cannot become the owner of land situate in a country where
the Mainmort legislation forbids such acquisition by corporations.[2]

Under English law the powers of a company are limited
by the Memorandum of Association. Any act done in the
name of the company outside the scope of those powers
(*ultra vires*) is void. No continental law contains a restriction of this kind; when the memorandum (statute) of a continental company designates the object of its enterprise this
does not mean that an act outside that object is void.[3] If then
an English company concludes a contract in Germany
beyond its powers as defined by the memorandum the act
is to be regarded as void both by the English and the German Courts.[4] If, on the other hand, a German company acts
in England beyond the scope designated in its statute the
act is valid because neither under German nor under English law is it *ultra vires*.[5]

285.
**(3) Organi-
zation and
(4) transfer
of the
company**

3. It goes without saying that the personal law governs
the organization of the legal person, the duties and powers
of directors and other officers, the meetings of shareholders,
the alteration of memorandum and articles, the admissibility of preference shares or privileged voting rights, &c.

---

[1] *Risdon Iron & Locomotive Works* v. *Furness*, [1906] 1 K.B. 49, 56. See
American *Restatement*, § 191.

[2] *Great West Saddlery Co.* v. *The King* (1921), 37 T.L.R. (P.C.) 436, 445.
American *Restatement*, § 165.

[3] Cf. Düringer-Hachenburg, *Commentary to the Handelsgesetzbuch*, III. 1,
§ 201, n. 46. It is surprising that in 1872 an English judge (Wickers, V.C.) in
Pickering v. *Stephenson* (14 L.R. Eq. 322, 340) thought that the *ultra vires*
doctrine 'is not a mere canon of English law, but a great and broad principle
which must be taken, in absence of proof to the contrary, as part of any given
system of jurisprudence.' See Rabel II. 158–9.

[4] Probably, however, a German court would apply art. 7 § 3 of the Introduct.
Law to the Civ. C. by way of analogy: according to this the incapacity of a
natural person is to be disregarded if the person is capable under the law of the
place of contracting. Against this analogy: Düringer-Hachenburg, loc. cit.

[5] English law applies the *ultra vires* doctrine only to certain groups of
English corporations.

The contract by which the company appoints a person as managing director or other officer is subject to its own proper law, which however will usually be the same as the personal law of the company.

4. The personal law of the company decides whether a transfer of the central place of management to another country is possible or not. Under English law such transfer does not entail any change in the personal law, but it can be achieved only if the law of the new centre permits.

5. In respect of instruments issued by the company a distinction must be drawn between share certificates on the one hand, and bonds, debentures, bills of exchange, promissory notes and the like, on the other. As share certificates are only concerned with rights of membership, their creation, their nature, and their transfer from a shareholder to a purchaser are governed by the personal law of the company; the same law decides whether such transfer is permissible. The method of transfer differs according to whether the instrument is issued to bearer or to a shareholder designated by name. We shall deal with this *infra*, s. 520. Bonds, debentures, promissory notes, and other instruments issued by a company and embodying a debt are governed by their own proper law and not by the personal law of the company.

6. The personal law of the legal entity governs its dissolution and the effects of the dissolution. Any foreign country will treat the dissolution as valid unless it has to be disregarded for reasons of public policy. This had to be considered after 1918, when the Soviet Russian Government by a series of 'Nationalization Decrees' dissolved all corporations and confiscated their property. The text of these decrees was so ambiguous that in the earlier English cases the court decided that no dissolution had been effected.[1] Later, however, it was recognized that the legal existence of the corporations had been destroyed.[2] A deci-

286.
(5) Instruments

287.
(6) Dissolution of legal persons

---

[1] *Russian Commercial & Industrial Bank* v. *Comptoir d'Escompte de Mulhouse*, [1925] A.C. 112. *Banque Internationale de Pétrograd* v. *Goukassow*, [1925] A.C. 150. *Employers' Liability Insurance Corp.* v. *Sedgwick, Collins & Co.*, [1927] A.C. 95. The same view was adopted in some decisions in the United States and in a German decision; see Makarov in *Zeitschr. f. osteuropäisches Recht* 1936, 569.

[2] *Lazard Bros. & Co.* v. *Midland Bank*, [1933] A.C. 289. *Russian & English*

sion of the New York Appeal Court of 1934 held that the 'arbitrary dissolution of a corporation . . . is contrary to our public policy and shocking to our sense of justice and equity', and therefore regarded these legal persons as still existing.[1] French, Swiss, German, and Swedish decisions, on the other hand, recognized the validity of the dissolution,[2] and so have the English courts since 1933.[3] Although the dissolution caused destruction of the personality, French and English courts admitted the winding-up of these corporations with regard to the business they had carried on in France and England respectively. The French courts declared very aptly that, though the corporations no longer existed in law, their French *succursales* (branches) continued to exist in fact, as 'sociétés de fait', and were governed by French law, 'having their activity on French soil'.[4] The English courts had much greater difficulty in coming to a satisfactory solution. True, the Companies Acts had for many years before the extinction of the Russian corporations allowed the winding-up of unregistered companies, but not until 1929[5] was it enacted that a company incorporated outside Great Britain which has been carrying on business in Great Britain and then ceases

Bank v. Baring Bros., [1932] 1 Ch. 435; [1936] A.C. 405. In re Russian & English Bank, [1932] 1 Ch. 663. In re Russian Bank for Foreign Trade, [1933] 1 Ch. 745. In re Russo-Asiatic Bank, [1934] Ch. 720.

[1] Vladikavkazski Railway Co. v. New York Trust Co., 189, N.E. 456, quoted by Makarov, loc. cit., p. 569, n. 25. See Wortley, 14 Brit. Y.B. (1933), p. 1 et seq.

[2] Makarov, loc. cit., p. 570.

[3] See the quotations in the preceding footnotes, and compare the decision of the Privy Council in Dairen Kisen Kabushiki Kaisha v. Shiang Kee, [1941] A.C. 373.

[4] J. Clunet 1934, 663; Makarov, loc. cit., 572. Here a difficult question arises: can the property of the dissolved company situate in France be seized by all the creditors of the former Russian company, or should it be reserved to its French creditors and to such creditors as have made their contracts with the French branch ? The correct answer to this seems to be that in principle the property should be distributed among all the creditors of the company (the French, the English, the German, &c., alike). But it might be justifiable to exclude those and only those creditors who were Russian nationals at the time of the dissolution of the company, the dissolution and the confiscation having been decreed by the Russian state in the interest of Russia and her subjects. This solution might be based on the French doctrine of ordre public. Cf. Travaux du Comité français, II (1935) 11. See also supra, p. 89.

[5] Companies Act, 1929 (19 & 20 Geo. V, c. 23), s. 338 (2). See Companies Act, 1948 (11 & 12 Geo. VI c. 38) s. 400. Comp. American Restatement, s. 162.

to do so may be wound up as an unregistered company not-withstanding that it has been dissolved under the laws of the country where it was incorporated. This rule was applied to the Russian corporations, though their dissolution had occurred before the rule was made. Was such a company, which under its personal (Russian) law no longer existed, capable of suing and being sued in this country during the winding-up proceedings? The House of Lords by a majority of three to two answered this question in the affirmative.

'A legal system', said Lord Macmillan, 'which for so long admitted as suitors in its courts those wholly fictitious persons John Doe and Richard Roe, who were in much worse case than the Russian & English Bank, for they never existed at all, might be expected to suffer with equanimity the apparition of a dissolved company as a plaintiff.'[1] There is—even apart from this witty comparison—nothing illogical in the admission of an extinguished company as still existing for certain purposes.[2] True, those who believe that a corporation is a 'living' being may regard it as un-thinkable that a being 'dead' in Russia 'lives' in England and that its English life is restricted to acts preparing its English death. But for those jurists who decline to follow the 'organism doctrine' there is no diffi-culty in treating a body as a person in some respects and as a non-person in others.[3]

It has been argued that if a state dissolves a corporation and at the same time confiscates its property we have here something analogous to the transmission of property left by a deceased natural person and that the confiscation might therefore be governed not by the *lex situs* of the pro-perty but—in so far as tangible or intangible movables are concerned—by the *lex domicilii* of the dissolved corporation; hence in the case of a dissolved Russian company Russian law would be decisive, and if Russian law ordains that the whole of the movable property of the company belongs to the Russian state, irrespective of where the movables are situate, this would be binding on the courts of the *situs*.[4] This inference from analogy is, however, out of place, since under no legal system is the murderer allowed to succeed to the property of his victim. And even if the *lex domicilii* of the murdered company were to permit such succession, should not the English or American court regard such a provision as inconsistent with public policy?

[1] *Russian & English Bank* v. *Baring Bros.*, [1936] A.C. 405, 438.
[2] Under continental laws there is no difficulty in recognizing the survival of an extinguished company as long as there is property belonging to that company. Cf., for example, German Supreme Court, *Official Coll.*, 134, 94.
[3] Cf. 54 *L.Q.R.* (1938), 511.
[4] See on this W. Herzfeld, *Nationalization of Foreign Corporations, Contemporary Law Pamphlets*, ser. 9, no. 1, New York, 1943, p. 9.

288. Na-
tionality
of legal
persons

IV. It is usual to speak of the *nationality* of legal persons, and thus to import something that we predicate of natural persons into an area in which it can be applied by analogy only. Most of the effects of being an 'alien', or a 'citizen' of the state are inapplicable in the field of corporations: duties of allegiance or military service, the franchise and other political rights do not exist. Nevertheless the concept of a corporation of French or German nationality cannot be dispensed with. In many countries aliens are prevented from acquiring land, from purchasing ships or shares in ships, from carrying on a commercial or industrial enterprise. Or they are bound when bringing an action in court to give security for costs. In cases of this kind it does not matter whether the alien concerned is a natural or a legal person. The test of nationality is further important in Public International Law. A state can give diplomatic protection only to its own nationals, whether they are natural or artificial persons.[1]

In English private international law the question of nationality of corporations does not arise, but it arises in foreign rules on the conflict of laws, and where by way of *renvoi* a foreign conflict rule is to be applied by an English court, it follows that the court becomes concerned with the problem of the legal person's nationality.

According to most continental laws this nationality is determined by the real centre of management, under English (and Anglo-American) law by the law under which the incorporation was made. The rule that a natural person is a citizen of the state X only if X regards him as a citizen applies equally to legal persons.

If, for example, a company has been incorporated in France but has its centre of management in England, it is neither an English company under English law nor a French company under French law. It is stateless and would therefore enjoy neither English nor French diplomatic protection. On the other hand, one legal person may have two nationalities. An example of this is a company incorporated in England but having its real centre in France.

289. The
corporation
as enemy
alien

V. The question whether a corporation has 'enemy' character in war-time should be distinguished from that of its

[1] E. Borchard, *Diplomatic Protection of Citizens Abroad*, p. 617.

nationality. The former problem requires that the screen of legal personality should be drawn aside; the natural persons who stand behind the legal person and actually control it must be discovered. The leading case on this subject is *Daimler Co.* v. *Continental Tyre and Rubber Co.*[1] There the question was whether a company incorporated in England and therefore of British nationality, with a British secretary, but with all its shares in the hands of enemy aliens, could be looked upon as an enemy company within the meaning of the prohibition of trade with the enemy. The Court of Appeal denied this on the ground that the company had 'a separate existence which cannot be swept aside as a technicality'. The House of Lords, however, reversed the decision. Lord Parker pointed out that if a company was regarded as British on account of its place of incorporation, this would not suffice to answer the question whether it had enemy character. The corporation, he said, is 'itself incapable of loyalty or enmity. . . . The qualities of enmity and amity . . . are attributable only to human beings; I know not from what human beings that character should be derived if resort is not to be had to the predominant character of its shareholders.'[2] It is, however, submitted that it is not always the shareholders that are the decisive factor. Sometimes the human beings from whom the character of enmity is to be inferred are to be found in the members of another corporation holding all, or practically all, the shares of that corporation; sometimes the dominating persons are outsiders controlling the company by nominees. The same principle obtains in peace-time when a state wishes to prevent its national industry, commerce, or agriculture from passing into the hands of aliens; the law then is bound to penetrate the screen of legal personality.[3]

---

[1] [1915] 1 K.B. 893; [1916] 2 A.C. 307. The City Court and the Supreme Court of New York decided the question in the opposite sense; *Fritz Schulz jun. Co.* v. *Raymes & Co.* (1917), 164 N.Y. Suppl. 455, and 166 N.Y. Suppl. 567. The Mixed Arbitral Tribunals, established by the Peace Treaties, varied in their decisions. Cf. Feller, *Bruns' Z.*, II. 2, p. 55.   [2] [1916] 2 A.C. at p. 340.

[3] A good example is the Swedish legislation of 30 May 1916 and 18 June 1925, against the acquisition of land and mines by companies which though constituted in Sweden are in fact controlled by aliens. German industrial magnates, screened by Swedish companies and Swedish dummies, had purchased Swedish forests and mines to an extent prejudicial to Swedish national economy.

290. Super-national legal persons

VI. *Super-national* legal persons may be created by state treaties.[1] Thus the legal personality of the League of Nations was, and the personalities of the United Nations Organization and of the Pan-American Union are based on the agreement of all their Member-States. As a rule, however, corporations aiming at international activity acquire legal personality only through their formation in one particular state. Thus the Bank for International Settlements, though based on a State Convention of 1930 between a number of states, was actually brought to birth by a Swiss Act which put into force the Constituent Charter of the Bank; it is a company limited by shares, incorporated and having its seat in Switzerland;[2] it is therefore of Swiss nationality both in the continental and the English sense.

291. Private international corporations

Private associations with 'international' aims have been created during the last century in ever-increasing number. They are either commercial and industrial associations working for profit, or associations 'formed for the purpose of promoting art, science, religion, charity, or any other like object not involving the acquisition of gain'.[3] Under the prevailing law it is in neither case possible to constitute them apart from their connexion with a particular state, in other words as really 'international' corporations. This can only be achieved by a Convention *ad hoc* between the various states involved.

No general Convention on the subject has yet been reached, though since 1910 many projects have been drafted by the World Congress of International Associations, by the International Law Association, by the Institute of International Law,[4] and the International Chamber of Commerce. Most of these projects are limited to associations not aiming at profit; the most remarkable among them is the plan drafted by the Greek lawyer Politis.[5] None of these endeavours have led to any practical results.

Similarly international companies working for profit are

---

[1] W. Friedmann, 6 *Mod. L.R.* (1943), 185. Wright, 43 *Amer. J.* (1949), 509.

[2] See the Hague Convention respecting the Bank for International Settlements of 20 Jan. 1930, art. 1, and the Statutes of the Bank, art. 1 and 2. Fischer-Williams, *Am. J.I.L.* 1930, 665.

[3] Companies Act, 1948, s. 14, subs. (1). The first international association of this kind seems to have been the British & Foreign Anti-Slavery Society, created between 1835 and 1840.

[4] See *Annuaire*, 25 (1912), 466; 30 (1923), 97 et seq.

[5] *Annuaire*, 30, 111 et seq.

always created as national bodies under the law of one single state. Their foreign branches are sometimes nothing more than dependent places of business, where mercantile agents are appointed to carry on the enterprise. Or they are in the hands of legally separate companies, but the shares in the subsidiary company are owned either by the same persons as control the principal company, or mainly by the principal company itself. Or it may be that in each of the territories concerned a separate company is constituted, economic unity being produced by a holding company which owns practically all the shares in the various local companies, while the shares in the holding company are possibly made the subject of Stock Exchange transactions.

International cartels[1]—that is combinations with monopolistic tendencies for the restriction of competition, established between industrial or mercantile enterprises which retain their separate entity—seldom have legal personality themselves. If they have, it goes without saying that under English conflict rules their organization depends on the law under which they have been incorporated. Most of the cartels, however, are merely contracts producing a series of duties between the contracting parties, particularly duties to abstain from certain acts of competition, such as the selling of products at a lower or the buying of raw materials at a higher price than that fixed under the cartel contract, or to restrict production to a specified amount. Such cartel contracts are subject to their proper law, mainly determined by the intention of the parties. The uniformity of legal treatment throughout the world which thus seems to be reached is, however, substantially jeopardized by the fact that the national rules on public policy prevailing in the various countries differ largely from each other, in particular those rules which concern the limit to which a restraint of trade is valid,[2] or the reasons for which a party is entitled prematurely to rescind the contract.[3]

[1] Geiler, loc. cit., 196, and in Düringer & Hachenburg, *Commentary to the Commercial Code*, II. 1, 474 et seq. (with bibliography).

[2] Cf. *Nordenfelt* v. *Maxim Nordenfelt Co.*, [1894] A.C. 535, 565. French *code pénal art.*, 419.

[3] See, for example, German Cartel Decree of 2 Nov. 1923, s. 8.

BIBLIOGRAPHY

FARNSWORTH, *The Residence and Domicil of Corporations*, 1939 (on this: LORENZEN, 49 *Yale L.J.* (1940), p. 1350). FARNSWORTH, *J. Comp. Legisl.*, 1938, 183. RABEL II. 1–225. E. J. SCHUSTER, 'Nationality and Domicil of Corporations', 2 *Grotius Soc.*, 1916, 59. WEIDENBAUM, 36 *Michigan L.R.* (1938) 881. VAUGHAN-WILLIAMS & CRUSSACHI, 49 *L.Q.R.* (1933) 334. GOODRICH 71. PILLET, *Des personnes morales en droit internat. privé*, 1914. MAMELOK, *Die Jurist. Person im I.P.R.*, 1900. NIBOYET, *Traité*, II 255 V, 558–644. ARMINJON, *Rev. Ghent*, 1927, 360. GUTZWILLER and GEILER, *Mitteilungen der Deutschen Gesellschaft für Völkerrecht*, 12 (1933), pp. 116, 177, 227. BEITZKE, *Juristische Personen im I.P.R. und Fremdenrecht*, 1938. RÜHLAND, 45 *Rec.* (1933 III) 391. MAMELOK, *Staatsangehörigkeit der jur. Person*: Report for the Swiss *Verein für internat. Recht*, 1918. STREHL, *Staatsangehörigkeit bei jur. Personen*, 1933. MAZEAUD, *J. Clunet*, 1928, 63. LEVEN, *De la nationalité des sociétés en France*. DOMKE, 8 *Nouv. R.* (1941) 69 et seq. JESSUP, *Modern Law of Nations* (1949) 84. M. TRAVERS, 33 *Rec.* (1930 III) 5. NEUMEYER, *Internat. Verwaltungsrecht*, I, p. 106. SERONI, *La cittadinanza degli enti morali nel diritto internazionale*, 1934. LANDAU, *J. Clunet*, 1931, 610. *Travaux du Com. franc. de dr. intern. pr.*, III (1937) 11 (recognition of foreign companies in France). E. LEBÉE, 'Trusts et Cartels internationaux', 19 *Rec.* (1927 IV) 147. FARNSWORTH, 'The enemy character of corporations', 7 *Modern L.R.* (1944) 80.

CHAPTER XXII

MARRIAGE

IN the doctrine and practice of private international law 292. Preliminary observation problems concerned with marriage and divorce have attained special prominence. The municipal laws of the various countries differ in these matters much more than in any other legal sphere, in particular more than in the field of commercial intercourse. The rules relative to the conclusion, the conditions, the nullity, and the dissolution of marriage are so closely connected with morality, religion, and the fundamental principles of life prevailing in a given country that their application is often regarded as a matter of public policy. It follows that the creation of a 'harmony of laws', which is one of the ultimate goals of private international law, is more difficult of achievement in questions of marriage and divorce than in any other branch of the law. Unfortunately, for example, it often happens that the same couple is looked on in one country as validly married, while in another the marriage may be void or voidable, or may have been dissolved by a divorce decree not recognized elsewhere. The attempt made by the Hague Conventions of 1902[1] to attain unity on European conflict rules proved a complete failure: few states adhered to the Conventions, and of these some withdrew very soon and for good reasons. Great Britain was never a party to them.

We shall deal firstly with the conception of marriage, secondly with the admissibility of a marriage between two given persons (the conditions upon which the conclusion of the marriage is permitted), thirdly with the form of the celebration of marriage, and fourthly with the consequences of a defect either in the conditions of a marriage or in the form of its conclusion.

THE CONCEPTION OF MARRIAGE

I. Among the manifold kinds of union between man and 293. Types of regular marriages woman that have developed in the course of ages there is one in every community (nation, state, caste, tribe, religious

[1] See *supra*, s. 40.

community) which has stronger legal effects (within that community) than any other. This is the regular 'marriage', distinguished everywhere from other unions between persons of different sex.

It is hardly possible to supplement this rather formal—though not vague—description of the regular marriage by enumerating the effects it produces or by describing the forms in which it comes into existence; for both effects and forms of marriage differ so greatly in the various countries and the several periods of their history that no factor common to them all can be discovered. Marriage may or may not influence domicile, nationality, legitimacy, succession on death, property law, tax law, criminal law, and judicial procedure. It may or may not create unilateral or reciprocal obligations.[1] It may be based on forcible abduction (capture), or on sale or barter between the bride's father or guardian and the bridegroom, or on free consent. In the case of such consent any declaration of the parties to the marriage may be sufficient, or something more may be necessary, such as a religious or tribal ceremony or a declaration before a state official or the chieftain of a tribe. Marriage may be monogamous or polygamous, and a polygamous marriage may be either polygynous, as under Muhammedan law, or polyandrous, as in Tibet and some parts of India, where several men, mostly brothers, may have one wife in common. Polygyny may be of different kinds: sometimes all the wives have equal rank and position, sometimes one of them, usually the first to be married, holds a higher position and is regarded as the principal wife, while the others are inferior wives though not concubines.[2] Marriage may have the character of a merely worldly institution[3] or of a sacrament. It may be dissoluble

[1] *Contra*: Vinogradoff, *Outlines of Historical Jurisprudence*, i. 203.

[2] E. Westermarck, *History of Human Marriage* (5th ed. 1921), iii. 1 et seq., 107 et seq. Whether the much-discussed 'group-marriage' concluded between a group of men and a group of women, which is alleged to be found in Ceylon, Tibet, and parts of India, should be called a marriage remains doubtful. Cf. Westermarck, iii. 223 et seq.

[3] It was particularly Luther who emphasized that 'marriage is something external and secular subjected to temporal authority like clothing and victuals, house and home' (Luther, *Von Ehesachen*, 1530, Weimar edition, vol. xxx, sect. 3, p. 205).

or not, and where dissolution is admitted the law of the country may render it extremely difficult or again facilitate it: it may allow divorce by mutual consent of the parties or even by a unilateral and arbitrary declaration of one of the spouses.[1]

There are, however, in many countries certain kinds of **294. Other** union between a man and a woman which entail some **unions** though lesser effects than those produced by marriage of the normal type. In the case of persons belonging to the 'high nobility' German common law before 1919 admitted a full marriage only where the other party was of equal birth; a union between a German prince or a member of his family and a commoner could be concluded as a so-called 'left-handed' or 'morganatic' marriage, but its effects fell short of those of a full marriage: the wife did not acquire the husband's name or title, the children, though legitimate, bore their mother's name and could not succeed to the family property.[2] In some countries a mere concubinage entails certain of the legal effects of a full marriage. Thus under English regulations of 1939, 1940, and 1941 certain war pensions and allowances were granted to an 'unmarried wife', as she has been called,[3] that is, an 'unmarried dependant living as a wife', provided that she has been wholly or substantially maintained by the man 'on a permanent bona fide domestic basis continuously from a date not less than six months prior to the commencement of the war'.[4] Under the Mexican Code of 1928 a concubine who has lived for the last five years with the deceased has a right of succession on intestacy if both parties were unmarried and she was the only woman with whom he lived.[5] Under some other laws the children born in a concubinage are in a better position as regards alimony and succession than other illegitimate

---

[1] As was the case in ancient Roman law and is again the case in Soviet law.

[2] In 1540 Luther even allowed Prince Philipp the Magnanimous of Hesse to conclude a left-handed marriage without dissolving the marriage with his normal wife; and King Frederick William II of Prussia followed his example with the sanction of the clergy. But the validity of these marriages can hardly be maintained.

[3] For example, Order in Council sanctioning Retired Pay, Pensions, Allowances, &c., 1939, S.R. & O., 1939, No. 1221, ss. 43, 58.

[4] ibid., s. 14 (2) (c).

[5] *Código Civil*, 1928, art. 1635.

children.[1] In France the *union libre* creates mutual natural obligations, and it has even been held that the concubine is entitled to damages in case of the death of her consort through a railway or motor-car accident.[2]

295. Sub-normal marriages and concubinages

It is not easy to distinguish marriages of an inferior order from concubinages, as both have some, but not all, legal effects of full marriages. Whether a union belongs to the first or the second group depends on the law of the country where it was concluded. Where under this law most of the effects of a full marriage (as determined by the law of the country) come into existence, the term used for the normal type of marriage is also used for the sub-normal type; thus in the case of the German morganatic marriage. Where, on the other hand, the union entails legal effects only exceptionally and to a very small degree, the law of the country avoids the word marriage, thereby showing that it regards it as a mere concubinage.

296. So-called Christian marriages

II. Not all the various kinds of marriages existing in different parts of the world are recognized as marriages by English law. European civilization grants full effects of marriages only to what English lawyers have called 'Christian marriages', that is 'voluntary unions for life of one man and one woman to the exclusion of all other connubial unions'.[3] This needs explanation in respect of four points:

1. The term 'Christian marriage' does not exclude marriages concluded between Jews, Chinese, and Japanese parties[4] in the form of their respective religions, or non-religious marriages, such as those concluded before a registrar or by informal consent.[5] It means marriages 'formed on the same basis as marriages throughout Christianity'.[6]

---

[1] Thus in Roman law: *Nov.* 18, c. 5, and *Nov.* 89, c. 8–10, 12.

[2] See Josserand, *Cours de droit civil*, i, nos. 1177, 1178, 1180, and *Dalloz, Hebdom.*, 1932, Chron. 45; Nast, *Vers l'union libre ou le crépuscule du mariage légal*, ibid., 1938, Chron. 37. *Trib. de la Seine, Dalloz, Pér.*, 1931. 2. 57.

[3] *Hyde* v. *Hyde* (1866), L.R. 1, P & D., 130, 133. *Re Ullee* (1885), 53 L.T. (N. Ser.) 711. *In re Bethell* (1888), 38 Ch.D., 220, 234. *Brinkley* v. *Att.-Gen.* (1890), 15 P.D. 76.

[4] *Brinkley* v. *Att.-Gen.* (*supra*).

[5] *Examples*: marriages concluded in Soviet Russia (cf. *Nachimson* v. *Nachimson*, [1930] P. 217; *Way* v. *Way*, [1949] 2 A.E.R. 959), or in some of the states of U.S.A. (e.g. Texas), or before 1938 in Scotland.   [6] *In re Bethell* (*supra*).

Among Jews, however, polygamy is still practised in certain parts of Africa (Morocco, Algiers) and perhaps of Asia. Though based on the Scriptures, such marriages are now rare, and it would not be justifiable to treat Jewish marriages concluded in those countries in the forms and rites of Jewish custom as polygamous, unless the husband has, in fact, taken a second wife.

2. The union must be for life. Whether it is for life does not depend upon the individual intention of the parties, but upon the typical and distinctive scope of the union as determined by law. A concubinage does not become a marriage because the parties intend to remain united till death; nor is a marriage a nullity because the parties merely wish to effect a change in the woman's nationality or to give her her husband's title, and have agreed to part immediately after leaving the register office. The facility or otherwise with which a union can be dissolved is immaterial; even where the marriage can be dissolved by the unilateral declaration of one party it must be borne in mind that before dissolution it was according to its distinctive idea a 'union for life', and the dissolution is regarded as an exception both by law and by custom.[1]

3. The union must be to the exclusion of all other connubial unions. Though many millions of British subjects in Asia and Africa practise polygamy, and their courts as well as the Privy Council have to recognize polygamous marriages, English law does not treat them as marriages in the sense in which this term is used in Europe. The question arises: what constitutes a polygamous marriage? American law seems to regard as polygamous only marriages concluded while one of the spouses has a living undivorced spouse,[2] and continental European laws apparently take the same view, though it has seldom been pronounced.[3] Therefore the first marriage concluded between two Muhammedans in Pakistan is valid under American and continental European laws, and only the second, the third, and the fourth marriages are disqualified. English law

297. Polygamous marriages

---

[1] *Nachimson v. Nachimson*, loc. cit. See *Warrender v. Warrender* (1835), 2 Cl. & Fin. 488, 533.

[2] Restatement, § 132, comment (c).

[3] Valéry, p. 845; Frankenstein, iii. 94, n. 138, and others. As to English law, Lord Brougham in *Warrender v. Warrender* (*supra*, at p. 532) seems to look at it in the same way.

differs from this and brings out the true character of polygamy as understood in Asia and Africa much more nearly than the American rule. A marriage is polygamous if according to the law under which it is concluded another valid marriage may be (or may have been) concluded. The four marriages allowed to a Muhammedan are not converted into one valid, as it were monogamous, marriage with the first wife and three defective marriages; but all four marriages are of the same quality—and different, for instance, from a fifth marriage which under Muhammedan law would be a nullity; they are all polygamous, differing in principle from European marriages, and it would be unjust for a European court to treat the first wife and her issue more favourably than the others in respect of domicile, nationality, and succession. Even if one of the wives is the 'principal wife' and the others are inferior in rank, this does not make one of the unions a monogamous marriage and the rest concubinages.[1]

298. Their distinction from monogamous marriages

The problem remains: on what does it depend whether a marriage is monogamous or polygamous?[2] The answer is:

(a) *Not* on the *intention* of the parties. If two Muhammedans marry in Pakistan and the husband firmly intends to exclude any other marital union and carries this intention through, their marriage is nevertheless polygamous, because he remains at liberty to change his intention and enter into a second marriage which notwithstanding any promise made to his first wife would be valid under his personal law.[3]

(b) *Not* on the *race or religion* of the parties. *Examples*: Two Indians of Muhammedan faith may conclude a monogamous marriage before a London registrar.[4] A marriage concluded by an Englishman in Bechuanaland according

---

[1] In *Cheang Thye Phin* v. *Tan Ah Loy*, [1920] A.C. (P.C.) 369, 373, the deceased was a Chinese from Penang who had four *t'sais*, i.e. principal wives, and one *t'sip*, i.e. secondary wife. They all succeeded to the husband's property in equal parts.

[2] Cf. Lorenzen, 394–401.

[3] *Hyde* v. *Hyde* (1866), L.R. 1, P. & D. 130. Beckett, 48 *L.Q.R.* (1932), 341, 356; *Contra*: Vesey-Fitzgerald, 47 *L.Q.R.* 253.

[4] Examples in *Chetti* v. *Chetti*, [1909] P. 67, and *R.* v. *Hammersmith Superintendent Registrar, ex parte Mir-Anwaruddin*, [1917] 1 K.B. 634, 642.

to the rites of the Baralong tribe was regarded as polygamous though he never married a second wife.[1]

(c) *Not* on the domicile of the husband or the *matrimonial domicile*.[2]

(d) *Not* even on the *formalities* of marriage or the observation of certain rites. True, a marriage celebrated according to the rites of the Baralong tribe[3] cannot be monogamous, but whether it is polygamous or no marriage at all depends on where it is celebrated; if it is celebrated within the country of that tribe it is a (valid) Baralong polygamous marriage, if in Natal or England, it is no marriage. It must further be borne in mind that the rites and formalities of marriage are sometimes immaterial for its validity. A Muhammedan marriage, for example, is valid if the spouses (or their fathers or guardians) have expressed their consent in the presence of a certain number of witnesses; no religious act, no registration, no declaration before a Kadi or other official is required.[4] If two Muhammedans domiciled in Syria thus conclude a marriage by consent in the presence of witnesses in New Jersey, this is a valid monogamous marriage; if they conclude it in Egypt it is a valid polygamous marriage; if finally the declarations are made in England the marriage is void for lack of the local form.

(e) The decisive test for the character of the marriage is as W. E. Beckett has proposed:[5] the *place* at which the marriage was *celebrated*: if this place is in England, the marriage cannot be polygamous, but is either monogamous or a nullity. If the place of celebration is in Egypt, Iran, or Iraq, the decision depends on whether it was concluded according to the Foreign Marriages Act, 1892,[6] or any corresponding law of other European countries, i.e. within the precincts of an embassy, consulate, &c. If so, it is monogamous, if not, polygamous.

---

[1] See *In re Bethell* (1888), 38 Ch.D. 220, 234.

[2] *Aliter*: Cheshire, pp. 409–12. See, however, Dicey–Morris, p. 226, n. 75.

[3] The bridegroom has to kill an ox and send its head to his mother-in-law. See *In re Bethell* (*supra*).

[4] See Faiz Badruddin Tyabji, *Principles of Muhammedan Law* (2nd ed., 1919), p. 88; Vesey-Fitzgerald, *Muhammedan Law* (1931), pp. 37, 45.

[5] 48 *L.Q.R.* (1932), 356. *Contra*: Cheshire, p. 411.

[6] 55 & 56 Vict., c. 23.

The principle that the place of contracting is decisive for the monogamous or polygamous character of the marriage needs qualification. As an Islamic marriage can be validly concluded by mere consent and *verba de praesenti* without the observation of any of the usual rites, the question arises: how can such polygamous marriage be distinguished from a monogamous marriage concluded at the same place between Christians? For the answer to this all the circumstances of the case must be taken into account. If e.g. before 1939 a Scottish missionary, residing in some remote place of what is now called Pakistan, marries a Scottish girl by mere declaration of consent, their marriage is monogamous. If the same happens at the same place between two Muhammedans (or between a Muhammedan and a Scottish girl) the marriage is polygamous. It is submitted that in both cases the domicile of the husband is immaterial.

A marriage thus found to be polygamous is—like any other legal institution—either valid or voidable or void. Which of these it is will be decided by the law under which it was concluded: Muhammedan law, Hindu law, American Indian law,[1] &c. Since questions of capacity, as opposed to questions of form, are to be answered by the personal law of each party,[2] it is that law which has to decide whether the respective parties had the capacity to conclude a polygamous marriage. This was possibly the reason why in *Re Bethell*[3] the court held (erroneously, it is submitted) the polygamous marriage between a domiciled Englishman and a Baralong woman to be entirely void.[4]

299. Valid and void polygamous marriages

4. Though a polygamous marriage is not a marriage in the English sense, it does not follow that English law should treat it as a nullity, like a bigamous marriage concluded in England by a married Englishman. A marriage void for bigamy gives rise to proceedings for a nullity decree, but has no further effects. Its children are illegiti-

---

[1] In the new state of India the abolition of polygamy has been proposed. See Vesey-Fitzgerald, 29 *J. Comp. Leg.* (Nov. 1947), p. 30, and Deshmukh, ibid. 30 (May 1948), p. 111. On polygamous marriages of American Indians, with which American courts are often confronted, see Goodrich, p. 319.

[2] See on this *infra*, s. 309. There seems to be no reason why only the husband's domicile should be decisive, and not the wife's. Beckett, loc. cit., 360–1, takes a different view. He emphasizes that though English law rejects polygamy, this cannot prevent an Englishwoman from concluding a polygamous marriage because in such case *she* remains confined to one husband. But the prohibition of polygamy is intended to protect not only public morality but also the individual women.

[3] (1888) 38 Ch.D. 220.

[4] *Contra*: J. H. C. Morris, *Cases*, 88, 90.

mate.[1] If the husband dies intestate neither the second wife nor her children have rights of succession. The woman does not acquire her husband's domicile. The conclusion of the marriage is a criminal offence. The first wife can start divorce proceedings, &c. All this is different in the case of a valid polygamous marriage. Because it has not the character of a 'Christian' marriage (in the sense developed *supra*, s. 296), it cannot be validly concluded in England. English matrimonial remedies—proceedings for nullity, for divorce, for restitution of conjugal rights—are not open to the parties of a polygamous marriage. It is further true that under certain circumstances the recognition of a polygamous marriage would be 'repugnant to the moral principles of the people', as the South African Court said in *Seedat's Executors* v. *The Master (Natal)*.[2]

Example: Little girls of six or seven years are married to men in some barbaric country in accordance with the custom of the tribe. The example, however, which the South African judge found in *Seedat's Executors* v. *The Master (Natal)*[3] is ill chosen. The facts were these: A Muhammedan married a first wife in India, when he was domiciled there, and a second wife, also in India, when he was domiciled in Natal. He had four children by the first and six by the second wife. The court declared the children of the first wife to be legitimate, the children of the second wife to be illegitimate (because the father when domiciled in a monogamous country, Natal, was no longer capable of concluding a valid polygamous marriage). But the court denied both wives a right to succession, as this would be 'repugnant to the moral principles of the people'. It is submitted that this view is hardly justifiable. When the decision goes on to say that a recognition of the *first* marriage is 'reprobated by the majority of civilized peoples on the ground of morality and religion', the answer is that in most monogamous countries it is not the first but the second and following marriages which are considered to be offensive.

Apart from such exceptional repugnance to English public policy the principle ought to be and seems to be that the consequences of marriage are applicable to valid polygamous marriages. The opposite view would entail the preposterous consequence that millions of British subjects

---

[1] *Shaw* v. *Gould* (1868), L.R. 3 H.L. 55. See *infra*, s. 364.
[2] [1917] App. Div. 302, 307.
[3] In France it seems doubtful whether it is permissible to include the principle of monogamy in the conception of *ordre public*, because in Algeria those French nationals who live under Islamic or Jewish law are allowed to conclude polygamous marriages; Valéry, p. 1039.

in Asia and Africa must be treated by the English courts as illegitimate, and as being unable to produce legitimate issue. Some *dicta* of English judges show that if the courts had to decide on the secondary consequences of the non-recognition of polygamous marriages they would refrain from taking such an outrageous view. Lord Penzance said, in *Hyde* v. *Hyde*,[1] that 'it might be proper to accord to the issue of the polygamous unions . . . rights of succession or legitimacy', and Chitty, J., expressed *obiter* the same view in *Re Ullee*.[2] The three newest decisions recognize the status created by a polygamous marriage: the decision of Barnard, J., in *Srini Vasan* v. *Srini Vasan*,[3] the decision of the Court of Appeal in *Baindail* v. *Baindail*,[4] which approved the *Srini Vasan* decision, and the 'opinion', which Lord Maugham gave to the Privileges Committee of the House of Lords in the *Sinha Peerage Claim*:[5] Lord Maugham here stated that 'it cannot be doubted now that a Hindu marriage between persons domiciled in India is recognized in our courts, that the issue are regarded as legitimate, and such issue can succeed to property in this country' (with certain exceptions which need not be mentioned here).[6] It is, however, difficult to say how far the courts would go in admitting marriage-like effects of polygamous unions. With regard to legitimacy and succession rights of their issue there is no doubt, and it would seem incongruous to deny succession rights to the mothers of such legitimate children.[7] True, there are difficulties in adjusting those English laws which give rights to 'the surviving wife' to cases where the husband leaves more than one surviving wife. Shall each of the wives receive a full widow's share? Or shall they divide it between them?[8] The

---

[1] (1866), L.R. 1 P. & D. 130. See Cheshire, 402. *Contra*: Morris, *Cases*, 88 et seq.

[2] (1885), 53 L.T.R. (N.S.) 711.

[3] [1946] p. 67.   [4] [1946] p. 122.   [5] [1946] 1 A.E.R. 348 (n).

[6] See also *R.* v. *Rahman*, [1949] 2 A.E.R. 165, 168.

[7] See the South African Court in the *Seedat's Executors'* case, [1917] App. Div., 302.

[8] The latter view was taken, though not in an interpretation of an English statute, in *Cheang Thye Phin* v. *Tan Ah Loy*, [1920] A.C. (P.C.) 369, 373. Cf. Goodrich, 319. If the deceased had changed his domicile to England, the court would have to decide by application of the Administration of Estates Act (1925), s. 46 (1) (i) how the residuary estate is to be distributed. It is believed that equal

English rule that a wife always shares her husband's domicile will easily be applied to the wife or wives in a valid polygamous marriage, and Mr. Beckett[1] convincingly suggests the application of the British Nationality and Status of Aliens Act, 1914 (no longer in force): it would be incongruous to refuse British nationality to the Persian, Iraqi, or Arabian wives and legitimate children of a British Muhammedan.

Finally, if a polygamous marriage has been validly concluded in a foreign country, neither of the spouses is able to conclude with a third person a monogamous marriage in England; if he or she does so, the monogamous marriage is void.[2]

If, for example, an Englishwoman marries a Moslem in Pakistan, then returns to England after hearing that he has taken three other wives, and there marries an Englishman in London in due form, this marriage is void.[3] Whether she will be punished under s. 57 of the Offences against the Person Act (23–25 Vict. c. 100) depends on the interpretation of this Statute.

THE CONDITIONS OF MARRIAGE (IMPEDIMENTS TO MARRIAGE)

I. Under all legal systems permission to two given persons to marry is made subject to certain conditions (age, consent of certain third persons, absence of relationship within the prohibited degrees of consanguinity, affinity, or adoption,[4] or, as it is usually expressed in canon law and in modern doctrine, subject to the absence of certain *impediments*.[5] These

300. The various kinds of impediments

distribution between the two surviving wives would be unavoidable. It may however be that the courts hold the statute wholly inapplicable as inappropriate to the case of more than one widow.

[1] loc. cit. 342, 344; Cheshire, 402.

[2] See the *Srini Vasan* and the *Baindail* cases (*supra*).

[3] This would seem a correct though rather bold decision. Formerly one thought differently. The Egyptian Khedive Ismail Pasha had a rich Harem; one of his wives fell in love with a Neapolitan and fled (1880) to a small place in the province of Naples. The registrar doubted whether he ought to admit the marriage, but the Italian minister demolished his scruples; *J. Clunet* 7, 338. The English registrar would not be able to produce such a happy end unless that specific marriage with the Khedive suffered from such defects as to make the marriage repugnant to English principles of morality.

[4] Adoption of Children Act 1949 (12, 13 & 14 Geo. 6, c. 98), s. 11.

[5] English law, too, uses the term 'impediment'; Marriage Act 1836 (6 & 7 Will. IV, c. 85), s. 20; Stat. Order, 1909, no. 1332, IV. 2.

impediments are of various kinds according to their effect on a marriage concluded in spite of them:

1. The marriage concluded may be valid though not permissible, *illicitum sed validum*. Impediments of this kind are merely directory; they are called in canon law *impedimenta impedientia tantum seu prohibentia*; in Scottish law: 'impediments prohibitive'.[1] There are many of them in canon law and modern continental laws,[2] while in English law their number is small.

Examples: The absence of consent of parents or guardians in the case of an infant[3] and the existence of a prior invalid marriage which has not yet been declared void by a nullity decree.

2. Or, the marriage concluded in spite of the impediment may be void, as is the case where a spouse is still validly married to a third person.[4] Or, finally,

3. The marriage may be voidable,[5] for example, if concluded under the influence of an essential mistake or fraud.

The question is, what law is to determine the legal prerequisites upon which a marriage may be concluded? Most unfortunately the answer varies greatly from country to country.

301.
System of lex loci celebrationis

II. The first and oldest of the prevailing systems declares the law of the place where the marriage is celebrated to be decisive. 'A marriage valid where celebrated is valid everywhere, a marriage invalid where celebrated is invalid everywhere.' This system goes back to a doctrine of the statutists according to which the *lex loci actus* governs not only the form of any contract but also its essence. The system is

---

[1] Fraser, *Husband and Wife*, p. 49.

[2] *Continental examples*: A widow or divorced woman is not allowed to re-marry before the expiration of a certain time after the dissolution of the prior marriage (known to all continental laws, but not to canon or to English law). A marriage between guardian and ward is forbidden subject to exemption. Under canon law the marriage between a Roman Catholic and a non-catholic Christian is as a rule prohibited. Many laws forbid the marriage between uncle and niece, aunt and nephew, but the marriage, if concluded in spite of the prohibition, is (in contrast with English law) not invalid.

[3] See *R. v. Inhabitants of Birmingham* (1828), 8 B. & C. 29, 34. *Simonin* v. *Mallac* (1860), 2 Sw. & Tr. 67. *Ogden* v. *Ogden*, [1908] P. 46.

[4] In canon law these prohibitions are designated as *impedimenta dirimentia*; in Scottish law, 'impediments irritant' (a term which will be adopted here).

[5] Unknown to canon and Scottish law. See *supra*, s. 74.

simple and easy to apply, because the place at which a marriage has been celebrated can mostly be ascertained without difficulty. Only in the case of a marriage concluded by correspondence between persons in different countries —a case which can only happen where the common-law marriage by mere consent is law—do certain difficulties arise.[1] One of the great disadvantages of the system of *lex loci celebrationis* is that it induces persons to marry in a country where the impediments established by the law of their domicile do not operate and thus to evade domestic prohibitions. In the United States, where the system of *lex loci* is common law, the dangers which it creates are avoided to a certain degree by statutory provisions. Thus the Uniform Marriage Evasion Act, 1912—which, however, was accepted only by a small number of American states—and certain Acts of individual states[2] provide that no marriage shall be concluded in the state to which the Act applies by a couple domiciled elsewhere, if such marriage would be void or voidable under the law of the domicile, and that a marriage concluded in spite of such prohibition is void. The intention to evade the domiciliary law need not be proved.—The system of the *lex loci celebrationis* has also been accepted by a number of Latin-American states, such as Argentina, Paraguay, Peru, Guatemala, Nicaragua, and in particular by the Convention of Montevideo.[3] In Europe only the Soviet Union, and to a certain degree Denmark and Switzerland, have adopted the *lex loci* principle, but in the Soviet Union its application is limited to marriages concluded within the Union; no foreign impediment unknown to Russian law is there regarded as prohibitive or irritant.[4]

The second system declares the *personal law* of the parties competent to govern the conditions of their marriage. This may be the law of the domicile, as in Denmark,

302.
System of
personal
law

---

[1] The case, though rare in peace, is not infrequent during a war, when a soldier fighting in a foreign country wishes to marry a woman at home. Vernier, *American Family Laws*, I. 143; Lorenzen, 379–93. The American *Restatement*, § 125, applies in such cases the law of the state from which the acceptance is dispatched—just as in the case of a commercial contract concluded between persons in two different states (*Rest.*, § 326 (b)).

[2] See Vernier, *Amer. Family Laws*, I. 3 et seq., 209.

[3] Rabel I. 247 et seq.

[4] Makarov, *Conception du droit intern. privé russe*, pp. 88, 89, 92.

Norway, and some of the Latin-American states, or the national law, as in most other countries.

303. Mixed systems Finally, some countries have developed systems which are mixtures of the basic types just mentioned; either combinations of the national and the domiciliary law, or combinations of one of them and the law of the place of celebration. Such mixed system was in particular developed by the Hague Convention concerning Marriage, 1902.[1] The leading principle of this convention is the rule of the national law of each party; but the *lex loci celebrationis* has a twofold influence: it may allow the conclusion of the marriage in spite of such prohibitions in the national law of either party as are based on religious grounds; and it may on the other hand refuse to allow it on the ground of certain impediments of its own municipal law, unknown to the national laws of the parties, such as impediments of consanguinity or affinity, or religious prohibitions.

304. English law. Principle: *lex loci celebrationis* III. English law also possesses a mixed system which, however, is far from being unambiguous.

Its starting-point was the old statutist rule, taken over from the Dutch school[2] and its American adherents: the law of the place of celebration was exclusively decisive; *locus regit actum*. This rule was originally meant to apply both to the form and the substantial conditions of marriage. Old English decisions even based the rule of the *lex loci celebrationis* on the 'common consent of nations' and on *ius gentium*.[3] Though this way of justifying it has been abandoned in modern times, the rule itself was maintained as a 'general principle'.[4] We shall see that with regard to the capacity of the parties a different principle—the rule of the *lex domicilii*—has been adopted; but 'putting aside capacity' the old rule remained in force,[5] not only in respect of form

---

[1] Other examples of mixed systems in Mexico and Esthonia. See *RVgl.HWB.* IV. 399; Rabel I. 259 et seq.

[2] Ulric Huber, *De conflictu legum*, I. 3, 10.

[3] *Scrimshire* v. *Scrimshire* (1752), 2 Hagg. Consist. 395. See also *Herbert* v. *Herbert* (1819), 3 Phil. 58, 63.

[4] *Brook* v. *Brook* (1861), 9 H.L.C. 193, 205. *Sottomayor* v. *De Barros* (No. 2), 5 P.D. 94, 100, and others.

[5] Cf. Lord Dunedin's dictum in a case from Quebec, *Berthiaume* v. *Dastous*, [1930] A.C. (P.C.) 79, 83: 'If there is one question better settled than any other

but also in respect of any point of substance except capacity. Is this still the law? Three groups of problems must be examined separately.

1. First group: cases where the substantial validity of the marriage act itself (apart from capacity) is in issue. Examples: one party did not know that the act was in the nature of a marriage, or there was an *error qualitatis*, or fraud, or coercion of one party, or mental defects, or impotence. According to the prevailing view, all these questions should be answered by the *lex loci celebrationis*. This solution is open to objection.

305. substantial validity?

This becomes particularly clear in the case of mental defects or impotence. In many countries following canon law impotent persons are regarded as incapable of concluding a valid marriage, while in other countries, for example, in Germany, impotence is a bar to marriage only if the other party was at the time of the marriage ignorant of the facts. There is a similar divergence where one of the parties is of unsound mind or subject to recurrent fits of insanity. If under the *lex domicilii* the defect is one that causes incapacity to marry or restricts full capacity this law will be applicable; if, on the other hand, the law of the domicile regards the defect as something not curtailing capacity, the law of the place of marriage will decide the effect of such personal qualities. It is sometimes difficult to say whether a given legal provision should be classified as concerned with an *error qualitatis* or with capacity. The English Matrimonial Causes Act, 1937,[1] for example, says that a marriage 'shall be voidable on *the ground* that . . . either party to the marriage was at the time of the marriage of unsound mind or a mental defective . . . or subject to recurrent fits of insanity', but adds that 'the court shall not grant a decree unless it is satisfied that the petitioner was at the time of the marriage ignorant of the facts alleged'. Does this provision establish incapacity (unless the petitioner knew the facts) or avoidability based on error? The wording seems to suggest the former solution. But it is regrettable that the differentiation made by the conflict rule should compel the lawyer to study and answer such absurd questions—which call to mind Warwick's strictures on 'these nice sharp quillets of the law'.

The situation has now been clarified by the decision in *Way* v. *Way*.[2] Hodson, J., examined the question as to what law applies where some point of substantial validity, except capacity, is in issue, notably where marital consent of the

in international law, it is that as regards marriage, putting aside the question of capacity, *locus regit actum*.'

[1] (1 Edw. VIII & Geo. VI, c. 57), s. 7, subs. (1).
[2] [1949] 2 A.E.R. 959, 963.

parties is doubtful. He applied not the *lex loci celebrationis*, but the personal law of the parties and found some support for this in two *dicta* in *Apt. v. Apt.*[1] If, as may be hoped, this is the correct view, the unfortunate distinction between capacity and other points of substantial validity disappears, and an atavistic English rule is satisfactorily replaced by the rule prevailing in other countries.

306.
consent of
third
persons

2. The *lex loci actus* is undoubtedly decisive where the consent or advice of third persons, such as parents, grandparents, or guardians plays a part. The law of the domicile of one of the parties often requires such consent or advice by declaring either that without the consent the marriage is not permissible, or even that the unsanctioned marriage is voidable.[2] In both cases English law disregards the provisions of the laws of the domiciles; it applies only the law of the place of contracting. This has been decided in cases where domiciled English parties have married abroad (*Gretna Green Cases*),[3] and also several times in the converse situation where persons domiciled abroad have married in England without consulting their parents in defiance of the provisions of their domiciliary law. The leading cases of this type are *Simonin v. Mallac*[4] and *Ogden v. Ogden.*[5]

In the case of *Simonin v. Mallac* a marriage had been concluded in England in 1854 between two domiciled French parties aged twenty-nine and twenty-two respectively. This marriage offended against two rules then forming part of the French civil code: it had been concluded without the previous *publications* (banns), which should have been made by the registrar in a prescribed form,[6] and without the three *actes respectueux et formels* by which a man under thirty and a woman under twenty-five years had to seek advice (*conseil*) though not consent from their parents.[7] The

---

[1] [1948] P. 93, 88.

[2] Under the German Marriage Law, 1946, s. 35, the lack of consent of the legal representative (who may be the father or the mother or a guardian) renders the marriage voidable.

[3] Runaway marriages of English infants concluded in Scotland, where the consent of the parents required by English law was no condition of marriage. U. Huber speaks of 'adolescentes furtivos amores nuptiis conglutinare cupientes'. The leading case is *Compton v. Bearcroft* (1769), 2 Hagg. Consist. 444.

[4] (1860), 2 Sw. & Tr. 67.

[5] [1907] P. 107; [1908] P. (C.A.) 46.

[6] *Code civil*, art. 63, 170.

[7] *Code civil*, art. 151, 152, 170 i.f.

French code declared that each of these deficiencies precludes the validity of a marriage concluded by a French subject outside France. The French court accordingly pronounced the marriage null and void. The English court upheld the marriage; it based its view on the general rule of the *lex loci actus*, as applied in *Scrimshire* v. *Scrimshire*, 'not merely to the question of form and ceremonial'.[1] It stressed the 'impossibility of having any rule applicable to all cases, save that the law of a country where the marriage is solemnized shall, in that country at least, decide whether it is valid or invalid'.[2] The suggestion that the law of the domicile should be applied was rejected for the reason that if the parties had had different domiciles each of their respective states would have 'an equal right to claim respect for its law', and 'both cannot be observed'.[3] Unconvincing though the last argument is—in all continental states the conflict rules show that there is no difficulty in applying both laws—the judgment in *Simonin* v. *Mallac* is good authority for the rule that an English court applies the *lex loci actus* not only where the form of the marriage is to be examined but also where some essential conditions of the marriage, apart from capacity, are in issue.

Ogden v. *Ogden*[4] follows this rule, but goes one step farther. In this case a domiciled Frenchman of nineteen and an Englishwoman of twenty-five went through a ceremony of marriage in the English form in England. As in *Simonin* v. *Mallac*, the French court annulled the marriage, the English court upheld it; again the reason was that the question should be answered not by the law of the French domicile, but by the English law of the place of contracting. The difference, however, was that this time the man lacked capacity under French law, since his capacity to marry was conditioned on his father's *consent*.[5] Nevertheless, the defect was disregarded both in the Divorce Court and in the Court of Appeal. The result is that where under the law of domicile, but not under the law of the *locus celebrationis*, the validity depends on the consent of a third person the *lex loci celebrationis* is applicable. Unfortunate and illogical though this rule may be,[6] it is the prevailing law.

It applies to any kind of consent of a third party, irrespective of whether it is required in the private interest of one of the parties to the marriage, or in order to maintain the respect due to the third party (the father or the chief of the family),[7] or in the public interest (military service,[8] state policy, &c.). In cases of the last kind, however, there is still

---

[1] *Simonin* v. *Mallac (supra)*, at p. 80.
[2] Ibid, p. 85.   [3] Ibid., p. 84.
[4] [1907] P. 107; [1908] P. (C.A.) 46.
[5] *Code civil*, art. 148; see art. 182.   [6] Cf. Cheshire, p. 289.
[7] The *acte respectueux et formel* of the civil code, art. 151, 152 (*supra*, p. 328, n. 7) is an instance of this.
[8] Thus in Germany the members of the armed forces needed the consent of their superior officers until 1945.

another reason for disregarding the foreign rule, viz., the non-applicability of foreign public law.[1]

307. The Sussex Peerage Case

In all those cases where in a foreign monarchy there is a rule that no member of the reigning family may marry without the Sovereign's consent, this rule would be disregarded by the courts of any other state as embodying a principle of foreign constitutional law, even if the ordinary conflict rule of the forum required the application of that foreign law in all questions of capacity. On the other hand, the courts of the country where the Sovereign's consent is required will hold a marriage invalid which was concluded without that consent, irrespective of whether the *lex loci actus* or the *lex domicilii* would apply the rule or disregard it. This is probably the reason for the decision in the *Sussex Peerage* Case.[2]

The Royal Marriage Act[3] provides that no descendant of King George II shall be capable of concluding a valid marriage without the consent of the Sovereign in Council. One of the sons of George III, Prince Augustus Frederick, a British subject domiciled in England, married in 1793 the daughter of the Earl of Dunmore without consent; the marriage was celebrated in Rome. According to Italian law the marriage was valid, but in spite of the rule of the *lex loci celebrationis* the English court invalidated the marriage.

This decision was by no means based on the English domicile of the prince or on his British nationality; it would have been the same if he had been a domiciled Italian. It was founded solely on the interest of the state, to which a marriage of any member of the Royal Family 'might be detrimental'.[4]

308. directory rules

3. The *lex loci actus* is (probably) decisive where the question concerns merely foreign directory rules, *impedimenta impedientia tantum*, that is, where the problem is not whether a marriage already concluded is valid, void, or voidable, but whether a marriage not yet concluded is permissible. There is no authority on this problem, and the question will rarely arise before the courts. It is a question

---

[1] See *supra*, s. 162, 164.
[2] (1844) 11 Cl. & Fin. 85.
[3] (1772) 12 Geo. III, d. 11.
[4] *Sussex Peerage* Case (*supra*) at p. 147.

for the registrar to decide,[1] and only if he refuses to issue the marriage certificate or licence and the Registrar-General dismisses the appeal, may the problem be brought before the court by way of *mandamus*.[2] Up to the present no reported case has been concerned with a refusal on the ground of a merely directory prohibition.[3] The fact that the courts are silent on this point has caused English text-book writers to refrain from discussing the problem at all. On the Continent there is no doubt that the personal law of the parties to the marriage (either their national or their domiciliary law) governs all impediments no matter whether they are irritant or directory; the registrar is not allowed to proceed to the marriage ceremony until it has been proved that no impediment to the marriage exists under the personal law of either of the parties.[4] English law requires that before the marriage certificate is issued both parties make a solemn declaration that they 'know not of any lawful impediment why (they) may not be joined in matrimony to' each other;[5] but it is not said what law decides whether there are lawful impediments. It would seem safe to assume that with regard to *impedimenta impedientia tantum* the old rule according to which the *lex loci actus* is decisive is still in force, and that the law of the domicile is irrelevant.

Illustrations: A domiciled French widow wishes to marry before the English registrar three months after her husband's death. The marriage is permissible; the directory rule of French law under which a remarriage is forbidden to a woman until a period of three hundred days has passed since the dissolution of the prior marriage,[6] is not applicable in this country. Again, a marriage between guardian and ward is forbidden by Spanish law; but the marriage is valid if concluded in spite of that prohibition. There seems to be no bar to the conclusion of such marriage in England by a domiciled Spanish guardian.

[1] In the case of a register-office marriage.

[2] See *R. v. Hammersmith Superintend. Registrar, ex parte Mir-Anwarrudin*, [1917] 1 K.B. 634.

[3] In the *Hammersmith Case* (*supra*) the ground for refusal was the existence of a prior valid marriage, an impediment irritant.

[4] In most countries foreigners who wish to marry have to bring a certificate, issued by the state to which they belong, declaring that under the law of that state no impediment exists.

[5] Stat. Order 1909, No. 1332, s. IV, 2.

[6] *Code civil*, art. 228.

309. Capacity tested by domicile

IV. Questions of *capacity* are in general governed by the law of the domicile.

First a few words on the conception of capacity within the meaning of this rule. There are two kinds of incapacity: absolute incapacity, derived from a certain status owing to which the *incapax* is unable to conclude *any* valid marriage (for example, nonage), and relative incapacity, independent of status and existing only between certain persons (for example, consanguinity within the prohibited degrees). No incapacity is created by a mere prohibition to marry if a marriage concluded in spite of the prohibition is valid.

310. First step: where the domicile is English

The rule that the *lex domicilii* is decisive for all questions of capacity has developed very slowly. The first step was taken in the case of incestuous marriages. Impediments unknown to the *lex loci celebrationis* but existing under the *lex domicilii* were recognized as invalidating a marriage in cases where the marriage is forbidden (at the domicile) as 'contrary to religion, morality, or to any other fundamental institution'.[1] This rule was applied in particular where the *lex domicilii* was English, the place of contracting foreign, and the English prohibitions on the ground of consanguinity or affinity were more stringent than the corresponding rules at the place of celebration: cases of marriage in Denmark between two domiciled English persons, a widower and his deceased wife's sister,[2] or of marriage in Germany between a domiciled Englishman and a German woman, again his first wife's sister,[3] or conversely a marriage concluded in Germany between a domiciled Englishwoman and a domiciled German who had previously been married to her sister,[4] or a marriage in Germany between uncle and niece both having an English domicile (under German law marriages between uncle and niece are allowed).[5] Does the same principle obtain where the law of the domicile is not English and neither the *lex fori*, that is,

---

[1] *Brook* v. *Brook* (1861), 9 H.L.C. 193, 212.

[2] *Brook* v. *Brook*, ibid. (under English law of that time a marriage could not be validly concluded between them).

[3] *Mette* v. *Mette* (1859), 1 Sw. & Tr. 416.

[4] *In re Paine*, [1940] Ch. 46.

[5] *In re De Wilton*, [1900] 2 Ch. 481.

English law, nor the *lex loci celebrationis*—which may be English or the law of a third country—limits the parties' capacity? It is difficult to glean an answer from the confusing authorities on this point.

The problem is mainly one of construction of the hardly satisfactory decisions in *Sottomayor* v. *De Barros*.[1]

311. The Sottomayor v. De Barros cases

The facts were as follows: A girl of fourteen and a half and a boy of sixteen went through a marriage ceremony in England; they were first cousins, both of Portuguese nationality; under Portuguese law as it then stood a marriage between first cousins was void unless concluded with a Papal dispensation, for which no application had been made; the parents of both parties had approved and even encouraged the marriage for business reasons; the marriage was never consummated. The domicile of the parties was doubtful. The case was first decided upon the assumption that both parties were domiciled in Portugal[2] and came up for decision again two years later after it had been ascertained that only the girl was domiciled in Portugal while the husband had an English domicile.[3]

In the first case Phillimore, J., declared the marriage to be valid. He held that English law as the *lex loci actus* was decisive, that the disregard for the Portuguese impediment did not result in the recognition of a marital union which would be 'incestuous, unnatural, or destructive of civilized life', and that the impediment was merely one 'of positive law'.[4] The Court of Appeal unanimously reversed that judgment by applying the 'well-recognized' principle[5] that, at least where both parties have the same domicile, their capacity to marry each other depends on the law of that domicile. This view was sharply attacked in the 'second' Sottomayor case by Sir J. Hannen, P., who emphasized that the application of the law of domicile to questions of capacity was by no means 'well-recognized', and that the old principle of the *lex loci actus* still prevailed, at least where one of the parties was at the time of the ceremony a domiciled Englishman and the marriage was celebrated in England. Otherwise—so he reasoned in pursuance of a hint given in Sottomayor No. 1 by the Court of Appeal[6]—

---

[1] (1877) 2 P.D. 81; (1877) 3 P.D. (C.A.) 1; (1879) 5 P.D. 94.
[2] Judgments in 2 P.D. 81 and 3 P.D. 1 (called *Sottomayor* v. *De Barros*, No. 1).
[3] Judgment in 5 P.D. 94 (called *Sottomayor* v. *De B.*, No. 2).
[4] At pp. 86, 87, loc. cit.
[5] 3 P.D., at p. 5 (*per* Cotton, L.J.).
[6] 3 P.D., at p. 7, and 5 P.D. at p. 104.

'injustice might be caused to our own subjects if a marriage were declared invalid on the ground that it was forbidden by the law of the domicile of one of the parties'—a startling reason to be advanced in this undefended case of a non-consummated marriage concluded between two children and instigated by their parents for some business interest. However well-founded the criticism may be that can be raised against the judgment in the *Sottomayor Case* No. 2, and however true it may be on the other hand, that in the *Sottomayor Case* No. 1 the Court of Appeal described as 'well-recognized' a principle which at that time was by no means recognized, both decisions have made law. The maxim that capacity to marry, just as capacity to conclude other contracts, is governed by the law of domicile is well recognized to-day, though mainly by *dicta*. The latest judgment delivered on this subject, the judgment in *Re Paine*,[1] relies on the unanimous opinion of eminent writers; the learned judge was able to quote Dicey's and Westlake's text-books and the article on 'Conflict of Laws' in Halsbury's *Laws of England* in favour of the law of domicile. On the other hand, the unfortunate exception to the domicile principle pronounced in Sottomayor No. 2 has never been overruled and also constitutes a precedent. The result seems to be the following:

(*a*) The capacity of two persons to marry each other is governed not by the *lex loci celebrationis* but by the *lex domicilii*.

(*b*) To this rule there are two exceptions:

(i) Whether capacity depends on the consent of third persons is decided by the law of the place of celebration.

(ii) Impediments of a foreign *lex domicilii* based on consanguinity or affinity between the parties are disregarded in an English court if one of the parties has an English domicile *and* the marriage has been celebrated (or is to be celebrated) in England.

312. What is the lex domicilii? One question remains to be examined: what is meant by *lex domicilii*? Three different answers have been proposed: first, the law of the husband's domicile; secondly, the law

[1] [1940] Ch. 46.

of the matrimonial domicile; thirdly, the laws of the domiciles of both parties.

1. The first answer, much advocated in former times, in particular by Savigny,[1] is based on the conception of the husband as the head of the family; but the moment in which the incapacity of a woman to marry becomes important is pre-nuptial; at that time there is no 'husband', there is no 'family'.

2. The second answer is advanced notably by Dr. Cheshire[2] and favoured by *Brook* v. *Brook*.[3] This decision designates as decisive the law of the domicile which the husband will have 'once the couple are settled in the country in which the matrimonial residence is contemplated'.[4] Dr. Cheshire's formula is more precise. His view is that the capacity of both parties to conclude a marriage is governed by the 'law of the intended matrimonial home', and that there is a rebuttable presumption that the husband's domicile at the time of the marriage is the matrimonial home. There are some objections to this doctrine. Marriage may create a matrimonial domicile (or home); but whether marriage itself has come into existence should not be tested by a not yet existent matrimonial domicile. In support of the doctrine of matrimonial domicile an opinion of Ulricus Huber, the great Dutch jurist, has been proffered. Huber attempted to combine the *lex-loci-actus* doctrine and the *lex-domicilii* principle by explaining that the 'locus matrimonii contracti non tam is est ubi contractus nuptialis initus est, quam in quo contrahentes matrimonium exercere voluerunt'.[5] The objection to this is that such identification of the place of conclusion with the place of performance is purely fictitious.

In support of his doctrine of the matrimonial home, Cheshire finds an analogy in the rules for the choice of law concerning contracts: the 'proper law of the contract', that is, the law with which the contract is most closely connected is in the case of marriage the law of the intended home. But

1 VIII., sect. 379 (pp. 325, 326).
2 at pp. 269 et seq, 651.
3 (1861) 9 H.L.C. 193, 207. See also the *De Reneville* case, [1948] P. 100, 114.
4 Graveson, 20 *J. Comp. Leg.* (1938), 55, calls it very aptly 'a domicil of hope, of desire, of sincere intention, a domicil of the uncertain future'.
5 *Warrender* v. *Warrender* (1853), 2 Cl. & Fin. 488. The rule is based on the famous passages in the *Digest* 42, 5. 3 and 44, 7. 21. See on this *infra*, s. 414.

capacity is not dependent on any proper law of the contract. It depends on the *lex domicilii* and in mercantile contracts partly on the domicile, partly on the *locus celebrationis*.[1]

The decisive point is, however: Is Dr. Cheshire's doctrine desirable? It is believed that it is not. An unmarried woman who is about to marry must be protected against the non-observation of those laws which are still her laws. If a Spaniard who suffers from venereal disease in a communicable form wishes to marry a healthy Swedish girl this must be prevented, although Spanish law allows such marriage, and only the girl's domiciliary law forbids it.[2]

313.
Domicile
of each of
the parties
decisive

3. The only sound solution—and that which has been accepted in practically every country where the personal law of the spouses governs the problem of their capacity—is that the personal law of *each* of them must be taken into equal consideration. The law of the domicile of each party decides his or her capacity to marry the other party.[3] When *M* has a French and *W* a Spanish domicile, French law decides whether *M* can marry *W*, and Spanish law whether *W* can marry *M*. If French law denies to *M* the capacity to marry *W* the marriage is invalid irrespective of whether Spanish law allows it or not. On the other hand, if *M* is capable under French law but would not be capable under Spanish law of marrying *W* this does not prevent the marriage from being valid. It may happen, however, that the law of *M*'s domicile permits his marriage to *W* only if certain conditions are fulfilled with regard to *W*, although the law of *W*'s domicile does not require those conditions. Example: Swedish law does not allow the marriage of epileptics, French law does. If a domiciled Frenchman suffering from epilepsy intends to marry a Swedish woman (who knows the facts) this offends against Swedish law, which obviously intends to forbid Swedish subjects both to marry when epileptic themselves and to marry non-Swedish epileptics. The same is true in respect of the impediment of impotence known to the other party. Such impediment is to be found, for example, in canon law, English and Spanish law, but not in German or French law. It invalidates a marriage between a Spanish woman and a

[1] *Supra*, s. 261 et seq.
[2] On other reasons: Dicey–Morris, p. 762–3.
[3] *Re Paine*, [1940] Ch. 46, and Dicey–Morris, Westlake; further Halsbury's *Laws of England* at the passages quoted by the Court.

domiciled German, and it is immaterial whether the Spanish woman or the German husband is the impotent party. It must, however, not be supposed that all impediments have such a two-sided character. When, for example, the law of Massachusetts allows a girl of twelve to marry, while English law fixes the age at sixteen, this does not mean that an Englishman could not conclude a valid marriage with a Massachusetts girl under sixteen.[1]

Capacity must be existent at the time of the marriage. A marriage validly concluded does not become void when the husband later acquires a domicile under which he would not have been able to marry. Conversely an invalid marriage does not become valid through a change of domicile, although under the new domicile the marriage would have been validly concluded. If, for example, a domiciled Englishman marries his divorced wife's sister in Denmark, the invalid marriage remains invalid even if the spouses settle in Denmark and there acquire a new domicile.

314. Date decisive in respect of capacity

V. Lastly, the English Matrimonial Causes Act, 1937,[2] has introduced a new impediment to marriage, which seems to be unknown to any other legal system and which might create some difficulties in the field of private international law. A marriage is voidable 'on the ground that it has not been consummated owing to the wilful refusal of the respondent to consummate the marriage'. The peculiar feature of this impediment consists in the voidability being based on a post-nuptial fact. One would have expected a right to sue for divorce in the case of refusal of consummation, such as exists in many other countries. There is, however, much to be said for an equal treatment of wilful refusal to consummate the marriage and of impotence;[3] both preclude the physical effects of a normal marriage, and a wilful refusal may often cover impotence.[4] It is therefore sub-

315. Impediment of wilful refusal of consummation

---

[1] If the girl is only twelve the marriage may be regarded as offending against morality (but that does not affect the question discussed here).

[2] s. 7, sub-sect. (1) (a).

[3] See on this *Inverclyde* v. *Inverclyde*, [1931] P. 29, and *supra*, pp. 82–3.

[4] In the Scottish case *G.* v. *G.*, [1924] A.C. 349, the House of Lords emphasized that impotence may come 'from some bodily defect or from hysteria or invincible repugnance', and several times the courts have assumed the existence of some latent impediment 'amounting to incapacity where there has been persistent

mitted that in English private international law it is proper to deal with the impediment of wilful refusal on the same lines as with real 'incapacity' and to apply the English rule if either party had an English domicile at the time of the marriage.

316. Cases of *renvoi* and of exclusion of foreign law (*ordre public*, &c.)

VI. It is important to bear in mind that all the rules on the law applicable to the conditions of marriage are subject to the general principles of private international law, in particular

1. to those on *renvoi*.[1] Where the law of the domicile remits the question of the applicable law to the law of the English forum or transmits it to a third country, the *renvoi* has to be accepted. Thus, if the parties are British subjects domiciled in Italy, or Spanish nationals domiciled in Italy, their capacity to marry is (under English private international law) governed respectively by English or by Spanish law.

2. to those on the *exclusion of a foreign law* which would normally be applicable.[2] Foreign impediments to marriage will very often be disregarded by the English registrar or the English court owing to the fact that they are 'penal' or that they belong to foreign administrative law or that they are inconsistent with English public policy. Impediments of this kind are very numerous. The main examples are the following:

317. Religious and racial impediments

(*a*) Impediments based on religious grounds, most of them of canonical origin, such as the prohibition of marriage between Christians and non-Christians,[3] or between Roman Catholics and other Christians,[4] or the impediments imposed on priests or monks,[5] or the incapacity of persons engaged to be married to marry any third person.[6]

---

refusal to consummate the marriage'; see, for example, *F. v. P.* (1896), 75 L.T. 192. Cf. Eversley, *Domestic Relations*, p. 24.

[1] See *supra*, s. 178 et seq.

[2] See *supra*, s. 163.

[3] The *impedimentum disparitatis cultus*, which in canon law is even irritant; *cod. iur. can.*, c. 1070.

[4] The *impedimentum mixtae religionis*; *cod, iur. can.*, c. 1060.

[5] *Impedimenta ordinis* and *voti, cod. iur. can.*, c. 1072, 1073.

[6] *Impedimentum sponsalium de futuro*, particularly maintained by the Orthodox Church, but cancelled by the *cod iur. can.*

(b) Prohibitions founded on diversity of races or castes.

In 33 states of the United States of America inter-racial marriages have been forbidden, mostly between white persons and negroes or mulattos, in some states also between white persons and Indians, Mongolians, Malayans, Chinese, or Japanese. Louisiana also bars inter-marriage between negroes and Indians, and Maryland between negroes and persons of the Malay race. An inter-racial marriage which is against the law of the state of domicile of either party is regarded by the law of other American states as invalid,[1] by English law as valid. For the same reasons English registrars and courts allowed marriages offending against the racial laws of national-socialist Germany. The diversity of castes, though an impediment in India, was disregarded in *Chetti* v. *Chetti*.[2]

(c) Marriage restrictions of a *penal* character have been mentioned before.[3] They are for the most part concerned with the right of divorced persons to marry again; where they affect equally the innocent and the guilty spouse, they are not penal; but in no court anywhere do they render a marriage void or voidable, and *impedimenta impedientia tantum* of foreign law are immaterial if a marriage is concluded in England.[4] Where such prohibitions affect only the guilty party, or the guilty party more strongly than the innocent spouse, they are of a penal nature. So are provisions forbidding an adulterous spouse to marry his partner in adultery after the divorce.[5]

318. Impediments of a penal character

(d) Restrictions belonging to foreign *administrative* or other public law. Examples are provisions requiring the consent of military authorities or of the Sovereign.[6] It seems doubtful whether impediments based on eugenic considerations should also be classed among rules of a purely territorial nature. It is suggested that this depends on the scope of the foreign impediment: if a state prohibits the marriage only in the interest of its own people, as was the case with the German (Nazi) Law of 18 October 1935 for the 'Protection of the Hereditary Health of the German People', the rule will be inapplicable elsewhere; if it has no such

319. Administrative restrictions

---

[1] According to the *Restatement*, § 132 (c). On the South-African Prohibition of Mixed Marriages Act, 1949, see 3 *Intern. L.Q.* 91-6.

[2] [1909] P. 67, 78.　　　　　[3] See *supra*, s. 163.

[4] See *supra*, s. 308.

[5] This impediment prevails in Belgium, the Netherlands, Spain, and other countries, and formerly prevailed in Germany.

[6] *Supra*, s. 307.

limited national aim its application outside the state might be unobjectionable.

320.
Incapacity under *lex loci actus*

3. Conversely: a type of incapacity known to the *lex loci actus* but not to the law of the domicile will be taken into consideration if the disregard of such incapacity would offend against morality, religion, or public policy. In Germany and Sweden a marriage between a divorced man and his wife's sister is permissible; under English or French law it is void. If a domiciled German subject and the (German) sister of his divorced wife wish to marry in this country, it would not be allowed, and if in spite of this they go through a marriage ceremony in England, their marriage would probably be treated as void. Had they married in Germany there is no doubt that such marriage would be recognized in England (or France).

BIBLIOGRAPHY

CHESHIRE, 397–496. DICEY–MORRIS, 758–87. COOK, 442–56. RABEL, I. 197–288. GOODRICH, 298–322. LORENZEN, *Répert.*, VI. no. 263, 264. E. AUDINET, 'Conflits de lois en matière de mariage et divorce', 11 *Rec.* (1926 I), 175. AUDINET, *J. Clunet*, 1930, 319. TRAVERS, *Rev. Darras*, 1910, 24, 362. KESSLER, *Rabel's Z.*, 1,858 (American law). UNDÉN, *Internat. äktenskapsrätt* (Sweden), 1922. PLAISANT, *Conflits dans les Traités*, 330 et seq. BATIFFOL, *Traité*, 446–66. NIBOYET, *Traité* V. 309–51. On the Hague Convention: KAHN, *Abhandl.* II. 37. R. REY, *Le mariage d'après la convention de la Haye*, 1916. FLEMING, 3 *Intern. L.Q.*, 9–27, 228–42.

THE FORMALITIES OF MARRIAGE

321. The rule *locus regit actum* ambiguous

I. The form of a marriage is governed by the law of the place at which it is concluded. *Locus regit actum.* This maxim, which has been called one of the most firmly established rules of Private International Law, is not free from ambiguity. In many countries it means only that for the valid conclusion of a marriage it is *sufficient* but not necessary to observe the forms prescribed by the *lex loci celebrationis*; the parties have the choice between the *lex loci* and their personal law. In other countries it is obligatory to obey the law of the place of celebration; there the rule *locus regit actum* has an imperative character.

The first view was predominant in the epoch of the statutists[1] and was rightly favoured by many of the most

---

[1] See von Bar, I. 353, n. 44.

eminent authors of the last century, in particular by Savigny and von Bar.[1] This sound conception was weakened under the influence of leading ideas of the French Revolution and of the movement tending to a separation of Church and State. In France, Belgium, Germany, and other states which proclaimed civil marriage as the compulsory form of marriage there arose an inclination to prohibit on their own territories any religious form of marriage even if the personal law of the parties provided for or required a religious form. The technical instrument of the prohibition was the doctrine of *ordre public*. The optional character of the rule *locus regit actum* was thus partly eliminated. In each of these states the rule became imperative for marriages concluded within its own territory; it remained optional only for marriages concluded abroad. And this is still the law prevailing on the continent. Take, for example, two Greek subjects, faithful members of the Orthodox Church, who marry in France or Germany in the religious form prescribed by their personal law but do not go through a civil ceremony before a registrar. If the marriage is concluded in Germany, German law regards it as non-existent; under Greek law it is valid, and French law, respecting the Greek view as that of the personal law of the parties, also treats it as valid. If, on the other hand, the marriage is concluded in France, it is a nullity in the eyes of the French courts, though a valid marriage under Greek and German law.[2] The reason for these surprising divergencies lies in the maxim that no country may apply foreign rules of *ordre public* even if they coincide with its own.[3]

English and American laws avoid this unsatisfactory result. But they replace it by a solution which is possibly worse. They take the principle *locus regit actum* to be imperative in every case. 'A marriage invalid where concluded is

322. English view: always imperative

---

[1] Savigny, VIII. 358, 381; von Bar, I. 353, 461 (Engl. transl., pp. 274, 358).

[2] See German Introd. Law to the Civ. Code, art. 13 § 3, 11 § 1. The same rule prevails in Switzerland, Poland, Hungary, Sweden, Japan, and (though not supported by statute) in Belgium and many other countries. In French (and Spanish) Colonial Law the maxim is always optional: the marriage is valid if concluded either in the form of the *lex loci actus* or in that of the personal law of the parties.

[3] See on this, *supra*, s. 176.

invalid everywhere.' No distinction is made between the case where the *locus celebrationis* is English and that where the marriage is concluded abroad. No conception of public policy was introduced to support the rule. In the earliest reported case, *Scrimshire* v. *Scrimshire*,[1] two British subjects domiciled in England had married in France in English form. The marriage was declared to be void because the form of French law had not been observed.[2] The rule was adopted in numerous later cases.[3] It was derived from the principle that when the parties chose a French place as place of contracting they thereby subjected questions of validity of their marriage in every respect, with regard to both formalities and to essentials, to French law. True, such voluntary submission to foreign law was nothing but a fiction. But the judge could point out that a refusal to apply the principle *locus regit actum* would lead to the inconvenient result that the marriage would be regarded as valid in England and as invalid in France, that if the husband were to contract a second marriage in France this would be valid under French and void under English law, that the children of the first marriage would be legitimate in England and illegitimate in France, while the children of the second marriage would be bastards in England and legitimate in France. Of course the objection to this reasoning is that the danger of 'limping marriages', as they have been called,[4] is by no means averted, since most continental courts do not regard the principle *locus regit actum* as imperative. If, for example, an Italian court had to adjudicate upon the validity of the Scrimshire marriage it would declare it to be valid as concluded in accordance with the personal law of the parties,[5] that is, English law.

The most serious objection to the imperative character

---

[1] (1752) 2 Hag. Cons. 395, 408, 415, 417. Cf. *Roach* v. *Garvan* (1748), 1 Ves. Sen. 157.

[2] A continental court would in such case hardly apply the rule *locus regit actum*.

[3] *Dalrymple* v. *Darlymple* (1811), 2 Hag. Cons. 54, 59. *Warrender* v. *Warrender* (1835), 2 Cl. & Fin. 488, 530. *Berthiaume* v. *Dastous*, [1930] A.C. (P.C.) 79, 83.

[4] *Matrimonia claudicantia*: Endemann, *JurW.*, 1914, 113.

[5] A German (or Polish) court would by way of 'transmission' from English to French law declare the marriage to be void.

of the rule lies in the lack of consideration it shows for the couples belonging to the Roman Catholic or the Orthodox church. Both churches treat a marriage between Christians concluded without the assistance of a priest as a nullity, as a mere concubinage. In their view the religious ceremony is not a mere 'form' but belongs to the essence, to the soul of the sacrament. The *codex iuris canonici* speaks with a certain scorn of the civil marriage as 'matrimonium civile ut aiunt',[1] and sincere adherents of the Roman or the Eastern church must regard a civil contract concluded before a civil registrar, usually in a business-like fashion, as an act of irreverence to the Holy Sacrament. The ecclesiastical view has become state law in the Città del Vaticano, in Malta, in Bulgaria, Yugoslavia, Greece, and other eastern countries. All the objections that in the sphere of municipal law can be offered to the compulsory civil form of marriage can be raised in private international law to the imperative rule of the *lex loci celebrationis*. It is, however, easy to understand that a country which has adopted the strict rule in municipal law is likely to adopt the similar, strict conflict rule. It is difficult, on the other hand, to explain why England, a country which in internal law wisely refrains from accepting the narrow French-German principle and allows a certain, though limited, number of religious marriage forms, does not adopt an equally liberal attitude in the field of private international law. Here English law even surpasses the French-German rule in stringency. While France and Germany recognize marriages concluded outside their respective territories in the forms of the personal law of the parties, England insists on the compulsory nature of *locus regit actum* even in such cases.

The law of the place of contracting is decisive in this country irrespective of whether that place was chosen honestly and in good faith, or with the purpose of evading the more stringent rules of the law of domicile. This has been firmly established in the Gretna Green cases.[2]

II. *Where* is the marriage deemed to have been concluded?

---

[1] *Cod. iur. can.*, s. 188, no. 5; s. 646, § 1, no. 3; s. 2356.
[2] See *supra*, s. 137.

Generally there is no doubt about the place. Some exceptional cases, however, are worth mentioning.

1. Some laws (e.g. Spanish law, Argentine law, &c.) permit a marriage *by proxy*, after the model of Canon law, which requires for a *matrimonium per procuratorem* a 'special mandate' to conclude a marriage with a *certa persona subscripta a mandante*.[1] The procurator is not an agent but a mere messenger, ordered in writing to give an oral message.

Marriages by proxy have proved expedient, particularly in war-time, when the bridegroom is on active service in a distant country. It is then sufficient and necessary that the proxy should make his declaration at a place where marriages by proxy are admitted. The place at which the principal has appointed his proxy is immaterial because the proper law of the 'appointment' is the law of the place where the marriage is to take place.[2]

2. Common law marriages (by mere consent) may be concluded *by correspondence* (so it seems). The contract is completed *when* the acceptance of the offer of marriage is dispatched. Can it be inferred from this that it suffices if the law of the place *where* the acceptance is dispatched permits marriage by correspondence? Certainly not. The marriage contract demands two valid declarations; it is therefore necessary that marriage by correspondence should also be admitted by the law of the place where the 'offerer' is staying at the time when he sends his offer.

3. Scottish law recognizes marriages *by habite and repute*. As such a marriage is constituted not by a single act, but by a series of facts extending over a long time, a requirement of validity must surely be that both parties should have their ordinary residence, their habite, in Scotland[3] and that they should there be regarded as husband and wife by their neighbours and friends.

---

[1] See *Cod. iur. can.* c. 1088, 1089, 1091.

[2] *Apt* v. *Apt*, [1948], p. 83 (C.A.). See: 55 *Yale L.J.* (1946) 735, 748; Lorenzen, *Select. Art.* 379–93. See *infra*, s. 424.

[3] *In re Green* (1909), 25 T.L.R. 22, Swinfen Eady, J., said that a foreign marriage concluded by repute should be regarded as valid in England if it is valid by the law of the 'domicile' of the spouses. With all respect a doubt must be expressed as to the correctness of this view.

4. The situation is different in a case like the following, decided by a New York court:[1]

The parties were married in Ontario by a so-called 'ceremonial Jewish marriage', that is without the presence of a rabbi or magistrate; under the law of Ontario such marriage becomes valid if followed by cohabitation for three years. The couple lived together for three years, but it was doubtful whether they spent the whole period in Ontario or part of it in New York. The court regarded this doubt as immaterial and held the marriage to be valid. This seems well-founded, since the Ontario ceremony constituted a valid marriage subject to the condition of cohabitation during a certain period; the place of fulfilment of the condition is just as immaterial as in the case of a conditional mercantile contract.[2]

III. What legal rules respecting the conclusion of marriage are concerned with form as opposed to substance? It would be for the conflict rule to answer this question, but there is no relevant conflict rule in any country. Since under the English conflict rule it is the law of the place of contracting which governs the marriage form, it is probably the same law that decides what belongs to form. The various municipal laws differ widely on this point. English law, for instance, looks on the consent of third parties (parents, guardians) as a matter of form, while continental laws consider it to be part of the substance of the marriage.[3] German law classifies under the rules relating to form the provisions that the marital consent of the parties must be unconditional and not restricted to any particular period, and that such consent must not be declared by proxy,[4] while the *codex iuris canonici* of 1917 more correctly deals with the question of conditional marriages and of marriages concluded *per procuratorem* in Chapter V *de consensu matrimoniali*, and not in Chapter VI *de forma celebrationis matrimonii*.[5]

324. Form and substance

[1] Quoted by Beale, II. 672, n. 1.

[2] The same would be true in respect of a similar German provision. Under German law a marriage formally invalid but duly registered becomes valid by continuous cohabitation during a prescribed period (Marriage Law of 20 Feb. 1946, s. 17). This rule applies if the defective marriage is concluded in Germany (or Austria), irrespective of the place of the subsequent cohabitation.

[3] See on this *supra*, ss. 148, 306.

[4] The German Civil Code, s. 1324, expressly spoke of the 'form required by s. 1317', and s. 1317 included the prohibition of a conditional or limited consent and of a declaration by proxy. See also s. 1699 § 2, and the Marriage Law of 20 Feb. 1946, ss. 13 and 17.

[5] *Cod. iur. can.*, c. 1092, no. 3, 1088 et seq.

325. Exceptions

IV. In some exceptional cases, however, English law recognizes the validity of a marriage which has not been concluded in accordance with the form of the *lex loci celebrationis*. Some of these exceptions fall under common law rules, others under statute, viz. the *Foreign Marriage Act*, 1892.[1]

326. under common law

I. Common Law rules cover the following cases:

(*a*) Marriages between two British subjects can be concluded outside the British Dominions within the mansion of a British ambassador in the form of English law; and generally any marriage between two subjects of the same state[2] is valid if concluded according to the forms held valid by such state within the precincts of its embassy, whether in England or in a third state. This rule was originally derived from the conception that the ambassador's mansion is to be treated as if it were part of the country which he represents. Though modern writers recognize the exaggeration implied by this fiction, the rule based on it stands.

(*b*) Marriages on board ship are formally valid if they are concluded in the forms of the law of the country to which the ship belongs; in the case of a British ship,[3] therefore, a common law marriage is possible. The marriage must, however, be concluded while the ship is on the high seas; only in the case of a warship may it be celebrated in a foreign port.

It makes no difference whether the parties to the marriage are British or not, or whether they are of the same nationality; their domicile is likewise immaterial. Nor is it of any consequence whether the law of their domicile or their nationality or the law of the harbour where the warship was at the time of the marriage recognizes the validity of such marriage or not.

(*c*) In some countries in the East it was a common practice, carried out with the express or implied consent

---

[1] 55 & 56 Vict., c. 23.

[2] Under common law it is not sufficient that one of the parties is a subject of that state. See *Pertreis* v. *Tondear* (1790), 1 Hag. Cons. 136, 138. Contrast Foreign Marriage Act, 1892, s. 1.

[3] As to the question which of the laws prevailing in the British Empire applies if British subjects marry on shipboard, see *supra*, p. 131.

of the government, to allow foreigners to marry according to the law of their home country provided the marriage is celebrated in their trade (or industrial) settlement. The validity of such marriages is recognized in England.[1]

Though this rule is much older than the doctrine of *renvoi* it may now be looked upon as a simple case of application of that doctrine. When English law declares the law of the place of contracting to be decisive this includes a remission from that law to the national law of the parties.

(*d*) The rule *locus regit actum* is inapplicable where there is no local form, as in an unoccupied part of the earth (North-Pole expedition), or where the local form presents insuperable difficulties of either a legal or a moral nature, as where the country is inhabited by savages, or where the only local form available is a religious one and the parties belong to a different religion or to none at all.[2] If then the parties are British subjects (or at least one of them is) the marriage may be concluded validly in the form of English common law.

It is not within the scope of this book to examine what the form required by English common law is. According to the famous judgment in *Reg.* v. *Millis*,[3] which dealt with a marriage celebrated in Ireland, a common law marriage requires the intervention of an episcopally ordained priest; but this judgment is of doubtful value and at any rate not binding on the courts in cases where the marriage was not concluded in Ireland, but in a country where the use of a local form is impossible: it seems that there the mere consent of the parties to become husband and wife is sufficient.[4] If the parties to the marriage are not British subjects and if in absence of a local form available to them they have married by mere consent, it will probably depend on their personal law whether such marriage is to be regarded as valid by the English court.

2. The Foreign Marriage Act, 1892,[5] adopts principles similar to those developed in several continental statutes. It regulates three categories of marriages:

327. under the Foreign Marriage Act

---

[1] *Wolfenden* v. *Wolfenden*, [1946] P. 61. See Dicey–Morris, p. 769 (b).

[2] *Ruding* v. *Smith* (1821), 2 Hagg. Cons. 371, 385. *Kent* v. *Burgess* (1840), 11 Sim. 361, 376. *Catterall* v. *Catterall* (1847), 1 Rob. Ecc. 580. *Lightbody* v. *West* (1902), 87 L.T. 138. Cf. also *Lord Cloncurry's Case* (1811), quoted in the *Sussex Peerage Case*, 11 Cl. & Fin. 92; see Cruise, *On Dignities* (1823), p. 276 § 85.

[3] (1844) 10 Cl. & Fin. 534–907. See on this Lord Campbell in *Beamish* v. *Beamish* (1861), 9 H.L.C. 274, 337.

[4] *Catterall* v. *Catterall* (1847), 1 Rob. Eccl. 580. *Wolfenden* v. *Wolfenden*, [1946] P. 61.   [5] 55 & 56 Vict., c. 23.

(*a*) marriages solemnized by or before a British Ambassador, Consul, Governor, High Commissioner, Resident, consular, or other officer, at their respective official residences in a foreign country. Such marriages, usually called 'diplomatic' and 'consular' marriages, are as valid as if they had been solemnized in the United Kingdom 'with a due observance of all forms required by law'.[1] The formalities to be observed before the ambassador, consul, or other marriage officer, are laid down in the Act,[2] and they replace those rules which would have been applied if the marriage had been concluded in England. Questions relating to the substantial validity of the marriage will be answered in the same way as if the place of celebration had been in England; that is, capacity and certain other substantial requirements are tested by domicile.[3] The ambassador, consul, or other officer has power to solemnize marriages only if one of the parties is a British subject. If after the ceremony it is ascertained that neither of them was British the marriage is void, and it remains void even if both parties acquire British nationality. The Act does not require both parties to be British nationals. English law thus seems to adopt the dangerous solution given by many continental laws. The danger consists in the attitude possibly taken either by the state where the marriage is concluded or by the state to which the other spouse belongs by nationality: one or other of them may refuse to recognize the marriage, which consequently becomes 'limping'.[4] English law, however, avoids that danger to a certain degree, first, by general Marriage Regulations made by Order in Council, and, secondly, by the rule that a marriage officer shall not allow a marriage to be solemnized in his presence if in his opinion the solemnization thereof would be 'inconsistent with international law or the comity of nations'.[5]

[1] s. 1 of the Act.

[2] ss. 12–16 of the Act and Foreign Marriage Order in Council, 1913, S.R. and O. 1270, amended 1925 (S.R. and O., No. 92); 1933 (975); 1947 (2875).

[3] See *supra*, ss. 304, 309.

[4] Comp., for example, *Hay* v. *Northcote*, [1900] 2 Ch. 262: marriage concluded in France before the British consul, void in France, valid in England. See also *Este* v. *Smyth* (1854), 18 Beav. 112, 121.

[5] s. 21, subs. (1) (a) of the Act.

(*b*) A marriage duly solemnized on board one of H.M. ships on a foreign station by or before the commanding officer thereof is valid if one of the parties is a British subject. This rule does not affect the common law rule mentioned sub (1) (*b*) (*supra*, p. 346), which certainly retains its importance, first, in case of marriages celebrated on board any British merchant ship or alien ship; secondly, if the marriage is concluded on board a ship of the Royal Navy not 'on a foreign station' but on the high seas; and probably, thirdly, in the case of a British couple marrying on a ship of the Royal Navy in English common law form, that is, by mere consent or in the presence of an ordained priest.[1]

(*c*) A marriage within the lines of a British army may be solemnized 'by any chaplain or officer, or other person officiating under the orders of the commanding officer of a British army serving abroad'.[2] No special form is required. The rule applies not only to marriages of British subjects but also to marriages between aliens.   ·

[1] This follows from s. 23 of the Act, according to which the Act does not affect the validity of marriages solemnized beyond the seas otherwise than as provided in the Act.
[2] s. 22 of the Act. Cf. *R.* v. *The Inhabitants of Brampton* (1808), 10 East 282, and *The Waldegrave Peerage Case* (1837), 4 Cl. & Fin. 649, 656.

BIBLIOGRAPHY, see p. 340.

CONSEQUENCES OF A DEFECT IN THE MARRIAGE

I. The consequences of a defect are determined by the legal system that has been violated. As capacity is tested by domicile the law of the domicile decides whether the marriage concluded in spite of the lack of capacity is void, voidable, or valid. As the law of the place of contracting governs the forms, this includes the decision on the effects of any non-observance of those forms.

Where several legal systems have been violated, it goes without saying that under English law the marriage is void even if only one of these systems declares it to be void. The marriage is valid only if under all systems involved the rule transgressed was merely directory. Sometimes an

328.
Principle
and
examples

impediment that is irritant under all systems can be cured according to one system but not according to the others. In such case the marriage would still be regarded as void though the cure has been effected.

(*a*) A domiciled Frenchman marries his niece, a domiciled Swiss woman, in Germany; under German internal law the marriage would be valid, under Swiss and French law it is void; but under French, though not under Swiss law, a dispensation is permissible. The marriage is incurably void in France as well as in Switzerland, and is so looked upon in Germany and England.

(*b*) A bigamous marriage is void under all systems concerned, but under Swedish internal law it becomes valid when the first spouse of the bigamous partner dies. This rule is not applicable if only one of the spouses of the bigamous marriage is a domiciled Swede, while the other is English.

329.
'Limping' marriages

II. It is unfortunately not rare for the violation of the legal system of one country to be disregarded in another, owing either to a divergence of conflict rules, or the non-recognition of foreign divorce or nullity decrees, or to the principle that a court does not apply foreign law inconsistent with the public policy prevailing in the country of the court. The results are limping marriages, as they have been called,[1] i.e. marriages which are valid in one country and nullities in another.

Illustrations: (*a*) The marriage between two domiciled Greeks, celebrated in London before a Greek priest, is valid in Greece, Germany, and France, invalid in England. (*b*) The marriage between the same persons, concluded in London before a registrar, is valid in England, Germany, and France, invalid in Greece. (*c*) The marriage between a domiciled German, who had been divorced by his first wife on the ground of his adultery, and his partner in adultery, concluded in England, is valid in England, but was void in Germany under the *BGB*. (*d*) The marriage of an Austrian priest or monk celebrated in England before August 1938 is valid in England, Germany, France, but void in Austria. (*e*) The marriage between two Italian nationals domiciled in England and divorced here has ceased to be a marriage in England but remains a valid marriage in Italy.

The existence of limping marriages leads to the curious phenomenon of one person being 'monogamously' married to more than one spouse. If nullity of his marriage with Anne has been pronounced in Germany but the nullity decree is not recognized in England, he may marry Berta in Germany; he will then, when in England, be married to

---

[1] See *supra*, p. 342, n. 4.

Anne, when in Germany, to Berta. Both are his wives and both his concubines.

III. The legal *effects* of a *void* marriage are not the same everywhere. German law, for example, grants the wife in the case of a void marriage a right to maintenance against her husband provided that he knew, and she did not know, that the marriage was void. French law gives her the same right. Again, Swiss law, and since 1938 German law, refuse retroactive effect to a nullity decree; it merely destroys in most respects the marriage *ex nunc* as if it were a case of divorce.[1] Under most other legal systems a nullity decree extinguishes all marriage effects *ex tunc*. What law determines the legal effects of a void marriage? The answer is: the law that annuls it. Where the marriage is void for the violation of several legal systems it can obviously produce only those marriage effects that are common to all the systems. If an Englishman marries his Swiss niece the Swiss rule under which the marriage is to be treated as valid during the period between its conclusion and the nullity decree is inapplicable in an English court.

330.
Effects of
void
marriages

The following questions are doubtful:

(*a*) In determining the effects of a void marriage is the law of the country where the nullity decree was pronounced immaterial? An English court decrees the nullity of a marriage which two domiciled Swiss nationals have concluded in Switzerland, on the ground of an infringement of Swiss law. Does the marriage thereby become void *ab initio*, according to English law, or void *ex nunc*, according to Swiss law? It is suggested that the former alternative is correct, because an English nullity decree can hardly have a meaning unknown to English law.

(*b*) Which law is decisive if after the conclusion of the defective marriage the spouses have changed their domicile (or nationality)? It would seem correct to disregard the change.

A marriage between a Swiss uncle and his Swiss niece should not become valid by the fact that both spouses acquire German nationality and domicile, although under German law they could have concluded a valid

[1] Swiss Civ. Code, s. 132 et seq. German Marriage Law of 20 Feb. 1946, s. 30 et seq.

marriage. Or: two Americans concluding a marriage by mere consent on English soil then returning to New Jersey remain unmarried.[1] They may conclude another common law marriage with each other in New Jersey, and if they continue living together as husband and wife this may constitute an implied declaration of marital consent. See *supra*, s. 314.

(*c*) The problem whether and under what conditions a child born in a void marriage is to be treated as legitimate is not primarily concerned with the effects of an invalid marriage but with 'legitimacy', that is, a legal relationship between parents and children. The answer depends therefore upon the law of the father's domicile. If the father has changed his domicile between the invalid marriage and the child's birth, say, from England to Scotland, it is for the law of the new domicile to say whether a child born in an invalid marriage is to be treated as legitimate.[2]

(*d*) There is a similar difficulty where contractual relations with third parties depend on the validity of a marriage. Under many laws a husband can in certain defined circumstances dispose of goods belonging to his wife or to both spouses. If then the marriage turns out to be void, some legal systems, for example German law, provide that such nullity cannot affect the title of a bona fide purchaser without notice of the nullity.[3] Is this (German) rule, intended to protect commercial intercourse, only and always applicable if the nullity of the marriage is based on a violation of German law? Certainly not. Whether the vendor of goods to which he is not entitled may dispose of them to a bona fide purchaser depends on the law governing the alienation of the goods; this may be the proper law of the contract, or the *lex situs rei*; it is not the law governing the invalid marriage of the vendor.

[1] English law does not admit a marriage by mere consent, while the law of New Jersey admits it.
[2] Children born in 'putative' marriages are treated as legitimate in Scotland. As to England, see *infra*, p. 385, n. 1.
[3] German Marriage Law of 20 Feb. 1946, s. 27.

CHAPTER XXIII

THE EFFECTS OF MARRIAGE

ITS EFFECTS UPON THE PERSONAL RELATIONSHIP BETWEEN HUSBAND AND WIFE

THE personal relationship between husband and wife is not often subject to judicial supervision, and if questions arising out of it are brought before the court there is a very natural tendency everywhere to apply the law of the forum. If under the personal law of the spouses the husband is entitled to beat his wife, no English, French, or American court will allow him any such right; and if a French rule permits him to supervise his wife's correspondence while she has no such right with regard to his,[1] it might be difficult to find a court in a civilized country outside France prepared to recognize so repugnant a rule. Russian law denies the spouses the right to demand restitution of community of life; the German Supreme Court has declared,[2] and an English court would probably declare, that rule to be inapplicable. The extent to which the legal system of any country recognizes the liability of a person to maintain his or her spouse will be regarded by the courts of that country as a maintenance minimum, so that a foreign rule granting a lesser right of maintenance would be excluded.[3] In brief, most of the rules governing incidents of marriage are, to borrow the continental phrase, rules of *ordre public*.

331. Decisive either *lex fori*

But not all of them.

332. or *lex domicilii*

Examples: How does marriage influence the woman's name?[4] Is she bound to use her husband's name, is she entitled to a combination of her husband's name and her own? Does marriage diminish her capacity to conclude contracts, to sue, to carry on a trade or enter a profession?[5] Are

[1] Planiol & Ripert, *Traité prat.*, II., no. 374, 381 et seq.
[2] *IPRspr.*, 1926–7, no. 68.
[3] Niboyet, *Manuel*, no. 628, no. 3.
[4] Whether this question concerns primarily the 'personal effects of marriage' or a 'personality right' of the wife (see *supra*, s. 274) is controversial; Frankenstein, III. 230. Under English law the answer is in both cases the same: the law of the wife's domicile, which coincides with the husband's domicile, is decisive.
[5] Here, too, the classification ('personal effects of marriage' or 'capacity'?) is subject to many doubts. Under English conflict rules the answer is the same in either alternative.

gifts between husband and wife valid, as under English and German law, or void, as under Roman and Roman-Dutch law? Is a husband allowed to enter into a partnership with his wife or to sell goods to her (under French law such contracts are void)?

The answer to these and similar questions must be given by the personal law of the spouses, and if they have changed this during marriage, by the later personal law. The application of this rule is easy in England, Scotland, South Africa, and all other countries where the personal law is the law of the domicile and the wife necessarily shares her husband's domicile, but not so in countries where the personal law is determined by nationality, since the spouses may be of different nationality. In that case the correct answer—which for that matter becomes material in English law in cases of *renvoi*—seems to be in most countries that the national law common to both spouses governs the case; if they are of different nationalities then they are subject to the national law common to them before one party changed it. If they never had a common nationality, for example, where a Frenchwoman marries a citizen of the United States, three solutions have been proposed.

1. The husband's national law should decide.

2. The marriage produces only the effects common to both national laws.

3. The marriage imposes on each spouse the duties and only the duties established by his or her national law.[1]

None of these solutions is satisfactory, and when drafting the Hague Convention of 1905 on the effects of marriage, the Contracting Powers did not reach agreement on this point, so that the question was left unanswered. The third solution is to be rejected at once; it creates an inequality hardly compatible with the nature of marriage. The second answer would possibly be accepted if reason alone were decisive; but it is not. The prevailing opinion is in favour of the husband's national law. It relies mainly on historical grounds and on the Scriptures ('vir caput mulieris'). Weak though this support may be, the result is not necessarily unfair to the wife, since the national law of the husband may or may not be more favourable to her than her national law.

[1] Thus: Frankenstein, III. 241.

The rule that the personal relationship between husband and wife is determined by the law of their domicile by no means implies that their relationship to third parties must also be determined by the law of domicile. Under most laws marriage gives the wife authority to act on behalf of her husband or of both spouses in all household matters. In the various legal systems this power differs in foundation, in extent, and in many details, such as the way in which the husband may withdraw the authority. What law governs these matters? **333. The wife's power in household matters**

(*a*) The question whether the wife has the right as against her husband to pledge his credit is one which concerns merely the internal relations between the spouses. See on this: s. 332.

(*b*) The question of her authority *vis-à-vis* the third party validly to conclude a contract binding on her husband concerns the relationship between the husband and the third party and will therefore be governed by the law of the place where the wife's authority (if any) is exercised. If, for example, the couple resides in Germany where the law gives the wife power to conclude very extravagant contracts on behalf of her husband[1] and to borrow money to cover household debts, a contract concluded in Germany within the limits of that power is valid, though it may be *ultra vires* according to the law of their, say, Dutch domicile.[2] The protection of commercial intercourse demands this solution, just as in the case where a person incapable under his personal law but capable under the *lex loci contractus* concludes a commercial contract.

MATRIMONIAL PROPERTY SYSTEMS; SURVEY

The legal systems governing property in matrimony are so numerous and varied that a general survey can do no more than describe the fundamental types, ignoring deviations from them as well as the various mixed systems. As marriage under English internal law does not (since 1883) entail any change in the property of the parties, it is easy to understand that English lawyers should find themselves in **334. Survey**

[1] German Supr. Court, *Off. Coll.*, 61, 81.
[2] Raape, *Commentary*, p. 359.

some difficulty when they encounter foreign matrimonial property systems in the sphere of private international law. The fundamental types are the following:

1. The English common law system of *coverture*, as it prevailed before the reform of 1882. The woman's property, apart from certain exceptions in respect of immovables, passes to the husband. He also acquires ownership of such goods as accrue to her during the marriage.

2. The modern English system of *separation of goods*, first fully developed on the Continent—where it was and still is in force in Austria, Hungary, Italy, and the Balkan states—and adopted in nearly all common law countries of the British Commonwealth, as well as in most states of the United States of America. Each spouse remains owner of his or her property, retaining the right to manage and dispose of it as if he or she were not married. This is modified only by certain obligations, such as the husband's duty to maintain his wife and to defray the expenses of the household, and the woman's duty to contribute to that burden. Husband and wife are each liable for their respective debts; neither is liable for those of the other.

3. The system of *marital administration*, prevailing in Germany, Switzerland, parts of the Baltic states, and in Japan. Here, too, the property of each spouse remains his or her own; the husband retains the administration of his own property as if he were unmarried. But the right of the wife to administer her own property passes to the husband, and this applies even to property the wife acquires during the marriage.[1] He also has the right of an usufructuary to take the income from his wife's property. These rights of the husband to administration and enjoyment are *iura in patrimonio alieno*, encumbrances not on particular things but on the whole of the property.

4. The system of *community of all goods*, prevailing in the Netherlands, South Africa (under Roman-Dutch law), the Isle of Man, Portugal, Brazil. All property belonging to husband or wife at the time of marriage or acquired later by

---

[1] Apart from privileged property, for example, property acquired by the wife through her work or through any trade carried on by her independently of her husband.

either spouse becomes the common property of both.[1] The spouses become co-owners of the whole without any act of transfer such as conveyance, registration, or assignment, by the mere fact of marriage, *uno actu*. The acquisition is similar to the 'universal succession' upon death. The 'couple' succeeds the husband, the 'couple' succeeds the wife. It is essential in private international law to bear in mind that co-ownership in the husband's property vests in the wife from the very moment of the celebration of the marriage,[2] or in respect of goods acquired later from the time of their acquisition. Though both spouses are co-owners of the common goods, or, as French lawyers call it, the *communauté*, their management belongs to the husband alone,[3] and, apart from certain exceptions, he, not his wife, is entitled to dispose of it.

5. The *community of acquests*, or of income and profit (*communauté réduite aux acquêts*), is the legal system in Spain, Soviet Russia, Malta,[4] most of the Latin-American states, and fourteen states of the United States of America.[5] Everything acquired during the marriage by the work or trade of husband or wife or by the use and enjoyment of his or her property accrues to the community and belongs from that time jointly to both spouses; this applies to immovables as well as movables.

6. Systems of *community upon death*. Here the community, which may be a community of all goods (*supra* (4)) or a community of acquests (*supra* (5)), does not begin with the conclusion of marriage but with its dissolution, particularly at the death of one of the spouses. At that moment

---

[1] Again, apart from privileged property (which may be constituted by contract or will). But the wife's earnings through her work or trade do not as a rule belong to her privileged property.

[2] The difference between such 'real proprietary right' and a mere 'hope of a certain distribution upon the husband's death' was very clearly stressed by Lord Halsbury in *De Nicols* v. *Curlier*, [1900] A.C., at p. 27.

[3] Some jurists have wrongly inferred from this that the husband, being the sole administrator of the common goods, is in reality their only owner. This mistaken view was adopted by Lord Eldon in *Lashley* v. *Hog*, 4 Paton at p. 617.

[4] art. 1360 of the Maltese Code (1868).

[5] Not only in Texas, New Mexico, Arizona, Louisiana, and California, but even in Idaho, Nevada, Washington, and (recently) Oklahoma, Oregon, Michigan, Pennsylvania, Nebraska, and Hawaiian Isl. See de Funiak, 22 *Tulane L.R.* (1947), 264 et seq.

the goods either become the common property of the
spouses or their successors and are distributed amongst
them according to certain quotas; or they are not made
'common' property at all, but are divided between the two
spouses (in case of dissolution by divorce) or between the
surviving spouse and the successors of the deceased. This
system is to be found (in various forms) in the Scandinavian
states and Finland, in Austria, Hungary, Switzerland,[1] and
—as it seems—in Scotland.[2]

7. The *community of movables and of acquests* is the legal
system in France, Belgium, Luxemburg, and Lower
Canada (Quebec).[3] It includes everything belonging to
either party except immovables not acquired during the
marriage as income or profit.

The applicable Law, apart from Marriage Property Agreements

What law determines the legal system applicable to the
matrimonial régime of a given couple?

335. Legal or merely conventional conflict rules? I. In most countries there exists a fixed conflict rule established by statute or customary law, such as the German
rule according to which the national law of the husband at
the time of the marriage is decisive. The parties to the
marriage have the right to choose the applicable law only
within the limits fixed by the municipal law to which that
conflict rule points. German spouses, for example, cannot
choose Danish law to govern their matrimonial régime
unless they have their ordinary residence in Denmark. The
fact that most of their property lies in Denmark would not
suffice. The conflict rules of England and France differ
from this. French law does not establish any fixed conflict
rule independently of the will of the parties, but leaves the
decision entirely to them; if they have not chosen any law,
then to their presumed intention. This enables the French
courts to apply according to circumstances the law of the
matrimonial residence or the national law or any other law

---

[1] Kaden, *RVglHWB*, IV, 1 et seq. Marg. Berent, *Die Zugewinnstgemeinschaft*, 1915.　　　　　　　　　　　　　　　　[2] *Infra*, s. 338.

[3] It is called *communauté légale*.

with which the case under review has the closest connexion.[1] Under English law, too, the parties are at liberty
to determine the applicable law just as in the case of mercantile contracts.[2] But in contrast to French law, English
precedents have established a legal conflict rule (though
its content is very doubtful), which becomes operative if
the parties have not chosen any law, or if they disagree in
respect of the applicable law.

II. In the absence of a choice of law by the parties the
English conflict rule differentiates between movables and
immovables.[3] The rights of husband and wife are determined as regards movables by the law of the domicile, as
regards immovables by the *lex situs*.[4] This system of
'scission'—which also prevails in the United States and
Argentina, and has often been followed in France, Italy,
and Austria—sometimes leads to technical difficulties, particularly in respect of the parties' creditors and, after the
dissolution of the marriage, in respect of the distribution of
the matrimonial property between the spouses or their successors. But these difficulties are not insurmountable;[5] and
it is a sound basic idea that the law of any country should
decide what *iura in rem* can be and have been created on any
piece of land in that country. Nevertheless most countries
have rejected the scission, mainly because it is founded on
feudal conceptions and feudalism is (or ought to be?) dead.
They have developed a 'unity' system under which the
personal law governs movables and immovables alike, and
which conforms more closely to the dominating conceptions founded on Roman law in respect of succession on
death. Some of the modern systems, such as German law,
have however made a substantial concession to the scission
system. Where part of the matrimonial property consists of
land situate abroad the German courts apply the *lex situs* if
the *lex situs* is applicable according to its own conflict rule.[6]

336. Unity
or scission
system?

---

[1] Planiol & Ripert, *Traité prat.*, VIII. s. 9; Niboyet, *Manuel*, no. 715.
[2] See *infra*, s. 400.
[3] On this distinction see *infra*, s. 482 et seq.
[4] See Dicey–Morris, pp. 535, 539.
[5] This will be dealt with in the law of succession; see *infra*, s. 539 et seq.
[6] See *supra*, s. 201.

337. Law of the husband's domicile

III. As regards movables the husband's domicile is decisive. But which one? Three answers have been advanced.

1. The domicile at the date of the marriage.

2. The domicile the husband intends to establish and does indeed establish immediately after the conclusion of the marriage, called the 'matrimonial domicile'.

3. The domicile from time to time, i.e. whenever the domicile is changed, the new domicile.

The second of these answers is hardly satisfactory.[1] Compare the case of an English husband who intends to settle in Capetown, and who with his bride boards a ship bound for South Africa immediately after the wedding, with that of another Englishman who spends the first month of his married life with his wife at his English domicile of origin and then decides to change his domicile from England to South Africa. In the latter case the spouses are undoubtedly governed by English law until they arrive at the Cape. Why should they be treated otherwise in the former case and be subjected to South African law while *in itinere* although intention alone is not sufficient to produce any change of domicile?[2] *If* any change of domicile is to be taken into consideration it should be immaterial, first, whether such change was contemplated at the time of the marriage or subsequently, and secondly, whether the change takes place immediately after the marriage or later.

338. Change of domicile; mutability or immutability?

Thus the choice lies between the first and the third answer. Whether the legal system regulating the property of husband and wife at the time of their marriage remains decisive till death or divorce, or whether it should be replaced by a different system if the domicile changes, is one of the most discussed problems in private international law. It is, to borrow the expression used by the statutists, the 'quaestio famosissima'.

To-day the principle of immutability prevails nearly everywhere. The

---

[1] It was propounded by Story and accepted by Westlake, s. 36, Cheshire, pp. 192, 651, and Dicey–(Morris), p. 789.

[2] See *supra*, s. 102. The unsound retroactivity involved by Story's doctrine ought also to be considered: during their voyage to Africa they are governed by English matrimonial law, and if one of them dies on board English law obtains irrevocably. But if they both arrive, they would be treated as if they had lived under South African law from the date of their marriage.

law of the husband's first domicile—or where the nationality principle obtains, the law of his nationality at the time of marriage—remains applicable under all modern codes, from the French code and the systems influenced by it to the German and Swiss codes and to the Hague Convention, 1905, the Convention of Montevideo, and the Código Bustamante. This is also the law in the Scandinavian countries.

English law favours the opposite view. The matrimonial system established not by agreement of the parties but by law changes with a change of domicile. This was laid down in a Scottish case, *Lashley* v. *Hog*,[1] where the House of Lords held that a change of domicile from England to Scotland entails the application of Scottish law to the matrimonial régime. In the English case *De Nicols* v. *Curlier*[2] the House of Lords started from the same rule. Here the change of domicile was from France to England, and only because it was thought[3] that under French law the French 'legal' system of community was to be treated as a contractual system did the court decline to apply the rule adopted in *Lashley* v. *Hog*.

The correct interpretation of the decision in *Lashley* v. *Hog* is, however, controversial. Westlake and Cheshire advanced the view that the matter turned on 'testamentary and not on matrimonial' law.[4] Indeed, the case deals with the distribution of a person's property after his death. But this is not sufficient to prove that the question is one of inheritance. There exist many systems of matrimonial community where the husband as administrator of the property is (or was) regarded as its owner to the effect that it is (or was) *his* property which at his death was to be distributed.[5] And there are numerous systems, so-called community systems 'upon death',[6] where at the moment of death the matrimonial property is to be united and divided in a particular way, without having ever been 'common goods' of the spouses. Whether such rules on distribution of matrimonial property are to be classified as concerned with inheritance or with matrimonial property, has often been discussed with regard to older German customs and particular local statutes. The prevailing and preferable view favours their classification as matrimonial property.[7]

The mutability doctrine would, however, be intolerable if it were to result in a destruction of rights acquired under

339. The mutability doctrine

---

[1] (1804) 4 Paton 581.
[2] [1900] A.C. 21 (see *supra*, s. 149).
[3] *Aliter*: Bartin, *Principes*, II., p. 249 i.f., 250.
[4] Westlake p. 74; Cheshire pp. 654–5.
[5] *Supra*, p. 357, n. 3.
[6] *Supra*, sect. 334, no. (6).
[7] Marg. Berent, *Die Zugewinnstgemeinschaft*, 1915, pp. 88–91.

the old domicile. These rights—irrespective of their nature as rights *in rem* or *in personam*—remain in force under the new law. Illustrations:

1. A Dutch domicile has been replaced by an English one. The co-ownership of husband and wife in goods which before the change were their common property remains what it was. The distribution of the common property which each of the spouses can now demand takes place in the same way as if at the time of the change the marriage itself had been dissolved by divorce. The husband receives one moiety of the common goods as his (separate) property, the wife the other moiety. The husband's power to dispose of goods which have now become the wife's property ceases *ex nunc*. If neither husband nor wife demands the distribution at the time of the change this does not destroy his or her right to demand it: the distribution may not, and often does not, take place until the marriage is dissolved; but even in that case it retains the character it had under Dutch law. Such rights, however, as are acquired by either spouse after the change fall under the law of the new, the English, domicile.[1]

2. The converse case is simpler: spouses with an English domicile and therefore living under the separation system change their domicile to Holland; then the community system comes into existence *ex nunc*. Husband and wife pool their property, just as if they had come unmarried to Holland and had married there.

If a year later they abandon their Dutch domicile and return to England this does not result in a restitution of the ownership of the property as it was before they made their first change. The difference of the two changes lies in this; the change from separation to community entails an alteration of existing proprietary rights, while the change from community to separation does not.

3. A testator with a Dutch domicile, and therefore living in community of goods, makes a will which, in disregard of his wife's legal rights to a certain portion of his property, leaves the whole of his property to a stranger, and later acquires a domicile in England, where he dies.[2] The change

---

[1] American *Restatement*, § 290.

[2] Case discussed by Dr. Cheshire in the 2nd ed. of his *Priv. Int. L.* at pp. 493, 494.

to a new *lex domicilii* does not deprive the wife of her proprietary right, that is of her right to a moiety of the common
goods. The husband can dispose only of his moiety of what
was formerly common property.

4. The spouses were domiciled in a country where gifts
between husband and wife are invalid or at least revocable,
e.g. in South Africa. They later change their domicile to
England. According to *Dicey(-Keith)*[1] 'their rights (thereby) would be varied, such gifts becoming in future irrevocable'. This is not unassailable. If a wife made a donation
to her husband when the spouses were domiciled in South
Africa, she has a right to revoke it until it is confirmed by
her death. This right is a 'well-acquired' proprietary right,
and she is entitled to bring an action for recovery. She does
not lose her right when the marriage is dissolved by divorce;
it is difficult to believe that she should lose it because the
husband changes his domicile from Africa to England.

5. German spouses, domiciled in Germany, refugees
from Nazi oppression, emigrate to England, where the
wife's parents have lived for 40 years. They become domiciled in England. Then the wife's father dies intestate and
his daughter succeeds to his property. Under the mutability system all the wife's property is, from the time of the
acquisition of the English domicile, strictly separated from
her husband's. Only the income of the wife's property
which the husband has legally acquired before becoming
domiciled in England remains his property. Under the
immutability system the husband would retain all the rights
which German matrimonial law grants him, that is, the
right to management and usufruct of the wife's whole
property.

The mutablility system has been adopted by the United States, by
Argentina, and by Paraguay. Before the coming into force of the German
Civil Code (1900) it prevailed in some parts of Germany.[2] It obtains
in the Baltic states in a very unsatisfactory form: under the Baltic Code
of 1864[3] a change of domicile even entails the destruction of vested rights
of the spouses; the code protects only the vested rights of third parties.

---

[1] Fifth ed., at p. 767. His view has been abandoned in Morris's 6th ed.
[2] See Gierke, *Deutsches Privatrecht*, I. 238, n. 100, 101.
[3] Art. XXIX (printed in Makarov, *Quellen des Internat. Priv. Rechts*,
p. 42).

340. Protection of third parties?

IV. Does the protection of commercial intercourse demand a restriction of the effects of foreign matrimonial property systems as against third parties? If, for example, a domiciled German couple resides in England and the wife sells some goods of her own without her husband's consent, is it justifiable to deny ownership to the purchaser on the ground that under German matrimonial law the right of administration of the wife's property belongs not to her but to her husband?[1] A few continental systems grant protection to the bona fide purchaser by declaring all foreign matrimonial régimes to be inoperative as against him unless the spouses have made their property régime publicly known, either by registration in particular lists or by an announcement to certain authorities, and the like.[2] The Hague Convention of 1905 refrains from establishing such restrictions but allows the Contracting Powers to require particular formalities for making the matrimonial system effective against third persons.

Experience, however, has shown that the need of protecting trade against the effects of foreign matrimonial property systems is not so great as might have been expected.[3] The so-called publications by registration do not attain their aim. Nobody looks at them. Small wonder that England, like France and most other continental countries, does not pay much attention to the problem.

---

[1] German Civ. Code, s. 1396, 1405.

[2] This is the case in German law (art. 16, Introduct. Law), and Swedish law. Swiss law goes even farther. There the law of the actual residence is applicable where third persons are concerned, and the spouses are unable to avoid this result and to make their foreign matrimonial system operative by any registration or publication.   [3] See Frankenstein, III. 360.

BIBLIOGRAPHY

CHESHIRE, pp. 653–8. DICEY–MORRIS, pp. 796–98. RABEL I. 328–81. GOODRICH, 323–33. H. BATEMAN, *La détermination de la loi applicable au régime matrimonial*, 1938. BATIFFOL, *Traité* 628–47. NIBOYET, *Traité* V, 351–422. AUDINET, 'Conflits relatifs aux effets patrimoniaux du mariage', 40 *Rec.* (1932 II), p. 241. AUDINET, *Rev. Darras*, 1906, 102; 1910, 289. A. TEICHMANN, *Über Wandelbarkeit und Unwandelbarkeit des gesetzlichen ehelichen Güterrechts*, Basel, 1879. SAVATIER, 20 *Rev. trimestrielle d. dr. civ.* (1921), 93. I. M. BAAK, *De rechtsgevolgen van het huwelijk in het internat. privaatrecht*, 1928. NEUNER, 5 *Louisiana L.R.* (1943), 167. See *RVglHWB*, IV, 412.

The Regulation of the Matrimonial Property Régime by Agreement

I. Under most continental laws a pact between husband and wife or between persons engaged to be married, regarding their future property relations, a *convenzione matrimoniale*, an *Ehevertrag*, is admissible only within the limits established by the legal rules on matrimonial property. For example, under German law or the Hague Convention, 1905, the legal matrimonial system is determined by the national law of the parties. It therefore depends on that law whether a matrimonial pact may be concluded at all, whether if so it must be concluded before marriage (as in French law[1] and the legal systems derived from it), or is equally permissible during marriage (as in Austrian, German, and Swiss law); further, what types of matrimonial property régime may be chosen by the parties, and which are excluded; Italian law, for example, does not allow any community system except the community of profits and income.[2]

English law differs from this. It allows the parties to subject their property relations to the legal system of any country and even as it were to create by agreement a property system of their own invention, provided that such pact does not offend against British public policy. Matrimonial property pacts are not contracts in the narrow sense in which this term is mostly used; as a rule they create not only obligations of the parties—as does a contract—but may include the creation of *iura in rem* and the transfer (assignment, conveyance, &c.) of existing rights.[3] But the rule established for contracts, that they are governed by their proper law, holds good for matrimonial property pacts also.[4] Proper law is the law of the country with which in the view of the parties the pact has a most real connexion. In so far as the pact includes the creation or transfer of *iura in rem*, certainly in the case of immovables, but

341.
Autonomy of the parties

---

[1] *Code civil*, art. 1395.

[2] *Codice civile* (1865), art. 1433; (1938, 1942), art. 213.

[3] Therefore the new Italian civil code (1938–42) rightly replaces the term *contratto di matrimonio* by *convenzione matrimoniale*; see art. 160.

[4] See *Marlborough (Duke)* v. *Att.-Gen.*, [1945] 1 Ch. 78, 88 (C.A.).

possibly also of movables, the *lex situs* is to be regarded as the proper law.

342.
Admissibility of the pact

It depends on the law governing the matrimonial property régime whether the pact is admissible. If, for instance, the parties, both Italians by nationality but domiciled in London, have made a pact some years after their marriage by which they agree to pool their profits and income—i.e. to establish the Italian *communione degli utili e degli acquisti*, as regulated by art. 213 of the new code of 1938 (1942)— Italian law will have to decide whether such a pact replacing the previous régime by a new one can lawfully be made after marriage. Such change was disallowed by the code of 1865, but is permitted by the new code.

343.
Capacity

II. The *capacity* to make a matrimonial property pact depends,

1. in so far as the agreement is intended to create or transfer rights to land, on the *lex situs*;

2. in all other respects, in particular with regard to movables and to liabilities of spouses towards third persons and to each other, on the *lex domicilii*. If the pact is post-nuptial the common domicile of the spouses at the time of concluding the pact is decisive; if it was made before the celebration of the marriage—as is usual—the capacity of each party is tested by his or her domicile at the time of making the pact.

The first of these propositions is not disputed. It springs from the principle that all rights to land are determined by the law governing that land. That was stated by Story and has been repeated over and over again since his time. It was the basis on which *Bank of Africa* v. *Cohen*[1] was decided.

The second rule, too, applies a general principle. If it is true that a person's capacity to make himself liable by contract or to conclude a valid marriage depends on his domicile at the time of the contract or marriage,[2] there is no reason to depart from the underlying principle in the case of a matrimonial property pact. The result at any rate is sound, and it is worth mentioning that it corresponds to the continental conflict rules and doctrines. It has further

[1] [1909] 2 Ch. 129, 135, 143. See 26 *J. Comp. Leg.* (1944), 75.
[2] See on this *supra*, s. 262–4.

become the predominant English doctrine.[1] Three English decisions either support it or are at least reconcilable with it. In all of them pre-nuptial conventions or settlements had been made by a woman who under the law of her pre-nuptial domicile was an infant; and in all of them the court held the arrangement void, voidable, or revocable.

In the first of these cases there is no room for doubt: *In re Cooke's Trusts*[2] is expressly based on the woman's incapacity under the law of her pre-nuptial domicile, and the court relied on the analogous rules governing capacity to marry and to conclude 'other contracts'.[3] The second decision, *Cooper v. Cooper*,[4] applies the law of a country which was both the bride's domicile and the place of contracting; Lord Watson and Lord Macnaghten did not state which of these two qualities was decisive, while Lord Halsbury applied the domicile rule as such. The third case *Viditz v. O'Hagan*[5] has a bearing on the capacity problem only in so far as the court decided that the incapacity of the woman under the law of her pre-nuptial domicile to conclude an irrevocable contract caused the contract to be revocable.

III. The *form* of the matrimonial property pact is governed by the rule *locus regit actum*. Here, however, the rule is optional, not imperative as in the case of the conclusion of the marriage. It is sufficient if that form is observed which the proper law of the agreement requires. Thus the parties have the choice between the proper law and the law of the place of contracting.[6] The same alternative is to be found in most of the continental legal systems and in the Hague Convention of 1905.

344. Form

IV. The substantial validity, apart from capacity, and the interpretation and effects of a marriage property pact are governed by the proper law of the pact.[7] This law also answers the question whether the contracting parties are competent to modify or cancel their agreement. If they cancel it without replacing it by a new agreement the statutory system becomes operative as such and not as a

345.
Validity
and effects

---

1 Westlake, s. 2; Foote, p. 102 et seq.; Halsbury, VI, § 314. *Contra*: Dr. Cheshire, 292 et seq.; J. H. C. Morris, 54 *L.Q.R.* (1938), 78–86, and *Cases*, pp. 298 299 (and in Dicey–Morris, pp. 790–1).
2 (1887), 3 T.L.R. 558; 56 L.T. 737.
3 See *Sottomayor* v. *De Barros* (no. 1), (1877), 3 P.D. 1, 5.
4 (1888), 13 A.C. 88, 99, 106–8.
5 [1899] 2 Ch. 569; [1900] 2 Ch. 87.
6 *Van Grutten* v. *Digby* (1862), 31 Beav. 561. *In re Bankes*, [1902] 2 Ch. 333.
7 *In re Bankes*, loc. cit. *Re Fitzgerald*, [1904] 1 Ch. 573.

system constituted by implied contract.[1] This distinction is important in case of a change of domicile; see s. 346.

346.
Change of
domicile

V. A change of domicile during marriage does not entail any change in the matrimonial property system in so far as this is based on an express or implied agreement.[2]

As we have seen before,[3] it is otherwise where the spouses have made no agreement and their property is therefore regulated by the statutory system: in the case of change of domicile the statutory system of the old domicile is superseded by that of the new domicile.

The maintenance of a contractual matrimonial régime in spite of a change of domicile may be contrary to the law prevailing at the new domicile. If, for example, a domiciled German couple establishes by matrimonial pact a community of all goods and later becomes domiciled in Italy where such system is not permissible, it might be that for this reason Italian courts would treat the agreement as rescinded. English courts would not concur in this view.

[1] Morris, loc. cit., p. 79; *Cases*, pp. 283–4. He relies for this on *Re Groos*, [1915] 1 Ch. 572. It is, however, doubtful whether this decision is to the point; it deals with testamentary capacity in a case of change of domicile.

[2] *Anstruther* v. *Adair* (1834), 2 My & K. 513. *Este* v. *Smyth* (1854), 18 Beav. 112. *Duncan* v. *Cannan*, ibid., pp. 128, 142. *De Nicols* v. *Curlier*, [1900] A.C. 21, 46. *In re Fitzgerald*, [1904] 1 Ch. 573.

[3] See pp. 361–3.

BIBLIOGRAPHY, see p. 364.

CHAPTER XXIV

DIVORCE AND JUDICIAL SEPARATION

I. Who can pronounce a divorce *a vinculo*, or a separation from bed and board? The answer is given by the law of the country where the divorce or separation is sought. In England, as in most countries, only the Courts of Law and the Legislature are competent to pronounce such decree. But this is not the case everywhere. Denmark and Norway admit a divorce by the King or some administrative body. In some Eastern countries the decision lies with ecclesiastical courts or other religious authorities. In Japan divorce as the *contrarius actus* to marriage is carried out before the registrar; similarly in Soviet Russia, where until 1936 informal mutual consent or even unilateral repudiation by either party was sufficient to dissolve the marriage. Jewish law requires the sending of a letter of repudiation with the co-operation of several rabbis.[1] Ireland, Quebec, and Newfoundland admit divorce by a special Act of Parliament only.

347.
Judicial and extra-judicial divorces

1. If a divorce has been pronounced by a person who according to the *lex loci* has no power to do so, the act is a nullity in that country, though it might be valid under the personal law of the parties.

If, for example, Lithuanian Jews, resident or domiciled in this country, execute an act of divorce here in accordance with Jewish law, it will be null and void in England and in third countries, though possibly Lithuanian law will treat it as valid. The result is a 'limping' marriage.[2]

2. If conversely a divorce is pronounced by a person who according to the *lex loci actus* has the power to do so the divorce is effective where pronounced, though it may not be effective elsewhere. Take the case of a Lithuanian couple domiciled in England; an English divorce might have no effect in Lithuania. Some doubts exist in respect of *extra-judicial* divorces carried out in a foreign country in accordance with the law there prevailing.

---

[1] Allerhand, 4 *Zeitschr. f. Ostrecht* (1930), 460 et seq.; 5 ibid. (1931), 10.
[2] See on this p. 350.

B b

Examples: A Russian couple has obtained a divorce in Russia by a declaration before the Russian registrar. Or, a Serbian Jew has divorced his wife in Belgrade by sending her a Hebrew letter of divorce with rabbinical intervention. These divorces are, of course, effective in Russia and Serbia respectively. Are they to be recognized elsewhere?

If, according to the applicable conflict rule, Russian law is the personal law of the spouses, the Russian extra-judicial divorce is effective; for example, in Germany or France[1] when the parties are of Russian nationality, in England when they are domiciled in Russia. If, on the other hand, the parties are nationals of or domiciled in a third country, there will be no recognition unless the third country recognizes the divorce. It has sometimes been contended that a non-judicial divorce should never be recognized in countries where the municipal law requires a judicial divorce decree. The answer to this is that you cannot infer from a compulsory rule of municipal law the existence of a similar conflict rule. The rule 'no divorce without a judicial decree' belongs—to use the continental terminology[2]—to the *ordre public interne*,[3] not to the *ordre public international*. The opposite view is inconsistent with other features of divorce law. A legal system which recognizes judicial divorce decrees of foreign courts, even if they are based on mere consent or on a unilateral declaration of one of the parties,[4] should not invoke the doctrine of public policy where such consent or declaration has been sufficient to produce the dissolution of marriage. Hundreds of thousands of honest and law-abiding persons all over the world have obtained divorces under their personal law and within their home country by simple agreements, letters of divorce, declarations of administrative or religious authorities, and the like. There is no reason why England should treat them as still married, should punish them for bigamy if they remarry in this country, and should regard their second

---

[1] See in particular Lewald, pp. 125, 126; Arminjon, III. 35.

[2] See *supra*, s. 159.

[3] Even this has sometimes been doubted in France. French courts have allowed foreign Jewish couples to divorce on French soil in Jewish form, i.e. by letter of divorce; Niboyet, *Manuel*, 870; Arminjon, III. 35, note 3.

[4] Or on any other fact not admitted as ground of divorce by English municipal law; see *Mezger* v. *Mezger*, [1937] P. 19; *Pastre* v. *Pastre*, [1930] P. 80, 82.

marriage as void, even if they have concluded it in their home country.

All this would possibly have been accepted in England without question if it were not for the unfortunate authority of the *Hammersmith Case*:[1] here it was laid down that a foreign divorce not decreed by a court will not be recognized in this country. The facts were the following: A Muhammedan domiciled in India, who had concluded a monogamous marriage with an Englishwoman in England, divorced her in India by a letter of divorce (*talaknama*), that is, in a way provided by Muhammedan law for the dissolution of a Muhammedan (polygamous) marriage. The English courts declared the divorce to be ineffective in England, and it is impossible to quarrel with the result. A means of dissolving a polygamous marriage cannot be used for the dissolution of a marriage of a different character (as the courts convincingly explained). This is the true reason on which the decision should have been based;[2] the other reason, previously mentioned, that only judicial divorces should be recognized, is open to exception.

348. The Hammersmith Case

II. Only such unions are divorceable as are regarded as *marriages* in the country where the divorce is sought.

1. The English court must on the one hand decline to pronounce a divorce decree if a union which is treated as a valid marriage in another country is regarded as a nullity in England. The Greek couple that went through a marriage ceremony in England before a Greek priest cannot obtain divorce in this country.

349. Divorce of defective marriages

In *Nachimson* v. *Nachimson*,[3] Hill, J., declined to pronounce a decree of separation in the case of a Russian marriage because he held that a marriage concluded under Soviet law, though valid in Russia, was not a marriage in the sense of English law; the Court of Appeal reversed the judgment on the ground that the marriage was to be recognized in England, but did not deny that the indispensable condition for an English decree of separation was the existence of a marriage recognized in this country.

2. The English court will, on the other hand, be pre-

[1] R. v. *Hammersmith Superintendent Registrar, Ex parte Mir-Anwarruddin*, [1917] 1 K.B. 634.
[2] See Dr. Cheshire's impressive criticism (pp. 484 et seq.) of the decision.
[3] [1930] P. 217.

pared to pronounce a divorce decree if the union, though no marriage under the personal law of the parties, is a marriage under English law. If two Greeks have married in England before the registrar such a marriage is divorceable here notwithstanding the fact that under Greek law the parties are not married.

350. Jurisdiction

III. The test of *jurisdiction* of the English court for the purpose of granting divorce or judicial separation has been examined above, s. 71, 79. On the conditions under which the English court recognizes the jurisdiction of a foreign court to pronounce divorce or separation decrees see *supra*, s. 240.

351. Applicable law. Comparative survey

IV. What *substantive law* is applicable if the court entertains divorce or separation proceedings? In particular, what legal system determines the ground for divorce and separation, the influence of condonation, connivance, and collusion, the weight to be attached to contributory guilt on the part of the petitioner or to his wilful neglect or misconduct?

1. Most of the European and Latin-American laws decide in principle in favour of the national law of the spouses or the husband; but they modify this by ordaining the application of the *lex fori* where public policy is in issue. The Hague Divorce Convention, 1902, for example, permits a divorce *a vinculo* only if both the national law of the spouses and the *lex fori* include this institution, and if furthermore under both legal systems there is a ground for divorce in the case before the court.[1] Where the spouses are of different nationality, some legal systems have recourse to the last common nationality, others apply the husband's national law. Both these solutions are open to objection. They lead to injustice against the wife in those cases where before the marriage she was the subject of a state which

---

[1] Hague Convention, art. 1. 2, formulated on the model of German law, art. 17 Introd. Law. Similarly Swedish, Swiss, Chinese, and Japanese law. Under all these systems the function of the law of the forum is precisely determined. As a rule, however, the domain of public policy, and therefore the degree to which the *lex fori* applies, is left to the discretion of the court; thus in France, Belgium, the Netherlands, Roumania, Poland, Portugal, Spain, and in respect of separation from bed and board, Italy.

permits divorce and by marriage became the subject of a state like Italy, where no divorce is admitted. In that case she cannot obtain a divorce decree, even if she leaves her adulterous husband, returns to her old country, and succeeds in reacquiring her pre-nuptial nationality. It was a great achievement when the French Supreme Court in the famous *Ferrari Case*[1] refrained from drawing this conclusion and granted divorce to a Frenchwoman who had married an Italian, obtained a separation decree in Italy, and after being repatriated in France started divorce proceedings in the French court. This was justifiable by reason of *ordre public*.[2] Other states—Switzerland, Sweden, and Germany—have followed the French example[3] and thus removed some of the most regrettable consequences of the application of the husband's national law.

2. Some other legal systems apply the *lex fori*, or the *lex domicilii* which as a rule coincides with the law of the forum. This is the case in Soviet Russia, Estonia, Latvia, Austria, Greece, Denmark, Norway, and in some Latin-American states, such as Chile, Ecuador, and Uruguay.[4] In English and Anglo-American law the *lex fori* system prevails.

3. It is difficult to say whether the English court applies English law because it is the law of the place where the proceedings take place, or because it is the law of the domicile and therefore the personal law of the parties. The American *Restatement*[5] stresses the latter view, but this does not seem to dispose of the question in all its aspects, at any rate for English law. The English court when entertaining divorce or separation proceedings applies nothing but English law because the question of the conditions under which

352. English law

---

[1] *Dalloz Pér.* 1922. 1. 137.

[2] Outstanding French jurists, however, have attacked the *arrêt Ferrari*; for example, Pillet, *Rev. Darras*, 1922–3, 461; Niboyet, *Rev. crit.*, 1934, 134.

[3] By withdrawing from the Hague Convention: Switzerland 1929, Sweden and Germany 1933; in Sweden and Germany new statutes were promulgated: Sweden, 23 March 1934, Germany, 25 January 1935. Cf. *Rabel's Z.*, 8, 639; 9, 876.

[4] See *Código Bustamante*, art. 52, and the startling rule in the Montevideo Convention, art. 13b, that the ground of divorce must be admitted by the law of the place where the marriage was concluded—as if parties to a marriage concluded as it were a partnership agreement subject to the implied condition that the contract should not be dissolved for any reason not contemplated at the time of conclusion.

[5] s. 135, comment.

the nuptial tie may be loosened or destroyed touches fundamental English conceptions of morality, religion, and public policy. There can therefore be no doubt that where in exceptional cases the English court is not the court of the domicile it is nevertheless English law that applies and not the law of the foreign domicile.

353. Cases where *lex fori* is not *lex domicilii* Such exceptional cases are of three kinds:

(*a*) The English court has jurisdiction to entertain *separation* proceedings if the parties are resident, though not domiciled, in this country.[1] The court will not make a decree for judicial separation on grounds recognized by the foreign law of domicile (*e.g.* mutual consent).

(*b*) Under the Matrimonial Causes Act, 1937,[2] s. 13, the English court has jurisdiction to entertain divorce or other proceedings in matrimonial causes where a wife has been deserted by her husband or the husband has been deported, if the husband has changed his domicile from England to a foreign country. When the English court exercises this jurisdiction it will disregard the law of the foreign domicile. Example: a husband on deserting his wife acquires a Belgian domicile and there commits adultery; the wife can sue him immediately in an English court, not for desertion, because the period of three years required by English law[3] has not yet elapsed, but for adultery, although under the Belgian *lex domicilii* the husband's adultery would not be a ground for divorce unless he had kept his concubine in the marital home. The change of domicile on the part of the husband is, so to speak, ignored in favour of the deserted wife.

(*c*) The Law Reform (Miscellaneous Provisions) Act, 1949,[4] s. 1, established an important extension of the jurisdiction of the English Court in the interest of the wife. The court can entertain matrimonial proceedings, notably divorce proceedings, although the husband (and therefore the wife) is domiciled abroad if she is *residing* in England and has been ordinarily residing here for three years immediately preceding the proceedings. As in the case (*b*) the

[1] See *supra*, s. 79. [2] 1 Edw. VIII and 1 Geo. VI, c. 57. See *supra*, s. 73.
[3] Matrimonial Causes Acts, 1925 and 1937, s. 176 (b).
[4] 12, 13 & 14 Geo. VI, c. 100.

wife's petition can only be based on the English *lex fori*, and not on the *lex domicilii*.

Example: An Italian has married an English woman, and they reside in Italy where they are domiciled. The husband commits adultery, and the wife leaves him settling in England. After three years she can bring a petition for divorce although the law of her domicile does not allow divorce.

V. Apart from these three exceptions the law of the English forum—if there is an English forum—coincides with the law of the domicile. But this does not mean that the *lex fori* covers the whole ground and that the conception of domicile plays no part in determining the substantive law applicable to divorce. The *lex domicilii* becomes important in two cases: first, before any forum has been established; secondly, where the forum is not English.

354. Importance of *lex domicilii*

1. Suppose that no divorce proceedings have yet been initiated in any court, but an event has occurred which would justify them in the courts of country X, but not in those of country Y. Which law answers the question whether the event has created a 'right to divorce'? The *lex domicilii* alone applies. There can be no question of a *lex fori*, because there is no forum. This becomes important when the domicile is changed before a petition for divorce is brought. *Example*: While the couple was domiciled in Brussels the husband committed adultery outside his home; according to Belgian law that adultery gave his wife no right to divorce him, and if she were to bring a petition against him after a change of domicile to France, Germany, Switzerland, or any other country where simple adultery is a sufficient ground for divorce, the French, German, or Swiss court would dismiss it.[1] Would it be otherwise if their new domicile were English? Should an immoral but legally immaterial act become a ground for divorce merely through a subsequent change of domicile? The answer is no.

355.
(1) before a forum has been established

It cannot, however, be concluded from this that in the converse situation the wife retained the right to divorce acquired under the law of her old (Belgian) domicile, but not recognized by her new law; if, for example, the husband while domiciled in Belgium has been sentenced to a severe and degrading punishment,[2] and then becomes domiciled in England, she will not be allowed to sue on this ground.

[1] See, for example, Hague Convention, art. 4; German Introductory Law, s. 17 § 2; Swiss Civil Code, Final Title, art. 61 7 h § 2. *Código Bustamante*, art. 52, 54.   [2] This is no ground for divorce under English law.

There is an even more doubtful situation when an act which under the law of the old domicile (Italy) has created merely a right to judicial separation, under the law of the new (English) domicile gives the innocent party a ground for divorce. Can then the change of domicile from Italy to England transform the right to separation into a right to divorce? It is suggested, though with considerable hesitation, that such alteration should be admissible.[1] The adultery committed in Italy has there generated a claim to a loosening of the marriage tie in the highest degree conceded by Italian law. That this maximum is lower than that granted by English law should not prevent the court from applying the more trenchant English rule.

In two cases under English law the 'right to divorce' does not arise from a single fact (as from adultery or cruelty), but from a set of facts covering a long period: three years in the case of desertion, five years in that of insanity.[2] In many continental laws where desertion and insanity are recognized as grounds for divorce[3] the required period is shorter. If during this period the husband changes his domicile from the continent to England, the years which have run under the old domicile law may be taken into account in computing the longer English period.[4] In the case of insanity English law requires that during the whole period the respondent 'has been continually under care and treatment';[5] and he 'shall be deemed to be under care and treatment' if the provisions of certain English statutes have been complied with. A literal construction of the passage would lead to an unfortunate result; viz. even if the requirements of corresponding foreign provisions have been fulfilled this would not suffice in England. Bearing in mind that the Matrimonial Causes Act does not deal with difficulties arising out of the conflict of laws one might be

---

[1] See, for example, German Introd. Law, s. 17 § 2; Hague Convent., s. 4.

[2] Matrimonial Causes Acts, 1925 and 1937, s. 176 (b) and (d).

[3] Both are, for example, recognized in Germany, Switzerland, the Netherlands, Estonia, Latvia, Greece.

[4] Is the same true when the law of the old domicile does not admit divorce for insanity, as, for example, France? The answer should be in the affirmative.

[5] Matrimonial Causes Acts, 1925 and 1937, s. 176 (d). See Law Reform (Miscellaneous Provisions) Act, 1949, s. 3.

entitled to construe the passage less narrowly than is usually permissible under the rules of interpretation of statutes.

2. The law of the domicile is ·further decisive where there is no English but a foreign forum and where the foreign court recognizes the doctrine of *renvoi*. Suppose a British subject, domiciled in France, marries a German woman and lives with her in Germany, without establishing a German domicile. The marriage being unhappy, she becomes renaturalized in Germany and brings a divorce petition in a German court.[1] This court has to apply the national law of the husband (English law), but has to consider *renvoi* rules. The question is: does the English conflict rule *re*mit the decision to German law, as this is the *lex fori*? Or does it *trans*mit the case to French law, that is, to the *lex domicilii*? It cannot be doubted that the second alternative should be chosen. The English rule: *English* courts apply English divorce law, is not a derivative of a wider English conflict rule to the effect that 'every court applies the divorce law of the forum'. No such 'all-sided' rule[2] exists. As divorce affects status, and status depends on domicile, it is to the law of the domicile that English law refers in a case of *renvoi*.

VI. The *effects* of divorce are determined by the law governing the act of divorce, be it a judicial decree or an ecclesiastical or private act. We have seen that the dissolving effect of divorce is limited to the country where the divorce has been pronounced and to those foreign countries where it is recognized, and that this is one of the sources of the unfortunate type of limping marriages. The exact moment at which the marriage is dissolved is also determined by the law that governs the divorce proceedings, that is, the *lex fori* or, in the case of an extra-judicial divorce, the law under which the divorce agreement or the unilateral repudiation has become effective. In the normal case of a judicial decree the law of the Divorce Court determines the time at which the marriage ceases to exist: this may be the moment when the decree is pronounced, or the date after which it can no longer be reversed by way of appeal or *cassation*, or when it

356.
(2) where there is a foreign forum and *renvoi*

357.
Effects of divorce

---

[1] The court has jurisdiction under a German law of 25 Jan. 1935, s. 2.
[2] On the meaning of this term see *supra*, s. 89.

becomes absolute, or the moment at which subsequent to the judicial procedure the dissolution is entered on the marriage register.[1]

The law under which the divorce has been granted, normally the *lex fori*, also governs the secondary effects of the divorce. It decides whether the divorced wife is obliged, allowed, or forbidden to use her former husband's name,[2] whether, on what conditions, and to what degree one of the spouses is bound to maintain the other, and the like. As to the right of using a particular name, this is open to controversy, because the right to a name is one of the attributes of personality and is as a rule subject to the personal law, that is here the law of the domicile of the divorced wife. If she therefore acquires a domicile of her own after the divorce, some jurists hold that the law of that domicile should determine what her name is.[3] But the question whether she is obliged, forbidden, or allowed to use her marriage name concerns the relationship created between her and her former husband by the divorce and affects both her duties and her rights towards him; the change of her domicile can neither increase her rights nor relieve her of her duties. Similar considerations apply to maintenance duties arising out of divorce. Once they have come into existence under the divorce law they cannot be affected by a mere change of domicile. Even if there is a subsequent change in the relative pecuniary situation of the parties, only the law under which the claim to alimony was established can decide whether the claim is affected by such change or not.

358. Remarriage after divorce
According to some legal systems the divorce court is empowered or even bound to impose on the parties a disability to conclude a new marriage within a specified period. Such disability based on foreign law must be respected in England unless it is imposed only on the guilty party and its penal character is thereby evinced.[4] If it affects both

---

[1] This was the French system until amended by a law of 26 June 1919. It is still the system prevailing in Belgium, Roumania, and the Netherlands.

[2] See, for example, the very detailed regulation of this question in the German Civil Code, s. 1577; Swiss Civ. C., s. 149.

[3] Thus Frankenstein, III. 574 et seq.

[4] *Scott* v. *Att.-Gen.* (1886), 11 P.D. 128. See *supra*, s. 163 (p. 172, n. 6).

parties equally it constitutes, as Dr. Cheshire points out,[1] something analogous to the marriage disability imposed on domiciled English spouses in the period between the decree *nisi* and the decree absolute.[2]

Apart from this, the capacity of a person to remarry after the dissolution of a former marriage is governed not by the law under which the divorce was granted, but by the law of his or her domicile at the time of the new marriage. *Example*: Two Italian subjects domiciled in England have been divorced in an English court; the ex-husband then returns to Italy and there acquires a new domicile. Italian law does not permit him to conclude a new marriage, because Italy does not recognize divorce decrees in respect of Italian subjects. Should he therefore return to England for a few months in the hope of concluding his second marriage here, he would do so in vain. Such marriage would be void because the law of his new domicile renders him *incapax* owing to the *impedimentum ligaminis*.[3] He is in a state of secular celibacy—unmarried and incapable of marrying.

The Berlin Court of Appeal had to deal with an instructive and thorny case showing the predicament of courts faced with limping marriages.[4]

The facts are as follows: A German couple was divorced in an American court. As that court had no jurisdiction in the eyes of German law, the decree, though valid in the United States, was invalid in Germany. Then the husband married an American woman in the United States. This marriage would consequently have been void in Germany but for the fact that between the divorce decree and the second marriage he had acquired American nationality. Owing to this change his second marriage was valid both in America and in Germany; an American citizen, validly divorced according to American law, could not be prevented from concluding a valid second marriage in America; and it could no longer matter that the American divorce decree was not recognized in Germany. The question arose: does the first marriage still continue to exist from the German point of view, in spite of the validity of the second marriage? Certainly not. Because the second marriage has to be recognized the first must have been dissolved by the conclusion of the second, and this is the result at which the Court of Appeal arrived, though its reasoning was unsatisfactory. If this is true it leads to a rule of municipal law which must be recognized by any state that rejects polygamy: a first marriage is dissolved if one of the

---

[1] *Priv. Int. L.*, pp. 490–1.   [2] See *Warter* v. *Warter* (1890), 15 P. 152.
[3] See, for example, Frankenstein, III. 101. *Contra*: Reichel, loc. cit.; Zitelmann, II. 772.   [4] *JurW.* 1925, 2146. See Melchior, 414.

spouses concludes a second marriage, and if this second marriage is valid under the legal system under which the first marriage was valid till the date of the second.[1]

It is open to grave doubt whether an English court would reach the same decision in an analogous case, that is, where the couple, when divorced in America, was domiciled in England and the husband acquired a bona fide domicile in America before concluding his second marriage in America with a domiciled American woman. If the English court feels itself bound to follow *Shaw* v. *Gould*[2] and *In re Sterling*[3] it will regard the first marriage as still valid and therefore the second marriage as void, although the latter was concluded by two domiciled Americans in America and in accordance with American law—a rather unfortunate result.

[1] Instances of this rule can be found in internal German, Austrian, and Canon Law. (1) If a man has been untraceable for a long time and the German court has made a declaration of death, his wife may marry again unless she knows that he is actually living. The remarriage has the effect of dissolving the former marriage. German Civ. Code, s. 1348; German Marriage Law, 1946, s. 38. (2) Before 1938 Austrian Roman Catholics were unable to obtain a divorce *a vinculo* under Austrian law. If they were separated from bed and board the marriage tie remained. The Republican Government, however, tried to 'help' them by issuing to petitioners under s. 83 of the Austrian Civ. Code dispensations from the *impedimentum ligaminis*. More than fifty thousand Catholic Austrians obtained such permits to conclude a so-called 'dispensation marriage'. The effect of these marriages was doubtful. If they were valid, as many lawyers thought (Hofmannsthal, *Die Dispensehen*, 1920; Lenhoff, *Auflösung der Ehe und Wiederverehelichung*, 1926), the first marriage must have been dissolved by the conclusion of the second, because it cannot be supposed that both are simultaneously valid. (3) Under Canon Law the valid and consummated marriage between two non-Christians is dissolved if one of the spouses becomes baptized and concludes a valid marriage with a person of Catholic faith. The second marriage is valid under certain conditions in virtue of the *privilegium Paulinum* (1 Cor. vii. 12-15). See *Codex iuris canonici* c. 1216: 'Vinculum prioris coniugii, in infidelitate contracti, tunc tamen solvitur cum pars fidelis reapse novas nuptias valide inierit.' Comp. German Supreme Court, *Off. Coll.*, 152, 31.

[2] (1868) L.R. 3 H.L. Cas., 55; cf. (1865) 1 L.R. Eq., 247. See on this *infra*, s. 364.   [3] [1908] 2 Ch. 344.

BIBLIOGRAPHY

CHESHIRE 470–96. DICEY–MORRIS 236. GOODRICH 334–69. RABEL, I. 383–534. BATIFFOL, *Traité* 473-86. NIBOYET, *Traité*, V. 422-58. LORENZEN, *Répert.*, VI. 340. Cf. *RVglHWB.*, IV. 419. F. SCHÖNDORF, 75 *Jhering's Jahrb.*, 77. REICHEL, 124 *Arch. f. d. civilist, Praxis*, 204. BATES, *Divorce and Separation of Aliens in France*, New York, 1929. SALVIOLI, *Riv. d. dir. internaz.*, 1927, 354. DELAUME, 37 *Rev. Crit.* (1948), 205–34. PLAISANT, *Conflits dans les Traités*, 384 et seq. On Jewish divorces: MESSECA-FARA, 3, *Nouv. Rev.* 685. To the Hague Convention: ANZILOTTI, *Riv. d. dir. internaz.*, 1908, 315. TRAVERS, *La Convention de la Haye relative au divorce*, 1909.

CHAPTER XXV

PARENTS AND CHILDREN

LEGITIMACY

I. The question whether a child is legitimate by birth is answered under most European and Latin-American laws by the personal law of the mother's husband, i.e. in some countries his national law, in others the law of his domicile. If he has changed his nationality or domicile during the marriage the decisive date is that of the birth of the child, and if the child is born posthumously that of the father's death. In some instances Danish courts have held that the critical time should not be the date of the birth of the child but the date of its conception; French authors have expressed the same view.[1] But this solution, though logically unassailable, is hardly satisfactory; it is not advisable to make legal effects dependent on circumstances which in most cases will be impossible to ascertain, and the danger that the mother's husband might change his personal law between the child's conception and birth with the purpose of influencing legitimacy is too remote to be worth serious consideration.

359. The various systems, notably the English system

The test of legitimacy by the personal law of the mother's husband has been rejected in France.[2] French courts apply the personal law of the child.[3]

Under English law the personal law of the mother, her husband, and the child almost always coincide, as wife and child share the domicile of the husband and father. There is no doubt that the law of that domicile governs the case. It has, however, not yet been decided which law applies in those rare cases where the mother's domicile differs from that of her late husband, e.g. in the case of a posthumous child if the widow has changed her domicile between her husband's death and her confinement. Some English judges have spoken *obiter* of the father's domicile,[4] others

---

[1] Veith, *RVglHWB*, IV. 421.   [2] See Frankenstein, IV. 28, n. 5.
[3] The same rule is to be found in the *Código Bustamante*, art. 57.
[4] See *Re Goodman's Trusts* (1881) 17 Ch.D. 266, 292 (Cotton, L.J.); *Re Andros* (1883), 24 Ch.D. 637 (Kay, J.).

of the child's domicile[1] as decisive. It is probable that the courts would accept the former view. 'Legitimacy is not a unilateral matter affecting the child alone. If an illegitimate child is legitimated it is not only the status of the child that is affected; the status of the putative father is also changed.'[2] Legitimacy is concerned with the relationship between child and father, and this relationship is governed by the law of the father's last domicile. In the case of a posthumous child the law of the father's last domicile will decide whether it is to be regarded as his legitimate offspring, and the child's mother cannot be allowed to alter the answer by establishing a new domicile of her own before her confinement.

Is it sound, at least, to subject the question whether the child is its mother's legitimate offspring to the law of the mother's domicile?—a question which arises both in the case of a posthumous child and in that of a child born after the divorce of its parents within the period of gestation. The answer is in the negative. A child which is his father's bastard, according to his personal law, or which is not the child of its mother's husband, cannot be its mother's legitimate offspring; and conversely, a child which is its father's legitimate offspring cannot be its mother's illegitimate child.[3] In respect of both parents the status of legitimacy is tested only by the father's domicile.[4]

360. The details

II. The prerequisites of legitimacy vary very much in different countries. There is unanimity, at least in all countries of European civilization, on one fundamental principle: a child conceived in lawful wedlock is legitimate if it is *certainly or possibly* begotten by the mother's husband. Then there is a second rule on which most modern laws, though not French law, agree: a child born in wedlock but begotten before wedlock by the mother's subsequent husband is legitimate.[5] But the operation in detail of these two

---

[1] *Birtwhistle* v. *Vardill* (1835), 2 Cl. & Fin. 571, 573; *In re Don's Estate* (1857), 4 Drew, 194, 197.

[2] Greene, M.R., and Luxmoore, L.J., in *Re Luck*, [1940] Ch. 864, 882.

[3] *Contra: Restatement*, s. 137, 138; Beale, II. 704 et seq.

[4] *Aliter* Welsh, 63 *L.Q.R.* (1947), 65 et seq.

[5] French law seems to treat children of this kind not as legitimate but as legitimated by subsequent marriage. Planiol, I, no. 1366, 1559; Colin & Capitant, 8th ed., I, no. 242. *Contra: Cour de Cass., Dalloz Pér.* 1930. 1. 51.

leading principles differs widely from country to country. In all continental laws there exists a legally fixed period of gestation; not so in English law. In many legal systems the right to dispute the legitimacy of a child borne by a married woman is reserved to her husband; it is denied both to the child and its mother in spite of the vital interest they may have in seeing the natural status recognized.[1] Often the right of the mother's husband is limited in point of time, and if it has not been exercised within the legal period the child is irrevocably treated as his legitimate child unless he dies before the period has elapsed.[2] English law contains no restrictions of this kind; not only can the father at any time contend that the child is not his, but any person interested in the discovery of the truth—for example, for reasons of succession—is entitled to do so; and in England the mere fact that the husband takes no steps to establish his non-paternity does not suffice to render legitimate a child not begotten by him.

Which of these conflicting rules applies is (probably) to be determined by the husband's personal law, that is, the law of his domicile. This view, which prevails in continental laws, is however not beyond doubt. As we have already seen,[3] English private international law is much more inclined than are continental laws to regard foreign rules as merely procedural. It might be argued that all the manifold rules determining the period of gestation or excluding the right of third parties to show the true relationship between the child and its mother's husband are nothing but rules on evidence or procedure and for this reason inapplicable in an English court. This argument might be supported by the wording of continental provisions: if the mother's husband has not taken proceedings in due time to dispute the legitimacy of a child not begotten by him, the child is to be treated as legitimate; the German Civil

361. Procedural rules?

---

[1] *Example*: The woman's son wishes to marry her husband's daughter by a previous marriage and should therefore be able to rebut the presumption that the latter is his 'sister'.

[2] Therefore the legitimacy of a posthumous child can be impugned by anybody, even under the German Civil Code; see s. 1593 et seq. (changed by a statute of 12 April 1938, art. 2).

[3] *Supra*, s. 170, 218 et seq.

Code, however, carefully avoids calling it a legitimate child, it speaks of an illegitimate child whose illegitimacy 'cannot be alleged'.[1] Nevertheless it would be wrong to rely on such inappropriate terminology; for if nobody is allowed to allege that the child is illegitimate this means that legally it is legitimate. The German Code[2] gives the husband to the exclusion of other persons a genuine substantive right to establish his non-paternity. If he exercises this right he thereby alters the child's status: he changes a voidable legitimacy into illegitimacy. If, on the other hand, he does not exercise it in due time, the voidable legitimacy becomes a fully valid legitimacy. These are effects of a substantive, not of a procedural, character.

Much more doubtful is the question whether rules establishing fixed *periods of gestation* are merely procedural. They vary from country to country. When, for example, French law determines the commencement of gestation as not earlier than the 300th nor later than the 180th day before the birth of the child, this may be regarded as a rule on evidence to ascertain whether the child was, or was not, begotten by the husband. But the French provision also contains a substantive rule, viz. that a child born later than three hundred days after the dissolution of the marriage is illegitimate even if it is certain that it was begotten by the husband.[3] The tendency of English courts to regard substantive rules as merely procedural[4] might be operative in respect of the period of gestation;[5] and the result is not contrary to justice, since the system of English municipal law—which avoids a fixation of the period—is possibly preferable to the continental system.

362.
Valid
marriage

III. Under English municipal law legitimacy requires

[1] 'Die Unehelichkeit des Kindes kann nicht geltendgemacht werden.' The French civil code (art. 312 §2, 313) also uses procedural terms.

[2] The same is true of the French civil code.

[3] *Code civil*, art. 312. Under German law (s. 1592, civ. c.) the 300th day has been replaced by the 302nd day, and the period of gestation may even be extended beyond this. It therefore seems justifiable to regard the German rule as merely procedural in the English sense.

[4] See *supra*, s. 170.

[5] The French *code civil*, on the other hand, distinguishes rules concerned with evidence permissible in paternity cases (such as art. 319 to 326) from substantive rules. The former are of course inapplicable in an English court.

birth during a valid marriage or within a certain period
after its dissolution; the issue of a void marriage is illegitimate. Many other legal systems grant the position of
legitimate offspring to children born in an invalid marriage,
the nullity of which has not yet been pronounced; their
legitimacy is recognized provided that both spouses were,
or at least one of them was, acting in good faith at the time
of the marriage (putative marriages);[1] under some other
laws the children are treated as legitimate even if both
parents knew that their marriage was void.[2] Whether the
narrower English view or one of the wider foreign notions
of 'legitimacy' is to be applied by English courts depends
on the connexion in which the notion is used.

Examples: (*a*) *S*, born in a void marriage, the nullity of which neither
of the parents *F* and *M* knew, had two great-uncles, one a domiciled Scotsman, the other English. Both gave by will a share of residue to 'the
children' of their niece *M*. Whether *S* is legitimate or illegitimate depends
on the *lex successionis*, that is the domiciliary law of the testator. Therefore
S is legitimate in so far as the legacy of the Scottish great-uncle is concerned,
and illegitimate in respect of the British bequest.

(*b*) *S*, a British subject, who at the time of his birth was domiciled in
Scotland but is now domiciled in England, applies by petition to the
English court, praying for a decree declaring that he is the legitimate
child of his parents *H* and *W*, who at the time of the birth of *S* were
domiciled in Scotland, but later acquired an English domicile. The
marriage of his parents *H* and *W* was (and still is) void, but both parents
were in good faith. The English conflict rule points to Scottish law as the
law of *H*'s domicile at the birth of *S*. Therefore the petition is well-founded.

A much more thorny problem arises where legitimacy is
not content with a putative marriage. Which law then
decides whether the union between the parents of the *propositus* is a valid marriage? The question becomes important notably in the case of limping marriages. Suppose that
two domiciled Greeks have married in England before a
Greek priest, and that the English court has to decide on
the legitimacy of a child born in this union. Under English

363.
Limping
marriages

[1] This system prevails in Scotland, Germany, Austria, France, Italy, Belgium,
the Netherlands, and South Africa. Under English law children of the parties to
a voidable marriage are treated as legitimate; not so if the marriage is void *ab
initio*, Law Reform Act, 1949, 12, 13 & 14 Geo. VI, c. 100, s. 4.

[2] Thus in Switzerland, Sweden, Norway, Greece, and some states of the
United States of America; on California see the Connecticut case *Moore* v.
Saxton, in Lorenzen, *Cases*, 776.

law the marriage is void, though valid under Greek law. As legitimacy depends on the law of the father's domicile, that is, Greek law, and under Greek law the child is legitimate, it is submitted that the English court would also regard it as legitimate. A person who is legitimate in the country of his father's domicile will as a rule be considered legitimate in any country which tests legitimacy by domicile. This rule, however, though generally correct, suffers an exception, as previously shown:[1] there are cases where the recognition by the English court of the validity of the marriage would involve a violation of principles of justice. In such cases the English court under its own conflict rule treats the marriage as void and therefore denies the legitimacy of the child.

364. Shaw v. Gould   This seems to be the basis on which two difficult English cases might be explained:

(a) The case *Shaw* v. *Gould* (or *In re Wilson's Trust*).[2]

The main facts were as follows. A testator Wilson, domiciled in England, bequeathed funds in trust for the 'children' of his great-niece Elizabeth Hickson. In 1828 Elizabeth, when a girl of sixteen, was induced by fraud to marry a domiciled Englishman, Buxton. Immediately after the marriage her friends interfered and took her away from her husband; no marital intercourse took place. Buxton was convicted and sentenced to three years imprisonment. Sixteen years later Elizabeth became engaged to be married to Shaw, a domiciled Englishman. As under the English law of the time no divorce was obtainable she and Shaw devised a scheme to procure a dissolution of her first marriage by the Scottish Court of Sessions. They induced Buxton to live for forty days in Scotland, whereby according to Scottish law the jurisdiction of the Scottish court, a so-called *forum domicilii*, was established. In 1846 the Scottish court pronounced a divorce decree, and Elizabeth married Shaw in Scotland, where he acquired a genuine domicile. Buxton remained domiciled in England. Elizabeth had three children by Shaw during Buxton's life. As under an English rule of construction of wills the term 'children' is to be interpreted as legitimate children, the question arose whether those children were Elizabeth's legitimate children. The House of Lords unanimously[3] affirmed the decision of Kindersley, V.C., to the effect that the children were illegitimate and could not take under the will.

[1] See *supra*, s. 200.

[2] *In re Wilson's Trusts* (1865), L.R. 1 Eq. 247 (Kindersley, V.C.), and under the designation *Shaw* v. *Gould* (in the House of Lords) (1868), L.R. 3 H.L.Cas. 55 to 99. See also the case *In re Paine*, [1940] Ch. 46.

[3] Lord Colonsay agreed only with great hesitation and remarked that it was difficult to 'reconcile (the judgment) with general principles of jurisprudence or the generally recognized rules of international law' (at pp. 96, 97). He did not, however, say to what principles and rules he referred.

The reason for this startling decision—which under the circumstances of the case was particularly unsatisfactory—was that though legitimacy was to be tested by the (Scottish) law of the father's domicile, and though under Scottish law the marriage of 1846 was valid because the Scottish divorce decree was unobjectionable from the Scottish point of view, the English court saw no way of recognizing that decree and consequently the validity of the second marriage. The judges inferred the nullity of the divorce partly from *Lolley's Case*,[1] according to which an English marriage could not be dissolved by a foreign judgment on grounds on which it was not liable to be dissolved in England,[2] partly from the fact that the divorce had been obtained by fraud or by a 'reconcerted arrangement',[3] and partly from the consideration that the Scottish law in so far as it permitted a divorce decree to be pronounced in a *forum domicilii* after forty days residence in Scotland involved a violation of 'rules of international public law',[4] because it caused the Scottish court to 'usurp the rights and functions of sovereignty over the subjects of another country'. Lord Cranworth reasoned further that if after the second marriage Buxton and Elizabeth had again cohabited and there had been issue that issue would have been legitimate, and 'it cannot be argued that the issue of both unions should share together'.[5] None of the reasons given seems convincing. *Lolley's Case*, which never was a good authority,[6] lost all value with the English Divorce Act, 1857. The non-recognition of the Scottish divorce decree by English courts follows simply from the fact that under English law the Scottish court had no jurisdiction, irrespective of

[1] (1812) Russ. & Ry. 237, 239; and in *McCarthy* v. *De Caix* (1835), 2 H.L.Cas. 569, 570.

[2] According to Lord Brougham (in *Warrender* v. *Warrender* (1835), 2 Cl. & Fin. 488, 541, 549) *Lolley's Case* was decided on an even wider principle: 'no foreign proceeding in the nature of a divorce can affect an English marriage'.

[3] Thus Lord Chelmsford at p. 79, while Lord Cranworth refused to decide the case on the ground of fraud (p. 69).

[4] Thus Lord Westbury at pp. 81, 82, following Kindersley, V.C. (1 L.R. Eq. 257).

[5] loc. cit., at p. 71.

[6] See the criticism by Lord Brougham, loc. cit., and Dr. Lushington in *Conway* v. *Beazley*, 3 Hagg. Eccl. Rep. 639, 644.

whether the decree was procured by fraud and preconcerted arrangement or bona fide. That Scottish law should be reproached with having violated rules of international law is hardly understandable. There is no rule of international public law which obliges the European nations (or countries) to grant jurisdiction in divorce cases only to the court of domicile in the English sense of this term. Finally, the unsatisfactory consequence as set forth by Lord Cranworth is not worse than the situation of Elizabeth's children treated as legitimate in Scotland and as bastards in England. It is suggested that the authority of *Shaw* v. *Gould* is restricted to those cases in which legitimacy is based on the divorce decree of a foreign court lacking jurisdiction and where the recognition of the remote consequences of the decree by an English court would be particularly repugnant to English principles of justice owing to the circumstances in which the decree was obtained.[1]

365. *In re Bischoff-sheim*

(*b*) The case *In re Bischoffsheim*.[2]

The main facts were these: A domiciled Englishman gave a share of residue to his granddaughter Nesta for her life with remainder to her 'children'. Nesta married first *X*, and after his death his brother George, who was a domiciled Englishman. The second marriage took place in New York in 1917. At that time a marriage of a widow to her deceased husband's brother was void under English law, though valid under the law of New York. In 1920 both Nesta and George had acquired a domicile of choice in New York. In that year Nesta gave birth to a son Richard, of whom George was the father. Is Richard Nesta's legitimate child with the effect that he can share the testator's residue? As already seen[3] the answer is: yes, if Richard is his father's legitimate child, and no, if he is his father's bastard.

Romer J., decided in favour of legitimacy, and though the judgment has been heavily criticized,[4] it is submitted that it is correct. English law, as the *lex domicilii testatoris*

---

[1] *Shaw* v. *Gould* is thus an illustration of the rule developed *supra*, ss. 196–200, concerning the treatment of incidental questions. The decision has been gravely criticized by Dr. Cheshire, p. 508 (see, on the other hand, J. H. C. Morris, *Cases*, p. 188). It was referred to in *Re Stirling*, [1908] 2 Ch. 344. But this case was not decided on the basis of *Shaw* v. *Gould*; in *Re Stirling* the decree which dissolved the first marriage was invalid not only at the first husband's, but also at the second husband's domicile as well as at the place of celebration of the second marriage, so that the court had only to decide upon the question whether the marriage was to be regarded as a putative marriage or not.

[2] [1948] Ch. 79. See 2 *Int. L.Q.* 48–53.   [3] *Supra*, p. 386.

[4] Welsh, 63 *L.Q.R.* 74 et seq.; Mann, 64 *L.Q.R.* 201–2; Falconbridge, 1949 *Can. B.R.* 1163.

(and therefore the *lex successionis*) disposes that under the English rule of construction of wills, 'children' means 'legitimate children';[1] but the rule does not indicate the conditions required for the status of legitimacy. Which law decides whether a child is legitimate or not? Under the English conflict rule[2] the law of the father's domicile at the time of the child's birth, that is in this case the law of New York, is decisive. Under New York law the marriage of Nesta and George has been valid since its conclusion, according to the rule that a marriage valid where concluded is valid everywhere. Therefore the child is legitimate. It is believed that the decision *in Re Bischoffsheim* is not inconsistent with *Shaw* v. *Gould*. Nesta's first marriage had been dissolved by death before she married again, while Elizabeth's first marriage was dissolved by a divorce decree of a foreign court the jurisdiction of which was not recognized by the House of Lords.

THE RELATIONSHIP BETWEEN PARENTS AND LEGITIMATE CHILDREN

Most legal systems subject the relationship between parents and children born in lawful wedlock to the father's and after his death to the mother's personal law. Very few laws, among them notably the *Código Bustamante*,[3] declare the personal law of the child to be decisive. But all laws agree that in so far as the parents' rights and duties regarding the person of the child are concerned the *lex fori* must have considerable influence; continental courts justify this influence by the requirements of *ordre public*.

English law is not quite clear. Most of the problems which have arisen elsewhere have not yet been brought before English courts. As the father's and the child's

366. The principle

---

[1] *Hill* v. *Crook* (1875), L.R. 6 H.L. 282, 276; *Dorin* v. *Dorin* (1875), L.R. 7 H.L. 577; *Re Wohlgemuth*, [1949] 1 Ch. 14.

[2] It would hardly be justifiable to limit the term 'legitimate' to its interpretation under English municipal law. The question is the same as where the testator has bequeathed a fund to his nephew 'provided the nephew has attained majority at the time of my death'. 'Majority' does not always mean 21 years; if the nephew is a domiciled Swiss he can take under the will as soon as he is *capax* under Swiss law, that is when he is 20. See Wengler, 8 *Rabel's Z.*, 150.

[3] Art. 69, 70 of that code.

domicile coincide during the latter's infancy it is difficult to say which of them is decisive when the child has attained majority and established a domicile of its own.[1] It seems probable that the court would decide in favour of the father's domicile, since the child's domicile of origin is derived from it.

367.
Details

1. The father's rights and duties in respect of *immovable* property are undoubtedly governed by the *lex situs*. His rights and duties in respect of the child's *movables* are tested by the law of the father's domicile. It is this law which will say whether he is entitled and obliged to administer such property, whether he has a usufructuary right (a right of enjoyment) over it or any part of it,[2] whether a daughter is legally entitled on her marriage to a dowry, a trousseau, or the like from her parents.[3] The father's *lex domicilii* also governs his rights and duties with regard to the child's *person*. But these rights are limited as long as the child is in England to such powers as English law gives an English father.[4] Thus a foreign father who in punishing his son exceeds the limits of what English law regards as reasonable chastisement cannot rely on his personal law which may allow such punishment. The exercise of the father's powers is further subject to the right of the English court to intervene in the interest of the child or for reasons of public policy. Thus a German father who during the war of 1914–18 sought to remove his children, British subjects, from England, was deemed to be overstepping his powers;[5]

---

[1] It need hardly be mentioned that the legal relationship between parents and child does not come to an end with the child's coming of age. Though the so-called 'paternal power' which all continental laws have developed and the 'parental power' of French, German, and Swiss law end when the child attains its majority, many duties remain which are independent of the child's age: reciprocal duties of maintenance, for example, or the duty of parents (under German law) to give their daughter a dowry on marriage.

[2] See the facts in *Gambier* v. *Gambier* (1835), 7 Simons Rep. 263. The decision, however, is not helpful: the judge mentions first the law of the country 'where the children happen to be', then 'their residence', ultimately 'their domicile'—all of them were identical in the case before the court—without indicating which test is decisive.

[3] See, for example, German Civ. C., s. 1620 to 1623, as opposed to the French rule 'ne dote qui ne veut' (art. 204 French c.c.), and to English laws.

[4] Westlake, p. 44, s. 4; Dicey–Morris, rule 117.

[5] *Uhlig* v. *Uhlig* (1916), 33 T.L.R. 63.

on the other hand, in *Nugent* v. *Vetzera*[1] the court declined to prevent an Austrian from removing to Austria his children of Austrian nationality who were being educated in England.

2. The law of the father's domicile sometimes requires the co-operation of a court in the exercise of parental power. The court's consent is, for example, necessary when a father concludes certain contracts on behalf of his child. Or, the court may be empowered to regulate in detail the respective rights of divorced parents to custody, and the like. These rules based on the public duty of the Sovereign to protect *homines minus potentes* are territorial in character and therefore (if foreign rules) not applicable in England. They will be replaced by the corresponding rules of English law.

3. The father's personal law also decides in what circumstances parental power ceases to exist. In all European laws the power is extinguished when the child ceases to be a minor, but the question of the age at which a person attains his or her majority is answered by the law of the child's, not the father's, domicile. If a domiciled English daughter while an infant marries a domiciled Swiss citizen and thereby acquires Swiss nationality and domicile she automatically comes of age according to Swiss law[2]—which is applicable both under English and Swiss conflict rules. Under her father's personal law, i.e. English law, marriage does not entail majority; nevertheless, the father loses his paternal power.

368. Extinction of parental power

When the father dies, his last domiciliary law decides whether his powers pass to the child's mother or whether a guardian must be appointed. If she acquires the 'parental power' its content is determined by the law of her domicile.

369. Change of domicile

4. The applicable law changes if the father (or the mother) changes his (or her) domicile. The principle of mutability obtains here just as in respect of the legal personal effects of marriage.[3] It is accepted even by those

---

[1] (1886), L.R. 2 Eq. 704, 713. The authority of this decision has fortunately been rendered doubtful by *Re B.'s Settlement*, [1940] Ch. 54. See *infra*, p. 410, n. 3.
[2] Swiss Civil Code, art. 14 § 2: *Heirat macht mündig.*
[3] *Supra*, pp. 360-2.

continental laws which in matrimonial property law prefer the immutability system.

370. Maintenance duties

5. It is doubtful what law applies to duties of maintenance other than those between father and child.[1] In most countries ascendants and descendants are bound to maintain each other in certain circumstances. The French code recognizes mutual maintenance duties even between parents-in-law and children-in-law.[2] Under English law a stepfather is bound to support his wife's child as if it were a member of his own family.[3] The Italian code declares brothers and sisters to be under an obligation to maintain any of their number unable to maintain himself (or herself) owing to a mental or corporeal defect,[4] and the Swiss code establishes a maintenance duty between brothers and sisters without any restriction.[5] On principle it is reasonable to subject maintenance duties to the domiciliary law of the person from whom maintenance is required. Thus the law of the father's domicile decides whether he has to support his child after it has come of age,[6] and the law of the son's domicile determines whether he is obliged to support his father or not. Though this is the prevailing opinion everywhere, it has sometimes been contended that a claim for support should be allowed only if it is recognized by both the personal law of the defendant and that of the claimant. Under this contention the claim of a domiciled Englishman who cannot maintain himself to support by his rich Swiss brother would have to be dismissed because in the converse situation of a rich Englishman and his poor Swiss brother no claim to support could be maintained. It is, however, hardly possible to advance any sound reason for this view. In particular, it ought not to be founded on the conception of reciprocity, first because in many legal systems the duty of maintenance is entirely one-sided—in England, for

[1] See Gutteridge, 2 *Intern. L. Quarterly* (1948), 155, on the very important question of the enforcement of foreign maintenance orders. Cf. Anonym., 47 *Columb. L.R.* (1947), 279.

[2] *Code civil*, art. 206, 207.

[3] s. 14 (3) Poor Law Act, 1930 (20 Geo. V, c. 17). The same rule obtains in Sweden and the Netherlands.

[4] *Cod. civ.*, art. 433, 439.

[5] Art. 328, 329.

[6] *Coldingham Parish Council* v. *Smith*, [1918] 2 K.B. 90.

example, grandparents have to maintain their grandchildren, but not grandchildren their grandparents[1]—
secondly because no real reciprocity exists, even in the
sphere of purely municipal law, the maintenance duty never
being effective for both parties at the same time.[2]

For these reasons it seems right to confirm the prevailing
opinion according to which only the law of the debtor's
domicile is decisive. But whether an English court would
admit any action for support based on foreign law must be
regarded as doubtful. All maintenance duties between relatives are treated in this country as parts of Poor Law; their
aim is to relieve the parish. If an English court has jurisdiction it will therefore apply English law even if the person
bound to maintain another person is domiciled abroad. The
same view is taken in France, Belgium, Italy, and Switzerland[3] and based on the requirements of *ordre public*.

LEGITIMATION

There are various ways in which illegitimate children 371.
can be legitimated. In most countries legitimation is Various
kinds of
effected by the subsequent marriage of the child's parents, legitima-
sometimes subject to a previous recognition of the child tion
by the father (France), but mostly by the mere fact of the
marriage.[4] Many legal systems admit legitimation by the
Sovereign,[5] or any other competent authority.[6] This
method is particularly useful where a marriage between the
parents is not possible (for example, when the mother is
dead, or one of the parties has marrried a third person), or
where the father cannot be expected to marry the mother.

[1] s. 14 (1) Poor Law Act, 1930.

[2] Zitelmann, II. 908.

[3] Bartin, II. 365. *Cour de Cass.*, Sirey, 1923, 1. 27. See Frankenstein, IV. 211,
d. On Swiss law: Schnitzer, *I.P.R.*, II. 403–4.

[4] Thus in Roman, Roman-Dutch, and Scottish law, in German, Austrian,
Hungarian, and in the Scandinavian laws, and, since the Legitimacy Act, 1926,
in English law.

[5] The legitimation *per rescriptum principis* (*seu Papae*) originates in Roman and
Canon law. It is still to be found, particularly in Italy, the Netherlands, and the
Scandinavian states.

[6] The judge (Switzerland), the President of the Court (Germany), the Minister
of Justice (Greece), &c. French law does not admit such legitimation by act of
state.

In most countries legitimation so achieved does not entail quite the same consequences as legitimation by subsequent marriage.[1] Finally, mere recognition on the part of the father suffices under some legal systems to legitimize a bastard. Such legitimation by recognition may be accomplished by means of adoption; sometimes it is merely called 'adoption', the term being used loosely, not with its usual connotation.[2]

What law governs legitimation?

372. Legitimation by marriage. Common law   I. Legitimation by subsequent marriage is tested by the personal law of the father. If he has changed his domicile between the child's birth and the marriage, the domicile at the date of marriage is decisive under the Legitimacy Act, 1926.[3] Before this Act came into force, English common law deemed no legitimation valid unless it was allowed by the law or laws of both domiciles—the domicile at the date of the birth and that at the date of the marriage.[4] The reason given for this rule by English courts was that the child must at its birth have had 'the capacity of being made legitimate by subsequent marriage', as Cotton, L.J., expressed it,[5] or in L.J. Fry's words, 'the capacity to change the status of illegitimacy for one of legitimacy'.[6] But neither of these statements explains why a person must be born with such 'capacity'; is there any other capacity in the world which functions only if it existed at the time of birth? It seems as if the reasoning of the courts covered the desire to make more difficult the recognition of foreign legitimations; a comprehensible tendency at a time when English municipal law admitted no legitimation of bastards.

373. Statutory rule   The Legitimacy Act, 1926, while improving English municipal law, also replaced the old conflict rule by one

---

[1] Under German law, for example, no legal relationship between the legitimated child and the wife of the father or his relatives comes into existence as a result of legitimation by act of state, while legitimation by subsequent marriage puts the child in exactly the same position as if it had been born in wedlock; s. 1737, German Civ. Code.

[2] See *In re Luck*, [1940] Ch. 864, concerning Californian law.

[3] 16 & 17 Geo. V, c. 60, s. 8 (1).

[4] *Re Wright's Trusts* (1856), 25 L.J. Ch. 621; *Re Goodman's Trusts* (1881), 17 Ch.D. 266; *Re Grove* (1888), 40 Ch.D. 216.

[5] *Re Grove (supra)*, p. 232.

[6] Ibid., p. 238.

framed on the principle of continental private international law.[1]

The law of the father's domicile at the date of the marriage decides[2]

(a) whether the prerequisites of legitimation are fulfilled, in particular whether recognition of the child by the parents is necessary and, if so, whether it was expressed in due form. If the recognition was declared in a country different from that of the domicile, it depends on the law of the domicile whether the formalities of the *lex loci actus* are to be observed. On the model of canon law[3] many legal systems deny the privilege of legitimation to children born in adultery or incest; thus French, Italian, Spanish, Scottish, South African laws. Others, such as German, Swiss, and Scandinavian laws, do not exclude from legitimation issue born in adultery, or even *liberi incestuosi* in those rare cases where in spite of the incest the marriage between the parents is valid.[4] The English Legitimacy Act, 1926,[5] takes the former view: the offspring of an adulterous union cannot be legitimated by subsequent marriage. But this is merely a rule of English municipal law. Where under English private international law the law of the father's foreign domicile applies, the English rule against the legitimation

---

[1] Probably the old common law rule was based on the canonical theory of fictions. Commentators on the *Corpus iuris canonici* (for example, *Panormitanus ad* c. 6 X. 4, 17) justified legitimation by subsequent marriage by treating the marriage as if it had been concluded at the time of the birth of the child: 'fingitur matrimonium a principio fuisse contractum'. But retroactivity according to the doctrine assumed that the act would have been possible at the earlier date—in other words, that at the time of the birth the parents would have been able to conclude a valid marriage. See Esmein, *Le mariage en droit canonique*, II. 44, n. 3. De Becker, *De sponsal. et matrimonio* (Brussels, 1896) 374. Kogler, 25, *Zeitschr. d. Savigny Stiftung (German Abt.)* 94. Modern canon law rejects any retroactive effect of the legitimation; c. 1116, 1117 *cod. iur. can.*; see Triebs, *Handbuch des kanon. Eherechtsist.* IV (1932), 677.

[2] As to acquisition of British nationality by legitimation see s. 23 (2) British Nationality Act, 1948.

[3] Now: *cod. iur. canonici*, c. 1116.

[4] For example, where, as in Portuguese law, the marriage between first cousins was prohibited as incestuous at the time of the birth of the child, but owing to a change of legislation was allowed at the time of the marriage between its parents. Another example may be found in modern English law, when a divorced husband begets a child on the body of his former wife's sister and marries her after his first wife's death.

[5] s. 1 (2).

of *adulterini* is inapplicable, and it depends solely on the law of domicile whether the *adulterinus* is legitimated[1] or not.

The law of the father's domicile also governs

374. Effects of legitimation

(*b*) The effects of legitimation. It decides above all whether legitimation creates a status of full legitimacy from the date of the marriage or with retroactive effect from the time of the birth. Retroactivity is perhaps[2] the English rule, while most continental rules reject it. Nearly everywhere legitimate and legitimated children have identical legal status. But there are some exceptions, for example, in respect of property passing with a dignity or a title of honour,[3] and the exclusion of a legitimated person from succession to land as an 'heir'[4] or to fiefs.[5] Such exceptional rules concerning succession to land apply if they are embodied in the law of the *situs fundi*. Whether a legitimated child acquires its father's nationality or not is a question for the law of the state to which the father belongs.[6] Whether it can succeed to its father's property on intestacy depends on the legal system governing succession, that is, for immovables the *lex situs* and for movables the law of the father's last domicile. If according to these rules a legitimated child can succeed, the question whether the child is legitimated is (probably) answered by the law applicable according to the conflict rule of the legal system governing succession.[7]

375. Legitimation by rescript or recognition

2. The question what law governs the legitimation by rescript of the Sovereign or state and the legitimation by simple recognition of paternity is not yet definitely settled. Continental conflict rules point either to the father's per-

---

[1] *In re Askew*, [1930] 2 Ch. 259; *Collins* v. *Att.-Gen.* (1931), 47 T.L.R. 484. In the former case both the birth of the child and the marriage of its parents took place before the coming into force of the Legitimacy Act; in the latter case both birth and marriage took place after it had come into force.

[2] If Scott, L.J., in *Re Luck*, [1940] Ch. 864, 898, 899 is right (?)

[3] See s. 10 of the English Act. *Codex iur. canon.*, c. 232, § 2, no. 1; c. 331 § 1, no. 1; c. 320 § 2.

[4] Cf. *Birtwhistle* v. *Vardill* (1826), 5 B. & C. 438; (1830), 2 Cl. & Fin. 571, 582; (1840), 7 Cl. & Fin. 895, 940.

[5] See *Libri feudorum* (twelfth century) II. 26 § 1: 'naturales filii, licet postea fiant legitimi, ad successionem feudi nec soli nec cum aliis vocantur'. *Contra*: German feudal law; see German Supreme Court, *Offic. Coll.*, 12, 239.

[6] *Abraham* v. *Att.-Gen.*, [1934] P. 17, 25.

[7] See F. A. Mann, loc. cit., at p. 127 et seq., and *supra*, s. 196.

sonal law at the date of the purported legitimation (German system) or to both the father's and the child's personal laws (French, Swiss, and Italian systems). Neither group takes into consideration the law at the time of the child's birth. In this English law differs from both. The question was raised in *Re Luck*.[1] The facts were as follows: David Luck, a bastard, was born (1906) in California, where his mother was domiciled, while his father had an English domicile. Later (1925) the father acquired a Californian domicile, married a woman not the mother of his son, and by an act called adoption recognized the boy as his legitimate child, thereby causing him to become legitimate from the time of his birth according to Californian law. The Court of Appeal by a majority decision (Scott, L.J., dissenting) held that he had remained a bastard. It applied by way of analogy the old Common Law rule established for cases of subsequent marriage. Consequently a legitimation by recognition would require that the father's personal law both at the time of the child's birth and at the date of recognition should permit legitimation by recognition.[2] Whether this analogy is justifiable is, however, open to doubt. Scott, L.J., denied it in his dissenting judgment; in his view only the date of recognition should be taken into consideration. It is suggested that this view is preferable at least in those cases where the act of recognition has no retroactive effect.[3]

The law of the father's domicile determines also the effect of a valid legitimation by rescript or recognition. Children legitimated in one of these ways do not as a rule acquire the full legal position of legitimate children,[4] as do the children legitimated by subsequent marriage.

[1] [1940] Ch. 323 and (C.A.) 864.
[2] In the case of legitimation by rescript the old Common Law rule is certainly not applicable.
[3] See *supra*, p. 395, n. 1.
[4] Different: Swiss Civil Code, s. 263. Cf. *supra*, p. 394, n. 1.

BIBLIOGRAPHY

R. S. WELSH, 63 *L.Q.R.* (1947) 65–93. F. A. MANN, 57 *L.Q.R.* (1941) 112. GOODRICH, *Confl. of Laws* 370–80; 22 *Mich. L.R.* (1924) 638 et seq. CHESHIRE, 514–30. DICEY–MORRIS, 496–511. RABEL, I. 571–609. POLLOCK, 26 *Cornell L.Q.* (1941) 460. VEITH, *RVglHWB* IV 432 et seq. See also 59 *Harv. L.R.* (1945) 128. TAINTOR, 18 *Can. B.R.* 589. KEITH, 22 *J. Comp. Leg.* (1940) 231.

ADOPTION

376. Great differences in the various municipal laws I. Legitimation is the legalization of a natural relationship, of genuine consanguinity. Adoption constitutes an artificial relationship, a fictitious consanguinity. Its conditions, its aims, and its effect differ widely in the various countries and under the various types of civilization. In Eastern Asia adoption serves to maintain ancestor-worship; in ancient European laws it was a means of strengthening weakened families. In modern Europe adoption serves the individual interest of childless persons and is encouraged by various states in the case of parentless children, notably after great wars. In many countries a father is permitted to adopt his own illegitimate children,[1] though this is not the main aim of the institution of adoption and is even prohibited under some modern systems (Italy,[2] Bulgaria, and, until 1914, Austria). English and Swedish law only permit adoption in the case of minors; but in most countries no such restriction obtains. The age at which one is allowed to adopt a person varies from country to country.[3] The Roman law rule that adoption imitates nature and therefore the adopter must be considerably older than the adopted person prevails everywhere, but there is much diversity in detail.[4] Methods of adoption also vary greatly. Most countries require an adoption agreement between the adopter and the person to be adopted or his legal representative; as a rule the consent of other persons (the child's parents, the adopter's spouse) and confirmation of the adoption by the court or other authority are necessary, and while under most legal systems (England, Italy, Spain, Switzerland, the Scandinavian states) it is within the discretion of the court to grant or refuse confirmation, German and Austrian law give the parties the right to claim judicial confirmation if all the legal prerequisites of adoption are fulfilled.[5]

[1] Thus now in England; Adoption of Children Act, 1949 (12, 13, 14 Geo. VI, c. 98), s. 1. On Californian law, see *Re Luck*, [1940] Ch. 864.

[2] Italian *Codice civile*, s. 293.

[3] 50 years, Germany; 45, Spain; 40, Switzerland, France, Austria; 25, England (s. 2, Adoption of Children Act, 1949) and Scandinavian states.

[4] The difference in age is mostly 18 years (Germany, Italy, Switzerland, &c.); in England 21 years.

[5] An exception to this is to be found in the German law of 23 Nov. 1933.

An even greater variety is to be found in respect of the effects of adoption. Generally the rights and duties of the natural parents or the guardian in relation to custody and education are extinguished and replaced by corresponding rights and duties on the part of the adopter; only in Italy does the parental power remain with the natural parents, the adopter acquiring merely the right to grant or refuse the parental marriage consent. English law, on the other hand, even looks on the natural parents' duty of mainten-ance as entirely extinguished and replaced by the adopter's obligation.[1] Everywhere the adoption creates a kind of relationship between the adopter and the adopted child; a few laws extend this relationship to the issue of the adopted child (Italy, Austria, and, with certain limitations, Germany). There are, finally, manifold solutions of the difficult problem of intestate succession. Most European laws grant the child succession both to the property of its natural parents and to the adopter's property, while on the child's death only the natural parents succeed *ab intestato*, and not the adopter. The English Act, 1926, differed from this in so far as here the adoption order did not 'confer on the child any right to property as a child of the adopter'. But the Adoption of Children Act, 1949,[2] provides that adopted persons are treated as children of the adopter for the pur-poses of intestacies, wills, and settlements. In many states of the United States of America adoption extinguishes all succession rights between the child and its natural family and creates full reciprocal rights of succession between the adopter and the adopted child.

II. Conflict rules concerning adoption usually declare the adopter's personal law to be decisive.[3] In France the ques-tion is controversial; by way of a wrong analogy drawn from legitimation some authors—and for that matter some decisions—accept the rule of the adopter's personal law. The prevailing opinion in France, however, points to a

377.
Applicable
law

---

[1] Adoption of Children Act, 1926 (16 & 17 Geo. V, c. 29) s. 5 (1)—a sur-prising rule unknown to continental laws.
[2] 12, 13 & 14 Geo. VI, c. 98, s. 9.
[3] Thus in Germany, Switzerland, Austria, Poland, Denmark.

cumulation of the law of the adopter and that of the adopted person, and this view is better founded.[1] It has been accepted by the laws of Norway, Sweden, Finland, and the Código Bustamante. Legitimation allows the child's personal law to be entirely disregarded, because as a rule it improves the child's position by legalizing an existing factual relationship. Adoption possibly worsens it, because it destroys or loosens the child's ties with its natural parents and grants dangerous powers to a stranger in blood—unless the adopter is the natural father or mother or other relative of the adopted child.

378. English law   English law has not yet developed a comprehensive conflict rule. Before the Adoption of Children Act, 1926, the institution of adoption did not exist in English municipal law, and foreign adoptions were not recognized in this country. The statute of 1926, amended by two Acts of 1939 and 1949,[2] only contains a rule dealing with the jurisdiction of the English court to issue an adoption order. It seems that thereby the application of the English Act has been implicitly determined; viz., only if the adoption order is to be made by an English court is the adoption governed by English law, and no other law is apparently applicable. The English court has no power to make an adoption order if the adopter is not resident in England or Wales and is not domiciled in England and Wales or in Scotland. The order can be made (since 1950) in respect of any infant who is or is not a British subject and who is resident in England or in Wales.

Example: Adopter and child are domiciled in England, but resident in Denmark. The English court has no jurisdiction to make the order.

379. Recognition of foreign adoptions in England?   Are *foreign* adoptions to be recognized by English courts? The Act is silent on this point. Probably the answer is:

(i) *no* if the English court has jurisdiction to make the order. Example: a German adopter domiciled in England but resident in Germany, the child being of British nationality and resident in England, concludes an adoption agreement valid in Germany and obtains the confirmation of the

[1] See on all this Mann, 57 L.Q.R., 123.
[2] Adoption of Children (Regulations) Act, 1939; 2 & 3 Geo. VI, c. 27; Adoption of Children Act, 1949, 12, 13 & 14 Geo. VI, c. 98.

German court.[1] The adoption will (probably) not be recognized in this country. It is, of course, open to the adopter to make a new application for an English adoption order if the conditions of English municipal law are fulfilled.

(ii) *yes* in other cases, that is, where neither party has an English domicile or residence; provided however that the foreign adoption has been made in conformity with the laws of both (the adopter's and the child's) domiciles. An adoption not permissible under one of these domiciliary laws would probably not be recognized in this country, and only the effects common to both these laws can take place. This seems to be a very severe—perhaps too severe—restriction on the recognition of foreign adoptions. But one must consider that until 1926 foreign adoptions were under no conditions whatever recognized in this country, and one may even doubt whether such recognition is allowed now.

One exception to the principle proposed here should however be accepted. In the case of a father adopting his illegitimate child the child's personal law need not be consulted; for such adoption being nothing but a legitimation by recognition should not be treated differently from any other form of legitimation. That such exception is justifiable is shown by the decision of the Appeal Court in *Re Luck*.[2]

Where the domicile of the adopter or of the child has changed before the adoption is completed the time at which the adoption is completed is decisive. Nobody will be inclined to take the date of the child's birth into consideration, as does the majority decision of the Court of Appeal in *Re Luck* in a case of legitimation. If, for example, the child is born in Portugal as a Portuguese subject (Portugal allows no adoption) and later becomes a domiciled Spanish national, adoption thereby becomes permissible, and there is no reason to think that a child should be capable of being adopted only if it had at the time of its birth the 'capacity of changing its status for one of being an adopted child', to use (slightly altered) the phrase framed by an English court in the case of legitimation.[3]

380.
Change of domicile

---

[1] This is in accordance with German law. See German Introduct. Law, s. 22; German Law on Voluntary Jurisdiction (of 17 May 1898), s. 66.

[2] [1940] Ch. 864.   [3] *Supra*, p. 394.

If after a valid adoption the adopter's or the child's domicile is changed, the relationship thus created is governed by the new law. The principle of mutability obtains here, just as in the case of the natural relationship between parents and children. The protection of the adopted child, however, demands one limitation to this rule. If by the law of the new domicile the adopter has more extensive rights than under the law under which the adoption was made, such rights must not be exercised; thus in a case where under the law of the old domicile (for example, under English law before 1950) the adopter had no right of administration or usufruct over the child's property, while the new law (for example, German law) gives him administration and usufruct,[1] no such rights may be exercised. If the law of the new domicile does not allow adoption—as was the case in England before 1926—the adoption becomes ineffective for the time being, though not void.

A dissolution of the adoption relationship is governed by the law of the domicile at the time of dissolution.

BIBLIOGRAPHY

FÜRER, *Adoption, Legitimation und Kindesanerkennung im internationalen Recht*, 1926. F. A. MANN, 57 *L.Q.R.* (1941), 112. RABEL, I. 632–58. GOODRICH, 381–87. NIBOYET, *Traité* V 492–8. Cf. *RVglHWB*, II. 43; IV. 435, and *supra*, p. 397.

ILLEGITIMATE CHILDREN

381.
Notion of illegitimacy

I. A child is illegitimate if there is no man under whose personal law it would be deemed to be his legitimate child. In order to ascertain the legitimacy or otherwise of a given person, therefore, recourse should not be had to the personal law of that person. This is particularly so in England, where the personal law is determined by domicile and the domicile of a child is dependent on its being legitimate or not. It is the personal law of the alleged father that must provide the starting-point of investigations. If under the law of his domicile the child is his legitimate child it is irrelevant that under the law of the mother's domicile it would be illegitimate. And if under the personal law of a

---

[1] S. 1757, 1767, German Civ. Code.

man the child is not his, or is not legitimate, it must be ascertained whether there exists any other male person whose domiciliary law affirms his paternity and the child's legitimacy. If there again the answer is *no*, the child is illegitimate.[1]

Illegitimacy exists also in respect of the child's relationship to its mother. Though under most modern laws the relationship between a bastard and its mother is nearly the same as that between a legitimate child and its mother,[2] there are differences. Under German law, for example, the mother of an illegitimate child has no 'parental power';[3] and if a testator bequeaths funds to the legitimate children of a woman any child of hers would be excluded which is not looked upon as her husband's legitimate offspring by *his* personal law, even though *her* personal law affirms its legitimacy and her husband's paternity.[4]

This does not mean, however, that if a person is a legitimate child of the man *A* it is necessarily regarded as his legitimate child everywhere. Thus in *Shaw* v. *Gould*[5] the House of Lords, though deeming Elizabeth's children illegitimate, conceded that a Scottish court would be bound to regard them as legitimate. Another illustration: an Italian national domiciled in England is subject to English law (as his personal law) in this country, and to Italian law in Italy; a child begotten by him in a marriage which is valid in England but void in Italy is legitimate here and a bastard there. Limping marriages lead to limping legitimacies.

382. 'Limping' legitimacies

It is hardly necessary to add that the unfortunate discordance which arises from the differences between the various legal systems and from the non-recognition of many foreign divorce decrees may have the startling result

---

[1] See *supra*, s. 101.

[2] For example, in respect of the mother's right to custody, of succession, &c. See the French adage, 'nul n'est bâtard de par sa mère.'

[3] German Civ. C., s. 1707.

[4] Example of different personal laws: both spouses are domiciled in Italy, where the personal law is determined by nationality. If then the husband is a national of the state *X*, and the wife of *Y*, they have different personal laws. Owing to the rule of *renvoi* this is so even in England.

[5] (1868) L.R. 3 H.L.Cas. 55. See *supra*, p. 386. Cf. also Lord Brougham's observation in *Birtwhistle* v. *Vardill* (1835), 2 Cl. & Fin. 582, 595.

that the same person is the legitimate child of *A* according to the law of *A*'s domicile and the legitimate child of *B* under the latter's domiciliary law. This would have happened, for example, in the case *Shaw* v. *Gould* if the facts were altered in one point.

As stated above, p. 386, Elizabeth Hickson married first the Englishman Buxton and later, after a divorce in Scotland, the Englishman, later domiciled Scotsman, Shaw. The divorce was not recognized in England, but was to be regarded as valid in Scotland. If she had had sexual intercourse with both her 'husbands' during the period of gestation, her children would *prima facie* be treated as legitimate children of Buxton in England and as legitimate children of Shaw in Scotland.

383. Child and mother

II. The relationship between an illegitimate child and its *mother* is in most countries determined by the mother's personal law, which usually coincides with the child's personal law. The *Código Bustamante* declares the child's law to be decisive, and Italian law requires observance of the provisions both of the mother's and of the child's law. English law has not yet answered the question. It is probable that an English court would accept the prevailing continental view and apply only the law of the mother's domicile, from which after all the child's domicile *of origin* is derived. If later the mother's domicile changes the law of the new domicile applies.

The exercise of the mother's rights and duties in respect of the child's person, in particular custody and education, is everywhere controlled, corrected, and complemented by the law of the country where the child is living, just as is the exercise of the father's power over the person of a legitimate child.

384. Child and father. Various systems

III. Whether a legal relationship between the bastard and its *father* comes into existence, and what rights and duties such relationship includes, is one of the most discussed questions in private international law. Every imaginable point of contact has been recommended by legal writers, considered by courts, and introduced into modern codes. In the foreground of these controversies is the problem of the father's duty to maintain the child.[1] The old judicial

---

[1] Gutteridge, 2 *Internat. L.Q.* (1948), p. 155 et seq.

practice in German common law regarded extra-matri-
monial sexual intercourse as a delict or quasi-delict[1] and the
father's duty to maintain the offspring of such intercourse
as a delictual obligation to pay damages. This view cannot
explain the *child's* right to damages, as it is extravagant to
treat a person as injured by the fact of having been brought
into existence. The doctrine led to the application either of
the *lex fori* or the law of the place where the delict was committed, that is, where the child was begotten.[2] Most legal
systems rightly recognize to-day that the source of the duty
of maintenance is the natural blood-relationship, the consanguinity existing between father and child. From this
point of view one is likely to come to the conclusion that
either the father's personal law or the child's personal law
should prevail, since it is between these two persons that a
relationship has been created. Many modern laws have
chosen the father's personal law (Swiss, Spanish, Danish,
Baltic laws, &c.), because the law of a putative debtor is the
appropriate system to decide whether, under what conditions, and for what amount the obligation exists. French
law,[3] Polish law, and the *Código Bustamante*[4] prefer the personal law of the child, because it is the child's status from
which the obligation arises. Some French decisions tend
towards a cumulation of the two legal systems and rule that
the duty of maintenance exists only if and in so far as it is
recognized by both. This doctrine, which at first sight
appears more equitable than any other, is in reality—as
Niboyet rightly says—'too perfect, and this renders it
unjust'. Such cumulation of prerequisites may make it
very difficult to establish any liability on the part of the
father. There is no justification for the system adopted
by the German code,[5] under which the maintenance
duty incumbent on the father is governed neither by the
father's nor by the child's but by the mother's personal law
at the time of the birth of the child. Only the fact that

---

[1] Windscheid, *Pandekten*, II. § 475, n. 18.
[2] See Gierke, *Deutsches Privatrecht*, I. 242, n. 119.
[3] Though this is subject to controversy; Niboyet, *Manuel*, 762.
[4] Art. 64 (see, however, art. 63).
[5] Introduct. Law, art. 21.

in most (though not in all)[1] cases the mother's personal law coincides with the child's makes the German rule tolerable.

385. In particular: *lex fori* doctrine

Finally, there are countries where all (or the main) questions concerning the father's duty to support his bastard are governed by the *lex fori*. This is based on one of two reasons:

(*a*) On the conception of *ordre public*. Rules such as the French 'la recherche de la paternité est interdite' are founded on the conviction that in the interest of morality legal claims and judicial proceedings built on extramatrimonial intercourse should be excluded,[2] and that the admission of such claims would entail blackmail and a disturbance of family life. Where, on the other hand, the French code and the French statute of 1912 permit inquiry into paternity (for example, in the cases of rape, seduction, or concubinage) *ordre public* according to some French decisions demands application of the French rule, even where under the personal law of the parties inquiry is forbidden.[3] In German law considerations of public policy have led to the principle that a German court must not enforce claims for the support of bastards which go beyond those admitted under German municipal law.[4]

386. English system

Or (*b*) on the conception of bastardy law as part of the *Poor Law*. That is the starting-point of English and Anglo-American law on the subject. The father's duty to maintain his illegitimate child is regarded only as a natural obligation, and common law provides no means for its enforcement. Those foreign laws therefore that grant the child a maintenance action against its father would be regarded in England and the United States as inapplicable, though no English decisions on this point have been reported. The American *Restatement*[5] declares that 'no action can be

---

[1] The present writer's attention was directed to a case where a Scottish waitress resident in Berlin had given birth to a child begotten by a German national. The relationship between the stateless bastard and the German father had to be determined by Scottish law!

[2] Thus Savigny, VIII, p. 279 (Guthrie's transl., p. 255).

[3] See Niboyet, loc. cit., and *supra*, p. 170.

[4] Introductory Law, art. 21 i.f.

[5] s. 454.

maintained on a foreign bastardy statute', and the same is probably true for English law. But in both countries bastardy proceedings against the father, initiated by the state or a public corporation or by the mother, have become permissible on the basis of statutory law. Their aim is to relieve the parish, the state, the town, and ultimately the taxpayer of their burden of supporting the bastard. The relevant statutes are concerned with public (administrative) law, viz. with the organization of public assistance to destitute persons.[1] The English Poor Law Acts give the Justices of the Peace jurisdiction at Petty Sessions to compel the father by a bastardy order to make certain contributions to the maintenance of the child. But the child itself has no civil action against its father, and no legal duty rests on him until a bastardy order is made. The right of an illegitimate child under foreign law to claim *perpetual* maintenance against its father was regarded by an English court as contrary to public policy, and recognition of a foreign judgment based on such right was refused.[2]

The jurisdiction of the justices to make a bastardy order presupposes that the father is 'present' in this country, and that

(*a*) either the child was born in England or Wales[3] or on a British ship[4] (the place of sexual intercourse, the parents' domicile or residence, and their nationality[5] have no bearing on the matter);

(*b*) or, in the case of a child born abroad, that the mother is domiciled in this country, so that 'no other than English law has to be considered' in ascertaining the child's status.[6] The mother's nationality or residence and the father's nationality, residence, or domicile are immaterial.

Where one of these prerequisites of jurisdiction is lacking, no action lies in this country. The result is highly

---

[1] *Reg.* v. *Blane* (1849), Ad. & E. 13 Q.B. 769, 772.

[2] *In re Macartney*, [1921] 1 Ch. 522.

[3] *Reg.* v. *Blane*, loc. cit.

[4] *Marshall* v. *Murgatroyd* (1870), L.R. 6 Q.B. 31.

[5] *Hampton* v. *Rickard* (1874), 30 L.T. (N.S.) 636 (*per* Cockburn, C.J., and Blackburn, J.).

[6] *R.* v. *Humphreys*, [1914] 3 K.B. 1236, 1240, where Bankes, J., explained (or rather corrected ?) the old judgment in *Reg.* v. *Blane, supra*.

unsatisfactory. It is difficult to understand why English law lays stress on the place of the child's birth.

Take, for example, the following case: Father, mother, and child are resident in England. The mother has a French domicile of origin and being herself a minor cannot acquire an English domicile of choice. She goes to Belgium for her confinement, intending to return to England with her child. Then nothing can be done in this country to make the father liable for any payment. Another case: a German father, obliged under German law to maintain his illegitimate (German) child, came as a refugee from Nazi oppression to England; the mother and the bastard followed him (without acquiring an English domicile of choice); then all duty of maintenance ceases and the father's legal obligation becomes an unenforceable natural obligation.

BIBLIOGRAPHY

RABEL, *Conflict of Laws*, I. 610–31. REXROTH, *RVgl HWB*. VI. 633–76. VEITH, ibid. IV. 427–32. NIBOYET, *Traité*, V. 476–89.

CHAPTER XXVI

GUARDIANSHIP

I. Continental laws distinguish between parents and guardians. The conception of guardianship (*tutela*) is confined to cases where 'parental power' is lacking, in particular where orphans or lunatics are in need of protection. English law differs from this. It reckons the parents among the guardians, they are 'guardians by nature and nurture'. In matters of detail, however, their position is slightly different from that of testamentary guardians or guardians appointed by the court. 387. Different conceptions of guardianship

There is another dissimilarity between the continental law systems and English law. While under both the guardian has the custody and tuition of the ward and to a certain degree the possession and management of the ward's property, only under continental laws is he the infant's legal representative. This enables him to conclude contracts on behalf of and binding on the infant, to represent his ward in lawsuits, and to validate contracts concluded by the latter by giving his consent in advance or by subsequent ratification. Under English law the guardian is never the ward's representative; where he acts in the ward's interest, he acts in his own name as a trustee, *domini loco*, as Paul and Justinian put it.[1] Nor is he able by his consent or ratification to supplement his ward's incapacity to contract.

As under all legal systems the aim of guardianship is to shield persons in need of protection on account of their infancy, lunacy, or other defects, it is obvious that everywhere the personal law of the ward, i.e. in England the law of his domicile,[2] governs all questions arising out of the ward's need for protection. The main questions are the following: 388. Applicable law: the ward's domiciliary law

1. How does a guardianship come into existence? Example: under some laws a person called by will to be a guardian becomes a guardian by the death of the testator; under other laws by an appointment by the court, to which

---

[1] *Dig.* 26. 7. 27.
[2] See, for example, *Monaco* v. *Monaco* (1937), 157 L.T. 231. Cf. Mann, 59 *L.Q.R.* 54, notes 58, 59.

he may or may not be legally entitled. The question as to which of the various laws decides this is answered by the personal law of the ward, and not by that of the testator at the time of his death.[1]

2. What are the effects of an existing guardianship? In particular, what are the rights, powers, and duties of a guardian in relation to his ward and to third parties?

3. When does an existing guardianship come to an end?

All these questions are answered by the ward's domiciliary law.

389. Encroach-ments on domiciliary law

II. The domain of the ward's personal law is, however, restricted by a series of factors.

1. Any state feels itself responsible for the welfare of children and insane persons who are actually *present* within its territory, irrespective of where they are domiciled or resident. If therefore an infant or a person of unsound mind is on English soil the English court will have to consider whether the protection given to the ward by his or her domiciliary law is sufficient, and how the public should be protected against a dangerous lunatic. This examination is, of course, subject to the law of the court. Thus the court will have to decide according to English law whether the right to custody and control over a foreign ward present in this country should be given to its father or to its mother (if the parents are divorced). The domiciliary law of the ward is superseded by the imperative rules of the English Guardianship of Infants Act, 1925,[2] which regards 'the welfare of the child as the first and paramount consideration, whatever orders may have been made by the courts of any other country'.[3]

---

[1] A different question is that of a person's right to refuse to be appointed guardian. This certainly does not depend on the ward's personal law. It is mostly thought that it depends on the personal law of the person declining to be nominated. It seems sounder to say that it is for the state which appoints the guardian (or where guardianship comes into existence) to say what persons within its territory are bound to accept such appointment.

[2] 15 & 16 Geo. V, c. 45, s. 1.

[3] *Re B.'s Settlement*, [1940] Ch. 54, 64. The 'weight to be attached to orders of the foreign court depends on the particular circumstances of the case'. The view taken by two older decisions—*Nugent* v. *Vetzera* (1866), L.R. 2 Eq. 704, and *Re Savini* (1870), 22 L.T. 61—in so far as it is contrary to the principles of the Guardianship of Infants Act, 1925, s. 1, was expressly disavowed by *Re B.'s Settlement*, loc. cit.

In one case it is not the (High) Court but the Secretary of State who appoints a guardian; Guardianship (Refugee 'Children) Act 1944.[1] This concerns children under 16 arriving in the United Kingdom after 1936 in consequence of war or of religious, racial, or political persecution if neither of its parents is in the United Kingdom. The High Court, however, is allowed to remove a guardian appointed by the Secretary of State and to appoint another guardian in his place.

2. Another question which has often been discussed in this country is whether a guardian appointed under the law and in the state of the ward's foreign domicile is entitled to act as such in England without having been reappointed by the English court. The answer to this is that the foreign guardian (curator, committee, and the like) has no 'right'; but his power to act will as a rule be recognized by the English court unless the refusal of recognition is more beneficial to the infant.[2] In any case, the powers of a foreign guardian to act in England are subject to a twofold limitation:

390. The power of foreign guardians

(*a*) He has no greater power than is granted to guardians under the law of the country where he was appointed. If the powers of an English guardian are wider than his, he cannot use them unless he is also appointed by the English court.

(*b*) He has no greater power than an English guardian has in the case of an English ward.[3] This refers both to the person and to the property of the ward. He can therefore not act as the 'legal representative' of the ward, even though under continental laws he is capable of binding the ward and not himself by contracts he concludes on behalf of his ward. His power to take possession of and manage the ward's movable property, and to claim payment of money due to a foreign ward, is subject to the discretion of the court.[4]

---

[1] 7 & 8 Geo. VI, c. 8, s. 1.

[2] 'The benefit of the infant which is the foundation of the jurisdiction must be the test of its right exercise'; *Johnstone* v. *Beatty* (1843), 10 Cl. & Fin. 42, 122; *Stuart* v. *Bute* (1861), 9 H.L. Cas. 440, 463. *Re D. (Infant)*, [1943] 1 Ch. 305. *Re X Settlement*, [1945], Ch. 44, 46.

[3] *Johnstone* v. *Beatty*, loc. cit., at pp. 113, 114.

[4] As to infants, see: *Re Hellmann* (1866), L.R. 2 Eq. 363; *Re Brown's Trust* (1865), 12 L.T. 488; *In re Chatard's Settlement*, [1899] 1 Ch. 712, 716; comp. *Scott* v. *Bently* (1855), 1 Lay & J. 281. As to lunatics: *In re Sottomaior* (1874), L.R. 9 Ch. App. 677, 679; *In re Burbridge*, [1902] 1 Ch. 426; *Didisheim* v. *London Westminster Bank*, [1900] 2 Ch. 15, 51; *Pélégrin* v. *Couts*, [1915] 1 Ch. 696.

If the English court in the exercise of its discretion appoints a guardian, or in the case of a lunatic a curator or a committee, the foreign guardian or curator loses his *locus standi* here.[1]

391.
British wards

3. All these encroachments on the domiciliary law of the ward apply equally to the case of a ward of British nationality not domiciled, resident, or even present in England.[2] It is regarded as 'one of the incidents of a British-born subject that he is entitled to the protection of the Crown as *parens patriae*', as Lord Cranworth, L.C., said in *Hope* v. *Hope*.[3]

392. *Lex situs*

4. Finally: the guardianship in so far as immovable property is concerned is entirely governed by the *lex situs*, therefore by English law if the immovables are situate in this country.[4] This rule, unknown to continental laws, may result—in the case of land situate on the continent—in the application of the personal law of the ward by way of *renvoi* from the *lex situs* either to the *lex patriae* or to the *lex domicilii*.

---

[1] Examples (in the case of lunacy): *Re Bariatinski (Princess)* (1843), 1 Phil. 375; *Re Burbidge, supra*; *In re R.S.A.*, [1901] 2 K.B. 32.

[2] *Johnstone* v. *Beatty* (1843), 10 Cl. & Fin. 42, 120, 122. *Hope* v. *Hope* (1854), 4 De G.M. & G. 328, 345, 346. *In re Willoughby (An Infant)* (1885), 30 Ch.D. (C.A.) 324. *In re Bourgoise* (1889), L.R. 41 Ch.D. (C.A.) 310, 318–21. See the Irish case *Re Pavitt*, [1907] 1 Ir. Rep. 234.

[3] *Supra*, at p. 345.

[4] Dicey–Morris, 537, n. 50.

BIBLIOGRAPHY

ROBERTSON, 59 *Juridical Rev.* (1947), 70 et seq. (contrasts English and Scottish law). KEITH, 22 *J. Comp. Leg.* (1940), 234.

PART V

OBLIGATIONS

CHAPTER XXVII

CONTRACTS

THE CHOICE OF LAW BY THE PARTIES

THE term 'contract' is used here in the narrow sense attributed to it by English jurisprudence. It means an agreement between two or more parties which, in accordance with their intention, imposes a duty on at least one of them, the promisor, and creates for the promisee a right to claim fulfilment of the promise. Agreements creating a status, such as marriage or adoption, and agreements transferring or extinguishing *iura in rem*, such as the conveyance of property, the assignment of a debt, or the creation of a mortgage, are not contracts.

And yet the conflict rules relative to contracts, notably the principle that the parties are entitled to choose the legal system that shall govern their contract, are also applied to certain agreements or unilateral acts-in-law which are not —or not entirely—in the nature of contracts. Marriage settlements in particular, which do not, or do not only, create obligations *inter partes*, but *iura in rem* effective *vis-à-vis* everybody, are governed by the law chosen by the party or parties.[1] Similarly in the case of a deed of arrangement made in Scotland by a domiciled Englishman who resided in Scotland, the question whether the deed was to be registered was answered by reference to the law which the debtor had in view when signing the deed. English law required registration, Scottish law did not; the court applied Scottish law in accordance with the presumptive intention of the debtor.[2]

I. What law pronounces on the validity and determines

393. Meaning of the term 'contract'

394. Two divergent views on the applicable law

---

[1] *Chamberlain* v. *Napier* (1880), 15 Ch.D. 614. *In re Hewitt's Settlement*, [1915] 1 Ch. 228, 232. *Re Fitzgerald*, [1904] 1 Ch. 573, and others.

[2] *Re Pilkington's Trust*, [1937] 3 A.E.R., 213, 218.

the effect of a contract? There are two divergent opinions on this. Some legal writers, particularly in France, Germany, and Italy, advocate the doctrine that the answer (as in other departments of law) must be sought in the conflict rules of the forum. Other writers, and the courts in nearly all countries, assign the task of choosing the applicable law to the *contracting parties*. Just as the parties are permitted to create rights and duties between themselves as they please, and thus to 'make law for themselves',[1] so it is for them to determine the law governing their contract.

395. The autonomy doctrine. Objections

This doctrine of the 'autonomy' of the parties has often been branded as illogical. The objectors say: before we can state that an agreement between the parties determines the law governing the contract, we must first ascertain what law determines the validity of that agreement itself. The answer to this objection is simple: the rule stating that the parties have the power to determine the 'proper' law of their contract or, to put it differently, that the *lex voluntatis* governs the contract, is a legal rule forming part of the private international law of most countries. Another objection raised against the doctrine of autonomy is that here private individuals are entrusted with a task which is normally fulfilled by the law, namely, that of determining the applicable law. Indeed, the autonomy of the parties is an emergency solution arising out of the difficulties encountered by any law when it attempts to submit contracts to any particular fixed system of legal rules. Such attempts have often been made. Some authors[2] and the American *Restatement*[3] test the validity and the effects of a contract by the law of the place of contracting; often however it is a matter of chance whether the contract was concluded in this that or the other country, for example when the con-

---

[1] Cf. art. 1134 *code civil*: 'les conventions légalement formées tiennent lieu de loi à ceux qui les ont faites.' This article of the civil code has been used in France (with regard to *contrats internationaux*) as foundation for the thesis that the parties may exclude the subjection of their contract to *any* law, so that the contract is the only *loi* governing their relations. See J. Donnedieu de Vabres, *Évolution de la jurisprudence*, pp. 516–53. Cf. the present writer's article in *Grotius Soc.* 1950.

[2] In particular French and Italian scholars (Foelix, Laurent, Brocher, Fiore).

[3] s. 332 et seq., 346, 347. Similar: Polish Law of 1926, s. 8, 9; Italian *cod. civ.* (1865) art. 9 § 2, new *cod. civ.* (1938, 1942) *Dispos. prelim.* art. 15 § 2.

tract was made by telephone between London and Paris or by correspondence in which over a long period the parties make proposals and counter-proposals before they reach agreement, and where it is often difficult to say which of them was ultimately the 'offerer' and which the 'acceptor'. Many authors, particularly in Germany, regard the law of the place of performance or the law of the debtor's residence[1] as the most appropriate test. But both these doctrines lead to an unsatisfactory scission of the contract in all cases where both contracting parties are debtors (as in the case of a contract of sale) and where they reside in different countries and each party has to fulfil his obligation at his own place of residence. The most inadmissible of all doctrines hitherto set up is Zitelmann's,[2] accepted by Frankenstein;[3] in their opinion the contract should be governed by the national law of the debtor. The reason given for this is the arbitrary contention that only the state of which a person is a member (national) is entitled to issue orders to him.

The over-rigidity of all these formulas is beginning to be acknowledged even by some of those who are opposed to the autonomy of the parties, and many efforts have been directed to finding a more elastic formula. It has been proposed that the *judge*, taking into consideration all accompanying circumstances, should in each individual case before him establish the law with which the contract has the most real connexion, and that the law thus found by the judge should be the proper law of the contract. Nowhere, however, has this doctrine been accepted by the courts. According to almost universal practice it is the task neither of the law nor of the judge to determine the proper law of the contract. It is for the parties themselves to select from the various legal systems that system which shall govern the contract. This doctrine is beyond doubt the prevailing law in England. Numerous decisions have pronounced that, as Dicey formulated it, the proper law of a contract is the law by which the contracting parties intended it to be

396. Determination of the law by the judge?

---

[1] Thus: von Bar, II. 13 (Engl. transl., p. 543).
[2] Zitelmann, II. 366.
[3] Frankenstein, II. 126.

governed.[1] Perhaps even preferable is the formula framed by Lord Mansfield:[2] it is decisive whether 'the parties, at the time of making the contract, had *a view* to (the laws of England or to) a different kingdom'.

This rule is a wise one. It is often a difficult matter to find the local centre of gravity of a contract containing foreign elements. Opinions of the best legal or commercial experts may differ widely. The contracting parties' own interest in the matter makes them the best judges.

397. Application of all parts of the chosen law

By choosing a particular legal system the parties subject their contract to *all* legal provisions embodied in that system. These provisions, however, are either compulsory (imperative or prohibitory; *ius cogens*) or optional (*ius dispositivum*), that is, subject to alterations by the contracting parties. Most legal rules relating to the effects of contracts are of the second kind; and if the parties have chosen a legal system, it goes without saying that they may exclude any of the optional rules which form part of that legal system, for example, rules on the warranties or the passing of the risk to the buyer. Not so in respect of compulsory rules. Once the parties have chosen their law, they are subject to all compulsory rules embodied in it.

An example of this: The parties concluding a contract of carriage by sea from England to the foreign country *A* agree that the contract shall be governed by English law. English law has adopted the Hague Rules, under which the liability of the carrier for negligence of the master or servants cannot be validly excluded. If nevertheless parties have agreed to exclude such liability the exclusion is void, even if such exclusion is permissible under the law of the country *A*.

398. Limits of autonomy

II. The autonomy of the parties has its limits. One of these limits is beyond doubt and recognized everywhere: the parties have no power to exclude by their choice of law the rules of public or distinctive policy of the forum. A contract offending against the interest of the British state or against the English conception of morality cannot be enforced in an English court, even though it may be valid under the proper law chosen by the contracting parties.

Another limitation of the autonomy of the contracting

[1] Dicey–Morris 579. See, for example, the statement of Lord Wright in *Mount Albert Borough Council* v. *Australasian Temperance Society*, [1938] A.C. (P.C.) 224, 240.   [2] In *Robinson* v. *Bland* (1760), 2 Burr. 1077.

parties follows from the rule that the parties can only choose an existing municipal legal system. They are not at liberty to subject their contract to a legal system which is no longer in force, or to the draft of a foreign code or to a system which they have freely invented. Further, they cannot declare that their contract shall be governed only by the rules of public international law, that is by those rules which the International Court of Justice would apply.[1]

The opposite view has been 'tentatively' proposed for 'commercialized contracts, between states or between a state and individuals (e.g. international loans).[2]

As to other limitations of the autonomy of contracting parties there is some diversity of opinion, though closer examination shows that the difference is not so great as appears at first sight.

1. According to prevailing *continental* doctrine and practice the parties can subject their contract only to a system of law with which it is *internally connected*, for example, to the law of the place of contracting, or of the place of performance, or of the domicile or nationality of one of the parties, and the like. They cannot set up as the proper law of their contract a system of law with which the contract has no connexion. Two domiciled Englishmen make a contract while travelling in France and decide on New York as the place of performance; they may select English, French, or New York law, but not, for instance, Chinese law. If they choose a law unconnected with their persons or their contract the proper law of the contract must be ascertained as if the parties had made no choice of law.[3] Suppose English law to be the system with which the contract has the most real connexion. This does not mean that Chinese law, on which the parties have agreed, is not applicable at all. But its application depends on whether it contravenes any of the *compulsory* (imperative) provisions of the proper, i.e. here English, law. As in contractual matters compulsory legal provisions are not frequent, the result will be as a rule

399. The continental doctrine

[1] Art. 38 of the Statute of the Intern. Court: application of the general principles recognized by civilized nations; decision *ex aequo et bono*.

[2] By Mann, *Brit. Y.B.* 1944, p. 11 et seq. Ph.C. Jessup, *A modern Law of Nations* (1948), 139. Cf. the present writer's article in *Grotius Soc.*, 1950.

[3] How this is to be done will be explained, *infra*, p. 482 et seq.

that the law chosen by the parties is applicable, even if internally it is not connected with the contract. This was, for example, the case in *Vita Food Products Inc.* v. *Unus Shipping Co.*[1] decided by the Privy Council. Here a transaction between residents in Newfoundland and New York relating to the carriage on a Canadian ship of goods from the former to the latter country had been subjected by agreement to English law. Although the contract contained nothing to connect it in any way with English law, the choice was considered to be fully valid and effective. This decision seems to be correct, because the law of Newfoundland—which would probably have been applied if the parties had not chosen English law—does not apparently contain any compulsory rule incompatible with English law.

That the parties must have the power to replace optional rules of the proper law by rules taken from any other legal system hardly needs proof. The choice of a foreign code in such cases is nothing more than the curtailment of clerical work; the articles of the code, instead of being set out in full, are simply referred to. As early as 1703[2] this was rightly recognized in a case where the contract declared the Custom of Paris of 1580 to be applicable; this reference in the contract was 'as much as if the custom had been recited at large'; and the Lords emphasized that it 'by no means involved an attempt to introduce foreign laws'.[3]

400. English law

2. *English* law starts from the principle of *unlimited autonomy* of the contracting parties. 'The intention expressed in the contract . . . will be conclusive' (Lord Atkin).[4] 'That the intention of the parties to a contract is the true criterion by which to determine by what law it is to be governed is too clear for controversy' (Lord Lindley).[5] 'The only question to be determined (is) the question what was the law which the parties contemplated as being the law governing the contract' (Lord Halsbury).[6] No principle of

---

[1] [1939] A.C. (P.C.) 277.
[2] *Foubert* v. *Turst,* 1 Brown Parl. Cas., 129.
[3] At that time English courts did not adjudicate cases under foreign law.
[4] [1937] A.C. 500, 529. (*R.* v. *International Trustee*).
[5] [1902] A.C. 446, 450. (*Spurrier* v. *La Cloche*).
[6] (1889) 42 Ch.D. 321, 336. (*In re Missouri Steamship Co.*).

English private international law has been expressed so often.

In *Vita Food Products* v. *Unus Shipping Co.*[1] the question was discussed whether this statement of the prevailing law was exhaustive or whether 'some qualifications are necessary'. The Privy Council (*per* Lord Wright) answered that 'it is difficult to see what qualifications are possible, provided the intention expressed is *bona fide* and legal, and provided there is no reason for avoiding the choice on the ground of public policy'. Of these three provisos the last is self-evident: a contract governed by a foreign legal system chosen by the parties but contrary to the public policy of the forum cannot be enforced at that forum.[2] The two other requirements, *bona fides* and legality, are not free from ambiguity. Is *bona fides* only excluded where the parties did not really intend what they declared to be their intention, where their declaration was feigned? Or also where they selected the law with the intention of evading some imperative or prohibitory rule of the legal systems internally connected with the contract? Probably the simple intention of eliminating certain compulsory rules which would normally be applicable is neither necessary nor sufficient to constitute *mala fides*; English law, as opposed to French law, has no objection to any artificial creation of points of contact, as explained above.[3] Something more than the desire to escape imperative provisions will be necessary under English law to make an intention *mala fide*, some morally impeachable or some anomalous and unreasonable choice of law is probably required.[4] Where some 'sound idea of business convenience and common sense'[5]

401.
Formula in
*Vita Food
Prod.* v.
Unus

---

[1] [1939] A.C. (P.C.) 277, 290, *per* Lord Wright. See also *Ocean Steamship Co.* v. *Queensland &c.*, [1941] 1 K.B. 402. Dicey–Morris, 581.

[2] It must be borne in mind that not every compulsory rule of the *lex fori* has the character of a rule of public policy (*ordre public*) in the meaning of Private International Law. The lack of consideration, for example, is a bar to the validity of a contract under English law, not under Italian law. Thus an Italian contract, under which the promise to pay money for services rendered in the past is valid, can be enforced in England. *In re Bonacina*, [1912] 2 Ch. (C.A.) 394.

[3] See *supra*, pp. 143–4.

[4] Anzilotti, *Il principio dell' autonomia* (*Diritto commerc.* XXII, 1904) aptly speaks of a *saggia e normale volontà*, as opposed to a *capricciosa*.

[5] Cf. *Jacobs, Marcus & Co.* v. *Crédit Lyonnais* (1884), 12 Q.B.D. (C.A.) 595.

may be behind the choice of law English courts will uphold the choice, even if there is no internal connexion between the contract and the selected system. Still more inexact is the requirement that the 'intention expressed' be *legal*. J. H. C. Morris and G. C. Cheshire rightly object that it is not stated by what law the legality of the intention is to be tested.[1] Does it merely mean that if a contract or its performance is illegal under the municipal law of the place of contracting or of the place of performance respectively, such illegality stands, whatever law the parties may have chosen?[2]

402.
Differences between the two views
The difference between the continental and the English doctrine is after all not so great as might appear at first sight. The continental doctrine permits the choice by the parties of any legal system with which the contract is internally connected and indeed, where no compulsory rules are concerned, of any legal system. The English doctrine allows the choice of any legal system on earth which may seem convenient for business purposes and reasonable. The difference is practically negligible if the conception of internal connexion is not too rigidly framed. When, for example, the Polish code of 1926 restricts the choice to five possible points of contact, viz. the place of contracting, the place of performance, the place where the object of the contract is situate, the domicile, and the nationality of either of the parties,[3] such restriction is too narrow. A merely economic connexion of the contract in question with some other previous or simultaneous contract or contracts, even with contracts made by other people, may be a sufficient reason for shifting the centre of gravity of the contract to the law of that other contract or contracts.

The American corn trade is accustomed to make use of the La Plata Grain Contract forms issued by the London Corn Trade Association which subject the parties to English law (and an English Arbitral Tribunal). If a German importer of American corn resells the goods bought under that contract to a German in Germany, he must also be able to have the resale

[1] 56 *L.Q.R.* (1940) 335. See Cheshire, 326 et seq. Cheshire, *Intern. Contracts* 31, Dicey–Morris 585. Cook 419–32. Falconbridge, 353–5.
[2] Cf. *The Torni*, [1932] P. 78, 88; *Ralli Bros.* v. *Compañia Naviera*, [1920] 2 K.B. (C.A.) 287, 304.
[3] Polish Law, 1926, art. 7.

governed by English law,[1] even if some imperative rule of German law thereby becomes inapplicable. Another example: in an Oriental settlement mainly inhabited by English traders it may be usual for them to conclude contracts of certain types with the natives under English law; if there are French merchants living in that settlement it will be understandable and reasonable that they too should submit their contracts with the natives to English law.

In some branches of commerce and transport there is a tendency towards international standardization or unification—it finds expression in the famous slogan: 'the law of the ocean must be one'. The goal, apart from international conventions, can be reached only by the subjection of all important contracts of a certain type to the same law, irrespective of nationality or residence of the contracting parties, of the place of contracting or performance, or of the flag of the ship. Though the *isolated* contract as such may have no 'internal connexion' with the chosen law, such connexion becomes manifest if one views that contract as a part of world economy. In those branches of commerce and transport where the contract forms generally used are written in English and drafted according to the customs of English commerce, a reference to English law is natural and reasonable; an internal connexion between each contract thus concluded and English law should therefore not be denied.[2]

3. In certain special circumstances, however, one more point remains to be considered:

403. Choice of the *lex fori*

No restriction whatever of the autonomy of the parties to a contract will be recognized in those cases where the law of the *forum* coincides with the law chosen by the parties. The court in which an action on a contract is brought will be only too glad if the parties when they concluded the contract agreed that the law of that court should apply. If, for example, by a contract of employment a Roumanian employee has promised the German employer to refrain for three years after the termination of the employment from competing in the employer's trade, and if the parties have expressly declared that the contract shall be governed by English law, though there is no internal connexion with English law, the English court, if seized of the matter, will

---

[1] See Haudek. loc. cit. 39 (who, however, dissents).
[2] See 49 *Jurid. Rev.* (1937), 120, 121.

probably apply English law—under which the clause of non-competition may be regarded as valid if the restraint is reasonable.[1] The court will neither look at German law, according to which a restraint for more than two years is ineffective, nor at Roumanian law under which any clause of non-competition seems to be void.

Another example: Two domiciled Italian nationals conclude in Lugano a contract which they submit to English law, because they wish to escape from certain imperative Italian rules. The English court will apply English law as the proper law of the contract and therefore disregard any Italian rules; if it finds that the contract has no valid consideration, it will declare the contract to be void, though Italian, and for that matter Swiss, law does not require consideration.

Such attitude of the courts of all countries is based not only on the natural inclination of every judge to apply the law of his country, but also on the rule that parties to a contract can always agree to the jurisdiction of a foreign court,[2] irrespective of whether the case is in any way connected with the country of that forum or not. It would hardly be understandable if the parties were not empowered to grant to the court they choose the right to administer its own law. In the English case, *N. V. Kwik Hoo Tong Handel Maatsch. v. James Finley*,[3] the House of Lords even held that 'parties in submitting their contract to an English forum impliedly consented that the law which was to regulate the decision was the law of the forum'.

Further: if the contract is undoubtedly subject to a foreign law and has no connexion with English law, the parties can by agreement make English law applicable by pleading that they agree that the foreign law is identical with English law.[4]

404.
Choice of
more than
one law

III. The contracting parties are allowed to subject different parts of their contract to different laws. They then choose not one single proper law, but several laws to govern their relationship. Examples of this are frequent.[5] In a contract of sale the parties may agree, either expressly or by

---

[1] See *Nordenfelt* v. *Maxim Nordenfelt Guns Co.*, [1894] A.C. 535.
[2] See on this rule: Neuner, *Internationale Zuständigkeit*, 28, 39. Cf. also *infra*, p. 437.
[3] [1927] A.C. 604.
[4] See *supra*, p. 219.
[5] *Jacobs* v. *Crédit Lyonnais* (1884), 12 Q.B.D. 589, 600. *British South Africa Co.* v. *De Beers Cons. Mines*, [1910] 1 Ch. 354, 382.

implication, that the duties of each party shall be governed by the law of the place where they are to be performed. In Germany such separation of the seller's and the buyer's duties is indeed so prevalent that it is the legal rule applied where the parties themselves have failed to designate the applicable law.[1] Very often the parties, though determining a single law for their transaction as a whole, make certain exceptions in respect of special points: they agree, for example, that the period within which the purchaser is bound to examine the goods delivered to him and to give notice of any defect shall be determined by the law prevailing at the place of delivery.[2] Further, in international loan indentures a clause is frequently included which provides for repayment of the capital and interest at the option of the creditor in one of two or more countries in the currency of the chosen country; and in such a case it is often agreed between the parties that the law of the country chosen by the creditor shall answer all questions relative to the amount to be paid and the method of payment.[3] In a contract of agency the relations between the principal and the agent can be governed by a law different from that which determines the creation, the scope, and the revocation of the agent's power to bind his principal *vis-à-vis* third parties.[4]

Therefore, strictly speaking, it is not quite exact to use the term 'proper law of the *contract*'. One ought to speak of the proper law of 'contractual obligations'. Thus if there is more than one obligation arising from the contract there may be several proper laws.

IV. By the choice of the 'proper law' of the contract the parties submit their contract to a particular legal system *as a whole*, a system with which in their view the contract has a vital connexion.

405. Changes in the chosen law

If such law is subsequently altered by some compulsory rule, the law applies in its altered form and the parties are

---

[1] Neuner, in *Rabel's Z.*, 2, 108; 7, 850. Haudek, loc. cit., 72; Niederer, 9 *Nouv. Rev.* (1942), 480; C. Knapp, ibid., 10 (1943), 404. The scission of a unitary contract leads to many difficulties and great inconvenience. See *infra*, s. 436.

[2] Examples: German Supreme Court (*Offic. Coll.*) 46, 195; 73, 390; 81, 273.

[3] *Rex* v. *International Trustee*, [1937] A.C. 500, 574. See *infra*, s. 437.

[4] *Chatenay* v. *Brazilian Submarine Telegraph Co.*, [1891] 1 Q.B. (C.A.) 79, 83. *Maspons y Hermano* v. *Mildred* (1882), 9 Q.B.D. (C.A.) 530, 539. On agency in Private International Law, see *infra*, p. 442, n. 2.

bound by the new provision. Suppose an English debtor
has expressly submitted his gold-dollar loan, floated in New
York in 1930, to the law of New York. Then the creditors,
after the abrogation of the gold clauses in contracts by the
Joint Resolution of 1933, cannot demand to be paid gold-
dollars or their value in paper-dollars.[1] The submission of
a contract to a particular law does not mean submission to
its provisions at the date of contracting, but to a living and
changing body of law.[2] This was the basis of the judgment
in *Re Chesterman's Trusts*.[3]

In 1911 a German had borrowed a certain sum from a Dutch bank in
marks; the loan was governed by German law; at the outbreak of war
Germany went off the gold standard, and when the debt fell due the
intrinsic value of the mark was next to nothing. The Court of Appeal held
that the creditor could not claim to be paid as he would have been paid in
1911, i.e. in goldmarks or their value. The applicable German law 'must
be the German law as it is from time to time, and the (creditors) cannot
take that law as it exists at one time and claim that their rights must be
regulated by its then state, however it may be changed in the future'.

**406. Revo-
lutionary
changes**
It is doubtful whether this is true also of such revolutionary alterations of the law as amount to the destruction of
a whole body of law and the introduction of a different
system, as was the case in the Russian revolution. It must
be assumed that the part played by the law of the parties'
choice is not taken over by the new law. Mere changes in
the law do not affect the identity of the legal system as a
whole, a revolutionary overthrow of the existing law and its
replacement by something new does. Of course, the well-
known difficulty remains of distinguishing with precision
between revolution and evolution, change of identity and
retention of identity in spite of altered features; we are
accustomed to such uncertainty on the border-line between
two conceptions and recognize that it is inevitable. The
principle in any case is clear. Where the parties have submitted their contract to a particular legal system, thereby
manifesting that the contract is closely connected with it,
the submission stands in spite of alterations as long as the
system exists. But it comes to an end where the chosen

[1] *Infra*, s. 452.
[2] 49 *Jurid. Rev.* (1937), 123, 124.
[3] [1923] 2 Ch. 466, 478.

system is replaced by a new one, albeit for the same territory and the same state.[1] If consequently the submission to a legal system becomes inoperative, the contract will be governed by that law which would apply if the parties had made no choice of law. The new law prevailing in the old territory can be regarded as governing the contract only in those cases where the contracting parties continue to reside in that territory, or the contract retains some connexion with the territory.

We are faced with a question similar to that arising out of the extinction of a legal system when *sovereignty* over a territory is transferred from one state to another by international treaty. The following case, which was decided by the German Supreme Court,[2] shows the issue:

407. Change of sovereignty

> Before 1914 a debt was incurred in the then Prussian province of Posen on the basis of a loan given in Posen and to be repaid there; the contract was governed according to the intention of the parties by the *lex loci solutionis*. The debt matured after the war, when the Posen territory was under Polish sovereignty. Does the repayment fall under the German revalorization law or under the Polish law, which differed from it? The court declared German law to be applicable, and this was the correct view. The reference in the contract to a particular town in the province of Posen does not mean its localization in the group of buildings forming that town, but its submission to the system of law prevailing at that town at the date of contracting. When the debt fell due, this system of law, though no longer in force in that formerly Prussian town, was not extinguished but continued to exist and to develop in Germany, and this was the law chosen by the parties. It cannot be assumed that the parties intended to replace by Polish law the German law which had governed their contract before the war. Such substitution would only be justified if both parties (or at least the debtor) had resided in that former Prussian province and continued to reside there after the war; for only if the debt is to be regarded as situate in the now Polish territory has the Polish state the right and the power to alter the incidents of the obligation.

---

[1] The wisdom of Westlake's formula—as opposed to Savigny's and Gierke's [see *supra*, p. 37, n. 2]—is very evident here. He says that the contract is governed by 'the *law* with which' it has the most real connexion. He does not say, as did his precursors, by the law of 'the *country* where' it has its seat or centre of gravity. Contracting parties who in 1913 subjected their contract to Russian law did not point to Russian territory or any part of it; nor did they have in view the Russian State (which after 1917 remained identical with the Russian State of 1913 in spite of its new government). Their submission was to a particular body of *law*, and that has disappeared.

[2] German Supreme Court, *Offic. Coll.*, 121, 344; compare ibid., 107, 121; 123, 134; 131, 46, 48.

408. Substitution of one legal system for another

V. Are the contracting parties at liberty to conclude a new agreement by which they submit their old contract, which till then had been governed by the legal system X to the law of country Y? The answer to this must be given by the law X which first governed the contract. English law would not raise any objection to an affirmative answer,[1] provided the new choice is '*bona fide* and legal'[2] and no retrospective effect is intended. In an undecided case, which came to the present writer's knowledge, the parties had in their first contract designated a foreign place as the place of performance and declared that the transaction should be governed by the law of the place of performance. They had later by a new agreement shifted the performance to another country. The question was whether they had thereby substituted the law of the new place of performance for the law previously governing their contract. It might be contended in favour of such substitution that the law of the first place of performance was no longer connected in any way with the contract. But even those authors who would place considerable restriction on the liberty of the parties to choose their law do not demand that the most real connexion between the contract and a particular legal system should endure throughout the whole period in which the contract is operative. The correct answer seems to be that a mere change of the place of performance cannot entail a change of law. The presumption that legal situations once created remain what they were can only be rebutted by clear evidence that the parties have made a new agreement on this point.

409. Express choice

VI. After having examined *what* law or laws the parties to a contract are permitted to choose, we have to describe the *manner* in which such choice may be made.

Express stipulations of the applicable law are not very frequent. They occur in particular where the contract is framed with the help of legal advisers, or where typical forms, mostly drafted by lawyers, are used by the contracting parties. But it is a surprising fact that even such typical forms or general business conditions as are used or referred

[1] Comp. *Kremezy* v. *Ridgway*, [1949] 1. A.E.R. 662.
[2] to use the terminology of Lord Wright in the *Vita Food case*, *supra*, p. 419.

to by insurance companies, shipowners, railway companies, banks, and other large commercial enterprises often fail to indicate the law applicable to the transaction; and still more startling is it that such omissions occur even in international loan contracts made by sovereign states.[1] In individual contracts concluded between two merchants express clauses determining the governing law are rare.

Where an express stipulation is lacking, it is sometimes **410.** possible to infer from the text of the contract an *implied* Implied choice agreement between the parties as to the proper law. A contract between an English and a Scottish party contained several legal expressions pertaining to Scottish and unknown in English law. Another contract where German and English parties were concerned used (1891) the terms 'Act of God' and 'the Queen's Enemies', which, particularly the second, are meaningless in German law. In both cases the parties showed by their language what law they had in view when making their contract: in the first case Scottish, in the second English, law.[2]

Possibly even more impressive is a German case:[3] In a contract between a German and an Austrian, to be performed in Germany, it was said that the contracting parties 'expressly waive the right to claim rescission of the contract and restitution *in integrum* in case of *laesio enormis*'. German law embodies neither the notion of restitution *in integrum* nor that of *laesio enormis*, while the Austrian code contains both conceptions and expressly mentions that rescission and restitution on the ground of 'lesion' does not take place if one of the parties to the contract has expressly waived it.[4] Hence it is beyond doubt that they had Austrian law in mind for their contract.

Sometimes it is uncertain whether an express agreement on the law applicable to some particular points in the contract includes an implied subjection of the whole of the contract to that law. This was one of the problems in *The Torni*:[5] there the bill of lading issued in Palestine contained the clause that the contract should be 'construed according to English law'. The Court of Appeal denied (*per* Scrutton,

---

[1] *Rex* v. *International Trustee*, [1937] A.C. 500, 531, 557.
[2] *Re Hewitt's Settlement*, [1915] 1 Ch. 228, 233; *The Industrie*, [1894] P. 58, 72, 73.
[3] Not reported.
[4] Austrian Civil Code of 1811, s. 934, 935.
[5] [1932] P. 78, 84.

L.J.) that this meant that the contract as a whole was 'governed' by English law, and declared Palestinian law to be the proper law. But in a later (Canadian) case[1] the Judicial Committee of the Privy Council rejected this distinction as 'merely verbal and too narrow to make a substantial difference'.

BIBLIOGRAPHY

CHESHIRE, *Priv. Internat. L.*, 301–56. CHESHIRE, *International Contracts*, 1948. DICEY–MORRIS, 579–656. RABEL II. 355–591. LORENZEN, 261–321. GOODRICH, 258–97. HAUDEK, *Die Bedeutung des Parteiwillens im Intern. Priv. Recht*, 1931. COOK, 389–441. BATIFFOL, *Les conflits de lois en matière de contrats*, 1938. NIBOYET, *Rec.* 16 (1927 I.) 5 et seq. NIBOYET, *Traité* V. 1–145. JOS. JITTA, *La substance des obligations* I. 1906. M. CALEB, *Essai sur le principe de l'autonomie de la volonté*, 1927. JACQUES DONNEDIEU DE VABRES, *Évolution de la jurisprudence française*, 516 et seq. AUDINET, in *Mélanges Pillet* (1929) I. 57. HOLLAND, *J. Clunet*, 1936, 112. ANZILOTTI in *Diritto commerciale* 32 (1904). v. SZASZI, *Rev. Crit.* 1935, 676 et seq. PLAISANT, *Conflits dans les Traités*, 271 et seq. LENHOFF, 45 *Mich. L.R.* (1940) 39. BARBEY, *Le conflit des lois en matière de contrats dans le droit des États-Unis*, 1938. NUSSBAUM, 51 *Yale L.J.* 893. ALGOT BAGGE, *Les conflits de lois en mat. de ventes*, 25 *Rec.* (1928 V.), 129. STEIN, *Le droit internat. des assurances*, 19 *Rec.* 125. MANN, 3 *Internat. L.Q.*, 60. MORRIS, ibid. 197.

ABSENCE OF CHOICE OF LAW BY THE PARTIES

411. Two views I. In the great majority of contracts the parties make no choice of law either expressly or implicitly. What-law is the judge then to apply? There are two answers to this question:

1. that the judge must ascertain what law the parties *would have chosen* if their attention had been called to the point. Here the place of an express or implied intention is taken by a merely *hypothetical* intention, often wrongly called a presumptive and more wrongly an implied intention. The task of finding out what the parties would have done if they had thought of the importance of determining the applicable law has been assumed by the courts in all countries. Legal writers, however, have for the most part objected to this and framed a different rule, viz.:

2. that the judge should find the solution on the objective facts of the case before him. He should, as Westlake

---

[1] *Vita Food Products* v. *Unus Shipping Co.*, [1939] A.C. 277.

aptly puts it,[1] examine with what law the contract has the *most real connexion*.

The question which of the two formulas is preferable, the subjective or the objective, is not of great significance. If one tries to find out what the parties would have meant, one must ascertain where they as reasonable men would have considered the centre of gravity to lie, and this is in most cases the same as the judge will find by applying the objective formula. There is only one difference, which however has not yet been considered by any court. What is the law if the contracting parties would not have agreed on any of the laws which might be appropriate? It is conceivable that each of the parties takes for granted the application of his own law. Is it really to be decided in such a case that in the absence of a hypothetical agreement in respect of the applicable law the contract itself has not been legally concluded because it would not be subject to any law? This would be a welcome solution to the party which, because prices have risen or declined, wishes to be free of its obligations. In cases of this kind the objective formula shows its superiority. On the other hand, it would be wrong entirely to dismiss the subjective formula, which is everywhere used in the courts. Its value lies in the fact that it compels the judge seeking the centre of gravity of the contract to visualize the actual parties at the date of their contracting and not to rely on that abstract and ideal creature called the reasonable man.

II. In order to elicit the law with which the contract has the closest connexion and on which therefore the parties would probably have agreed when making their contract, the judge will have to study carefully all the circumstances of the particular case. A good guide 'is to be found in applying sound ideas of business, convenience and sense to the language of the contract itself'.[2] But this is not the 'only certain' guide; all the surroundings of the contract and its economic aim considered from the standpoint of the

412.
Means of
eliciting
the proper
law

---

[1] *Westlake*, s. 212; Cheshire, *Internat. Contracts*, p. 27; Morris, 56 *L.Q.R.* 337. See *Jurid. Rev.*, 1937, 121.

[2] *Jacobs* v. *Crédit Lyonnais* (1884), 12 Q.B.D. (C.A.) 589, 601.

parties are equally material. The strict rules of English law
on the interpretation of contracts are not applicable where
the judge seeks to ascertain not what the parties *had* in view
when contracting but what their view *would* have been if
they had made a choice. It is hardly possible to enumerate
all the circumstances which may give a clue and which the
judge will have to weigh against each other. Lord Atkin in
Rex v. *International Trustee*[1] mentions four typical facts
which may lead to a 'prima-facie inference' of the applicable
law, all of them 'capable of being overcome by counter indi-
cations':[2] the place where the contract is made, the place
where the contractual duties are to be performed, the place
where the immovable forming the subject-matter of the
contract is situate, and the flag under which a ship sails. The
first two facts are general, every contract having a place of
contracting and a place of performance, and the choice
between them is sometimes difficult if there are no other
circumstances pointing to either. On the other hand, both
may have to give way to some predominant third test, such
as the two special tests which Lord Atkin mentions: the
situs of an immovable and the flag of a ship.

413. Lex
loci actus

I. *The place where the contract was concluded.* The presumption in favour of the *lex loci actus* is old. It goes back to
the doctrine of the statutists, whose maxim *locus regit actum*
pointed not only to the form but also to the substance of the
contract. It passed into some modern bodies of law, notably
the Austrian civil code of 1811, the Portuguese commercial
code of 1884, the Polish statute of 1926, the old and the
new Italian civil codes (1865, 1942), the *Código Bustamante*,
and some of the Latin-American codes.[3] The paramount
importance of the *lex loci actus* is furthermore recognized in
practice by the French, Belgian, Dutch, and Spanish courts
as well as by the laws of many states of the United States of
America.[4] English law, which formerly took the same view,
has in recent decades tended to an increasingly lax application of the *lex loci actus* principle. Though it has been stated

[1] [1937] A.C. 500, 529.
[2] See also Lord Wright in *Mount Albert Borough Council* v. *Australasian
Temperance Society*, [1938] A.C. (P.C.) 224, 240.
[3] *RVglHWB*. IV. 375, 376.
[4] *Restatement*, s. 332 et seq.

that the prima facie rule in its favour can only be refuted by proving 'an express intention' of the parties,[1] English courts in fact follow a much more liberal practice.[2] Indeed, if the only pointer to the law of a given country is that the contract was concluded there, if there is no additional clue pointing to the place of contracting, such place can hardly be regarded as a sufficient test. Just as the capacity of a person and his status are not tested by the place of his temporary sojourn but by a home of great stability, and just as *iura in rem* are not governed by the law of a merely transitory situation of the chattel,[3] so the conclusion and the effects of contracts are determined by the place of contracting only if there is some stronger connexion between it and the contract: for example, if the residence or business office of one of the parties to the contract is situated at such place, or if the goods are produced there, or if it is likewise the place of performance of any essential contractual obligation. In particular, the identity of the place of performance and the place of contracting has always been regarded as a strong indication that the law of that place should be applied.[4]

It happens, however, in the case of transactions concluded at international fairs, markets, exhibitions, and the like, that neither of the parties knows or cares about the residence, nationality, or place of business of the other party. In such cases the *lex loci actus* is the only possible criterion. Transactions at fairs or markets, or on stock exchanges, have a character all their own. Each is one of hundreds of similar contracts and all are more closely connected with the place where they are concluded than any other contracts. This peculiarity dates back to the Middle Ages; it was at the international fairs held in the Champagne[5]

---

[1] *Jacobs* v. *Crédit Lyonnais* (1884), 12 Q.B.D. 589, 600. See *South African Breweries* v. *King*, [1900] 1 Ch. (C.A.) 273; *Lloyd* v. *Guibert* (1865), L.R. 1 Q.B 115, 112.

[2] See, for example, *Maritime Insurance Co.* v. *Assekuranz Union*, 52 Ll.L.R. (1915) 16, 19 (the policy was executed by one party in Hamburg, by the other party in Liverpool: in such case the 'place of contracting' cannot be decisive).

[3] See on *res in transitu: infra*, s. 494, 495.

[4] *Chatenay* v. *Brazilian Submarine Telegraph Co.*, [1891] 1 Q.B. (C.A.) 79, 82. *Hamlyn* v. *Talisker Distillery*, [1894] A.C. 202, 212.

[5] Lagny-sur-Marne, Bar-sur-Aube, Troyes, Provins; later the fairs of Lyons. See Lewin Goldschmidt, *Universalgeschichte des HandelsRs*, p. 224 et seq.

that a uniform mercantile law applicable to all transactions concluded there originated.

414. Lex loci solutionis

2. *The place of performance of the contract.* The predominance of the *lex loci solutionis* was advocated particularly by Savigny and adopted by German and Swiss law.[1] But a leaning towards this doctrine is already to be found in the epoch of the statutists. Always desirous of supporting their views by passages in the *Digest*, they invoked *Dig.* 44, 7, 21[2] and 42, 5, 3.[3] These sections suggested that a contract should be regarded as having been made not where the transaction took place but where the debtor was to perform his obligation. Thus the place of performance was treated as a fictitious place of contracting. This way of putting the solution was accepted by Ulric Huber and other Dutch jurists and through them found its way to England.[4] It helped considerably to lessen the importance of the real *locus actus* in favour of the place of performance. English courts mostly apply the *lex loci solutionis* in respect of any duty to be performed outside the place of contracting.[5] And indeed the *lex loci solutionis* has much to recommend it as compared with the *lex loci actus*. Performance is the final aim of the contract; thus it is understandable that the place where performance is due should be regarded as the real centre of the obligation. In a contract to marry, the term 'performance' must not be understood in a narrow sense. Strictly speaking the contract is performed at the place where the marriage is celebrated, but the parties will as a rule have had their future matrimonial home in mind,

[1] Savigny, p. 208. See Lewald, p. 224 et seq. German Supr. Court, *Off. Coll.*, 6, 131; 9, 227; 12, 36; 46, 199; 54, 316; 55, 117, &c. Swiss Federal Court, *Off. Coll.*, 32, II. 264; 50, II. 27, and others.

[2] 'Contraxisse unusquisque in eo loco intelligitur in quo ut solveret se obligavit.'

[3] 'Contractum . . . non utique eo loco intelligitur quo negotium gestum sit, sed quo solvenda est pecunia.'

[4] Cf. for example, *Warrender* v. *Warrender* (1835), 2 Cl. & Fin., 488, at p. 509. See *supra*, s. 312.

[5] *Adelaide Electric Supply Co.* v. *Prudential Assurance Co.*, [1934] A.C. 122, 151. *Chatenay* v. *Brazilian Submarine Telegraph Co.*, [1891] 1 Q.B. 79, 83. *Rouquette* v. *Overmann* (1875), L.R. 10 Q.B. 525, 536, 537 (the surety liable under the same law as the principal debtor, whose obligations are determined by the law of the place of performance). *Benaim* v. *Debono*, [1924] A.C. 514, and others.

and it is the law of that home that will, in the view of the
parties, have to govern the contract.[1] The place of contracting often depends on chance; the place of performance
does not. On the other hand, the determination of the place
of performance is difficult in some cases: a contract of
carriage from country X to country Y with transit through
Z can only be performed in all three countries. A contractual duty to refrain from competing with the other
party's business in Europe covers more than thirty countries and is to be performed in each of them. The main objection to the place of performance shows itself in bilateral
contracts, where possibly the respective obligations of the
two parties are not to be performed at the same place.[2] Such
objections, however, merely prove that it is impossible to
discover a test appropriate to all contracts alike. In some
cases the place of contracting, in others the place of performance is preferable; the choice largely depends on the
circumstances of the case.

The following facts gave rise to an instructive decision of the German
Supreme Court: During the Russian revolution a Russian citizen, domiciled and resident in Russia, but about to emigrate, borrowed from a
Russian woman, also still living in Russia and anxious to leave it, a certain
sum and gave her a cheque for 1,000 dollars drawn on his account at an
American bank in New York; at the same time he delivered to her a
written acknowledgment of his obligation to pay her the sum of 1,000
dollars in American currency if the American bank should refuse payment.
The bank refused, and after the emigration of both parties the creditor
brought an action based on this written promise in a German court, the
debtor having meanwhile established a German domicile. Under Russian
law the whole transaction between the parties was void as offending
against the currency decrees of the Soviet Government. The German
court[3] refused the application of Russian law, not for reasons of German
public policy, but because the parties, if their attention had been called
to the question of the applicable law at the time of the transaction, would
certainly have agreed that Russian law should not apply, despite the fact
that it was the law of the place of contracting and of the common domicile
and residence of both parties. In this case it was much easier to say what
law the parties would *not* have selected than to ascertain the law of their
probable choice.[4] The German court, having to choose between German

---

[1] *Kremezy* v. *Ridgway*, [1949] 1 A.E.R. 662.
[2] *Supra*, s. 404.
[3] *Offic. Coll.*, 108, 241.
[4] See the similar situation in the decision of the German Supreme Court
published in *Juristische Wochenschrift*, 1928, 1196.

and American law, decided in favour of German law, because it held that the contractual place of performance was the debtor's future domicile, unknown at the time of the transaction. Though the exclusion of Russian law would probably be approved by the courts of many countries, the German court's choice is hardly well founded. The facts that the cheque was drawn on an American bank and payable in New York and that the debtor had expressly promised to pay in American currency point to New York as the contractual place of performance.

415. *Lex situs fundi*

3. *The situs of immovables.* We shall see, in dealing with property law, that the conveyance of immovables situate in country X or the granting of mortgages, rent-charges, or other real rights is governed exclusively by the law of the situs. Such compulsory rule does not exist in respect of contracts by which one of the parties promises to convey his property or to grant a *ius in rem* to the other party. The contracting parties may subject such contract to the law of a different country; but a strong presumption in favour of the *lex situs* does exist.[1] This presumption may be displaced by the circumstances of the contract. Three brothers, all of them domiciled Englishmen, having an interest in a piece of land in Chile, made a contract by correspondence by which two of them sold their shares in that land to the third. The English court held that the contract was to be governed by English law, because all parties had an English domicile, though the buyer was resident either in Peru or in Chile.[2] Although this decision may be open to criticism,[3] there are indeed situations where the prima facie inference in favour of the *lex situs* is overcome by counter-indications.

Example: English co-heirs, anxious to avoid a lawsuit concerning the construction of the English testator's will, make an arrangement with each other, under which the whole of the property of the deceased is distributed among them in a certain way. The property consists mainly of valuable English securities deposited with an English bank and a small piece of land in Scotland. The contract will be governed by English law, even in respect of the Scottish immovable.

---

[1] *Lloyd* v. *Guibert* (1865), L.R. 1 Q.B. 115, 122.
[2] *Cood* v. *Cood* (1863), 33 L.J. Ch. 273, 278 (*per* Romilly, M.R.). See also *Campbell* v. *Dent* (1838), 2 Moore P.C. 292, 307.
[3] Is the (unconscious) reason for this decision to be found in the predilection which every court shows for its own law? If the three brothers had been domiciled Chileans, one of them resident in England, and the land had been situate in this country, would the English court have applied Chilean law?

4. *The flag under which a ship sails.*[1] The law of the flag is prima facie applicable to all maritime contracts. It is, however, easily displaced by counter-indications in the case of contracts concluded before the ship sails,[2] particularly contracts of affreightment. Where a German ship is chartered by English charterers under an English charter-party and an English bill of lading, and the port of delivery of the cargo is English, the contract will be governed by English law and not by the law of the flag.[3] The inference from the flag is much stronger 'in respect of such contracts as the master may be driven to make by necessity in the course of the voyage',[4] particularly bottomry contracts[5] and contracts of sale of cargo in a port of distress.[6] The third party with whom the master makes the contract must be able to trust in the master's authority to conclude the contract within the framework of the law of the flag. Contracts concluded on board ship are treated as concluded in the country of the flag, so that where the *lex loci actus* would be decisive, the law of the flag is substituted for it.[7]

Apart from these four main clues there are numerous other circumstances which must be considered when one tries to ascertain the applicable law, for example:

5. *the residence, the domicile, the place of business of the parties,* or at least of the debtor. Many eminent writers, for example, von Bar and Gutzwiller,[8] even advocate the predominance of the law of the debtor's residence or, where the debtor is a merchant, of his place of business. Though this goes too far, there are indeed certain situations in which the place of business of one of the parties is the most appro-

416. Law of the flag

417. Residence, domicile, place of business

---

[1] See *supra*, p. 100 (4).

[2] See *Chartered Mercantile Bank of India* v. *Netherlands India Steam Navig. Co.* (1883), 10 Q.B.D. (C.A.) 521, 529.

[3] *The San Roman* (1872), L.R. 3 A. & E. 583, 592, 593. See also *The Industrie*, [1894] P. (C.A.) 58, 72, where the contract had been negotiated by English brokers on behalf of the German shipowner and British shippers and the charter-party was made in English form: the Court of Appeal excluded the law of the flag and applied English law.

[4] *The Njegos*, [1936] P. 90, 107.

[5] *Lloyd* v. *Guibert* (1865), L.R. 1 Q.B. 115, 125. *The Gaetano and Maria* (1882), 7 P.D. (C.A.) 137, 142.

[6] *The August*, [1891] P. 328, 339.

[7] *The Adriatic*, [1931] P. 241, 246.

[8] v. Bar, II. 23 (Engl. transl., pp. 551, 552); Gutzwiller, 1607, 1608.

priate test. Insurance contracts, except contracts of re-insurance between companies, will in case of doubt be governed by the law of the insurer's place of business.[1] The same is probably true of most other kinds of contracts that are concluded under typical conditions set up by great industrial, commercial, or railway companies, contracts 'where one will predominates, dictating its law not to single individuals but to an undetermined collectivity and leaving to those who want to enter into an engagement nothing more than unreservedly to accept the terms of the contract, to *adhere* to them' (contracts of adhesion, as they have been called).[2] Such mass contracts, concluded under identical conditions and 'approaching much more the *lex*' than an agreement of two or more parties working together at the framing of the contract, can maintain their uniformity only if they are all governed by the same law, and there is a strong inference that this is the law of the place of the enter-prise. Again, solicitors, or other advocates, notaries, and similar persons exercising a profession[3] may be supposed to subject the service contracts they conclude with their clients to the law of the place where they regularly exercise their profession, irrespective of where they are to fulfil the task entrusted to them.[4] It has been stated that the fact that one of the parties is a sovereign state suffices to make the law of that state applicable to all contracts it concludes, or at any rate to any international loan it may enter into.[5] But this view was rejected by the House of Lords in *Rex* v. *International Trustee.*[6]

Here the British Government had issued bonds in New York; the

---

[1] Cp. *Spurrier* v. *La Cloche,* [1902] A.C. 446, 450.

[2] Saleilles, *De la déclaration de la volonté,* 1901, p. 229, who was the first to call attention to this kind of 'contracts', named them very aptly *contrats d'adhésion.*

[3] Is this true for the medical profession ? Hardly. If a foreign physician is summoned to an English patient in this country, he probably concludes the contract under English law; he may claim fees as if he were a Harley Street man; and should he belong to a country where doctors' fees are even higher than in Harley Street, he cannot claim the higher amount.

[4] The Polish statute on Private International Law of 1926, art. 8, no. 6, contains an express rule to this effect; but the same rule is probably correct for all other legal systems.

[5] *Smith* v. *Weguelin* (1869), L.R. 8 Eq. 198, 212. *Goodwin* v. *Robarts* (1876), 1 App. Cas. 476, 495.

[6] [1937] A.C. 500, 530, 553, 554. Dicey–Morris, p. 591.

money lent had been paid in dollars; any registered bonds were to be registered in New York and were transferable by registration there; the payments were to be made (on one option) in America; finally the loan was secured by a pledge agreement made and performed in America. Upon these facts Lord Atkin declared it to be an 'irresistible inference' that the proper law was American.

6. English law apart, *the nationality of the contracting parties*, at any rate if it is the same for both, is an important circumstance in testing the applicable law. In Italy, both under the old liberal code of 1865 (which on this point was influenced by Mancini's ideas) and under the fascist code of 1938 (1942), the common nationality of the parties is the main test; and so in Germany too, provided that both parties are German nationals.[1] In England common nationality seems of little importance, since British nationality never suffices to indicate the applicable (English, Scottish, South African, &c.) law.

418. Nationality?

7. A much more decisive factor for establishing the applicable law will be derived from a contractual agreement that disputes arising between the parties shall be submitted to the tribunals of a certain country or to arbitration.[2] The old phrase 'qui eligit iudicem eligit ius' still has some value, though the inference from such clauses is not conclusive. Perhaps it is correct to distinguish between the submission to a regular court of a foreign country and the arbitration clause. In the former case it may be justifiable to construe the clause to the effect that the foreign court should apply its own conflict rules in order to find the proper law of the contract. In the case of an arbitration clause such reference will hardly ever correspond to the presumptive intention of the parties. If, for example, they refer the matter to arbitration by the London Corn Exchange[3] they probably expect the arbitrator to decide it just as if it were a purely English case, i.e. to apply English municipal law as he understands

419. Submission to jurisdiction

---

[1] German Supreme Court, *Offic. Coll.*, 68, 207; 120, 72.

[2] *Hamlyn & Co.* v. *Talisker Distillery*, [1894] A.C. (Scot. C.) 202, 212. *N.V. Kwik Hoo Tong Handel Maatsch.* v. *James Finlay & Co.*, [1927] A.C. 604. *The Njegos*, [1936] P. 90, 100. Cf. also *Vita Food Products* v. *Unus Shipping Co.*, [1939] A.C. (P.C.) 277, 290, and *supra*, p. 422. See Dicey–Morris, p. 589. On the choice of law in the case of submission to a foreign court or to arbitration, see Ernst Wolff in *Schönke's Internat. Schiedsgerichtswesen*, II. 53, 54.

[3] *Hamlyn & Co.* v. *Talisker Distillery* (*supra*), at p. 208.

it. The task of finding out which law the High Court would apply to the case is beyond what should be demanded from an ordinary arbitrator.

420. The most effective law?

8. It has often been said that there is a presumption in favour of that law which is most effective.[1] This is based on the general maxim on interpretation of contracts and wills 'ut res magis valeat quam pereat'. This presumption, how-ever, unless cautiously applied, is apt to lead to unfortunate results. Take the case[2] that a Frenchman buys a ticket from a French navigation company for the carriage of his family and his luggage from Madagascar to Southampton, that the ticket contains a clause exempting the company from liability for loss of luggage, that—as was formerly the case—that clause is valid by English and void by French law, and that the parties have neither expressly nor by implica-tion determined the law governing the contract. Every-thing points to French law, except the English port of destination. Is the fact that under French law the exempt-ing clause is void a sufficient reason for the court to declare English law to be the proper law of the contract, the law with which the contract has the most real connexion? It is submitted that it is not. The rule in favour of the most effective law is sensible in those cases where a reasonable man can doubt which of two legal systems is more closely connected with the contract, but not where there can be no hesitation about the correct choice and where only the thinnest of threads binds the contract to English law.

[1] *P. & O. Steam Navigation Co.* v. *Shand* (1865), 3 Moo. P.C. (N.S.) 272. *Hamlyn* v. *Talisker Distillery (supra)*, at p. 215. *South African Breweries* v. *King*, [1899] 2 Ch. 173, 181. *In re Missouri Steamship Co.* (1889), 42 Ch.D. 321. *The Njegos*, [1936] P. 90, 107. *Brit. South Africa Co.* v. *De Beers*, [1910] 1 Ch. 381, 2 Ch. (C.A.) 512.

[2] Inverted from *P. & O. Steam Navigation Co.* v. *Shand (supra)*. In that case nearly everything pointed to the application of English law, except that the last short part of the voyage had to be made in territory under French law. The Privy Council applied English law for many obvious reasons and for one much less obvious reason, i.e. because under French law the clause in question would be void. See Rabel, II. 474, Dicey–Morris 591, n. 48.

BIBLIOGRAPHY, see *supra*, p. 428.

THE VALIDITY OF THE CONTRACT

I. The law that decides whether a contract was validly con- 421. Law
cluded is that law which regulates its effects if in fact it was ^{applicable} ^{to offer and}
validly concluded. This law, the proper law of the contract, acceptance
decides therefore

1. whether there are two declarations, an offer and
an acceptance, directed to the conclusion of a contract,
whether in particular the offer was accepted in due time and
in the right way. If, for example, the English offeree posted
the acceptance immediately after receiving the offer, but
the letter never reached the German offerer, the contract is
validly completed under English municipal law, but void
if German law applies. And the proper law which governs
the contract *if* it is valid is the one that must be applied to
test the validity.[1] The question, however, whether a particular declaration or course of conduct (for example,
silence of one of the parties) has the character of a legal act
at all, or whether it is something legally immaterial, cannot
reasonably depend on the proper law of the putative contract. The contrary view would lead to grave injustice,
notably in the case of silence of the offeree.

Example: Under all Scandinavian laws the courts are inclined to regard
silence as acceptance if the offerer could expect that the offeree, had he wished
to refuse, would make an express declaration to that effect.[2] English law
has no such rule.[3] Suppose a Danish merchant makes a written offer to an
English merchant with whom he had had previous transactions; his offer
contains among other clauses the clause that the contract shall be governed
by Danish law. The English party does not answer. Can his silence be interpreted as acceptance because under Danish law it would be regarded as
such and because the letter referred to Danish law? It cannot.

The silence of a person can be deemed to be an act of legal
significance only if that is so under the law of that person's
residence or place of business.

2. The proper law answers the question whether and
how long an offer is irrevocable, and whether the death of
the offerer before acceptance, or the death of the acceptor

---

[1] *Aliter* Cheshire, *Internat. Contracts*, pp. 53–4.
[2] Rabel, *Recht des Warenkaufs*, I, p. 97.
[3] Cf. *Felthouse* v. *Bindley* (1862), 11 C.B. (N.S.) 869.

before his letter of acceptance reaches the offerer, hinders the completion of the contract. The various laws differ widely on these points. In England and the United States the offer is always revocable until the contract is completed; in Germany, Switzerland, the Scandinavian states, Austria, and Hungary it is binding during a certain period, in French law it is binding only if the offerer has fixed a term for acceptance. The offerer's death before acceptance destroys the offer under French and English law, not so under German law.

422. Defects of consent

3. The proper law (probably) determines the influence of mistake, misrepresentation, fraud, coercion, and similar *defects of consent* on the validity of the contract. This is however subject to some controversy. It has been proposed by eminent German and French scholars that such defects should be treated on the same lines as a lack of full capacity, that therefore the personal law of the party whose declaration is defective should be applied. There is much to be said in favour of such equality of treatment.[1] But the courts have not often accepted this view.[2]

423. Defects as to the essence

4. There is no doubt that as a rule the influence of defects other than defects of consent on the validity of the contract is determined by the proper law. The defects in question are those concerning the essence of the contract. Examples: (a) An Italian debtor, a discharged bankrupt, by a contract, the proper law of which was Italian, promised one of his creditors to repay a pre-bankruptcy debt. The contract was valid under Italian law, while under English law there was no consideration to support it. The English court held that this was 'no bar to its validity'.[3] (b) The validity of an arbitration clause in a contract depends on the proper law. Under the law of Jersey the clause was void, under English law valid. The owner of a stamp collection in Jersey concluded a fire insurance contract with an English insurance company which contained a submission to English arbitration. The clause was deemed to be valid

---

[1] Lewald, p. 239; Pillet, *Traité prat.* II. 289. See Sichel, Ἀρχεῖον Ἰδιωτικοῦ Δικαίου, I. (1934) 11. Bartin, *Principes*, II. 29, 60. Perroud, *J. Clunet*, 1933, 289. Maury in *Travaux d. Com. franç.*, III. (1937) 91.

[2] See the catalogue in Lewald, 240, 241.

[3] *In re Bonacina*, [1912] 2 Ch. (C.A.) 394.

because the proper law of the contract was English.[1]
(c) The parties, an English and a Swedish insurance company, concluded a re-insurance contract in respect of a ship. Under English law it was invalid in so far as it exceeded a time limit of twelve months; under Swedish law it was valid. As the court regarded English law as the proper law of the contract it declared the contract to be invalid beyond the time limit.[2] (d) Contracts of affreightment very often contain clauses—or did so at least before the Hague Rules came into operation—exempting the carrier from liability for his servants' negligence; the validity of such clauses should be tested by the proper law.[3] (e) A service contract concluded between English parties living and working in South Africa contained a clause by which the employee agreed not to engage in any brewery business in South Africa within ten years after the termination of his engagement; the clause was valid under English, void under South African law. Since South African was the proper law the English court declared the clause to be void.[4] (f) Where the question is whether the contract is void for offending against morality the proper law decides; if under the proper law the contract is valid, as for example in the case of a foreign champertous agreement, the English court will reject it as contravening English public policy.[5] If conversely a contractual engagement is *contra bonos mores* in the eyes of its proper law no court will enforce it, even though according to the *lex fori* contracts of the same kind could be validly concluded.

Example: In France a promise of marriage is regarded as legally not binding on the ground that it would be immoral to restrict the 'liberty of marriage'; hence it is unenforceable in this country too, though under English law such contracts can be validly concluded.

[1] *Spurrier* v. *La Cloche*, [1902] A.C. (P.C.) 446. See also *Hamlyn* v. *Talisker Distillery*, [1894] A.C. 202.
[2] *Royal Exchange Assurance Corp.* v. *Sjöforsäkrings Aktiebolaget Vega*, [1901] 2 K.B. 567, 574; [1902] 2 K.B. (C.A.) 384.
[3] *P. & O. Steamship Co.* v. *Shand* (1865), 3 Moo. P.C. (N.S.) 272. *The Chartered Mercantile Bank* v. *The Netherlands India Steam Navig. Co.* (1882), 9 Q.B.D. 118; 10 Q.B.D. (C.A.) 521. *In re Missouri Steamship Co.* (1889), 42 Ch.D. 321. *Jones* v. *Oceanic Steam Navig. Co.*, [1924] 2 K.B. 730.
[4] *South Afric. Breweries* v. *King*, [1899] 2 Ch. 173; [1900] 1 Ch. (C.A.) 273.
[5] *Grell* v. *Levy* (1864), 16 C.B. (N.S.) 73.

424.
Validity
dependent
on third
parties

5. The validity of a contract often depends on the *declarations of third persons*. Under many continental laws an infant from a certain age upward is capable of concluding any contract if his father, mother, or guardian consents. The necessity of such consent is tested not by the proper law of the contract, but by the law governing the capacity of the infant, that is, his domiciliary law,[1] the function of the consent being to grant capacity to an *incapax*. The same is (probably) true of the validity of the consent, which should depend neither on the proper law of the contract to which the consent was given nor on the personal law of the consenting father, mother, or guardian.

A different problem arises where the person who makes a contract, though not *incapax* or restricted in his capacity, needs the consent of a third person. The main case of this kind is that of an agent acting on behalf of his principal, where the validity of the contract depends on the validity of his authority. What law decides whether such authority was validly given and whether it was still in force at the time of contracting? If the principal *P* appoints *A* as his agent and *A* upon the authority vested in him makes a contract with *X* on behalf of *P*, the validity, the scope, the duration, and the revocability of the authority are governed neither by the proper law of the contract which *P* concludes with *X* nor by that of the agency contract between *P* and *A*, but by the law of the country in which the delegated authority is to operate, i.e. in which *A* is entitled or bound to exercise it.[2] The third party *X* must be able to rely on the assumption that a foreign agent has the same power as similar agents have under the municipal law of the country where the contract is made. If, for example, the contract of agency contains the clause that the powers shall be irrevocable for a certain period, and such clause is invalid under the proper law

---

[1] This is qualified by the rule (see *supra*, s. 263, 264) that a person cannot rely on his incapacity under the domiciliary law if he is capable under the *lex loci actus*. (The proper law of the contract as such has no bearing on the question whether consent creates full capacity.)

[2] *Chatenay* v. *Brazilian Submarine Telegraph Co.*, [1891] I Q.B. (C.A.) 79, 83, 84. *Sinfra Ltd.* v. *Sinfra Akt. Ges.*, [1939] A.E.R. 675; see on this: Falconbridge, *Essays*, 368–74. On *Apt* v. *Apt*, *supra*, p. 344. On agency and the authority of the agent in priv. internat. law: Rabel in his Z., III. 807; Zitelmann, II. 206; Breslauer, 50 *Jurid. Rev.*, 1938, 282.

of the agency contract, but valid under the law of the country where the agent acts, P's contractual obligation *vis-à-vis* X is valid. In cases where the agent has been appointed to act in several countries, the interpretation and the effect of his authority may be different in each of them. Powers created and determined not by contract but by operation of law may have their centre of gravity in a country other than that in which the power is to be exercised. Thus the authority of the master of a ship to sell or mortgage cargo during the voyage is governed by the law of the flag.[1]

II. The problem of illegality of contracts calls for particular examination. Under all continental systems of private international law the answer is easy and undoubted. The proper law of the contract governs the question, and no other conflict rule must be considered. Under English private international law the same rule prevails in principle. If a contract is void under its proper law on the ground of illegality the nullity is recognized. But if the contract is legal (and valid) under its proper law it is doubtful whether it is necessary to consult in addition two other legal systems, viz. (1) the law of the place of contracting, and (2) the law of the place of performance. Each of these systems has been considered decisive.[2]

    425. Illegality

1. The rule that a contract is void if 'the making thereof is unlawful by the law of the country where it is made' is not unassailable. Suppose an American citizen borrows a sum of 1,000 dollars from another American, promises repayment in gold value in London, and the parties subject the contract to English law. Under the proper law of the contract, i.e. English law, the contract is unobjectionable, it does not contravene any English prohibitory rule. But it violates the American Joint Resolution of 1933, which enacted that every dollar obligation shall be discharged upon payment, dollar for dollar, in any coin or currency which at the time of payment is legal tender. Is the fact that the contract was made in New York a sufficient reason for applying the Joint Resolution to it? This is open to doubt.

---

[1] See *supra*, s. 416.
[2] Dicey–Morris, 632, 639, n. 83. See F. A. Mann's helpful criticism in 18 *Brit. Y.B.* (1937), p. 100 et seq.

True, the *lex loci contractus* is often identical with the proper law of the contract and, as mentioned before, there is a strong presumption in favour of this. But when the presumption has been rebutted, or the parties have expressly chosen a different legal system, there remains only one possible argument—and not a convincing one—in favour of the alleged rule, that is, that nobody should be allowed to derive rights from an act which was illegal at the place where it was done. Is there such a rule? Does international comity demand that an act which violates the law of the country where the act is done should be regarded all over the world as incapable of producing rights to the benefit of the malefactor? The suggested rule becomes, as Dr. Mann stresses,[1] preposterous where there is no connexion between the transaction and the place of contracting, for example, where two Englishmen while travelling from Holland to Switzerland make a contract in the dining-car somewhere near Cologne by which they violate a prohibitory rule of German law. The exception is not supported by authority, but only by a few dicta in *Re Missouri Steamship Co.*[2] and in *The Torni*.[3] It is tacitly rejected by *Spurrier* v. *La Cloche*.[4]

2. The second rule runs: a contract, though lawful by its proper law, is invalid in so far as its performance is unlawful by the law of the country where it is to be performed.[5] This rule seems intended to cover all kinds of unlawfulness: illegality existing when the contract was concluded as well as supervening illegality;[6] illegality known to both contracting parties or to one of them or neither; permanent or merely temporary illegality. These

---

[1] Loc. cit., p. 104.

[2] (1889) 42 Ch.D. 321, 336 (Lord Halsbury).

[3] [1932] P. 27, 78, 88 (Greer, L.J.).

[4] [1902] A.C. (P.C.) 446, 451.

[5] Dicey–Morris, l.c. Cheshire, *Internat. Contracts*, p. 70 et seq. *Adelaide Electric Supply Co.* v. *Prudential Assurance Co.*, [1934] A.C. 122, 151. *Ralli Bros.* v. *Compañía Naviera Sota y Aznar*, [1920] 2 K.B. (C.A.) 287. *De Beéche* v. *South American Stores*, [1935] A.C. 148. *International Trustee* v. *The King*, [1936] 3 A.E.R. (C.A.), 407, 429. Other decisions in Dr. Mann's article, pp. 107–13.

[6] Example: A Dutch contract embodying a gold clause was concluded in 1932, and the place of performance was New York. In 1933 American law abrogated all gold clauses.

various forms of illegality have, however, very different consequences under the various municipal laws. The contract may be void or may subsequently become ineffective, and the nullity may be irreparable or it may be cured by an authoritative act of ratification; or again the contravention, though a punishable misdemeanour, may not affect the validity of the contract as between the parties.[1] Again, if only one of the parties has acted in contravention of the law of the foreign country, the other party may be treated by that law as if he had made a valid contract, and so forth. The rule under discussion here does not affect any of these consequences. If it says that a contract unlawful by the *lex loci solutionis* is 'invalid', this is surely over-simplification. The law which pronounces a contract to be illegal is the only one able to determine the influence of that illegality on the validity of the contract. Not the proper law of the contract but the law of the place of performance determines the effects on the contract of the violation of a prohibitory rule prevailing at that place. But once these effects have been ascertained—for example, if under the *lex loci solutionis* the contravention has brought about incurable nullity of the contract—the proper law of the contract steps in and decides all the questions which arise out of such nullity. Suppose, e.g., one of the parties knew the transaction to be illegal, while the other party did not, is the innocent party entitled to damages? Or is a liberal interpretation of the contract permissible to the effect that the place of performance agreed on by the contracting parties is to be disregarded and that the creditor may claim performance in a country where such performance is not forbidden?[2]

[1] Example: Under the German law on currency restrictions of 12 December 1938, s. 10 § 1, the acquisition and transfer of foreign money or of foreign money debts was prohibited, and severe penalties were imposed for contravention of that rule; but such contracts, though unlawful, were valid (s. 64 of that law). In certain other cases the law provided that the contract is void but that such nullity may not be relied upon to the prejudice of a *bona-fide* party to the contract; s. 64 § 3.

[2] Whether such change of the place of performance is permissible depends, for example, under German law on what 'good faith (*Treu und Glauben*) requires', s. 242 German Civ. C. The German Supreme Court once allowed the change, though in a very special case; *Jur.W.* 1924, p. 1357. English law does not allow the court 'to vary the terms of the contract in any way'. See *Re Parana Plantation*, [1946] 2 A.E.R. 214.

III. *Capacity* to conclude a contract does not depend on the proper law of the contract, but on the personal law. On this see *supra*, s. 264.

426. *Locus regit actum*. General observations

IV. What law governs the *form* of the contract? There is no doubt that a contract is formally valid if the formalities prescribed by the *lex loci actus* have been observed. But it is open to controversy whether these formalities must be observed, or whether it is sufficient to comply with the formalities established by the proper law of the contract. The controversy is nearly as old as the phrase *locus regit actum*.[1] That maxim was regarded by some of the statutists as imperative (where it applied to the form of an act), and some modern legal codes have adopted this view. In particular the civil codes of Spain, Portugal, Argentine, and Peru,[2] and the draft French civil code, embodied a rule making the *lex loci actus* compulsory.[3] But it was not included in the final form of the French code, and the predominant practice of the French courts is to allow the parties to choose between the *lex loci actus* and the law governing the essentials of the contract. This was and is also the view upheld in German, Swiss, Austrian, Hungarian, Norwegian, and Swedish law.[4] There is no doubt that the right of option between the proper law and the law of the place of contracting is preferable to the compulsory application of the latter law. Why should two Englishmen travelling on the Continent be debarred from concluding a contract (to be governed by English law) in the English way? Why should they be compelled to ascertain the law of the country in which they happen to be? As the whole contract, its conclusion, its interpretation, and all its effects are governed by the proper law, is there any reason for making an exception of the formalities of its conclusion? It would be much more reasonable to formulate the question the other way round, i.e. to ask: Must the parties make their

---

[1] See Neumeyer, *Gemeinrechtliche Entwicklung des I.P.R.*, II. 84, 135; Gutzwiller, p. 1585.

[2] On this see Rheinstein, *RVglHWB.*, IV. 360.

[3] 'La forme des actes est réglée par les lois du lieu où ils sont faits'; see Gutzwiller, 1586.

[4] Rheinstein, loc. cit., 361.

contract in the form of the proper law, or are they permitted to observe exclusively the form prescribed in the country in which they conclude their contract?[1] For it is this alternative, and not the sovereignty of the proper law, which needs justification. Where it is sufficient to observe the formalities of the place of contracting the reason for this is that the parties are not always able to obey the rules of the proper law in a foreign country. Thus the purpose of the *locus regit actum* principle is to facilitate the conclusion of the contract.

The optional character of the *lex loci actus* is, or might be, particularly important in the case of transactions other than contracts in the strict sense of the term; for example, wills,[2] pacts relative to succession,[3] and adoptions. How should, for example, two domiciled Germans *A* and *B*, while sojourning in England, make a pact by which *A* irrevocably appoints *B* as his 'heir', unless they are permitted to conclude that pact in the form of German law? (There cannot be any English rule on the formalities of such a pact because the institution of *Erbvertrag* is unknown in English law.)

Although these considerations make it highly desirable that the rule should be given an optional character, it is doubtful whether English law has conceded this. Over and over again up to the middle of the nineteenth century the courts stressed its imperative character. 'There seems no room for reasonable doubt', said an English judge as late as 1851.[4] In particular, marriages celebrated in the form of the domiciliary law of the parties and not in the local form were always held to be invalid.[5] So were contracts for lack of the stamps prescribed by the local law.[6] The marriage cases, however, do not prove much, since marriages are not

427. The English view

---

[1] This is the way in which the problem is formulated, for example, in German law; see art. 11 Introd. Law.

[2] *Infra*, s. 559.

[3] *Infra*, s. 577.

[4] Bruce, V.C., in *Guépratte* v. *Young*, 4 De G. and Sm. 217, 228. This is the view adopted by Foote and Westlake. It was Dicey's view, *aliter* Morris, in the 6th edition of Dicey's work, pp. 625–8.

[5] For example, *Kent* v. *Burgess* (1840), 11 Sim. 361.

[6] *Alves* v. *Hodgson* (1797), 7 T.R. 241. *Clegg* v. *Levy* (1812), 3 Camp. 166. *Bristow* v. *Sequeville* (1850), 5 Ex. 275.

contracts—they create a status not an obligation—and even countries where the optional character of *locus regit actum* is recognized make the rule compulsory in the case of marriages.[1] It is more difficult to deal with the second group, the stamp cases. If the absence of a formality so purely technical as stamping (to comply with the foreign *lex loci actus*) destroys the validity of an English contract, other formalities naturally pertaining to the contract should be of still greater weight, and their omission should entail the nullity of the contract with still greater certainty. But such argument *a fortiori* is open to objections. Stamping a contractual instrument is a formality the purpose of which is not to endow an instrument with greater authority in evidence or to make the parties aware of the serious nature of their engagement, but to secure revenue to the state in the territory of which an instrument is signed and delivered. When English law, on the one hand, refuses directly to enforce foreign revenue laws[2] and, on the other hand, recognizes the nullity under foreign law of a contract concluded abroad and not duly stamped, such recognition is as it were an act of friendliness *vis-à-vis* the foreign country, and it is hardly justifiable to draw from this special case any conclusion with regard to the general problem of the imperative nature (or otherwise) of the *lex loci actus* in regard to contractual formalities.

Therefore there is no cogent authority in favour of the imperative character of the *locus regit actum* maxim. Authors who take a different view themselves admit that there exists a series of exceptions to the compulsory nature of the rule.

428.
Dicey's doctrine

Dicey and Keith (in Dicey's fifth edition[3]) have indicated two exceptions, viz.

I. The formal validity of a contract concerned with immovables depends on the proper law of the contract; and, as has been seen above,[4] there is a rebuttable presumption that the law of the location is the proper law.

Keith, the editor of Dicey's fifth edition, even contended that contracts on immovables *must* be made in the form of the proper law, and that there is no alternative admitting the *lex loci actus*. This view is not supported by

---

[1] *Supra*, s. 322.　　　　　[2] See *supra*, s. 164.
[3] pp. 644–6.　　　　　[4] See *supra*, s. 415.

authority.[1] If it were, this would represent an exaggeration in favour of the proper law similar to the exaggeration which in the case of other contracts favoured the *lex loci actus*. How unfortunate the result of such view would be becomes particularly evident where the *lex situs* and the *lex loci actus* coincide but the proper law of the contract differs. If a French owner of an English piece of land sells it in England to a Frenchman and the parties agree that their contract shall be governed by French law, it would be preposterous to compel them to observe the forms of French law; it must suffice for them to comply with the rules of English law.

2. A second exception set up by Dicey concerns such contracts as are 'intended to operate wholly' in the country of the proper law. In cases of this kind the parties have a choice between the formalities prescribed by the *lex loci actus* and those of the proper law of the contract.[2] Example: a contract concluded in France between a domiciled Englishman and a domiciled Frenchman to be carried out wholly in England is valid if made either in French or in English form. The question remains: is there any sound reason for restricting the applicability of the proper law to the case where the parties intend to carry out the contract 'wholly' in the country of the proper law, i.e. where the proper law coincides with the *lex loci solutionis*? And for excluding the proper law where one of the obligations created by the contract has to be performed in a third country? Such distinction can hardly be based on any reasonable ground; and it is suggested that what Dicey regarded as an exception to an unsatisfactory rule is in truth the application of a sound general rule to the effect that the formalities of any contract are governed either by the law of the place of contracting or by the proper law of the contract. No significance, it appears, attaches to the fact that in the cases supporting the rule the proper law was identical with the *lex loci solutionis*.[3]

It should be borne in mind that even if the doctrine of the compulsory character of the *lex loci actus* were correct, this

---

[1] It is submitted that neither *Adams* v. *Clutterbuck* (1883), 10 Q.B.D. 403, nor *Bank of Africa* v. *Cohen*, [1909] 2 Ch. (C.A.) 129, justify the rule.

[2] *Van Grutten* v. *Digby* (1862), 31 Beav. 561, 568. *In re Bankes*, [1902] 2 Ch. 333, 342.

[3] The optional character of the *lex loci actus* has been advocated in particular by G. C. Cheshire, *Priv. Intern. Law*, 302, 306, *Internat. Contracts*, 60–3. Further: Morris (in Dicey[6], 625–9); Lorenzen, 239, and others.

would mean that the whole law prevailing at the place of contracting, including its conflict rules, is to apply; hence if these conflict rules, like most of the continental rules, refer to the proper law of the contract the formalities prescribed by the proper law apply by way of *renvoi*.[1]

430. What is the *locus actus*? Where the *lex loci actus* is to be applied, the question: What is the place of contracting? is referred first to the applicable conflict rule, but as the conflict rules are silent on this point, the answer will have to be derived from the municipal law; i.e. a contract is concluded at that place where the last act necessary to create a binding agreement is performed.[2] Thus, for example, an obligation created by deed under English law comes into existence when the instrument has been signed, sealed, and delivered; therefore the place of delivery is the *locus actus*.[3] A contract by correspondence is according to English law completed at the time and place when and where the offeree posts his acceptance.[4]

431. Form and Procedure V. In the above discussion relating to the form or the formalities of a contract we have had in mind only such formal provisions as must be observed in order to create a valid contract. There are other rules on 'formalities' which are relative only to procedure, such as s. 4 of the Statute of Frauds: if certain forms are not observed, though the contract is valid, no action can be brought upon it until the omission is made good. Rules on forms of this kind, like all procedural rules, are applied by the courts of the country in which they have been established, irrespective both of the *locus actus* and of the proper law of the contract; and conversely, foreign rules concerned with the necessity of 'written evidence' are not applied by the courts of this country.[5]

[1] See *supra*, s. 179, 180.
[2] Goodrich, 218.
[3] See *Chapman* v. *Cottrell* (1865), 34 L.J. (Ex.) 186.
[4] *Benaim* v. *Debono*, [1924] A.C. (P.C.) 514, 520. See *supra*, s. 132.
[5] *Leroux* v. *Brown* (1852), 12 C.B. 801. See *supra*, s. 218.

BIBLIOGRAPHY

BEALE, 23 *Harv. L.R.* (1910), I, 79, 194, 260. K. NEUMANN, *Vertragsgültigkeit und Parteiwille*, 1930. Cf. *supra*, Bibliography, p. 435. For the form of contracts: LORENZEN, 228–60. E. SILZ, *Du domaine de l'application de la règle 'locus regit actum*', 1933. ARMINJON, *Rev. Darras*, 1925, 489; 1926, 161. AUDINET, *Répert.* X. 388. DICEY, 'Locus regit actum', 26 *L.Q.R.* (1910), 277. NIBOYET, *Traité*, 203–38.

THE EFFECTS OF A CONTRACT

I. The *interpretation* of a contract is governed by the proper law of the contract.[1] This does not mean—as has been suggested—that the technical legal terms included in the text of the contract must necessarily be interpreted as in the proper law. If, for example, the parties have expressly agreed that the proper law of a contract made in America with the assistance of American lawyers shall be English law, it may nevertheless be appropriate to understand the legal expressions used in that contract in the sense of American and not of English law. It is the *rules of interpretation* of contracts—rules different in the legal systems of the various countries—that must be taken from the proper law of the contract.[2] For example, the narrow English rule of construction according to which words are to be understood in their plain and literal meaning unless 'from the context of the instrument a definite meaning can be collected which gives a broader interpretation to specific words than their literal meaning would bear',[3] must not be applied in interpreting a contract governed by French, German, or Swiss law.

432. Interpretation

II. The proper law of the contract governs all its effects, no matter whether they have been foreseen and intended by the parties or whether they come into existence by operation of law.

433. Effets and suites

In France the old distinction between these two groups of consequences, the first called *effets*, the second *suites du contrat*, has the support of many eminent scholars,[4] the seller's duty, for example, to deliver the goods sold to the purchaser being subjected to the law chosen by the parties, while the

---

[1] Dicey–Morris, pp. 646–8.

[2] *In re Société Intercommunale Belge*, [1933] Ch. 684, 690. *St. Pierre* v. *South American Stores*, [1937] 3 A.E.R. 351, 355.

[3] Anson, *Contracts* (19th ed.), 301; *Mallan* v. *May* (1843), 13 M. & W., 517. Cf. Lord Wensleydale's rule in *Grey* v. *Pearson* (1857), 6 H.L. Cas. 61, 106.

[4] Foelix, *Traité*, I. 231; Valéry, *Manuel*, 987, 988. Against this doctrine: Weiss, *Traité*, IV. 392, and others.

obligation to pay damages in case of breach of contract would be governed by the law of the place of performance. Under English law no such differentiation exists: both consequences are governed by the proper law of the contract.

434.
Changes in the obligation

1. The proper law therefore governs all the *changes* which the contractual obligations undergo owing to a failure of performance on the part of the debtor, or to facts which make the performance impossible, or to the creditor's refusal to accept the goods tendered to him. The proper law decides whether in the case of a breach of the contract the creditor can claim interest and at what rate, whether he is entitled to reparation of the immaterial damage he has suffered, what is the influence of contributory negligence on the part of the creditor,[1] and so forth. It may happen that the damaging fact constitutes both a breach of contract and a delict (tort); in such case the proper law of the contract may differ from the legal system which regulates the consequences of the delict.[2] Thus, if the seller of specific goods maliciously destroys them in England and the contract of sale is governed by French law, the English court will (it is submitted) apply the French law of sale and the English law of torts.

435. Effect of contract on ownership

2. Only the *obligations* imposed on the parties are governed by the proper law of the contract. Whether the contract has the effect of transferring ownership or other *iura in rem* must be decided by the *lex situs rei*.[3] Equitable interests created by a contract are—on the ground that equity looks on that as done which ought to have been done —obligations of a peculiar type, that is, obligations which are effective not only *vis-à-vis* the other contracting party but also *vis-à-vis* a third purchaser who is aware of the conflicting equitable interest.[4] Whether a contract creates such equitable right is answered by its proper law, and (it seems) not by the law of the situs. Example: A contract to

---

[1] Continental laws also apply the concept of contributory negligence in the case of contractual damage, not only where the damage has been caused by a tortious act.

[2] That is the *lex fori*; see *infra*, s. 476.

[3] On this see *infra*, s. 488 et seq.

[4] *Quaere*: is not the equitable right (for example, of a *cestui que trust*) by its structure similar to the *ius ad rem* of medieval canon and feudal law and of the Prussian *Allgemeines Landrecht* I. 10 § 25; I. 19 § 5?

execute a legal mortgage of land abroad, the proper law of which is English, produces an equitable mortgage within the meaning of English law, and all the English equitable rules, for example the rule against clogging the equity of redemption, are applicable.[1]

3. We are faced with grave difficulties in cases where a contract is *split up* to the effect that the obligations of one party (for example, the seller) are governed by one law, and those of the other party (the buyer) by a different law. Such scission is the normal rule under German and Swiss law in the case of contracts of sale or other reciprocal contracts, where each debtor is subject to the law of the place where he has to perform his obligations, unless the parties have chosen a unitary law for the whole of the contract. But it may occur in English law too, although here in the case of sale the duties of both parties are normally to be performed at the same place, viz. the seller's place of business. Such splitting up of the contract into seller's duties and buyer's duties leads to strange and unsound results.[2] Whether in the case of breach of a condition or warranty the buyer can claim damages or delivery of goods free from defect is decided by the law governing the seller's duties; whether he is entitled to repudiate the contract or to reduce the price of defective goods, or whether the risk passes to him at the moment of concluding the contract or not till the time of delivery, will be answered by the law governing the buyer's duties, &c. In the case of an unpaid seller his right of stoppage *in transitu* and his lien are governed by the buyer's law in so far as they are effective against him; but the question whether these rights, if existing under the buyer's law, can be exercised against third purchasers depends (probably) on the situs of the goods at the time of the acquisition by the third purchaser.[3]

The case in which the contract is split up into two equal

436. Splitting up of a contract

---

[1] *British South Africa Co.* v. *De Beers Consolidated Mines*, [1910] 2 Ch. (C.A.) 502, 513 (reversed on appeal on another point: [1912] A.C. 52). *Ex parte Pollard* (1840), Mont. & Ch. 239, 250. *In re Smith*, [1916] 2 Ch. 206. On trusts see *infra*, s. 506.

[2] See on this (in detail), on the one hand, Neuner, *Rabel's Z.*, 2, 108; 7, 850; on the other, Haudek, loc. cit., 72 et seq. *Supra*, s. 404.

[3] Cf. *Inglis* v. *Usherwood* (1801), 1 East 515, 524, and *infra*, s. 492.

parts, corresponding to the duties of one or the other of the parties, must be distinguished from the much more frequent case where the contract as a whole is governed by a unitary law, its proper law, but where certain particular matters are to be determined by a different legal system which thus becomes 'incorporated' into a contract, as English judges have aptly expressed it. Two examples of this:

(*a*) It may happen that while the contract as a whole is governed by one legal system, its 'construction' or 'interpretation' is to be carried out in accordance with a different legal system. This was the case in *The Torni*,[1] where the Court of Appeal held the contract of affreightment to be governed by Palestinian law as the proper law, in spite of the express clause that the construction of the contract was to be determined by English law. True, this point in the judgment in *The Torni* was gravely criticized by the Privy Council in the case of *Vita Foods Products* v. *Unus*;[2] but that criticism affects only the presumptive meaning of the contractual clause that the construction of the contract shall be determined by the law of X;[3] it does not challenge the right of the contracting parties to differentiate expressly between the contract as a whole and its construction.

437. Mode of performance (*b*) There is a presumption in English law that whatever is the proper law of the contract as a whole, the 'mode or method of performance' and its 'incidents' are nevertheless governed by the *lex loci solutionis*, and not by the proper law.[4] This has often been expressed by the antithesis 'obligation' and 'performance', the former being governed by the proper law, the latter by the law of the place of performance. Similarly, continental courts have often contrasted the contract itself and the act of performance, the *Zahlungsgeschäft*,[5] and have subjected—as in England—the act of performance, at least where it consisted in the payment of

---

[1] [1932] P. 78, 84. [2] [1939] A.C. 277.

[3] Apart from the fact that the view of the Court of Appeal in *The Torni* is still the law.

[4] *Lloyd* v. *Guibert* (1865), L.R. 1 Q.B., 115, 126. *Jacobs* v. *Crédit Lyonnais* (1884), 12 Q.B.D. 589, 604. *Auckland City Council* v. *Alliance Assurance Co.*, [1937] A.C. (P.C.) 587, 606, and others.

[5] German Supreme Court, *Offic. Coll.*, 118, 374; 126, 205; and Haudek, loc. cit., 69. As to French law: Niboyet, *Manuel*, p. 814, and *Rev. Darras*, 1925, 161 et seq.

money, to the law of the country where such payment was to be made.

It will be observed that the English contrast between obligation and performance is rather rough and ready and far from precise. If a person promises to pay £1,000 in Sydney, Australia, on 1 July, the question whether the obligation exists and is to be performed depends on the proper, say English, law; but the question whether there is an obligation on the debtor to pay English pounds or only Australian pounds,[1] and whether he has to pay exactly on the first of July or is to be allowed some days of grace, is answered by the law of the place of payment, that is, Australian law. The correct antithesis is not obligation and performance, but main obligation and subsidiary obligations (and rights), that is, obligations concerning the details of performance.

THE EXTINCTION OF OBLIGATIONS

The proper law of the contract answers the question whether the contractual obligation still exists or whether it is extinguished.[2] It governs the different ways of extinguishing an obligation, in particular:

438. The different ways of extinguishing obligations

1. by performance—subject to the presumption that obligations concerning the mode of performance are governed by the law of the place of performance (see s. 437). Where the performance demands transfer of ownership of a thing the question whether such ownership has been transferred to the creditor is answered not by the proper law or the *lex loci solutionis*, but by the law of the situs of the alienated thing.[3]

2. by a substitute for the promised performance: the debtor instead of paying the due sum of money gives to his creditor and in agreement with him a motor-car in lieu of performance. Whether this new agreement is valid and what are its effects *inter partes*, for example in the case of defects in the car, will be determined by the proper law of the new agreement, which may differ from the proper law of the old contract. But whether it extinguishes the original obligation and therefore exonerates sureties and brings mortgages to an end is decided by the proper law of the

---

[1] *Adelaide Electric Supply Co.* v. *Prudential Assurance Co.*, [1934] A.C. 122.

[2] *Ralli* v. *Dennistoun* (1851), 6 Ex. 483, 493. *Taylor* v. *Hollard*, [1902] 1 K.B. 676, 682. *Swiss Bank Corp.* v. *Boehmische Industriebank*, [1923] 1 K.B. 673. *Perry* v. *Equitable Life Assurance Soc.* (1929), 45 T.L.R. 468.

[3] *Infra*, s. 491 et seq.

original contract. This becomes important where the substituted thing is defective or turns out to have been stolen
from the true owner; for under some laws the creditor can
still revert to his old claim,[1] even against sureties, while
most legal systems declare the substitution and therefore
the extinction of the debt to be final.[2]

3. By lodgement with a public authority, for example
deposit in court.[3] The proper law decides whether and in
what circumstances the debt is thereby discharged. The
'mode' of lodgement and the place where the deposit is to
be made are determined by the law of the country where it
takes place.

4. The proper law governs further the extinction by
waiver on the part of the creditor. It decides in particular
whether a unilateral declaration by the creditor is sufficient[4]
or whether the waiver demands an agreement between him
and the debtor; further, whether the waiver is valid only if
made with valuable consideration or by deed.

5. Novation, which only plays a small part in modern
practice, is to be treated in the same way as performance in
lieu of promised performance.

439. In particular: set-off

6. The extinction of debts by *set-off* is under English law
regarded as an act of the court and therefore as a matter of
procedure.[5] In this, English law differs from most other
legal systems; under these the extinction is either brought
about by a private unilateral declaration of one of the parties
addressed to the other, or by operation of law through the
mere fact that a debtor is his creditor's creditor. The first
method prevails in Germany,[6] the second in France[7] and
under many laws derived from French law. Hence English

---

[1] e.g. in Roman law: *si quis aliam rem pro alia volenti solverit et evicta fuerit res, manet pristina obligatio*; Dig. 46, 3, 46 pr.

[2] See *RVgl.HWB*. III. 158.

[3] *De Beéche* v. *South American Stores*, [1935] A.C. 148.

[4] According to Haudek, *RVgl.HWB*. III. 160, this is so in Hungary and Japan.

[5] *Supra*, s. 220.

[6] s. 388 German Civ. Code. See also Swiss Law of Oblig., s. 124.

[7] Code civil, art. 1290; this rule (*ipso iure compensatur*), however, operates only if one of the parties relies on it; when the creditor brings an action in court the debtor must *opposer la compensation*; see art. 1299 and Planiol & Ripert, *Traité prat.*, VII, p. 623, n. 1. Similarly: the Austrian Courts in respect of s. 1438 Austrian Civ. Code.

courts apply the *lex fori*,[1] continental courts the proper law of the contracts in which the debts arose.[2] Such difference of classification does not, however, exclude the application of foreign substantive rules on set-off in an English court, or conversely the application of English rules in a foreign court. True, if *A* has a claim against *B* on the ground of a wilful delict committed by *B*, if *B* has a claim against *A* based on a contract, if the contract is governed by German law, and if *A* sues *B* in an English court, the court is at liberty to admit the set-off, though German law expressly provides that 'against a claim arising from an unlawful act committed wilfully no set-off is permissible'.[3] But the English court does not assume that if under the foreign proper law of the contracts in which the reciprocal debts arose the debts have been extinguished in the way prescribed by the said law, such extinction should be regarded as non-existent.

Take, for example, the following case: Under two German contracts each of two persons *A* and *B*, while living in Germany, had a claim against the other; in accordance with German law, *B* by a simple extra-judicial declaration addressed to *A* expressed his intention of setting off his claim against his debt: by this declaration both claims were entirely extinguished (provided that both had been valid at the time of the declaration). Later, however, *A* brings an action in the English court against the Englishman *E*, who had become surety for *B*'s debt by a contract which is also governed by German law. As German law allows the surety to avail himself of all defences to which the principal debtor is entitled, *E* must be allowed to plead extinction of the principal debt by *B*'s extra-judicial unilateral declaration.[4] It does not matter whether *B* made the declaration in Germany or in England.

7. In principle the proper law governing a debt answers the question whether the discharge of the debt under the *bankruptcy law* of a foreign country is a valid discharge in England.[5] If a debtor whose debt is governed by the law of

      440. Discharge of a bankrupt

---

[1] *Meyer* v. *Dresser* (1864), 16 C.B. (N.S.) 646, 664.

[2] If the two debts have different proper laws some scholars (for example, Zitelmann, II. 397) admit a set-off only if both proper laws allow it. Convincingly against this view see Lewald, p. 283.

[3] s. 393 German Civ. Code.

[4] See *Allen* v. *Kemble* (1848), 6 Moore, P.C., 314, 321 (extinction of the debt by *compensatio* according to Roman-Dutch law). *Supra*, s. 220.

[5] *Potter* v. *Brown* (1804), 5 East 124. *Gardiner* v. *Houghton* (1862), 2 B. & S. 743. *Ellis* v. *McHenry* (1871), L.R. 6, C.P. 228, 234. *Gibbs* v. *Société Industrielle* (1890), 25 Q.B.D. (C.A.) 399. *Bartley* v. *Hodges* (1861), 1 B. & S. 375.

country X has been made bankrupt in X and discharged there, he is no longer a debtor. The law of a different country 'to which the contract does not belong'[1] cannot discharge him. An exception to this principle however exists in favour of a discharge made under English, Scottish, or Irish bankruptcy law; such discharge is operative in any part of the British Empire even if the proper law of the debt is French or German.[2]

Limitation of action is not a means of extinction of debts. See on this *supra*, s. 219.

SUBSTITUTION OF ONE DEBTOR FOR ANOTHER. SEVERAL DEBTORS

441. Substitution of a new debtor

I. The substitution of one debtor for another[3] is treated either as a novation, that is, an extinction of an existing debt by the creation of a new one, or as a true succession into an obligation which remains in force. The first method, developed on the basis of Roman law, is to be found in English and French municipal laws; the second method prevails in German law and has been adopted in the legal systems of Austria, Switzerland, and Poland.

In both cases the question whether the old debtor is discharged by the entry of a new debtor depends on the proper law of the debt. But whether the entry of a new debtor has taken place must be determined by the law with which that entry is most closely connected; this may be the new debtor's personal law or the law of his place of business, unless he and the creditor have agreed on a particular legal system.

Under some legal systems when a commercial enterprise

---

[1] Lord Esher, M.R., in *Gibbs* v. *Société Industrielle*, loc. cit., at p. 406, in using these words points very clearly to the proper law of the contract. Older decisions mostly speak of the law of the country in which the debt has been contracted or 'has arisen' (for example, *Ellis* v. *McHenry*, loc. cit.) or where it is to be paid. But it will be remembered that the *lex loci contractus* or *loci solutionis* is presumably the proper law, and that formerly the courts were even more inclined than now to assume that the *lex loci contractus* is the proper law.

[2] See Dicey–Morris, pp. 444–7; Westlake, ss. 241 242; Cheshire, pp. 648–50.

[3] The substitution of one creditor for another, the assignment of debts, is regarded by English law as a transfer of intangible property. Hence the question which law governs the assignment will be dealt with under Property Law (*infra*, s. 511).

is transferred from *A* to *B* the law operates to make *B* liable for all debts incurred in the course of the business. The law of the place where the enterprise has its centre will decide whether or not *B* has been made so liable.

II. Where there are *several debtors* to one debt it may be that the obligation of one of them is governed by a law different from the law to which the others are subjected. In such cases it is difficult to say which law is to decide whether the joint debtors as between themselves are each liable in equal shares, and whether, if one of them has paid the whole amount of the debt, he can claim contribution from the others. It is suggested that a right to recover from his co-debtors exists only if and in so far as all the proper laws regulating the respective obligations of the various debtors grant such right.[1]   *442. Several debtors*

A collateral security for a debt,[2] in particular a suretyship, is not necessarily governed by the law regulating the principal obligation. The creditor and the surety may subject the contract of suretyship to a different law. If, for example, a French merchant gives credit to his French debtor on the security of a suretyship which a domiciled and resident Englishman gives by an instrument signed and delivered in London the duties of the surety will be governed by English law. But as the suretyship is valid only if the principal debt is valid, it is necessary to ascertain whether this is the case, and that must be done by reference not to the law governing the suretyship but to the proper law of the principal contract.[3]   *443. Principal debtor and surety*

[1] At any rate it is not the *lex fori* that ought to be applied; see *supra*, s. 227.
[2] Cf. also *Moulis* v. *Owen*, [1907] 1 K.B. 746: as a security for a French debt a cheque was drawn by the debtor on an English bank; the cheque was intended to be governed by English law.
[3] See *supra*, p. 207 (*d*).

CHAPTER XXVIII

MONEY OBLIGATIONS

444.
Principle

I. THE contractual obligation to pay money—like all other duties arising from a contract—is governed by the proper law of the contract; the 'mode or method' of performance and its incidents are, however, determined by the law of the place of payment unless the contracting parties have agreed to apply a different law to these matters.[1]

445.
'Option de place' and *'option de change'*

The place of payment is not always finally fixed at the time of contracting, but often depends, in particular in the case of public loans, on certain options granted to the creditor. Such option may be given in the form '£100 payable at the creditor's choice in London or New York or Amsterdam'. Or it may run: '£100 payable in London, or at the creditor's choice U.S.A. dollars 280 payable in New York or &c.' The first is called an option of place, the second an option of change (or of payment).[2] In both cases the place of performance and therefore the law applicable to the mode of payment remains unsettled till the creditor has made his choice.

446. What kind of money owed

The proper law governing the duty to pay decides what kind of money (English or French or Canadian, &c.) is owed.[3] Where the contractual denomination of the currency is ambiguous, it is for the proper law to indicate the rules on interpretation under which the doubtful expression is to be explained. Example: the contract speaks of a certain sum in 'dollars', but it is doubtful whether U.S.A. dollars or Canadian or Mexican dollars are meant. If the proper law is English it is presumed that such ambiguous designation of the money due points to the money of the

---

[1] See *supra*, s. 437, and Mann, *Legal Aspect of Money*, p. 155.

[2] These options must be distinguished from a mere 'option of collection': '£100 payable in London and collectable in New York or Amsterdam.' Here only London is the 'place of payment' in the technical sense of the term; and if the creditor demands and receives payment in New York this does not alter the place of payment. The law applicable to the mode and method of payment is therefore English law. The pounds to be paid in London and collected in Amsterdam are English pounds, and the payment cannot be made in Dutch guilders.

[3] Dicey–Morris, p. 734 et seq.

place of payment,[1] and the same rule seems to exist in other countries.[2] Of course, this presumption is of no help if the currency circulating at the place of payment differs from all those which the parties may have had in view;[3] if then the intention of the parties cannot be ascertained by the circumstances of the case, the contract is void on the ground of uncertainty.

II. Is a debt expressed in foreign money to be paid in foreign money? There are three possible answers to this. First, an unqualified affirmative; the debtor of 100 Canadian dollars payable in London always and only fulfils his obligation if he pays his creditor 100 Canadian dollars. Second, the debtor is obliged, if the creditor so demands, to pay an equivalent sum in pounds sterling. Third, the debtor is entitled to discharge the debt by paying in pounds sterling even against his creditor's wish. The correct answer depends on the proper law of the contract;[4] for the question to be decided does not merely concern the mode and method of payment, but deals with the very essence of the obligation. Therefore if the contract is an English contract, English municipal law decides the question of conversion,[5] no matter whether the place of payment is English or not. If, on the other hand, the contract is governed by a foreign law, the decision lies (apart from *renvoi*) with the internal foreign law even if the payment is due in England.

447. Conversion of a foreign money debt

This statement must, however, be modified owing to an

---

[1] See in respect of pounds (English, Australian, and New Zealand pounds) the cases of *Adelaide Electric Supply Co.* v. *Prudential Assurance Co.*, [1934] A.C. 122, 145, 151, and *Auckland City Council* v. *Alliance Assurance Co.*, [1937] A.C. (P.C.) 587, 599, 606; Mann, pp. 165, 169, 170.

[2] See Mann, p. 165, n. 2.

[3] *Example*: a Frenchman promises a Swiss firm to pay '1000 francs' in London. See Mann, loc. cit., p. 167, n. 3.

[4] Mann, 250, 251, where the different view of other authors is criticized.

[5] But English municipal law is not quite clear on this question. Probably every monetary obligation *can* be discharged in the currency of the place of payment if the debtor chooses to do so; see Lord Wright's remark in *Rhokana Corp.* v. *Inland Revenue Commissioners*, [1937] 1 K.B. (C.A.) 797; *Andersen* v. *Equitable Assurance Society* (1926), 134 L.T. (C.A.) 557, 562. But can the creditor *refuse* to be paid in the currency expressed in the contract? There seems to be no authority supporting such an unfortunate result. (Mann, pp. 243–5, grants the creditor such right.)

English rule of procedure, viz.: English courts 'have no jurisdiction to order payment of money except in the currency of this country'.[1] The question of the rate of exchange at which a foreign money debt should be converted into English currency is not yet settled.[2] The predominant doctrine and some decisions apply the rate current on the day when the debt falls due.[3] The rate at the date on which judgment is delivered was regarded as decisive by an old decision of the Privy Council; and this view was contemplated in several dicta of the Court of Appeal; for a very special case it was accepted by the Foreign Judgments (Reciprocal Enforcement) Act, 1933.[4] In the case of *Marrache* v. *Ashton*[5] the Privy Council took yet another date, viz. the date when the writ was issued. It is suggested that conversion at the rate on the judgment date is more satisfactory than any conversion at a previous date; and yet it is not fully satisfactory, since it ignores the possibility of a change of value between the date of judgment and that of the actual payment. The creditor should obtain the sum in sterling which it would cost him to purchase in the market the amount of the foreign money which the debtor was bound to deliver to him.[6] Hence it would be sound to declare the debtor to be discharged only if he pays the equivalent of the foreign money due at the rate current on the day of payment.[7]

III. Alterations and disturbances of the monetary system, with which all nations are confronted in times of economic crises, are of one of two kinds:

1. They may be alterations of the legal organization of

[1] *Manners* v. *Pearson*, [1898] 1 Ch. 581, 587; *Di Ferdinando* v. *Simon, Smits & Co.*, [1920] 3 K.B. 409, 415; *S.S. Celia* v. *S.S. Volturno*, [1921] 2 A.C. 544, 560; *Madeleine Vionnet* v. *Wills*, [1939] 4 A.E.R. 136; *Graumann* v. *Treitel*, [1940] 2 A.E.R. 188, 198. Similarly the law of the United States. None of the continental laws forbid actions or judgments for foreign money; Mann, p. 280.
[2] See on this subject notably Mann, 8 *Mod. L.R.* 177.
[3] Mann, *Legal Aspect of Money*, p. 291 et seq.
[4] 23 Geo. V, c. 13, s. 2, sub-sect. (3).   [5] [1943] A.C. (P.C.) 311, 318.
[6] See *Marrache* v. *Ashton*, loc. cit., p. 318.
[7] This is the German rule (s. 244, Germ. C.C.). Of course, the judgment can convert the foreign money only at the rate on the judgment date. But if the amount turns out to be insufficient, the creditor may bring a second action for the surplus due to him owing to the increase of value (of the foreign money) between judgment and payment.

the monetary system, such as the introduction of new coins or new notes,[1] the reduction of the weight of coins, the transition from a silver to a gold standard, the endowment of banknotes with the character of legal tender (*cours légal*), or the introduction of inconvertibility (*cours forcé*). As long as the *metallistic doctrine* prevailed, money was regarded as a certain quantity of metal with an impression on it certifying weight and fineness,[2] paper money such as banknotes being looked upon not as money but as a substitute for it. The relationship between the monetary systems of different countries or of the same country in different periods was mainly determined by the amount and fineness of metal contained in the standard unit of one country or period as compared with that of another country or period, and in the case of different standard metals (gold, silver) by the value of one metal as compared with that of the other. If the monetary system changed within a country the legislator would often lay down a rule on conversion of monetary debts expressed in units of the old system into monetary debts of the new style. Where such rule was based on the metallic relationship between the old and the new money it was also decisive in international intercourse; not so where the new coins were of a lower metallic content although an equal paying power was officially attributed to them.

The metallistic doctrine has disappeared entirely; *nominalism* prevails everywhere; i.e. a debtor of money is bound to pay in whatever at the date of payment is legal tender in the country whose money is in issue, and he has to pay so many pieces of that money that if one adds together the units of measurement as indicated on those pieces their sum equals the sum of money owed. The question what chattels are money and what is their nominal value (or better, their nominal amount) is answered by the

449. *Lex pecuniae* decisive

---

[1] Or the declaration that the old (*peseta*) notes shall retain their character as money only if they are accompanied by a certificate (*guia*) of a certain kind; thus during and after the Spanish revolution: see *Pyrmont Ltd.* v. *Schott*, [1939] A.C. (P.C.) 145, 156.

[2] That is what one of the most distinguished German jurists (E. I. Bekker, *Couponsprocesse der österreichischen Eisenbahnen*, pp. 93, 121) still thought in 1881.

law which creates them or endows them with the quality of money and a precise nominal value (*lex pecuniae*).[1] No other than English law *can* answer the question what ten English pounds are. Though the obligation to pay ten pounds may be governed by French law as the proper law of the contract, French law cannot indicate what is meant by the term 'ten English pounds'. A pound sterling is no longer defined by any legal system as a certain weight of gold bullion.

Therefore, if the monetary system of country *A* is replaced by another, if, for example, country *A* abandons the gold standard and adopts a system of inconvertible paper money, it is solely the law of *A* that establishes the rule under which old monetary obligations expressed in its currency are to be converted. The proper law of the contract has no say in the matter. This has sometimes been doubted on the ground that laws on compulsory tender (*cours forcé*) should not have extraterritorial effect. But no such rule exists. If in August 1931 two Germans concluded a contract of sale in Germany to be performed there, but agreed that the price should be expressed and paid in English money, there is no reason why the seller should not suffer from the English departure from the gold standard in September 1931 in the same way as an Englishman who makes an English contract. The seller who distrusts the value of his own country's money and places his trust in a foreign currency must take the rough with the smooth.

This was stated by the Privy Council in *Ottoman Bank* v. *Chakarian*:[2] 'The currency in any particular country must be determined by the law of that country, and that law is naturally in terms limited to defining what is legal tender in that country. But when that is fixed by the local law it determines what is the legal tender of that country for purposes of transactions in any other country, so that a foreign court will, when such questions come before it, give effect to the proper law of legal tender so determined.'

The problem of the applicable law was most thoroughly discussed in the lawsuits which German creditors brought against Austrian railway companies after 1876.

---

[1] See *In re Chesterman's Trusts*, [1923] 2 Ch. 466, 478; *Pyrmont Ltd.* v. *Schott*, [1939] A.C. (P.C.) 145, 157. Cf. Ehrenberg's *Handbuch des Handelsrechts*, IV. 1 (1917), 637.

[2] [1938] A.C. 260, 278; Mann, pp. 193, 194.

Before 1871 the defendants had issued bonds payable either in Austrian (silver) guilders or in German (silver) thalers, 200 guilders being equal to 133⅓ thalers. After the introduction of the gold standard in Germany the price of silver dropped heavily; the relation between gold and silver changed in a short time from 1:15½ to 1:19, which caused a considerable depreciation of the Austrian guilders. Under German law the debts expressed in thalers were converted into mark debts at the rate of 1 mark to ⅓ thaler.[1] The defendants denied their obligation to pay the plaintiffs in German money. If it was true that they had engaged themselves to pay Austrian or German money at the choice of their creditors,[2] the problem of private international law was this: is the German rule on conversion (at the rate of 1 to ⅓) applicable even though the proper law of the contract was Austrian law?[3] This was rightly answered in the affirmative by nearly all German courts.[4]

2. Fluctuations in the purchasing power of money must be treated differently from changes in the monetary system, though they may represent the economic effect of some such change, for example, of a transition from the gold standard to paper currency. In principle the debtor of foreign money must pay, and the creditor must accept, the nominal amount according to the rules of legal tender and conversion prevailing in the country of the monetary system involved, and if the debtor so pays, his obligation is thereby extinguished irrespective of whether between the date of the contract and the date of payment the purchasing power of the money has remained the same, or has decreased for example by inflation, or has increased by deflation.[5] There are, however, some legal systems—of countries in which a catastrophe or at least a very considerable decrease of the purchasing power of the currency has taken place (Germany, Poland, Danzig, Hungary, Lithuania, Czechoslovakia)—which have provided for a revalorization of old debts either by special statutes or by applying

*450.
Changes in purchasing power (inflation, &c.)*

---

[1] The depreciation of silver caused the Austrian silver guilders to sink so low that 200 guilders were equal to about 345 German marks, that is 115 thalers according to the German rate of conversion.

[2] This was doubtful, but was in most cases affirmed.

[3] Whether the proper law was Austrian or whether it depended on the law of the place of payment was also subject to doubt.

[4] German Supreme Commercial Court (*Off. Coll.*), 23, 205; 25, 41; Supreme Court (*Off. Coll.*), 6, 126; 19, 48. Bibliography: see Ehrenberg's *Handbuch des Handelsrechts*, IV. 1, 643, n. 30.

[5] See the decisions in *Re Chesterman's Trusts, supra,* and *Pyrmont Ltd.* v. *Schott, supra,* s. 448, 449.

the general rule of the law of obligations according to which 'a debtor must fulfil his obligation in accordance with the demands of good faith'.[1]

451.
Revaloriza-tion laws

What is the international scope of such revalorization rules? Are they part of the *monetary* system of the country where they are enacted, and therefore applicable wherever money of that country is due, or is their application dependent on the proper law governing the debt? The latter answer is the correct one. Take the law of Germany which (after the first world war) provided the chief example of revalorization. When in 1924[2] the old *Mark* was replaced by the *Reichsmark* the relationship between the former and the latter was fixed at 1,000,000,000,000 : 1. This relationship (or, as the economist F. Knapp formulated it, the 'recurrent link', which in truth defines the new currency by recurring to the old)[3] was not altered by the revalorization laws. These established different revalorization rates for various groups of monetary obligations and charges— for example, a mortgage of 10,000 Marks if constituted in 1917 was revalorized at 2,500 Reichsmarks, but if constituted in December 1919 was revalorized at only 260 Reichsmarks; bearer bonds for 10,000 Marks issued in 1917 were given a value as high as 1,500 Reichsmarks, but the debtor could apply for lower revalorization; and so forth. Does that imply that the meaning of the term 'Reichsmark' was different in the different cases, that the inscription '1,000 Reichsmarks' on a Reichsbank note changes its meaning according to the use made of the note? The revalorization alters the content of monetary obligations and not the currency law. Hence, German, Polish, Hungarian (&c.) revalorization laws could only be applied to a debt if the debt was governed by German, Polish, or Hungarian law respectively. A debt of 1,000 Marks created between Englishmen in 1913 and governed by English law is revalorized neither under the German revalorization decree nor under the general German rule which requires that the debtor shall discharge his obligation in accordance

---

[1] German Civ. Code, s. 242.
[2] Monetary Law of 30 Aug. 1924, s. 5 § 2.
[3] Knapp, *Staatliche Theorie des Geldes*, 1905, p. 12.

with the demands of good faith. Whether it can be re-valorized depends solely on English municipal law, and in this country no right to revalorization exists.[1] This view has been accepted by the courts of all countries where the problem has been decided. The leading English case is that of *Anderson* v. *Equitable Assurance Society of the U.S.A.*,[2] unanimously decided by the Court of Appeal, where Atkin, L. J., framed the rule that 'it is the debt that is valorized and not the currency' and derived from this the non-applicability of the German revalorization law to an English mark-debt.

IV. Contracting parties often attempt to protect themselves against fluctuations in the value of money by inserting into their contract a *gold clause* or some other stipulation which links the sum of money owed to some commodity (silver, rye, wheat, &c.) in the stability of which they have more confidence. Gold clauses are either gold coin clauses or gold value clauses.[3] In the first case the money debt is to be paid in gold coins, and if owing to a change of the monetary legislation gold coins cease to be money, the performance of the money debt becomes impossible. In the second case the money debt must be paid in whatever chattels have the character of money at the time of payment (banknotes, treasury certificates, &c.), but to such an amount that the creditor can buy with it the indicated quantity of gold.[4] Whether a phrase in the contract which mentions an amount of gold in connexion with the amount of the debt is a gold clause, or merely a reference to the gold standard on which the legal currency is based, depends on the construction of the contract.[5] And if owing to that construction

452. Gold clauses

[1] See on English municipal law *British Bank for Foreign Trade* v. *Russian Commercial & Industrial Bank* (1921), 38 T.L.R. 65, and Mann, op. cit., p. 208.

[2] (1926), 134 L.T. 557, 566. Later cases (which are not so clear) are *In re Schnapper*, [1936] 1 A.E.R. 322, 326, and *Kornatzki* v. *Oppenheimer*, [1937] 4 A.E.R. 133. See on them: Mann, loc. cit., 205–7.

[3] A duty to pay a certain amount of gold of a certain fineness is not a money debt at all, but is just like any other obligation to 'pay' in commodities (rye, wheat).

[4] See in particular the decision of the Permanent Court of International Justice in the case of Serbian Loans, *Coll. of Judgments*, Ser. A, No. 14, pp. 32, 41.

[5] *St. Pierre* v. *South American Stores*, [1937] 3 A.E.R. 349, 352. See Mann, 219 and 93–8 on the two Privy Council cases of *Ottoman Bank* v. *Dascalopoulos*, [1934] A.C. 354, and of *Ottoman Bank* v. *Chakarian*, [1938] A.C. 260, 268.

the clause is in the nature of a gold clause the decision whether it is a gold coin or a gold value clause will be given by the proper law of the contract.[1] Clauses such as '$100 in gold coin of the United States of America of or equal to the standard of weight and fineness existing on 1 September 1928', or '£100 in gold coin of the United Kingdom or in so much current legal tender of the United Kingdom that every pound comprised in the nominal amount of such payment represents the price in London in sterling (calculated at the date of maturity) of 123·27447 grains of gold of the standard of fineness specified in the First Schedule to the Coinage Act, 1870' are regarded in the United States and in this country as gold value clauses.[2] Gold value clauses are valid unless invalidated by special statutes. The validity of gold coin clauses is open to doubt in England[3] and in some other countries.

Gold clauses are economically superfluous as long as the monetary system is stable and operates smoothly; they become important when the monetary system of a country is seriously shaken. It is justifiable and from the point of view of economic policy even desirable that in such a period of financial insecurity or disaster all creditors should be treated alike, and that none should be allowed to exercise any privilege arising from a gold clause to the prejudice of others. Hence the abrogation of gold clauses in many countries[4] just at the time when they should have become operative.[5] This should be borne in mind in discussing

[1] Cf. Mann, 220.

[2] Ibid., 100 et seq. *Feist* v. *Société Intercommunale Belge*, [1934] A.C. 161. *The King* v. *International Trustee for the Protection of Bondholders*, [1937] A.C. 500, 566. *British and French Trust Corp.* v. *New Brunswick Railway Co.*, [1937] 4 A.E.R. (C.A.) 516; [1938] 4 A.E.R. (H.L.) 747.

[3] Owing to the observations by Farwell, J., in the *Feist Case (supra)*, [1933] Ch. 684, 692. See Mann, 104–8.

[4] During the First World War: in Germany, Austria, Belgium, Hungary, Roumania, Italy, Greece, Egypt. After the war, notably since 1931: in the Scandinavian states, Poland, Estonia, Mexico, Costa Rica, the United States (1933), Canada (1937; the text of the Gold Clauses Act is to be found in *All Engl. Rep.* 1938, 4, 752, and in *J. Comp. Leg.* 1941, Part II, 46), Brazil, Cuba, Guatemala, Columbia. See Nussbaum, 44 *Yale L.J.* 61; Mann, 111, 112.

[5] It has been said that such abrogations are unfair to the saver who wants and needs protection. The best answer to this is given by a distinguished French jurist: 'La meilleure protection de l'épargne c'est la conscience des risques qu'elle

whether a court should apply abrogation laws of foreign countries or not. The conception developed by shrewd business men and their lawyers that foreign abrogations of gold clauses must be inapplicable outside the state where they were enacted is narrow-minded and utterly unsound. If England was able in 1931 to control monetary disturbances without abrogating the gold clauses, the reason for this is that such clauses are rare in this country. Suppose (for a moment) that in 1931 all English contracts had contained the gold clause: this would have defeated the whole policy of abandoning the gold standard.

As to the international scope of laws abrogating gold clauses the only problem with which this book deals is this: What law answers the question whether a court should apply foreign abrogation laws? Three solutions come into consideration. The decisive law may be, firstly, the law of the monetary system concerned (*lex pecuniae*); or secondly, the *lex loci solutionis*; or thirdly, the proper law of the contract in which the debt originated. The first solution has been accepted only in Poland, Germany, and Austria.[1] It is open to objection. True, the abrogation of gold *coin* clauses has as a rule the effect of altering the currency by destroying the money character of gold coins; in so far the currency law is indeed concerned. But its further effect of making performance impossible must be regulated by the proper law of the contract like any other ground for discharging the debtor or altering his obligation. The abrogation of the gold *value* clause, on the other hand, immediately creates a substantial change in the amount of the debt, a partial reduction of it. Thus there remains the choice between the second and the third solution, that is, between the proper law of the contract and the law of the place of performance (governing the mode and method of payment). Take, for example, the case of a loan of Canadian dollars under Canadian law repayable in London and subject to a gold value clause. Is the court to apply the Canadian

453. International scope of gold clause abrogation laws

court, parce qu'on court des risques dès qu'on possède quelque chose et qu'on veut le garder.' (Hamel, *Travaux du Comité français d. dr. int. pr.*, III (1937), 126.)

[1] Poland, Law of 12 June 1934; Germany, Law of 26 June 1936; Austria, Law of 4 Apr. 1937. See Mann, 221, n. 3.

Gold Clauses Act, 1937 (which abrogated the gold clauses)? The answer depends on whether the proper law of the obligation or the law of the place of payment governs the question. The correct answer (it is suggested) is the former. The abolition of the gold-value clause does not result in an alteration of the 'mode and method of payment', but in an alteration of the main content of the obligation; the debtor has to pay less than before because he 'owes' less than before. The Court of Appeal, however, in *British & French Trust Corporation* v. *New Brunswick Railway Co.*[1] seems to have taken a different view, the court holding that not only the mode and method but also the measure of payment falls to be determined by the law of the place of payment. The objection to this reasoning is that the measure not of the payment but of the debt is in issue; the debtor has to pay what he owes—as soon as the amount of the debt is fixed, there is no doubt about the measure of payment. Fortunately the authority of the decision of the Court of Appeal is weakened by the fact that in the case before the Court the sum to be paid in London was expressed in pounds sterling and that the payment had to be made not in Canadian currency but in gold coin of Great Britain. The court may have based its view on the conception that the parties intended to subject the question of the amount of the debt to English law.

The result is this: the law of a country *X* which abrogates gold clauses is applicable in England only if the proper law of the debt is the law of that country *X*.

Where this is the case it is of course for the abrogating law to determine the scope of its application and to answer questions like the following: Does the abrogating law intend to abrogate *all* gold clauses? Or only those which refer to the currency of the country? Does it apply only to parties domiciled or resident in the country, or to its nationals? Or is it applicable to foreign as well as to domestic creditors? Does its application presuppose that the *locus*

---

[1] [1937] 4 A.E.R. 516, 525, 528, reversing the decision of Hilbery, J. ([1936] 1 A.E.R. 13). See Mann, op. cit., pp. 224–7. (The decision of the Court of Appeal on the main point was affirmed by the House of Lords, [1939] A.C. 1; but the reasoning was different.)

solutionis is within the country where the abrogation was enacted? The answer to all these questions depends on the interpretation of the abrogating law. It bristles with difficulties, particularly in the case of the most important of all foreign laws abrogating the gold clauses, the American Joint Resolution of 5 June 1933. But it is not a matter to be examined in a book on Private International Law.

The only remaining point of importance here is the question whether the application of a foreign law abrogating gold clauses offends against the public policy of the forum. Such offence has sometimes been asserted in Germany and the Netherlands,[1] and also in France, with the particular argument that in view of public policy a foreign abolition of gold clauses must be regarded as a measure with strictly territorial effect.[2] The courts of this country and most other countries have refused to apply the conception of public policy.[3] If what was said above about the economic unsoundness of gold clauses is correct, it is difficult to see why any country should object to their invalidation. Only if the abrogation of gold clauses were directed solely against creditors of foreign residence or nationality would the courts be likely to refuse application.

454. Gold clauses and public policy

V. *Moratoria*, i.e. statutory postponements of the stipulated date of payment of certain debts, are not infrequent in war-time, during a revolution, or in grave economic crises. Their international scope is doubtful. In foreign countries they are often regarded as strictly territorial, and their application by the courts of another country has been refused on the ground of public policy.[4] English law differs. The courts in this country do not object to applying a foreign moratorium, provided the place of payment is in the territory in which the moratorium was enacted.[5] A debtor should not be required to pay his creditor in a country where owing to a general moratorium he could not

455. *Moratoria*

---

[1] German Supreme Court *Jurist. Wochenschrift*, 1936, 2058 (*J. Clunet*, 1936, 951). On the Dutch cases: Mann, 231, n. 2.

[2] Example: *Dalloz Pér.* 1936.2.88. Mann, 229, 230.

[3] Mann, 232.

[4] Nussbaum, p. 248 *ad not.* 4.

[5] *Rouquette* v. *Overmann* (1875), L.R. 10 Q.B. 525, 535. *In re Francke and Rasch*, [1918] 1 Ch. 470, 482. Beale, II. 1270.

collect debts owing to him. It makes no difference whether the proper law of the contract in which the debt originated is identical with or different from the law of the place of payment.

456.
Currency
restrictions

VI. *Foreign currency restrictions* have been enacted in the course of the last thirty years in most countries.[1] They are of various types: their general trend is strict government control over all exportation or importation of money and over the conclusion and discharge of contracts which may influence the value of money. The most elaborate and increasingly stringent rules were enacted in Germany, soon after the collapse of the Austrian *Credit-Anstalt* and of some important German firms in 1931. The German interference with the freedom of international payments— even before the war of 1939—went so far as to forbid German debtors to make payments to foreign creditors, except by payment of German Reichsmarks into a blocked account within the German Reich, or to pay debts to foreigners out of funds held by the debtor abroad.

457. Their
application
abroad

Are such currency restrictions to be applied by any court outside the territory of the state that has enacted them? The question is in principle subject to the proper law of the contractual debt. At least this is the English view,[2] while the American *Restatement* prefers the *lex loci solutionis* where this differs from the proper law.[3] Under English law we must therefore distinguish: where the proper law is the law of the country in which the currency restrictions have been enacted these restrictions will be applied by an English court. Where, on the other hand, the proper law differs from the law prevailing in the restricting country the currency restrictions are inapplicable. It must however be

[1] Even before the war of 1939 thirty-six countries had currency restrictions against twenty-nine where freedom of exchange still prevailed; Freutel, 56 *Harv. L.R.* 30. Great Britain introduced a series of restrictions, notably by the Exchange Control Act, 1947.

[2] The English rule can be deduced from *De Beéche* v. *South American Stores*, [1935] A.C. 148 and *St. Pierre* v. *South American Stores*, [1937] 1 A.E.R. 206, 215, where the proper law of the contractual debt was Chilean law, though the payment had to be made in England; the court applied the Chilean currency restrictions.

[3] *Restatement*, §§ 358, 363, 370, and Freutel, loc. cit.

examined whether these two principles are in any way
qualified by the nature of the currency restrictions.

1. Are foreign currency restrictions always applicable **458.** (1) if
where the law of the restricting country is the proper law the re-
of the contractual obligation? Their application may be law is the
incompatible with their so-called territorial nature or con- proper law
trary to the public policy of the forum.

In a series of very forceful judgments the Swiss Federal Court[1] rejected
the application of the German currency restrictions as being 'attacks on the
rights of creditors repugnant to fundamental principles of Swiss law' or
'measures of force taken unilaterally by a foreign state to protect her own
economic interests to the detriment of those of other nations'. French courts[2]
reached the same result by stressing the fact that such restrictions are *adminis-
tratives*, *pénales*, and *politiques* and should therefore be strictly territorial.
The most emphatic language against the German currency restrictions
was however used by American courts (even before the United States
entered the war); in one instance they were stigmatized as 'highly repugnant to our sense of honour and decency' and as 'reflecting financial
sadism at its worst'.[3] Their application in the United States would indeed
have led to highly objectionable and immoral results. Examples are to be
found in those actions for money had and received which were brought by
German Jewish refugees against German steamship companies, such as the
North German Lloyd and the Hamburg-America Line. The plaintiffs
sought to recover the price they had paid for steamship passages from
Germany to the United States; the passage by German ships had become
impossible owing to the outbreak of war, and the plaintiffs (who as Jews
were practically forced to leave Germany) had succeeded in reaching the
United States by ships belonging to neutral countries. The defendant companies recognized their duty to return money received, but contended that
by virtue of German law they could repay the money only within Germany,
and only into a blocked account. They offered to make such payment. But
since the plaintiffs could not return to Germany or use their German
'blocked accounts' in America, these offers were of no value to the plaintiffs.
The American courts refused to apply the German currency laws.

The English courts have had no opportunity of deciding
cases similar to these.[4] In *Graumann* v. *Treitel*[5] both parties,

---

1 See *Offic. Coll. of the Decisions of the Fed. Court*, 60, II. 294; 61, II. 242;
63, II. 42.

2 Paris App. Court, *J. Clunet*, 1933, 963 and others.

3 *Pan-American Securities Corp.* v. *Fr. Krupp Aktiengesellschaft*, 169 Misc. 445
(1938), and others. See B. Hollander, *Confiscation, Aggression and Foreign Funds
Control* (1938), p. 93–6; 96, n. 10.

4 In the English case *Ginsberg* v. *Canadian Pacific Co.* (1940), 66 LL.L.R. 20,
the contract was not a German contract; therefore the German currency rules
were inapplicable.

5 [1940] 2 A.E.R. 188, 195.

former partners, were German refugees from Nazi oppression; the claim on which the action was based had originated while both were still in Germany, where they had obeyed the German currency provisions; after emigrating to England neither was bound further to observe them, and neither sought to rely on them here. The court was therefore able to give judgment without investigating whether the duty to obey such rules would be obnoxious to English public policy. In *De Beéche* v. *South American Stores*[1] and in *St. Pierre* v. *South American Stores*[2] the proper law of the contract was Chilean law; Chilean currency restrictions forbade the debtor to pay the due sum of pounds sterling in London, as he had promised; and the debtor, in accordance with Chilean law, had paid the due sum in pesos in the Chilean court, thereby discharging his debt according to Chilean law. The English court dismissed the creditors' actions for payment in pounds sterling. The inevitable inference from this is a general rule to the effect that foreign currency restrictions must always be applied where the proper law of the contract is the restricting law. Exceptions will, however, be admitted where in the particular circumstances of the case before the court the result of an application of a particular restriction enacted by a particular state offends against English principles of justice—as is likely in the circumstances of the American steamship cases. A general repudiation of all foreign restrictions would seem particularly unfair where the municipal law of the forum has enacted an exchange control similar to that of the foreign state.

The newest development of the problem is connected with the Bretton Woods Agreement. It has become evident that from the point of view of economic morality or decency the imposition of currency regulations may be either laudable or the very reverse. One type may indeed be characterized, as Swiss and American courts did, as repugnant to 'fundamental principles or to our sense of honour and decency'. The other type is represented by the postwar attempt to start an organized international—if possible,

[1] [1935] A.C. 148.
[2] [1937] 1 A.E.R. 206, 215, and (C.A.) 3 A.E.R. 349, 355.

global—economy. Under the Bretton Woods Agreement Act, 1945,[1] and the Order made under that Act[2] contracts inconsistent with the currency regulations of any member-state shall not be enforceable, provided such regulations are in accordance with the Bretton Woods Agreement.[3]

2. Where the law of the restricting state is the law of the place of payment, though different from the proper law of the contract, foreign currency restrictions may be taken into account on the basis of the rule that the English courts refuse to enforce a contract if the performance would be illegal according to the law of the place of performance.[4]

459. (2) if it is the lex loci solutionis

3. Where the law of the restricting state is neither the proper law of the contract nor the *lex loci solutionis*, the foreign currency restrictions will be disregarded. Though this goes without saying, debtors have sometimes relied on currency restrictions established by the law of their domicile or residence or their place of business. Thus in the case of *Kleinwort, Sons & Co.* v. *Ungarische Baumwolle Industrie Aktiengesellschaft*[5] the plaintiffs sued on a contract the proper law of which was English and which was to be performed in England. The Hungarian debtors in their defence fell back on Hungarian law, under which they were forbidden to pay their creditor in London, asserting that they could not be expected to break their domestic law. The defence was held to be bad. A debtor who under his personal law is not allowed to pay what he owes resembles any debtor who cannot fulfil his obligations because he has been robbed by a gang of highwaymen of all he possesses.[6]

460. (3) if different from proper law and lex loci solutionis

4. It goes without saying that offences against *English* currency regulations will not be condoned by an English court.[7]

---

[1] 9 and 10 Geo. VI, c. 194.   [2] S.R. and O. 1946, No. 36.

[3] *Frankman* v. *Anglo-Prague Creditbank* (per Cassels J.), [1948] 1 K.B. 730. (The Court of Appeal reversed the decision for different reasons.) The House of Lords, where the case was designated as *Zivnostenska Banka National Co.* v. *Frankman*, [1950] A.C. 57, restored Cassels' judgement. *Kahler* v. *Midland Bank*, [1950] A.C. 24 (H.L.) The decisions are based on the assumption that the contracts were governed by Czech law, which is not unassailable.

[4] *Ralli Brothers* v. *Compañia Naviera*, [1920] 2 K.B. (C.A.) 287; *supra*, s. 425.

[5] [1929] 2 K.B. 678, 683, 690.

[6] See also the American cases referred to by Hollander, loc. cit., p. 92.

[7] *Boissevain* v. *Weil*, [1949] 1 A.E.R. 146 (C.A.).

VII. The rules developed for contractual money obligations are applicable also to money obligations arising out of legacies, tort, quasi-contract, maintenance duties, or any other legal relationship.

BIBLIOGRAPHY

F. A. MANN, *The Legal Aspect of Money*, 1938, particularly p. 117 et seq. (the main work on the subject). NUSSBAUM, *Money in the Law* (Chicago), 1939, *passim*. DICEY–MORRIS, 718–53. NIBOYET, *Rev. Darras*, 1925, 161.

WORTLEY, 17 *Brit. Y.B.* (1936), 112. NUSSBAUM, 43 *Rec.* 559 (1933). J. REISS, *Portée internationale des lois interdisant la clause-or*, 1936. BAGGE, 18 *Rev. Ghent* (1937), 457, 786. E. COHN, 52 *L.Q.R.* (1936), 474; 55 L.Q.R. (1939), 552. R. R. NEUMANN, *Devisennotrecht und internationales Privatrecht*, 1941 (1938). E. C. FREUTEL, 56 *Harv. L.R.* (1942), 30. RASHBA, 41 *Michig. L.R.* (1943), 777, 1089. GUTZWILLER, *Der Geltungsbereich der Währungsvorschriften*, 1940. MANN, *Problems of the Rate of Exchange*, 8 *Mod. L.R.* (1945), 177.

CHAPTER XXIX

BILLS OF EXCHANGE, PROMISSORY NOTES, AND CHEQUES

THE Geneva Conventions concerning Bills and Notes, 1930, and those relating to Cheques, 1931, unfortunately did not succeed in establishing a unitary world law on those negotiable instruments.[1] The Geneva law was not adopted in particular by Great Britain, the British Commonwealth of Nations, and the United States of America. The English-speaking world and its commerce were well accustomed to the rules which commercial practice had created in the course of centuries and which had been clarified and laid down in the British Bills of Exchange Act, 1882. There was not the slightest reason why the nations within the British Commonwealth should depart from that well-established and as it were venerable law and give up many institutions, such as the bearer bill, introduce distinctions hitherto unknown, such as the distinction between bill of exchange and cheque, and replace numerous simple and liberal rules by much stricter and vexatious regulations. The same is true of the United States, where in 1896 a Uniform Negotiable Instruments Act was set up (essentially on the British model), which has been adopted by all the states of the Union.[2]

Among the six Geneva Conventions—three concerned with bills and notes, and three with cheques—there are two dealing with the 'Settlement of Certain Conflicts of Laws', one relating to bills and notes, the other to cheques. The delegates at Geneva were fully aware of the fact that Great Britain and America would refuse to introduce the substantive Geneva laws on bills, notes, and cheques. But there was apparently a widespread hope that they would at least adopt the conflict rules. Even this hope vanished. England possessed in her Bills of Exchange Act, 1882, a small number of conflict rules,[3] and though some of these had met

461. The Geneva Conventions and the British Commonwealth

[1] See *supra*, s. 41.   [2] See Hudson and Feller, 44 *Harv. L.R.*, 1931, 333, 347.
[3] The American Negotiable Instruments Act does not embody rules on private international law.

with sharp and well-deserved criticism, and are indeed partly 'obscure and even verging on the unintelligible',[1] the English legislator preferred the preservation of this unfortunate situation to an adoption of the Geneva conflict rules, which had all the defects of compromises. If I have the choice between my own defective rules and foreign rules which have other defects I am well entitled to retain my old rules. The Geneva conflict rule subjecting capacity to the national law of the person was particularly inconsistent with one of the fundamental principles of English law, viz. the domicile principle.

The rules which the English Bills of Exchange Act, 1882, established with regard to private international law are contained in its s. 72. In the present chapter we are dealing only with the *obligations* arising from drawing, accepting, or indorsing a bill of exchange (or from making or indorsing a promissory note). The *transfer* of rights embodied in the instrument will be dealt with in a later part of this book,[2] in connexion with the transfer of intangible property.

462.
Capacity

I. *Capacity*. The Act, which is by no means exhaustive, does not answer the question as to what persons are capable of entering into an engagement by drawing, accepting, or indorsing a bill of exchange. In many municipal laws the capacity to sign bills of exchange does not differ from the general capacity to conclude contracts. In others there exist special rules designed to protect debtors unacquainted with commercial intercourse against the danger of losing their pleas owing to the negotiability of bills; hence infants, women, soldiers, peasants, clergymen, state officials, and others have often been declared to be incapable of validly signing bills of exchange. The conflict rule, however, does not differ from that prevailing in respect of ordinary contracts. In England capacity depends on the personal, i.e. domiciliary, law; but it suffices that a person is capable according to the law of the place of contracting.[3]

---

[1] Thus: G. C. Cheshire, p. 363.
[2] ss. 526–30.
[3] See *supra*, s. 261 et seq.

II. The *formal* validity of the various contracts which may be embodied in one instrument must be ascertained for each one separately. It depends entirely on the observation of the *lex loci actus*. Thus the obligation of the drawer is formally valid if the law prevailing in the country where he signed and delivered the instrument was observed, while the validity of the acceptor's or any indorser's obligations requires observation of the formalities prescribed respectively at the places where they made their contract.

463. Form of the contracts

The *locus regit actum* principle prevails in respect of negotiable instruments imperatively, and not optionally, as is the case with other kinds of contract.[1] This difference between ordinary commercial contracts and the issuing or negotiating of bills, notes, and cheques obtains also on the Continent. But the *locus actus* is determined differently in continental laws and the Geneva Conventions on the one hand, and in English and American law on the other. Under Geneva law it is 'the territory in which the contract has been *signed*'. Under English law it is the 'place where such contract is made', and this means the place of 'delivery'; the Act defines 'delivery' as 'transfer of possession, actual or constructive, from one person to another'. If this transfer is made by letter containing the instrument, delivery and therefore the contract is completed where the letter is posted.

The place of delivery is decisive even if it does not appear from the text of the instrument. If the drawer signs the bill in France and dates it correctly from Calais, but posts it to his creditor after having crossed to Dover, the formal validity of the bill depends on English law, though only the stamp on the envelope shows whence the letter came. Luckily such discrepancies are very rare. If they occurred frequently the English solution would be inferior to the Geneva solution (which it is not).[2] Owing to their rarity it seems justifiable to assume two rebuttable presumptions to the effect, firstly, that the place named in the text of the instrument as the place of signature really is the place of signature, and secondly, that the place of signature is the

464. Locus scriptus and locus verus

---

[1] *Supra*, s. 426–8.
[2] See Gutteridge, op. cit., p. 71.

place of delivery.[1] It seems much more doubtful whether a person who in signing names a wrong place is allowed to rebut the first of these presumptions *vis-à-vis* a *bona-fide* purchaser of the instrument.[2] If, for instance, the bill signed at or dated from Calais and posted in England is valid under French law but formally invalid under English law the drawer should by his conduct be excluded from relying on the invalidity of his obligation under English law. But it would be an exaggeration to frame a general rule pronouncing that a *bona-fide* purchaser may be entitled in all respects to treat the *locus scriptus* as *locus verus*, for example, in order to obtain higher interest in the case of a delay of payment.[3]

465. Exceptions to lex loci actus

The rule that the formalities are governed by the *lex loci actus* is subject to two exceptions:

1. A foreign bill issued outside the United Kingdom is not invalidated by any violation of foreign stamp laws.

2. If a bill of exchange issued outside the United Kingdom is formally invalid under the *lex loci actus* but valid under English law it is to be treated as valid, but only

(*a*) between persons who negotiate, hold, or become parties to it in the United Kingdom;[4] and

(*b*) only for the purpose of enforcing payment.[5]

The same rule, though this is not stated in the Act, will probably prevail in respect of formally invalid indorsements and acceptances. The Geneva Convention has no such rule. It includes a provision which on the one hand goes farther, on the other not so far: it lays down that if an obligation in a bill is formally invalid according to the *lex loci actus* but in conformity with the laws of any territory in which a subse-

---

[1] Cf. Dicey–Morris, p. 688, n. 4.

[2] On American Law see Raiser, p. 41, nn. 5–7.

[3] Suppose the *locus scriptus* is Berlin, the *locus verus* Paris. In France the legal rate of interest (in the case of bills of exchange and cheques) is 6 per cent., while in Germany it may be higher: it is 2 per cent. over the official bank-rate. Art. 48, no. 2, and 49, no. 2 of the Geneva Uniform Law on Bills of Exchange; art. 13 of Annex II; German Law of 3 July 1925. Arminjon and Carry, pp. 418, 419. Cf. the article in the *Festgabe* to Karl Wieland edited by the Law Faculty of Basle: *Beiträge zum Handelsrecht*, 1934, pp. 458–60.

[4] If the plaintiff has acquired the bill in France and brings it to England, where he now 'holds' it, it thereby becomes valid. Is this validity destroyed again when he returns with the bill to France? *quaere*. The correct answer (it is submitted) is that the bill remains valid.

[5] See *Guaranty Trust Co. of New York* v. *Hannay*, [1918] 1 K.B. 43.

quent contract has been entered into, the formal invalidity of the previous contracts does not entail the invalidity of the subsequent contract. But the previous contracts remain invalid (the provision differing in this from English law).[1]

III. The *interpretation* of the various contracts, including their essential validity and their effects, is, according to the unambiguous text of the Act[2] 'determined by the law of the place where such contract is made'. Thus the *lex loci actus* and not the *lex loci solutionis* has been expressly declared decisive. This rule is based on Story's formulation. But Story, in declaring that the *lex loci actus* obtains, contended that 'correctly considered' this rule is 'entirely in conformity' with the sovereignty of the *lex loci solutionis*. In this he was certainly mistaken. The language of the Act, however, does not allow Story's formula to be replaced by Story's real meaning. The best solution would probably be that which after long and thorny discussions the Geneva lawgivers accepted: the obligations of the acceptor of a bill of exchange and of the maker of a promissory note are determined by the law of the place where the instrument is payable; any other obligation, for example of the drawer or an indorser, is determined by the law of the country where the signature was affixed.[3] This seems to have been the English solution before the Bills of Exchange Act came into force. The old rule 'contraxisse unusquisque in eo loco intellegitur in quo ut solveret se obligavit',[4] which through the Dutch writers came to America and to England and which was understood as identifying the *locus actus* with the *locus solutionis*, was applied to the obligation of the acceptor,[5] while the obligations of the drawer and the indorsers were tested by the law of the country where each of them 'made his contract'.[6]

466.
Effects of the contracts

---

[1] Art. 3 § 2 Geneva Convention.

[2] s. 72, sub-sect. (2). The proviso in sub-sect. (2) concerns the transfer of existing obligations only; see on this *infra*, s. 526 et seq.

[3] Art. 4 of the Geneva Convention. On this sound solution: Gutteridge, loc. cit., 15.

[4] D. 44, 7, 21. See *supra*, s. 414.

[5] *Allen* v. *Kemble* (1848), 6 Moore, P.C., 314; *Rouquette* v. *Overmann* (1875), L.R. 10, Q.B. 525.

[6] Thus *Allen* v. *Kemble, supra.* See Raiser, p. 29 et seq.

The law which according to these rules governs the particular contract is applicable to all incidents of the contract, such as the amount of interest in the case of delay of payment, the question of damages or recovery of costs, the problem whether the drawer and the indorsers are liable only where the drawee refuses payment or turns out to be insolvent, and so forth. With regard to the date of payment the English Act[1] refers expressly to the law of the place where the bill or note is payable.

467. Presentment, protest, and notice

IV. If the drawee fails to accept or to pay the bill, certain obligations or burdens fall on the holder of the instrument. He has as a rule a right of recourse against the drawer and the indorsers. But the exercise of this right presupposes some preliminary steps to be taken by the holder. Of these the most essential are (*a*) the presentment of the bill to the drawee, either for acceptance or for payment, (*b*) a formal protest to be made by certain officials at the place of payment or at the residence or place of business of the drawee, and (*c*) a notice of dishonour to be sent by the holder either to the drawer and to all the indorsers, or only to the last indorser, who under some laws is in such case bound to pass on the notification to his indorser, and so on. For the most part these burdens are not 'duties', as their violation does not produce any claim for damages,[2] but merely conditions precedent, on which the exercise of a right depends. What law is to decide whether these measures are necessary, and how they are to be discharged? The Bills of Exchange Act gives an answer which it is difficult to understand:

'The duties of the holder with respect to presentment for acceptance or payment and the necessity for or sufficiency of a protest or notice of dishonour, or otherwise, are determined by the law of the place where the act is done or the bill is dishonoured.'

Thus presentment, protest, and notice of dishonour are subjected alternatively to one of two laws: either to the law

---

[1] s. 72, sub-sect. (5).

[2] A true duty exists under art. 45 § 6 of the Geneva Law on Bills of Exchange, where it is said: 'A person who does not give notice within the limit of time . . . is responsible for the injury, if any, caused by his negligence, but the damages shall not exceed the amount of the bill of exchange.'

of the place where an act *has been* done, or to the law of the place where a certain act *has not been* done and therefore the bill has been dishonoured. It would be meaningless to contend that the question whether an act (which has not been done) *ought to* have been done should be answered by the law of the place where 'the act is done'. Therefore the two alternatively applicable legal systems should be apportioned as follows: Whether and where one of the three acts mentioned (presentment, prctest, and notice of dishonour) has to be done can only be decided by the law of the place where the bill is dishonoured, that is, the place where the drawee is expected or bound to pay.[1] But how the act is to be done will be answered by the *lex loci actus*, according to the rule *locus regit actum*.

V. The right of contracting parties to choose the law applicable to their contract is mentioned neither in the English Act nor in the continental codifications; but neither do they exclude it, and there is no doubt that it exists as in other contracts. As however the negotiability of the instrument includes a protection of *bona-fide* purchasers, a choice of law by the contracting parties, for example by an agreement between drawer and acceptor or between an indorser and the indorsee, must be contained in the text of the instrument in order to be effective against such purchaser. Unless the parties do this their choice of law has effect only as between themselves and *vis-à-vis* a purchaser who at the time of acquiring the instrument had knowledge of the agreement.[2] Can an implied choice of law be inferred from an untruthful statement in the text of the instrument in respect of the place of issue of the bill? Example: an Englishman draws a bill in France but dates it 'London, 1 June 1949'. The answer is doubtful. An affirmative answer is impossible where the misstatement was caused by a mistake of the writer, and arbitrary where he knew what he was doing.[3]

468.
Autonomy of the parties

---

[1] 'expected' as long as he has not yet accepted the bill; 'bound' if he has accepted it.

[2] *Contra*: Dicey–Morris, pp. 681–2.

[3] Raiser, p. 50.

BIBLIOGRAPHY

DICEY–MORRIS, 678–93. CHESHIRE, 357–66. LORENZEN, *Conflict of Laws relating to Bills and Notes*, New Haven, 1919. GUTTERIDGE, 'The Unification of the Rules of Conflict relating to Negotiable Instruments', 16 *J. Comp. Legisl.*, 1934, 53. FALCONBRIDGE, *Essays*, 269–329. L. RAISER, *Die Wirkungen der Wechselerklärungen im Int. Pr. R.*, 1931. VEITH, *RVgl.HWB.* IV. 489. ARMINJON and CARRY, *La lettre de change*, 1938, p. 447.

CHAPTER XXX

TORTS

As in contracts so in torts the *lex loci actus*—here the law **469.** The of the place at which the tort was committed—plays an various systems important part. If an act is illicit under that law and has created an obligation at the place where it was done it seems at first sight a matter of course that such obligation should be recognized and enforced wherever the wrongdoer may be found. Indeed, in most countries the *lex loci delicti commissi* governs the conditions and the effects of torts. But it is not the only decisive law: it is everywhere complemented by the *lex fori*, because every state reserves to itself the right to supervise the civil consequence of a wrongful act committed abroad, in order to exclude from application such consequences as might be inconsistent with the requirements of public policy. Some eminent jurists, such as K. G. von Wächter[1] and Savigny,[2] went even further—they were in favour of making the *lex fori* alone decisive for the conditions and effects of civil wrongs. Herein they were approximating the conflict rule on torts to the rule governing crimes: a person who commits a punishable crime in one state may thereby create a 'right' on the part of that state to punish him, but justice does not require other states to protect such right (if it is one). An equal treatment of civil tort and crime—which would indeed lead to the subjection of torts to the *lex fori*—is, however, hardly justifiable; and the pure *lex fori* doctrine has been adopted nowhere, though English law has been considerably influenced by it.[3]

If then in all countries the applicable law depends on the 'combined effect' of the *lex loci delicti* and the *lex fori*, the proportion in which the respective weight of these rules is distributed varies in the different countries. Sometimes the part played by the public policy of the forum is left entirely

---

[1] *Archiv f. d. civilistische Praxis*, 25, 389.

[2] *System*, VIII. 278 (transl., p. 253).

[3] Frankenstein, II. 362, has developed the doctrine that the national law of the wrongdoer should be decisive. He even considers this to be 'the only possible solution'. No country has adopted it.

to the discretion of the court (for example in France); sometimes the scope of public policy has been precisely determined by the legislator, for example in Germany, where foreign law is excluded in so far as it imposes on a German national greater liability than he would incur under German law.[1] Finally, there are legal systems where the relationship between *lex loci delicti* and *lex fori* is reversed: instead of starting from the foreign *lex loci delicti*—and limiting its application to a certain degree by the influence of the *lex fori*—the *lex fori* is applied, but a certain influence is granted to the *lex loci delicti*.

470. The English system

English law follows the last of these three systems. Since the leading case of *Mostyn* v. *Fabrigas*[2] actions for foreign torts may be brought in an English court. In this case the court applies English law, the *lex fori*, and not the law of the place where the tort was committed. But this application of the English rules depends on two conditions: first, the act must be 'of such a character that it would have been actionable if committed in England', and second, 'the act must not have been justifiable by the law of the place where it was done'.[3]

Let us first examine the two conditions separately, and then study their effect.

471. 1. Tort actionable in England

I. The two conditions. 1. No action for tort lies in England if the act, though it is a tort under the *lex loci delicti*, would not be an actionable tort if it had been committed here.

Examples: (i) Under Belgian law the defendant, a shipowner, was liable for faulty navigation due to negligence of a pilot whom he was compelled to employ; under English law (as it stood in 1868) he was not liable. Though the negligence occurred in Belgian waters and therefore created an obligation under the *lex loci delicti*, no action could lie in England.[4] (ii) The defendant by constructing and selling engines in France violated a patent right granted in France to the plaintiff. The plaintiff brings an action in an English court. The action fails because if such

---

[1] Art. 12 Introductory Law.

[2] (1775) 1 Cowp. 161.

[3] This is the formula framed by Willes, J., in *Phillips* v. *Eyre* (1870), L.R. 6 Q.B. 1, 28. It was repeated in *Machado* v. *Fontes*, [1897] 2 Q.B. (C.A.) 231, 233, and by Lord Macnaghten in *Carr* v. *Fracis, Times & Co.*, [1902] A.C. 176, 182.

[4] Decision of the Privy Council in *The Halley* (1868), L.R. 2 P.C. 193.

violation of a French patent had occurred in England there would have been no tort, owing to the strict territoriality of patents. (iii) *X* commits a homicide in France, for which under French law he would be bound to pay damages, while his act, though punishable in England, would not give rise to an action for tort under English common law.[1] No such action lies here under common law. (iv) *X* publishes in Germany a defamatory statement concerning a deceased person; in Germany the deceased's son can sue him.[2] No such tort is recognized by English law; hence no action lies here.

2. The influence of the *lex loci delicti* is confined to the requirement that the act must not be 'justifiable' under that law. The term 'justifiable' however is not free from ambiguity. In *The Mary Moxham*[3] James, L.J., said that a person is not answerable here for an act which 'by the law of the foreign country is lawful or . . . excusable or . . . has been legitimized by a subsequent act of the legislature'. At first sight this seems a sound definition of the term 'justifiable'. An act is indeed justifiable

(*a*) if it is lawful, that is, if it is the permitted exercise of a 'right', such as the right of self-defence or self-help. If, for example, a German exercises in Germany the extraordinarily extended right of self-help which German law grants him,[4] and if in the exercise of it he overcomes the resistance of the other party (e.g., the debtor) by force, his act, lawful in Germany, cannot operate as a tort in this country, although if it had been done here, it might have been tortious. The 'exercise of a right' is lawful by definition. There are, however, cases where under the foreign *lex loci actus* such exercise is accounted a delict as involving an *abus de droit* (French law),[5] or as serving only to injure another

472.
Condition
2: Act not
justifiable
under *lex
loci delicti*

---

[1] According to the rule in *Baker* v. *Bolton* (1808), 1 Camp. 492 (which, however, has been almost extinguished by legislation).

[2] German Penal Code, s. 189; see German Supreme Court Civ. Cas., *Offic. Coll.*, 91, 357.

[3] (1876) 1 P.D. 107.

[4] A right of self-help arises under s. 229 German Civ. C., if the enforcement of a right is in danger of being frustrated or substantially hindered by failure to take immediate steps for its protection, and if the assistance of the public authorities cannot be obtained in time. In any such case the person whose rights are jeopardized is not only permitted to take or destroy things, but may even restrain the liberty of persons against whom the right operates and use force in order to prevent any person from resisting an act he is bound to allow.

[5] Josserand, *De l'abus des droits*, 1905, and in his *Cours d. droit civil*, II, no. 428.

person (German law).¹ In such situations the correct view is that the vexatious act, because forbidden by the law, goes beyond the exercise of a right.

473. Liability for dangerous acts and acts of third persons

The rule that every 'lawful' act is 'justifiable' needs qualification. There are some types of *dangerous acts* which are lawful in the sense that they are not contrary to law and which yet owing to their dangerous character entail claims for damages under the *lex loci actus* if they lead to injury. All modern legal systems include such cases of absolute or strict liability based on the conception that the risk must be run by the person who creates the dangerous situation. Everyone has the 'right' to keep a dog, a horse, or a cow, even if he knows the animal to be mischievous; and yet under many legal systems the possessor becomes liable for any harm it may do to other persons though he may have taken care to observe all possible precautions. Running a factory, a mine, or a railway is lawful, though the owner knows that in the course of years some unforeseen accident may happen through the fault of an employee or of an outsider, or without any traceable fault. All the modern laws which make him strictly liable base such liability neither on intention nor on negligence nor on 'unlawfulness', but solely on the dangerous character of the act. Such lawful but dangerous acts when leading to injuries are not 'justifiable acts' in the sense of the conflict rule here under examination.

Illustration: a German harbours in Germany an animal which in spite of all precautions escapes and injures a person; under German law he is liable; if the events had taken place in England he would possibly be liable under the English *scienter* rule. The injured person must be allowed to sue him in an English court (if he is present in this country).

Such dangerous acts as create (under the law of a given country) a duty to pay damages are sometimes characterized as torts or delicts, sometimes as facts very similar to delicts, 'quasi-delicts'. It does not matter which of these designations is chosen; for quasi-delicts are in all respects treated as if they were delicts, i.e. unlawful acts.

---

¹ German Civ. C., s. 226; see Swiss Civ. C., art. 2 § 2. 'The manifest abuse of a right is not protected by law.' On other legal systems: Riezler, *RVgl.HWB.*, VI, 1 et seq.

All these considerations concerning liability for dangerous acts apply equally where under the *lex loci actus* a person is liable for mischievous acts of *other persons*, such as servants, agents, apprentices, infants. To employ a servant carefully chosen and supervised is a lawful act; if nevertheless the master is responsible for damage done by the servant the set of facts—lawful act of appointment plus unlawful act of the employee—is to be treated as if the employer had committed an unjustifiable act.

(*b*) An act is further 'justifiable' if though contrary to law it is 'excusable', i.e. if there is no *mens rea* (negligence or intention to injure) and the act does not give rise to an absolute liability.

474. Excusable and legitimized acts

(*c*) Finally, the defendant's act may have been unjustifiable at the time when it was done but have become justifiable subsequently owing to an act of the legislator. This happened, for example, in 1865 in Jamaica, where during a revolution the Governor Eyre imprisoned a man Phillips. This was a tort under the law of Jamaica, just as it would be a tort under English law. But later an Act of Indemnity was passed by the local legislature, whereby the Governor's Act became retrospectively 'justifiable'; the fact that the defendant in his capacity as Governor of the colony himself played a part in the passing of that Indemnity Act was not regarded as an impediment to its validity or to the excusability of his action.[1] Similarly in Germany Hitler and two of his supporters, the state ministers Frick and Guertner, made a Law on 3 July 1934[2] by which they declared the assassinations and other crimes committed from 30 June to 2 July 1934 (by Hitler himself and other members of his party) to be acts of 'self-defence on the part of the state' and therefore lawful. Would an English court apply this Indemnity Act if the heirs of one of the murdered persons—assuming they were able to sue—actually should sue the murderer here? Or would it refuse application on the ground of immorality, thus distinguishing *Phillips* v. *Eyre*? *Quaere.*

---

[1] *Phillips* v. *Eyre* (1869), L.R. 4 Q.B. 225; affirmed by the Exch. Chamber, 1870, L.R. 6, Q.B. 1, 28.

[2] *Reichsgesetzblatt*, 1934, I. 529.

If the two conditions—actionability under English municipal law, lack of justification under the foreign *lex loci actus*—are fulfilled, the English court allows the action of the injured person. No further conditions have been laid down; it is in particular

475.
Action-
ability
under the
lex loci
***actus* not**
required

3. not required that the unjustifiable act should under the *lex loci actus* create an *actionable* duty to pay damages.[1] It has been declared sufficient that the act is punishable where committed. This is founded on the decision of the Court of Appeal in *Machado* v. *Fontes*.[2]

> The defendant in that case had published a libel against the plaintiff in Brazil and was sued for damages in England. His defence was that by Brazilian law no action lay for recovery of damages in respect of that libel, although a criminal prosecution was possible. The defence was held to be bad since actionability in England did not presuppose actionability in Brazil.

True, according to this rule of English Private International Law, the injured person can recover damages in an English court which he would not be able to obtain in a Brazilian court. But this result, unsatisfactory though it is, follows from the regrettable principle that the English court is required in actions for tort to apply English law and not the *lex loci delicti*.[3] It is, however, difficult to explain the decision of the Privy Council in *McMillan* v. *Canadian Northern Railway Co.*[4] An employee of the defendant company had been injured in the course of his employment in Ontario; he sued the company for damages in Saskatchewan. Under the law of Saskatchewan (the *lex fori*) the defendants had no legal defence. Under the law of Ontario (*lex loci laesionis*) they had two defences. One: the plea of common employment; the injury was due to the negligence of a fellow-servant. Two: the Workmen's Compensation Act of Ontario gave the employee a right of 'compensation' against the employer according to a fixed scale and ordained that all claims should be heard and determined by a special Board. The first plea (of common employment) was undoubtedly good, and the action was bound to fail for this

---

[1] G. C. Cheshire advances the opposite opinion (pp. 375–82), which, indeed, would be preferable, but seems inconsistent with *Machado* v. *Fontes*.

[2] [1897] 2 Q.B. 231.   [3] *Infra*, s. 476.

[4] [1923] A.C. 120.

reason. But the decision of the Privy Council rested also on the second plea, and we are here concerned only with this part of the judgment. Dr. Cheshire understands the (very short) decision in the sense that the Privy Council was decisively impressed by the 'fact that the injury to the workman was not actionable by the *lex loci delicti*'.[1] But with all respect to the eminent author, this does not seem to be what the decision says. It stresses another fact, viz. that the claim granted by the statute has not the character of a claim for tort, and is not a claim for damages, but leads only to a 'compensation strictly limited in amount'. The court thus takes the whole matter of the workmen's compensation out of the sphere of tort. It may have been influenced by the previous decision in *Walpole* v. *Canadian Northern Railway*,[2] where the duty to pay compensation under the Act of British Columbia was indeed the effect of the contract of employment, which by law had been complemented by certain statutory duties.[3] Further: it would not seem correct to say that the statute for Ontario had created a 'non-actionable duty' on the part of the employer. It merely said—as is frequent in enactments of this kind—that until the special Board had 'determined the claim' the injured workman had not yet acquired a 'right' to be paid the compensation. So it was not for lack of actionability that the action was dismissed.

II. If the two conditions are fulfilled, i.e. if the act is not justifiable under the *lex loci actus* and is actionable under the English *lex fori*, the English conflict rule ordains the application of English municipal law, and not of the *lex loci delicti*. This principle, which coincides with what Savigny

476. Effects of delict governed by *lex fori*

---

[1] G. C. Cheshire, p. 381.   [2] [1923] A.C. 113.

[3] In the case of *Walpole* v. *Canadian Northern Rly.* (*supra*) the accident had happened in British Columbia, while the action was (again) brought in Saskatchewan. The case differed from the *McMillan case* in that under the Workmen's Compensation Act of British Columbia the contract of employment was subject to the double qualification (1) that the employee who had suffered an accident should be entitled to compensation out of a fund contributed to by the employers, but had no claim against the employer himself; (2) that he should have no other remedy. Thus here it was evident the employer was not liable at all, and that the liability of the fund was not based on delict or quasi-delict but on a legal incident of the contract of employment.

thought to be the desirable solution, has not been accepted anywhere on the European continent or in America.[1] Its defect is—as is the case with other matters of substantive law if they are governed by the *lex fori*—that an injured person who has no right to damages under the law of the place where the injury was done can acquire such right by suing the wrongdoer in England. And whether he can sue him here depends on the wrongdoer's presence in this country, a matter of pure chance. That this is the law is shown by *Machado* v. *Fontes*,[2] as explained before. Even if we suppose that both parties, the slanderer and the slandered, were of Brazilian nationality, resident in Brazil and in no way connected with England, and if it were true (what in the Machado case was ascertained as 'fact') that Brazilian law declares the slanderer punishable but not liable to pay damages, the slandered person can recover damages provided the slanderer pays a visit to this country. It follows from this that under the English conflict rule English municipal law, and not the law of the place of the wrongful act, decides whether reparation must be made for *dommage moral* as well as material damage, whether contributory negligence merely diminishes or entirely destroys the claim, whether lost profits have to be taken into consideration, whether the causal nexus between the act and the damage is to be denied on the ground of remoteness, and the like.[3] In so far as the detrimental act is directed against a particular 'right', such as ownership or a copyright, the question whether that right exists is governed neither by the *lex fori*

[1] In the United States O. W. Holmes's *obligatio* theory obtains: if at the place of the act under the law prevailing there an *obligatio* has arisen, that *obligatio* 'follows the person and may be enforced wherever the person may be found'. The source of such obligation is the law of the place where the tort was done; Lorenzen, 362. This sound doctrine is not the English doctrine, though some utterances of great English judges have been made along similar lines. Cf. Willes, J., in *Phillips* v. *Eyre*, L.R. 6 Q.B. 1, 28: the civil liability arising out of a wrong is brought to birth by the law of the place, and its character is determined by that law. Unfortunately the courts have not accepted the consequences of this view.

[2] [1897] 2 Q.B. 231. *Supra*, s. 475.

[3] See on the question whether the measure of damages is a matter of procedure, *supra*, s. 226. The question whether the English court can grant an injunction though the *lex loci actus* would not allow it is clearly one concerned with procedure; therefore *Baschet* v. *London Illustr. Standard Co.*, [1900] 1 Ch. 73, 78, is not a case in point.

nor by the *lex loci delicti*, but by the law governing such right, for example, the *lex situs rei*.

To sum up: the orbit within which the *lex loci delicti* is operative is very limited; it is restricted to the question: is the act that caused the damage justifiable? All other questions must be answered by the (English) *lex fori*.

III. The little importance thus attributed to the locality of the act may be the reason for the surprising fact that English courts have never been concerned with one of the most controversial questions in the conflict of laws on tort as discussed on the Continent and in America, viz. what place is regarded as the *locus delicti commissi*?[1] Three main answers have been given. First: it is the place where the defendant acted either himself or through an agent who may be *bona fide* (e.g. the postman who brings the slanderous letter to its addressee) or *mala fide* (e.g. the employee who by his employer's order makes false representations knowing that they are false). This doctrine (theory of the place of action) has been advanced mainly by German authors[2] and accepted by Swiss and Scandinavian practice and by the predominant French and Italian doctrine.[3] A second doctrine declares the *locus delicti* to be the place where 'the last event necessary to make an actor liable takes place', as the American *Restatement* has formulated it.[4] This 'theory of the place of the first effect' has been adopted by the law of the United States. A third doctrine, followed by the German Supreme Court,[5] permits the injured person freely to choose as *locus delicti* any country where any part of the tortious set of facts (including both acts and effects) has taken place.

Some examples may illustrate the issue:

477. What place is the *locus delicti?* Various doctrines

[1] See notably Rheinstein, 19 *Tulane L.R.* (1944), 165, and *Rabel* II. 301–35.

[2] Von Bar, II. 120 (Engl. transl., pp. 634, 638); and others.

[3] If the wrongdoer has acted at several places (e.g. has chloroformed his victim in a railway compartment in Massachusetts and thrown him out of the train in Connecticut) the decisive place is probably that where he finished his action (though the German Supreme Court holds every place in which he acted equally decisive; Lewald, p. 262).

[4] s. 377. The assumption that this is the prevailing American rule has been shaken by Rheinstein, loc. cit. See also W. W. Cook, 345; Goodrich, 222.

[5] See Lewald, p. 261.

(i) The *Kansas–Oklahoma case.*[1] The plaintiff's farm bordered the Kansas–Oklahoma state line and was situate wholly on Oklahoma territory. The defendant's railway engine was on the Kansas side; sparks from it set fire to the farmhouse.

The (American) court decided that the tort was committed in Oklahoma. The predominant French doctrine of the place of action would declare Kansas to be the *locus delicti*. The German Supreme Court would decide that the delict was committed in both countries, and that the plaintiff could rely on either law.

(ii) The defendant sends poisoned food to X from state A to state B; X consumes it in state C, while travelling by rail. He falls ill in state D and dies as the train arrives in state E. Under the doctrine of the place of action the *locus delicti* is in A, under German law it is in each of the five states (and the plaintiff has the choice); under American law the decisive place is in D, because it was here that harm was first caused.[2]

(iii) The following example—the most important in practice—gives rise to especially grave doubts: the defendant publishes a statement defamatory of the plaintiff by a newspaper, copies of which are sold and read in all European countries. The first question is here: has the defendant committed one libel only, or is each sale of a copy a new publication giving rise to a separate cause of action? If the former view is adopted the libel has been committed according to the German doctrine both where the newspaper was edited and in every country where a copy was sold, while the American formula creates some difficulties: 'the last event necessary to make the defendant liable' is (probably) the first sale of a copy to a person who will read it. If, on the other hand, the doctrine that each sale of a copy contains a new publication is accepted, the 'last event' is in each country where a copy is sold.

478. English view still uncertain

What place is the *locus delicti commissi* under English law? In principle, it is suggested, English courts would accept the theory of the place of action rather than any other doctrine. The reason is that all an English court wants to learn from the *lex loci delicti* is whether the defendant's

---

[1] *Otey* v. *Midland V.R.R. Co.* (1921), quoted by Beale, II. 1287.

[2] Thus, at any rate according to the *Restatement*, illustration 2 to s. 377 (p. 456). But *quaere*. Poisoning was indeed completed in D (or in C?), but murder was not completed till the victim reached E.

behaviour is or is not justifiable. Only the law of the place at which the defendant acted[1] is competent to characterize his behaviour. If he acted lawfully at the place of action, he is justified, and his act does not become illegal on the ground that it has effects in a foreign country where that act would have been illegal if it had been done there. Suppose A in state X writes to B who sojourns in state Y a letter containing a defamatory statement in respect of C; under the law of X, but not under that of Y, the defamatory statement would be justifiable by a plea of fair comment. A's act should be regarded as justifiable. Often however the law of the country in which the defendant acted will treat as unlawful such acts as have effect in a different country under the law of which they are lawful. Thus it always depends on the law of the country where the alleged wrongdoer acted whether the act is justifiable or not.

This view is apparently supported by a single decision of the Court of Appeal in *George Monro Ltd*. v. *American Cyanamid and Chemical Corporation*.[2]

In this case the defendants had committed a tortious act in New York: they had sold a substance without warning the plaintiffs of its dangerous qualities; the plaintiffs had then sold the substance in England to a farmer who had suffered injury by its use and who recovered from the plaintiffs. The plaintiffs asked leave, under Order XI rule 1(*ee*) of the Rules of the Supr. C., to serve notice of the writ upon the defendants in New York. The English court had to decide whether the action was based on a 'tort committed in England.' The Court of Appeal answered in the negative and thus adhered to the theory of the *place of action*; but this view was limited to the question of assuming jurisdiction under the R.S.C.

Still more remote from our problem are several decisions dealing with the *locus delicti* in connexion with *criminal* law. In *Reg*. v. *Peters*[3] the prisoner, an undischarged bankrupt, resident in Newcastle, had obtained credit from an Irish farmer by buying a horse without disclosing his status. The contract had been made by correspondence. The prisoner had posted the offer in Newcastle; the farmer had accepted it in Ireland. The horse was then sent to Newcastle and

---

[1] In the case of a tort committed by omission the *locus delicti* is the place where the defendant had a duty to act.

[2] [1944] K.B. (C.A.) 432, 437, 440. On the case of *Bata* v. *Bata*, see *infra*, p. 609.   [3] (1886), 16 Q.B.D., 636, 639.

received there. The court decided that the credit had been obtained in Newcastle, so that the prisoner could be tried in England; it left open whether the Irish court would also have jurisdiction. This decision, at least in its result, is compatible with the doctrine advocated here. The decision in *Reg.* v. *Ellis*[1] differs: the prisoner had obtained property by representations false to his knowledge; he had made the false representations in Scotland, but had thereupon obtained the property in England. The court held that the place where the goods were obtained was decisive, as the false representations were 'antecedent to and not part of the obtaining of the goods'; the decision thus seems to have been based on the view which prevails in the United States. In the old case *R.* v. *Sir F. Burdett*[2] it was stated that a person who writes a libel in one country with the intent to publish it, and publishes it in another country, has committed the misdemeanour in both places and can be indicted in either. The decision in *Kroch* v. *Rossell*[3] concerned merely the question whether jurisdiction of the English court should be assumed[4] in a libel action against publishers of a Belgian and a French newspaper of which a small number of copies had been brought to England and distributed here; the court refused to use its discretion for assuming jurisdiction, but there seems to have been no doubt that 'the publication of a libel in a newspaper takes place every time a copy is sold'.[5]

It is suggested that these decisions, apart from the fact that they are not based on any expressed doctrine and are of a somewhat tentative character, are not of a nature to serve as a foundation for determining the law that decides whether in an action for tort the defendant's act is justifiable or not. Jurisdiction and criminal law have too little in common with the problem discussed here; analogous application should be based on intrinsic similarity.

479. Torts on the high seas IV. As to torts committed on the high seas, that is, outside territorial waters, certain distinctions must be made:

1. Acts on board ship are treated as torts by an English

---

[1] [1899] 1 Q.B. 230, 233, 236, 237.
[2] (1820), 3 B. & Ald. 717; 4 ibid. 95, 170.   [3] [1937] 1 A.E.R. 725.
[4] R.S.C., XI. r. 1 (ee).   [5] See Mr. G. O. Slade's (now J.) argument at p. 726.

court if they are actionable in England and not justifiable under the law of the flag. This law replaces the law of the country where an act is committed.

2. It is not settled which law governs acts external to a single ship, caused by disputes between the crews of two ships, e.g. concerning the capture of a whale or the salvage of a wreck, or affecting persons or property not on board, for instance the destruction of a maritime cable. Dicey formerly took the view that the same rule as in case 1 applies.[1] But where the ships concerned carry different flags difficulties arise: is the act justifiable if it is so under the law of one of the ships, or only if under both? The main objection to any recourse to the *lex loci actus* is— as Dr. Cheshire points out convincingly[2]—that no foreign sovereign has exclusive jurisdiction over the high seas,[3] so that the reason for taking into consideration the *lex loci actus* ceases. Cheshire's view according to which the 'general maritime law' as administered by English courts applies seems preferable.[4]

3. The most important instances of torts committed on the high seas are the cases of collision between two ships. The substantive law applicable in such cases has been established nearly completely by the International Convention for the Unification of certain Rules with respect to Collisions between Vessels,[5] to which all European and many extra-European maritime states are parties. Therefore questions of private international law seldom arise. But if they do, for example if one of the ships concerned carries the flag of a state that is not a party to the Convention,[6] the question whether an act of navigation which led to the collision on the high seas is justifiable must be answered by the *lex fori*, that is, English law, for the reasons mentioned above, in 2.

[1] See Dicey (5th ed.), p. 778.

[2] At p. 390. Morris in Dicey (6th ed.) has accepted Cheshire's view.

[3] *Chartered Mercantile Bank of India* v. *Netherlands India Steam Navigation Co.* (1883), 10 Q.B.D. 521, 536 (*per* Brett, L.J.).

[4] See *Lloyd* v. *Guibert* (1865), L.R. 1 Q.B. 115, 125.

[5] Concluded in Brussels, 23 Sept. 1910. The transformation of this convention into English municipal law was effected by the Maritime Conventions Act, 1911 (1 & 2 Geo. V, c. 57).

[6] See art. 12 of the Convention.

BIBLIOGRAPHY

G. C. CHESHIRE, 367–91. DICEY–MORRIS, 799–807. LORENZEN, 360 et seq. A. H. ROBERTSON, 4 *Modern L.R.* (1940) 27. O'RIORDAN, ibid., 214. M. HANCOCK, *Torts in the Conflict of Laws*, 1942. LORENZEN, 44 *Columb. L.R.* 454. HANCOCK, 3 *University of Toronto L.J.* (1940), 400; 22 *Canad. B.R.* (1944) 843 et seq., 23 ibid. 348. FALCONBRIDGE, 23 ibid. 309. SCHMITTHOFF, 27 ibid. 816. RABEL, II. 229–354. COOK, 311–46. NIBOYET, V, 146-91.

CHAPTER XXXI

QUASI-CONTRACTS

THE notion of quasi-contract was conceived by Roman jurists to cover a series of obligations created neither by contract nor by delict, but having—so it was thought—a certain similarity to particular contract types: obligations arising out of *negotiorum gestio* or out of guardianship were regarded as akin to those originating in a contract of mandate; the *communio incidens* was analogous to a contract of partnership, and actions for unjust enrichment were supposed to resemble those founded on a loan.[1] English lawyers have adopted this classification in the case of certain legal obligations known to English law and have made the unhelpful Roman conception even worse by identifying 'quasi-contracts' with 'implied contracts'.

480. Concept of quasi-contract

As to the applicable law, no firm rule can be established, and in no country have the courts had much opportunity of developing any principles by which the choice may be regulated. Not without great hesitation are the following suggestions made:

481. Applicable law uncertain. Suggestions

1. Sometimes the quasi-contractual obligation originates in connexion with a transfer of ownership or other rights. Claims on the ground of unjust enrichment, for example, are usually the technical means adopted to restrict the effect of the act which caused the enrichment. Some illustrations:

(*a*) In order to safeguard commercial intercourse, many laws—when regulating sale and transfer of ownership—provide that ownership shall pass to the purchaser by agreement, whether the underlying contract of sale is valid or not, and that the invalidity of that contract, the lack of a *causa*, shall only create a claim for retransfer of ownership. It seems sound that in such cases the claim for retransfer should be governed by the law under which the defendant acquired ownership.

(*b*) Under Roman law and under all European continental laws, as well as under South African law, a donor has

---

[1] On the history of the notion of quasi-contract from Gaius to the modern continental laws, see the instructive study by H. Vizioz, *La notion du quasi-contrat*, Bordeaux, 1912, and Vizioz, 'L'école du droit naturel et le quasi-contrat' in the *Rev. critique de législation et de jurisprudence*, 1913.

the right to revoke his donation for grave ingratitude on the part of the donee or for certain other reasons. This right and the donor's claim for restitution of the gift still in the possession of the donee will be subjected to the same law as the gift itself.

(c) According to a strange German rule the finder of lost property becomes its owner if during one year after the find no notice of the loss has been given to him or to the local police; but within a further period of three years the former owner can bring an action for unjust enrichment against the finder.[1] The claim on the ground of such enrichment must be governed by the law under which the finder had acquired ownership, i.e. the law of the situs.

2. The obligations existing between co-owners of a tangible or intangible thing are governed, if the co-owner-ship arose out of a contract, e.g. a partnership, by the proper law of that contract. If there was no valid contract, as when co-ownership originates in a merger of things belonging to different persons,[2] the relationship between the partners should be determined by the law of the country where the merger took place, i.e. where the things were situated at the time of the act.

3. If a person voluntarily does work or spends money for the preservation of another person's property,[3] he is (under English municipal law) as a rule not entitled to recover his expenses. Continental laws, like Roman law, allow him to claim them. What law decides the matter? On the Continent the question is controversial. According to some authors the law of the place where the *dominus negotii* has his ordinary residence is decisive.[4] Pillet thinks that either the *lex situs* or the national law of the *dominus* should apply.[5] It seems hardly possible to cover all cases of *negotiorum gestio* by a single answer. If a contractual relationship exists between the *gestor* and the *dominus*, e.g. where the *gestor* is an agent of the *dominus*, and the work done or the money spent by him in the principal's interest does not fall

---

[1] German Civ. Code, s. 973, 977.

[2] *Example*: art. 573 French civ. code; 'mélange de plusieurs matières appar-tenant à différents propriétaires'.

[3] *Negotiorum gestio, gestion d'affaires, Geschäftsführung ohne Auftrag.*

[4] Windscheid, *Pandekten*, I. § 35 nr. 3; Zitelmann, II. 513.

[5] Pillet, *Traité prat.* II. 310, 311. (It is difficult to see why the national law of one of the parties should be of importance.)

within the orbit of his contractual duties and rights, it will be reasonable to regard the proper law of the contract as that legal system with which the *negotiorum gestio* has the most real connexion. Where there is no such contract capable of providing a connecting factor it would seem correct to assign the problem to the law of the country where the *gestor* acted and where therefore the claim (if any) arose. The same law will answer the question whether conversely the principal acquires a claim against the *gestor*. The *gestor* may, for instance, be liable for negligence in the same way as if he had acted under a contractual mandate. This leads in certain circumstances to a conflict between the English *lex fori* and the foreign law of the place of action. If under English law the act of the *gestor* is in the nature of a tort, the English court will apply the English rules on tort, because it takes the foreign law into consideration only for the purpose of ascertaining whether the act was justifiable or unjustifiable; and unjustifiable it is, though not as a tort, but as a breach of a quasi-contractual duty. If, however, under English law the act does not amount to a tort, and creates under the foreign law a quasi-contractual duty to repair a damage done by the *gestor*, the English court applies the foreign rule on quasi-contract. This was recognized, though not in a case of *negotiorum gestio* (in the strict sense of the term), in *Batthyani* v. *Watford*.[1]

Here the possessor of a *Fidei-Kommiss* (entailed property) situate in Austria was under an obligation to hand over the property to his successor in as good a state as when he received it; he was, on the one hand, liable for deterioration, on the other, entitled to be indemnified for improvements he had made. The English Court of Appeal held that Austrian law on *Fidei-Kommiss* applied, and that according to that law the successor's claim was 'not in the nature of damages for default, but a claim under an obligation to keep the property in a (certain) good condition', that is a claim under an implied contract, as Cotton, L.J., called it.

[1] (1887), 36 Ch.D. 269, 278. The decision is, incidentally, a sound though unconscious contribution to the correct doctrine of classification: the Court of Appeal classified the foreign legal rule according to the views of the foreign legal system.

BIBLIOGRAPHY

GUTTERIDGE and LIPSTEIN, 7 *Cambridge L.J.* (1941), 80. DICEY–MORRIS, 754–7. FALCONBRIDGE, 356–67. ZWEIGERT, 2 *Süddeutsche J.Z.* (1947), 247. NIBOYET, *Traité*, V. 192–9. RABEL, II. 540–1. ARMINJON II. 335–50.

PART VI

LAW OF PROPERTY

CHAPTER XXXII

MOVABLES AND IMMOVABLES

482. Importance of this distinction   I. To say of a tangible thing that it is movable or immovable may mean solely that it can or cannot be moved from one place to another. This natural, extra-juridical distinction is everywhere the starting-point for the legal distinction. But only the starting-point. Legal technique applied to the economic relationship of things may in some cases make it necessary to treat as immovables things which are in actual fact movable. Thus, for instance, fixtures in a house or fishes in a pond, or wild animals in a forest.[1] Conversely, things which cannot be removed without being destroyed —for example, temporary buildings, such as exhibition halls—are treated in some legal systems as movables.[2] Many legal systems even extend the distinction between movables and immovables to intangible things, such as debts, shares, commercial or industrial enterprises, hypothecs, rent-charges, and other rights. Here the original meaning of the words mobility and immobility has disappeared entirely.

The distinction between movables and immovables is important in various branches of the law.

Under most legal systems the transfer of ownership of movables, or the creation of a mortgage on them, differs considerably from similar transactions in immovables. The period of usucapion (prescription) is not the same in the case of movables as in that of immovables. The inalienability of the *fundus dotalis* in Roman law has been extended by several modern laws to all immovable but not to the movable parts of the dowry.[3] French law gives the seller of an immovable, not of a movable, the right to rescind the contract if the price was less than five-twelfths of its value.[4] There

---

[1] Thus in Austrian law (Civ. Code, 1811, s. 295 to 297).

[2] They are movables under German law (Civ. Code, s. 95; German Supreme Court, *Offic. Coll.*, 55, 284; 59, 21; 97, 106, and others).

[3] e.g. French *code civil*, art. 1554.

[4] Ibid., art. 1674.

exists in France and elsewhere a matrimonial property system which includes in the community of goods the movables, but not the immovables, owned by either of the spouses at the time of the marriage or devolving on him or her by way of succession.[1]

The distinction between movables and immovables is especially important in private international law. In England, the United States of America, France, Belgium, Roumania, Austria, and Hungary, the succession upon death to movable property is governed by the personal law of the deceased, while in the case of immovables the *lex situs* is decisive. See s. 483.

Unfortunately movables and immovables are not everywhere distinguished alike. Mortgages on immovables are regarded as movables under French and German law,[2] and as immovables in this country. Movables serving the use and exploitation of a piece of land are 'immovables by destination' in France, while German law treats them as movables in some respects and as immovables in others.[3]

II. What law determines whether a thing is movable or immovable? In most countries the leading text-books and the decisions of the courts declare the law of the *situs* to be decisive, while in the case of intangible things—which have no real *situs*—the answer lies in the law of the place which presents 'a close analogy' to the *situs* of a tangible thing.[4] It is not easy to accept this view without certain qualifications.

483.
Decisive law.
Various answers

Many conflict rules concerned with succession, with matrimonial property, or with the rights of guardians over the property of their wards, themselves distinguish between movables and immovables: in the case of movables they apply the personal law[5] of the deceased, the husband, or the

---

[1] Ibid., art. 1404.

[2] Ibid., art. 526 (which mentions as incorporeal immovables only the usufruct of immovables, the servitudes, and the actions for recovery of immovables); German Civ. C., s. 1551 § 2.

[3] French c.c., art. 524. In German law the *Zubehör* of land (and houses) is in general treated as a movable; but it passes to the purchaser of the land and is subject to usufruct and mortgages as if it were part of the land. German Civ. Code, ss. 926, 1031, 1062, 1093, 1120; also ss. 1096, 314, 1551; and code of civ. procedure, s. 865. Cf. Cook, 284–310; 252 et seq.

[4] See *infra*, s. 515.

[5] That is, either the law of the domicile or the national law of the person.

ward respectively, while the rights over immovables are governed by the *lex situs*.[1] In all such cases the conflict rule will either itself elucidate the distinction by stating what things are to be regarded as movable and what as immovable; or the conflict rule may abstain from answering this question and leave the answer to some other legal system, in particular to the *lex situs rei*.

An example of the first method occurs in Austrian law. The German Supreme Court[2] had to decide on the succession to an industrial enterprise situate in Germany but belonging to the estate of a deceased Czecho-Slovak citizen. If the industrial enterprise were held to be movable, succession would be regulated by Czecho-Slovak law, i.e. the Austrian Civil Code of 1911; if immovable, it would under the Czecho-Slovak conflict rule[3] be governed by the *lex situs*, i.e. the German law of succession. The German Supreme Court held that the Czecho-Slovak conflict rule was decisive, that under this conflict rule an industrial enterprise was movable, and that it was immaterial whether or not it would be treated as immovable under the German *lex situs*. There can be no doubt that this decision was correct;[4] and it is submitted that an English court, if called upon to apply the Czecho-Slovak conflict rule by way of *renvoi*, would reach the same solution.

The *second* method is however much more usual. Most conflict rules leave it to the law of the *situs* to decide whether a thing is movable or not. This is the method advanced particularly by French writers and usually accepted by French courts. The predominant German doctrine is to the same effect.

484. The English rule

Under English law[5] there is not even a doubt that this solution is correct: the character of a thing as movable or immovable is determined by the law of the *situs*. It must however be borne in mind that if the law of the *situs*, say French law, decides that the thing in issue is movable, this does not mean that the case itself should be governed by French municipal law or that French private international law should determine the applicable law. The help given by French law is limited to one small component of the

[1] Thus the conflict rules of England, the United States, France, Austria, Hungary, and many others.

[2] *Offic. Coll.*, 145, 85.

[3] The Czecho-Slovak conflict rule was applicable by way of *renvoi*.

[4] See Lewald, p. 175.

[5] *Johnstone* v. *Baker* (1817), 4 Madd. Rep. 474 n. *In re Hoyles*, [1910] 2 Ch. 333, 341; [1911] 1 Ch. (C.A.), 179.

problem: after having made known to the English court that the thing situate in France is movable as understood by French law, that law withdraws, and the English court will apply the English conflict rule concerning movables.

Example: a 'domiciled' Englishman, ordinarily resident in France, dies intestate owning a mortgage (*hypothèque*) of a French piece of land; under French law his 'heir' would be X, while his next-of-kin according to English law would be Y. Under English law a mortgage is immovable,[1] under French law it is movable; English law applies the *lex domicilii* to movables, the *lex situs* to immovables. In such case French law is decisive on the question of the mobility of the mortgage; the English court accepts that decision and applies its own conflict rule on succession to movables: hence the law of the domicile in the English sense of that term applies, and judgment will be given for Y.

III. The question *where* the *situs* of a given thing is to be found—particularly doubtful in the case of debts, shares, and other intangible things—is answered solely by the English conflict rule. Thus heritable bonds, that is, bonds for a sum of money secured by a conveyance of pieces of Scottish land, are under English law deemed to be situate in Scotland, even if the bonds themselves are deposited with an English bank. Scottish law considers such bonds to be immovable, and English courts accept this view as that of the law of the *situs*.[2] When slavery existed in Antigua the law of that country decided whether the slaves living there were to be regarded as immovables; they were.[3]

485. Where is the *situs*?

IV. The English distinction between movables and immovables is not identical with the difference between real and personal property. The two sets of conceptions overlap, particularly in two respects:

486. Real and personal property

1. All rights and interests in land are immovable, whether they are legal estates or interests or equitable interests.[4] A leasehold interest, in particular, is an immovable, though

[1] *In re Hoyles*, loc. cit. *Jerningham* v. *Herbert* (1829), 4 Russ. 388.

[2] *In re Fitzgerald*, [1904] 1 Ch. (C.A.) 573. *Johnstone* v. *Baker*, loc. cit. *Jerningham* v. *Herbert*, loc. cit.

[3] *Ex parte Rucker* (1834), 3 Dea. & Ch. 704. See also with regard to negroes in Louisiana: *McCollum* v. *Smith* (1838), in Beale's *Cases*, II. 8.

[4] On rent-charges: *Chatfield* v. *Berchtoldt* (1872), L.R. 7 Ch. A.C. 192. On mortgages, see *supra*, p. 503, n. 2.

(in the sphere of English municipal law) it is not real but personal property.[1]

2. The English equitable doctrine of conversion has no bearing upon the distinction between movables and immovables. According to that doctrine real property which is to be sold and turned into money becomes personal property on the testator's death before it is sold. But it is not treated as a movable.[2] And conversely: money to be employed under testamentary direction for the purchase of land becomes real property before being so employed, but remains movable. In *Berchtoldt's Case*[3] a domiciled Hungarian died intestate. He had been entitled to freeholds situate in England but subject to a trust for sale. The freeholds, which had not been sold, were treated as immovable though they were personal property. Succession to them was therefore regulated not by the Hungarian law of the deceased's domicile, but by the English rules concerned with the succession to and distribution of personal property.

The distinction between movables and immovables plays a part only in English private international law, not in English municipal law.[4] Conversely the distinction between real and personal property belongs solely to English municipal law. There is, however, one exception to this. Under the Wills Act (Lord Kingsdown's Act), 1861, a will made by a British subject in the form of the *lex loci actus*, though not in the form of the domiciliary law, is valid only in so far as it regulates the succession to personal property.[5]

---

[1] *Freke* v. *Lord Carbery* (1873), L.R. 16 Eq. 461, 466. *Duncan* v. *Lawson* (1889), 41 Ch.D. 394. *In re Berchtoldt*, [1923] 1 Ch. 192, 199. *Pepin* v. *Bruyère*, [1902] 1 Ch. (C.A.) 24.

[2] *In re Berchtoldt*, loc. cit. Cf. the Irish case *Murray* v. *Champernowne*, [1901] 2 Ir. Rep. 232, 236, 237. On *Re Cutcliffe's Will Trusts*, [1940] Ch. 565. See G. C. Cheshire, p. 533–4, Dicey–Morris, 526 (*aliter* Falconbridge, p. 515).

[3] [1923] 1 Ch. 192, 199.

[4] *In re Hoyles*, [1911] 1 Ch. (C.A.) 179, 185.

[5] See *infra*, s. 560 et seq. and *In re Lyne's Settlements Trusts*, [1919] 1 Ch. 80; *In re Cartwright*, [1939] Ch. (C.A.) 90, 100, 108.

CHAPTER XXXIII

THE LAW APPLICABLE TO REAL RIGHTS
(*IURA IN REM*)

I. OWNERSHIP of an immovable and other interests (rights) in immovables are subject to the *lex situs*. This principle, developed in the Italian doctrine of the Middle Ages, has become the common law of all European countries. In some modern codifications it has been expressly stated; thus in the Austrian Civil Code, the Italian Code, and the Polish Statute on Private International Law. The French Civil Code mentions it only in respect of immovables situate in France,[1] and many European and American codes which depend on the French code have adopted this form. But there is no doubt that in spite of such restricted mention the principle prevails unreservedly. 487. Rights in immovables

The very nature of immovables—their immobility—provides the reason for the application of the *lex situs*. Immovables are part of the country and so eternally and closely connected with it that all rights over them have there their natural centre of gravity. *Iura in rem* are rights valid against everybody and to be respected by everybody. If land ownership were determined by the personal law of the actual owner, the law governing rights over a piece of land would change with any change of ownership; the incidents of ownership, e.g. in the relationship between neighbours, would be altered by any alienation of the immovable to a foreigner or by a change of domicile on the part of the owner. It goes without saying that this would result in confusion.

The *lex situs* is decisive for *all* questions relative to rights *in rem immobilem*; see on this *infra*, p. 522 *et seq*.

II. Much more doubtful is the question what law governs ownership (or other rights *in rem*) of *tangible movables*. The Italian statutists of the Middle Ages and their followers in France, Holland, England, Scotland, and Germany have 488. Chattels the old rule: *mobilia personam sequuntur*

---

[1] *Code civil*, art. 3.

developed the rule that such rights are subject to the law of the domicile of the owner or the possessor: *Mobilia personam sequuntur* or *mobilia ossibus inhaerent*.[1] The corresponding English phrase runs: '*Personalty*[that is personal property] has no locality.' This rule was adopted by a number of modern codifications, such as the Prussian General Code of 1794, the Austrian Civil Code of 1811, the Baltic Code of 1864, the old Italian Civil Code of 1865,[2] the Spanish Código Civil of 1888, and the Civil Code of Lower Canada. Nineteenth-century theory, however, led by Savigny, overthrew the old statutist rule or at least restricted its sphere of application to the case of succession to movables upon death and to the matrimonial property system, while in respect of the creation and transfer of real rights in isolated things the principle of *lex situs* was applied. The texts of the Prussian, the Austrian, and the Italian codes were so interpreted by the courts and by scholars as to restrict the application of the *lex domicilii* to movables transferred or encumbered as parts of a person's whole property (*patrimoine, Vermögen*).[3]

489. The old rule ceasing to prevail in England?   English and American law retained the old rule of the statutists longer than did other legal systems. This is probably due in the first place to Story, whose famous 'general rule', repeated over and over again, ran: 'A transfer of personal property, good by the law of the owner's domicile, is valid wherever else the property may be situate.'[4] Nevertheless, American law no longer follows this doctrine; it has adopted instead the modern continental view under which the *lex situs* regulates rights in movables.[5] The development in England was slower. Old decisions, like *Bruce* v. *Bruce* (1790),[6] *Sill* v. *Worswick* (1791),[7] *Philips* v.

---

[1] The German doctrine, however, as early as the sixteenth century developed the rule that the law of the *situs* is decisive for movables and immovables alike; thus Everardus (d. 1532), Andreas Gail (d. 1587), Joachim Mynsinger (d. 1588). See on this Waechter, *Archiv f. d. civilist. Praxis*, 24, 274.

[2] The new Italian Code (1938, [1942] art. 12, *Dispos. Prelim.*) abolished the rule and replaced the personal law by the *lex situs*.

[3] See *supra*, p. 36, n. 3.

[4] Story, s. 384.

[5] American *Restatement*, s. 255 et seq.

[6] 2 B. & P., 229.

[7] 1 H. Blackst., 665.

Hunter (1795),[1] *Somerville* v. *Somerville* (1801),[2] and the very emphatic judgment in *Re Ewin* (1830)[3] could be quoted and have often been quoted in favour of the *lex domicilii*.[4] Even in recent times (1895) the rule was applied in the case of an assignment of isolated things, where the litigation concerned the title to goods situate in Scotland and both parties were domiciled Englishmen. This case, *North Western Bank* v. *Poynter*,[5] a Scottish case, does not however carry much weight, for Scottish and English law were agreed on the crucial point, and the remarks made in the House of Lords regarding the application of the domiciliary law were therefore mere *obiter dicta*.[6] Apart from this case, the *lex domicilii* principle has been applied in recent times only in a few situations:

1. where the thing in question had no real *situs*, e.g. a ship on the high seas.[7]

2. in cases of general (universal) assignments of all movables, e.g. succession on death[8] and assignment of all the debtor's property to a trustee for the benefit of his creditors.[9]

3. The domiciliary law is probably applicable in respect of capacity to dispose of movable property. See *infra*, s. 499.

The result is that English law is practically at one with modern continental laws in rejecting the domicile principle where isolated things are alienated, pledged, or otherwise disposed of.

There is indeed little to be said in favour of the domicile

490. Objections to the domicile principle

[1] 2 H. Blackst., 402, 406.
[2] 5 Ves. Jun., p. 749a.
[3] 1 Cr. & J., 151, 156: 'personal property follows the person, and it is not in any respect to be regulated by the *situs*; and if in any instance the situs has been adopted as the rule by which the property is to be governed, and the *lex loci rei sitae* resorted to, it has been improperly done' (*per* Bayley, J.).
[4] See *Liverpool Marine Credit Co.* v. *Hunter* (1868), L.R. 3 Ch. App. 479, 483; *Dulaney* v. *Merry & Son*, [1901] 1 Q.B. 536, 541.
[5] [1895] A.C. 56.
[6] See Lord Herschell, L.C., at p. 66; Lord Watson at pp. 75, 76.
[7] See *Liverpool Marine Credit Co.* v. *Hunter, supra.*
[8] *Provincial Treasurer of Alberta* v. *Kerr*, [1933] A.C. 710, 721.
[9] *Dulaney* v. *Merry & Son*, [1901] 1 Q.B. 536, 541. The general rule on which Channel, J., based his judgment is, however, not unassailable. The judge says that 'a transfer good according to the law of the domicile of the owner, and made there' is valid even if 'not conforming to the law of the country where the goods are situate'.

principle. As in the case of immovables, so here rights *in rem* are effective against anybody coming into contact with the thing in question. The owner's domicile, however, may not only change any day, but it is frequently unknown to purchasers or creditors who are not in a position to ascertain it. Moreover, if such purchasers or creditors are aware that the owner has a foreign domicile they cannot be expected to delve into the intricacies of foreign law. Thus the domicile principle appears calculated to hamper commercial intercourse, in particular if one bears in mind that the domicile of a person under English law often differs from his ordinary residence.[1] The basic idea on which the domicile principle is founded, viz. that movables follow the person of the owner, would be correct if the *omnia sua secum portans* were the ordinary type of man, which he is not.[2] True, the owner's domicile may be a good point of contact with regard to those things which he usually carries with him or which serve his personal needs.[3] Of an artificial set of teeth it may indeed be said that such *mobilia ossibus inhaerent*; but questions of conflict of laws do not arise in respect of them. In the old case of *Philips* v. *Hunter*[4] the court justified the rule *mobilia personam sequuntur* by a consideration of national economy: 'In a country a great part of whose commercial capital is employed abroad it is peculiarly proper that such capital over which the trader has a disposing power, although situated out of the Kingdom, should be considered as referable to the *domicilium* of

---

[1] Wharton, s. 308 and G. C. Cheshire, pp. 561–2, raise a further objection to the domicile principle: they urge that it is impossible to rely on the *lex domicilii* where the title to goods is disputed by two claimants with different domiciles. But to test *iura in rem* by the domicile of the owner means that *if A* is the owner of a thing and wishes to transfer ownership or to pledge the thing to *B*, this must be done in accordance with the rules established by the law of *A*'s domicile. It does not mean that the question *whether A* is the owner is to be answered by the law of *A*'s domicile. Whether *A* when buying the thing from *X* became its owner is decided by the domiciliary law of *X*; whether he has lost ownership by the domiciliary law of *A*.

[2] The *Código Bustamante*, art. 106, establishes a presumption to the effect that a thing is 'normally or ordinarily' situate at the owner's residence, and if there is no owner, at the possessor's residence. There is hardly any reason for such presumption.

[3] The Argentine and Brazilian codes rightly recognize this; they declare the domiciliary law to be decisive in those two cases.

[4] (1795) 2 H. Blackst., 402, 406.

the owner.' This may have been true in 1795 in the case of colonial trade or trade in uncivilized countries. But where British trade on the European continent is concerned the subjection of *iura in rem* to the law of the domicile might be more likely to weaken than to strengthen the English merchant's disposing power.[1]

Modern continental laws have practically everywhere replaced the rule *mobilia personam sequuntur* by the rule of the *situs*. This principle obtains in particular in France and all the legal systems dependent on French law, such as those of Belgium, the Netherlands, Roumania, and Italy; furthermore in Germany, Switzerland, Austria, Hungary, Poland, and Greece. There is, however, no unanimity on the reason why the law of the *situs* should be decisive. Savigny's opinion that the owner presumably wants to have his right subjected to the *lex situs*[2] is hardly more than a fiction. Some authors base the principle on the rule of public international law according to which the dominion of a sovereign state over things situate in its territory must be recognized by other states.[3] But, first, no such sweeping rule exists; secondly, if it existed it would not justify the conclusion drawn from it; thirdly, it might lead to unsatisfactory results in the case of goods *in transitu* (for example, sent from Portugal to Holland via Spain, France, and Belgium). The predominance of the *lex situs* in questions of *iura in rem* is better based on the nature of the *ius in rem*, on its efficacy *vis-à-vis* third parties. Real rights should be as manifest as possible; third parties who intend to acquire a right in a thing must be protected against the risk that such thing might be subject to a foreign law under which the acquisition would be void. While under the law of contracts the contracting parties have a choice as to the applicable law

491. *Lex situs* decisive?

---

[1] See the remark made by Maugham, J., in *Re Anziani*, [1930] 1 Ch. 407, 420, in favour of the *lex situs* principle: 'Business could not be carried on if that were not so.'

[2] Savigny, VIII. 169.

[3] Zitelmann, I. 133 et seq. Frankenstein, II. 5, 7, thinks that the principle follows 'necessarily from nature itself'; 'between a thing and the law there exists no legal relationship except the relationship of the local situation', because 'the part played by the thing is merely passive, the thing being unable to determine its destiny'. If this were true a ship on the high seas could not be subject to ownership.

because they alone are affected by the contract, the acquisition of a right *in rem* is something which concerns or may concern a great number of unknown strangers. As the place where a thing is situate is the natural centre of rights over it, everybody concerned with the thing may be expected to reckon with the law of such place. This view seems justifiable at least where the thing has a situs *of a certain duration* in one country. In this respect the *situs rei* can rightly be compared with the domicile of a person. Just as the place where a person is actually 'present' for a short time does not determine his personal law, so real rights are not centred in a place of transit: goods sent from Portugal to Holland are not 'situate' in Belgium when passing through. As, on the other hand, the mere presence of a person in England suffices to make him amenable to English jurisdiction, so it is possible (though not imperative) to subject things to the law of any temporary location: they may, for example, be arrested by creditors. Finally, just as in the doctrine of domicile it is not a person's ordinary and permanent residence at a certain spot but his residence in a certain country that matters—a person is domiciled in England even if he has no home[1]—so things constantly brought from one place to another within the same country are situate in that country even though they may have no fixed resting place.

492. English authorities doubtful
The dominion of the *lex situs* has been accepted by modern English law. This at least is the predominant opinion of English writers (Westlake, Dicey,[2] Foote, and others),[3] and it has been expressed several times by English courts,[4] though mostly in cases which would have been decided in the same way if a different doctrine had been accepted.

1. In the old case *Inglis* v. *Usherwood*[5] an English merchant had instructed a factor in Russia to procure certain goods; this the factor did and delivered the goods to a ship

---

[1] See *supra*, p. 106, n. 2.

[2] Morris in Dicey[6], pp. 558–70 concedes some influence to the *lex actus*.

[3] But not Dr. Cheshire, p. 564 et seq.

[4] Also by the British-German Mixed Arbitral Tribunal in *Luttges & Co.* v. *Ormiston & Glass, Ltd.* (1926), Recueil VI. 569, which stated that under English Private International Law the transfer of ownership is governed by the *lex situs*.   [5] (1801), 1 East 515, 524.

chartered by the English merchant; before the ship left the Russian port the merchant became insolvent, and the factor stopped the goods. Under English law ownership would have passed to the merchant and the factor would have no right of stoppage; under Russian law he had remained the owner and was allowed to stop the goods. Russian law was applied, probably because the *lex situs* was Russian; at any rate, it was not stated that the factor's domicile was Russian.

Dr. Cheshire,[1] however, argues that Russian law was applicable because it was 'the proper law of the contract by virtue of which the agent had procured the goods', that is, the contract between the English merchant and his factor. But first, the facts reported are not sufficient to show beyond doubt that that contract was governed by Russian law. Secondly, it is difficult to see why a contract which only created duties between the contracting parties should be the test for the passing of ownership. We shall see later[2] that in the field of Private International Law contract and conveyance must be strictly separated from each other.

In any case the court based the application of Russian law on the fact that the delivery of the goods on board ship took place in Russia.[3]

2. The next case, often quoted in favour of the *lex situs* doctrine, *Freeman* v. *East India Co.*[4] (1822), is consistent with the doctrine, but not more than that; the two legal systems between which the choice lay, English and Roman-Dutch law, were in harmony with each other.

3. The first clear case where it was expressly said that the *lex situs* applied is *Cammell* v. *Sewell*.[5]

There a Russian *A* had sold goods to the English merchant *B* and shipped them to England; ownership had passed to *B*. The vessel was wrecked off the Norwegian coast, and the goods were sold by public auction in Norway by the master *C* to *D*, who brought them to England and sold them there to *E*. Under English law the master *C* was not entitled to alienate the goods, and the transfer of ownership to *D* was void. Under Norwegian law the transfer was valid. The court held that Norwegian law applied, and the reason given by the court was that the law of the *situs* was decisive.

4. This principle was confirmed in *Liverpool Marine Credit Co.* v. *Hunter*.[6]

---

[1] At p. 568.   [2] *Infra*, s. 505.
[3] See loc. cit., pp. 524, 525. (True, the *lex situs* is here identical with the *lex loci actus* (*traditionis*).)   [4] 5 B. & Ald. 617, 624.
[5] (1858), 3 H. & N. 617; (1860), 5 H. & N. 728, 742, 744, 746.
[6] (1867), L.R. 4 Eq. 62; (1868), L.R. 3 Ch. App. 479.

A British subject *A* mortgaged his ship in England to *B*, another British subject, without giving him actual possession of the ship. When the ship was at New Orleans, Louisiana, *C*, another creditor of *A*'s, also a British subject, resident in England, arrested the ship, and the question arose whether *C* had to respect *B*'s mortgage, though under the law of Louisiana the mortgage was invalid.

The House of Lords affirming the decree of the Vice-Chancellor held that the law of Louisiana applied: the mortgagee, who in England had obtained a good title, lost his right, because the *lex situs* did not recognize a pledge without possession, and this despite the fact that all parties concerned had an English domicile. The reasons given by the House of Lords may be assailable, but the result was correct.

5. In *Hooper* v. *Gumm*[1] the facts were as follows:

A had been building ships in America, mortgaging them to his creditor Hooper by registration, indorsing the mortgages on the certificates of registry and sending the ships to England, where they were sold. As the indorsements hindered sales in England, *A* and Hooper agreed that the mortgages should not be indorsed in future. Thereafter a new ship was built, mortgaged to Hooper (by registration in America), and sent to England. Hooper acquired a good title according to American law. When the ship was in England it was sold to Gumm, and it was a question of the law of the new *situs* (England) whether the transfer of ownership to Gumm was valid in spite of Hooper's mortgage. Under English internal law this was the case.

The decision was in accordance with the *lex situs* principle, but it is true that the decision would have been the same if the effects of the sale to Gumm had been governed by the *lex loci actus*, and the court stated expressly that the sale to Gumm was made and completed in this country.[2]

6. In *Castrique* v. *Imrie*[3] Blackburne, J., recognized the authority of *Cammell* v. *Sewell*,[4] though only by a *dictum*.

7. In *Re Queensland*,[5] North, J., left it open whether it would suffice for the law of domicile to have been observed, and held that at any rate it was sufficient that the transaction conformed to the *lex situs*.

8. The judgments in *Alcock* v. *Smith*[6] and *Embiricos* v.

---

[1] (1867), L.R. 2 Ch. App. 282, 290.
[2] Ibid., p. 289.
[3] (1870), L.R. 4 H.L. 414, 429.
[4] *Supra*, p. 513 (3).
[5] [1891] 1 Ch. 536, 545.
[6] [1892] 1 Ch. (C.A.) 238, 255, 266, 267.

Anglo-Austrian Bank[1] deal with the transfer of ownership in negotiable instruments, such as bills of exchange and cheques. In the first case an English bill of exchange, drawn by and upon English firms and payable in England, had been indorsed in Norway to *X*, and a creditor of *X*'s seized it; it was eventually sold by public auction in Norway to *Y* and delivered there. Under Norwegian law *Y* had become the owner, under English law he had not. The court stated that the domicile of the debtor was immaterial, that therefore English law did not apply, but that 'the law of the country where the transfer takes place' is applicable, i.e. the *lex loci actus*, which however coincided with the *lex cartae sitae*. In the *Embiricos Case* a cheque had been stolen in Roumania, the thief had forged an indorsement and sold the cheque to an Austrian bank; the question was whether the bank had acquired a good title. The court applied Austrian law as the *lex situs cartae*; but both the King's Bench Division and the Court of Appeal mentioned that the *lex situs* was also the *lex loci actus*.[2]

9. In *Inglis* v. *Robertson*,[3] a Scottish case, the *lex situs*, as distinct from the *lex loci actus*, was applied by the Scottish courts and the House of Lords. The goods belonging to a domiciled Englishman but stored in a warehouse in Scotland had been mortgaged by the owner to another domiciled Englishman, the plaintiff, but contrary to Scottish law no notice of the 'hypothecation' was given to the warehouse-keeper. Subsequently the defendant, who was a personal creditor of the owner's, attached the goods and thereby acquired a *ius in rem* according to Scottish law. It was held that the defendant had a better right; the *lex situs* was applied and it was pronounced that a judgment disregarding this would be 'contrary to the elementary principles of international law'.

10. In *Dulaney* v. *Merry*,[4] as we have seen (*supra*, p. 509[9]), the law of the domicile was decisive because the owner had assigned the whole of his property for the benefit of his creditors. It was there stressed, however, that even in such

---

[1] [1904] 2 K.B. 870; [1905] 1 K.B. (C.A.) 677.
[2] Loc. cit. [1904] 874 (*per* Walton, J.), [1905] 683 (*per* Vaughan-Williams, L.J.).   [3] [1898] A.C. 616, 625.   [4] [1901] 1 Q.B. 536, 541, 542.

a case the *lexsitus* cannot be disregarded entirely, viz. where 'English law enacts rules as to the passing of property situated in this country'; 'the property in goods situated here which has been dealt with by foreign owners in accordance with the law of their domicile shall not pass by such dealing unless certain formalities are also complied with'. The term 'certain formalities' is by no means unambiguous. Undoubtedly, rules on the necessity of registration or indorsement, or of a notice to be given to a third possessor, are included in it; but is a rule of the *situs* which requires delivery of possession to a purchaser or pledgee to be held to relate to 'certain formalities'? If so, it would be difficult to discover any rule of English law which could be disregarded where English law is the *lex situs*. And does the same principle apply where the *situs* of the goods is in a foreign country? It may be hoped that the answer to this is in the affirmative.

11. The two decisions *In re Korvine's Trusts*[1] and *In re Craven's Estate*[2] deal with *donationes mortis causa*. The first held that the gift had to be treated as one *inter vivos* and that therefore the validity of the gift and the transfer of ownership did not depend on the law of the domicile (as in the case of a will), but on the *lex situs*, which, however, was identical with the *lex loci actus*. The second decision declared the question of the validity of the gift to be 'to some extent' a question of administration of the estate (?) and therefore subject to the law of the domicile of the testatrix; but the question whether the testatrix had effectively parted with the ownership and transferred it to the donee was declared to be a matter for the *lex situs*.

It was possibly a slight exaggeration when Maugham, J., in *Re Anziani* said *obiter*: 'I do not think that anybody can doubt that with regard to the transfer of goods the law applicable must be the law of the country where the movable is situate.'[3] But at least this *dictum* states the goal to which the development of English law tends and which it has probably attained.[4]

---

[1] [1921] 1 Ch. 343, 347.　　　　[2] [1937] 3 A.E.R. 33, 39.
[3] [1930] 1 Ch. 407, 420.
[4] See also *supra*, p. 511, n. 1, and p. 512, n. 4.

A different view is taken by G. C. Cheshire;[1] he regards **493. *Lex loci actus?*** the *lex loci actus* as decisive in the following two cases:

(*a*) where questions arise only 'between parties to a transfer'. It must, however, be doubted whether any transfer of ownership has this character. A contract creating mere obligations between the parties is of no concern to third parties; a transfer, an alienation, or the creation of a charge upon the goods concerns everybody, since it is in the nature of a *ius in rem* to be effective against everybody.

(*b*) where a third person is involved who 'is driven to rely upon the original transfer'.[2] If the thesis (*a*) were correct, the thesis (*b*) might be correct too.

Take however as an example *Inglis* v. *Usherwood*,[3] where an English merchant *A* had given his factor *B* in Russia a mandate to procure certain goods. Suppose—as Dr. Cheshire does—that both the mandate and the transfer of ownership to *A* are subject to Russian law. Does it follow that rights which a third party *C* claims to have derived from *A* should be governed by the same law? It is submitted that the answer should be: no. Whether *A* has acquired ownership is determined not by the law governing the mandate between *A* and *B* but by the Russian *situs* of the goods, and whether *C* has acquired ownership depends on the *situs* which the goods have at the time of the transfer from *A* to *C*. If, for example, *A* had not acquired ownership under the law of the Russian *situs*, it might happen that the *situs* is changed subsequently and that under the law of the new *situs C* would be able to acquire ownership from the non-owner *A* owing to his good faith.

Incidentally, G. C. Cheshire in declaring the *lex loci actus* to be decisive uses this term in a sense differing from the usual meaning of the word. While ordinarily *lex loci actus* designates the law of the country where an agreement has been made, Cheshire has in mind the law 'which is equivalent to the proper law of a contract' or 'with which a transaction has the most real connexion'.[4] There is no point in disputing this terminology, and it is incontrovertible that in all problems of private international law we have to look for the law of the country with which the question has the most real connexion. But which law is thus indicated in the case under review? The answer should be, not the *lex loci*

---

[1] p. 576.
[2] Cheshire, p. 580 et seq.
[3] (1801), 1 East. 515, 524. See *supra*, s. 492 (1).
[4] Cheshire, p. 564.

actus, but the *lex situs*. Only where formalities of transfer are in issue is the *lex loci actus* material.

Attention must, finally, be called to the obvious fact that the *lex loci actus* doctrine cannot present a solution to questions not connected with human acts. Where the purported acquisition of a *ius in rem* is based on the lapse of time, as in the case of prescription or usucapion, or where the incidents of a real right, for example of a right of pledge created by law, are to be determined, there is no *lex actus* which could possibly be consulted. The law of the *situs* will be decisive.

BIBLIOGRAPHY

CHESHIRE, 557–94. DICEY–MORRIS, 557–70. J. D. FALCONBRIDGE, 2 *Dominion L. Rep.* (1934), 1 et seq.; 13 *Canad. Bar Rev.* (1935) 265; 20 *Canad. Bar R.* (1942) 1, 109. COOK, 252, 301. NIBOYET, *Des conflits de lois relatifs à l'acquisition de la propriété*, 1912. NIBOYET, 60 *Rev. Darras*, 1933, 468. NIBOYET, *Traité*, IV. 197–476. BATIFFOL, *Traité*, 504–27. LOUIS ROUSSELL, *Du conflit des lois en ce qui concerne l'acquisition et la transmission entre vifs de la propriété*, 1893. DESBOIS, *J. Clunet*, 1931, 281. DIENA, *I diritti reali considerati nel dir. internaz. priv.*, 1895. DIENA, *Rev. Darras*, 1911, 561. K. DUDEN, *Rechtserwerb vom Nichtberechtigten im I.P.R.*, 1934. RABEL and RAISER, in *Rabel's Z.*, 3, 64. *Annuaire*, 23, 231, 249; 24, 368. ARMINJON, II 99–113.

CHAPTER XXXIV

GOODS *IN TRANSITU* AND MEANS OF TRANSPORT

THERE are two kinds of tangible movables for which the so-called *situs* is not the appropriate test: **494.** *Res in transitu.* Different doctrines

1. The *res in transitu*, that is, goods transported from one country to another. What law governs the question of the creation, transfer, and extinction of real rights in them? Dr. Niboyet, in his impressive study on the subject, has advocated the application of the law prevailing at the place of their destination, and a rule to this effect was adopted by the Montevideo Convention[1] in respect of ships' cargoes on the high seas. As goods in transit have no fixed resting-place, no *situs praesens*, the decisive place, so Niboyet suggests, should be the country where the rights created during transport will later become operative. The objection to this doctrine[2] is that it is by no means certain that the place of destination will become the *situs futurus*. The original destination may be altered while the goods are in transit, or the goods may perish or be stolen before reaching the country to which they are bound. Zitelmann[3] proposed that rights over goods *in transitu* should be constituted or transferred according to the law of the actual place where they are at the time of the transaction, and that if that place is unknown the general presumption in favour of the continuance of a previous legal position would solve any difficulty. But there he was mistaken. If, for example, the goods are being transported from Belgium, the owner's country, through France and Switzerland to his factory in Italy, and if he sells and alienates them to an Italian purchaser at a moment when the transport has *certainly* reached France and *possibly* reached Switzerland, Zitelmann's doctrine would entail the application of French law, though there is practically no relationship to France on the part of any of the persons

[1] Art. 28.
[2] See against it in particular Bartin, *Principes*, III. 223 et seq.
[3] II. 354 et seq.

concerned. Zitelmann's solution leads to unsatisfactory results; a mere place of transit is not the centre of gravity of rights *in rem*.[1]

495.
Recommendable solution

It seems impossible to set up a simple and comprehensive formula indicating the appropriate law. The answer must differ according to the various relationships. The three most important events that may occur during transport would seem to be the following:

(*a*) One of the owner's creditors seizes and arrests the goods *in itinere* with the result that the transport is discontinued for the time being. He thereby creates a resting-place, if only of a temporary nature. It will depend on the law of that place whether or not the seizure was lawful, and, if so, whether he has acquired a lien, a pledge, a *privilège* or a similar right, and what pertains to that right.

(*b*) Similarly, the owner of the goods *in transitu* may treat such temporary resting-place, for example an *interim* port, as if it were a real *situs*, and therefore transfer ownership or mortgage the goods according to the law of that place. If, for instance, the territorial law of the port allows him to mortgage the goods without giving notice to the shipowner or master, a mortgage thus constituted will be held valid. But the owner is not restricted to this method of disposal. Where according to the *lex loci actus* ownership can pass by mere consent or by an assignment of the seller's claim against the carrier, such consent or assignment will suffice, even if the law of the country where the goods are at that time is more exacting in its requirements. This is particularly important where the seller has in hand a bill of lading or a carrier's receipt and disposes both of such document and of the goods themselves: then the *lex situs cartae* coincides with the *lex loci actus*. It will further be permissible to substitute for the non-existent *situs praesens* the country of destination, provided that the goods arrive there; or again to act as if the transport had not yet started, that is, to have the transaction governed by the last real *situs* of the goods,

[1] See *supra*, s. 491. The Anglo-German Mixed Arbitral Tribunal rightly declared in *Luttges & Co.* v. *Ormiston & Glass, Ltd.* (Recueil VI, 564, 570): 'The casual and temporary situation of the goods during the passage through Holland cannot make Dutch law applicable as to the passing of the property.'

a *situs praeteritus*. Thus a measure of *choice* between several legal systems should be given to the owner who disposes of his goods during transport. And what is true of the owner is equally true of any person not the owner who has the right to dispose of them, such as a pledgee in possession of the goods who dispatches them to a foreign country and sells them during transport in order to recover the money due to him.

(*c*) The same cannot be said of a non-owner who alienates the goods during transport without authority to do so. The validity of such alienation to a *bona fide* purchaser should not depend on any other law than the law of the country where the goods really were at the time of the alienation.

2. The means of transport, such as railway trains, motor-cars, vessels, aircraft, have generally some fixed resting-place, in which they are as it were resident, even if temporarily absent. In the case of sea-going ships the law of the flag replaces the *lex situs*; in states consisting of several countries, for example the United Kingdom, the place of registry is decisive.[1]

496. Means of transport

Thus a ship while on the high seas or in a foreign port can be alienated or mortgaged according to the law of the flag or the port of registration. This, however, does not exclude the right of the owner or his creditors[2] to treat a vessel in foreign coastal waters or in a foreign port in accordance with the law of her location at the moment.

---

[1] Where, however, confiscation is in issue, a ship on the high seas is not to be regarded as a 'floating part of the flag-state'. *Chung Chi Cheung* v. *The King*, [1938] 4 A.E.R. 786; *Government of Spain* v. *National Bank of Scotland*, [1939] Sess. C. 413, 421, 426, 432.

[2] See *Liverpool Marine Credit Co.* v. *Hunter* (1867), L.R. 4 Eq. 62; (1868), L.R. 3 Ch. App. 479.

BIBLIOGRAPHY

Supra, p. 518, and H. WEIL, *Die kollisionsrechtliche Behandlung von Tatbeständen in Beziehung auf res in transitu*, 1933 (Dissert.). ARMINJON in *Mélanges Pillet*, II. 33, and *Précis*, II 120-7. HELLENDALL, 17, *Canad. Bar R.* (1939), 105. DICEY–MORRIS, 564-5. NIBOYET, *Traité*, IV. 476-625.

CHAPTER XXXV

THE DOMAIN OF THE *LEX SITUS*

It has been shown that, apart from certain exceptions, the law of the *situs* governs real rights over immovables and (tangible) movables. It now remains to indicate the scope of the *lex situs* in greater detail. The law of the *situs*, the *statutum reale*, as it was called by the statutists, covers the whole field of *iura in rem*.

497. What real rights are allowed? I. The law of the *situs* decides *what* real rights *can* come into existence. A type of real right unknown in country X cannot be created with regard to things situate in country X. Example: French law does not admit mortgages without possession (*hypothèques*) of movables. Therefore movables situate in France cannot be pledged without delivery, irrespective of whether this would be possible under the law of the place of contracting or under the domiciliary law of the creditor or the debtor.

498. Whether a particular right comes into existence? II. The law of the *situs rei* decides whether a *particular* right affecting a particular thing comes into existence, or passes to another person,[1] or changes its effects, or is extinguished.

1. The application of this principle is easy as long as the movable in question does not change its *situs*. If two domiciled Germans conclude a sale of ascertained goods situate in England, the ownership may pass without delivery of the goods to the purchaser, though under German law delivery or particular substitutes for delivery would be necessary. German law is not applicable; its content will only be taken into account by the court in order to ascertain whether, having regard to the specific circumstances of the transaction, the intention of the parties was directed to the exclusion of a transfer of ownership before delivery. Another example: A creditor and pledgee, expressly reserving his right, returns to his debtor the jewel pledged to him by the latter; the law of the country in which the jewel is decides whether the return of the pledge extinguishes

---

[1] *inter vivos*; on succession upon death, see *infra*, s. 539 et seq.

the right of pledge, or whether the reservation made by the creditor is effective.

The *lex situs* is generally applicable to *any* creation, transfer, or extinction of *iura in rem*. Such creation (&c.) may be based on a transaction between two parties or a unilateral voluntary private act-in-law, such as a dereliction by the owner. Or the right may come into existence by operation of law, as in the case of usucapion (prescription), or finally by an act of the state.

(*a*) Where a voluntary transaction or a unilateral act is in issue, the question arises whether the form of the act and the capacity of the persons concerned are governed by the *lex situs* or by any other law. A distinction must be made between movables and immovables. · 499. Capacity and form

(i) In the case of *movables* capacity is (probably) governed by the rules developed *supra*, s. 261 et seq. for contracts;[1] i.e. the law of the domicile applies; where, however, the party is capable under the *lex loci actus* but not under the law of his domicile, the *lex loci actus* is applicable. The *form* of the act seems to be regulated by the rules on mercantile contracts; therefore it is probably sufficient, though not necessary, that the *lex loci actus* be observed (as an alternative to the *lex situs*).[2]

(ii) A person's capacity to alienate *immovables* or to charge them with mortgages, easements, or other real rights, or to bring such rights to an end, or to acquire rights in immovables, is governed solely by the law of the *situs*, whatever his domicile may be.[3] The formalities of such

---

[1] There are, however, no authorities on the point. See the following note.

[2] In *Republica de Guatemala* v. *Nunez*, [1927] 1 K.B. (C.A.), 669, which deals both with capacity and formalities in an assignment of intangibles, there was divergence of opinion. Scrutton, L.J., held that the application of the *lex loci actus* was imperative (at p. 690), and Maugham, J., followed him in *Re Anziani*, [1930] 1 Ch. 407; while Lawrence, L.J., declared the *lex situs* to be imperative. At any rate there is no reason why the question should be answered differently in the case of conveyance of movables from what is (probably) the law in the case of a contract regarding movables. If it is correct that the formal validity of a contract depends on either the *lex loci actus* or the proper law of the contract, it should be correct that in the case of a transfer of movables the formalities of either the *lex loci actus* or the *lex situs* must be observed.

[3] *Bank of Africa* v. *Cohen*, [1909] 2 Ch. (C.A.), 129 (concerning capacity to mortgage land); see 26 *J. Comp. Legisl.* (1944), 75. *Birtwhistle* v. *Vardill* (1840), 7 Cl. & Fin. 895 (concerning capacity to acquire immovables). In this, English

transactions are also determined exclusively by the *lex situs*, and not by the law of the country where the transaction took place[1]. But it must be emphasized that both these rules (on capacity and formalities) restrict the exclusive application of the *lex situs* to transactions of a 'real' character, that is, transactions which immediately create, transfer, or extinguish a *ius in rem*. They do not apply to 'contracts', i.e. to transactions which impose on one party a duty to constitute, to transfer, or to terminate such right.[2] The owner who agrees to sell his land does not alienate it, but merely promises to do so. In respect of capacity the contract—like any other—is governed either by the law of the domicile or the law of the place of contracting, and in respect of formalities by the 'proper law' of the contract, as an alternative to the law of the place of contracting.[3] It is therefore neither necessary nor sufficient that the form prescribed by the *lex situs* as such has been observed. Only if the *lex situs* is the

and American law differs from most legal systems, in which capacity to dispose of immovables is governed by the personal law of the parties. See Raape, *Comment.*, 87 sub IV. In France the old doctrine established by d'Argentré, that the law of the *situs* determines capacity with regard to immovables, had been maintained even under the *code civil*, but it has been abandoned by the courts for over fifty years. See Valéry, p. 848.

[1] The rule *locus regit actum* is therefore inapplicable where the conveyance of immovables is the subject of the transaction. *Adams* v. *Clutterbuck* (1883), 10 Q.B.D. 403; *In re Hernando* (1884), 27 Ch.D. 284. The decision in *Bank of Africa* v. *Cohen*, [1909] 2 Ch. 129, is partly concerned with formalities (the warning to married women according to the *Senatusconsultum Velleianum* is a 'formality', though the validity of the mortgage depends on it). The English principle that the formalities of a conveyance are exclusively governed by the *lex situs* has been accepted and extended to movables by German, Polish, and Japanese laws. Most of the continental legal systems have refused to adopt this (very sound) exception to the rule *locus regit actum*. Instead, some of them have developed the principle that a *ius in rem immobilem* can only be validly created within the territory where the property lies, so that the *lex situs* and the *lex loci actus* coincide. Thus with regard to mortgages, French *c.c.*, art. 2128. *RVgl.HWB.*, IV. 394.

[2] See *infra*, s. 505. This distinction between the form of a contract and the form of a conveyance is to be found in continental laws too. See German Introd. Law, art. 11 § 2 (very meticulously drafted), Lewald, 71; Niboyet, *Manuel*, p. 635. Only Polish law subjects contracts relative to immovables in respect of form to the same rules as conveyances; Pol. Internat. L., 1926, art. 6 § 3; Pol. Interloc. L., 1926, art. 8 § 3.

[3] See *supra*, ss. 261, 427. German courts have often pronounced that land situate in Germany and belonging to a German can validly be sold abroad without observation of any form, for example, orally, if the *lex loci actus* does not require any formalities; Lewald, p. 71. Under English law a different treatment may follow from the procedural character of the rule of the Statute of Frauds.

proper law of the contract—and this is frequently the case
—is it sufficient for the parties to observe the form determined by that law. Where the contract forms part of an
instrument covering the alienation of the land, such alienation is, of course, void if the form of the *lex situs* has not been
observed; but in such a case the contract having been concluded in the correct form, the owner remains bound to
transfer ownership[1] unless the contract is vitiated by the
nullity of the act of alienation. Whether this is the case or
not is tested by the proper law of the contract.

(*b*) The *lex situs* covers real rights based on *usucapion*[2] or
on an act of state, in particular *confiscation* and *expropriation*.[3]
The state in the territory of which a thing is situate will
decide whether the decree of confiscation or expropriation has effectively transferred ownership to the state.
The answer may be different in the cases of confiscation
and expropriation respectively.

500. Confiscation

(i) Confiscations are 'penal' or financial or political in
character and the owner affected by them is not entitled to
compensation. Therefore they will not be enforced in this
country in so far as they bear upon things situate outside
the territory of the confiscating state. Illustrations of this
are to be found in the cases of *Lecouturier* v. *Rey*[4] and of
Banco de Vizcaya v. *Don Alfonso de Borbon y Austria*.[5]

In the former case certain religious corporations had been dissolved by
a French statute; their property had been confiscated and their members ex-
pelled from France. Among them there were some Carthusian monks who in
England continued to manufacture the liqueur called Chartreuse, according
to a secret formula. The French confiscation could not prevent them from
exploiting the reputation which that liqueur enjoyed in England; the
property situate in this country was made up of that reputation, the English

---

[1] Whether the purchaser thereby acquires an equitable interest depends not on
the *situs*, but on the proper law of the contract.

[2] See on this *infra*, s. 503.

[3] Dicey–Morris, 155–60. Wortley, *Problèmes soulevés par la législation sur
l'expropriation*, 67 *Rec.* (1939), I. 343. Walter Herzfeld, *Nationalization of
Foreign Corporations*, New York, 1943 (*Contemporary Law Pamphlets*, ser. 9,
no. 1). Gordon, *Expropriation of Foreign owned Property in Mexico* (*Mod. L.R.*
1946, 207).—Beitzke, *Enteignung im Int. Priv. R.*, in the *Festschrift f. Raape*,
1948, p. 93 et seq. Petersen, *Tagung deutscher Juristen*, 1947, 127 et seq.

[4] [1910] A.C. 262, 264.

[5] [1935] 1 K.B. 140. See also the Scottish case, *Government of the Republic of
Spain* v. *National Bank of Scotland*, [1939] Sess. C. 413.

trade-marks, and the secret formula. The French statute had no power to
confiscate such extra-territorial property. In the case of the *Vizcaya Bank*
against the former King of Spain the Spanish Republican Government had
decreed that King Alfonso's property, including any property deposited
with Spanish banks, should be confiscated. Certain securities which he had
bought with his own money had been deposited with an English bank to
the order of the King's agents, the Bank of Vizcaya. The claim of this
bank to the securities situate in London was not successful, since they were
situate outside Spain and the penal nature of a confiscation prevents it
from operating outside the territory.[1]

In so far as the confiscation decree affects property
situate *within* the territory of the confiscating state its
effect is the transfer of the title to the state, and this will be
respected everywhere, even if the confiscated things did not
belong to a national of that state. Take the example of a
British national residing in Russia during the revolution
and deprived of his property situate in Russia by confiscation. If the Soviet Union sends some of the confiscated
goods to England and sells and delivers them here, the
purchaser, though he may know their origin, acquires
an unimpeachable title as against the previous owner. It
makes no difference whether the state has confiscated

---

[1] Cf. *Folliot* v. *Ogden* (1789), 1 H. Blackst. 123, 135; *Barclay* v. *Russell* (1797),
3 Ves. jun. 423, 429 ('confiscation in a foreign country cannot operate upon
property here', for 'no nation executes the criminal judgments of another');
Luther v. *Sagor & Co.*, [1921] 3 K.B. 532, 545; *The Jupiter (No. 3)*, [1927]
P. 122, 140; 250, 253 (C.A.): the Russian 'nationalization' decrees had no effect
on property situate outside Russia; *Princess Paley* v. *Weisz*, [1929] 1 K.B. 718;
In re Russian Bank for Foreign Trade, [1933] Ch. 745, 767 (where Maugham, J.,
stresses the strictly territorial character of nationalization decrees and mentions
that even the Russian Republic does not claim extraterritoriality for its decrees);
Bank of Ethiopia v. *National Bank of Egypt*, [1937] 3 A.E.R. 8. *Tallina Laevau-
hisus* v. *Tallin Co.* (1946), 175 L.T. 285. *Frankfurther* v. *Exner Ltd.*, [1947] Ch.
629. The same view was taken in Germany, but not in France. On this see: A. N.
Makarov in *Zeitschr. für Ostrecht* 7 (1933), 436–8; André-Prudhomme, *J. Clunet*,
1937, 487. A surprising decision was delivered by the United States Supreme
Court in the case of *United States* v. *Pink* (printed in 36 *American Journ. of
Internat. Law* (1942), p. 309). Property located in the United States and belonging
to Russian companies which were dissolved by the nationalization decrees had
been confiscated by these decrees in favour of the Russian state, and after the
recognition of the Russian revolutionary government the Russian state had
assigned its rights in that property to the United States. If the confiscation by
Russia of property situate outside Russia was valid the assignment was valid also;
if the confiscation was *ultra vires*, the assignment to the United States could not
make it valid. The Supreme Court held the assignment valid; but in a forceful
dissenting opinion Stone, C.J., showed the defects of the majority decision
(p. 332). Cf. the criticism of the decision by E. Borchard, ibid., 275.

specific goods by taking them into possession, or whether a general confiscation decree concerns all goods of a certain kind, which provisionally remain in the possession of the former owner. If in the latter case the former owner against whom a confiscation order has been issued brings the goods to England, this does not extinguish the ownership of the confiscating state, since the goods were in Russia at the date of confiscation. The Soviet State therefore can give a good title to a purchaser in this country without ever having possessed the goods.[1] But if the former owner sells the goods in England in market overt to a *bona fide* purchaser for value the latter will acquire a good title.[2]

(ii) Expropriation has no penal character; it is the acquisition by law of things which are needed for a certain enterprise of public utility, usually against adequate compensation. Until recently it was generally assumed that in every country the law allows only such things to be expropriated as are situate in that country. This assumption was based, not, as in the case of confiscation, on any penal character of the act, but on a principle of public international law: it was thought inconsistent with the respect due to the sovereignty of state X that state Y should be permitted to expropriate things situate in X for the purpose of promoting its own public interest. This old principle of strict territoriality of expropriation decrees has, however, proved unsuited to wartime needs. The Norwegian Government, shortly before they left Norway, and the Dutch Government, when residing in London, issued decrees by which they vested in the state the title to certain tangible property (vessels) and to certain claims connected therewith, belonging to nationals of the state and situate outside their respective territories. The Dutch decree was recognized by the New York Court of Appeals in *Anderson* v. *Transandine Handelsmaatschappij*,[3] in so far as intangible property situate in New York was concerned; and this decision was based on the 'comity of nations' and on the consideration that the decree was designed to prevent property from

501. Expropriation

---

[1] *Contra*: Foster, *La théorie angl.*, p. 109.
[2] Sale of Goods Act, s. 22.
[3] 36 *American Journ. of Internat. L.* (1942), 701, 706.

falling into the hands of the common enemy and thus to protect the rights of the former owners. The same view was adopted in the English case of *Lorentzen* v. *Lydden & Co.*[1] The decision concerned certain claims against the defendants, belonging to Norwegian subjects and 'situate' in England, which had been requisitioned and transferred to the plaintiff as 'curator' and representative of the Norwegian Government. The learned judge founded his judgment on three grounds: first, the Norwegian decree was intended to operate *extra territorium*, and was not confiscatory in character, because it provided for a compensation to be fixed in accordance with Norwegian law; secondly, the recognition of the decree was required by the comity of nations, and thirdly, it was supported by considerations of public policy. The second of these reasons would seem to suffer from the ambiguity of the term 'comity of nations' and is therefore hardly convincing. The third argument introduces an entirely new and rather dangerous conception of public policy: the judge invokes it, not in order to exclude foreign law which would normally be applicable, but to allow foreign law to impose itself although it would normally not be applicable.[2] The first reason has greater force though it needs some qualification. The judge distinguishes between confiscations and other state acts depriving a person of property (that is, expropriations). In the case of confiscations the *lex situs* is decisive, and under this a foreign confiscation decree has no extra-territorial effect.[3] But in the case of expropriations extra-territorial effect is to be granted to a foreign decree, provided, first, that the decree itself is intended to have such effect and, secondly, that its application is not contrary to public policy. The decision thus evolves a new rule of private international law, viz. that the question whether ownership of property situate in England passes to a foreign state by an act of expropriation of that state is to be answered by the law of

[1] [1942] 2 K.B. 202, 216 (*per* Atkinson, J.).

[2] See F. A. Mann, 5 *Modern L.R.* (1942), 262.

[3] Why, however, did the judge endeavour to show that in the Russian cases, which were cases of confiscation and not of expropriation, the foreign decrees were not intended to operate outside the territory? Would it be different if the decrees had been so intended?

that state unless such transfer of ownership is inconsistent with English public policy. A rule of this kind is sound and satisfactory.

In the New York case of *Anderson* v. *Transandine* the application of the Dutch expropriation law seems to have been restricted to the case of expropriation of *intangible* goods; in the English case no such distinction was made. The reason for the exclusion of tangible property in New York may have been that tangible goods have a real *situs*, to the law of which they should be exclusively subjected, while the so-called *situs* or quasi-*situs* of intangibles is more or less fictitious; it is therefore better to replace the law of the *situs* by the law of the state which has issued the decree. The extension of the rule to tangible goods is, however, justifiable: it would be startling if the expropriation of ships by a foreign decree were to be excluded but the expropriation of claims connected with the use of the ships recognized.

2. Which *lex situs* governs *iura in rem* if the *situs* of a chattel changes from one country to another? It may be

**502.
Change of
situs**

(*a*) that a *ius in rem* has come into existence under the law of the *situs* and that subsequently the chattel is transported into a country where it would not have been possible to create the right in the same way. In such cases the right 'acquired' elsewhere usually remains in force.

Illustrations: (i) A specific chattel situate in England has been sold; ownership has passed though possession was not transferred. Later the chattel is brought to Germany, where transfer of ownership requires delivery of possession or certain substitutes for delivery. The ownership acquired under English law is not invalidated.

(ii) Stolen goods belonging to *O* are sold in England in market overt to a *bona fide* purchaser *P*; he takes them to Germany. Under German law he would not have acquired ownership, but he retains the right previously acquired. While the goods are in Germany, the thief is discovered in England, prosecuted, and convicted. According to English law this causes the property to 'revest in the person who was the owner', i.e. *O*.[1] Is this rule applicable although acquisition of ownership now depends on the law of the new *situs* (Germany)? The answer should be Yes. *P* when becoming owner under English law acquired not an unqualified ownership, but ownership subject to a subsequent (resolutive) condition, and *O* retained ownership subject to a precedent (suspensive) condition.

(iii) Chattels situate in Cape Town are mortgaged by notarial deed duly registered but unaccompanied by delivery. They are subsequently taken to Germany or France. In principle the mortgage continues to exist, though under German or French law no mortgage would have come into existence owing to the lack of delivery. But it may be that German or French law is

---

[1] ss. 22 (1), 24 (1) Sale of Goods Act.

opposed not only to the *creation* of a mortgage without possession, but also to its *existence* if it was validly created under a foreign *lex situs*. This is a question for German and French internal law respectively: under German law the mortgage would continue to exist and to be operative. Not so under French law,[1] where the mortgage cannot be exercised as long as the goods are in France.

(*b*) Conversely: If, according to the *lex situs*, a transaction has not created the intended *ius in rem*, the transport of the goods to another country (where the transaction would have led to a different result) will not cure the defect.

Example: An Englishman buys in good faith a stolen chattel in an open market in Berne; he does not acquire ownership. Bringing the chattel back to England does not make him the owner. He only keeps the right acquired under Swiss law to retain possession as against the true owner until he recovers the price he has paid in Berne.[2]

503. Acquisitive prescription (usucapion) (*c*) What law is to apply if not one single fact but a series of successive facts may have created (or transferred or extinguished) the intended *ius in rem*, and if during the period concerned the *situs* of the chattel has changed? This question arises in particular where ownership is based on acquisitive prescription (*usucapion*), or where the loss of a real right is founded on acquiescence during a long period. In principle the law of the last *situs* is decisive, the law under which the set of facts, still incomplete at a former *situs*, has been brought to a close. Though all the requirements of the last *situs* must be fulfilled, it is not necessary that all of them should be fulfilled under the rule of the last *situs*. Facts which have occurred before the change now take on the 'legal value'[3] the new law gives them.

Examples: (i) In France usucapion of movables is accomplished in three, in Switzerland in five years. *X* possesses a chattel in France in good faith for two years; he takes it to Switzerland, where he continues to possess it for a further three years; he thereby becomes the owner.[4]

(ii) Conversely: having possessed the chattel in Switzerland for three years, the possessor takes it to France. Under French law he becomes the

[1] 'Les meubles n'ont pas de suite par hypothèque' (*c.c.*, art. 2119).
[2] Swiss Civil Code, art. 934 § 2.
[3] Expression Zitelmann's ('Rechtswert').
[4] A different doctrine asserts that the time passed at the old *situs* must be taken into account proportionately to the legal period required by the law of such old *situs*. The possessor having been in possession for two-thirds of the French legal period would have to remain in possession during one-third of the Swiss period, that is, one year and eight months (von Bar, I. 638, Meili, I. 397). This

owner as soon as a true *situs rei* has been established in France. If he merely travels from Switzerland to France for a week and then returns taking the chattel with him, he cannot claim usucapion.

(iii) Usucapion of movables is unknown to English municipal law. If a *bona-fide* possessor takes to Switzerland a chattel he has possessed in England for three years and if he continues to possess it in Switzerland for a further two years, the usucapion is perfected. The fact that the first three years ran in a country where usucapion is unknown is no obstacle.[1]

(iv) It may happen that under the law of the old *situs* the possessor has acquired more than a mere hope (*spes*) of ownership, though not yet a *ius in rem*. Under many continental systems this arises if the owner of a chattel has lost and another person has found it. German and Swiss law gives the 'finder' a 'right' of expectancy; that is, if the owner remains unknown during a certain period the finder acquires ownership, irrespective of whether he is still in possession or not, and whether he is in good or bad faith. This 'right of expectancy' is more than a merely factual expectancy such as the possessor has where a period of usucapion has begun to run. It has the nature of a right.[2] It will therefore not be extinguished if during the period in question the chattel becomes situate in a country where acquisition of ownership by a finder is unknown.

Example: *X*, while boarding a ship bound for England in Hamburg harbour, finds a jewel, duly gives notice of his find to the police, and takes it with him to England; the true owner remains unknown. Under German law *X* becomes owner after the lapse of a year; under English law he never acquires ownership. German, not English, law is applicable, because *X* found the thing in Germany and thereby acquired a 'right' not to present ownership but to ownership after a year, unless the former owner should become known before that time.[3] It would be different if the law of the new *situs* included a positive rule inconsistent with the right duly acquired by the finder, for example to the effect that ownership of all things lost vests in the state.

III. The law of the *situs* is applicable to all rights which 504. Possession

solution would perhaps be correct if the possessor after having been in possession for two years in France had acquired two-thirds of the ownership; Zitelmann, II. 348. On other doctrines: Arminjon, *Mélanges Pillet*, I. 28 et seq.

[1] *Contra*: Frankenstein, II. 80.

[2] The finder may alienate it, pledge it to his creditor, &c. A personal creditor may seize and arrest it. If the finder dies it passes to his successor.

[3] Cf. the case decided by the Hamburg Court of Appeal in 1904, in Falkmann and Mugdan, *Entscheidungen der Oberlandesgerichte*, 10, 114.

according to that law are *iura in rem*. It applies also to possession,[1] and it does not matter whether possession is regarded as a right or merely as a fact. Where a servant has the factual control over a movable, it may be that under the law of the *situs* he is regarded as its possessor,[2] while under the law of the master's domicile the latter is looked on as sole possessor;[3] in that case the *lex situs* is decisive. The law of the *situs* also answers the question whether, besides the direct possessor, for example the bailee, a second person, the bailor, is in more remote, indirect, 'constructive' possession, or whether he has only a personal contractual claim. It does not matter whether the proper law of the contract between bailor and bailee does, or does not, recognize the institution of 'indirect' possession. An Austrian in the course of comprehensive business relations with a German merchant which were expressly subjected to Austrian law once pledged some securities deposited with a German bank in Berlin; though there is no such thing as indirect possession in Austrian law, the German *situs rei* caused the Austrian to be regarded as 'mediate possessor' in the sense of German law. The law of the *situs* decides further whether and by what means possession may pass from one person to another. In some legal systems, such as the German and the Swiss, possession passes *ipso iure* to the successor in the case of the possessor's death; similarly under English law, where the successor obtains at least constructive possession. In other legal systems, such as Roman law, possession does not pass to the heir. Which of these rules applies is not decided by the law governing succession on death, i.e. by the law of the deceased's domicile, but by the *lex situs*;[4] for the law of succession only decides who succeeds to the heritable property, but not what is included in it.

505. *Lex situs* not decisive for contracts

IV. The *lex situs* governs only *iura in rem* (and possession). It is not the test for contracts connected with the thing in

---

[1] Thus expressly the new Italian civil code (1938, 1942), *Dispos. prelimin.*, art. 12.

[2] Pollock and Wright, *Possession*, 1888, pp. 60, 130, 138. *R. v. Harding* (1930), 142 L.T. 583.

[3] For example in Germany; s. 855 Civ. Code.

[4] See Zitelmann, II. 951.

question. As we have already seen,[1] a contract which imposes on one party the duty of transferring ownership to the other party is governed by its proper law—which is usually but not always the law of the *situs*. Further, a debt secured by pledge or mortgage or by a transfer of ownership may be governed by a legal system different from the law applicable to the security. If the owner of land borrows money and promises to mortgage the land, the contract, according to the presumptive intention of the contracting parties, will as a rule be governed by the law of the *situs*; but again, this is not necessarily the case. Where the security is a movable, or even several movables, an agreement of the parties to have the debt governed by the *lex situs* of the movable (or of one of them) points to the *situs* at the date of the contract. If the *situs* subsequently changes, the debt is governed by the law of the old *situs*, while the *ius in rem* is tested by the actual *situs* of the movables.[2]

Equitable rights or interests are not *iura in rem*; equity acts *in personam*. The law governing them is therefore not necessarily the law of the *situs*; it may be the law of the place of contracting or of the owner's domicile, or any other 'proper' law. This is particularly important where the right is an equitable mortgage of land situate in a country where such kind of mortgage is unknown,[3] or where foreign land forms part of trust property and the fiduciary relationship which might be created under the *lex situs* would confer on the beneficiary fewer substantial rights than English law gives the *cestui que trust*.[4]

506.
Equitable
interests

In the United States (according to the American Restatement) equitable interests are governed by the law of

---

[1] *Supra*, s. 435, and, in respect of capacity and form, s. 499.

[2] The fact that the security may be governed by a law different from that governing the debt sometimes leads to difficulties and unsatisfactory results. Cf., for example, the case of *Moulis* v. *Owen*, [1907] 1 K.B. 746.

[3] *Re Courtney, ex parte Pollard* (1840), Mont. & Ch. 239. *British South Afria Co.* v. *De Beers Consolid. Mines*, [1910] 1 Ch. 354, 387. *In re Smith*, [1916] 2 Ch. 206. *In re The Anchor Line* (1937), Ch. 483, 488. Cf. Cheshire, 746–60. W. W. Cook, 19 *Columb. L.R.* (1919), 486. Swabenland, 45 *Yale L.J.* (1936), 438. Croucher, 4 *Modern L.R.*, (1940), 111. Cavers, 44 *Harv. L.R.* (1930–1), 182. L. G. Hoar, 26 *Canad. Bar R.* (1948), 1415–36. (Land's book on *Trusts in the Conflict of Laws* [1940] was not available to the present writer. On it: Griswold, 55 *Harv. L.R.* (1941), 163.)

[4] See *infra*, p. 535.

the country where the land or the chattel affected is situate.[1]

507.
Servitudes:
***situs* of**
praedium
serviens
decisive

V. A *ius in rem* is tested by the *situs* of the thing in which the right in question exists. Every legal system includes rights which do not belong to a person individually designated but to the owner of a certain piece of land as such. Examples are easements, rent charges created in favour of land-owners, and the like. Such rights are governed by the *lex situs* not of the dominant but of the servient piece of land.

Under the Treaty of Versailles Germany renounced in favour of Belgium all rights and title over the territory of Eupen and Malmédy; thereby it happened that an easement ('servitude') which had been established under German law before the war belonged to a piece of land which was still German, while the land charged with the servitude was now on the other side of the border. It consequently became subject to Belgian law; the particulars of the *praedium dominans* are immaterial.

508. Inci-
dents of
iura in rem

VI. The law of the *situs* determines the *incidents* of all *iura in rem*. If the *situs* changes from one country to another the content of the real right may also change. Examples:

1. Under Spanish law *res sacrae* were inalienable. A *res sacra* was brought from Spain to France. Alienation became possible.[2]

2. A creditor-pledgee takes the pledge from country *X* to his new residence in country *Y*. From that time on the law of *Y* decides whether he has the right to sell the pledge by private act or only by public auction, whether he may sell it before the debt is due in case of an impending deterioration of the pledge or of a diminution of its value, whether instead of selling it he may keep it as owner, &c. True, if he exercises the rights which the law of the new *situs* grants him he may thereby offend against the contract concluded between the parties; for this contract—i.e. the *contractus pigneraticius* of Roman law—is governed by its own proper law, which is not altered by a subsequent change of the *situs* of the pledged thing.

3. Sometimes the legal system of the new *situs* does not embody exactly the same type of right as has been created

---

[1] *Restatement*, s. 239 et seq., 294.
[2] 'Tribunal de la Seine', *J. Clunet*, 1886, 593.

under the law of the old *situs*. It is necessary then to seek in the new law the type of right approximating most closely to the old. The restricted ownership of an English trustee does not exist in German law. Therefore if trust property is taken to Germany the rights English law gives to the *cestui que trust* can only continue to exist within the limits recognized by German law. The trustee becomes a fiduciary, that is, an owner who, though not allowed to dispose of the goods against the beneficiary's rights and interest, and responsible for any breach of duty, has nevertheless the power so to dispose; an alienation even where illicit is valid.[1]

509. Equivalence

The question whether an institution known to the law of one country is *equivalent* to a similar institution developed in the legal system of a different country, in the sense that in private international law one of them may be replaced by the other, bristles with difficulties.[2] In a comparison between them their historical origin must be left out of account—the English trust and the Islamic *Wakf* are very similar to each other in spite of the difference of the civilizations which have created them.[3] Nor will their legal structure be primarily decisive: there is no objection to replacing the rights of an English testamentary executor by those of a German *Testamentsvollstrecker*, though the English executor is owner of the property, while his German counterpart is not (the latter having only a right to administer property owned by the heir). The question of chief importance is whether and to what degree the substituted type fulfils the *economic* and *social* functions of the type it serves to replace.

510. Protection of real rights

VII. Under all continental laws the *lex situs rei* also covers the *protection* of real rights. This is not the view of English law. Probably the courts of this country would prefer to apply the *lex fori*, owing to the very wide application of the ambiguous term 'remedy'. A few examples may illustrate the issue:

---

[1] According to s. 137 German Civ. C.
[2] See also *infra*, s. 567.
[3] Cf. on *fideicommissum* and trust: *Abdul Hameed* v. *de Saram*, [1946] A.C. (P.C.) 208.

1. A person ousted from possession in France or Germany brings an action in England against the offender. Which law determines the period within which the action must be brought?[1] The court will probably apply English law. Which law decides whether the defendant is allowed to rely on his own right to possession?[2] Again English law will probably be applied.

2. The owner of a chattel stolen from him in Germany and now possessed by a *bona fide* purchaser in Germany brings an action against the latter in England. He is thereby relying on his ownership (*rei vindicatio*). Under German substantive law he has a claim to recovery of the chattel itself and not to restitution of its value.[3] Is this rule applicable in an English court? It must be feared that it is not.[4]

---

[1] Under German law the action must be brought within one year. Failing this the former possessor loses his substantive right, and not only the remedy, as in the case of limitation of action. German Civil Code, s. 864.

[2] Compare, for example, German Civ. C., s. 863, where the *exceptio ex iure possidendi* is excluded, with Swiss Civ. C., s. 927, where this *exceptio* is admitted if the defendant can prove his right at once.

[3] Civil Code, s. 985.

[4] See, however, *In re Moses* [1908] 2 Ch. 235.

BIBLIOGRAPHY

See *supra*, p. 518.

CHAPTER XXXVI

ASSIGNMENT OF INTANGIBLES

I. SIMPLE DEBTS

In England, as in many other countries, the law regards a **511.** Preliminary observations claim by one person against another not only as a 'right', but also as the subject-matter of another right, that is, as an incorporeal thing of which the creditor has the 'ownership'. There has been much discussion among continental jurists about the usefulness of such a view; it seems an unnecessary and illogical duplication to describe the creditor as the owner of his claim. Sometimes, however, this way of looking at the situation, or better, of expressing it, facilitates understanding. Where, for instance, a creditor *A* pledges his claim against his debtor *B* to his creditor *C*, it renders matters easier if we view the pledgee *C* as having a *ius in re incorporali aliena*, as opposed to *A*, who may then be called its owner, its *dominus*. The same is true where a judgment creditor garnishes as part of his debtor's property a claim by his debtor against a third person. Similarly in the case of assignment of debt it may be permissible to call the debt an incorporeal 'thing' passing from the ownership of *A* into that of *C*. In private international law it is material to ascertain whether this mode of expression conveys the true legal situation or is only a figure of speech, an image as it were. Sober and unbiased reflection leads to the simple result that an assignment merely has the effect of making the debtor from the date of assignment liable to *C* instead of to *A*, that therefore the assignment changes the debtor's duty. When other changes are made affecting a debt, when, for example, the place or time of performance is changed or an unconditional duty is made subject to a condition, such changes are brought about by a new agreement between the creditor and the debtor. An assignment is different: its effect may possibly be produced without the debtor's co-operation, an agreement between the assignor and the assignee being sufficient. But this difference does not matter so far as private international law is concerned.

512. Proper law of assigned debt decisive?

I. In view of the character of an assignment as an alteration of the content of the debt it would appear reasonable for it to be governed by the same law as governs the assigned debt, that is, if the debt was created by a contract between the assignor and the debtor, by the proper law of that contract. This is indeed the common opinion expressed in German, Swiss, and Scandinavian laws;[1] and both Foote[2] and G. C. Cheshire[3] rightly recommend it as the only practical one. If the proper law of a contract is English the debt created by that contract should remain subject to English law throughout the whole of its existence. It follows that English law should decide to whom the debtor is liable.[4] The practical advantage of this doctrine is that if the creditor assigns the same debt twice and in different countries the same law applies to both assignments. A *renvoi* is, of course, possible: the proper law of the contract out of which the debt arose may refer for its assignment to a different legal system, for example to the *lex loci actus* (i.e. *cessionis*).

It cannot, however, be stated with certainty that the doctrine developed by Foote and G. C. Cheshire is that accepted by English courts. In so far as priorities between various assignees of the same debt are in issue, G. C. Cheshire relies on *Kelly* v. *Selwyn*.[5]

The facts were as follows: Selwyn, when domiciled and present in New York, assigned to his wife his equitable interest in certain trust funds administered in England; no notice was given to the trustees. The law of New York does not require notice, English law does. Three years later Selwyn assigned the same interest to his creditor Kelly, and notice of this was given to the trustees. The court held that English law applied, because the fund was an English trust fund, administered by the English court, and because the fund was 'constituted by an English testator who may be taken to have made his will with the English law in his mind'.

[1] Lewald, 270; Schnitzer, *Internat. Handelsrecht* (Swiss law), 218; also *RVgl.HWB.*, IV. 386.

[2] Foote, p. 296.

[3] pp. 599–602, 610.

[4] There is in particular no reason why an assignment should be treated so differently from a *stipulatio alteri*. If *A* and *B* conclude a contract according to which certain payments *B* has to make shall be made not to *A* but to *C*, the law governing this contract has to answer the question whether and on what conditions *C* thereby acquires a right to claim the money. It is difficult to understand why it should be otherwise, if under the contract the parties agreed that the money should be paid to *A*, and if *A* the next day assigns the debt to *C*.

[5] [1905] 2 Ch. 117, 121, 122.

The very short judgment thus gives two reasons, the first that English law applies as the *lex situs*, the second that it possibly applies as the proper law of the will in which the debt originated. Therefore all that can be said is that *Kelly* v. *Selwyn* is compatible with the doctrine that assignments are governed by the proper law of the transaction out of which the debt arose.

This doctrine is further the foundation on which *Lebel* v. *Tucker* is decided;[1] but the judgment is concerned with such a special case of bills of exchange that it is hardly justifiable to infer from it a general principle.

II. We reach a different solution of the problem if we take seriously the conception of the debt as being the subject-matter of rights. If an assignment of a debt is to be regarded as a transfer of ownership of an intangible movable, this leads—by way of analogy—to an application of the rules developed in respect of the transfer of ownership of tangible goods. We have already seen that these are far from being unambiguous, and that English judgments apply three different tests.[2] The same, if not a greater, uncertainty is found here.[3] The tests are again the *lex domicilii*, the *lex loci actus*, and the *lex situs*. In examining these various tests in what follows, we shall omit the rules relative to capacity and formalities, and consider only the law applicable to the essential validity and the effect of an assignment. The rules on capacity and form do not differ from those applicable to the conclusion of contracts.[4]

(a) Corresponding to the old rule *mobilia personam (domini) sequuntur*, we find here the doctrine that the domicile of the owner of the debt is decisive, or as French jurists have formulated it: 'nomina personae creditoris inhaerent'. From the sixteenth to the eighteenth century, from

513. *Lex domicilii* decisive?

---

[1] (1867), L.R. 3 Q.B. 77, 83. See *infra*, s. 527, no. (3).

[2] *Supra*, s. 488, 491, 493.

[3] Scrutton, L.J., in *Republica de Guatemala* v. *Nunez*, [1927] 1 K.B. 669, 688, emphasizes the fact that 'the English authorities are scanty and unsatisfactory', and many writers feel themselves bound to express the same disappointment.

[4] See *supra*, s. 499. Capacity is tested by domicile; but if under the domiciliary law capacity is lacking, it suffices for the validity of the assignment that capacity exists under the *lex loci actus*. As to formalities there is a doubt whether the *lex loci actus* is exclusively decisive or whether an alternative exists in the law governing the essentials of the assignment.

Dumoulin to Froland, that rule was accepted in France, though not without encountering well-founded opposition. Modern French doctrine and practice have abandoned it entirely.[1] Story, however,[2] and under his influence some English writers, adopted it. Fortunately no English decision supports this theory. It is subject to the same objections as the domicile doctrine in respect of tangibles.

514. Lex loci actus decisive? (*b*) The second possible test is the *lex loci actus*, the law of the place where the assignment is executed. According to the American *Restatement*[3] this is the test adopted by American law, and only the assignability of a contractual right is determined by the law of the place of contracting.[4] English courts have on several occasions adopted the same test, sometimes alone, sometimes as an alternative to the law of the domicile. The main authorities in point are: *Lee* v. *Abdy*,[5] *Republic of Guatemala* v. *Nunez* (judgments of Greer, J.,[6] and in the Court of Appeal of Scrutton, L.J.),[7] and *In re Anziani*.[8]

In *Lee* v. *Abdy* a husband, domiciled and resident in Cape Colony, had assigned to his wife (also resident there), apparently as a gift, his rights arising out of a life assurance contract with an English company; the assignment was made in Cape Colony. Under South African law gifts between husband and wife are invalid, under English law they are valid.

The court applied South African law, because it was the *lex loci actus*. But both judges (Day and Wills, J.J.) added that it was also the domiciliary law of the assignor and the assignee.

The decision in the *Guatemala Case* is equally uninformative; though the three judges in the Court of Appeal were unanimous in their conclusion, each gave different reasons.

The facts in the *Guatemala Case* were as follows: In 1906 Cabrera, then President of the Republic of Guatemala, deposited a sum of money

[1] Niboyet, *Manuel*, p. 819.
[2] Story, s. 362.
[3] ss. 348–50.
[4] In France, likewise, the *lex loci actus* has sometimes been applied; see *J. Clunet*, 1908, 1118. But this is not the predominant doctrine.
[5] (1886), 17 Q.B.D. 309, 313.
[6] (1926), 42 T.L.R. 625; 95 L.J. (K.B.) 955.
[7] [1927] 1 K.B. 669, 688.
[8] [1930] 1 Ch. 407, 420 (*per* Maugham, J.).

with a London bank; in 1919 he assigned his claim against the bank to his
illegitimate son Nunez as a gift. In 1920 he was deposed and imprisoned.
The Republic claimed the deposit, alleging that Cabrera had misappro-
priated state money, and Cabrera, possibly under duress, thereupon
assigned it to the Republic; but this assignment was held to be void. The
question before the English courts was the validity of the assignment to
Nunez. If English law were applicable it would have been valid. Under
Guatemalan law it was void for two reasons: first, because it was not made
in the form prescribed by Guatemalan law, and secondly, because Nunez
had not only not accepted the gift, but being an infant lacked capacity to
do so.

The English courts (Greer, J., affirmed by the Court of
Appeal) held that in both points Guatemalan law was
applicable. Scrutton, L.J., stated that either the *lex domicilii*
or the *lex loci actus* applied to the question of capacity[1] and
that the *lex loci actus* governed formalities.[2] The material
validity of the assignment was not in issue. But it seems that
later Scrutton's judgment was understood (by Maugham,
J.) to have covered not only the formalities but the substance of an assignment. At any rate, Maugham, J.,
adopted the rule that essentials of an assignment are
governed exclusively by the *lex loci actus*.

He applied it in *Re Anziani*,[3] where a married woman had assigned in
Rome an English claim against trustees resident in England; under Italian
law the assignment was deemed to be void, not only as regards formalities,
but in substance.[4]

Two further judgments,[5] often quoted in favour of the *lex
loci actus* principle, should be disregarded where the assignment of simple debts is in issue; both deal with negotiable
instruments, and in both the *locus actus* was identical with
the *situs cartae*.

In view of these English decisions it cannot be contended
that the subjection of assignments of debts to the *lex loci*

[1] This is unassailable; *supra*, s. 499.
[2] We have seen, s. 426–8, that the compulsory character of *locus regit actum*
can hardly be maintained.
[3] [1930] 1 Ch. 407.
[4] This, at least, is what the Italian lawyer who gave evidence on Italian law said.
The court surprisingly accepted this evidence though it found 'these matters
somewhat confusing from the point of view of an English lawyer' (at p. 418).
This is one of those decisions which show the unfortunate results of the rule that
foreign law must be treated as a fact.
[5] *Alcock* v. *Smith*, [1892] 1 Ch. 238. *Embiricos* v. *Anglo-Austrian Bank*, [1904]
2 K.B. 870; [1905] 1 K.B. (C.A.) 677. See *infra*, s. 528.

actus is well established in this country. And there is no reason to regret this. To test an assignment by the place where it was made is to choose the least important of all points of contact, to substitute fortuity for reason.

515. *Lex (quasi-) situs decisive?*

(c) The third possible test is the *lex situs*. As debts have no real *situs*, something corresponding to it in the sphere of intangibles must be sought. This has been called a *quasi-situs*, a 'quasi-locality', just as in the rules on possession the *quasi possessio* of servitudes in Roman law and of advowsons or other permanent rights in ecclesiastical law are compared with the genuine possession or physical control of corporeal things. As *quasi possessio* of a right lies in its enjoyment and exercise, so the *quasi-situs* of a right is to be found at the place where it is normally enjoyed or exercised. In the case of a debt, that is the place where the debt is 'properly recoverable'.[1] This is as a rule the place where the debtor is resident.[2] The debtor may have more than one residence, and there may be more than one place where recovery can be had; several courts may have jurisdiction to entertain an action against the debtor. The *situs* will then be found at the place where performance of the duty would normally be exigible or expected. If, for example, the debtor is a bank with branches in various countries the *situs* of a debt due from the bank to a customer is at the branch where his account is kept.[3]

The *situs* of debts is, for that matter, legally important not only for the purpose of establishing the law applicable to an assignment, but also for the exercise of jurisdiction, the grant of probate or of letters of administration, the interpretation of the Treaty of Peace Order, 1919,[4] or of a

[1] *Swiss Bank Corp.* v. *Böhmische Industrial Bank*, [1923] 1 K.B. (C.A.) 673, 678. *Sutherland* v. *Administrator of German Property*, [1934] 1 K.B. (C.A.) 423, 430, 431.

[2] *New York Life Insurance Co.* v. *Public Trustee*, [1924] 2 Ch. (C.A.) 101, 119. The predominant rule in French courts, too, points to the debtor's residence. See Niboyet, *Manuel*, p. 820.

[3] *R.* v. *Lovitt*, [1912] A.C. (P.C.) 212, 218, 219. *Joachimson* v. *Swiss Bank Corp.*, [1921] 3 K.B. 110, 127. *Richardson* v. *Richardson*, [1927] P. 228, 231, 232. *Clare & Co.* v. *Dresdner Bank*, [1915] 2 K.B. 576, 578.

[4] S. 1, sub-s. 16, dealing with 'all property, rights, and interests within His Majesty's Dominions or Protectorates belonging to German nationals'. See *Favorke* v. *Steinkopff*, [1922] 1 Ch. 174.

statute imposing a tax upon property situate in a given country. It is not a matter of course that the conception of 'quasi-locality' is the same whatever may be the connexion in which it is used. Rules developed in tax law cannot be mechanically transferred to the sphere of private international law, nor can judicial decisions made in one field be treated as binding precedents in another. In the United States, for example, a debt is deemed to be situate where the creditor resides if taxation of his property is in issue, while for granting letters of administration the *situs* is determined by the debtor's residence.[1] And in English revenue cases, shares in a foreign company are regarded as situate at the place of trading, while their transfer is determined by the law of the place where the register is kept.[2] The doctrine which proclaims the *lex situs* the true test for determining the law applicable to the assignment of debts is favoured in particular by Westlake.[3] It presents the best analogy to the *lex situs* doctrine as applied to the transfer of tangible goods. This was the basis of the judgment which Lawrence, L.J., delivered in the *Guatemala Case*.[4] In *Re Queensland*, North, J., left it open whether the law of the domicile was applicable, but pronounced that an assignment was certainly valid if it was so under the *lex situs*.[5] In the case of a debt attached by a judgment creditor and due to the judgment debtor by his debtor, the garnishee, the attachment places the judgment creditor in the position of an assignee, the assignment being replaced by the order of the court. There is no doubt that in such a case the *situs* of the attached debt is decisive;[6] but this *situs* mostly coincides with the place of the judicial assignment, the *locus actus*. Finally, *In re Maudslay*[7] was decided on the basis of the *lex situs* doctrine.

The facts were these: An English creditor *A* of an English company *B* took proceedings in France to attach a debt due to *B* from a French firm *C*.

[1] Goodrich, pp. 83, 401.
[2] *Bradbury* v. *English Sewing Cotton Co.*, [1923] A.C. 744, 753. See Companies Act, 1948, s. 119, 120 (4). [3] s. 150, p. 202.
[4] [1927] 1 K.B. 669, 695, 696.
[5] [1891] 1 Ch. 536, 545. (The decision of the Court of Appeal, [1892] 1 Ch. 219, 226, was guided by entirely different considerations.)
[6] *Swiss Bank Corp.* v. *Böhmische Industrial Bank*, [1923] 1 K.B. 673.
[7] [1900] 1 Ch. 602, 610, 611.

This debt was subject to French law and situate in France. The question was whether the attachment was good as against the claims of the debenture holders of *B*. Under English law the debenture holders had an enforceable charge upon all the assets of the company *B*, including the French debt, and there was an equity in their favour against the creditor *A* who attached the debt; but under French law *A*'s right prevailed, and French law was applied as the law of the 'locality or quasi-locality' of the debt.

The decision, however, is of no great assistance; for French law was at the same time the law of the place of attachment (*lex loci actus*) and the proper law of the contract in which the debt originated. A similar coincidence of the *lex debiti* with the *lex situs* is also to be found in *Kelly* v. *Selwyn*.[1]

516.
Summary

To sum up: The test by the law of the creditor's domicile is rejected, but it is still unsettled whether assignments are to be tested by the proper law of the transaction in which the debt originated, by the *lex loci actus*, or by the law of the *situs* of the debt. It is to be hoped that the first of these three will prevail in the end.

517.
Assignment and 'contract' between assignor and assignee

III. Whatever may be the proper test to be applied to assignments, one cause of confusion should be avoided. Just as in the case of tangible things the transfer of ownership itself is distinct from the underlying contract, so in the case of intangibles. The transferor may assign the debt he owns by way of sale, or barter, or as a gift, or in lieu of payment of a debt he owes to the assignee. As a rule the assignment and the contract of sale, &c., which forms its basis coincide temporarily; both are often expressed in the same instrument. But legally they are separate acts. And if it is correct that the assignment is governed by the proper law of the contract which gave rise to the assigned debt,[2] this does not apply to the *contract* between assignor and assignee. Such contract has its own proper law, which need not be the same as that governing the relationship between assignor and debtor.

An illustration may show the issue. *A* sells certain goods to *B* for £100 to be paid three months after delivery, and this transaction is governed by English law. Then *A* sells and assigns the debt to *C*, a Frenchman, in France, and *C* is to pay at once, in francs. The sale of the debt is subject to

---

[1] [1905] 2 Ch. 117, 122.   [2] As has been suggested, *supra*, s. 512.

French law. But English law decides whether *C* has become *B*'s creditor
for £100. Should *B*, however, fail to pay the sum and become bankrupt, it
is French law that decides what rights *C* has against *A*, whether he can
demand payment of £100, or restitution of the amount of francs paid, or
damages, whether he is entitled to interest, and to what amount, and so
forth.[1]

IV. What is true of an assignment by agreement is true also
of involuntary assignments of debts. Examples: a transfer
based on an act of the court; the substitution of a new
creditor for the previous creditor by operation of law, as
(apart from universal succession upon death or bankruptcy)
in many cases of particular succession to an isolated debt,
called *cessio legis* by continental lawyers. Such assignment
by operation of law is in particular to be found when a
surety pays the creditor and thereby acquires (*par subroga-
tion légale*) the creditor's rights against the principal debtor.
Though this principle or a similar one exists in nearly all
countries, the details are worked out in various ways.
Under Roman law and according to the Baltic Code of
1864 the surety does not acquire the creditor's claim *ipsa
lege*, but is only entitled to demand an express assignment
from the creditor; he has a *beneficium cedendarum actionum*.[2]
Under most laws the transfer takes place by operation of
law.[3] According to Swiss law the surety cannot waive
his right until he has paid the creditor;[4] all other legal
systems recognize the validity of a waiver unconditionally.
What law determines these and many other details? The
lex loci actus principle is here obviously inapplicable, since
there is no *actus* of transfer (unless the payment made to the
creditor be regarded as such an act). The doctrine of *lex
situs* leads to the law of the principal debtor's residence, and
this usually coincides with the solution believed to be the
best, i.e. that which tests an assignment by the proper law of
the transaction in which the debt of the principal debtor
originated.

518.
Assign-
ment by
operation
of law

[1] Best treatment of this thorny problem by Lewald, p. 274 et seq.
[2] *Dig.* 46, 1, 36.
[3] English law: Mercantile Law Amendment Act, 1856 (19 & 20 Vict., c. 97),
s. 5. *Re McMyn* (1886), 33 Ch.D. 575. French law: *code civ.*, art. 2029, 1251, 3.
German law: Civil Code, s. 774.
[4] Swiss Law of Obligations, s. 505, 2.

2. OTHER RIGHTS

519.
Assignment of obligations other than debts

I. The rules developed for simple debts apply equally to other rights. Both their assignability and their assignment probably depend—or should depend—on the law under which they arose and to which they are subjected. This applies particularly

1. to obligations other than debts, such as obligations arising from tort, quasi-contract, or the right to maintenance. Whether these rights are assignable, and if so to what amount, can only be decided by the law governing the legal relationship out of which they originated. If a tort is committed in England the right to damages is not assignable,[1] even if all parties concerned are domiciled Germans and the assignee sues in Germany.

520.
Assignment of shares

2. to rights of membership (or shares) in a company. These are governed by the personal law of the company[2] and are assignable only if the said law permits, and in the way prescribed by that law. If in accordance with the personal law of the company the share has been incorporated in an instrument the same law determines the legal significance of such instrument. Where instruments are issued to bearer,[3] the personal law of the company usually leaves all questions relating to their transfer to the law governing the transfer of tangible movables;[4] the right embodied in the instrument is treated as if it were itself a corporeal thing; and if it is correct to subject the transfer of corporeal things to the law of the *situs*[5] the transfer of such shares will be governed by the *lex situs cartae*. It therefore depends on the *situs* of the instrument whether ownership passes to a buyer without delivery, as under English and French law, or whether delivery is essential, as in Germany.[6] The *lex situs cartae* further decides whether stolen share certificates can be validly transferred to a *bona fide* purchaser without notice, as in most modern laws, or not. Where the share

---

[1] Cf. Winfield, *Text-book of the Law of Torts*, s. 192.

[2] On this see *supra*, s. 279–81.

[3] as is the common practice in Germany and other continental countries.

[4] *Colonial Bank* v. *Cady* (1890), 15 L.R. App. Cas. 267, 283.

[5] See on this controversy, *supra*, s. 491, 492.

[6] See, on the one hand, Sale of Goods Act, 1893, s. 18, r. 1; French *code civil*, art. 1138 § 2; on the other hand, German Civ. C., s. 929.

certificates designate the shareholder by name, the share is under most legal systems transferable by indorsement, delivery, and registration. Here again the personal law of the company will leave the details of the transfer to be regulated by the law of the place where the 'right of membership' is situate. But, in contradistinction to bearer certificates, shares which pass by indorsement, delivery, and registration are deemed to be situate at the place where the register of the shareholders is kept.

If there is more than one register (branch registers) the register at which this particular share can be transferred is decisive,[1] and only if there is a choice between two places where such transfer can be made will the location of the certificate itself determine the issue.[2]

3. to patents, designs, trade marks, and copyrights. The old doctrine, which prevailed when for the first time rights of this type came into existence, regarded them as having the character of individual privileges or monopolies granted by the sovereign or the state. Though this doctrine has fortunately been abandoned, one of its consequences has been preserved, viz. a state will protect only such patents, designs, trade marks, and copyrights as it has itself granted, either by particular act (privilege) or by general statute. No state applies foreign law to questions of patents, copyrights, and the like, or recognizes rights of this class created under foreign law. An inventor who obtains a patent in country X will be protected in X only. If he wants protection for his invention in country Y he may apply in Y for a second patent, and not for recognition of the first. The same invention may thus be covered by several patents, each of which is operative within a particular territory only and is governed by the law of the state which granted it.

The law under which a patent right is created applies to its assignment, and the same is true of copyrights, trade marks, and designs. The disposal of such rights—by alienation or by pledge, or by the grant of a sole licence (for example, to use the invention in a particular district)—can

§ 521.
Assignment of patents, copyrights, &c.

---

[1] *Att.-Gen.* v. *Bouwens* (1838), 4 M. & W. 171, 191. *Brassard* v. *Smith*, [1925] A.C. 371. *Erie Beach Co.* v. *Att.-Gen. for Ontario*, [1930] A.C. (P.C.) 161, 167, 168.

[2] *R.* v. *Williams*, [1942] A.C. (P.C.) 541, 549.

certainly not depend on the *lex loci actus* if the disposal happens to have taken place in a foreign country. The law governing the patent (&c.) is, for that matter, always identical with the *lex situs*.[1]

522.
Assign-
ment of
iura in rem

4. Real rights (*iura in rem*) can also be the subject-matter of an act of disposal. The permissibility of such a transaction, the method of disposal, and its effect are doubtless governed by the law governing the *ius in rem*; the *situs* of the *ius in rem* coincides with the *situs* of the corporeal thing in which the right exists.

Examples: (*a*) A German landowner creates, in favour of his English creditor, a *Grundschuld*, that is, a mortgage independent of the existence of a debt; the creditor receives an instrument from the German Land Registry which enables him to dispose of the mortgage by an act of assignment and delivery. There can be no doubt that the transfer, though executed in England, is governed by German law and is to be regarded as valid in England, even if the debt secured by the *Grundschuld* is not transferred to the transferee of the *Grundschuld*.

(*b*) *A* pledges a jewel to his creditor *B* by delivery in country *X*; *B* takes the jewel to country *Y*, where he pledges his right of pledge to his creditor *C*. The question whether *C* thereby acquires a valid *subpignus* (a pledge of a pledge) is answered by the law of *Y*, since the *situs* of *B*'s right is identical with the *situs rei pigneratae*. The same law determines the incidents of the *subpignus*.

523.
Written
instru-
ments
(1) for evi-
dence only

II. At first sight a qualification of these simple rules would seem necessary in cases where the debt (or other right) is contained in a *written instrument*. Such instrument may have been issued and delivered to the creditor for any of the following reasons:

1. merely to furnish *evidence*. Example: a receipt mentioning the obligation to repay. Such a piece of paper is unimportant for the purposes both of internal substantive law and of private international law. If the creditor assigns his right to a third party, the validity of the assignment does not depend on the delivery of the instrument to the

---

1 The judgments in *Smelting Comp. of Australia* v. *Commissioners of Inland Revenue*, [1896] 2 Q.B. 179; [1897] 1 Q.B. (C.A.) 175, are only concerned with revenue law and the interpretation of s. 59 Stamp Act, 1891. The text of this Act is so framed that the Court of Appeal could declare (*per* Lord Esher, M.R.) that a patent 'is incapable of being said to exist in any locality'; [1897] 1 Q.B. at p. 180. The decision does not affect the question which law is applicable to the transfer of patent rights.

assignee.[1] The applicable law is determined as if no such paper had been issued. Or:

2. the document *creates* the obligation; for instance, a deed in the case of a gratuitous promise. Or, if a valid oral contract already exists, the contractual obligation is merged in the deed, that is, the old obligation is extinguished by the instrument and a new obligation takes its place. Examples of this are to be found in the case of a deed repeating a pre-existent obligation, or of a judgment which under English and possibly under Roman law substitutes the 'judgment debt' for the old debt.[2] Two separate questions arise here. First, has the deed or judgment the effect of renewing the obligation? The answer to this is given by the proper law of the old obligation (which decides whether or not the latter is extinguished) in conjunction with the law of the deed or of the court delivering the judgment (which determines whether the deed, or the judgment, creates a new obligation).[3] Secondly, if the merger has taken place, by what law is an assignment of the new obligation to be tested? The English conflict rule apparently answers: by the law of the *situs* of the instrument (the deed or judgment) at the moment of the creation of the deed or the delivery of the judgment.[4] It must be open to doubt whether such a conflict rule—unknown elsewhere—is reasonable. Why should the *situs* of a document which is necessary only for the creation but not for the exercise and particularly not for the assignment of a right determine the law applicable to an assignment? It has been contended that 'a debt under seal or specialty has a species of corporeal existence by which its locality might be reduced to a certainty'.[5] This is hardly convincing. The debt specified in a deed is unaffected by the loss or destruction of the deed; if its previous existence

524.
(2) Instruments creating the obligation

---

[1] though there may be, and as a rule is, an obligation on the part of the assignor to deliver the document to the assignee.

[2] 'Novatur iudicati actione prior contractus'; *Cod. Just.* 7. 54, 3, 2; *Gai. Inst.*, III. 180. *Contra*: modern continental laws.

[3] Cf. Pillet, *Traité prat.* II. 214; Frankenstein, II. 285.

[4] *Toronto General Trusts Corporation* v. *The King*, [1919] A.C. (P.C.) 679, 683 (concerned, however, only with taxation). *Att.-Gen.* v. *Bouwens* (1838) 4 M. & W. 171, 191 (*per* Abinger, C.B.).

[5] *Commissioner of Stamps* v. *Hope*, [1891] A.C. 476, 480, 482.

and content can be proved, no harm is done, the right can be exercised without the deed. It can be transferred like any simple oral debt without delivery of the instrument. To ascribe a corporeal existence to the incorporeal thing would be a well-founded thought if the disposal of the thing required the disposal of the instrument. And this leads us to the third group of instruments:

525.
(3) Instruments issued for circulation

3. instruments created in the interest of *circulation and negotiation* (negotiable instruments in the wider sense of this term).[1] They may be issued to bearer or to the order of the first creditor. They are essentially a means of transferring the obligation they contain. An instrument of this type may indeed be called—by lawyers who prefer metaphor and word-painting to plain speaking—the 'body' of the incorporeal thing. The debt from being intangible becomes as it were tangible. At any rate, the creditor who wishes to dispose of the debt must dispose of his ownership in the piece of paper; the debt follows the instrument, and not the instrument the debt. In private international law two main questions must be answered:

(*a*) What law decides whether a given instrument is negotiable in that sense? The answer is: the law that governs the right embodied in the instrument. Under English municipal law a bill of exchange can be issued payable to bearer; it is then negotiable. Under German law the bearer clause on a bill is forbidden and renders the bill absolutely void. An English bearer bill would be negotiable in Germany, a German bearer bill is not negotiable in England; for no reasonable merchant would purchase

---

[1] In the strict sense of the term, an instrument is designated as negotiable only if (*a*) the transfer of the right set out in the piece of paper requires transfer of ownership of that paper, (*b*) the *bona fide* purchaser for value without notice has 'a good title notwithstanding any defect of title in the person from whom he took it', *and* (*c*) the *bona fide* purchaser is not affected by defences available against the claims of any prior holder. *Simmons* v. *London Joint Stock Bank*, [1891] 1 Ch. (C.A.) 270, 294; *Picker* v. *London & County Banking Co.* (1887), 18 Q.B.D. (C.A.) 515; *The Marlborough Hill*, [1921] 1 A.C. (P.C.) 444, 452 (concerning bills of lading). Dicey–Morris, rule 155. The conditions (*b*) and (*c*) are not always sufficiently distinguished from each other; there are in particular some instruments which fulfil conditions (*a*) and (*b*) but not (*c*), for example, share certificates of German law. In a wider sense all instruments fulfilling the condition (*a*) are negotiable, and the transfer of all of them is (probably) governed by the *lex situs cartae*.

it knowing that he cannot recover payment from the acceptor or the drawer. There is a further English rule to the effect that an instrument is negotiable in England only if it is made so by statute or by English trade custom.[1] It happens that bonds issued in a country where they are negotiable and governed by the law of that country are not recognized as negotiable by any usage of English trade or of the Stock Exchange;[2] they are therefore not negotiable in this country.

(b) What law decides *how* negotiable instruments and the rights merged in them are to be transferred, and what is the *effect* of a transfer? The choice lies between the proper law of the obligation to be transferred, the *lex situs cartae* at the time of the transfer, and the *lex loci actus*, i.e. *cessionis*, which has been advanced in *Alcock* v. *Smith* and in *Embiricos* v. *Anglo-Austrian Bank*[3] and leads to practically the same result as the *lex situs* doctrine. One thing is certain:[4] the answer must be uniform in respect of the transfer both of the obligation and of the ownership in the document. Divergent answers would be impracticable.[5] In principle the proper law of the obligation should be decisive, because it is not the valueless scrap of paper but the right embodied therein that matters, just as a key to a cellar where wine is stored is not delivered to the purchaser of the wine for its own sake. But on most points[6] the proper law of the obliga-

---

[1] Such custom may have grown up in a very short time. *Edelstein* v. *Schuler & Co.*, [1902] 2 Q.B. 144, 154.

[2] Certain Prussian bonds were regarded as negotiable, others as not negotiable in England. Comp. *Gorgier* v. *Mieville* (1824), 3 B. & C. 45, with *Picker* v. *London & County Banking Co.* (1887), 18 Q.B.D. (C.A.) 515.

[3] *Supra*, pp. 514–15. On the Bills of Exchange Act, 1882, see *infra*, s. 528.

[4] at least where the instrument embodies only one obligation, or where in the case of several obligations they are all governed by the same law.

[5] *Contra*: Frankenstein, II. 111 (see on this Duden, p. 68). The problem was thoroughly examined by the Institute of International Law; *Annuaire*, 21 (1906), 409.

[6] though not on all points. The most famous example is furnished by the French law of 15 June 1872, art. 12. Under this law the owner of a *titre au porteur* can in case of loss or theft make an *opposition* which is published in a particular way with the effect that no *bona fide* purchaser can become owner of the instrument. This applies to obligations governed by French law, even if the instrument is sold and delivered to the purchaser abroad, and if under the law of the *situs cartae* he would acquire ownership. In this conflict between the French proper law of the obligation and the foreign law of the *situs*, French law must prevail,

tion abdicates and refers to the *lex situs cartae*. If under the proper law of the obligation an instrument payable to bearer has been validly created, the law of the *situs* of the instrument determines the method of disposal, usually by declaring expressly or implicitly that the transfer of the paper and of the obligation must be made according to the rules on transfer of tangible goods.[1] Where, for example, the *lex situs cartae* rejects the principle *nemo dat quod non habet* in favour of a *bona fide* purchaser this benefits the transferee of rights contained in such instrument.

The situation is a little more complicated if the documents are not made out to bearer, but to a named person or his order, and can (under the proper law of the obligation) be transferred by indorsement and delivery to the transferee; or if a transfer of shares in a company of country X (under the law of X) demands indorsement, delivery, and a substitution of the purchaser's name for that of the transferor in the register of shareholders. In such cases the proper law of the right represented in the document leaves only part of the act of transfer to be regulated by the *lex situs cartae*. The law of the *situs* answers questions such as: what is necessary for a delivery? can the corporeal delivery be replaced by other means, for example, by an agreement of the parties to the effect that the transferor shall remain in possession of the instrument as pledgee or as depositary? But questions relative to the registration of the new shareholder[2] are probably answered by the law of the incorporation of the company.

BIBLIOGRAPHY

Supra, p. 518. FALCONBRIDGE, 415–31. NIBOYET, *Traité*, IV, 626–735.

3. THE TRANSFER OF BILLS OF EXCHANGE, PROMISSORY NOTES, AND CHEQUES

526. The problem. The Geneva solution

Obligations created by negotiable instruments have been discussed in Part V on the Law of Obligations (*supra*, s. 461–8). The problem of the *transfer* of negotiable instru-

since it is for French law to say when an instrument created under French law ceases to be a *titre au porteur*, and this is what the publication of the *opposition* entails. The contrary view held by Frankenstein, loc. cit., and Duden, 76, seems untenable.

[1] See, for example, German Civil Code, s. 929, 935 § 2, 1293.

[2] Cf. the case *Williams* v. *Colonial Bank* (in the House of Lords under the name of *Colonial Bank* v. *Cady*) (1888), L.R. 38 Ch.D. 388; (1890) 15 App. Cas. 267, 283. See *supra*, p. 526.

ments needs a few words here. A peculiarity of bills of exchange, and to a lesser degree, of notes and cheques, is the fact that the obligations of several persons, for example of the acceptor, the drawer, and a number of indorsers, are all contained in one instrument. These obligations may be governed by different legal systems.

Suppose a bill was drawn by A in England on B in France, payable in France to C or his order; B accepts it in France; the payee C indorses it in Belgium to D, and D again indorses it in Holland to E. In such case B's obligation as acceptor is governed by French law, A's obligation as drawer by English law, while the two indorsers C and D are liable under Belgian and Dutch law respectively.[1] If E then indorses the bill in blank in England and delivers it to F in this country, which law is to decide whether E thereby transfers his four claims against A, B, C, and D? If the rules developed for the transfer of simple debts were to be applied the answer would be: each of the four claims is transferred from E to F in accordance with the law which governs it. Under French law before 1922 an indorsement in blank did not effect a transfer of the rights embodied in the bill; as the obligation of the acceptor B is subject to French law, the indorsement in blank by E would therefore not transfer to F E's claim against B. Consequently F would acquire E's rights against A, C, and D only, while B's creditor would still be E.

Such inconvenient result can only be avoided by a *unitary rule* covering the transfer of *all* rights incorporated in the bill. The Geneva Convention of 1930[2] adopted a rule of this kind, providing that 'the effects of the signatures' are determined by the law of the country 'in which is situated the place where the signatures were affixed'.[3] In the example mentioned above this is the place where E signed the indorsement in blank; therefore English law applies. The phrase 'effects of the signatures' covers not only the *obligation* created by the signature (in our example the obligation of E to F) but also the *transfer* to F of all E's rights (against A, B, C, and D).

Great Britain has not adopted the Geneva rules. The solution in English law is less simple. Section 72 of the Bills of Exchange Act, 1882, in the main reproduced and to a certain degree clarified the content of the common law, as represented by the following five cases:

527. The English solution. Authorities before 1882

[1] See s. 72, sub-s. (2) Bills of Exchange Act.

[2] See *supra*, s. 41.

[3] Art. 4 of the Convention. Similar rule in the Geneva Cheque Convention, 1931.

1. *De la Chaumette* v. *Bank of England*.[1] An English promissory note (a banknote), made and delivered in England, was stolen in England, conveyed to France, and sold there to a *bona fide* purchaser for value. To decide whether the purchaser became owner of the note and creditor of the bank the court applied English law, that being the law of the transaction in which the obligation of the bank arose. Neither the *lex loci actus* (as later in *Alcock* v. *Smith* and *Embiricos* v. *Anglo-Austrian Bank*)[2] nor the *lex situs cartae* was considered.

2. *Trimbey* v. *Vignier*.[3] Here the promissory note on which the plaintiff sued was purely French: made in France by a Frenchman to the order of a Frenchman resident in France. The promisee indorsed it in blank in France; the plaintiff, who was resident in England, received it here. After the bill had matured the promisor became resident in England, where he was sued. Under French law the indorsement in blank was believed to be invalid, under English law it was valid. The court applied French law, because 'the interpretation of the contract' was governed by the *lex loci contractus*, and the court apparently looked on France as the country where the contract was made, although delivery to the plaintiff was made in England.[4]

3. In *Lebel* v. *Tucker*[5] the bill on which the holder sued the acceptor was drawn, accepted, and payable in England, but indorsed in blank in France to a Frenchman. Again the point was whether the indorsement was valid under English or invalid under French law. The court applied English law, reasoning that as the acceptor's obligation was governed by English law, so therefore was its transfer. It was left open whether or not the holder could have sued the indorser, the latter's liability being governed by French law (under which it did not exist). This decision is clearly based on the principle, which in the case of simple debts is to be preferred to all others, viz. that the transfer of a debt

1 (1831), 2 B. & Ad. 385.
2 *Infra*, s. 528.
3 (1834), 1 Bing. N. Cas. 151.
4 Under the Bills of Exchange Act indorsement means an indorsement completed by delivery.
5 (1867), L.R. 3 Q.B. 77, 83.

should be tested by the proper law of the transaction which gave rise to the debt.[1]

4. In *Bradlaugh* v. *de Rin*[2] the facts lie midway between the two cases just discussed. While in *Trimbey* v. *Vignier* the note was purely French and in *Lebel* v. *Tucker* the bill was purely English, here the bill was mixed, drawn in France (or Belgium)[3] upon England and accepted in England; it was indorsed in blank in France (or Belgium). The court by a majority judgment followed *Trimbey* v. *Vignier* and applied French law as the law of the place where the indorsement was made. The court so decided in order to avoid a 'splitting of the liability' which would contravene the rule that no partial indorsement is admissible. Montague Smith, J., in a dissenting judgment adopted the rule in *Lebel* v. *Tucker* and applied English law as the proper law of the transaction in which the acceptor's obligation originated.

5. The decision in *re Marseilles Extension Railway & Land Company*[4] deals with a bill drawn (in 1866) in France upon an English company, payable and accepted in England. The indorsement in blank was held to be valid in respect of the acceptor's obligation, because the latter arose out of an English contract. In other words, the 'splitting doctrine' in *Lebel* v. *Tucker* was here adopted.

The main result of this development was disappointing. It remained unsettled whether the unitary doctrine, as explained in *Bradlaugh* v. *de Rin*, was to prevail, or the 'splitting doctrine', as in *Lebel* v. *Tucker*.

The *Bills of Exchange Act*, 1882, attempted to reconcile these divergent views. In respect of the transfer of bills and notes by indorsement it distinguishes between 'requisites in form'[5] and the 'interpretation of the indorsement'.[6] The term 'interpretation', apparently taken from *Trimbey* v. *Vignier*,[7] includes both the essential validity of the indorse-

528. The Bills of Exchange Act, 1882

---

[1] See *supra*, s. 512.
[2] (1868), L.R. 3 C.P. 538, 542.
[3] Thus according to the facts as reported in L.R. 5 C.P. 473.
[4] (1885), 30 Ch.D. 598.
[5] s. 72, sub-s. (1) of the Act.
[6] s. 72, sub-s. (2).
[7] (1834), 1 Bing. (N.C.) 151.

ment and its legal effects as deduced from the interpretation.[1] The Act does not deal with the transfer by simple delivery, as in the case of bills or notes to bearer, or instruments validly indorsed in blank. Nor does it determine the law applicable to a transfer by judicial arrestment.[2] It may be questioned whether the Act indicates the applicable law on the acquisition of ownership by a *bona fide* purchaser of the bill when the indorser has no title. The courts in *Alcock* v. *Smith* and in *Embiricos* v. *Anglo-Austrian Bank* seem to answer this question (implicitly) in the negative, since these judgments do not refer to the Bills of Exchange Act, but are given on general principles.[3]

529. Form of indorsement

I. As to the *form* of a transfer by indorsement, s. 72, sub-s. (1) provides: '. . . the validity as regards requisites in form of the . . . indorsement . . . is determined by the law of the place where such contract was made'.[4] As previously explained (p. 479), the principle *locus regit actum* has here the character of an imperative rule. It is sometimes doubtful whether a defect in an indorsement relates to its form or to its substance. Is the French rule (now repealed) that an indorsement in blank is merely an act of *procuration* and transfers no rights to the indorsee concerned with form or with substance? The correct answer is: with substance.

In *Koechlin* v. *Kestenbaum*[5] the bill on which the indorsee sued was drawn in France upon London, accepted and payable in London, and indorsed in France; the indorsement, however, was not made by the payee himself but by the drawer, and the payee's consent to this was not mentioned on the instrument. Under French law the indorsement was valid if the payee had given his consent, under English law it was not. As the divergence between French and English law relates only to the way in which the consent was to be expressed, the point is one of form; the three judges in the Court of Appeal were agreed on this, though Sargent, L.J.,

---

1 This is the view taken by Romer, J., in *Alcock* v. *Smith*, [1892] 1 Ch. at p. 256. Doubts as to the correctness of this view were expressed in particular by Walton, J., in *Embiricos* v. *Anglo-Austrian Bank*, [1904] 2 K.B. 870, 875, 876, and by Vaughan Williams, L.J., in the Court of Appeal, [1905] i K.B. 677.

2 as in *Alcock* v. *Smith*, *supra*.

3 According to these judgments the applicable law is the *lex loci actus*. In the case of bills, notes, and cheques, however, this practically always coincides with the *lex situs cartae*.

4 That is: where the indorsed instrument was delivered to the purchaser. See on this *supra*, p. 479 *in fine* (s. 2 of the Act).

5 [1927] 1 K.B. 616; reversed, [1927] 1 K.B. (C.A.) 889, 898.

cautiously observed that even if it were not a matter of form, the result in the case before the court would be the same.

2. With regard to interpretation (including essential validity and legal effects), s. 72, sub-s. (2) provides that '. . . the interpretation of the . . . indorsement . . . of a bill is determined by the law of the place where such contract is made.[1] Provided that where an inland bill is indorsed in a foreign country the indorsement shall as regards the payer be interpreted according to the law of the United Kingdom'. Thus the Act distinguishes between inland bills and foreign bills. Inland bills[2] are those which are, or on the face of them purport to be, either drawn *and* payable within the British Islands, or drawn within the British Islands upon some person resident therein. Foreign bills are all others.

(*a*) The Act subjects the transfer of *foreign* bills without restriction to the unitary rule. The law of the place of indorsement decides on the transfer both of the ownership in the instrument and of the various rights embodied in it, irrespective of the laws governing the transactions in which all those rights originated. The rejection of the 'splitting' doctrine harmonizes with the corresponding rule in continental laws and in particular with the Geneva Convention. The objections which the majority decision in *Bradlaugh* v. *de Rin*[3] raised against the splitting of liabilities are recognized as sound.

(*b*) In the case of *inland* bills the unitary rule is adopted in principle, but subject to one exception. The unitary doctrine prevails in respect of the transfer of the obligations incumbent upon the drawer and all indorsers: these obligations are transferred according to the law of the place of indorsement, and it is submitted that the transfer of ownership of the instrument is subject to the same law. But in respect of the obligation of the 'payer'—that is, the acceptor in the case of a bill of exchange, and the maker in the case of a promissory note—its transfer is governed by the law

---

[1] and not by the law of the place where the contract is to be performed. Cf. *Banku Polskiego* v. *Mulder*, [1941] 2 K.B. 266; [1942] 1 K.B. 497 (C.A.).
[2] s. 4 of the Act.
[3] (1868), L.R. 3 C.P. 538, 542.

of the United Kingdom, even if the indorsement was made in a foreign country. Thus the method developed in *Lebel* v. *Tucker*[1] of splitting the various liabilities is here maintained to a certain degree.

The logical soundness of treating an acceptor differently according to whether the bill is an inland or a foreign bill may be doubted, and Dr. Cheshire, stressing a (very cautious) remark by Sargent, L.J.,[2] holds that the result is scarcely satisfactory to the commercial world.[3] On the other hand, there is something to be said in favour of the view that an Englishman who accepts a bill payable in England which another Englishman has drawn upon him in England, may reasonably expect a transfer of his obligation to be wholly governed by English law. But should not the analogous case of a Frenchman accepting a purely French bill in France be dealt with on the same lines?

---

[1] (1867), L.R. 3 Q.B. 77. See *supra*, p. 554 (3).
[2] In *Koechlin* v. *Kestenbaum*, [1927] 1 K.B. 889, 898.
[3] Cheshire, p. 622–3.

BIBLIOGRAPHY

Supra, pp. 518, 552, and GUTTERIDGE, *J. Comp. Legisl.*, 1934, pp. 67, 78. RAISER, *Wirkungen der Wechselerklärungen im I.P.R.*, 1931, 91, 99. CHESHIRE, 615–23. DICEY–MORRIS, 678–707. FALCONBRIDGE, 269–329.

CHAPTER XXXVII

BANKRUPTCY

GREATLY as the various legal systems on bankruptcy differ in innumerable details, there is one rule common to them all, viz. the appointment by the court of an administrator. He replaces the debtor in so far as he has to administer the debtor's property in the interest of the creditors, to convert it into money, and to distribute the proceeds among the creditors. He may be a trustee, as under English and Anglo-American law, so that the ownership of the whole property vests in him, or he may merely acquire the exclusive right to administer property which remains vested in the debtor's person, a *ius in patrimonio alieno*, as is the case under all continental European and Latin-American laws. The difference between the English and the continental type—which is similar to the difference between an English testamentary executor and a continental one[1]—does not prevent the courts from treating them as equivalent in so far as private international law is concerned. If, for example, the English trustee in bankruptcy sues one of the bankrupt's debtors in a French court, he will be treated there as a *syndic* of French law.

531. Preliminary observation

The central problems arising in the field of private international law are the following:

I. When the debtor has been adjudged bankrupt in one country, does this prevent his being made bankrupt in some other country? There can be no doubt that the answer is in the negative; there is no such thing as *unity* of bankruptcy.[2] Only by an international convention of all states can a plurality of bankruptcies be avoided. To reach such a convention and thus to obtain a working principle of unity— whether based on the doctrine that priority decides, or on the predominance of domicile—is an unattainable aim, and hardly even a desirable one.[3] The attempt to come to such

532. Unity or plurality of bankruptcies?

---

[1] See *supra*, s. 509, and *infra*, s. 567.
[2] G. C. Cheshire, p. 631.
[3] Pillet, *Traité pratique*, II. 872 et seq.

an agreement was made at the Fifth Conference on Private International Law at The Hague, 1925, where a draft of a unitary system was discussed, but not accepted.

533. Universality or territoriality? II. A different problem is: *universality* or *territoriality*? When in state X the debtor has been adjudged bankrupt, and proceedings have thereupon been initiated, does the whole property, irrespective of where it is situate, pass to the trustee in bankruptcy (administrator, curator, *syndic*, or whatever he may be called)? Or only that part of his property that is situate in state X? Some eminent jurists are in favour of a strict system of territoriality, and such attitude, apparently fair and moderate, seems at first sight to tally better than any other with the postulates of the comity of nations. Its drawback is that it causes unnecessary inconvenience and expense. If, for example, the debtor has taken property into various countries X, Y, and Z, and is subsequently adjudged bankrupt at his domicile X, the creditors under a territoriality system would be bound to apply for bankruptcy proceedings in each of the other countries Y and Z, though it might be quite easy for the trustee appointed in X to collect the assets situate in Y and Z; and if he does so, this implies no disrespect to the foreign sovereignty.

The territoriality system obtains, though not without certain qualifications, in the United States of America. Most states have adopted a combination of the two systems, for example, universality as effect of an adjudication in their own domain, territoriality for all foreign adjudications. This system, which at first sight owing to its inequality appears unfair (without being so), has been accepted by German, Swiss, and Dutch law. The principle of universality, advanced in particular by Italian and French authors, prevails in French law and most of those systems which are under French influence.

534. English law As to English law, it has adopted the universality doctrine both for domestic and foreign adjudications in bankruptcy, except for immovables situate in England.[1]

1. An adjudication in bankruptcy by the *English* court

[1] Similarly Austrian law.

is governed by English law. According to the Bankruptcy Act, 1914,[1] the property passing to the trustee in bankruptcy includes real and personal property, 'whether situate in England or elsewhere'. The effects of an English adjudication in other countries must be distinguished as follows. In Scotland, Northern Ireland, and the Republic of Ireland the adjudication is operative in all respects as if it had been made in one of these countries. The same is (probably) true[2] for all other countries forming part of the British Commonwealth. In all of them the adjudication of a debtor as bankrupt, made by an English court, automatically transfers property situate in one of them to the English trustee. It is different in the case of property situate in non-British countries. Though the English legislator has expressly ordained that property situate anywhere shall upon adjudication pass to the trustee in bankruptcy, such change of ownership cannot take place in the teeth of the *lex situs*. Only if the law of the *situs* accepts the British rule does the English adjudication *ipso iure* transfer ownership of foreign property to the English trustee. In other cases the universality principle can only be put into operation in a weakened form: the foreign property *is* not vested in the trustee but *shall be* vested in him; the debtor in bankruptcy is under a duty to transfer his title to the trustees in the way provided by the *lex situs*. He is bound to deliver possession of the movables to the trustee, to convey to him his foreign pieces of land, to assign the debts he owns abroad, &c. The English trustee can enforce these claims by bringing an action against the debtor in the English or the foreign court according to where jurisdiction lies. Under English law the trustee is entitled to act on behalf of the creditors; but if he sues in a foreign court it depends on the law of that court whether or not he can exercise such power.

The universality principle, if strictly applied, further leads to the result that English law forbids any of the bankrupt's creditors to recover payment abroad. But if a creditor

535.
Creditors
who have
received
payment
abroad

---

[1] (4 & 5 Geo. V, c. 59), ss. 53, 167.
[2] See *Callender* v. *Colonial Secretary of Lagos*, [1891] A.C. (P.C.) 460, 467. *Contra*: Westlake, s. 137, p. 178 (in respect of real property).

acts in contravention of this, the question arises whether the trustee in bankruptcy has a claim against him and may bring an action for money had and received in an English court (provided the creditor is present in England when sued). The answer is very doubtful. The German Supreme Court in a remarkable decision[1] has refused to accept that consequence, in spite of the fact that German law has adopted the universality principle in cases of a debtor adjudged bankrupt by a German court. Indeed, this seems a sound solution, provided the payment made to the creditor abroad was in conformity with the law of the country where it took place. As to English law, the following distinction must be drawn:

(*a*) One rule, derived from the equity maxim 'he who asks for equity must do equity', is clear: If the creditor has recovered payment abroad and wants to prove in the English bankruptcy for any further claims he may have, he must bring into hotchpot what he has recovered in the foreign country. This rule, based on Lord Eldon's reasoning in *Selkrig* v. *Davis*,[2] was firmly established by Lord Cairns in *Banco de Portugal* v. *Waddell*.[3] It is sound; a person who has acted in country X in accordance with the law of X and has thereby profited in a way he would not have done under the law of Y must not be allowed the benefit of both laws: he cannot rely later on the law of Y which he has previously violated.

(*b*) What is the law if the creditor does not prove in the English bankruptcy? Lord Eldon and Lord Cairns made their view quite clear: the creditor, even if personally present in England, is 'not obliged to bring the sum [he had received abroad] into the common fund—he might keep it if he liked—he might ignore the English bankruptcy proceedings altogether if he pleased'.[4] Nevertheless, the view predominates that even a creditor who does not participate in the English bankruptcy must in certain circumstances pay to the trustee in bankruptcy what he has

---

[1] German Supr. Court, *Offic. Coll.*, 54, 193.
[2] (1814), 2 Dow. 230, 249.
[3] (1880), L.R. 5 App. Cas. 161, 167.
[4] In *Selkrig* v. *Davis*, and *Banco di Portugal* v. *Waddell*, *supra*.

received. But on what ground and in what circumstances? This predominating view is based on three old decisions of 1791 and 1795,[1] that is, decisions previous to the quoted *dicta* in the two decisions of 1814 and 1880.[2] All three judgments were delivered in actions for money had and received.

In *Sill* v. *Worswick* the creditor was a domiciled Englishman who had recovered the debt due to him by the English bankrupt by an action brought in the British West Indies but 'founded on' and even 'commenced by' an affidavit made in England. On this point and on the debtor's English residence the decision was based. In *Hunter* v. *Potts* the creditor was resident in England and had through his attorney in America obtained money due to the bankrupt, although he knew of the assignment under the commission in bankruptcy; he had thus knowingly 'in order to gain a priority' acted 'in violation of the rights of the rest of the creditors'. It is impossible to say which of these facts Lord Kenyon, C.J., in giving judgment for the assignees, regarded as decisive. His short judgment is mainly concerned with the question whether the assignment in bankruptcy under the commission has the same effect as if the bankrupt had assigned the debt he owns 'by his voluntary act', and the learned judge comes to the conclusion that it has. But that is hardly to the point here. The majority decision in the case of *Philips* v. *Hunter*[3] was based on the ground that if a British creditor of the bankrupt had recovered the money due to him under an American judgment from a debtor of the bankrupt, such recovery must be taken to be for the use of the assignees (i.e. the trustees in bankruptcy) because otherwise the recovery would be 'in violation of an Act of Parliament; no residence in foreign parts can exempt a British subject from the operation of an Act of Parliament'; the judges stressed the fact that the bankrupts were English traders, that all of them resided in England, apart from one of the partners, who however resided in America only for a 'special and temporary purpose'.

What may we deduce from these three decisions? First, a rule of private international law, viz.: The question whether in an English bankruptcy a creditor is liable to refund what he has recovered abroad in accordance with the law of the foreign country is answered solely by English law, and neither by the law of the country where he has recovered nor by the proper law of the debt owed to him or

---

[1] *Sill* v. *Worswick* (1791), 1 H. Blackst. 665, 689; *Hunter* v. *Potts* (1791), 4 Term Rep. 182, 192; *Philips* v. *Hunter* (1795), 2 H. Blackst. 402.

[2] viz. *Selkrig* v. *Davis*, and *Banco di Portugal* v. *Waddell*, *supra*. These dicta, pronounced by two great judges, could not, it is true, overrule those old judgments, but they may weaken their authority.

[3] Eyre, C.J., dissenting (in a forceful and convincing judgment, p. 409, et seq.).

of the debt owed to the bankrupt. Secondly, under English municipal law the creditor is liable to refund if his act of recovery abroad was a violation of a duty under English law to refrain from recovering abroad. Such violation has been based on the English domicile, the English residence, the English place of business, or the British nationality of the creditor, or on the fact that his act of recovery abroad had been begun or at least prepared on English soil. These are examples; the underlying principle is that in the conflict between right and duty—the right to recover (under foreign law) and the duty to refrain from recovering (according to English law)—a non-exercise of the creditor's right can be expected only where a particular tie binds him to England. The fact that he is the creditor of a person who has been adjudged bankrupt by the English court is not sufficient.[1]

536.
Foreign adjudications in bankruptcy. Effects in England

2. An adjudication in bankruptcy by a *foreign court*[2] is governed by the law of that court. Only its effect in England will be examined here. Scottish and Irish adjudications have full effect in England, even in so far as immovables situate in England are concerned: the property vests in the Scottish or Irish trustee in bankruptcy as if it were situate in Scotland or Ireland.

As to the adjudications in other foreign countries, the English court recognizes them, irrespective of whether they have been made in the country where the bankrupt is domiciled (or resident) or elsewhere. But the foreign administrator (trustee, curator, *syndic*, &c.) must have been appointed in proceedings to which the debtor was a party, i.e. which were not made in his absence.[3]

The power of the foreign administrator in England differs for movables and immovables.

(*a*) He is not entitled to administer English *immovables*. The English court may, however, at its discretion allow him

---

[1] See on this much-disputed problem: Westlake, s. 142, 143; Dicey–Morris, pp. 330–1; Cheshire, pp. 641 et seq. Cf. *supra*, p. 226.

[2] Or the corresponding concept of foreign law, such as the *ouverture de la faillite*, the *Konkurs-Eröffnung*.

[3] *In re Davidson's Settlements* (1873), L.R. 15 Eq. 383; *In re Lawson's Trusts*, [1896] 1 Ch. 175; *In re Anderson*, [1911] 1 K.B. 896, 902; *Bergerem* v. *Marsh* (1921), 91 L. J. (K.B.) 80, and others.

to do so, and in particular to sell land for the benefit of the creditors.

(b) Regarding the *movables* situate in England the principle of universality has been recognized. It applies, of course, on the one hand only if it has been established also in the foreign country where the bankruptcy proceedings take place; if in that country a strict territoriality rule obtains, as in the United States, the foreign (American) trustee cannot acquire any right to chattels situate in England. The application of the universality principle, on the other hand, causes the English chattels to 'pass to the foreign trustee', as it is customary to say, or, to put it more correctly, the foreign administrator acquires by operation of law the same rights over the chattels as those he obtains over the movables situate in his own country, that is, in the case of continental bankruptcies a mere *ius in patrimonio alieno*, and not ownership.[1] If during the foreign bankruptcy a single creditor of the bankrupt attaches property situate in England, the title he may thereby acquire is invalid as against the foreign administrator.[2]

3. It happens, though not often, that the same person is adjudged bankrupt in two countries.[3] Then the later bankruptcy cannot destroy the effects produced by the earlier. Illustrations:

537. Ad-judications in two countries

(a) A debtor has been adjudged bankrupt first in New York, and subsequently in England. According to the American territoriality principle only the assets situate in New York pass to the American trustee in bankruptcy. The English trustee—in spite of the universality principle—acquires only the assets situate in Great Britain and in any third country. Not until the New York bankruptcy ends does the English bankruptcy extend to assets which the debtor may have acquired later in America.

(b) The first bankruptcy takes place in England, the second in Germany. According to the English universality principle the English trustee has a claim under English law

---

[1] See *supra*, s. 531.
[2] See the early cases in *Solomons* v. *Ross* (1764), and *Jollet* v. *Deponthieu* (1769), 1 H. Blackst., p. 131, n., p. 132, n.
[3] Example: *In re Temple*, [1947] 1 Ch. 345.

to a transfer of the property situate in Germany.[1] But the claim can hardly be enforced, except in respect of that part of the German property which is not subjected to the German curator's administration, for example property the bankrupt has acquired after the 'opening' of the German bankruptcy proceedings.[2]

538.
Administration in bankruptcy

III. The administration in bankruptcy is governed by the *lex fori* (*administrationis*). This is true not only of the undoubtedly procedural parts of the administration, but also of its effects in substantive law, such as the annulment of transactions of the bankrupt for fraudulent preference or fraudulent conveyance,[3] or the question of priorities between the creditors. When, however, the proceedings end by the bankrupt's discharge (as is the case under English law), such discharge extinguishes the debt only if the extinction is effective under the proper law of the obligation.[4]

[1] See *In re Temple*, loc. cit.

[2] Under German law property acquired subsequent to the opening (for example by legacy) does not belong to the bankruptcy assets.

[3] See for English municipal law: Bankruptcy Act, s. 44, and Law of Property Act, 1925, s. 172.

[4] See *supra*, s. 440.

BIBLIOGRAPHY

CHESHIRE, 626–50. DICEY–MORRIS, 276–91, 327–34, 437–49, 805–10. BURGIN, 9 *Grotius S.* (1923), 71. NADELMANN, 5 *Univers. of Toronto L.J.* (1944), pp. 324 et seq., 67–72; *J. Clunet* (1940–5), pp. 64–74; 91 *Univ. of Pennsylv. L.R.* (1943), 601; 93 ibid. (1944), 54; 38 *Americ. J.* (1944), 470; 59 *Harv. L.R.* (1946), 1025–59; 11 *Law and Contempor. Problems* (1946), no. 4, 696–712.

A. ROLIN, 'Des conflits de lois en matière de faillite', 14 *Rec.* (1926), 5. TRAVERS, *Droit commercial internat.*, VII. (1935). W. v. SIMSON, *RVgl.HWB*, IV. 528. *Travaux d. Com. franç.*, IV. (1938), 9. JAEGER, Comment. to the German *Konkursordnung* (1935), II. 960.

PART VII

SUCCESSION UPON DEATH

CHAPTER XXXVIII

LEADING PRINCIPLES

I. THE law applicable to succession on death is determined on the basis of one of the two following principles:

1. The law may distinguish between *immovables* and *movables*. This distinction has its historical roots in feudal law. The feudal lords could not allow the descent of their land to be affected if one of their vassals should acquire a foreign domicile. This conception led to the principle of *scission*. The deceased's movable property was regulated by his personal law, i.e. the law of his domicile, while his immovables were inherited under the law of their *situs*. *Quot sunt bona diversis territoriis obnoxia tot sunt patrimonia.* This system obtains in all parts of the British Commonwealth,[1] in the United States of America, in Russia, in France, Belgium, and Luxemburg, though in France there is some controversy on the subject.[2] In some other countries where the scission principle has been maintained the law of the domicile in respect of movable property has been replaced by the national law of the deceased; thus in Austria, Hungary, and Roumania. In some South American states the scission has even been extended by application of the *lex situs* principle to movables; in particular the Montevideo Convention[3] abandoned the subjection of all movables to a single legal system (law of the domicile or national law), every movable or immovable being inherited according to the law of its location.

2. Or a *unitary* law is applied to the whole of the deceased's property. This principle is founded on the conception of *universal succession* as developed in Roman law.

---

[1] See, for example, *Freke* v. *Lord Carbery* (1873), L.R. 16 Eq. 461.
[2] Lewald, *Successions*, p. 19 et seq.
[3] Art. 44, 45.

It has been justified in different ways. Universal succession was often based on Justinian's mystic idea that the deceased and his heir are in a certain sense (*quodammodo*) one person,[1] that the heir continues the personality of the deceased[2]—an idea the abstruseness of which is particularly evident in the case of co-heirs. It is better founded on practical reasons, such as the interest of the creditors, and means no more than that a person's property, including his debts, passes to his heir or heirs as one whole: the heirs succeed *per universitatem*, and not by a series of particular acts to each item. The principle of a unitary law obtains to-day in a great majority of modern laws, partly under the influence of Savigny, who was responsible for its adoption in German law; many legal systems, even those which in general were modelled on the French code, have accepted the unitary rule. Thus, for example, the laws of Italy, the Netherlands, Spain, Portugal. For movables and immovables alike the applicable law is the personal law of the deceased, in most countries, therefore, his national law (thus in Italy, Spain, Portugal, the Netherlands, Sweden, Germany, Poland, Egypt, Japan, China, and, since the code of 1940, Greece), in a few countries, such as Switzerland, Norway, Denmark, and the Argentine, the law of the deceased's 'domicile', i.e. of his ordinary residence.

540. Advantages and defects of both systems

II. There are advantages and defects in both systems. To criticize the scission system on the historical ground of the disappearance of feudalism from which it derived is to misinterpret the function of history; many sound institutions survive their historical basis. Similarly it would be a mistake to reject the unity principle (as regards English law) on the ground that the Roman rule on universal succession has no place in the municipal law of this country. The advantage of the unitary rule is its greater simplicity. Where the deceased leaves several immovables in different countries,

---

[1] Justinian, *Nov.*, 48 *pr.*

[2] Even one of the most modern writers on the subject adopts this conception and regards it as the root of the unitary rule in private international law. He speaks of 'the continuation of the person in infinite duration' and of the 'deep and audacious conception of universal succession which perpetuates the man and not his particular right' (Frankenstein, IV. 282).

these together with his movable property form a single mass, all parts of which are treated alike. All co-heirs are co-owners of any asset belonging to the estate, and the whole estate is liable for the debts of the deceased in the same way as during his lifetime. If, while the testator was alive, one of the co-heirs had received certain gifts, for example as an advance or on marriage, for which, according to the personal law of the deceased, he is accountable on division of the property, such 'hotchpot liability' is easy to fulfil where there is a single mass into which the gifts are to be brought. Complications are thus avoided which arise when several groups of property in one estate are to be distributed under different rules. Under the unitary system a will is either valid or invalid; under the scission system the same court may regard the same will as valid in respect of land situate in country X and as void in respect of land in country Y or of movables situate anywhere.

The simplicity of the unitary solution is, however, counterbalanced by a considerable disadvantage. If the succession law of state X is to be applied to the whole estate, including land situate in state Y, and if the succession law of Y is at variance with the law of X, the rights acquired under the law of X with regard to the foreign land are merely nominal; the courts of X have in fact no power to enforce them. Is it consistent with justice to establish rules which are necessarily ineffective? In the case of movables situate abroad no such inconsistency exists. True, the law of the domicile may be temporarily inoperative so long as the *situs* of the movables is outside the territory in which the domicile lies. But as the *situs* may be changed at any time, there is a chance that the domiciliary law will at some period become operative.

Two examples may illustrate the defect of the unitary rule:

(1) A Dutchman domiciled in Denmark and owning houses both in Copenhagen and Amsterdam, dies leaving a will which is valid under Dutch and void under Danish law. According to Dutch private international law Dutch municipal law applies; the heir W appointed by will must therefore be regarded by a Dutch court as owner of all assets, including both houses. The Danish court, on the other hand, will apply Danish municipal law according to the Danish conflict rule; the deceased will consequently be deemed in Denmark to have died intestate, and the

statutory heir S will succeed to both houses. Have the claims of W to the house in Copenhagen and of S to the house in Amsterdam any reality outside the lawyers' files?

(2) An Italian subject domiciled in Italy leaves land in England and in Italy. Under the Italian conflict rule, the heir determined by Italian law succeeds to both pieces of land. Under the English conflict rule English law applies to English land and Italian law to Italian land. There should be no doubt that the English rule is the more reasonable. But, in fact, most continental writers reject the scission de lege ferenda.

541. Inconveniences of the scission system in particular III. The English *scission system*, however, entails certain inconvenient results in respect of (1) liabilities, (2) the validity of a will, (3) the distribution of the assets where the deceased had granted advances to one of the beneficiaries, (4) the application of the English doctrine of election, and in some other cases.

As early as 1813 in *Brodie* v. *Barry*[1] Sir W. Grant very clearly recognized the problem arising in cases 'where land and personal property are situated in different countries governed by different laws, and a question arises upon the combined effect of those laws'. He goes on to state the difficulty in determining 'what portion of each law is to enter into the decision of the question; it is not easy to blend both together'.

But the difficulty is not insurmountable, as the following may serve to show. Suppose a domiciled Englishman leaves both immovables and movables in England, France, and Germany. The English conflict rule splits the whole of the property into three masses: one mass governed by English law, comprising the immovables situate in England and all the movables wherever situate; a second mass governed by French law, consisting of the French immovables; and a third ruled by German law including the immovables situate in Germany.[2]

[1] (1813), 2 Ves. & B. 127, 129, 133.

[2] Whether a thing is movable or immovable is determined (under English private international law) by the law of the *situs* at the date of death. See *supra*, p. 504. It may be remembered that the distinction between movables and immovables differs from that between personal and real property, and that particularly leaseholds, though personal property, are immovable, *supra*, p. 505. Suppose a domiciled Frenchman died intestate in 1920 and left a freehold and a leasehold, both in England. Both estates being immovables, their succession would be regulated by the *lex situs*, i.e. English law. As the freehold is real property it would devolve on the 'heir' (after having passed to the personal representative for administration). The leasehold, being personal property, would be distributed according to the Statute of Distribution. *Duncan* v. *Lawson* (1889), 41 Ch.D. 394; *Freke* v. *Carbery* (1873), L.R. 16 Eq. 461, 466. Cheshire, p. 551.

1. As regards the *liability* of the three masses for debts and legacies, the situation is the same as if, in a case of purely municipal law, three domiciled Englishmen, each liable as a partner for the debts of all, had died simultaneously. Their common creditors, just as they could have done during the debtor's lifetime, may enforce their claims against whichever estate (mass) they choose; provided that the procedural law of the forum does not forbid enforcement against immovables until enforcement against the movable part of the estate has proved unsuccessful. Whether the heir to one of the three masses after having paid the whole of the debt due from the deceased has a claim for reimbursement against the other two masses will depend in the first place on the will of the deceased.[1] But if there is no will or if the will does not deal with the matter, the decision is very doubtful. Westlake contends[2] that the *lex situs* of the immovables (which, if more than one?) determines the reimbursement. Dicey seemed to think that the answer should be left to the law of the country where the personality is administered. But outside English and Anglo-American law a fixed place for the administration of property does not always exist; the co-heirs, who possibly live in different countries, may regulate the distribution of the assets among themselves by correspondence or meetings, say in Switzerland. It seems more satisfactory to ask: what mass would the deceased reasonably have chosen if he had still been alive when the debt fell due? It is justifiable to assume that he would have paid the sum out of ready money or by selling bonds, shares, or other movable property, unless special reasons existed for preferring the sale or mortgaging of an immovable. Such a reason might be that the sum was so large as to create an uneconomic exhaustion of his personalty; or again, the particular debt might be closely connected with one of the immovables, as would be the case if it were secured by a mortgage upon that immovable. Thus the centre of gravity with regard to any claim for reimbursement by one mass against the others is normally to be found with the movable property. Claims against movable pro-

542.
Liability of the various masses

---

[1] *In re Smith,* [1913] 2 Ch. 216, 221.
[2] s. 118.

perty by the other masses are commoner than the reverse, and the law governing succession to the movable property will be decisive. In the unusual case that the heir to one of the immovable masses (for example, the German) claims repayment out of another immovable mass (the French), the *lex situs* of the latter will be applicable.

543.
Hotchpot
provisions

2. Certain difficulties stand in the way of hotchpot regulations.[1] If a man dies intestate, having previously made over some of his property to one of his children, the question arises: in which mass—if any—must the gift or its value be brought into account? The answer is: in that mass which has become poorer by the gift, that is, the mass to which the alienated property would have belonged had there been no gift. Take the hypothetical case mentioned above, p. 570: The deceased *A* was a domiciled Englishman with landed property in England, France, and Germany. And suppose he gave *inter vivos* to his daughter *D* a dowry and to his son *S* a sum of money, both out of the proceeds of a sale of part of his German estate, while his other son *N* received nothing; then *A* died intestate. The dowry to *D* and the gift to *S* will be brought, if at all, into the German mass; and whether they are to be brought into hotchpot *at all* will be for the German law exclusively to decide. Under German law the dowry must be so brought in, while the gift to *S* is (as a rule) not subject to hotchpot.[2] If French law were applicable, the gift to *S* would fall under the hotchpot rule; but French law does not apply to the distribution of the German mass, and the French mass is not the one out of which the gift to *S* was made. Hence German law rules alone. It also regulates all questions of detail,[3] such as the following:

(*a*) Does the hotchpot rule affect the distribution only between issue of the deceased, or is the surviving spouse included in its application?

(*b*) Is it applicable where there is a will in existence or only in a case of intestacy?

[1] See Lewald, *Successions*, pp. 83, 84.
[2] Cf. German Civ. Code, s. 2050 §§ 1 and 3.
[3] These questions are answered very variously in the different laws. Cf. English Administration of Estates Act, 1925, s. 47, sub-s. (1) (iii), German C.C., s. 2050–7, French *c.c.*, art. 843–69.

(c) Is the adjustment to be made by restitution *in natura*
of the specific gift received, or by bringing in its value to
reduce the recipient's share on the division of the mass?[1]

3. No serious difficulty arises—it merely constitutes an
anomalous feature—when a will is considered by one and
the same court to be valid in so far as the law of the domicile
applies, and void on points governed by the *lex situs*.[2]

544. Vali-
dity of will

4. The English equitable *doctrine of election*, unknown
to continental laws, deals with the case where a testator *A*
leaves some of his property to *B* and by the same will some
of *B*'s property to *C*. In that case *B* is put to his election: he
may either take under the will, or keep against the will. In
the first case, that is, if he accepts the legacy, he must allow
C to take his (*B*'s) property as prescribed by the testator.
If *B* keeps his property against the testator's will he loses
his legacy to the extent required to compensate *C* for the
failure of his legacy. This rule applies also if the property
left to *C* belonged to the testator *A* when he made his will,
but passed on *A*'s death wholly or partly to *B* by operation
of law, as where *B* is *A*'s son and heir. A problem of private
international law arises where the testator leaves immovables outside the country of his domicile. In particular, does
the English rule of election apply (*a*) if the domicile is
English, *or* (*b*) if the immovable belonging to *B* but devised
to *C* is situate in England? The correct answer is: the law
of the domicile must be decisive.[3]

545.
Doctrine
of election

If *A* is possessed of immovables situate in Paraguay and leaves them to
C in toto, though by the law of Paraguay he can only dispose of one-fifth
(four-fifths being his child's *porción reservada*), and if by the same will he
bequeaths to his only child *B* a certain sum of money, the English rule of
election is applicable, because the testator had an English domicile.[4] The

---

[1] Or, to use the French expression (art. 858), is the 'rapport' to be made 'en
nature' or 'en moins prenant'?

[2] *De Fogassieras* v. *Duport* (1881), 11 Ir. Rep. 123, 126; *In Goods of Gentili*
(1875), Ir. Rep. 9 Eq. 541; *Murray* v. *Champernowne*, [1901] 2 Ir. Rep. 232,
236; *In re Rea*, [1902] 1 Ir. Rep. 451, 461; *In re Moses*, [1908] 2 Ch. 235.

[3] The decision *Re Allen's Estate*, [1945] 2 A.E.R. 264 is (it is submitted)
untenable, as Morris has shown (27 *Can. B.R.* 528, Dicey–Morris, pp. 550–6,
833–5).

[4] See *In re Ogilvie*, [1918] 1 Ch. 492, 502. The old rule that an English heir-
at-law of English freehold cannot be put to his election (*Hearle* v. *Greenbank*
(1749), 1 Ves. Sen. 298, 306) is not a rule of private international law, but of
English internal law.

legacy to C of the immovables is void as regards four-fifths, the only question being how the nullity of that legacy influences the legacy made to B; and this can only be answered by the law governing the valid legacy to B, that is, the law of the testator's domicile. The legal position would (probably) be changed if the legacy to B were not a sum of money but a second immovable situate, for example, in Germany: then German law would have to decide whether or not B may only take the German immovable if he allows C to have the land in Paraguay. As there is no rule in German law similar to the English equitable doctrine, B would not be compelled to elect.

546. The legitim

5. The scission doctrine creates no embarrassing problem as far as the *legitim* and the *quotité disponible* are concerned. If a domiciled Englishman leaves bank accounts in London, Paris, and Bonn, and a house in each of these towns, and if he devises and bequeaths all he possesses to a friend F, without leaving anything to his only son S, the will is valid under English and German law, and partly valid (to the amount of the *quotité disponible*, that is a moiety)[1] under French law. F therefore acquires the three bank accounts, the houses in London and Bonn, and a half-share in the Paris house, but is obliged to pay to S in cash half the value of the Bonn house,[2] to which F can restrict his liability.[3]

Thus the alleged inconveniences of the English scission system shrink into insignificance on close examination.

547. A concession to *lex situs*

IV. Some of the legal systems which in principle subscribe to the unitary rule have made a valuable concession to the scission rule prevailing in other countries. In particular, the German Introductory Law to the Civil Code[4] ordains that the German unitary rule, according to which the national law applies, is inapplicable as regards property situate outside the national state of the deceased if under the conflict rule of the *situs* the municipal law prevailing at the *situs* applies.

Example: A domiciled German national leaves landed property in England and in Italy. Under the ordinary German conflict rule the whole of his property is regulated by German law. But because England applies

[1] *Code civil*, art. 913.
[2] German Civ. C., s. 2303.
[3] Under German law the liability *is* not restricted, but *can* be restricted by some act of his own; s. 1967, 1975 German Civ. C.
[4] Art. 28. See *supra*, pp. 211-12.

to immovables the *lex situs*, the German unitary rule gives way to the English scission principle in the case of the English immovable. In respect of the Italian immovable the situation is different, because Italy is governed by the unitary principle; here the German court will apply German law. This partial German departure from its leading principle is as good a concession to reason as half-measures can be.

V. The English conflict rule on succession—as it will be called for convenience in the following pages—thus distinguishes between movables and immovables: the *lex ultimi domicilii* obtains in respect of movables, the *lex situs* in respect of immovables. Both tests, however, are substantially modified by the doctrine of *renvoi*. In the sphere of succession this doctrine applies with special frequency if the nationality of the deceased differs from his last domicile (for example, if a British subject dies domiciled in Italy), or if an immovable is situate in a country where the succession to both immovables and movables is determined by the national law of the deceased (for example, in the case of immovables situate in Italy and left by a British subject who is domiciled in England). The *renvoi* rules of English law have been discussed *supra*, s. 178 et seq. *548. Renvoi and succession*

VI. The English conflict rule on succession is very rarely disturbed by the conception of *public policy*, or by the principle of non-application of foreign penal law. If, however, any country still existed in which civil death (*mort civile*) were a recognized institution, or in which a monastic vow created incapacity to take a legacy, such rule would not be applied in an English court. Continental courts have sometimes excluded from application the rules established by Soviet Russia in respect of succession;[1] not so English courts. A rule prohibiting a prodigal from making a will would not take effect in this country, because it is regarded as penal.[2] *549. Public policy and succession*

The German law of 5 November 1937, which precluded all persons deprived of their German nationality from acquiring any property of a German subject by way of succession, was inapplicable in England.

[1] Lewald, *Successions*, pp. 41, 42. See Makarov, *Z.f. Ostrecht*, 7 (1933), p. 438; *Z.f. Osteuropäisches Recht* (N.F.) 2 (1936), p. 586.
[2] Cheshire, pp. 194–5; Dicey–Morris, p. 467.

BIBLIOGRAPHY

H. Lewald, 'Questions de droit international des successions', 9 *Rec.*, 1925. W. Breslauer, *The Private International Law of Succession in England, America, and Germany*, 1937. Goodrich, 431–62. Bentwich, *The Law of Domicile in its Relation to Succession*, 1911. Falconbridge, 469–79; *Rev. Darras*, 1932, 254, 451. Lorenzen, in 7 *Rabel's Z.* (1933), 495. A. Tiran, *Les successions testamentaires en droit international privé*, 1932. Niboyet, *Traité*, IV. 735–931. Arminjon, III. 110–179. Lepaulle, 'Succession ab intestat', 10 *Nouv. Rev.* (1943), 60 et seq., 277 et seq. Plaisant, *Conflits*, 229–69. Batiffol, *Traité*, 648–85.

CHAPTER XXXIX

THE SCOPE OF THE CONFLICT RULE ON SUCCESSION

I. WHETHER and how a given person succeeds as heir or legatee to the deceased's property or parts of it, and whether he is liable for the debts of the deceased—these are the questions which fall within the scope of the conflict rule on succession.

The first problem that comes up for consideration concerns *capacity*. A person's capacity to acquire property by succession is tested not by *his* personal law, but (according to the conflict rule on succession) by the domiciliary law of the deceased or in the case of immovable property by the *lex situs*.

550. Capacity in its strict sense

The opposite view has been based on two decisions: in *Re Hellmann's Will*[1] and in *Re Schnapper*.[2] In both cases legacies had been bequeathed to persons who under their personal law, though not under English law, had capacity to conclude valid contracts and perform other valid legal acts; but the issue was in neither case whether the legacies had been validly acquired by the legatees, but whether the legatees were capable of *exercising* the rights they had validly acquired, that is, whether the bequeathed sums could be paid to them. Thus the two decisions are irrelevant to the question in point.

Certain problems under this head have evoked much discussion.

1. What law decides whether a given person is *unworthy* to take as beneficiary on the ground of certain crimes committed against the deceased, such as murder or manslaughter?[3] The correct answer is that the conflict rule on succession must apply.[4] It might be otherwise if such 'unworthiness' to succeed referred to a 'status', an incapacity inherent in that person. But that is not the case; a murderer remains capable of succeeding to the property of any third

551. Unworthiness

---

[1] (1866), L.R. 2 Eq. 363.

[2] [1928] Ch. 420.

[3] Cf. the German adage: 'Blutige Hand nimmt kein Erbe.' See further Chadwick, 30 *L.Q.R.* (1914), 211. English law: *Cleaver* v. *Mutual Reserve Fund Life Association*, [1892] 1 Q.B. (C.A.) 147; *In re Hall*, [1914] P. 1, 5, and others.

[4] Lewald, *Successions*, p. 57, n. 2.

P P

person. The English courts have based on public policy the exclusion of a person who has feloniously killed the testator.[1] They would therefore indubitably apply the English rule, if the conflict rule on succession did not pronounce the slayer unworthy.

552. Status   **2.** Even where a person's status is in issue, such as that of a legitimated bastard, English law determines the capacity to acquire land by the *lex situs*, and not by the law of the bastard's domicile.[2] Continental courts would reach a similar result; they apply the law applicable to succession (that is, the personal law of the deceased).

553. Capacity of unborn child. Capacity of corporations   **3.** The conflict rule on succession further answers the question whether an unborn child,[3] or a corporation in the face of mortmain legislation, can acquire by succession. If under the law of the testator's domicile a corporation is not capable of acquiring by will a sum of money exceeding a certain amount, or if under the *lex situs* the acquisition of an immovable by a corporation is prohibited, such prohibitions nullify the legacy.[4] If, on the other hand, the law applicable to succession contains no restriction of this kind, but the law of the country in which the corporation was constituted forbids the acquisition of land or money by corporations, it depends on the latter law whether the legacy is void on the ground of illegality, or valid despite the prohibition.

554. Pact of renunciation   **4.** Under some continental laws the future right of a person *A* to succeed to the property of *B* can be validly extinguished in *B*'s lifetime by a formal pact between *A* and *B*, in which *A* renounces such future right.[5] Most legal systems reject pacts of this kind, particularly French law and the legal systems based on the French Civil Code (for example, Belgian, Dutch, Italian, Spanish, and Portu-

---

[1] *In re Hall*, [1914] P., at p. 5.

[2] *Birtwhistle* v. *Vardill* (1840), 7 Cl. & Fin., 895.

[3] *Example*: Italian Civil Code, 1865, art. 764 § 2. See Lewald, *Successions*, p. 61, who rightly warns against the 'fallaciousness and equivocacy' of the term 'capacity'.

[4] *Att.-Gen.* v. *Mill* (1831), 2 Dow. & Cl. 393, 402; *Mayor of Canterbury* v. *Wyburn*, [1895] A.C. (P.C.) 89, 97; *In re Hoyles*, [1911] 1 Ch. (C.A.) 179; *In re Dawson*, [1915] 1 Ch. (C.A.) 626.

[5] Such pacts are permitted by the laws of Germany, Austria, Switzerland, and the Scandinavian states.

guese). Under English municipal law the institution is likewise unknown, but if the English conflict rule on succession points to a foreign legal system which approves the pact, such foreign law will be applied (and no consideration of English public policy is opposed to this).

In the famous Danish case *Arenstorff* v. *Giglioli*[1] the daughter of the deceased had made a pact with him by which she renounced succession to his property; the father was a domiciled Danish subject, the daughter was Italian by marriage and domiciled in Italy. The pact was valid under Danish, void under Italian law. The Danish court rightly applied Danish law as the law applicable to the succession.

II. Intestacy.

A person's right to inherit property may be based on rules regulating intestacy, on a will of the deceased, or on an inheritance pact. Intestacy and wills are provided for in all legal systems; not so inheritance pacts. 555. Relatives and spouses

To deal first with intestacy, it is obvious that the conflict rule on succession determines within what degree of relationship and in what order the relatives of the deceased are entitled to succeed, and what part of the estate, if any, devolves on the surviving spouse. It also answers the question whether a given person *A is* the relative thus entitled, and whether the woman *B* is the deceased's widow. If, for example, the deceased was a domiciled Frenchman and *A* purports to be his legitimated son, French municipal law decides whether a legitimated son is entitled to succeed, and, if so, the French conflict rule determines by what law the legitimation of *A* is to be tested.[2]

In default of next-of-kin, the universal rule is that the property goes to the state or the Crown or a township or some other public body—in Germany, Italy, and Switzerland as ultimate 'heir', in England, Austria, and Turkey by virtue of a *ius regale* over *bona vacantia*.[3] In the latter case the conflict rule on succession is not applicable because there is no 'succession' (inheritance). If, for example, a 556. State or Crown as heir

---

[1] Reported *J. Clunet*, 1904, 436. See Lewald, *Successions*, pp. 58, 59; Raape, *Commentary*, p. 681.

[2] See on that incidental question *supra*, s. 196 et seq.

[3] England: Administration of Estates Act, 1925, s. 46, sub-s. (1) (vi). Austria: Civ. Code, s. 760 (cf. *In re Barnett's Trusts*, [1902] 1 Ch. 847, 855). Turkey: *In the Estate of Musurus*, [1936] 2 A.E.R. 1666.

domiciled Austrian or Turk is unmarried, has no relatives, and dies intestate, leaving movable property in England, the law of the domicile of the deceased, that is, the conflict rule on succession, does not apply, since the right to 'heirless' property is governed by the *lex situs*.[1]

The succession can be founded on the *will* of the deceased. On this: the following chapter.

[1] See *supra*, s. 146.

CHAPTER XL

WILLS AND INHERITANCE PACTS

In the case of wills it will be convenient to distinguish capacity, formalities, and essential validity.

I. *Capacity* to make a will is determined by the conflict rule of succession. In the case of immovables no difficulties arise—capacity is tested by the *situs fundi*, and the *situs* does not change. In regard to movables capacity is judged by the law of the testator's domicile. As the domicile may change subsequent to the making of the will, the difficulty lies in deciding whether the domicile at the time of the execution of the will shall be decisive, or the domicile at the date of death. The English principle points to the last domicile,[1] and some continental authors[2] endorse this view. But it would be highly unsatisfactory entirely to eliminate the date when the will was made. If a domiciled German aged sixteen makes a will in Germany, which according to German law he is able to do,[3] and if subsequently he acquires an English domicile and retains it till the day of his death, it is hardly justifiable to treat that will as void.[4] Where a valid legal act has been performed, that act should not be vitiated by the fact that under the law of a different domicile capacity to make it would have been lacking. Against this it has been urged that the will creates no 'rights' previous to the death of the testator. That is true, but it would be a well-founded objection only if the recognition of foreign acts were solely justifiable from the point of view of protection of 'vested rights'. Therefore both English law and continental laws rightly take the date of the making of the will into consideration.

In England the common law rule under which capacity is tested by the *lex ultimi domicilii* is qualified by s. 3 of the

---

[1] *In the Goods of Maraver* (1828), 1 Hagg. Eccl. 498.
[2] Zitelmann, II. 968; Frankenstein, IV. 424.
[3] Civ. Code, s. 2229 § 2; Law on Testaments, 31 July 1938, s. 1 § 2.
[4] Cheshire, p. 681.

Wills Act, 1861 (Lord Kingsdown's Act).[1] According to this Act no will becomes invalid by reason of any subsequent change of the testator's domicile. This rule applies not only to the formalities of a will but also to the testator's capacity to make one.[2] It applies not only to British subjects as do the first two sections of the Act, but to any testator of whatever nationality and whatever domicile.[3] The result of this is:

(a) If the testator when making the will was capable of doing so under the law of his domicile at that time the will remains valid, though under the law of his last domicile it would have been void on the ground of his incapacity. In the example given above, therefore, the will made by a sixteen-year-old German in Germany should be regarded as valid, even if the testator dies domiciled in England.

(b) If conversely the testator when making the will was not capable of doing so under the law of his domicile at the time but would be regarded as capable under the law of his last domicile, the will is valid owing to the common law rule. This result is rather startling. An Englishman aged twenty makes a will and later acquires a Swiss domicile, which he retains until he dies. That will, though void when made, has become valid by the change of domicile,[4] even if he knows that at the time of making it he lacked testamentary capacity. He is treated like a person under municipal law who has made a valid will which he later erroneously believes to be void[5] and therefore never revokes.

(c) Finally: Does a person who under the law of his domicile is capable of making a will but has not made one, retain that capacity in spite of a change of domicile? Example: a domiciled German, aged sixteen, together with his father, flees from Germany to England, where they become domiciled; has the boy, who when in Germany had not made a will, retained his capacity to make one? This is

---

[1] 24 & 25 Vict., c. 114. See *infra*, pp. 584–8.

[2] This is, however, not certain, although the text of the provision is unambiguous. See Westlake, s. 75; Dicey (5th ed.), 822. *Contra*: Dicey–Morris, 842. No authority can be quoted either in favour of or against this view.

[3] Whether s. 3 applies to aliens is, however, doubtful. See *infra*, p. 588 (c).

[4] This, too, is doubtful. *Contra*: Story, s. 465.

[5] For example, owing to information given by a good friend and bad lawyer.

doubtful under German law, though the sounder answer is a plain negative. Under English law it is certain that no such preservation of capacity exists.

Continental writers have often debated whether the principles applicable to capacity are to be applied by way of analogy to the case where a legal act has been executed under mistake, misrepresentation, fraud, coercion, or undue influence. The degree to which such curtailments of free will affect the validity of the act has been regulated in a variety of ways under the different municipal laws. The act may be void, or voidable, or valid in spite of the defect; and if it is voidable the period within which the avoidance must be sought is not the same everywhere. What law governs these matters? In English law—as in most continental laws—the problem has not yet been decided or authoritatively answered. One rule only seems firmly established by statute—a will which in spite of mistake or misrepresentation is valid according to the law governing the will remains valid even if the testator subsequently changes his domicile and the will would be void under the new domiciliary law. This follows from the text of s. 3, Wills Act, 1861.[1] Where the will was made under the influence of fraud or coercion, the English court would (probably) apply the *lex fori* for reasons of public policy. If, on the other hand, the will was void or voidable under the law of the old domicile but valid under the law of the domicile at the time of the testator's death, the answer is much more doubtful. It is submitted, though with hesitation, that then, as in the case of incapacity, the *lex ultimi domicilii* must furnish the decision, since it is this law which in principle governs all incidental questions concerning succession to movables.

558. Will made under mistake, fraud, coercion, &c.

II. *Formalities*. Before 1861 a will had to be made in the form prescribed by the law of the testator's domicile at the time of death. Neither the law of his domicile at the time of the execution of the will nor that of the place where he made the will sufficed. The situation was highly unsatisfactory. A domiciled Englishman who falls ill while travelling

559. Form under common law

[1] See *infra*, s. 563.

abroad and wishes to make his will immediately may have difficulty in finding a lawyer who could assist him in making a will in English form, while it would be easy to use the local form. Again, a domiciled Englishman, of Scottish origin, who makes his will in English form, should be entitled to assume that the will is valid and will remain so. But under common law the validity depended on his maintaining his English domicile till death. If he left England for good in order to settle in Chile, and died during the voyage, the will was void because it was not made in Scottish form (as his domicile of origin had revived). Had he reached Chile and died there, the will would be void because it was not made in Chilean form. This disturbing situation became manifest in the case of *Bremer* v. *Freeman*.[1] The testatrix, a British subject domiciled in France, made a will in English form (in France). The will was held to be void because the forms prescribed by French law had been

560. Wills Act, 1861 disregarded.[2] This decision gave rise to the Wills Act, 1861,[3] (Lord Kingsdown's Act), which improved the legal situation considerably, though the text is not happily framed.

The first three sections of the Act need careful explanation. Sections 1 and 2 deal only with wills made by British subjects. The testator must be a British subject at the time of the execution of the will. It is not necessary that he remains British until death, nor is it sufficient that he is British at the date of his death.[4] The Act is further concerned only with dispositions of personal property, that is, movables and leasehold interests,[5] though it is difficult to understand why this relapse into the distinction between personal and real property was effected, seeing that no inconvenience had arisen from the subjection of wills dealing with leaseholds to the *lex situs*.

---

[1] (1857) 10 Moore, P.C., 306.

[2] This unfortunate result would have been avoided if the Privy Council had applied the *renvoi* doctrine, which had at that time been wholly developed. See *supra*, s. 183 et seq.

[3] 24 & 25 Vict., c. 114.

[4] See *In Goods of von Buseck* (1881), 6 P.D. 211, 212; *Bloxam* v. *Favre* (1883), 8 P.D. 101, 105, and (C.A.) 9 P.D. 130, 132.

[5] *In re Grassi*, [1905] 1 Ch. 584, 590.

Section 1 provides for wills made outside the United Kingdom (England, Wales, Scotland, and Northern Ireland),[1] while section 2 deals with wills made within the United Kingdom.

165.
Section 1 of
the Act

1. A will made under section 1 (i.e. outside the United Kingdom by a British subject) is formally valid not only

(a) if made in accordance with the common law rule that the formalities of the *lex ultimi domicilii* are to be observed,[2] but also if made in compliance with

(b) the law of the place where the will was made (*lex loci actus*), or

(c) the law of the place where the testator was domiciled at the time of the execution of the will (*lex praesentis domicilii*),[3] or

(d) the law of the domicile of origin (*lex domicilii originis*), if this domicile is situate within the British Dominions. This last possibility may be particularly useful where the testator, while travelling in a foreign country or on board a foreign ship, has some doubt about where he actually has his legal domicile.

This lengthy catalogue of testamentary forms is not even exhaustive. When under (b) the law of the place where the will was made is declared to be applicable, it must be remembered that this means not merely the municipal law of that place, but the whole of the law prevailing there, including its conflict rules. In *Goods of Lacroix*[4] the will made in English form by a British subject domiciled in France was held valid on the ground that the French conflict rule tests the validity of a will as regards formalities either by the *lex loci actus* or by the testator's national law.

2. A will made under s. 2 of the Wills Act (i.e. within the United Kingdom by a British subject) is formally valid not only

562.
Section 2 of
the Act

(a) if made according to the common law rule that the formalities of the *lex ultimi domicilii testatoris* are to be observed,[5] but also

(b) if the *lex loci actus* has been followed.[6]

---

[1] Not the Republic of Ireland, the Channel Islands, or the Isle of Man.

[2] s. 4 of the Act.

[3] Was this provision necessary? Does it not follow from the general rule of s. 3 of the Act? See on this *infra*, pp. 587, 588 (b).

[4] (1877), 2 P.D. 94. See *supra*, s. 187.

[5] s. 4 of the Act.

[6] See *Re Priest*, [1944] 1 Ch. 58.

Thus a will executed in Glasgow by a British subject domiciled till his death in Denmark is formally valid if the testator has observed the provisions either of Danish or of Scottish law.

An interesting point was raised in *Re Priest*.[1] A domiciled Englishman made a will in Scotland which contained a legacy to Mrs. X. In accordance with English law the will was attested by two witnesses; one of them was Mrs. X's husband. If the *lex domicilii* (English law) applied, the legacy to Mrs. X was void,[2] while under the *lex loci actus* (Scottish law) the legacy could be maintained as given by an unattested holograph.

The learned judge (Bennett, J.) held that the legacy was void because 'the testator did not intend to make an unattested holograph will'. Where, however, the law provides that a will is valid if it complies either with the law of the domicile or with the law of the place of making it, it seems not to matter what the testator thinks of the question what law governs the formalities of his will. His intention is merely to make a valid legacy. If he achieves this under the *lex loci actus* it is immaterial that he thought he was achieving it under the *lex domicilii*.

The decision has been sharply criticized.[3] Mr. J. H. C. Morris[4] tried to defend it by stating that the defect was more than a mere matter of form. This seems untenable. The English rule is to the effect that a beneficial interest in property cannot be given to a person by a will which is attested by that person or by his wife or her husband. This rule has nothing to do with the essentials or the substance of the legacy. It merely expresses that a specific form of the gift must be avoided. A rule concerns the 'form' of a legal act not only where the observation of a particular form is required, but also where the law forbids the use of a particular form.[5]

A comparison between the first and the second section of the Act seems to show that the testator has a more restricted choice under s. 2 than under s. 1, the facilities of the *lex praesentis domicilii* (*supra*, (1) (c)) and the *lex domicilii originis* (*supra*, (1) (d)) being excluded. The omission of the domicile of origin, in the case of a will made within the United

---

[1] [1944] 1 Ch. 58.
[2] According to s. 15, Wills Act, 1837.
[3] Kahn-Freund, 7 Mod. L.R. 238; Falconbridge, p. 476.
[4] 61 L.Q.R. 124; 62 L.Q.R. 172.
[5] See Zitelmann, II. 154.

Kingdom, is perfectly comprehensible: a British subject domiciled abroad but present in the United Kingdom can be expected, if he executes a will, to do so according to the formalities of the local law rather than to revert to his, say, South African domicile of origin. It is more difficult to understand why the law of the actual domicile of the testator has been omitted in s. 2. Does that omission really mean that this law is immaterial if the will is made in the United Kingdom? It is suggested that the application of the *lex praesentis domicilii*, in spite of its omission from the text of s. 2, is safeguarded by s. 3 (as will be shown below).

3. The third section of the Act deals with the influence of a subsequent change of domicile on the validity of a will.

563.
Section 3 of
the Act

It runs: 'No will or other testamentary instrument shall be held to be revoked or to have become invalid, nor shall the construction thereof be altered, by reason of any subsequent change of domicile of the person making the same.'

This is partly a repetition of the content of ss. 1 and 2: if the *lex loci actus* was observed by a British subject it does not matter where the testator was domiciled when he made his will or where he became domiciled subsequently. It also repeats the rule of s. 1, according to which the will made by a British subject out of the United Kingdom in the form regulated by the law of the testator's domicile at the time remains valid in spite of a subsequent change of domicile. But s. 3 goes much farther than ss. 1 and 2; namely:

(*a*) It ordains generally that a will which would be valid if the testator had not subsequently changed his domicile shall be valid in spite of such change. This seems to apply also to the case where the testator has made his will in the United Kingdom in the form not of the place of making the will, but of his domicile at the time.

Example: a domiciled Scotsman makes his will in England in Scottish form; later he abandons his Scottish domicile and dies domiciled in New York. The will then remains valid. It may be objected that it never was valid, because its validity depended on the domicile of the testator at the date of his death, and before that date the will could not be designated either as valid or as invalid. But the text of s. 3 expressly speaks of a will not '*becoming* invalid' by reason 'of any subsequent change of domicile'. Thus it appears to assume that under the old common law rule a will made in the form prescribed by the law of the testator's actual domicile is valid and becomes invalid by a change of domicile.

(*b*) Section 3 of the Act applies not only to the formalities of the will, as do ss. 1 and 2, but also to its 'construction' and to capacity,[1] and further to the effects of events which under some laws may be deemed to operate as a revocation of the will.[2]

(*c*) It applies to wills of aliens as well as to those of British subjects. This, however, has been disputed by eminent authors.[3] But while under ss. 1 and 2 of the Act the British nationality of the testator is a condition of the applicability of the respective rules, s. 3 refrains from any restriction. True, the title of the Act runs: 'An Act to amend the Law with Respect to Wills of Personal Estate made by British Subjects', and the genesis of the Act shows that the inconvenience caused by the decision in *Bremer* v. *Freeman*[4] to British subjects resident in France was the reason for altering the law. But neither of these arguments proves much. A statute aiming to improve the legal situation *x*, and saying so, may, apart from that, help to remove some other inconvenient rule *y*. And as to the genesis of a statute, to use it for the interpretation of the statute should be forbidden in any country, as it is happily forbidden here, on the ground that a statute frequently proves wiser than the legislator. The application of s. 3 to the will of a foreigner is supported by the decision in *The Estate of Groos*:[5] the judge could no doubt have based his decision on different grounds, viz. on the judgment delivered by Vaughan-Williams, L.J., in *Re Martin*;[6] but he did not do so, possibly because he doubted the correctness of Vaughan-Williams's *ratio decidendi*, which—it is submitted—is not unassailable.

564.
Testator of foreign nationality
According to the English conflict rule, a testator who is not a British subject is bound to make his will in the form prescribed by the law of his domicile. It is not sufficient that he should observe the rules prevailing at the place of

---

[1] Though this is doubtful. See *supra*, s. 557.

[2] See *infra*, s. 569, 570.

[3] In particular by Dr. Cheshire, p. 690–1, Dicey–Morris, 840, while Dicey–Keith (5th ed.), p. 820, and Westlake, s. 85, advocate the general application of s. 3.

[4] (1857), 10 Moore, P.C., 306.

[5] [1904] P. 269.

[6] [1900] P. (C.A.) 211, 240.

the execution of the will, unless the law of the domicile refers by way of *renvoi* to the *lex loci actus*. Sometimes the domiciliary law forbids its nationals to make use of certain forms when executing a will abroad.

Thus the famous art. 992 of the Dutch Civil Code of 1829 provides that Dutch nationals outside the Netherlands must not make holograph wills[1] except in a few unimportant cases. It is doubtful how far this rule should be taken into consideration by foreign courts. The rule constitutes an exception to the principle that the formalities of an act are governed (compulsorily or optionally) by the *lex loci actus*.[2] As the English conflict rule recognizes this principle only for wills made by British subjects, the holograph made by a Dutch subject in France or Germany will be regarded as void in England (and, of course, in the Netherlands), but as valid in France and Germany. Only where the testator is a *sujet mixte*, that is, both a British and a Dutch subject,[3] or where the *lex domicilii* coincides with the *lex loci actus*, or refers to it by way of *renvoi*, can the question arise whether that strange Dutch rule is to be applied by the English court. *Examples*: A Dutch subject makes his will in France, where he is domiciled, in holograph form as permitted by French law. Or he makes his will in Germany in German holograph form, though his domicile is in France. He leaves movable property in England. The correct answer is, as it seems, that the English court will admit the will to probate.

III. *Construction of Wills.* Under all legal systems the interpretation of a will must be directed to ascertaining the testator's intention as expressed in the document. But they differ in respect of the means to be adopted to this end. English law does not as a rule allow any intention to be taken into account which cannot be proved by the text of the will itself but is merely deducible from 'extrinsic' circumstances.[4] Continental laws recognize no such limitation. Most legal systems have established a series of rules of interpretation, or canons of construction, determining what is to be regarded as the *presumptive intention* of a testator who uses certain words such as 'next of kin',[5] 'children', 'issue', or makes certain dispositions.

565. Various canons of construction

---

[1] Similarly Portugal, Uruguay, and Greece; Fragistas, *Rabel's Z.* 4 (1930), 930.

[2] Lewald, *Successions*, p. 99. Fragistas, loc. cit. This problem has nothing to do with the problem of classification, as many French authors suggest.

[3] So that s. 1 of Lord Kingsdown's Act becomes applicable.

[4] See Lord Wensleydale in *Abbot* v. *Middleton* (1858), 7 H.L.C. 68, 114.

[5] *In re Fergusson's Will*, [1902] 1 Ch. 483: a domiciled Englishman had by

Two instances of this in English law: first, the equitable rule on satisfaction. If the testator leaves to his creditor by will a sum of money as great as, or greater than, the debt without referring to the latter, it shall be presumed that the legacy is made in satisfaction of the debt.[1] In continental codes the rule of construction in this case is just the opposite.[2] Second example: An Englishman domiciled in France executed a will in England in English form. In it he directed his executor to divide his residuary estate between ten named legatees; two of these died before the testator without issue. If the will was to be construed according to English law two-tenths of the residuary estate would devolve as on intestacy; if French law[3] governed the interpretation the whole of the residuary estate would be divided among the eight remaining legatees.[4]

566.
Applicable law

Which law applies? Although all such rules set up rebuttable presumptions and thereby regulate the burden of proof, it has never been suggested that they are of procedural character and that therefore the *lex fori* should govern. Their application depends on the conflict rule on succession. Foreign rules of interpretation are therefore applicable if the testator either leaves immovables abroad or if at the time of his death he had a foreign domicile. In the first case the rules prevailing at the *situs*, in the second case those of the *lex domicilii* apply; and if the testator's domicile changed subsequent to the execution of the will, s. 3 of Lord Kingsdown's Act expressly provides that the construction thereof shall not be altered by reason of such change. But as rules on interpretation are merely presumptions regarding the testator's intentions, it is open to a party affected by the will to rebut the presumption; this he can do not only by bringing evidence that the testator intended something different from the effect produced by the presumption, but also by showing that the testator when making his testamentary dispositions had in view some

his English will left a legacy to his domiciled German niece and, in case of her death, to her next of kin. Under German law the nearest relatives of the niece would not be the same persons as the next of kin under English law. The court decided for the English interpretation.

[1] *Campbell* v. *Campbell* (1866), L.R. 1 Eq. 383, 387.

[2] See French Civil Code, art. 1023: 'Le legs fait au créancier ne sera pas censé en compensation de sa créance.' The same rule in all codes framed after the French model, in Roman law (*Dig.* 37.7.4), in some German laws (cf. Prussian Code of 1794, I. 12 §§ 439, 440), &c.

[3] *Code civil*, art. 1044.

[4] *In re Cunnington*, [1924] 1 Ch. 68, 71.

legal system other than that of the domicile or the *situs*.[1]
Thus, to give some examples:

1. The testator disposes by one single will both of his movables, situate in country X where he is domiciled, and of his immovables situate in country Y. It cannot be supposed that he intended his unitary dispositions to be construed in one way for his movables and in another for his land. In such a case the law of the *domicile* will usually obtain, unless the deceased's movables were insignificant as compared with his landed property.

2. Where the domicile is in a country with which the testator has no real connexion it may be presumed that the rules of construction set up in the legal system of the testator's residence will fulfil his intentions better than those of the domicile. An instance of this is the will of a British-born woman who married a domiciled Italian, left him without divorce, and returned to England, where she made the will in the English language. Though she had an Italian domicile the will should be construed by reference to English law.

Difficulties arise where testamentary dispositions made under the law of country X are to be put into operation in country Y whose law embraces legal conceptions differing widely from those of the law of X. It is as if a concerto were to be played on two pianos that differ in pitch; the effect is an intolerable dissonance. Such a situation occurs particularly where the law of X is English or Anglo-American, while Y is any continental country the law of which is based mainly on conceptions of Roman law. The construction of an English will which is to become operative both in England and in France (or Germany) is not complete when the testator's intention as expressed in the will has been ascertained sufficiently to enlighten the English lawyer in regard to the appropriate legal conceptions. In order that the will may be carried out in France or Germany, it is necessary, as it were, to translate the conceptions of English law into French or German, to find the *equivalent* continental conceptions.[2] Take a typical English will by which the testator

567. Equivalent conceptions in foreign laws

---

[1] *In re Price*, [1900] 1 Ch. 442, 452.
[2] See Crichton, 40 *L.Q.R.* (1924), 472, and Breslauer, op. cit., p. 143 et seq. Cf. *supra*, s. 509.

appoints an executor and trustee, leaves a life interest to his wife, and orders that his personal property is to be distributed equally among his children after his wife's death. If the testator's last domicile was French or German, the construction of his English will, though perfectly clear under English law, gives rise to doubts on examination of the corresponding categories of French or German law. Under English law the executor and trustee becomes legal owner of the whole of the property; under continental laws the ownership vests immediately in the beneficiaries by universal succession, and an executor has merely a right of administration. Is it correct to translate the appointed executor and trustee into an executor of French or German law, or is it preferable to regard him respectively as the *légataire universel* of French, or *Erbe* of German law? Probably the first suggestion is the more correct.[1] Is the widow's life estate to be construed as *usufruct* (*Niessbrauch*),[2] or as ownership limited by a 'condition subsequent' (*Vorerbe* of German law), and are the children to be regarded as sole owners (heirs) whose rights are encumbered by the widow's *ius in rem alienam*, or as having only a qualified ownership (subject to a condition precedent, *Nacherben*)? The answer to questions of this kind cannot, however, be given by private international law, but only by comparing the two systems of municipal law.

568.
Effects of will

IV. *The Effects of a Will.* The effects of a will are determined by the conflict rule on succession. The law of the testator's last domicile, or as regards immovables the law of the *situs*, decides whether the testator's intention can be fulfilled or whether there are obstacles. Some of the problems arising here may be illustrated by the following examples:

1. The testator when domiciled in France makes a will by which he bequeaths the whole of his property to a charitable institution and leaves nothing to his son. If he dies while still domiciled in France, the bequest has no effect as regards half the property, which constitutes the reserved

---

[1] Cf. *In re Piercy*, [1895] 1 Ch. 83, 87: not the trustees, but the beneficiaries are the 'heirs'.

[2] Thus *In re Moses*, [1908] 2 Ch. 235 (in respect of Roman-Dutch law).

portion of his son. If, however, he changes his domicile and dies a domiciled Englishman, the will is wholly operative.[1] Even if he effected the change of domicile only in order to deprive his son of his French right to a legitim, the change entails the application of English law, because during his father's lifetime a son has no right to the succession either under French or any other law (his hope of succeeding might be destroyed at any time by his own death), and because the French doctrine of *fraude à la loi*—if fraud there were—would be rejected by the English court.[2]

2. The testator domiciled in France appoints X as his 'heir' and devises the piece of land he owns in Germany to Y. The question whether Y at once acquires ownership of that land (French law) or merely a claim against X for the transfer of ownership (German law) is to be answered in accordance with the *lex situs*. Hence Y only obtains a claim against X. The question would be more difficult if the testator had bequeathed to Y some movable property situate in Germany, for example, specified securities deposited with a German bank. Whether Y acquires ownership of the securities should at first sight be decided under the conflict rule on succession to movables, that is by the (French) domiciliary law. Under French law Y becomes owner at the date of the testator's death. Nevertheless, it seems very doubtful whether transfer of ownership of a specific thing without delivery can be allowed in the teeth of the law of the country where the thing is situate. It is submitted that it cannot; a French rule on singular succession cannot be applied to things outside France.[3]

3. Whether the testator can appoint several heirs or legatees in succession, one of them becoming entitled for a certain period or until the happening of a certain event (for example, his death), and the other then taking the place of the first, and how many substitutions of this kind are allowed, depends on the law governing the succession to the testator's property. If, for example, the testator T gives

---

[1] *In re Groos*, [1915] 1 Ch. 572, 576. Cf. *Thornton* v. *Curling* (1824), 8 Sim. 310; *Campbell* v. *Beaufoy* (1859), Johns, 320, 325.
[2] *Supra*, s. 136.
[3] *Supra*, p. 516.

A a life-estate and *B* a reversionary right (in respect of movable property) it is only the domiciliary law of *T* that matters, and it is immaterial whether the personal law of *A* allows such restriction of his rights as has been imposed under the law of *T*'s domicile.[1]

569.
Revocation of will. General rule

V. *The Revocation of a Will.* The revocation of a will is governed by its own law. Where, for example, the testator after having changed his domicile purports to revoke his will by a new will, the formalities of the new will must be consonant with the law of the new domicile. The interpretation of the new will must also be carried out according to the law of the testator's domicile at the time when he made it, and a second change of domicile subsequent to the execution of the new will remains immaterial. Sometimes it is doubtful whether the new will constitutes a complete revocation of the old will or not.

Under Swiss law, for instance, a new will, even if consistent with the old, is to be interpreted in case of doubt as a revocation thereof,[2] while under German law the opposite rule applies.[3] If the old will was made by a domiciled German who subsequently acquired a Swiss domicile and then made a second will, the question whether the old will is wholly revoked must be answered according to Swiss law.

570.
The rule 'marriage revokes the will'

Under English law and some laws derived from it a will is revoked by marriage, unless expressly made in contemplation of marriage.[4] This rule is regarded in England as part of matrimonial law[5] and is therefore applicable only (and always) if the spouses have an English domicile at the time of their marriage; the testator's domicile when he made his will and his domicile at the date of his death are immaterial. If a domiciled Scotsman makes a will formally valid according to Scottish and English law, and then having acquired an English domicile marries in this country, the will is revoked by operation of law. But if he marries while domiciled in Scotland and dies as a domiciled

---

[1] *Contra*: Frankenstein, IV. 479.

[2] Swiss Civ. C., art. 511.

[3] German Civ. C., s. 2258 § 1. German Law on Testaments, 31 July 1938, s. 36 § 1.

[4] Wills Act, 1837 (7 Will. IV & 1 Vict., c. 26), s. 18; Law of Property Act, 1925 (15 Geo. V, c. 20), s. 177.

[5] *In re Martin*, [1900] P. 211, 240 (*per* Vaughan Williams, L.J.).

Englishman the will stands.¹ The American Restatement differs from this; whether an act is effective to revoke a will relating to movables is determined by the *lex ultimi domicilii*.² The American rule seems preferable to the English rule, for it is difficult to agree with the English view that the rule 'marriage revokes the will' belongs to 'matrimonial law', seeing that the validity or nullity of a will does not operate until the testator dies, that is, until the marriage has ceased to exist.³

VI. *Some Particular Kinds of Wills*. **1.** Joint wills, in particular where made by married couples, are admitted in some legal systems (in English,⁴ Scottish, South African, German, and Austrian law); but most countries prohibit them, as, for example, France, Italy, Spain, Portugal, the Netherlands, the South American states, and Louisiana. Where joint wills are allowed, the dispositions made by the two testators in one instrument may or may not be interdependent. Interdependency means, firstly, that if one testator revokes his dispositions those of the other are likewise rendered ineffective; and secondly, that where one testator dies while the will stands, the dispositions of the survivor become irrevocable, at least, if the survivor has accepted some benefit under the will.⁵ In the case of such interdependence the peculiarity of the joint will is not merely one of form, but also one of substance. This is important where questions of private international law arise. Such legal systems as forbid joint wills may do so as a precautionary measure against undue influence. Or the prohibition may be based on the reluctance of the law to impose any restriction on the free revocability of wills. In the former case the prohibition of joint wills concerns the form of wills; this is the point of view of French law. In the latter case, as for example in

571. Joint wills

---

¹ Cf. *In the Goods of Reid* (1866), L.R. 1 P. & D. 74; *In the Estate of Groos*, [1904] P. 269.

² *Restatement*, s. 307.

³ It may be of some interest to call attention to the judgment of H. F. Jeune (Pres.) in *Re Martin*, loc. cit., p. 223, who classified the rule 'marriage revokes will' as concerning succession (reversed on appeal).

⁴ As to English law, see Jarman, *On Wills*, p. 43.

⁵ On South African law regarding this point, see R. W. Lee, *Introduction*, pp. 361, n. 6, 392.

Italy, the intrinsic validity of the will is in issue. Hence, if a domiciled French couple makes a joint will in Germany and in German form, the will should be regarded as valid in every country where the *lex loci actus* governs the form. If a domiciled Italian couple does the same, the invalidity of their will follows from the fact that the material validity is tested by the personal law of the testators.[1]

English law, which allows joint wills, and in the case of reciprocal dispositions provides for a certain interdependence,[2] would probably deal with foreign prohibitions in the same way as the foreign court would do.

572.
Powers of appoint-ment

2. Powers of appointment. Under English and American law, though not under continental laws, a testator T can by will or settlement give to some other person P a power to appoint by will or *inter vivos* the persons who in a particular eventuality, notably on P's death, are to succeed to T's property.[3] T is called the donor, P the donee of the power, and the person whom P appoints as successor is the appointee (A).[4] No difficulties arise in so far as the succession to immovables is concerned: all questions under this head are dealt with by the *lex situs*.[5] But in respect of movables the courts are often faced with the following problem: is the exercise of the power by the donee P governed by the domiciliary law of P or by that of the donor T? The answer given by English law is somewhat different according to whether the power granted to P is a 'general' or a 'special' power. General powers are those which the donee can exercise in favour of any person he pleases, including himself; special powers those where the appointee must belong to a certain specified group of persons, such as 'the issue of X'. In the first case the donee P, if he exercises the power by executing a will, makes his own will and is in principle treated as a testator; in the second case he is

[1] Lewald, *Successions*, 100, 101.

[2] *Dufour* v. *Pereira* (1769), 1 Dick. 419.

[3] On the continent the Roman rule prevails: the testator must not make a testamentary disposition in such a manner that it is left to another person to designate the person who is to receive the gift. (German C.C., s. 2065.) To this there are some exceptions where a very restricted power of appointment can be given; s. 2151, 2156, German C.C.

[4] See Dicey–Morris, 843–4.

[5] *In re Hernando* (1884), 27 Ch.D. 284, 296, 297.

mainly regarded as an agent, carrying out a mandate given to him by the donor.[1]

(*a*) *Capacity* of the donee to exercise by will a power of appointment. The donee, at least in the case of a special power, must be capable either according to his own domiciliary law or according to the law of the donor's last domicile. If, for example, the donor was a domiciled Englishman and the donee has a domicile in Spain and is twenty-two years old—hence a minor under his law—he can validly exercise his power by will. In the case of a general power[2] the will is (probably) invalid if the donee had no capacity under the law of his domicile.

573. Capacity to exercise the power

(*b*) *Formalities* of the will by which the power is exercised. Where the instrument conferring the power is governed by English law, the will by which the power is exercised is formally valid if either

574. Form of the donee's will

(i) it is valid under the ordinary rules of English *private international law*[3]—i.e. under the law of the donee's last domicile or of his actual domicile or (if the donee is a British subject)[4] under the *lex loci actus*, or, in the case of a will made outside the United Kingdom, under the law of the donee's British domicile of origin, *or*

(ii) the will of the donee has been made in the form of English *municipal law*. This is at first sight surprising; but in spite of some criticism it is now firmly established.[5] Where, for example, a domiciled Frenchman who has never had domicile or residence in England, has been given a power by an Englishman and makes a will in France in English form, exercising his power and at the same time

---

[1] See *In re d'Angibau* (1880), 15 Ch.D. 228, 243 (*per* Brett, L.J.); *Pouey* v. *Hordern*, [1900] 1 Ch. 492; *In re Pryce*, [1911] 2 Ch. (C.A.) 286, 297.

[2] *In re Lewal's Settlement*, [1918] 2 Ch. 391. The judgments in *Pouey* v. *Hordern* (*supra*), and *In re Pryce* (*supra*) do not deal with incapacity but with intrinsic invalidity (the right to dispose of a reserved portion). Probably, however, the principles developed there will be applied to capacity.

[3] *D'Huart* v. *Harkness* (1865), 34 Beav. 324, 327; *Re Price*, [1900] 1 Ch. 442, 452. *In re Wilkinson's Settlement*, [1917] 1 Ch. 620, 626. Cf. Cheshire, 696. As to the decisions in *Re Kirwan's Trusts* (1883), 25 Ch.D., 373 and *Hummel* v. *Hummel*, [1898] 1 Ch. 642, see Dicey–Morris, 848.

[4] Wills Act, 1861, s. 1 and s. 2, *supra*, s. 561, 562.

[5] *Tatnall* v. *Hankey* (1838), 2 Moore P.C., 342, 350. *In the Goods of Alexander* (1860), 29 L.J.P. & M. 93. *In the Goods of Hallyburton* (1866), L.R. 1 P.D. 90. *In the Goods of Huber*, [1896] P. 209. *Murphy* v. *Deichler*, [1909] A.C. 446.

disposing of his own property, the appointment he makes is valid, though the will in so far as it disposes of the donee's property is void. The reason given for this rule is that the donor's property passes to the appointee not so much by the donee's exercise of the power as by the donor's act in giving that power.[1] True, it is the donor's, not the donee's, property that passes to the appointee. True also that it would not pass without the donor's act in granting the power. But neither would it pass without the donee's act in exercising the power. From the truism that both acts are necessary to transfer the property to the appointee it ought not to be inferred that they must be tested by the same law.[2] The true reason seems to be the *favor testamenti*; 'the law takes a liberal view'—as Romilly, M.R., said in *D'Huart* v. *Harkness*[3]—where succession upon death is the issue.

(iii) The donor of the power often determines the mode in which the donee is to exercise it; he may, for instance, ordain that the donee's will must be attested by a certain number of witnesses. If then the donee does not comply with such terms, the appointment made in virtue of the power is formally invalid. An exception to this is to be found in the Wills Act, 1837, s. 10: if the donee's will has been executed in the form of English municipal law,[4] his non-compliance with additional forms prescribed by the donor does not entail the nullity of the appointment.[5]

If the instrument conferring the power of appointment is not governed by English law, but, for example, by Scottish or American law, the will by which the donee exercises it is formally valid only (as it seems) if the general rules of English private international law have been observed (that is, under the conditions explained *supra* (i)). There is no authority for an analogous application of the principle developed under (ii).

---

[1] *Tatnall* v. *Hankey* (1838), 2 Moore P.C. 342, 350. Cheshire, 698.

[2] Compare the following situation: The owner *A* of a movable thing gives *B* an authority to sell it and to transfer ownership to the buyer; *B* takes the thing from England to Germany and there sells it to *C* without delivery of possession to *C*. The transfer of ownership will be tested by German law, although *A*'s mandate to *B* may be subjected to a different legal system.

[3] (1865), 34 Beav. 324, 328.   [4] See *supra* (ii).

[5] Is this exception (s. 10, Wills Act, 1837) applicable also if the testator has no English domicile? Hardly. See *Barretto* v. *Young*, [1900] 2 Ch. 339, 343.

Example: a domiciled New York citizen wills to his daughter a power of appointment. Can the daughter, who is married in France to a domiciled Frenchman, exercise her power by a will she executes in France in the forms prescribed by the law of New York? It is submitted that the answer should be in the affirmative, since the 'liberal view', held by Romilly, M.R., in favour of the validity of a will is equally justifiable whether the donor is an American or an Englishman.

(*c*) As to the *interpretation* of the donee's will, English municipal law provides that if the donee has 'a general power of appointment' and makes by will a 'general' bequest of his personal property, this presumably includes the exercise of his general power of appointment.[1] It goes without saying that this rule applies if the donee is a domiciled Englishman who makes his will in English form. But does it apply in other cases also? The answer was formerly in doubt, but now seems to be well settled. The rule applies even if the donee is not domiciled in England, provided he makes his will either (i) in a form valid under his domiciliary law,[2] or (ii) in English form.[3] In the case of a special power given to the donee the rule is inapplicable.[4]

575. Interpretation of the donee's will

(*d*) The *effects* of a will by which a power of appointment is exercised are determined in the case of a general power by the law governing the will of the donee, and in the case of a special power by the law governing the will (or settlement) of the donor.[5]

576. Effects of the donee's will

Example: Under a marriage settlement made in England between British subjects domiciled in England the wife (the donee) had a special power of appointment in favour of her children. After her husband's death she marries a domiciled Frenchman and therefore becomes domiciled in France. She now exercises her power by will, appointing one of her children and disinheriting the others. Under English law this is valid, but not under French law in respect of the portion reserved to the other children. English law applies.

[1] Wills Act, 1837, s. 27.
[2] *In re Pryce*, [1911] 2 Ch. 286, 290. *In re Simpson*, [1916] 1 Ch. 502, 510. *In re Wilkinson's Settlement*, [1917] 1 Ch. 620. *In re Lewal's Settlement*, [1918] 2 Ch. 391.
[3] See *In re Baker's Settlement Trusts*, [1908] W.N. 161, and Dicey–Morris, 853–4.
[4] *Pouey* v. *Hordern*, [1900] 1 Ch. 492, 494.
[5] *Pouey* v. *Hordern*, [1900] 1 Ch. 492, 494. *In re Pryce*, [1911] 2 Ch. 286, 290.

Inheritance Pacts (Pacts on Succession).

577.
Inheritance
Pacts

An inheritance pact (*Erbvertrag, institution contractuelle*) is a pact[1] between *A* and *B* by which *A* appoints as successor to his property *B* or a third person *C*, and agrees that a revocation of that appointment shall be invalid without *B*'s consent. English law knows no such institution, and pacts concluded under foreign laws, notably under German or Swiss law, have not yet been the subject of English decisions. The admission in England of binding settlements, and the recognition of mutual wills which to a certain degree can become irrevocable,[2] seem to suggest that an English court would recognize a foreign pact if the domiciliary law of the person appointing his successor permits such pacts. The law of the domicile of the other partner to the pact seems immaterial, unless the pact is a mutual one, that is, a pact by which each of the partners appoints the other as his 'heir'. The capacity of the person whose estate is the subject-matter of the pact, and the formalities of the pact will probably be governed by the same rules as those developed by English common law for unilateral wills. English statutory law, in particular Lord Kingsdown's Act, 1861, will hardly be applicable. The capacity of the other partner probably depends on his domicile.

[1] It is no 'contract' in the English meaning of that term, since it creates no obligation.

[2] See Jarman, *On Wills*, p. 44.

CHAPTER XLI

THE ACQUISITION OF PROPERTY BY SUCCESSION

I. In respect of the acquisition of the property of a deceased person the various municipal laws have adopted one of the following systems:

578. The different systems of acquisition

1. The property becomes 'ownerless' at the death of its owner until those who are called upon to succeed as 'heirs' accept the inheritance. This system, developed in Roman law, is still in force where Roman law prevails. But all modern codes have abandoned it, except the Austrian Code of 1811,[1] the Baltic Code of 1864, and the Latvian Code of 1937.

Or, **2**, the property passes at the owner's death to the heir or heirs without acceptance but subject to his or their right to disclaim it. This is the predominating system on the European Continent, in Latin America, in Muhammedan laws, and in East Asia.

Or, **3**, the property passes first to the personal representative (executor or administrator) of the deceased; after having paid the debts for which the property is liable, he distributes and transfers the property or its proceeds to the beneficiaries (English, Scottish, and [Anglo-]American system).[2]

The main difference between the English system and the Continental systems (1 and 2, *supra*) consists in the obligatory interposition of an administrator or executor between the deceased and those who will ultimately succeed to his property. In Continental laws the administration of the estate and the payment of the debts is in principle a matter for the 'heirs' themselves, and though it is possible for a testator to appoint an executor, and such appointments are not infrequent, they are not the rule. Further, the executor

---

[1] In Austria ownership does not pass to the heir until the court delivers a formal decree to this effect.

[2] In South Africa the English system has superseded the Roman and Dutch system. Cf. Lee, *Introd. to Roman-Dutch Law*, p. 352 et seq.

of Continental laws has fewer functions than the English
executor;[1] in spite of his appointment the 'heirs' remain
liable for the estate debts. Where the testator has not
appointed an executor, the Continental courts cannot
normally order administration of the estate. On the Continent there is an essential difference between the heir and
the legatee,[2] the heir being liable to the creditors of the
deceased, while the legatee is not. Under the English system, on the other hand, the 'inheritance' is the 'net balance
of the estate which is left after the debts and legacies have
been paid, and which has to be handed over by the executor
(or administrator) to the heir';[3] the heir therefore 'is merely
a residuary legatee'.[4]

579. The
applicable
law

II. The law governing succession, i.e. the *lex situs* as regards
immovables and the *lex domicilii* as regards movables, determines *how* the persons called to succession acquire the
rights they are entitled to acquire. It answers such questions
as: Does acquisition presuppose an acceptance or, conversely, is a disclaimer necessary to exclude acquisition?
To whom are acceptance and disclaimer to be addressed?
Is a declaration of acceptance or disclaimer voidable on the
ground of mistake, misrepresentation, fraud, or coercion?
The law governing succession also indicates the various
kinds of debts for which the beneficiary is liable, particularly those debts which were never debts of the deceased
himself (funeral and testamentary expenses, the cost of an
inventory, and the like). The same law decides whether the
beneficiary (or heir or personal representative) is liable
ultra vires hereditatis, or whether the liability is limited to
the assets he acquires. If, for example, the deceased was
a French subject, domiciled in France and leaving movable

---

[1] Though it is an understatement to call 'the position of the executor merely
one of supervision'; *In re Achillopoulos*, [1928] 1 Ch. 433, 444, concerning Greek
law.

[2] This is so even in France, although the heir appointed by will is not called
héritier, but *légataire universel* (or, if he is a co-heir, *légataire à titre universel*);
code civil, art. 1002.

[3] That is, to what Continental systems call the heir.

[4] Maasdorp, *Institutes of South African Law*, I. 117, quoted by Lee, *Introd.*,
353.

property in France, England, and Germany, and if his heirs
are English, French municipal law answers the question of
their liability for the deceased's debts: they are liable with
the whole of their property unless they have accepted the
inheritance subject to 'benefit of inventory'.

CHAPTER XLII

ADMINISTRATION AND SUCCESSION

**580.
Concept of
administra-
tion**

I. THE dominion of the *lex domicilii* in questions of succession is, however, encroached on by the law under which the property of the deceased is to be administered. English and [Anglo-]American law make a clear distinction between administration and beneficial acquisition (succession).

Administration of property includes all factual or legal acts which are undertaken in the interest of its preservation. It covers primarily a series of duties; such as the collecting of debts owed to the deceased, the conversion of goods into money, the payment of debts. It embodies, on the other hand, some rights which the administrator needs in order to fulfil those duties, viz. rights to take possession of the property, to dispose of it, to conclude contracts by which new debts are incurred as a charge on the property, and so forth.[1]

**581. Law
governing
administra-
tion (as
different
from law
of succes-
sion)**

Administration is not governed by the law which governs succession (that is, the law of the deceased's last domicile), but by the law of the country where the administration takes place, and that is the law of the country from which the administrator 'derives his authority'.[2]

Example: The deceased was domiciled in France, so that succession to his movable property is governed by French law; the English court has granted letters of administration to X (see *infra*, II). Thus the grantee becomes personal representative of the deceased in the sense of English law; the property becomes vested in his person and the rule of the domiciliary law according to which the 'heirs' are universal successors of the deceased and legal owners of his property is infringed. The heirs are reduced to the position of mere legatees entitled only to the distribution amongst them of the surplus of the property after payment of the debts. Neither is the domiciliary law applicable to the payment of the debts, which is part of English administration. English law determines the manner in which the personal representative is bound to clear the property from debts; it decides on the priority of claims and even answers the question whether a specific debt is to be paid out of the estate.

---

[1] The power to postpone sale of parts of the personal estate for a certain period (s. 33, sub-s. (1) Administration of Estates Act, 1925) is also a power given to the administrator as such. *In re Wilks*, [1935] Ch. 645, 648.

[2] Dicey–Morris, rule 176.

In *re Lorillard*[1] the testator, domiciled in New York, with creditors both in England and in America, had left movable assets in both countries. Some of the debts were barred under the English Statute on Limitation, though not under American law. The English administrator rightly declined to pay them out of the property situate in this country; the American administrator wanted the surplus assets transferred to him for distribution among those American creditors whose claims were statute-barred under English law. But the English court, exercising its discretion, gave judgment against the American administrator, and the Court of Appeal rejected the appeal: the net assets were to be paid to the legatees.

The rules of the *lex domicilii testatoris* concerning limited and unlimited liability of the heirs are likewise excluded from application in England if the estate is administered here. This, however, does not prevent the application of these rules in a foreign country. Suppose the deceased was a domiciled Belgian leaving movable property both in Belgium and England, and the heir has accepted the succession 'purely and simply', that is, without benefit of inventory.[2] Then, quite apart from the English administration proceedings, the creditors are entitled to sue him in England— provided he is present here—for full payment of debts in accordance with Belgian law and 'irrespective of any question of assets'.[3] The judgment he obtains here may be enforced against the whole of the heir's property, and therefore against those parts of the deceased's property which have already been distributed by the English administrator or delivered to the heir. But it cannot be enforced against property which is still in the hands of the English administrator.

II. A few words may be added about the *jurisdiction* of the English court to take steps in the *administration* of the estate, particularly to make a grant of probate or of letters of administration.[4] The court has such jurisdiction if the deceased left immovables in England, or movables which at the time of his death are, or at any subsequent time

582. Jurisdiction concerning administration and succession

---

[1] [1922] 2 Ch. (C.A.) 638. See also *In the Estate of Goenaga*, [1949] P. 367 (cf. Morris, 3 *Int. L.Q.* (1950), 243); *In re Kloebe* (1884), 28 Ch.D. 175, 177.
[2] Art. 774, *code civil*.
[3] *Beavon* v. *Lord Hastings* (1856), 2 K. & J., 724.
[4] On American law, see Hopkins, 53 *Yale L.J.* (1944), 221 et seq.

become, situate in England, irrespective of where he was domiciled.[1]

Under the Administration of Justice Act, 1932,[2] the court has jurisdiction even if the deceased person has left no estate in England. It will in general exercise such jurisdiction if the deceased was domiciled here, but the Statute does not require an English domicile.[3]

Where the English court has jurisdiction in respect of administration, it also has jurisdiction to decide on questions connected with succession and distribution of movables.

If, for example, the deceased was domiciled in France and left movable property in England, the English court is competent to decide who is to take the property in case of intestacy, or how the will left by the deceased is to be construed, whether the will offends against the provisions of French law concerning the 'legitim' of children, &c.

583.
'Main' and
'ancillary'
administration

The jurisdiction of the English court is not exclusive in respect either of administration or of succession. The court of a foreign country has the same jurisdiction in the eyes of English law whether the property of the deceased lies in that country or whether the deceased was domiciled there. Administration may take place in more than one country. In such a case the main administration lies in the country where the deceased had his last domicile, or, in the case of *renvoi* from the domicile to the national law, in the country of which he was a subject. The administration in any other country is only 'ancillary'. Therefore, if the main administration is abroad, and there is an ancillary administration in England, the duty of the English administrator is only to administer the goods situate here, to collect the debts which are by English law deemed to have an English *situs*, to pay the English debts and all foreign liabilities of which he has notice, and ultimately to hand any surplus to the main administrator,[4] unless the English court exercises its dis-

[1] See Dicey–Morris, rule 49. *Att.-Gen.* v. *Hope* (1834), 1 C.M. & R. 530. *Preston* v. *Melville* (1840), 8 Cl. & Fin. 1, 12. *Enohin* v. *Wylie* (1862), 10 H.L. Cas. 1, 19 (Lord Cranworth), 23, 24 (Lord Chelmsford), while the view expressed in this case by Lord Westbury was disapproved in *Ewing* v. *Orr-Ewing* (1883), 9 A.C. 34, 39. *In Goods of Tucker* (1864), 3 Sw. & Tr. 585. *In Goods of Coode* (1867), L.R. 1 P. & D. 449.   [2] (22 & 23 Geo. V, c. 55) s. 2 (1).

[3] Dicey–Morris, 302–3.

[4] *In re Achillopoulos*, [1928] 1 Ch. 433, 445.

cretion to the effect that the payment has to be made direct
to the beneficiaries.[1]

III. The deceased's property situate in England can only 584. **Grant**
be administered by a person who has obtained an English **of probate and of**
grant of probate or of letters of administration.[2] Even if the **letters of**
greater part of the property is situate at the foreign domicile **admini-stration**
of the deceased and only a small part lies in England, a
separate grant in respect of the English property must be
applied for. It is within the discretion of the court to decide
in whose favour the grant shall be made. As a rule it will be
made to the person who administers the property situate
at the domicile, be it the testamentary executor appointed
by the testator himself, or a foreign 'administrator', or the
'heir' who under any continental law administers the estate
himself without judicial confirmation.[3] The court is of
course at liberty to depart from this rule and has often good
reason to do so. If, for instance, under the foreign (continental) law of domicile there are several co-heirs, who
abroad administer the estate between them, or if the only
heir is a minor,[4] or if the foreign executor or administrator
lives so far away that he is unable efficiently to manage the
English property, the court will appoint a particular
administrator living in this country.

The English executor or administrator is not restricted 585. **Con-**
to the administration of property situate in England. **current English and**
Whether he may obtain possession of goods situate out of **foreign**
England depends on the law of the place where they are. **admini-strators**
A foreign administrator, whether appointed by a foreign,
say American, court, or acting as heir, for example, in

[1] See *supra*, s. 581 about *In re Lorillard*.

[2] *New York Breweries Co.* v. *Att.-Gen.*, [1899] A.C. 62. An exception to this
rule exists in favour of grants (or Scottish 'confirmations') made in Northern
Ireland, Scotland, and many other parts of the British Commonwealth: these
grants or confirmations if re-sealed by the English court have the same effect and
operation in England as an English grant. Supreme Court of Judicature (Consolidation) Act, 1925 (15 & 16 Geo. V., c. 49) ss. 168, 169; Administration of
Justice Act, 1928 (18 & 19 Geo V., c. 26) s. 10; Colonial Probates Acts 1892 and
1927 (55 Vict., c. 6; 17 & 18 Geo. V., c. 43).

[3] *In the Goods of Earl* (1867), L.R. 1 P. & D. 450. *In the Goods of Hill* (1870),
L.R. 2 P. & D. 89. *In the Estate of Humphries*, [1934] P. 78. *In re Achillopoulos*,
[1928] Ch. 433. *In the Goods of Dhost Aly Khan* (1880), 6 P.D. 6, and others.

[4] *In the Goods of the Duchess d'Orléans* (1859), 1 Sw. & Tr. 253.

France or Germany, is not entitled to take and administer property situate in England. If nevertheless he obtains possession of assets in this country without a grant from the English court he acts wrongfully and can be made to account for the assets as executor *de son tort*.[1] A foreign administrator is further not entitled to sue a debtor of the deceased in an English court, or to accept money the debtor pays him here.[2] Whether the debtor from whom he receives payment is thereby discharged from liability seems to depend on the law of the *situs* of the debt.[3] If, for example, the debtor is resident in England and pays the American administrator to whom no letters of administration have been issued by the English court, English law decides whether he has to pay again, viz. to the English administrator.

A difficult problem arises if the deceased left chattels in two countries X and Y, some of which are brought from X to Y after his death. The administrator appointed in Y can undoubtedly administer them and take possession of them. But can the administrator appointed in X maintain a suit in the court of country Y against the possessor of the chattel, for example against the administrator in Y, to have chattels handed over to him (the plaintiff)? The answer seems to be: yes, if the plaintiff had taken possession of the goods before the change of *situs*; no, if he had not.[4]

[1] See *Coote* v. *Whittington* (1873), L.R. 16 Eq. 534. Compare *New York Breweries Co.* v. *Att.-Gen.*, [1899] A.C. 62.

[2] *Whyte* v. *Rose* (1842), 3 Q.B. (Ad. & E.) 493, 507. *Vanquelin* v. *Bouard* (1863), 15 C.B. (N.S.) 341, 370, 371.

[3] See Dicey–Morris, 456.

[4] The question has not yet been decided; but see *Whyte* v. *Rose* (1842), 3 Q.B. 493; Westlake, s. 95.

NOTE

Since the completion of the manuscript a number of statutes, judicial decisions, and articles relevant to the content of this book have been published. It was found possible to incorporate some of them in the text while the book was being printed. Others are mentioned in the following *Addenda:*

ad., p. 44, note 2:

The Czechoslovak Act on Private International and Interlocal Law and the Legal Position of Aliens was promulgated, according to the information given in *J. Comp. Leg.*, November 1949, p. 78, on 11 March 1948. It includes 75 articles mostly framed on the German model. An English translation has been published in the *J. Comp. Leg.*, loc. cit.

ad., p. 56, note 2:

On the conclusiveness of statements by the Executive, see Lyons, *Brit. Y.B.* 23, p. 240; 24, p. 116; 25, p. 160.

ad., pp. 59, 60:

On the termination of diplomatic immunity, see R. J. Jones, 25 *Brit. Y.B.*, p. 262.

ad., p. 110:

On the capacity to acquire a domicile, see notably R. H. Graveson, 3 *Internat. L.Q.* (1950), pp. 149–63.

ad., p. 133:

J. M. Jones's book on *British Nationality*, which appeared a year before the new Nationality Act, 1948, has been supplemented by the same author's article on the Nationality Act in 25 *Brit. Y.B.*, p. 158.

ad., p. 205:

On *renvoi* and the *désistement* doctrine (*supra*, pp. 198, 199) see further W. Raeburn, 25 *Brit. Y.B.*, p. 211.

ad., p. 277, note 7:

Under s. 1 (3) of the Law Reform (Miscellaneous Provisions) Act, 1949 (12, 13 & 14 Geo. VI, c. 100), the English court has jurisdiction to pronounce a decree of presumption of death and dissolution of marriage (according to s. 8 (1) Matrimonial Causes Act, 1937) in any case in which the petitioner is domiciled in England, and in the case of a petition by the wife if she is resident in England and has been ordinarily resident there for three years immediately preceding the commencement of the proceedings.

ad., p. 316, lines 2–4.

Since the decision of the French *Cour de Cassation* of 13 Feb. 1937 (*Sirey*, 1937, I. 153) this can no longer be maintained. See Colin et Capitant, *Traité élémentaire*, 11th edit. by Julliot de la Morandière, I, p. 132.

ad., p. 347, n. 5, and p. 349 (*c*):

The Foreign Marriage Act, 1892, was altered in several points by the Foreign Marriage Act, 1947 (10 & 11 Geo. VI, c. 33). Among other amendments it provides that the term 'Army' is to be interpreted to include the Navy and the Air Force, and the term 'British lines' to include 'any place where any part of the (said) British forces serving abroad is stationed'. Cf. Dicey–Morris, p. 772, n. 9; Joyce A. C. Gutteridge, 25 *Brit. Y.B.*, p. 390.

ad., pp. 494–6:

On the question as to what place is to be looked on as the *locus delicti*, see Z. Cowen, 25 *Brit. Y.B.*, p. 394. He relies mainly on the case of *Bata* v. *Bata*, [1948] W.N. 366, from which, however, it seems difficult to evolve a general solution.

INDEX

Except where otherwise indicated, the numbers given in this index refer to pages

s s

PRINTED IN GREAT BRITAIN
AT THE UNIVERSITY PRESS, OXFORD
BY VIVIAN RIDLER
PRINTER TO THE UNIVERSITY